THE
COIN
ATLAS

THE
COIN
ATLAS

THE WORLD OF COINAGE FROM ITS
ORIGINS TO THE PRESENT DAY

JOE CRIBB · BARRIE COOK · IAN CARRADICE

CARTOGRAPHY BY JOHN FLOWER

WITH AN INTRODUCTION BY THE
AMERICAN NUMISMATIC ASSOCIATION

Facts On File

New York • Oxford • Sydney

TO OUR PARENTS

THE COIN ATLAS
The world of coinage from its origins to the present day

Facts On File, Inc.
460 Park Avenue South
New York NY 10016
USA

Library of Congress Cataloging-in-Publication Data

Cribb, Joe
    The coin atlas; the world of coinage from its origins
to the present day/Joe Cribb, Barrie Cook, Ian Carradice.
        p.   cm.
    ISBN 0-8160-2097-3:
    1. Coins—History—Maps.   2. Coinage—History—
Maps.   I. Cook, Barrie, 1929–   II. Carradice,
Ian.   III. Title.
CJ59.C75   1989.
734.4—dc 19   89–1353
                                              CIP

Facts On File Books are available at special discounts
when purchased in bulk quantities for businesses,
associations, institutions, or sales promotions. Please
contact the Special Sales Department of our New York
office at 212/683–2244 (dial 800/322–8755, except in
NY, AK or HI).

EDITOR: Roger Tritton
COPY EDITOR: Mary Davies
ART EDITOR: Philip Lord
DESIGNER: Dave Goodman
PRODUCTION CONTROLLER: Ian Paton
PICTURE RESEARCHER: Sharon Hutton

Composition by Wyvern Typesetting Ltd
Manufactured by Toppan Printing Co. (S) Pte. Ltd.
Printed in Singapore

10 9 8 7 6 5 4 3 2 1

The publishers would like to thank the following agencies, libraries and
organizations for the kind permission to reproduce their photographs:

10 THE TELEGRAPH COLOUR LIBRARY; 12 © PHOTO: MICHAEL
HOLFORD; 13 SONIA HALLIDAY PHOTOGRAPHS; 15 PETER NEWARK –
NEWARK'S MILITARY PICTURES; 21 BRIDGEMAN ART LIBRARY; 24, 30, 33
left © PHOTO: MICHAEL HOLFORD; 33R ZEFA; 37 SONIA HALLIDAY
PHOTOGRAPHS; 38 © PHOTO: MICHAEL HOLFORD; 41 THE TELEGRAPH
COLOUR LIBRARY; 44 ARTOTHEK; 49 MARY EVANS PICTURE LIBRARY; 52
© PHOTO: MICHAEL HOLFORD; 55 THE IMAGE BANK; 57 BRIDGEMAN
ART LIBRARY; 60 MARY EVANS PICTURE LIBRARY; 65 THE TELEGRAPH
COLOUR LIBRARY; 70 BRIDGEMAN ART LIBRARY; 71 © PHOTO: MICHAEL
HOLFORD; 72–3 BRIDGEMAN ART LIBRARY; 76 THE IMAGE BANK; 78 ©
PHOTO: MICHAEL HOLFORD; 86 THE ANCIENT ART & ARCHITECTURE
COLLECTION; 91 SONIA HALLIDAY PHOTOGRAPHS; 96 MARY EVANS
PICTURE LIBRARY; 98 ANN RONAN PICTURE LIBRARY; 109 THE IMAGE
BANK; 123 JOHN MASSEY STEWART; 126 left, 126 right DAVID KING; 130 ©
PHOTO: MICHAEL HOLFORD; 132, 136 ZEFA; 139, 142 THE ANCIENT ART
& ARCHITECTURE COLLECTION; 147, 155 ZEFA; 169 THE J. ALLEN CASH
PHOTOLIBRARY; 175, 178 © PHOTO: MICHAEL HOLFORD; 179 THE
ANCIENT ART & ARCHITECTURE COLLECTION; 187, 188 © PHOTO:
MICHAEL HOLFORD; 190, 199 ZEFA; 206 THE TELEGRAPH COLOUR
LIBRARY; 210 PASCAL RONDEAU/ALLSPORT; 218 ZEFA; 220 WERNER
FORMAN ARCHIVE; 221 © PHOTO: MICHAEL HOLFORD; 223 ZEFA; 231
ALDUS ALDUS; 236 WERNER FORMAN ARCHIVE; 237 ALDUS ARCHIVE;
244 ROYAL COMMONWEALTH SOCIETY, PHOTO: JOHN FREEMAN; 255
FOTOMAS INDEX; 257 PICTUREPOINT – LONDON; 258 WERNER FORMAN
ARCHIVE; 259 HULTON/BETTMANN; 266 PHILADELPHIA NATIONAL
BANK; 268 left, 268 centre MARY EVANS PICTURE LIBRARY; 268 right
BRIDGEMAN ART LIBRARY; 272, 277, 279 MARY EVANS PICTURE LIBRARY;
292 BRIDGEMAN ART LIBRARY; 299 THE J. ALLEN CASH PHOTOLIBRARY;
301 MARY EVANS PICTURE LIBRARY; 303 © PHOTO: MICHAEL HOLFORD;
305 ANN RONAN PICTURE LIBRARY; 319 MARY EVANS PICTURE LIBRARY;
328 B & C ALEXANDER.
ALL COLOUR COIN PHOTOGRAPHY: REPRODUCTION COURTESY OF THE
TRUSTEES OF THE BRITISH MUSEUM. LONDON.

CONTENTS

List of Maps

INTRODUCTION

Coins have a history of over two and a half thousand years since they were invented in Turkey during the late seventh century BC. Having been mass produced and made of metal they survive in quantity to throw valuable light on the nations and rulers who have made and used them since then.

The coins excavated by archaeologists, dug up by treasure hunters or simply found by accident provide a tangible record of former civilizations and cultures, and particularly the extent of the role of money in international trade. Finds of Roman coins in Britain, Greek coins in Afghanistan, a Viking coin in North America, Arab coins in Scandinavia and East Africa, Spanish coins in China and Chinese coins in Indonesia all contribute to an understanding of a wider world history.

Coins also present through the designs on them a close up and detailed contemporary view of the world as perceived by their issuers. The most readily available official portraits of rulers from Alexander the Great, Julius Caesar and Cleopatra down to Philip II of Spain, Frederick the Great of Prussia and Napoleon are to be found on coins. Similarly, from ancient Greek, Indian and Islamic coins comes precise evidence of religious beliefs.

THE COIN ATLAS presents in a single volume the story of coinage throughout the world from ancient to modern times. Written with the non-specialist in mind, the use of technical numismatic terminology having been avoided, the book's novel arrangement should nevertheless make it an essential reference work for historians and archaeologists in particular.

Each country with full national status in the world today has a separate entry. These entries are arranged, within each continent, in groups according to their geographical, cultural and historical relationships. The coinage history of each country is described separately, but some countries, formerly united, but now politically divided, have their earlier coinages treated under one entry only.

Within each country the coins are normally discussed in chronological order. The dates used follow the common calendar and are AD dates unless otherwise indicated. The coin illustrations follow the same order as the text, providing a visual impression of the historical development of coinage in each country. The coin illustrations are all actual size. The maps, highlighting the location of mints and regions of coin circulation and identifying coin-issuing authorities, give a clear geographic context for the story presented in the text.

Given particular emphasis are the development of coin designs, the movement of coins in international trade and the response of coinage to the dynamics of political history. The result is a unique world-wide view of the origins, spread and evolution of coinage.

We would like to express our gratitude to our families, friends and our colleagues at the British Museum for their help and encouragement during the preparation of this volume for publication. Our special thanks are extended to our editor Roger Tritton, whose friendly direction has ensured its completion, also to his colleagues, particularly Philip Lord, art editor, at Macdonalds and to John Flower, cartographer, Mary Davies, copy editor, Dave Goodman, book designer, and our colleague Chas Howson for the colour photography.

THE AMERICAN NUMISMATIC ASSOCIATION

The AMERICAN NUMISMATIC ASSOCIATION is pleased to be associated with *The Coin Atlas*. Founded in 1891 and chartered by Congress in 1912, the American Numismatic Association is the world's largest, non-profit, educational organization dedicated to the collection and study of coins, paper money, tokens and medals. The ANA has nearly 35,000 members in the United States and throughout the world.

The Association annually organizes two educational conventions and money shows in different cities across the nation, sanctions money shows in the U.S. and throughout the world, conducts coin grading seminars each spring and autumn, presents a week-long summer numismatic study seminar, and provides correspondence courses.

The ANA's 102-year-old monthly magazine, *The Numismatist*, is a free membership service and contains articles of both a scholarly and popular nature.

The Association's Money Museum in Colorado Springs houses a world-class collection of some of the rarest and most valuable coins, paper money, tokens and medals.

The ANA's lending library offers members access to the world's largest collection of numismatic material, including books, magazines, slides and video tapes.

Members can have coins authenticated and graded, have them photo certified or encapsulated, and protected by comprehensive, low-cost insurance.

Information about collector services and membership in the ANA – the leading advocate for numismatic education – may be obtained by calling 1-800-367-9723 or by writing to the American Numismatic Association, 818 North Cascade Avenue, Colorado Springs, CO 80903-3279.

EUROPE

GOLD RIJDER *of the United Provinces, 1607.*

EUROPE has played a central role in the history of coinage. Although coins were invented in Asia (modern Turkey), it was the Greek and Roman peoples of southern Europe who gave to coinage the important role it has today. Under Greek influence coins quickly spread far afield, west to Spain, south to Arabia, north to Russia and east to India. The Roman Empire consolidated European coinage into a single tradition which survived the Dark Ages and developed in the medieval period as the distinctive states of the modern continent emerged.

In modern times European-style coinage has been spread around the world. European colonial and commercial expansion carried coins further into Africa and Asia, and to the Americas and Australasia. Under European influence local coinages were begun following European patterns. Where previously local coinages in the Islamic, Indian and Chinese traditions had flourished, they have now been replaced by coins in the European tradition.

THE PRESENT-DAY DENOMINATIONS OF EUROPE

ICELAND
KRONA

FINLAND
MARKKA

NORWAY
KRONE

SWEDEN
KRONA

USSR
RUBLE

DENMARK
KRONE

ISLE OF MAN
POUND

IRELAND
PUNT

UNITED KINGDOM
POUND

NETHERLANDS
GULDEN

GERMAN DEM. REP.
MARK

POLAND
ZLOTY

BELGIUM
FRANC

FED. REP. OF GERMANY
MARK

GUERNSEY
POUND

JERSEY
POUND

LUXEMBURG
FRANC

CZECHOSLOVAKIA
KORUNA

FRANCE
FRANC

LIECHTENSTEIN
SWISS FRANC

AUSTRIA
SCHILLING

HUNGARY
FORINT

ROMANIA
LEU

SWITZERLAND
FRANC

ITALY
LIRA

SAN MARINO
LIRA

YUGOSLAVIA
DINAR

BULGARIA
LEV

MONACO
FRENCH FRANC

ANDORRA
DINER

PORTUGAL
ESCUDO

SPAIN
PESETA

VATICAN CITY
LIRA

ALBANIA
LEK

GREECE
DRACHMA

GIBRALTAR
POUND STERLING

MALTA
POUND

CYPRUS
POUND

UNITED KINGDOM

FIRST COINS:	first century BC
FIRST DECIMAL COINS:	1971
MAIN MINT:	Royal Mint
CURRENCY:	pound

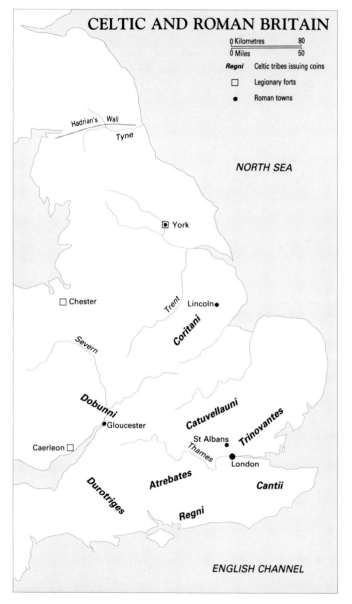

CELTIC AND ROMAN BRITAIN

0 Kilometres	80
0 Miles	50

Regni Celtic tribes issuing coins
☐ Legionary forts
● Roman towns

NORTH SEA

ENGLISH CHANNEL

T HE first coins used in Britain were potin (tin–bronze) pieces, produced by the Belgae in the area of Kent, and gold coins, usually called staters, issued by the Gallo-Belgic tribes of north-west France. These circulated in south and east England. By the time of Julius Caesar's expeditions to Britain (55–54 BC), the tribes of the south-east were striking their own gold coins. These have the same designs as the Gallo-Belgic staters: a head of Apollo and a two-horse chariot. Based originally on the fourth-century BC gold coins of Philip II of Macedon, the increasingly abstract style can make the designs difficult to recognize today.

The coinages of the ancient Britons included issues in silver and bronze as well as gold and potin. The various issues have been attributed to different tribes largely on the basis of the distribution pattern of coin finds (*see* map). Towards the end of the first century BC the coin designs began to show greater variation, often copying Roman coins and including names in Latin of tribal leaders. Some names identify known historical figures, such as King Cunobelin (Shakespeare's Cymbeline) of the Catuvellauni and his son Caratacus.

ROMAN BRITAIN

In AD 43 Britain was again invaded by Romans, this time under the Emperor Claudius. The result was incorporation into the Roman Empire. The Romans brought with them their own money and production of native coinages ceased. The Roman coins circulating in Britain soon after the conquest were made at the imperial mints at Rome and Lyon, but inadequacy of supply led to a widespread production of imitations, particularly of Roman bronze coins, identifiable as locally made pieces by their crude style.

As the Roman armies gradually pushed the frontier further west and north, so also the use of coinage advanced into regions that had never previously known it, including Wales, northern England and Scotland. In Scotland hoards of Roman silver denarii, issued mainly for the payment of troops, have been found. Some Roman bronze coins issued under Hadrian (117–38) and Antoninus Pius (138–61), who both had walls built across Britain's northern frontier, have designs referring to the province of Britannia, represented as a female figure seated on rocks. Because these coins are today found predominantly in Britain it is believed that they were sent direct to the province from the mint at Rome.

Hadrian's Wall, shown here near Housesteads Fort, Northumberland, marked the northern boundary of the Roman province of Britannia. The figure personifying Britannia appears on some of Hadrian's coins.

UNITED KINGDOM
1 GOLD STATER of ancient Britain.
2 GOLD COIN of Cunobelin, King of the Catuvellauni.
3 SILVER COIN of Caratacus, King of the Catuvellauni.
4 BRONZE AS of the Roman emperor Hadrian, depicting Britannia.
5 SILVER DENARIUS of Carausius.
6 BRONZE COIN of the Roman emperor Diocletian, London mint.
7 GOLD THRYMSA of the Kingdom of Kent, two emperors type.
8 SILVER SCEATTA, bird on cross type.

The most common coins circulating in Roman Britain during the first 200 years of occupation were the copper as and, later, the brass sestertius (= 4 asses); but from the 260s Britain was flooded with debased silver antoniniani, often known as radiates. Particularly common are issues of the Gallic usurpers Postumus (about 260–9), Victorinus (about 269–71) and Tetricus I and II (about 271–4), and the Roman emperors Gallienus (253–68) and Claudius II (268–70). Large numbers of locally struck imitations of these coins are found in Britain, as also are cast copies of third-century Roman coins and the moulds used for making them.

THE FIRST BRITISH EMPIRE

In 286 a separate British Empire, which also included northern France, was established by the usurper Carausius and continued after his murder in 293 by his successor Allectus. Both rulers issued Roman-style coins. Two of their mints were in Britain, one in London and another, so far unidentified, which marked its products with the letter c. In 296 Allectus was defeated by the Emperor Constantius I and Britain returned to the Roman Empire. However, the mint in London was allowed to remain open, now striking Roman coins with the same designs as all the other official mints in the empire.

END OF ROMAN BRITAIN

The London issues continued until about 326, after which most of the coinage circulating in Roman Britain came from the continental mints of Trier, Lyon and Arles. Roman bronze coins of the fourth century are extremely common finds in Britain, and, again, numerous contemporary local imitations exist. In the later fourth century good Roman silver coinage once more became available and many hoards have been found in Britain. However, the supply of official coinage to Britain suddenly ceased with the withdrawal of Roman government early in the fifth century. No new coins were issued, the silver coinage still in circulation was mutilated by clipping to remove silver, and by the middle of the century coinage was no longer being used in Britain.

ANGLO-SAXON COINAGE

In the late sixth century gold tremisses from Merovingian France were imported and, from about 600, the Anglo-Saxons began to copy these coins in Kent and the Thames region, though in small quantities. The gold content of these thrymsas, as they are known, or shillings (= 12 pence) was progressively reduced and from about 675 they were replaced by a larger number of silver pennies, known today as sceattas. The use of coins spread into the other Anglo-Saxon kingdoms: East Anglia, Wessex, Mercia and Northumbria.

Sceattas were produced for about a century. They were small, comparatively thick coins with a large variety of designs and mostly without inscriptions. Exceptions were the coins of East Anglia, under King Beonna (in power around 750), and of Northumbria, then the most powerful kingdom, where from the reign of Eadbert (738–58) they carried the name of the king and sometimes that of the Archbishop of York.

1 Castle Gotha	19 Wareham	37 Cissbury	54 Newport Pagnell	71 Hereford
2 Launceston	20 Shaftesbury	38 Steyning	55 Bedford	72 Bridgnorth
3 Lydford	21 Warminster	39 Lewes	56 Cambridge	73 Shrewsbury
4 Barnstaple	22 Bath	40 Hastings	57 Bury St Edmunds	74 Chester
5 Totnes	23 Bristol	41 Romney	58 Sudbury	75 Stafford
6 Exeter	24 Berkeley	42 Lympne	59 Maldon	76 Tamworth
7 Watchet	25 Malmesbury	43 Hythe	60 Colchester	77 Derby
8 Taunton	26 Wilton	44 Dover	61 Ipswich	78 Leicester
9 Langport	27 Salisbury	45 Sandwich	62 Norwich	79 Nottingham
10 Petherton	28 Southampton	46 Canterbury	63 Thetford	80 Peterborough
11 Crewkerne	29 Winchester	47 Rochester	64 Huntingdon	81 Stamford
12 Bridport	30 Bedwyn	48 Horndon	65 Northampton	82 Newark
13 Axbridge	31 Cricklade	49 Southwark	66 Warwick	83 Torksey
14 Ilchester	32 Oxford	50 London	67 Worcester	84 Lincoln
15 Milborne Port	33 Wallingford	51 Hertford	68 Pershore	85 Horncastle
16 Cadbury	34 Reading	52 Aylesbury	69 Winchcombe	86 Caistor
17 Bruton	35 Guildford	53 Buckingham	70 Gloucester	87 York
18 Dorchester	36 Chichester			

MINTS OF ANGLO-SAXON ENGLAND (973–1066)

The silver content of the sceattas gradually declined, and from about 770 a new type of penny was produced. Only in Northumbria was the old type retained, though it was increasingly debased as the ninth century progressed. These base coins, called stycas, usually had the name of both issuer and king.

Elsewhere the new penny was established, a broader, thinner coin, which henceforth bore the name and title of the king on the front, with the moneyer's name on the back. The first ruler to introduce it was Offa of Mercia (757–96), now the dominant power and to remain so until the early ninth century and the rise of Wessex. Until the early tenth century the archbishops of Canterbury and York and a number of other prelates issued coinage in their own names. The most productive southern mints were Canterbury, Rochester and London.

Viking raids began in the late eighth century, and in time the invaders conquered York, East Anglia and eastern Mercia to form the land of the Danelaw. They struck their own coinage, notably the St Peter coinage of York and the St Edmund Memorial coinage of East Anglia. Wessex alone remained independent and Alfred the Great (871–99) was accepted as king of all England outside the Danelaw. Alfred opened new mints and took the title REX ANGLORUM (king of the English) for his coins, the first time this had been done. He and his successors recovered the lost lands to found the kingdom of England.

By the mid-tenth century there were 35 mints in operation, and the capture of York from Eric Bloodaxe in 954 ended the independent Viking issues. From the reign of Eadred (946–55) comes the only known coin issued in the name of a Welsh prince, the unique penny of Hywel Dda. In 973 King Eadgar instituted a new, uniform coinage with all mints producing pennies to one design, which was changed regularly. However, a bust of the king remained the usual feature on the front of the coin. The name of the mint as well as the moneyer was included henceforth on all coins.

Viking raids began again under Ethelred II (978–1016), the Unready, and huge payments in English coins were made to the invaders as Danegeld. On Ethelred's death, Cnut, later king of Denmark, was accepted as king of England. He was succeeded by his sons, but in 1042 Edward the Confessor, of the old Wessex dynasty, was chosen king, to be succeeded briefly in 1066 by Harold II. All these kings continued the issue and regular change in the design of pennies. Royal control and organization of the English coinage were among the strongest in Europe and its standards were extremely high.

NORMAN COINAGE

The conquest of England by William of Normandy had little impact on the nature of the coinage. The Norman kings issued pennies in their

9 810–c.854
10 787–92
11 871–99
12 939–41
13 973–5
14 1056–9
15 c.1068–7
16 c.1131–4
17 1135–54

own names, continuing periodically to change the design. The most obvious difference was the tendency to use a facing bust instead of a profile. Under Henry I (1100–35) standards in production fell considerably and forgery and debasement became serious problems. A major reform in 1125 attempted to remedy the situation, inflicting drastic punishments on those who tampered with the currency.

The reign of Stephen (1135–54), nephew of Henry I, witnessed civil war between him and the supporters of Matilda, Henry's daughter. As well as the official coins of Stephen, of which there were a number of successive designs, coinage was issued in the name of Matilda, and several barons also struck coins in their own names, the only time this ever occurred in England.

LATE MEDIEVAL COINAGE

The reign of Henry II (1154–89), son of Matilda, saw a major change. Previously kings had introduced new designs after comparatively short intervals. Henceforth a design would be retained for a generation and only changed when the state of the currency made a wholesale recoinage desirable. The number of mints working consistently was gradually reduced, with others opening only when a major recoinage increased the workload.

The first of these long-lasting coinages was the Cross and Crosslets, or Tealby coinage, so-called because a vast hoard of them was found at

Left: Scene from the Bayeux Tapestry, Harold II's oath of loyalty to William of Normandy (the Conqueror).

Above right: *'The Deceitfulness of Riches', stained glass from Canterbury Cathedral. The Roman emperors Julian and Maurice are depicted with a pile of money and the inscription: 'These thorny ones are the rich and extravagant. They bear no fruit since they seek earthly things'.*

24 1344

19 1205–10

154–80

22 1280–1

20 1248–50

23 1280

1 1257–63

25 1369–77

26 1377–99

9 BASE-METAL STYCA of *Eanred, King of Northumbria.*
10 SILVER PENNY of *Offa, King of Mercia.*
11 SILVER PENNY of *Alfred the Great, London monogram type.*
12 SILVER PENNY of *Eadgar.*
13 SILVER PENNY of *Anlaf Gufrithsson, Viking king of York.*
14 SILVER PENNY of *Edward the Confessor.*
15 SILVER PENNY of *William I.*
16 SILVER PENNY of *Henry I.*
17 SILVER PENNY of *Stephen.*
18 SILVER PENNY of *Henry II.*
19 SILVER PENNY of *John, Short Cross coinage.*
20 SILVER PENNY of *Henry III, Long Cross coinage.*
21 GOLD PENNY of *Henry III.*
22 SILVER PENNY of *Edward I.*
23 SILVER GROAT of *Edward I.*
24 GOLD FLORIN of *Edward III.*
25 GOLD NOBLE of *Edward III, struck in Calais.*
26 GOLD ¼ NOBLE of *Richard II, struck in London.*

Tealby, Lincolnshire, in 1807. Tealby pennies, produced from 1158 until 1180, were very poorly struck and often almost square in shape.

The next change of type came in 1180 with the introduction of the Short Cross penny design, distinguished by the short double-cross on the back of the coins which continued to be issued until 1247 under Henry III. Throughout, the king's name is given as HENRICUS REX: there are no English coins in the name of Richard I (1189–99) and John (1199–1216). Standards of production gradually declined, but there was a large-scale recoinage in 1205 which did improve the appearance of the coins for a while.

By 1247, under Henry III, the coinage had again fallen into a bad state, with much of the currency consisting of worn, clipped and counterfeit coins. A new coinage was ordered and a number of changes were made. In a move intended to inhibit clipping, the cross on the back was extended to the edge of the penny, hence the name now given to the coinage, the Long Cross. The ordinal TERCI or III was added to the king's name on the front, a practice not repeated until Henry VII's reign. The other notable feature of this period was the attempt to introduce a gold coinage for the first time in 600 years. However, the new gold penny (= 20 silver pennies) was not successful.

Edward I succeeded in 1272 but ordered a new coinage only in 1279. It included two new denominations, halfpennies and farthings (= ¼ penny). Previously these had been provided by cutting pennies into fractions. He also launched the groat (= 4 pence), though it did not become established at this time. All the new coins had a design which was to survive on the silver coinage until the end of the Middle Ages: on the front an elegant, facing bust of the king shown beardless and on the back a cross with three pellets in each quarter. A reorganization of the minting system left a single official responsible for the whole coinage, so the moneyers' names disappeared from the coins. The new coinage was very popular internationally and rulers in the Low Countries, northern France and Germany copied the sterling design. So many of these imitations began to circulate in England that Edward ordered a major recoinage in 1299.

The next major development was the revival of gold, successfully achieved by Edward III (1327–77). His first attempt in 1344 produced

the florin (= 6 shillings), with its half and quarter, the leopard and helm. This issue was however not successful and was replaced that same year with the noble (= 6 shillings and 8 pence) and its half and quarter. The design of the noble was highly innovatory, featuring the king standing in a ship and holding a sword and shield. The ½ groat and groat also entered the currency in large numbers for the first time from 1351. The title 'King of France' was added to the coinage, to remain until 1801. From 1363 until the early fifteenth century a mint operated at Calais, using precious metal coming to England through the wool trade.

The denominational system established by Edward III survived until the sixteenth century, though under Edward IV the noble was replaced by the angel, so-called because of its distinctive design of the Archangel Michael fighting the Devil in the form of a dragon. The noble did however survive, slightly modified, as the rose noble, or ryal (= 10 shillings). The weight of the denominations was at times reduced but the English kings were opposed to debasing the coinage.

THE TUDORS

Under the Tudors English coinage went through its most drastic change. Most of the medieval designs disappeared, replaced usually by portraits in profile of the rulers on the front and a coat of arms on the back. Old coins were still issued but with different values, while the introduction of new denominations reflected rising prices and the new supplies of precious metal from Europe and the Americas. The pound (= 20 shillings) and shilling had previously been units of account only, worth too much to be useful as coins, but under Henry VII coins were issued to these values: the spectacular gold sovereign and the silver testoon. The latter introduced the first portrait to the English coinage in about 1504.

Sovereigns continued to be issued by later Tudor rulers, although the gold value of the coin increased until it was worth 30 shillings. A new 1 pound sovereign and its fractions, particularly the 5 shilling gold crown, were introduced alongside it by Henry VIII in his second coinage (1527–44). Henry's crowns bear the initials of the king and successive wives: κ for Katherine of Aragon, a for Anne Boleyn and ι for Jane Seymour. After 1537 this was changed to H R for Henricus Rex. The tiny silver farthing ceased to be produced in the mid-century. This development created a need for small change as many basic items still cost that little.

The ecclesiastical mints of Canterbury, York and Durham ceased to operate under Henry VIII, though not before Cardinal Wolsey had issued groats for the first time as Archbishop of York. Under Henry the coinage was exploited for profit, its traditional fine standards being undermined by debasement from 1544 until 1550. The silver coinage was affected particularly badly, with all good-quality coin driven out of circulation.

Henry's successors sought to restore the old standards and issued mostly good new coins. Edward VI (1547–53) introduced to England the threepence and sixpence and also the ½ crown and large silver crown (= 5 shillings), though these latter denominations were not then revived for 50 years. Other developments included the use of numbers to indicate value in pence on some of the silver coins, and the first appearance of dates (in 1551–3). Mary Tudor's coinage is notable for the portraits of herself and her husband, Philip of Spain, which appeared on her shillings. They are unusual because the figures face each other, the only time that this has happened in English coinage.

The old, debased money was finally removed from circulation by Elizabeth I in 1560. The silver coinage was returned to the sterling standard, though 'crown gold' of 22 carats began to be preferred to the virtually pure medieval gold coins. More denominations were issued under Elizabeth than under any other English ruler. There were also experiments in machine-made or 'milled' money, though only milled sixpences entered circulation in any quantity.

DENOMINATIONS ISSUED UNDER ELIZABETH I (1558–1603)

Fine gold	Crown gold	Silver
quarter-angel (2s.6d.)	half-crown (2s.6d.)	halfpenny
half-angel (5s.)	crown (5s.)	three-farthings
angel (10s.)	half-pound (10s.)	penny
ryal (15s.)	pound sovereign (20s.)	three-halfpence
sovereign (30s.)		half-groat (2d.)
		threepence
		groat (4d.)
		sixpence
		shilling
s: shillings		half-crown (2s.6d.)
d: pence		crown (5s.)

UNITED KINGDOM

27 SILVER GROAT of Henry VI, annulet issue, struck in Calais.
28 GOLD ANGEL of Edward IV, second reign, struck in London.
29 GOLD SOVEREIGN of Henry VII, with dragon mint mark.
30 SILVER TESTOON of Henry VII, with lis mint mark.
31 GOLD CROWN of Henry VIII, second coinage, with the initials of Henry and Katherine of Aragon.
32 SILVER SHILLING of Philip and Mary.
33 GOLD POUND SOVEREIGN of Elizabeth I, with tun mint mark.

27 1422–7
31 1526–9
30 1504–9
28 1471–83
29 1504–7
32 1554–5
33 1591–4

THE STUARTS

Large numbers of denominations in both gold and silver continued to be issued under the Stuarts. Under James I (1603–35) the title KING OF GREAT BRITAIN appeared for the first time and the union of England and Scotland is commemorated on the coins, particularly the 1 pound coin, now called a unite. From 1613 farthing tokens in copper were authorized to ease the shortage of small change caused by the lack of silver farthings.

During the latter part of Charles I's reign (1625–49) the coinage often reflected what was happening in the English Civil War. Local mints were revived, first at Aberystwyth in 1637 to exploit Welsh silver, but later by order of the king in various royalist strongholds (see map). The Tower mint, though under parliamentary control, continued to issue coinage in the king's name until 1649. Crudely-made emergency issues were struck on several occasions in towns under siege in order to pay the defending troops. These were Pontefract, Newark, Colchester, Scarborough and Carlisle.

After Charles I's execution, a republican coinage was issued under the Commonwealth. It was sometimes known as Breeches Money because the conjoined shields on the back of the coins resembled a pair of breeches. Coins showing Oliver Cromwell were prepared but never issued. In 1644 parliament had stopped the issue of farthing tokens but did not introduce any replacements. Instead a huge variety of locally-issued farthing and halfpenny tokens, mostly issued by merchants and shopkeepers, provided small change until 1672.

After the restoration of the monarchy in 1660 the coinage underwent a transformation, with the introduction of machine-manufacturing processes. There had been earlier milled issues, but a consistent supply of milled money began in 1662 under Charles II, though it was only in 1695 under William III that all the old handmade coins were finally replaced. Official copper coinage was also reintroduced under Charles II from 1672. A new pound coin became known as the guinea, a reference to the Gold Coast, source of the gold supply. The most long-lasting design feature introduced under Charles was the modern image of Britannia.

The Battle of Naseby, 14 June 1645, the last major battle of the Civil War, at which the royalist army was routed. Under the Commonwealth a republican coinage, sometimes known as Breeches Money, was introduced, while the use of locally-issued farthing and halfpenny coins flourished.

34 c.1613–14
35 1648
36 1652
39 1673
37 1660–70
38 1660–70

UNITED KINGDOM

34 COPPER FARTHING *token of James I, Harington issue.*
35 SILVER SHILLING *issued in the name of Charles I at the seige of Pontefract.*
36 SILVER SHILLING *of the Commonwealth.*
37 COPPER FARTHING *token of Robert Simons of Painswick, Gloucestershire.*
38 COPPER HALFPENNY *token of Lancelot Fenton of East Bergholt, Suffolk.*
39 COPPER FARTHING *of Charles II.*

SCOTLAND

□ Carlisle

□ Scarborough

York ▼

□ Pontefract

Chester ▼   Newark □

Shrewsbury ▼   Ashby ▽

Dyfi Furnace ▼   Bridgnorth ▽   ENGLAND
Aberystwyth ▼   Hartlebury ▽
WALES   ▽ Worcester
          Hereford ▼

Oxford ▽

Tower Mint, London ▼

▼ Bristol

Exeter ▼

Truro ▼

0 Kilometres 100
0 Miles 50

□ Parliamentarian area, Dec 1643
▼ Attested mint
▽ Probable mint
□ Siege issue

MINTS OF THE ENGLISH CIVIL WAR

15

UNITED KINGDOM
40 GOLD GUINEA *of Anne.*
41 COPPER 'CARTWHEEL'
PENNY *of George III, minted in Soho, Birmingham*
42 GOLD SOVEREIGN *of George IV.*
43 SILVER 'GOTHIC' FLORIN *of Victoria.*

40 1703

41 1797

43 1852

42 1824

EIGHTEENTH AND NINETEENTH CENTURIES

Throughout the eighteenth century the guinea remained the basic gold coin in England, with both multiples (2 and 5) and the ½ of the coin also being produced. Portuguese gold coins also entered circulation in some quantity. Due to the rising value of gold against silver, the value of the guinea was fixed at 21 shillings in 1717 until it was replaced by a new 1 pound coin, the sovereign, in 1816. The succession of the House of Hanover in 1714 brought German titles and devices onto the coinage until the succession of Victoria who, as a woman, could not inherit a German throne.

Supplies of precious metal varied greatly at times, producing shortages of official coins. From 1758 hardly any silver coins were

issued for the next 30 years, few copper coins were minted and, during the Napoleonic Wars, gold coins were temporarily replaced by paper money issued by the Bank of England. A revival in the issue of private tokens helped to ease the situation, most notably the tokens of the Parys Mining Company of Anglesey. In 1797 the Bank of England purchased Spanish silver 8 reals of Charles IV, countermarked them with the head of George III and issued them as dollars (= 4 shillings, 9 pence).

The early years of the nineteenth century saw the English coinage revived and restored. A copper coinage, manufactured by the new steam-presses developed by Matthew Boulton and James Watt at the Soho mint in Birmingham, put the petty coinage of pennies, halfpennies and farthings on a sound footing. From 1860 bronze replaced copper, being a harder and more durable material. Boulton presses were adopted at the Tower Mint itself. When the precious metal coinage was reformed in 1816, it was decided to base it on the gold standard alone, with the sovereign as the standard coin, to avoid the problems caused by the shifts in the relative value of gold and silver.

This left the silver coinage, though still consisting of fine metal, now effectively token. Silver denominations issued under Victoria consisted initially of the groat, sixpence, and shilling, with occasional issues of ½ crowns and crowns. The so-called 'Gothic' crown of 1847 was probably intended as a commemorative issue rather than a currency piece. From 1855 the 3 pence replaced the groat and in 1849 the florin (= 2 shillings = $\frac{1}{10}$ pound) was introduced in answer to those who wanted a decimal system. On the first florin the traditional phrase DEI GRATIA was omitted, earning it the nickname the 'Godless florin'.

The sovereign of 1816 had the famous image of St George and the Dragon designed by Pistrucci on the back and this has been retained on the coin to the present day. Gold multiples were rare in the nineteenth century. The 5 pound 'Una and the Lion' pieces were purely presentation coins given out by Victoria to highly honoured guests. In the year of the Golden Jubilee (1887), 2 and 5 pound pieces were issued, but were kept mainly as souvenirs. Changes in the legends and arms in the nineteenth century included the disappearance of the title 'King of France' from 1801 and the introduction of the imperial title under Victoria in 1893.

MODERN COINAGE
The main feature of modern coinage in Britain has been the abandonment of the use of precious metal in currency pieces. Its use survives in two forms; firstly the special silver Maundy money given by the monarch on Maundy Thursday as a symbol of charity, and secondly as gold bullion pieces: the sovereign and the Britannia (1987). Treasury notes replaced gold coins during the First World War, and the silver coinage was debased to 50 per cent fine metal in 1920 because of its rising price.

The last crown piece for general circulation was issued in 1902 and with the ending of coinage in gold the ½ crown remained the highest value current coin until decimalization. Since then crowns have been produced solely for collectors and as commemorative pieces, usually in honour of royal events. In 1933 very few pennies were minted, since large stocks with earlier dates were stored in the Royal Mint and thus available. Only eight examples are recorded. No coinage was issued in the United Kingdom in the name of Edward VIII (January–December 1936), since he abdicated before new issues were ready.

George VI's reign (1936–52) saw a number of innovations. In 1947

UNITED KINGDOM
44 SILVER SHILLING *of George V.*
45 NICKEL-BRASS THREEPENCE *of George VI.*
46 CUPRO-NICKEL 10 PENCE *of Elizabeth II after the introduction of decimal coinage.*
47 GOLD BRITANNIA *of Elizabeth II, made from 1 oz. of pure gold.*

44 1920

45 1938

46 1968

47 1987

SCOTTISH COINAGE

The production of coinage came comparatively late to Scotland. Finds of Roman coins have been made in the south, deposited when this region formed part of the Roman province of Britannia, and Anglo-Saxon and Viking coins were introduced by the Scandinavian settlements established on the western coast and isles after the Viking raids of the ninth century. Any need for coinage was most likely met by using English coin until the reign of David I (1124–53). He introduced the minting of silver pennies in imitation of the English coins of his contemporary, King Stephen. The names of moneyer and mint appeared on the back of the coins, the mints in operation being at Edinburgh, St Andrews, Roxburgh, Berwick and Carlisle (Northumbria and Cumbria were claimed by the Scots until the 1150s). David's son, Henry, Earl of Northumberland, also issued coins in his own name at Carlisle, Corbridge and possibly Bamburgh.

MEDIEVAL SCOTTISH MINT TOWNS

the use of silver was abandoned and it was replaced by copper–nickel, so that silver borrowed from the USA during the Second World War could be repaid. The threepenny piece was an exception. Instead of cupro-nickel, nickel–brass was used and the coin was made twelve-sided to make it easily distinguishable. Shillings were issued with two designs: so-called 'English' and 'Scottish' varieties, the latter showing the Scottish lion seated and holding a sword and sceptre on a Scottish crown. Unusually, different designs were used on the bronze denominations: Britannia on the penny; Sir Francis Drake's Golden Hind on the halfpenny; and a wren on the farthing. The title EMPEROR OF INDIA was relinquished in 1947 upon Indian independence.

In 1968 the Royal Mint moved from its ancient home on Tower Hill in London to Llantrisant in south Wales. Its first major task at the new site was to implement the most dramatic change of recent years: the abandonment in 1971 of the ancient system of pounds, shillings and pence in favour of a decimalized system in which only the pound survived at its original value. The new halfpenny, penny and 2 pence were in bronze and the other initial denominations in cupro-nickel: 5 and 10 pence (equivalent to the old 1 and 2 shillings) and the seven-sided 50 pence, the only coin to retain the Britannia design.

Subsequent additions to the coinage were the copper–nickel, seven-sided 20 pence in 1982 and the nickel–brass 1 pound coin introduced in 1983. The first 1 pound coin had the royal arms on the back, but gradually versions with different designs, referring to the four constituent parts of the United Kingdom, have been added: the thistle and diadem for Scotland, leek and diadem for Wales, flax for Northern Ireland and oak for England. In 1984 the halfpenny was removed from circulation.

The design of Scottish pennies was periodically changed, but a distinguishing feature for about two centuries was the use of a profile bust of the king, in contrast with the facing bust of English pennies. Otherwise the designs of Scottish coins tended to resemble the current English ones, though they were never outright copies. More importantly, the standards of weight and quality of the English coinage were also followed.

Malcolm IV (1153–65) carried on with the coinage that David I had begun. His brother, William the Lion (1165–1214), issued new coinages in about 1174, of the Cross and Pellets type, corresponding to the English Tealby issues, and in 1195, to echo the English Short Cross pennies. The latter continued under Alexander III (1249–86), but new designs were soon introduced to follow changes in England. A Scottish Long Cross coinage appeared early in the reign, and, in about 1280, a new Scottish penny, halfpenny and farthing, corresponding to Edward I's reformed coinage in England, were minted. Because of the similar appearance and standards of the English and Scottish coinages, the two were able to mingle freely in circulation. The much larger English issues provided a considerable proportion of the money circulating in Scotland, possibly more than that of its own kings.

The close links between the English and Scottish coinages continued despite the conflicts of the late thirteenth and fourteenth centuries. The next major innovation in Scottish currency came with the return of David III to Scotland after he was ransomed following capture at the Battle of Neville's Cross in 1346. He introduced gold coinage to Scotland, copying Edward III's noble for a short-lived issue. He also added $\frac{1}{2}$ groats and groats to the silver coinage on the English model, though the standards of the Scottish penny began to decline.

SCOTTISH COINS UNDER THE STUARTS

Under the Stuarts the design and standard of Scottish coinage diverged from the English pattern. Robert III (1390–1406) introduced two new denominations, the gold $\frac{1}{2}$ lion and lion (= 5 shillings). Both coins showed a crucified St Andrew on the back. The silver coinage on the other hand now more directly resembled the English design of a facing

royal bust, although it was increasingly debased. Changes in standards and revaluations became a feature of Scottish coinage and a wide range of silver denominations was used. Under James II (1460–88) the gold coinage began to be debased: his unicorn of 1484 was of 21 carat gold, not the traditional fine $23\frac{1}{2}$ carat standard. The base-silver plack replaced the old fourpenny denomination and purely base-metal farthings in copper and brass also appeared.

From the late fifteenth century there were three bands to the Scottish currency. The gold coins were usually lions and crowns of 20 and 22 shillings, with occasional larger pieces such as James V's 40 shilling ducat or 'bonnet-piece' of 1539–40 and Mary Stuart's 60 shilling ducat of 1558. The silver coinage of $\frac{1}{2}$ groat and groat was expanded by the introduction of large testoons, valued at 4 or 5 shillings Scots, under Mary from 1553, and even larger ryals of 30 shillings. The lesser coinage consisted of pennies, placks (= 4 pence), half-bawbees and bawbees (= 6 pence). The revival of portraiture on the coinage of Europe was reflected on some of these Stuart coins, as were Mary's marriages: to King François II of France and Henry, Lord Darnley.

James VI (1567–1625) took a strong personal interest in his coinage. He added new silver denominations, including the merk (16 shillings, 8 pence) and its fractions ($\frac{1}{8}, \frac{1}{4}, \frac{1}{2}$), and the thistle dollar (= 2 merks). He also produced several attractive new gold issues: a 20 pound piece in 1575–6 as well as more serviceable thistle nobles (= 14 shillings, 8 pence), lion nobles (= 75 shillings), ducats and 'hat-pieces' (both = 80 shillings), and the 100 shilling rider of 1593–1601.

When he succeeded to the English throne in 1603, James sought to

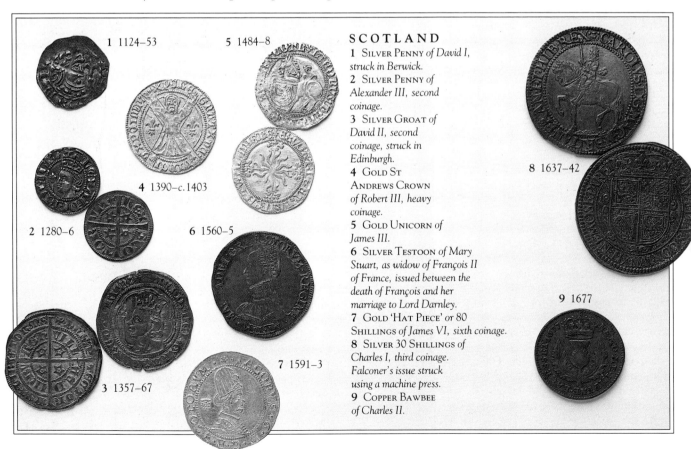

SCOTLAND

1 SILVER PENNY of David I, struck in Berwick.
2 SILVER PENNY of Alexander III, second coinage.
3 SILVER GROAT of David II, second coinage, struck in Edinburgh.
4 GOLD ST ANDREWS CROWN of Robert III, heavy coinage.
5 GOLD UNICORN of James III.
6 SILVER TESTOON of Mary Stuart, as widow of François II of France, issued between the death of François and her marriage to Lord Darnley.
7 GOLD 'HAT PIECE' or 80 SHILLINGS of James VI, sixth coinage.
8 SILVER 30 SHILLINGS of Charles I, third coinage. Falconer's issue struck using a machine press.
9 COPPER BAWBEE of Charles II.

Coin labels: 1 1124–53 · 5 1484–8 · 4 1390–c.1403 · 2 1280–6 · 6 1560–5 · 3 1357–67 · 7 1591–3 · 8 1637–42 · 9 1677

introduce equivalence to the English and Scottish coinages. Scottish coins of the same weight and fineness as English coins were issued, though the current ratio of £1 sterling to £12 Scots was maintained. The Scottish unit and crowns corresponded to the English unite and its fractions, and the silver coins, from the 1 shilling to the 60 shilling piece, paralleled the English coins from the penny to the silver crown. Differences in titles and heraldic designs differentiated the coinages. The smallest Scottish coins – 'turners' (= 1 penny), hard heads (= 2 pence) and placks in billon and copper – had no English equivalents.

The Scottish coinage was changed little under Charles I, the most notable development being the appointment of Nicholas Briot, the French engraver, to be master of the Edinburgh mint in 1635. He was responsible for some excellently produced coinage. After Charles's execution in 1649, his son was immediately accepted as king in Scotland, but the Edinburgh mint did not resume work until 1664, after Charles II was also established in England. A separate Scottish coinage was continued by the later Stuarts, the mint using improved machinery, but it was mostly in silver and copper. There was a revival of gold issues in 1701, when 6 and 12 pound pieces Scots were made using gold supplied by the Darien Company.

THE ACT OF UNION

Under Queen Anne the separate Scottish coinage came to an end. The Act of Union of 1707 provided for a uniform coinage throughout the United Kingdom. Some of the first issue was struck at the Edinburgh mint and distinguished by the initial E below the bust of the queen, but thereafter the Royal Mint provided all British coinage. Occasional issues have been produced with particular Scottish relevance, such as shillings with the Scottish arms issued under Elizabeth II until decimalization, and the current 1 pound coin, one variety of which has a thistle surrounded by a royal diadem. However, this is manufactured, like all the modern British coinage, in Wales.

1 1945
2 1987

JERSEY
1 BRONZE PENNY of George VI.　2 CUPRO-NICKEL 10 PENCE of Elizabeth II.

with the duchy of Normandy. French coins remained legal tender until the nineteenth century.

The first coins made especially for Jersey were silver 18 pence and 3 shilling tokens, produced in 1812 by the Royal Mint from Spanish dollars. Only in 1834 was English currency established as the sole legal tender, though until 1877 there were 13 Jersey pennies to the shilling. From 1841 until 1966 copper and then bronze farthings, halfpennies and pennies were intermittently issued. These coins had the sovereign's bust and the Jersey arms.

MODERN COINAGE

After the Second World War, when the Channel Islands were occupied by Germany, the pennies of 1949–54 had the phrase LIBERATED 1945 on them. Threepenny and 5 shilling pieces were issued briefly from 1957, but in 1971 Jersey had to follow the United Kingdom into decimalization, with coins corresponding to all the British denominations. Issues since 1982 have had new designs featuring different Jersey landmarks, such as the dolmen at Faldouet, instead of a coat of arms. A number of gold and silver coins have also been issued, commemorating anniversaries and royal events.

JERSEY

FIRST COINS:	1812
FIRST DECIMAL COINS:	1971
MAIN MINT:	Royal Mint
CURRENCY:	pound

THE earliest coins to be found in Jersey and the other Channel Islands are Celtic issues of the Armorican tribes from neighbouring parts of Gaul (see France). It is not certain whether this coinage, consisting mainly of base silver ¼ staters and staters, was used locally or if it was brought by refugees from the mainland, perhaps during Julius Caesar's invasion of Gaul, about 56 BC. Rome ruled the Channel Islands from the first to the late fourth century AD, though the territory was clearly of little significance to them; only a small number of Roman coins have been found.

Once Roman power in the west had declined, Frankish and French coinage provided the basic currency of Jersey for centuries, joined by English coinage after the Channel Islands passed to the English kings

GUERNSEY

FIRST COINS:	1809
FIRST DECIMAL COINS:	1971
MAIN MINT:	Royal Mint
CURRENCY:	pound

As on Jersey, coinage from the French mainland dominated Guernsey until the nineteenth century. Only since 1921 has sterling been the exclusive legal tender on Guernsey. There was a brief issue of 5 shilling silver tokens by the Bank of Guernsey in 1809, but these were soon banned. Local copper coinage began in 1830 with, eventually, coins of 1, 2, 4 and 8 doubles (from the French double tournois denomination). The 8 double piece was equal to one British penny and until 1921 there were 21 Guernsey shillings (2016 doubles) to the British pound. The Guernsey coins have the arms of Guernsey on one side and the date and value on the other. In 1864 bronze replaced copper and the size of the coins was reduced, but otherwise they stayed unchanged, as they had no ruler's head or title.

GUERNSEY
Copper 8 Doubles *of William IV*

1834

MODERN COINAGE

The smaller denominations were dropped from the currency in the coinage of 1956, to leave the 8 double piece (= 1 penny) and a new threepenny piece. A square 10 shillings in cupro-nickel was added in 1966 on the 900th anniversary of the Norman dynasty; this was the first Guernsey coin to show the ruler's head. Decimalization in 1971 finally brought the Guernsey coinage wholly in line with British issues. British denominations and materials were copied, though designs remained distinct, including the Guernsey lily on the 5 pence and Guernsey cow on the 10 pence. The new 1 pound coin of 1981, for example, is made distinctive by being square. There have been a number of commemorative crowns (25 pence pieces) issued for various royal occasions.

ISLE OF MAN

FIRST COINS:	eleventh century
FIRST DECIMAL COINS:	1971
MAIN MINT:	Pobjoy Mint
CURRENCY:	pound

UNTIL 1971, Manx coinage was intermittent and the bulk of the currency in use had been English and United Kingdom issues. Crude imitations of Irish Hiberno-Norse pennies were minted around 1020–30, but otherwise there were no local issues until 1709, when the Earl of Derby, heir to the island, issued copper halfpennies and pennies. These showed the Stanley family crest on the front and the three-legged symbol of Man on the back.

Claim to the island then passed to the Dukes of Atholl, under whom there was a further issue of halfpennies and pennies in 1758. Rights and privileges on Man were taken over by the British crown in two stages, in 1765 and 1829, and royal issues of halfpennies and pennies appeared in 1786, 1813 (made by Matthew Boulton) and 1839. Between 1811 and 1831 there was also a number of tradesmen's tokens produced in Douglas, Castletown and Ramsey.

A curiosity of the Manx coinage was that there were 14 pennies to the shilling. Through the 1839 coinage attempts were made to convert

the Manx coinage to the English reckoning of 12 pennies, but local opposition caused the coinage to be recalled to the mint. United Kingdom coins became prominent and remained the only current pieces until 1971, though brass tokens were provided during the Second World War for use in the internment camps established on the island.

MODERN COINAGE

Since decimalization in 1971, the Manx authorities have issued a complete range of coins corresponding to the English ones, but with distinct designs, such as the Legs of Man on the 10 pence and a Viking longboat on the 50 pence. New designs were introduced on the denominations in 1976, 1980 and 1984. Also a huge number of commemorative coins in gold, silver, platinum and other metals have been produced for collectors and tourists. These relate to sporting events (such as the Moscow Olympics and the Mexico Soccer World Cup), royal occasions, and anniversaries (in particular the millennium of Tynwald, the Manx parliament). The bullion coins include revivals of old English designs, such as the gold angel and the noble, though the Manx version is in platinum.

ISLE OF MAN
1 Copper Halfpenny Token *of the earl of Derby.*
2 Cupro-Nickel 25 Pence *of Elizabeth II.*
3 Bronze Penny *of Elizabeth II.*

IRELAND

FIRST COINS:	late tenth century
FIRST DECIMAL COINS:	1971
MAIN MINT:	Dublin
CURRENCY:	pound

THE issuing of coinage in Ireland has, until recently, usually been the prerogative of its conquerors and invaders. A few Roman coins made their way to the country, but comparatively extensive finds of coins first appear in the tenth century when Viking invaders brought

MEDIEVAL IRISH MINTS

Title page from the Book of Kells, c.700 AD. Early Irish manuscripts are the inspiration behind the most recent Irish coin designs.

with them quantities of Anglo-Saxon silver pennies. It was the Norse invaders who began the minting of coin in Ireland. They set up settlements in coastal areas, including Waterford, Wexford, Cork, Limerick, Carlingford and Dublin.

Nordic kings ruled in Dublin for three centuries and produced their coinage there. King Sihtric Silkenbeard began the issuing of coinage, the so-called Hiberno-Norse series, in about 995. His issues copied the contemporary English coins of Ethelred II: they were the Crux and Long Cross pennies. Sihtric's Long Cross coins bear his name and title: SIHTRIC REX DYFLIN. The Long Cross type remained the basic coin design for most of the eleventh century, though its inscriptions become unintelligible and the weight of the penny declined to half that of the English coin. Some late pennies have a crozier on them and probably represent an ecclesiastical issue, perhaps commemorating St Patrick. The Hiberno-Norse coinage ended in the mid-twelfth century, its last stage consisting of crude, uniface, base issues.

MEDIEVAL IRELAND

The revival of coinage in Ireland followed the invasion of Norman lords from England after 1169. King Henry II visited Ireland to secure the homage of these lords and some of the Irish chieftains. In 1172 he appointed John, his son, Lord of Ireland. Around 1185 a coinage of silver pennies was issued in John's name, to be followed in about 1190 by an issue of farthings and halfpennies from mints at Dublin, Waterford, Kilkenny, Carrickfergus and Downpatrick. John

1 995–1000 **2** 1207–11 **3** 1279–84

IRELAND

1 SILVER PENNY of Sihtric, King of Dublin, imitation of English Crux type, struck in Dublin.
2 SILVER PENNY of John, third coinage, struck in Dublin by the moneyer Roberd.
3 SILVER PENNY of Edward I, class I, struck in Dublin.
4 SILVER GROAT of Edward IV, anonymous 'Crown' coinage, struck in Dublin.

4 1460–3

de Courcy, a lord of Ulster, also issued a coinage in his own name around 1185–1205.

The thirteenth century saw a quite extensive coinage produced at intervals from Irish mints as the English kings established their power. The coins issued were all pennies of the English weight and silver content, together with equivalent farthings and halfpennies. The designs also corresponded to the current English issues. The first was of King John from between about 1205 and 1211, minted at Dublin, Limerick and Waterford, and it corresponded to John's renewal of the Short Cross coinage in England in 1205. The distinguishing feature on the Irish coins was a triangular border around the king's head on the front of the penny; this was retained throughout the century. The back of John's coins had a distinctive and unusual design of a sun, crescent moon and stars.

The next Irish coinage was much less original in appearance: it copied the English Long Cross design exactly, except that it kept the triangular border. The Dublin mint was active to produce this issue for three years from 1251. The Long Cross design was briefly revived in Ireland early in Edward I's reign in an issue produced by the moneyer Richard Olof, but in 1279 a new Irish coinage kept step with developments in England. The new design again copied Edward's English coins, but the distinctive Irish triangle still survives, though now inverted. Dublin, Waterford and Cork were at various times involved in the coinage, which consisted of farthings and halfpennies as well as pennies, until it ceased in 1302. Scarcely any activity is recorded for the Irish mints in the fourteenth century: only a few halfpennies of Edward III in 1339–40 produced in Dublin.

Only in the later fifteenth century did the English kings again think of issuing coins in Ireland. English coins were always legal tender in Ireland, and Irish coinage circulated readily in England. The late medieval developments were to change this. Under Henry VI there was a brief issue of pennies at Dublin from 1425 to 1426, but it was the Yorkists who really revived minting in Ireland on any scale. However, with Edward IV's coinage of 1460, debasement of standards was begun, the new coins being lighter than their English equivalents. The government stood to make a profit on issuing such lightweight coinage, though it sought to prevent it from circulating in England and weakening the English currency.

By 1467 the Irish penny was equal only to an English halfpenny. Pennies, ½ groats and groats were issued, with eventually a double-groat of 8 pence Irish to correspond to the English groat (4 pence). Mints operated at Dublin, Drogheda, Limerick, Waterford, Cork and Trim during this period. Several different designs followed each other under Edward IV and Richard III. These often featured a simple crown instead of a royal bust. The last Yorkist coinage, that of 1483–90, introduced a design of three crowns, and a small issue of groats of this type was produced at Dublin and Waterford for the pretender Lambert Simnel as 'Edward VI'. Production of the Three Crowns type continued under the Tudor Henry VII until 1494, when the king removed the Yorkist Earl of Kildare from power. A new coinage of the English type was then issued from Dublin alone.

SIXTEENTH CENTURY

For about 30 years the Dublin mint was inactive. Henry VIII produced an Irish coinage in 1534 but this was struck at the London mint. It consisted of ½ groats and groats with a new design: on the front the royal arms and on the back an Irish harp flanked by the initials of the king and his current wife. This coinage was much more base even than the earlier Irish issues, and the profits made as a result may have encouraged the king to commence debasement in England.

Minting at Dublin was revived under Edward VI to produce a coinage initially in the name of Henry VIII and still very base. Henceforth Tudor coinage for Ireland carried the ruler's portrait on the front. Shillings (= 12 pence) of an English design were introduced for the first time in 1552, these being also the first dated Irish coins. New issues continued under Mary with groats and shillings made after her marriage to Philip of Spain.

At first Elizabeth I continued the issue of base money but in 1561 she followed her reform of the English coinage with a recoinage in Ireland, which consisted of groats and shillings of over 90 per cent fine silver. However, this good start was not maintained and there were no further Irish issues until the end of the reign. In the meantime the Irish

IRELAND

5 Base Silver Harp Groat of Henry VIII, with the initials of Henry and Anne Boleyn.

6 Silver Shilling of Elizabeth I, 'Fine' coinage.

7 Silver Piece of Inchiquin money, marked 19 dwt. 8 gr. (19 pennyweights, 8 grains) struck with the authority of the Lord Justice of Ireland.

8 Copper St Patrick's Half-penny showing St Patrick on the front and King David playing the harp on the back.

5 1534–5

7 1642

8 1678

6 1561

9 1689

10 1760

currency came to consist of an array of English, Spanish and other foreign coins. The last Tudor coinage, of 1601, reverted to a very base issue of halfpennies, copper pennies and poor silver threepences, sixpences and shillings. James I minted fine silver sixpences and shillings for Ireland in London but after 1607 this ceased and English money became the standard currency.

SEVENTEENTH CENTURY

Apart from English coins, the mid-seventeenth century saw the use of a range of emergency money associated with the civil war. Emergency supplies from the royal government included the Inchiquin money, crudely formed lumps of metal stamped with their weight, as well as the Dublin money of 1643 and the Ormonde coinage of 1643–4, both of which had marks of value. There was a brief gold issue in 1646 and a well-made silver coinage of ½ crowns and crowns (= 5 shillings) issued in the name of Charles II in 1649 after the execution of his father, Charles I.

The royalist Confederation of Catholics produced copper farthings and halfpennies from their capital of Kilkenny in 1642 and, in 1643–4, so-called 'rebel money' of silver ½ crowns and crowns distinguished by a large cross. Emergency issues were also made by Parliamentary garrisons besieged in the ports of Munster. Meanwhile, as in England, a variety of private tokens were issued by inns and shops for use in small-scale local transactions.

Henceforth coinage issued in, or for use in, Ireland was almost always of base metal. It was some time before a royal coinage reappeared. Until 1679 private tokens remained in plentiful supply, joined in 1674 by the St Patrick's money: farthings and halfpennies made in Dublin of uncertain legal status. In 1680 royal halfpennies were introduced and the private tokens prohibited.

James II's attempt to regain the throne through Ireland in 1689–90 produced the famous Gunmoney: sixpences, shillings, ½ crowns and crowns made in base metal obtained by melting old cannon and scrap. These were to be redeemed in good money after the king's restoration and had the month as well as the year of issue on them, perhaps to stagger their exchange.

Issues of farthings and halfpennies were thereafter made intermittently: in 1692–4 under William and Mary, and in 1696 under William III alone; William Wood's unsuccessful brass issues, produced under royal patent in 1721; coins made in London under George II in 1736–55 and 1760 and in the later eighteenth century. Alongside the 1760 issue appeared imitation halfpennies, known as Voce Populi coins, because of the phrase which replaced the royal name on them.

English silver coinage was in short supply in Ireland and in 1804 the Bank of Ireland issued bank tokens made from restruck Spanish 8 real pieces produced by Matthew Boulton in Birmingham. The London mint provided some silver 5, 10 and 30 pence tokens in 1805–6, 1808 and 1813. New copper coins were supplied in 1805–6 (by Matthew Boulton) and 1822–3, after which only United Kingdom currency was permitted in Ireland.

MODERN IRELAND

With the creation of the Irish Free State in 1920, a new national coinage was needed. In 1928 this appeared in a range of silver and bronze denominations, from the farthing to the ½ crown, which had on the front the Irish harp and on the back a variety of animals, such as a horse, salmon and woodcock. The declaration of the republic had no immediate impact on the coinage, though from 1951 cupro-nickel replaced silver. A decimal currency system was adopted in Ireland in 1971 as in England. Some of the older animal images were retained for the cupro-nickel 5, 10 and 50 pence, whereas for the bronze ½, 1 and 2 pence pieces new bird designs have been produced echoing early Irish illuminated manuscripts.

DENMARK

FIRST COINS:	tenth century
FIRST DECIMAL COINS:	1873
MAIN MINT:	Copenhagen
CURRENCY:	krone

MORE Roman coins have been found in Denmark than in any of the other Scandinavian countries, which indicates that a fairly considerable trade must have existed with the empire. The most notable finds have been of silver denarii of the second century AD and of gold solidi of the fifth and sixth centuries. However, the coins were not used within Denmark as currency. They seem to have been regarded simply as precious metals, and some were used as jewellery, inspiring local copies, with designs on one side only.

VIKING PERIOD

The next influx of coin occurred in the tenth century. Viking trade with the Arab world via Russia resulted in a flood of silver dirhems which were, however, often remelted into rings and bars of metal. Yet trade with the Carolingian Empire had already inspired the beginnings of Danish coinage. Carolingian silver deniers were minted at Dorestad in what is now the Netherlands and these issues were imitated by

11 1966

12 1979

IRELAND

9 BASE-METAL HALF-CROWN of James II's Gunmoney coinage, made from old cannon, bells and other scrap metal.
10 COPPER HALFPENNY, Voce Populi coinage, the phrase 'by the voice of the people' replacing the king's name.
11 CUPRO-NICKEL SHILLING of the Republic of Ireland.
12 BRONZE TWOPENCE of the Republic of Ireland.

Men in a boat, from a Viking picture stone at Lillbjars, Gotland, eighth century. It was Viking success in trading, raiding and settlement which first brought the use of coinage to Scandinavia.

Viking rulers, apparently struck at the island of Hederby, the major Danish trading centre. Many of these early coins have a ship design, though others show buildings and animals. This type of coinage survived until about 990. From about 975 until 990 a group of coins with a cross design became common, perhaps struck in Jellinge in Denmark proper, rather than Hederby.

ENGLISH INFLUENCE

From 1000 the main influence on Danish coinage was England. The first Danish king to issue coins in his own name was Sweyn Forkbeard (985–1014). His coins, silver penninge, copied the Crux penny of Ethelred II of England (979–1016): a profile bust of the king and his titles and a cross with the letters CRVX (Latin for cross) in its quarters. It was Ethelred's issues which were paid to Sweyn in great quantities as Danegeld and it is even likely that Anglo-Saxon moneyers were responsible for Sweyn's coinage.

English influence continued under Cnut the Great, king of both Denmark (1019–35) and England (1016–35). His Danish coinage was large and struck at several mints: Lund, Viborg, Ribe, Orbæk and possibly Hederby. His son Harthacnut (1035–42) added Aalborg, Aarhus and Gori. Most of Cnut's coins have a royal bust on the front and a small cross in the centre of the back with the names of moneyer

and mint. Other coins have religious images: the Hand of God, the Lamb of God or the symbol of the Trinity. The Anglo-Saxon influence continued under Cnut's successors, though it was gradually challenged by Byzantine contributions under Sven Estridsen (1047–74), with issues bearing images of Christ, the Virgin and Byzantine crosses.

MEDIEVAL PERIOD

From the reign of Erik Lam (1137–46), the archbishops of Lund had a share in the issues of the Lund mint, the most productive in the kingdom. Issues showed the king on one side and the archbishop on the other. The bishops of Ribe and Roskilde also had a share in the coinage. Briefly in the mid-twelfth century bracteate coins replaced the usual two-sided penninge, but the latter was restored under Valdemar the Great (1157–70). The most common images on the coins continued to be busts of the kings and bishops, though St Lawrence, patron saint of Lund, appears on issues of that mint under Cnut IV (1182–1202). A novelty from the reign of Valdemar II (1202–41) is the first European coin to be dated, a penning inscribed ANNO DOMINI MCCXXXIIII (1234).

In the late thirteenth century symbols like a crown or sword and single letters often denoting the mint or ruler became the main coin-designs. Because of debasement the penning was by now virtually a copper coin. The coinage reached its low point under Christopher II (1319–32), and good foreign coins were sometimes used in its place, particularly hohlpfennige of the Hanseatic cities of northern Germany. Better money was needed for Baltic trade, and the cities of Flensborg and Ribe took the initiative with a new coin, a 4 penninge piece, the hvid, copying the German witten. Royal issues of hvids soon followed these city coinages, under Erik of Pomerania (1397–1439). He also issued 3 penninge sterlings (copying English pennies) and 1 penning coins in copper. Larger silver coins appeared: the soesling (= 6 penninge) and gros (= 9 penninge). The soesling bore the design of a shield on the front with the three Danish lions instead of the usual crown or letter on the back.

In the later fifteenth century Danish coinage had to respond to two more developments. First, the Hanseatic cities, Denmark's main trading partners, adopted a larger silver coin, the schilling of 12 pfennigs. Denmark followed suit in 1444 under Christopher of Bavaria: his skilling had the Danish lions in a shield on the front and his coat of arms on the back. Second, by this time gold coinage was familiar in the Baltic in the shape of florins from Lübeck, the Rhineland and Hungary and English nobles. The first Danish gold coin appeared under King Hans (1481–1513), the noble of 1496, a large and beautiful coin showing the king seated on a throne. He also issued more useful gulden, based on the Rhineland gulden (= 32 skillings), which showed St Cnut on the front.

SIXTEENTH AND SEVENTEENTH CENTURIES

In the sixteenth century Denmark followed the current trends of European coinage, introducing a large silver coin, the silver gulden, from 1514, alongside good silver skillings. In 1522 an even larger daler appeared, the image of Frederik I on the front making it the first Danish coin to carry a realistic portrait of the ruler. A period of civil war from 1533 saw coinage in the name of the Danish Privy Council and rival claimants to the throne: Christiern II and Christian III. A feature of this period was the issue of klippe ('clipped') coins, crudely cut and often debased small denominations. The bulk of the coinage was in very bad shape until a reform in 1540 improved standards.

From 1544 until 1873 the rigsdaler was the basis of the Danish monetary system, with marks and skillings (16 skillings = 1 mark; 3 marks = 1 daler) as lesser denominations. Occasionally special trade coins were produced for general European trade: gold portugalösers and Hungarian gulden; silver lion dalers for the Dutch trade and krones for the East India trade. Gold riders and Rhenish gulden were struck in quantities to pay troops during the Kalmar War (1611–13) and the Thirty Years War (1618–48). From the reign of Frederik III (1648–70) the silver krone (= 4 marks), popular in other states of northern Europe, became the principal coin. When Christian V succeeded Frederik in 1670, he began the custom of issuing an accession daler carrying portraits of both himself and his predecessor.

From around 1670 gold ducats (= 12 marks) began to be issued, some of them showing the Danish fortress of Christiansborg in Guinea. These coins became the major large denomination, with silver coins of ½, 1, 2, 4, 8, 12 and 16 skillings providing the lesser coinage and usually showing the king's portrait or monogram. Most were debased, following the pressures of the Great Northern War (1700–21). Paper money played an increasing role, though 3 million ducats were minted under

Frederik V (1746–66), as gold was the preferred pay of the army, and large quantities of dalers were issued under Christian VII (1766–1808). A new daler type, the Albert daler, was struck for Baltic trade and Spanish-style piastres were made for the Danish–Asiatic Company. The first large-scale issue of copper coins occurred in 1771, when ½ skillings and skillings were minted in this metal.

EIGHTEENTH AND NINETEENTH CENTURIES

In 1808–13 the Danish currency collapsed under the combined pressures of the Napoleonic War, the Continental System (Napoleon's attempt to exclude Britain from European trade) and wars with England in 1801 and 1807. A desperate appeal for people to give up their silver plate for coining produced the ⅙ rigsdaler of 1808, inscribed 'Voluntary Offering to the Fatherland 1808'. National bankruptcy followed in 1813. Gradually the coinage was restored, issued by the National Bank. The principal coin was the new rigsbankdaler (= 96 skillings) and early copper rigsbank tokens were soon replaced by rigsbank skillings and multiples (2, 3, 4, 8, 16 and 32 skillings). A little gold coinage was produced: Frederiks d'or (= 10 rigsdalers) based on French gold coins and intended mainly as trade coins. In the mid-

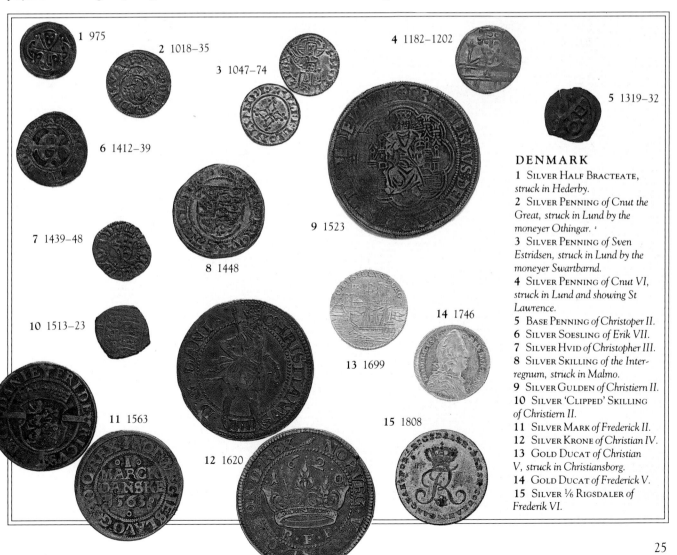

DENMARK

1 SILVER HALF BRACTEATE, struck in Hederby.
2 SILVER PENNING of Cnut the Great, struck in Lund by the moneyer Othingar.
3 SILVER PENNING of Sven Estridsen, struck in Lund by the moneyer Swartbarnd.
4 SILVER PENNING of Cnut VI, struck in Lund and showing St Lawrence.
5 BASE PENNING of Christoper II.
6 SILVER SOESLING of Erik VII.
7 SILVER HVID of Christopher III.
8 SILVER SKILLING of the Interregnum, struck in Malmo.
9 SILVER GULDEN of Christiern II.
10 SILVER 'CLIPPED' SKILLING of Christiern II.
11 SILVER MARK of Frederick II.
12 SILVER KRONE of Christian IV.
13 GOLD DUCAT of Christian V, struck in Christiansborg.
14 GOLD DUCAT of Frederick V.
15 SILVER ⅙ RIGSDALER of Frederik VI.

nineteenth century Danish coinage was fairly stable and uniform with older coins having been replaced. Paper money, convertible into silver, provided the higher denominations, though gold issues did not wholly cease.

In 1873 Denmark went onto the gold standard and adopted a decimal coinage based on the krone of 100 ore in concert with the other Scandinavian countries. The coins issued were the 1, 2 and 5 ore in bronze, 10 and 20 ore and 1 and 2 kroner in silver, and the 10 and 20 kroner in gold. From this time onwards the higher denominations had the ruler's portrait on one side, the remainder a crowned monogram.

MODERN COINAGE

During the First World War silver and bronze were replaced by cupro-nickel and iron. Bronze was restored in 1926, but cupro-nickel was retained for the 10 and 25 ore and aluminium-bronze introduced for the ½, 1 and 2 kroner coins. Gold ceased to be issued in 1931. As in many German-occupied countries, zinc was used for coinage during the Second World War and, unusually, was afterwards retained for the 1 and 2 ore until these coins ceased to be issued in 1972. During the war the Faeroe Islands, occupied by Britain, were provided with a Danish-style coinage struck in London.

Since the war, Danish coinage has remained relatively stable under Frederik IX (1947–72) and Margrethe II (1972–). The 5 ore is now the smallest coin produced, in copper-clad bronze, and, like most

DENMARK
16 SILVER KRONE of Christian IX.
17 ALUMINIUM-BRONZE
2 KRONER of Christian X.
18 CUPRO-NICKEL KRONE of
Margarethe.

denominations, is greatly reduced in size. The ½ and 2 kroner coins have been withdrawn, but cupro-nickel coins of 5 and 10 kroner have been added to the coinage. Danish commemorative coins are produced only to mark royal anniversaries and events, the most recent being the coming of age of the current crown prince in 1986.

GREENLAND

Denmark is responsible for the modern recolonization of Greenland, but coinage made specifically for the island has appeared only in the twentieth century. Previously Danish coinage was in use, but from

1910 a number of token issues were produced by companies active in Greenland: Thule-Kap York in 1910, Greenland Minedrift in 1911 and Cryolite Mining and Trade Company in 1922. In 1926 an official coinage was provided which consisted of cupro-nickel 25 ore, aluminium-bronze 50 ore and 1 and 5 krone. The coins were minted with the Danish arms on the front and a polar bear on the back. There have been a few subsequent issues of 1 krone pieces: minted in 1957, 1960 and 1964.

FINLAND

FIRST COINS:	about 1410
FIRST DECIMAL COINS:	1859
MAIN MINT:	Helsinki
CURRENCY:	markka

SMALL quantities of Roman coins have been found in Finland, but evidence for the use of coinage on any scale begins to appear only in the Middle Ages. The Swedish Vikings' trading links with the East brought numbers of Islamic silver dirhems and Byzantine coins to Scandinavia. There were some Finnish imitations of them, but these coins seem to have been intended as jewellery. In the tenth and eleventh centuries various western coins were imported, mostly Anglo-Saxon and German issues, though probably intended for use more as bullion than currency.

SWEDISH COINAGE

Only late in the Middle Ages does evidence of coinage use become relatively common. The area was incorporated into Sweden in the twelfth and thirteenth centuries and Swedish money came into general use, with some input also from Livonia and Denmark. The first local minting occurred from about 1410 until 1558, when coins in the name of Swedish kings were struck at Turku, though not continuously. The coins produced were mostly silver ortugs, then the largest Swedish denomination. They had simple designs: a shield, a king's initial, a crown or the initial A (for Aboa, the Latin name for Turku). All bore the king's name, except a regency issue in the name of St Henry, patron saint of Finland.

Gustavus I (1523–60) introduced larger, dated denominations into both Sweden and Finland: ores, marks and multiples of them. The new coins had a portrait of Gustavus and a heraldic shield. Minting at Turku in the 1550s was inspired by a war with Russia, which also accounts for simple, square coins being struck as well as the more usual round ones. These had a mark of value, but no portrait.

RUSSIAN GRAND DUCHY

Swedish rule ended in the war of 1808–9, after which Finland became a grand duchy under the Russian tsar. The ruble was proclaimed the monetary unit of the country. The new Bank of Finland began the issue of banknotes in 1811 but did not proceed with initial plans for a Finnish coinage. Instead Russian issues circulated, exchangeable with the notes, and Swedish money was also in common use. This compli-

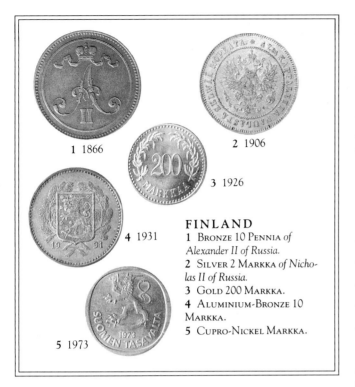

FINLAND
1 BRONZE 10 PENNIA of
Alexander II of Russia.
2 SILVER 2 MARKKA of Nicholas *II of Russia.*
3 GOLD 200 MARKKA.
4 ALUMINIUM-BRONZE 10
MARKKA.
5 CUPRO-NICKEL MARKKA.

with the new 1 markka equal to 100 old ones. Thus the new 1 penni equalled the old 1 markka. The design of the coinage was slightly altered to reflect this, but major new designs were only introduced on the markka in 1964 and the 5 markka in 1972 and 1979. The latter coin replaced the smallest value banknote. As in many countries, aluminium is now used for the smallest coins (1 to 10 penni), bronze for the medium range and cupro-nickel and aluminium–bronze for the highest value coins (markka and 5 markka). Finland also produces commemorative coins and was the first country to issue an Olympic commemorative, at the time of the 1952 Helsinki games.

SWEDEN

FIRST COINS:	late tenth century
FIRST DECIMAL COINS:	1874
MAIN MINT:	Stockholm
CURRENCY:	krona

As with the other Scandinavian countries, a little Roman coinage reached Sweden, presumably in exchange for such local goods as amber, furs and iron, and it would have been treated as treasure, not currency. It was, however, the Swedish Vikings who dominated the trade routes through eastern Europe and Russia to the Arab empire of the Middle East and who therefore played the leading part in the major importation of Islamic silver dirhems into Scandinavia in the ninth century. By the later tenth century the volume of Islamic currency in Sweden was diminishing, and German and Anglo-Saxon issues took its place almost entirely in the eleventh century. In particular payments of Danegeld by Ethelred II of England brought large quantities of English money into Scandinavia, as did the rule of King Cnut in both England and Denmark.

cated situation was ended by a reform in 1840 which prohibited the use of coinage other than the Russian and Finnish issues.

In 1859 the Russian government accepted the introduction of a separate monetary unit for Finland: the markka ($= \frac{1}{4}$ ruble), divided into 100 pennia. A mint was set up in Helsinki, and in 1864 Finland at last received its own currency of notes and coins in silver and bronze. Coin types were unchanged until 1917 except for changes in the tsar's initials in the crowned monogram shown on the bronze coins: the 1, 5 and 10 pennia. The silver coins, 25 and 50 pennia and 1 and 2 markka, showed the Russian imperial eagle. All coins had their value and date on the back. Gold coins of 10 and 20 markka were added in 1878, inscribed with their weights to signify Finland's adherence to the Latin Monetary Union. After the tsar's abdication in 1917, an uncrowned double-headed eagle was used on the coins.

INDEPENDENCE
With Finnish independence (6 December 1917) a new design was called for: the Finnish lion, standing on one sword and brandishing another. This has remained the main design for most Finnish coins. Cupro-nickel replaced silver in 1920, the first examples being produced by the Heaton Mint in Birmingham as the Finnish mint was at capacity production with the copper coinage. A small gold issue was struck in 1926, but Finland then came off the gold standard. Higher denominations in aluminium–bronze were introduced: 5, 10 and 20 markka in 1928 and 50 markka in 1952. From 1956 to 1960 silver coins of 100 and 200 markka were produced. During the Second World War, cheaper metals had been used: first copper and then iron.

MODERN COINAGE
Inflation had greatly reduced the value of the long-standing Finnish denominations and in 1963 a major reform established a new basis,

THE FIRST COINS
Meanwhile, the first local Swedish coins had begun to appear. Around 995 King Olof Skottkonung brought to Sweden Anglo-Saxon moneyers to strike coinage for him at Sigtuna. This coinage was interrupted but was resumed by his son, Anund Jakob (about 1022–50). As in Denmark, the first royal Swedish coinage copied the contemporary Crux penny of Ethelred II. These first local issues were small and there were no more for over a century, until about 1150. In the meantime, the bulk of coinage in use continued to be foreign imports. Furthermore, uncoined precious metal, as jewellery and ingots, was still used to make payments on a considerable scale.

SWEDEN
1 SILVER PENNING of Olof
Skottkonung

1 *c.995–c.1022*

MEDIEVAL PERIOD

The revival of minting in the mid-twelfth century produced two varieties of penningar. From about 1150 to 1260–70 a small, thin type of silver coin was manufactured probably on the island of Gotland, or else at mainland Kalmar. This had an image on each side while the other variety was a bracteate coin. This became the dominant type of penny in central and eastern Europe in the twelfth and thirteenth centuries and spread to Sweden from Germany in the reign of Knut Eriksson (1167–96). Uppsala seems to have been the main mint, with Lodose also important. The usual designs used in Sweden included a crowned head, letter (usually a royal monogram), animal, crown or sword, and occasionally an indication of the mint or king's name.

From about 1300 Sweden returned to the use of two-sided coins, though still striking only the penning, which was declining in value through debasement. A higher denomination was clearly needed and under King Albrekt of Mecklenburg (1364–89) the ortug (= 4 penningar initially) was introduced, minted principally at Stockholm and Kalmar. The first ortug showed the king's head and a cross, but under Erik of Pomerania the design of the shield of Sweden with its three crowns was introduced. The ½ ortug, or fyrk, was produced under Sten Sture the Elder (1470–97). The first dated Swedish coins also come from this period, inscribed 1478. It was at this time that foreign gold coins, mostly Hungarian and Rhenish gulden and English nobles, began to play a part in Swedish currency and in Baltic trade generally.

SIXTEENTH AND SEVENTEENTH CENTURIES

Major innovations occurred under Gustaf Vasa (1521–60), following current European trends. He introduced the larger silver riksdaler to Sweden, where it became the basis of the currency until 1873. Gustaf's daler (32 ore = 4 marks = 1 daler) showed the king holding a sword and orb on the front and his coat of arms on the back. The dalers of 1540–59 introduced a long-standing design to the back of the coin: a standing figure of Christ. Smaller silver coins, the 1 and 2 ore and the ½ mark and mark (= 4 and 8 ore respectively), made their appearance to fill the gap between the daler and the old-established denominations. In 1576–7 Gustaf also struck emergency rectangular klippe ('clipped') coins, multiples of the ore, as did successive Swedish kings in the sixteenth and seventeenth centuries.

Whereas the riksdaler's standards were maintained, because of its status as an internationally reputable coin, the other Swedish coinage was subjected to considerable debasement in the later sixteenth century, reaching its lowest point in the reign of Johan III (1568–92). The exception was the new gold coinage, based on the Hungarian gulden and also intended for a role in international trade. Designs employed on coins at this time, as well as portraits of the kings, both busts and full and half-length figures, included the badge of the house of Vasa of a sheaf of corn and, particularly on dalers of Karl IX (1598–1611), the name of Jehovah in Hebrew letters.

Great developments in Swedish coinage occurred under the country's most renowned king, Gustaf II Adolf (1611–32). Though he produced a substantial issue of traditional coins headed by the riksdaler, the pressures of his involvement in the Thirty Years War encouraged him to initiate the exploitation of one of Sweden's greatest resources for coinage purposes: her huge deposits of copper, in particular at Stora Kopparberg, the Great Copper Mountain, at Falun. He issued coins from the fyrk to the 2 ore in pure copper from mints at

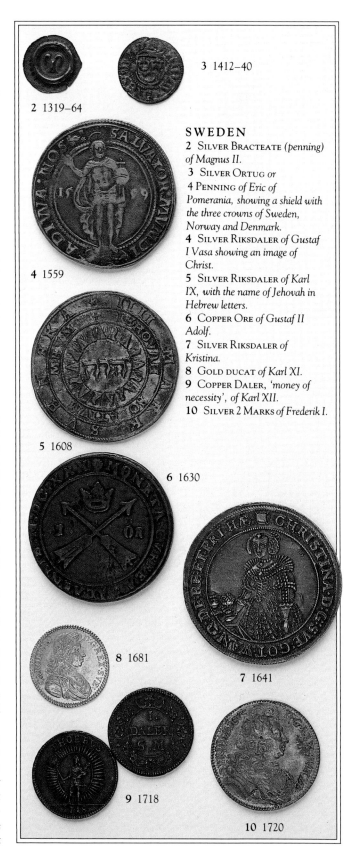

2 1319–64

3 1412–40

4 1559

5 1608

6 1630

8 1681

7 1641

9 1718

10 1720

SWEDEN

2 SILVER BRACTEATE (*penning*) of Magnus II.
3 SILVER ORTUG or
4 PENNING of Eric of Pomerania, showing a shield with the three crowns of Sweden, Norway and Denmark.
4 SILVER RIKSDALER of Gustaf I Vasa showing an image of Christ.
5 SILVER RIKSDALER of Karl IX, with the name of Jehovah in Hebrew letters.
6 COPPER ORE of Gustaf II Adolf.
7 SILVER RIKSDALER of Kristina.
8 GOLD DUCAT of Karl XI.
9 COPPER DALER, 'money of necessity', of Karl XII.
10 SILVER 2 MARKS of Frederik I.

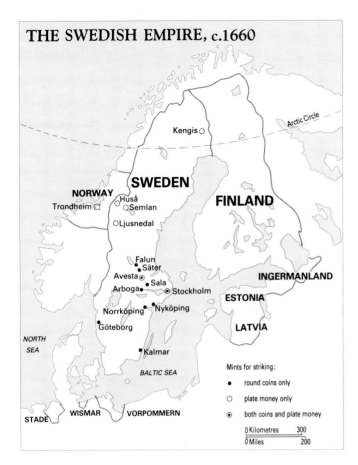

THE SWEDISH EMPIRE, c.1660

Kengis

Arctic Circle

SWEDEN

NORWAY
Trondheim   Huså
               Semlan

Ljusnedal

FINLAND

Falun
Säter
Avesta
Sala
Arboga   Stockholm

INGERMANLAND

Norrköping   Nyköping

ESTONIA

Göteborg

LATVIA

NORTH
SEA

Kalmar

BALTIC SEA

Mints for striking:
●   round coins only
○   plate money only
◉   both coins and plate money

0 Kilometres   300
0 Miles   200

STADE   WISMAR   VORPOMMERN

EIGHTEENTH AND NINETEENTH CENTURIES

Karl XII's reign (1697–1718) was a time of crisis for Sweden, witnessing her eclipse by Russia as the major northern power. The crown was put under great financial pressure and the coinage was revalued, with silver coinage withdrawn altogether, older plate money overstamped to higher values and an emergency token copper coinage of 1 daler pieces issued in 1715–19. The situation improved under Ulrika Eleanora (1718–20) and Frederik I (1720–51) and the old types of coinage were restored. Some of the gold coins of the mid-eighteenth century are marked to indicate the source of the metal used: the mines at Adelfors and Dalarna. The last plate money was manufactured under King Adolf Frederik (1751–71). It had never been exactly popular as currency, being much too cumbersome, and it was decided to abandon the system of plate money and paper notes, replacing the plate money with a currency predominantly of silver, with copper used only for small change.

The new coinage was based on the daler of 48 skillings, with 4 ore to the skilling. Thus the pattern of Swedish money in the late eighteenth and nineteenth centuries was much more similar to that of other European countries: petty coinage in copper, silver riksdalers and fractions and gold ducats. The types were also conventional: the royal portrait and coat of arms on the larger pieces and a crowned monogram and crossed arrows on the smaller silver and copper. The fineness of the coinage was lowered in 1830, and in 1855 a new riksdaler was introduced, in value a quarter of the old coin, which, known as the riksdaler species, was still issued as a high-value piece.

SWEDEN

11 Silver Krona of Oscar II.   **12** Cupro-Nickel Krona of Karl XVI Gustav.

Sater, Nynkoping and Arboga. Most had a design based on crossed arrows on the back.

His daughter, Queen Kristina (1632–54), took the development a step further. While maintaining silver marks and riksdalers, she authorized the issue of very large denominations in copper, produced from rectangular pieces of copper plate: the famous Swedish plate money. The denomination, date and ruler's monogram were stamped in the centre and at the corners of the large plates. These coins were not token as they contained their full value in copper. Kristina's issues included plates of 1, 2, 4, 8 and 10 dalers. Thereafter, the 8 daler was usually the largest piece issued. Part of the motive behind the use of copper coinage was that, by absorbing a proportion of the copper output internally, Sweden could keep the international price of the commodity relatively high.

For nearly 200 years most of the Swedish plate money was manufactured at the mint at Avesta, near Falun, by mechanical means developed by the mint master Marcus Koch and his sons in 1644. The practical inconvenience of the larger copper denominations encouraged the early use of paper money in Sweden and its use has been continuous from the 1720s. Coinage in silver was produced alongside the plate money and, under Karl XI (1660–97), minting in gold was revived with ducats (= 2 riksdalers) being struck to the internationally recognized standards until 1868. However, the precious metal coinage did not have wide internal circulation nor, of course, did the high-value presentation coins which were sometimes struck in the eighteenth century.

MODERN COINAGE

In 1872 Sweden helped set up the Scandinavian Monetary Union and introduced a corresponding new coinage based on the krona of 100 ore. The coins then issued were the 1, 2 and 5 ore in bronze, the 10, 20 and 50 ore and 1 and 2 kronor in silver (of different finenesses) and the 5 and 10 kronor in gold. The royal portrait appeared on the krona and larger coins, and the royal monogram on lesser issues. Gold ceased to be issued in 1925 and the 5 kronor is now the highest value currency coin produced. Iron was briefly used for the bronze denominations during the First World War. The use of base-silver lasted until the 1960s, when cupro-nickel gradually replaced it. Some denominations have not been produced in recent years: the 1 and 2 ore have not been struck since 1971, victims of inflation, and the 2 kronor has also disappeared. The use of precious metal is now confined to commemorative pieces, usually 100 kronors in silver.

NORWAY

FIRST COINS:	late tenth century
FIRST DECIMAL COINS:	1874
MAIN MINT:	Kongsberg
CURRENCY:	krone

Only very small numbers of Roman coins have been found in Norway. The first real influx of coinage into the land came with the Viking age, and even then the Norwegian Vikings concentrated their attention on non-coin producing areas: the Faeroes, Scottish islands, Ireland, Greenland, Iceland and North America. A few Anglo-Saxon and Frankish coins passed to Norway in the ninth century but were probably treated as jewellery. Islamic silver dirhems became more prominent and may have been used as means of payment. There is no Norwegian counterpart to the tenth-century issues of Denmark and Sweden, but Anglo-Saxon and German coins became increasingly important in the 980s and 990s and are found now all over the country. The English element in Norwegian currency dropped dramatically after 1050, but the role of Danish issues increased.

The Cuerdale hoard: part of the Viking hoard buried in Lancashire by a Norse raiding expedition around 904. The hoard included jewellery and silver ingots as well as large quantities of English coinage.

MEDIEVAL PERIOD

The minting of coins in Norway itself probably began under King Olaf Tryggvason (995–1000) with a copy of the Crux penny of Ethelred II of England. His coins and those of Olaf Haraldsson (1015–30), which also copied Anglo-Saxon designs, are very rare. The main Norwegian series began under King Harald Hardrade (1047–66) about 1047 with silver pennies of the mysterious Triqueta design, which seems to have had a religious or magical meaning. The issuing of pennies continued

under Harald's successors, although by the late eleventh century they had become very thin. More recognizable designs were used, usually a facing crowned bust. However, by the twelfth century the Norwegian penny was a bracteate, usually bearing simply a single letter.

Only under Magnus VI (1263–80) were coins with designs on both sides restored, with a penny design showing English influence in the facing royal bust and the cross on the back. Erik (1280–99) and Haakon V (1299–1319) maintained this larger penny. The Norwegian lion holding an axe appears on some of Erik's issues whereas Haakon's coins include some with the inscription MONETA DE ASLOIA, the first reference to a mint at Oslo. However, after this period the coinage reverted to small bracteates with a single-letter design until the end of Norwegian independence in 1387, when the Danish king inherited the Norwegian throne.

UNION WITH DENMARK

Norway remained in union with Denmark until 1815. Throughout this period the Norwegian titles and symbol of a lion and axe appeared on most Danish issues. At first the only coins struck in Norway were small base-silver hvids. Some larger silver coins were issued by the arch-bishop of Trondheim, Olaf Engelbrektsson (1523–37), and later in the sixteenth century a mint at Kongsberg began to strike coins equivalent to Danish denominations but with different designs, usually featuring

the king's bust or crowned monogram on one side and the Norwegian lion very prominently on the other.

In the later sixteenth and seventeenth centuries these coins generally included a range of silver issues from the skilling through the mark to the speciedaler and its fractions. There were very rare gold ducats minted under Frederik III (1648–70), whose Norwegian issues were fully parallel to his Danish ones, his output of Norwegian speciedalers being particularly large. The rich silver deposits at Kongsberg fuelled the large output of the Norwegian mint in this period. In 1704, 1732, 1733, 1749 and 1788 a special reisedaler or 'travel dollar' was struck in Denmark to pay for the current king's travels in Norway. These usually had some flattering reference such as

'Courage, Loyalty, Bravery and All That Gives Honour, Can the Whole World Learn among the Mountains of Norway' (1704). During the reign of the last Danish king to rule Norway, Frederik VI (1808–14), the mint at Kongsberg was still very active but its issues no longer carried distinctive Norwegian designs.

SWEDISH CONQUEST
In 1812 Norway was conquered by Sweden and until 1905 coinage was issued in the name of the Swedish kings. The denominations and designs used remained basically the same: the skilling and daler multiples and fractions mostly in silver, with some base silver and copper for the very smallest coins. In 1872 the Scandinavian kingdoms aligned their currencies in the Scandinavian Monetary Union. This produced a new decimal monetary system based on the krone of 100 ore. The new coins were of bronze (1, 2 and 5 ore), silver (10, 25 and 50 ore and 1 and 2 kroner) and gold (10 and 20 kroner).

KINGDOM OF NORWAY
The decimal system survived the establishment of Norway as a separate kingdom under Haakon VII in 1905, though some of the coin designs were changed, notably the introduction of the figure of St Olaf on the back of gold issues. However, gold coins ceased to be produced in 1910 and cupro-nickel replaced silver in 1920. From 1921 to 1951 the coins

ICELAND

FIRST COINS:	1922
FIRST DECIMAL COINS:	1922
MAIN MINT:	Reykjavik
CURRENCY:	krona

DESPITE Iceland's early existence as an independent republic (from 930 until 1262, when it came under Norwegian control), native coinage is an entirely modern feature, making an appearance only with the separation from Denmark in 1918. Previously its currency had been that of its mainland neighbours, Norway and Denmark, even before they had direct control of the island.

UNION WITH DENMARK
In 1918 Iceland became a virtually independent kingdom in union with Denmark. It issued its first coinage in 1922 with bronze, aluminium–bronze and cupro-nickel issues made in Copenhagen and marked with the monogram of the Danish King Christian X. The denominations consisted of the eyrir, 2, 5, 10 and 25 aurar, the krona

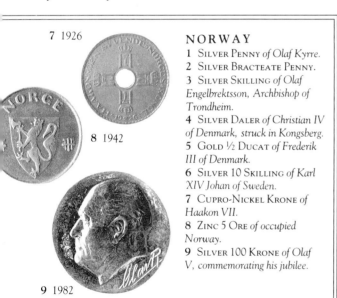

7 1926

NORWAY
1 SILVER PENNY of Olaf Kyrre.
2 SILVER BRACTEATE PENNY.
3 SILVER SKILLING of Olaf Engelbrektsson, Archbishop of Trondheim.
4 SILVER DALER of Christian IV of Denmark, struck in Kongsberg.
5 GOLD ½ DUCAT of Frederik III of Denmark.
6 SILVER 10 SKILLING of Karl XIV Johan of Sweden.
7 CUPRO-NICKEL KRONE of Haakon VII.
8 ZINC 5 ORE of occupied Norway.
9 SILVER 100 KRONE of Olaf V, commemorating his jubilee.

8 1942

9 1982

1 1926   2 1959   4 1981

3 1966

ICELAND
1 BRONZE 5 AURAR of Christian X of Denmark.
2 ALUMINIUM-BRONZE KRONA.
3 NICKEL-BRASS 2 KRONUR.
4 CUPRO-NICKEL 5 KRONUR.

had the distinctive feature of a hole in the centre in the middle of a cross formed by four crowned monograms. During the world wars unusual metals were used for coinage: iron in 1917–21 and zinc in 1941–5, while under German occupation. Some 1942 10, 25 and 50 ore pieces in nickel–brass were struck for the Norwegian government in exile in London.

Since the Second World War the Norwegian coinage has been fairly stable, in cupro-nickel and bronze. The 5 kroner coin was added in 1963 and the 10 kroner (in copper–zinc–nickel) in 1983 and new designs were produced in 1951, 1958 and 1974. A number of commemorative issues have been made, notably a silver 100 kroner minted in 1982 in honour of the 25th anniversary of King Olaf V's accession.

(= 100 aurar) and 2 kronur. They had the national coat of arms on the front and the value and name of the country on the back. In 1942 the issues that were sent from Denmark were of zinc: in countries under German occupation copper was too valuable a material to be used for petty coinage.

INDEPENDENCE
Iceland finally broke away to form a republic in 1944, while Denmark was under German occupation. Since full independence several new denominations have been added: 5, 10 and 50 kronur. In 1981 a new coinage was introduced, based on a revaluation of Icelandic money; the new krona was equal to 100 old kronur.

FRANCE

FIRST COINS:	fifth century BC
FIRST DECIMAL COINS:	1794
MAIN MINT:	Paris
CURRENCY:	franc

THE Mediterranean coast of Gaul (ancient France) was colonized by Greeks in ancient times, with the city of Massalia (Marseilles) founded about 600 BC. These Greek settlers produced the earliest coinage to be issued in France, dating from about 500 BC. The coins are small silver pieces, closely resembling contemporary coins issued by the Greeks of western Turkey, the homeland of the founders of Massalia. Many of these coins were discovered in a hoard from Auriol, so this word is used to describe the series.

Massalia continued to issue coins for centuries. From the late fourth century the typical coins of Massalia were silver drachms, with a female head on the front and a lion on the back, and smaller silver obols. Bronze coins were issued from the third century, and production of these and the silver coins continued after the Roman conquest of Mediterranean Gaul in the second century. The coinage of Massalia was widely used in southern Gaul and was imitated by some of the native Gallic peoples of the region. Massalia's coinage finally ceased in the middle of the first century BC.

To the west of southern Gaul, the major influence on the early native coinage was the money issued by the Greek colonies on the coast of north-eastern Spain, Rhode and Emporion. In particular, the rose design on the coins of Rhode was much imitated, though its shape was changed to that of a cross. These silver coins, called 'monnaies a la croix', circulated widely in southern and south-western Gaul in the second and first centuries BC. To the east of the Massalia region the earliest coins were silver pieces with horse-head designs imitating Carthaginian coins; then from the late second century BC Roman coins provided the prototypes for the native issues. Bronze coinage was also issued throughout southern Gaul from the second century BC.

CELTIC TRIBES

Away from the southern coastal regions most of ancient Gaul was inhabited by Celtic tribes, whose first contact with coinage came when their warriors fought as mercenaries for Mediterranean city-states and kingdoms, from as early as the fifth century BC. The major employers of Gallic mercenaries were the Greek cities of Syracuse in Sicily and Tarentum in Italy, Carthage in North Africa, and the kingdom of Macedon. When the Gallic tribes began to issue their own coinages, from the third century BC, they imitated the issues of these Mediterranean states.

The principal metal used for native coinage in most of Gaul was gold, and by far the most important influence was the gold coinage of Philip II of Macedon (359–336 BC). His gold stater with the head of Apollo and a charioteer on the back was the prototype for numerous Celtic imitations in the Rhineland, Gaul and Britain. Within Gaul the imitations show wide variations in style, from quite close copies on some issues of eastern and central Gaul to extravagantly barbarous versions further north. Some north Gallic issues have barely recogniz-

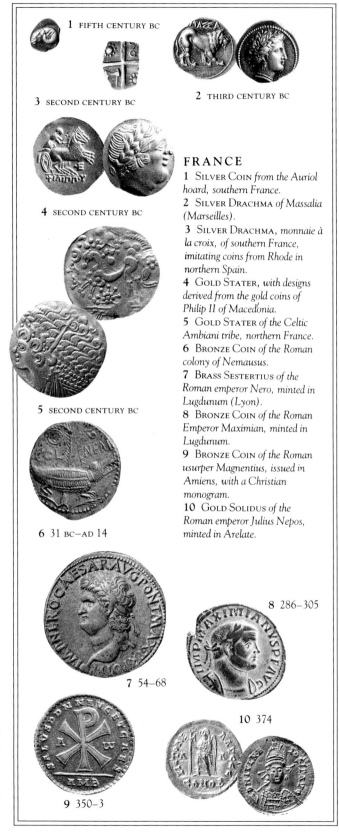

1 FIFTH CENTURY BC

2 THIRD CENTURY BC

3 SECOND CENTURY BC

4 SECOND CENTURY BC

5 SECOND CENTURY BC

6 31 BC–AD 14

7 54–68

8 286–305

9 350–3

10 374

FRANCE

1 SILVER COIN *from the Auriol hoard, southern France.*
2 SILVER DRACHMA *of Massalia (Marseilles).*
3 SILVER DRACHMA, *monnaie à la croix, of southern France, imitating coins from Rhode in northern Spain.*
4 GOLD STATER, *with designs derived from the gold coins of Philip II of Macedonia.*
5 GOLD STATER *of the Celtic Ambiani tribe, northern France.*
6 BRONZE COIN *of the Roman colony of Nemausus.*
7 BRASS SESTERTIUS *of the Roman emperor Nero, minted in Lugdunum (Lyon).*
8 BRONZE COIN *of the Roman Emperor Maximian, minted in Lugdunum.*
9 BRONZE COIN *of the Roman usurper Magnentius, issued in Amiens, with a Christian monogram.*
10 GOLD SOLIDUS *of the Roman emperor Julius Nepos, minted in Arelate.*

able abstract designs similar to those on the Celtic coins of Britain. The coins of Syracuse and Tarentum also influenced Gallic coinage, being copied in Armorica (Brittany) and again in northern France.

As well as issuing gold coins, many of the Gallic tribes produced silver and bronze coins from the second century BC. In the Armorican region bronze coins were not issued, but the gold and silver coins became increasingly alloyed with base metals. Debasement was also a characteristic feature of the gold and silver coins issued by the tribes of northern Gaul at the time of Julius Caesar's invasions. In the wake of the Roman conquest of Gaul production of native gold coinage ceased, but local silver and bronze issues tended at first to increase and Roman influence can clearly be seen in the spread of Latin inscriptions and Roman coin designs.

ROMAN GAUL

The first Roman coins to be issued in Gaul were silver denarii struck in 118 BC to mark the foundation of the Roman colony of Narbo Martius (Narbonne). Roman coins were also issued during the period of conquest in the first century BC, but it was not until the reign of Augustus (31 BC–AD 14) that mints were set up for regular production

demand in the first half of the first century AD there was widespread production in Gaul of locally made bronze imitations of Roman coins.

The Lugdunum mint of the early imperial period operated until the reign of Vespasian (69–79), by which time the use of Roman coinage was fully established throughout Gaul. Following the closure of the Lugdunum mint, for the next 200 years virtually all the coinage arriving in Gaul was minted in Rome. The only locally struck Roman coinage was that issued by Clodius Albinus (193–7) between 195 and 197, during a period of civil war.

LATE ROMAN EMPIRE

Minting resumed in Gaul in the 260s when the province was part of the secessionist empire of Gallic usurpers, and continued after the recovery of the western provinces by the official emperor Aurelian (270–5) in 274. The identities of the Gallic mints of this period are uncertain. The principal mints were in the Rhineland, not France, but Lugdunum probably produced some issues before and after Aurelian's reconquest, and later, from 313, an additional mint was opened at Arelate (Arles). It is also possible that the usurper Carausius (286–93) minted coins in northern France, which was part of his British-based empire; and later

Left: The Roman aqueduct at Nîmes, first century BC.

Below: The amphitheatre at Arles, first to second centuries AD.

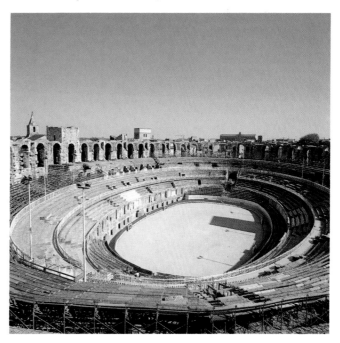

of Roman coinage. At the same time the last remaining native Gallic coinages came to an end.

The mints of Nemausus (Nîmes) and Vienne (Vienna, which struck only civic coinage) operated only under Augustus. Lugdunum (Lyon), on the other hand, became one of only two official Roman mints in the western half of the empire, the other being Rome. Lugdunum's purpose was to supply Roman coinage to the north-western provinces. When the supply of bronze coinage failed to meet

another usurper, Magnentius, established a mint at Amiens, which issued coins from 350 to 353.

The two official mints of the late Roman Empire in France, Lugdunum and Arelate, were operating through most of the fourth century, in the course of which they issued standard Roman coins in all three metals: gold, silver and bronze. Output declined early in the fifth century as the empire crumbled, but Arelate continued to issue rare gold coins for the officially recognized emperors down to the 470s.

CAROLINGIAN MINTS

0 Kilometres 300
0 Miles 200

● Mints of Pepin and Carloman
○ Mints of Charlemagne
□ Mints of Louis the Pious

BALTIC SEA

NORTH SEA

ENGLISH CHANNEL

Dorestad
Tiel
Maastricht Cologne
Thérouanne Tournai St Trond Aachen
Quentovic Condé Namur Liège Bonn Frankfurt
Arras St Gery Huy Dinant
Amiens Cambrai
Corbie Noyon Trier Mainz
Rouen Laon Mouzon Worms
Senlis Rheims Verdun Regensburg
Paris Chelles Roucy Metz
Meaux
Avranches
Chartres Ramerupt
Rennes Châteaudun Sens Troyes
Le Mans Orléans Langres Strasbourg
Angers Auxerre
Nantes Tours Besançon
Bourges Nevers Châlon
St Maixent Chur
Melle Alps
Brioux
Saintes Limoges Clermont Lyons Treviso
Angoulême Vienne Milan Verona Venice
Pavia Mantua
Bordeaux Piacenza Parma
Cremona
Agen Rodez Apennines ADRIATIC
Dax Uzès Avignon SEA
Toulouse Arles Lucca
Carcassonne Béziers Marseilles Pisa
Narbonne Siena
Pyrenees
Ampurias Rome
Gerona
Barcelona MEDITERRANEAN SEA
TYRRHENIAN SEA

Meuse *Scheldt* *Moselle* *Rhine* *Danube* *Seine* *Loire* *Saône* *Rhône* *Garonne* *Ebro* *Po*

11 EARLY SEVENTH CENTURY

12 c.670–750

13 751–814

14 814–40

15 840–77

FRANCE

11 GOLD TREMISSIS *of Merovingian France, struck in Banassac, Aquitaine.*
12 SILVER DENIER *of Merovingian France, struck in Paris.*
13 SILVER DENIER *of Charlemagne, struck at the mint of St Martin of Tours.*
14 GOLD SOLIDUS *of Louis the Pious.*
15 SILVER DENIER *of Charles the Bald,* XPISTIANA RELIGIO *type.*

Meanwhile, copies of late Roman gold coins were issued by Germanic invaders in Gaul, firstly the Vizigoths, whose kingdom in the fifth century was centred on Toulouse, and next the Burgundians, who ruled parts of Gaul from the mid-fifth century until their conquest by the Franks in 532–4. The Burgundians also issued small silver and copper coins in their own name.

MEROVINGIAN AND CAROLINGIAN COINAGE

By the beginning of the sixth century the kingdom of the Franks under Clovis, first of the Merovingians, dominated all France apart from a coastal strip in the south. The Roman Empire still provided the bulk of the coinage in use in the barbarian states of the west and its issues were copied when rulers began to produce their own coins. The first

Frankish ruler to do so was Theodebert I (534–48), who issued a Roman-type gold solidus distinguished by bearing his own name instead of that of the emperor. However, the real foundation of Frankish Merovingian coinage lies in late sixth-century Provence. Here were produced imitations of the Roman tremisses, the third of a solidus, though of a lighter weight and deviating somewhat in style from official Roman coins. The main mints producing these local issues were Marseilles, Arles, Uzès and Viviers in the period 574 to 628.

From about 620 the emperor's name on these Provençal tremisses was replaced by that of the Frankish king, Chlotar II (584–629). Meanwhile, other Merovingian kings had also begun to strike tremisses outside Provence before the seventh century and did so in their own names. However, most Merovingian coins did not in fact carry the name of a king, but showed only the name of one of the many mints and 1600 moneyers then active. The most notable of these moneyers was Eligius, St Eloi, patron saint of goldsmiths and moneyers. He was active around 620 to 640, producing coins for successive kings as well as in his own name. The design of the Merovingian tremissis reflected its Roman origin: a bust on one side, often in primitive style, and on the other a cross, monogram or other simple design, like the chalice on the plentiful issues of the mint at Banassac.

The Merovingian coinage began in good gold but in the seventh century it was becoming increasingly debased with silver. By the end of the century the coinage was solely made of silver: the first deniers. These became the basis of the long-lasting monetary system (12 denier = 1 sou; 20 sou = 1 livre). The design and organization of the coinage apparently remained as before, most coins just naming mint and moneyer, not ruler.

This situation changed with the replacement of the Merovingian dynasty by the first Carolingians, Pepin the Short (751–68) and Charlemagne (768–814). The coinage gradually came under royal authority, demonstrated by the royal name or monogram becoming a feature of all issues and single designs being used by many different mints. A new type of denier, broader, flatter and thinner, replaced the Merovingian type. Charlemagne reinforced uniformity with his reform of about 793–4. His new, heavier deniers had his name and title on the front and the mint name on the back with, in the centre, a cross and the Karolus monogram. Charlemagne's last coinage appeared after his coronation as emperor at Rome in 800; it carries the imperial title and has a profile bust with laurel wreath and military cloak. The back of the coin usually showed a church or temple and the inscription CHRISTIANA RELIGIO.

Charlemagne's denier designs were frequently re-used throughout the ninth century by his son Louis the Pious and later descendants who divided up the empire. Coins were produced at mints throughout the separated kingdoms, in Germany, Italy and the Low Countries as well as West Frankia. Most plentiful were the issues of Charles the Bald (838–77), in particular the GRATIA D-REX ('king by the grace of God') coins of 864–923, produced at 125 mints. The denier was always the most common, though there was some striking of halves, or obols, and a very small issue of gold solidi under Louis the Pious.

MEDIEVAL COINAGE

In the late ninth and early tenth centuries the royal monopoly of coinage began to be eroded. The right to coin was conceded by the Carolingian rulers of West Frankia to the counts, viscounts, abbots and bishops of the kingdom, though it was exceptional for minor lords to obtain minting privileges. The great age of these feudal coinages lasted from the tenth to the thirteenth century. Initially royal deniers were copied, but distinctive designs developed. Often a popular type remained unchanged for some time, especially if there were successive rulers of the same name. Sometimes a large number of local mints used similar designs, such as the very stylized head common in much of central France and originating in the issues of the count of Blois at Chinon. In other places, such as Languedoc, relatively few mints dominated large areas. Some of these feudal coinages became extremely important, for instance the deniers of the count of Champagne's mint at Provins known as provisini, which circulated widely in eastern France and Italy in the twelfth and early thirteenth centuries. The main feudal mints, listed by region, appear in the table.

Freed from centralized control, the local rulers could debase their

PRINCIPAL FEUDAL MINTS OF FRANCE

Northern France:
Royal mints: Paris, Pontoise, Mantes, Dreux, Senlis, Montreuil, Étamps.
Beauvais, bishops.
Corbie, abbey of St Pierre.
Abbeville, counts of Ponthieu.
Boulogne, counts.
Artois, counts.
Ypres, commune.
Douai, commune.
Lille, commune.
Orléans, viscounts.

Western France:
Nantes and Rennes, counts/ dukes of Brittany.
Guingamp, counts of Penthièvre.
Angers, counts of Anjou.
Le Mans, counts of Maine.
Rouen, dukes of Normandy.
Tours, abbey of St Martin.

North-eastern France:
Provins and Troyes, counts of Champagne.
Meaux, bishops.
Rheims, archbishops.
Auxerre, counts.
Dijon and Auxonne, dukes of Burgundy.
Châlon-sur-Saône, counts.
Cluny, abbey.

Berry and central France
Souvigny, abbey.
Bourbon, lords.
Charenton, lords.
Nevers, counts.
Sancerre, counts.
Gien-Donzy, lords.
Déols-Châteauroux, lords.
Issoudun, lords.
Bourges, viscounts.

Blois/Chartres:
Blois and Chartres, counts.
Châteaudun, viscounts.
Vendôme, counts.

Aquitaine:
Melle, counts of Poitou.
Bordeaux, dukes of Guyenne.
Marche and Angoulême, counts.
Limousin, viscounts and abbey of St Martial.
Auvergne, counts and chapter of St Clermont.
Le Puy, bishops.

Languedoc–Rousillon:
Toulouse, counts.
Albi, viscounts.
Cahors, bishops.
Rodez, counts.
Viviers, bishops.
Melgueil, counts (with counts of Montpellier, then bishops of Maguelonne).
Carcassonne, counts.
Rousillon, counts.

Kingdom of Arles:
Provence, counts.
Arles, archbishops.
Avignon, bishops.
Gap, bishops.
Valence, bishops.
Vienne, archbishops.
Lyon, archbishops.

Bar and Lorraine:
Lorraine, dukes.
Metz, bishops.
Toul, bishops.
Verdun, dukes of Bar.

coinages, whether through desire for profit or in the competition for limited amounts of bullion. The denier issues declined, resulting in coins of different values; for example, the deniers of Le Puy came to be worth only a quarter of those of Melgueil. Slowly the kings of France began to reassert their authority. The coinage of the early Capetians, kings from 987, were no more important than other feudal issues. Only with Philippe I (1060–1108) do coins from the royal mints become plentiful, though like the feudal coinages they were debased.

The great expansion of the role of the royal coinage began under

MEDIEVAL FRANCE

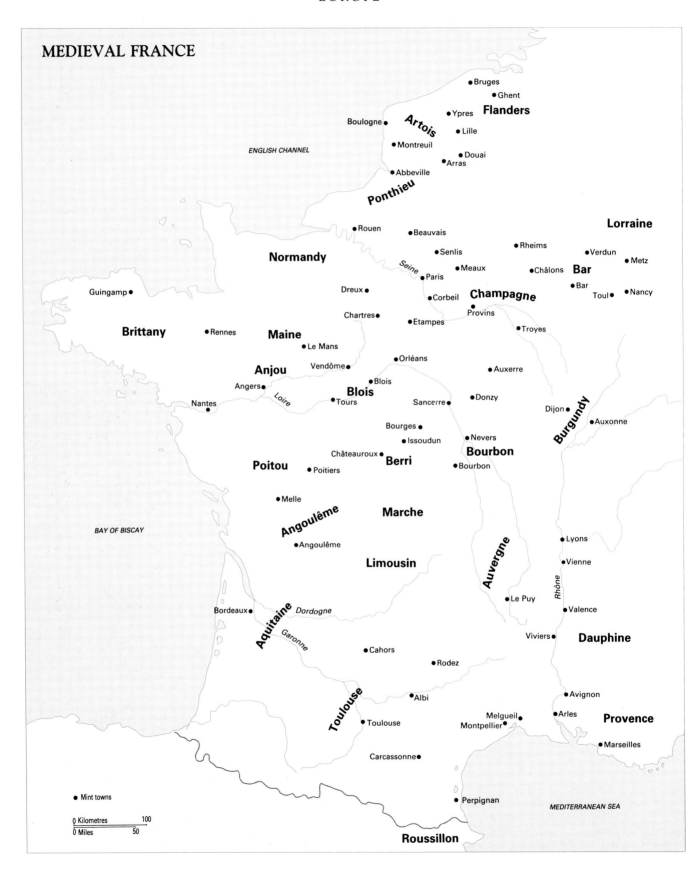

ENGLISH CHANNEL

Artois
Flanders
• Bruges
• Ghent
• Ypres
Boulogne •
• Lille
• Montreuil
• Douai
• Arras
• Abbeville

Ponthieu

Lorraine

• Rouen
• Beauvais
Normandy
• Rheims
• Verdun
• Metz
• Senlis
Seine
• Meaux
• Châlons
Bar
• Paris
Champagne
• Bar
• Nancy
Dreux •
• Corbeil
• Provins
Toul •
Chartres •
• Etampes
• Troyes

Guingamp •

Brittany
• Rennes
Maine
• Le Mans
• Orléans
• Auxerre
Anjou
Vendôme •
Burgundy
Angers •
• Blois
Blois
• Dijon
Nantes •
Loire
• Tours
Sancerre •
• Donzy
• Auxonne
• Bourges
• Issoudun
• Nevers
Poitou
Châteauroux •
Berri
Bourbon
• Poitiers
• Bourbon

BAY OF BISCAY

• Melle
Marche
Angoulême
Auvergne
Rhône
• Lyons
• Angoulême
• Vienne
Limousin
Bordeaux •
Aquitaine
Dordogne
• Le Puy
• Valence
Garonne
Viviers •
Dauphine
• Cahors
• Rodez
• Albi
• Avignon
Toulouse
• Arles
Provence
• Toulouse
• Melgueil
• Montpellier
• Marseilles
Carcassonne •

• Mint towns

0 Kilometres   100
0 Miles   50

• Perpignan
MEDITERRANEAN SEA

Roussillon

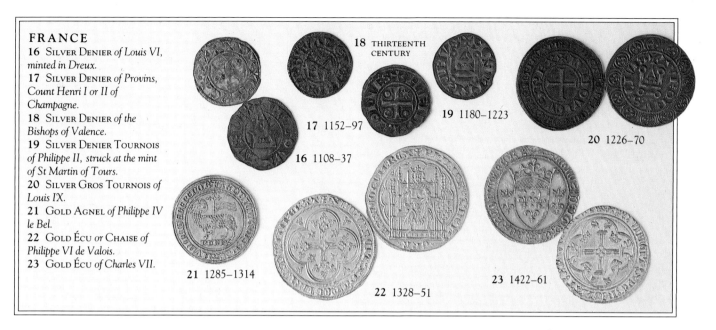

FRANCE

16 SILVER DENIER *of Louis VI, minted in Dreux.*
17 SILVER DENIER *of Provins, Count Henri I or II of Champagne.*
18 SILVER DENIER *of the Bishops of Valence.*
19 SILVER DENIER TOURNOIS *of Philippe II, struck at the mint of St Martin of Tours.*
20 SILVER GROS TOURNOIS *of Louis IX.*
21 GOLD AGNEL *of Philippe IV le Bel.*
22 GOLD ÉCU *or* CHAISE *of Philippe VI de Valois.*
23 GOLD ÉCU *of Charles VII.*

18 THIRTEENTH CENTURY
17 1152–97
19 1180–1223
16 1108–37
20 1226–70
21 1285–1314
22 1328–51
23 1422–61

Philippe II Augustus (1180–1223). The denier parisis, the issues of the main Capetian mint in Paris, and the denier tournois, taken over from the abbey of St Martin, became the most common coins of the kingdom. Coins with the parisis and tournois designs were struck at several mints. Reckoning based on the denier tournois was the most common way of reckoning in medieval France.

Louis IX (St Louis) (1226–70) further advanced the importance of royal money by establishing that all other coins were to have purely local currency, whereas the king's issues were valid throughout the kingdom. He also introduced the gros tournois, a large silver coin worth 12 deniers tournois. Gold coinage was successfully launched by his grandson, Philippe IV, the Fair (1285–1314), inaugurating a splendid and beautiful sequence of gold coins in the early fourteenth century, particularly under Philippe VI (1328–50), the first Valois king. Notable were the agnel (initially equalling 20 sou) with its Lamb of God design, and the écu (= 16 sou, 8 deniers) or chaise with its image of the enthroned king.

The fourteenth century also saw the beginnings of the Hundred Years War between England and France. This had a dramatic impact on the French coinage, as the resulting financial pressures encouraged the kings to debase their money in search of profits. As the existing silver denominations were debased with copper into 'black money', new silver coins were introduced to provide the higher-value pieces and restore confidence in the currency. Gold issues were relatively unaffected, though new types appeared, notably the franc à cheval (= 20 sou) of Jean II, struck to commemorate his release from captivity in England after the Battle of Poitiers.

The weakness of the French kings encouraged their most powerful nobles to begin coining gold and larger silver pieces. Most prominent were those with large territories outside France: the count of Flanders, the duke of Burgundy and the king of England, as duke of Aquitaine. The magnificent gold coins of Edward III and the Black Prince in Aquitaine rivalled those of the regal French series. Henry V of England's successes after Agincourt (1415) enabled him and his son, Henry VI, to issue coins as kings of France, particularly silver blancs

Medieval bankers: stained-glass from Chartres Cathedral. The representation of merchants, bankers and moneyers was common in Gothic art.

(= 10 deniers) and gold saluts (= 25 sou) from several mints, notably in Normandy, before the English were eventually expelled in the first half of the fifteenth century.

The restoration of peace under Charles VII (1422–61) enabled the French coinage to be reformed. Gold issues were dominated by the écu, showing the shield of France, and demi-blancs and blancs of various designs provided the silver. Small change existed as mailles tournois (= ½ denier), deniers and doubles (= 2 deniers) in billon. Louis XI (1461–83) introduced new lesser coins: the liard and hardi (both equalling 3 deniers). Stability in the coinage was largely retained for the rest of the Middle Ages. Regional versions of some coins were issued in Dauphiné, Brittany and Provence.

THE ANCIEN RÉGIME

The sixteenth century saw the impact of the Renaissance on French coins, encouraged by the participation of the kings in the Italian Wars. The new large silver teston (= 10 sou) was introduced in 1514 with a realistic portrait of the king, Louis XII (1498–1515). Under François I (1515–47) the complicated medieval system of secret marks which indicated the various royal mints was replaced by a system of single letters. Portraiture became well established on the larger silver coins, the teston, the ¼ écu (= 15 sou) and the silver franc (= 20 sou), introduced by Henri III (1574–89). This king also began coinage in pure copper instead of base silver with his machine-made doubles and deniers tournois from 1575, not at the main royal mint, where the moneyers resisted the introduction of mechanization, but at the separate Monnaie du Moulin.

With the succession of the Protestant Henri IV, the first Bourbon king, in 1589 a brief civil war erupted, during which the opposition Catholic League issued coins in the name of the Catholic claimant, Charles X, but Henri's renunciation of his Protestantism in 1594 eroded resistance to his rule. King of Navarre in his own right, Henry IV brought this title and coat of arms onto the French coinage. The minority of Louis XIII (1610–43) saw the last revival of non-regal coins as several great nobles produced copper issues, mostly doubles tournois, stoking inflation until their output was cut back in the 1630s

The War Salon at Versailles, showing Coysevox's wall relief of Louis XIV. The representation of the Sun King with classical symbols featured in all branches of artistic depiction under Louis' patronage, including his coinage.

FRANCE
24 Silver Teston *of Francois I.*
25 Silver Franc *of Henri III.*
26 Copper Double Tournois *of Henri IV.*
27 Copper Double Tournois *of Gaston, Prince de Dombes.*
28 Gold Louis *of Louis XIV*
29 Silver Écu *of Louis XV.*
30 Silver 30 Sols *of Louis XVI, monnaies constitutionelles.*
31 Copper 5 Centimes *of the First Republic, Year 8.*

and 1640s. The issues of the princes of Dombes were particularly extensive. A major reform of 1640–1 established the louis d'or (= 10 livres) as the main gold coin, with the king's portrait on one side, and the silver écu (= 60 sous) and its fractions for silver coinage.

ROYAL MINT-MARKS IN THE SIXTEENTH CENTURY

Paris	A	Bayonne	L
Rouen	B	Toulouse	M
Dieppe	B (1592–4)	Montpellier	N
Saint-Lô	C	Nantes	N T
Lyons	D	Dijon	P
Tours	E	Troyes	S
Angers	F	Bourges	Y
Poitiers	G	Rennes	Z 9
La Rochelle	H	Aix	7 & (from 1550)
Limoges	I	Marseille	7 ft
Bordeaux	K		

This coinage system remained virtually intact throughout the long reign of Louis XIV (1643–1715), successive portraits showing the king's progression from adolescent to ageing ruler, but although the coins issued did not change, the valuations given to them had to rise. Full mechanization of the minting system was achieved under the mint master Jean Varin at the start of the reign. The problem of small change had not been solved in the 1640–1 reform, and issues of 1, 2 and 4 sou pieces in billon and copper liards were produced, often overstruck on earlier coins or revalued because of the financial pressures of Louis's foreign wars.

The coinage of Louis XV's reign (1715–74) differed little in appearance and denominations from the well-established types. However, at first it was produced against a background of confusion caused by the extensive issue of paper money by John Law's Banque Royale. After a financial crash, a hard-currency system was restored in 1720. The year 1726 witnessed a review, after which the coinage

MINTS AND MINT MARKS OF THE NAPOLEONIC EMPIRE

29 1761

30 1791

31 1800

remained stable until 1785: the silver écu and gold louis were struck to consistent standards and the issue of the petty coinage of the country was kept under strict control.

REVOLUTIONARY AND NAPOLEONIC FRANCE

The course of the French Revolution was reflected on the coinage of the period. Louis XVI's portrait remained during the years of 'constitutional' kingship, but the royal coat of arms on the backs of the coins was replaced by designs illustrating the Spirit of France. In the turmoil of these years paper money was revived, *assignats* exchangeable with an issue of copper tokens, 'medals of confidence', most notably those of Monneron Frères in Paris.

In 1792 the republic was declared. In the new republican calendar, coinage was begun in year II (1793–4), the first French decimal coinage replacing the ancient system of livre, sou and denier with one of 100 centimes to the franc and a denomination system which has largely survived. In 1795–6 a female head wearing a cap of liberty, the personification of the republic, was first used on a copper coinage of 1, 5 and 10 centimes. Under the consulate and empire the head of Napoléon Bonaparte, increasingly represented in a Roman imperial style, was used on the coinage. New denominations were issued: $\frac{1}{4}$, $\frac{1}{2}$, 1, 2 and 5 francs in silver and 20 and 40 francs in gold. This coinage was made current throughout those lands under the direct rule of the emperor and was manufactured at mints in Turin, Rome, Utrecht and Geneva, as well as in nine French mints.

THE NINETEENTH CENTURY

Napoléon's range of denominations in precious metal was maintained after the Bourbon Restoration (1814–30) under Louis XVIII and Charles X, though the pre-revolutionary designs of the king's bust and the royal arms were revived. There were no monetary innovations under Louis Philippe's July Monarchy of 1830–48, though instead of the royal arms, the back showed simply the value of the coin within a laurel wreath. During the Second Republic (1848–52) the design of the coinage harked back to the Revolution, with the 20 franc piece illustrating first the Spirit of France and then the female head wearing the cap of liberty. The motto LIBERTÉ, ÉGALITÉ, FRATERNITÉ usually appeared on the backs of the coins, but on the silver 5 franc coin it appeared on the front along with a representation of the choices of Hercules. An innovation was the revival of copper coinage in the shape of 1 centime pieces.

Even before the proclamation of the Second Empire in 1852, Louis Napoléon had had his bust displayed on the coinage as president of the republic. He immediately had the coinage altered to portray him as the Emperor Napoléon III (1852–70). On the larger denominations his imperial coat of arms was shown on the back. The 5 franc piece became gold and denominations were added – 5, 10, 50 and 100 francs in gold and a range of base-metal coins in bronze of 1, 2, 5 and 10 centimes. The backs of the bronze issues carried an imperial eagle. There were still seven mints producing national coinage: Paris, Bordeaux, Lille, Lyons, Marseilles, Rouen and Strasbourg, though by the end of the empire, only Paris, Bordeaux and Strasbourg remained active. Very high-value issues were provided by paper money produced by the Banque de France.

France played the leading part in the foundation of the Latin Monetary Union at the Paris Exposition of 1865, an attempt to create currency acceptable across Europe. The countries involved, initially France, Italy, Belgium and Switzerland, agreed to harmonize their gold and silver currencies in shape, size and fineness. This involved no change in the French coinage as the French gold 5 franc was adopted as the basis of the system.

The Second Empire collapsed during the Franco-Prussian War (1870) and the new French regime, the Third Republic, looked back to the Second Republic for its coin designs, while maintaining the existing denominations. From that year also Paris alone was left as an active mint. In 1898 the appearance of the silver denominations was changed. The new design had on the front the figure of France before a rising sun and on the back an olive branch with denomination, date and motto. There was a new design for the bronze coinage also: a female head on the front and the figure of France protecting an infant on the back.

MODERN FRANCE

During the First World War paper money substituted for gold, though issues in silver were initially increased to compensate for the concern this aroused. Nickel and cupro-nickel replaced bronze in the lesser denominations (2 to 25 centimes) from 1915 to 1917 and a new design, first introduced for the nickel 25 centimes in 1914, was retained until 1939. The most distinctive feature of these coins was that they were pierced. In these years 1 and 2 centime coins ceased to be issued. During the war low-value banknotes, usually issued locally, eventually took the place of silver coinage. From 1920 until 1931 these were replaced by token issues in aluminium–bronze produced by the French Chamber of Commerce (50 centimes, 1 and 2 francs). In 1931 official issues were restored but the new metal was retained. Only the 10 and 20 franc coins survived with some silver content.

After the French defeat in the Second World War, coinage from 1941 consisted mostly of zinc (10 and 20 centimes) and aluminium (50 centimes, 1 and 2 francs) issued in the name of the Vichy French State, ÉTAT FRANÇAIS, with the design of a double-headed axe between wheat ears. The Americans minted a brass 2 franc coin at the Philadelphia mint for use during the Liberation. The new coinage issued by the Fourth Republic established in 1946 reflected the impact of twentieth-century inflation. The only coins in use were aluminium–bronze 10, 20 and 50 franc and cupro-nickel 100 franc pieces.

It was in 1961, three years into the Fifth Republic, that the range of

FRANCE
32 SILVER 5 FRANCS *of Napoleon I.*
33 SILVER 5 FRANCS *of the Second Republic with a design illustrating the choices of Hercules.*
34 GOLD 20 FRANCS *of Napoleon III.*
35 SILVER 2 FRANCS *of the Third Republic.*
36 ALUMINIUM 2 FRANCS *of Vichy France struck in Paris.*
37 NICKEL-BRASS 10 FRANCS *of the Fifth Republic.*

32 1813
34 1861
33 1849
35 1898
36 1944
37 1978

coins still in use today was introduced. Inflation had so eroded the value of the old denominations that a major revaluation was required, with 1 new franc equal to 100 old ones. The 1 centime was revived in chrome–steel, though continued inflation has again left it with little significance in currency. The remaining issues are: 5, 10 and 20 centimes in aluminium–bronze; ½, 1 and 2 francs in nickel; 5 francs, initially in base-silver but since 1970 in nickel-clad cupro-nickel; and 10 francs, also initially in silver and now in nickel–brass. The coins introduced in 1961 generally had designs which harked back to the Third Republic, but the 10 franc in 1974 took on a more novel appearance, showing a stylized map of France. Like most modern mints, the French produce commemorative coins, usually in precious metal. Recent examples have commemorated the work of Marie Curie and Émile Zola.

MONACO

FIRST COINS:	1640
FIRST DECIMAL COINS:	1837
MAIN MINT:	Paris
CURRENCY:	franc

Though the Grimaldi family have ruled Monaco since the thirteenth century, it was only under Honoré II (1604–62) that they took the title of prince and began the issue of coinage. Apart from a brief issue of Spanish-style billon coins in 1640, the issues of Monaco have always followed those of France, as was stipulated in 1643 when the principality came under French protection and the prince received the right to strike coinage. Official French coinage has always circulated legally in Monaco.

Once established, the mint of Monaco was active until 1739 under

Honoré II, Louis I, Antoine I and Honoré III, producing 5 and 10 sols, the equivalent of the French sou, and lesser coins in billon, silver ¼, ½ and 1 écu, and gold louis d'or to the French standards. The designs were straightforward: the portrait of the prince on the front and the Grimaldi arms on the back.

During the French Revolution the Grimaldis were dispossessed. The revolutionary government is recorded as issuing playing-cards which were authorized as money, but none of this is known to have survived. The Grimaldi were restored in 1814 but placed under the protection of the king of Sardinia, whose coins became current in Monaco alongside French issues. In 1837 Honoré V tried to revive the local coinage with copper 5 centimes and decimes (= 10 centimes) and silver 5 francs, but neither the French nor Sardinian authorities would accept the issue as valid.

In 1860 Monaco was restored to French protection, but as an independent state, although the coinage was still bound to conform to French issues. The only issues to appear were gold 20 and 100 franc pieces for use on the gambling tables of the new Casino. Coinage ceased again in 1904 until 1924, when the Crédit Foncier de Monaco

MONACO

1 BASE-SILVER 3 SOLS of Antonio I.

2 GOLD 100 FRANCS of Charles III.

issued aluminium–bronze and, from 1925, just aluminium ½, 1 and 2 franc pieces in line with the current French Chamber of Commerce issues. Hotel and gambling tokens survive from the inter-war period.

Under Rainier III (1949–) there was a coinage in 1950–6, corresponding to that of the Fourth Republic, and regular issues in line with the Fifth Republic since 1962. Denominations and materials follow the French model, though designs feature the portrait of the prince and the Grimaldi arms or monogram. Commemoratives have been issued in precious metal and as versions of the current base-metal denominations; for instance the cupro-nickel–aluminium 10 francs of 1982 showed Princess Grace rather than Prince Rainier.

The Casino at Monte Carlo, Monaco. In the late nineteenth century the only coinage produced by the princes of Monaco was intended for passing across the tables of the new Casino.

BELGIUM

FIRST COINS:	second century BC
FIRST DECIMAL COINS:	1830
MAIN MINT:	Brussels
CURRENCY:	franc

BEFORE the Roman conquest of Gaul and the Rhineland, the region now comprising Belgium and the southern Netherlands was inhabited by Celtic tribes, collectively labelled the Belgae, who also dominated northern France and south-eastern England. Celtic warriors returning from mercenary service in the Mediterranean region brought the first coins to the area. The earliest issues of local Belgic coinage from as far north as the Low Countries are gold staters and fractions, dating from the second century BC. Production reached its peak in the mid-first century BC, when the Belgic tribes were opposing Julius Caesar's invasion. Some of the issues of this period circulating in Belgium and the southern Netherlands resemble coins produced by German Celts, suggesting links between these peoples.

BELGIUM

1 GOLD STATER of the Nervii, a celtic tribe in Belgium.

1 c. 50 BC

Julius Caesar's Gallic conquests, completed in 49 BC, extended Roman domination over the whole of Belgium and the southern Netherlands as far north as the mouth of the Rhine, and most of the rest of the Netherlands was later incorporated into the Roman frontier province of Lower Germany. Under imperial rule, Roman coinage circulated in the region for the next 400 years and more. The Romans never established a mint in the Low Countries: most of the coinage, which arrived in the region principally to finance the Roman garrisons stationed there, was struck at the main imperial mints of Rome, Lyons and (later) Trier.

THE EARLY MIDDLE AGES

The lands of modern Belgium fell within the kingdom of the Franks. Merovingian gold tremisses without the royal name were struck locally, principally at Antwerp, Huy, Namur and Tournai. More mints operated under the Carolingians, striking royal deniers (see France), though much of the circulating currency came from mints outside the immediate area.

When the Carolingian Empire came to be divided between the descendants of Louis the Pious (814–40), the coastal lands, approximating to later Flanders, remained consistently within the West Frankish kingdom, with the main mints in the region being Bruges, Ghent, Courtrai and Tournai. The eastern part was included in the Middle Kingdom, Lotharingia, and had as its main mints Maastricht, Huy, Liège, Mons, Namur and Dinant. Lotharingia soon became a contested land, controlled at various times by the rulers of West and

East Frankia, but from 922 it came firmly under the authority of Henry the Fowler and his successors in Germany.

Not all the Carolingian mints operated consistently, particularly as they were in a region which suffered greatly from Viking attacks. Very little coinage at all was produced in the late ninth century. As elsewhere in the Frankish lands in the late ninth and tenth centuries, the local rulers came to acquire coinage rights in the emerging principalities. The power of the East Frankish rulers declined less swiftly and so deniers in the name of the German emperors from Otto I (936–73) to Henry III (1039–56) continued to be struck at Dinant, Liège, Thuin and Maastricht, after which time an imperial mint survived only in Maastricht.

MEDIEVAL PRINCIPALITIES

In the late tenth century the main principalities of the region – the counties of Flanders, Namur, Hainault and Limburg, the duchy of Brabant and the bishopric of Liège – were consolidated. All had extensive coinages in the later Middle Ages until the virtual unification of the area under the House of Burgundy.

In Flanders Baudouin II (883–918) may have issued Carolingian-style deniers from Bruges and Ghent before Viking assaults cut off all minting, but the main medieval series only began under Baudouin IV or V (1000–67), when deniers with a version of the Carolingian temple design were struck at Bruges and Ghent. The output of deniers in the name of the count continued throughout the eleventh century, struck also at St Omer, Arras and Lille. Theoduin of Bavaria (1048–75) was the first bishop of Liège to put his name and bust on deniers struck at Liège, Visé and Huy. In the twelfth century the dukes of Brabant followed suit with deniers mostly showing the ruler in armour.

In the twelfth and thirteenth centuries the characteristic coin of the region was an anonymous, very small denier issued from a great number of mints. In Flanders there were about 30 mints, each with its individual design, such as an armed man (Bruges), a shield (Ypres), a fleur-de-lis (Lille) or a helmeted head (Ghent). Similar coins were issued: in Brabant, sometimes with the inscription DVX (duke); in Hainault, with the Hainault monogram; and in Namur and Liège.

4 TWELFTH–THIRTEENTH CENTURIES

2 840–77

3 983–1002

5 1186–1235

8 1280–1305

6 1167–91

7 1244–79

9 1244–13

The need for larger coins in the flourishing commercial centres of the region, particularly in Flanders, began to be answered in the later thirteenth century. English pennies were increasingly common in the Low Countries and provided the model for new denominations. Marguerite of Constantinople (1244–79) issued the baudekin, equivalent to two English pennies, from the Alost mint as Countess of Flanders and from Valenciennes as Countess of Hainault. The coin was often known as a cavalier because of its design of a knight on horseback. John I of Brabant followed suit.

In the 1290s virtual copies of the English pennies of Edward I, known as sterlings, were issued in vast numbers by the rulers of Brabant, Flanders, Namur, Hainault and Liège. But the name of the actual issuing ruler was usually shown on them and the facing bust was not shown wearing a royal crown. Some more distinctive designs were also used, such as the lion shield of Brabant.

Also in the 1290s even larger gros or groten (the plural of groot), imitations of the French gros tournois, appeared in Brabant, Liège and Hainault, with Flanders following in 1302–3. Thus, the region had a coinage of fine-silver coins – sterlings, baudekins or ½ groten and groten – supported by the small debased deniers as small change. From the 1320s distinctive local versions of the groten replaced the tournois design; it bore, for example, the image of St Peter, patron saint of Louvain, on groten of Brabant; the helmeted lion of Flanders on the botdrager (a double groot) of Count Louis de Mâle (1346–84); and the griffin on groten of Liège.

The fourteenth century also saw the first gold coinage in the region. Louis I de Crécy of Flanders (1322–46) began with an imitation of the Florentine florin. In Hainault and Brabant florin imitations were also introduced. The larger Gothic-style French gold coins, however, provided a more lasting model. Louis II of Flanders was responsible for a splendid sequence of gold issues, admittedly as part of a policy of debasement designed to attract bullion from neighbouring mints. As well as direct copies of the French chaise and mouton, he issued more novel designs, such as the lion heaume, the helmeted lion of Flanders.

In Brabant gold pieters, showing St Peter, were issued under Joanna and Wenceslas (1355–83). The bishops of Liège issued gold coins both in the French style – chaises under John of Bavaria (1390–1418) and John of Heinsberg (1419–55) – and, like the archbishops of the Rhineland, florin-derived gulden which show the images of saints: Peter, John and Lambert. Hainault had moutons and gold riders, showing a knight on horseback, and William I of Namur (1337–91) issued a gulden showing the half-length figure of the Count.

THE HOUSE OF BURGUNDY

In 1384 the Valois dukes of Burgundy inherited Flanders. By 1433 they were also rulers of Namur (1429), Brabant and Limburg (1430), and Hainault (1433), as well as much of the northern Netherlands. Though independent, the bishops of Liège henceforth usually issued coinage in line with that of the ruler of the southern Netherlands. As count of Flanders Philippe le Hardi (1382–1404) introduced a new gold coin: the noble, an imitation of the English coin much prized for its fineness. The unification of the area was mainly the work of his grandson, Philip the Good (1419–67), who from 1434 instituted a common monetary system for the Low Countries. It was based on the Flemish gros (a unit of reckoning which, as a coin, was known as a patard or sol) which equalled 12 deniers and 24 mites, though local variants persisted.

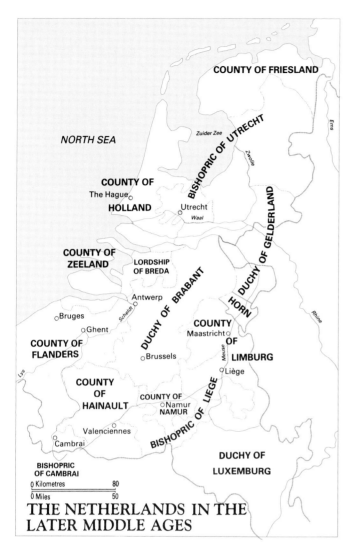

THE NETHERLANDS IN THE LATER MIDDLE AGES

10 1346–84

11 1355–83

BELGIUM

2 SILVER DENIER of *Charles the Bald, King of West Frankia, Bruges mint.*
3 SILVER DENAR of *Emperor Otto III, struck at Liège.*
4 SILVER DENIER *of Flanders.*
5 SILVER DENIER of *Henry I, Duke of Brabant.*
6 SILVER DENIER of *Raoul von Zäringen, Bishop of Liège.*
7 SILVER BAUDEKIN of *Marguerite of Constantinople, Countess of Hainault.*
8 SILVER STERLING of *Gui de Dampierre, Count of Namur.*
9 SILVER GROS of *John II, Duke of Brabant.*
10 GOLD HEAUME of *Louis II de Male, Count of Flanders.*
11 GOLD PIETER of *Joanna and Wenceslas, Duke and Duchess of Brabant.*

43

12 1378–89

13 1467–77

14 1467–77

15 1506–55

16 1506–55

17 1558

18 1584

The main coins produced were: in gold, the St Andrew florin, with the arms of Burgundy on the front and the image of St Andrew on the cross on the back; and in silver the patard and double patard, with the Burgundian arms on the front and a decorated cross on the back. Mites and double mites in base silver, so-called 'black money', provided small change. In 1474 Charles the Rash replaced the patard with the briquet, carrying the design of a seated lion holding the Burgundian coat of arms.

On the death of Mary of Burgundy in 1482 the Burgundian lands passed to her son, Philip the Fair (1482–1506). His son, the Emperor Charles V (1506–55), was heir to Spain and the Habsburg lands in Germany. In the sixteenth century the Low Countries thus formed part of the vast Habsburg Empire. Its coinage system, however, remained much as before, based on the local florin and the patard or briquet.

Occasional novelties were issued, such as the spectacular gold Austrian real of Philip the Fair, and the gold toison of Charles V, with its design of the Golden Fleece, the great Burgundian order of chivalry. Charles also changed the florin design, first to show St Philip on the cross and then, in 1521, he introduced portraiture, showing himself holding sceptre and globe on the gold real (= 60 sols or stuivers or 3 florins) and the new Karolus florin (= 40 sols). Other innovations of Charles's reign were the appearance of very large silver coins, the silver Karolus (= 20 sols), and substantial issues of pure copper coins, the courte or double mite.

When Charles abdicated in 1555, the former Burgundian lands passed to his son, Philip II of Spain. Larger copper coins were introduced, namely the gigot (= 6 mites) and the liard (= 12 mites). Portraiture remained dominant on the gold coinage, based on the real, and the silver, with ever larger denominations, like the écu Philippe or

'A Banker and His Wife', by Marinus van Reymerswaele, around 1490. The cities of the southern Netherlands, particularly Bruges, formed the most commercially developed part of late medieval Europe outside Italy. Merchants, bankers and money-changers were familiar figures and were often depicted by artists counting and weighing coins and making up accounts.

BELGIUM

12 GOLD GULDEN *of Arnold von Horn, Bishop of Liège.*

13 GOLD ST ANDREWS GULDEN *of Charles the Rash, Duke of Burgundy as Count of Flanders.*

14 SILVER DOUBLE PATARD *of Charles the Rash, as Duke of Brabant.*

15 GOLD REAL *of Charles V, as Duke of Brabant.*

16 COPPER COURTE *of Charles V, as Duke of Brabant.*

17 PHILIPSDAALDER *of Philip II.*

18 SILVER DAALDER *of the Estates of Brabant.*

19 SILVER DUCATON *of Albert and Isabella.*

20 SILVER 15 KREUZER *of Maximilian Emmanuel of Bavaria.*

21 SILVER KRONENDAALDER *of Maria Theresa.*

19 1619

21 1775

20 1711

Filipsdaalder (= 35 sols) with its splendid portrait of the king, encouraged by the silver of the New World imported by Spain. Fractions of the daalder were issued: $\frac{1}{40}$, $\frac{1}{20}$, $\frac{1}{10}$, $\frac{1}{5}$ and $\frac{1}{2}$.

Much of the silver was needed in the Netherlands to pay Philip's armies, for in 1572 the Dutch Revolt split north from south and threw the region into turmoil for a generation. Emergency money was issued by many cities under siege, including Brussels, besieged by the Spanish in 1579–80 and 1584–5, Tournai in 1581 and Ypres in 1579. The French prince François, Duke of Anjou, intervening in the struggle, struck $\frac{1}{2}$ daalders at Antwerp and Bruges in 1582 and the Independent States of Brabant also struck daalders at Antwerp in 1584–5.

THE SPANISH AND AUSTRIAN NETHERLANDS

The settlement of 1585 left the southern Low Countries under Spanish control. On Philip II's death, rule passed to his daughter Isabella and her husband and cousin, Archduke Albert of Austria, whose rule (1598–1621) saw the establishment of a monetary system which lasted with little change until the mid-eighteenth century, though the valuation of the gold and silver coins altered over time. When Albert died, Isabella acted as regent until she died in 1633 and the region reverted to rule by the Spanish kings until the end of the Spanish Habsburg Dynasty in 1700.

The new coinage system was established in 1612. It consisted of a range of coins: copper liards (= $\frac{1}{4}$ sol) as small change; billon patards (= 1 sol); the silver esclin or schelling (= 6 sols); two large silver coins, the patagon (= 48 sols) and the ducaton (= 60 sols) with their divisions (usually $\frac{1}{8}$, $\frac{1}{4}$ and $\frac{1}{2}$); and the gold sovereign and its divisions ($\frac{1}{2}$ and $\frac{2}{3}$) and double sovereign. The silver coins showed the portrait of the ruler or coat of arms, while the gold showed the portrait of the ruler. Most had the arms of Austria-Burgundy on the back. The main mints of the seventeenth century were Brussels, Antwerp, Bruges, Tournai, Maastricht and Bois-le-Duc, with Arras, Dôle and Luxemburg in lands outside modern Belgium. It was under Charles II (1665–1700) that the full mechanization of coin manufacture was introduced to these mints.

The first Bourbon king of Spain, Philip V, was able to issue coins in the Spanish Netherlands until 1711, though after 1706 Namur was the only mint under his control. In 1711–14 he surrendered Namur to his supporter, Maximilian Emmanuel of Bavaria, who minted in his own name. During the war of the Spanish Succession (1703–13), the Austrian archduke Charles, rival for the Spanish throne, invaded the province and issued coins as Charles III from Antwerp and Bruges. In 1711 he became Holy Roman Emperor as Charles VI (1711–40) and from 1714 the area passed to the Austrian Habsburgs.

Under Maria Theresa (1740–80) this control was briefly interrupted (1740–48) by French occupation which inhibited the issuing of local coinage. Otherwise, the monetary output remained comparatively stable, with Brussels the only operating mint from 1757. The main innovation was the introduction of the silver $\frac{1}{4}$, $\frac{1}{2}$ and 1 kronenthaler (= 54 sols) to replace the ducaton and its divisions. The only disruption resulted from political dissatisfaction with the reforms of the Emperor Joseph II (1780–90). The Republic of the United Belgian States was set up briefly in 1790 and issued a small coinage of gold lions and silver florins before the new emperor, Leopold II, revoked the offending laws and restored Austrian control.

In 1792, a month after the accession of the Emperor Francis II, war broke out between Austria and revolutionary France and in 1794 the Austrian Netherlands and Liège were occupied by French forces and declared annexed to France. The Brussels mint was immediately closed down. This annexation remained in force until 1814, with French coinage as the only legal tender. After the downfall of Napoleon, the Low Countries were united in 1814 as the Kingdom of the Netherlands under the Dutch House of Orange. Coinage in the name of William I was minted at Brussels from 1816 in a new monetary system of the gulden, or florin, of 100 cents. Older issues still circulated for a while, being given valuations in the new florins. The new copper coins consisted of $\frac{1}{2}$ and 1 cent pieces; the silver of 5, 10 and 25 cents and $\frac{1}{2}$, 1 and 3 florins; and the gold of 5 and 10 florins. There were also gold ducats made for international commerce, not for internal circulation.

THE KINGDOM OF BELGIUM

In 1830 the southern, Catholic Netherlands revolted against rule by the Protestant Dutch, establishing a new kingdom with Leopold of Saxe-Coburg as the first king of the Belgians (1831–65). The monetary system remained basically the same, though based on the franc of 100 centimes. Denominations produced were: in copper, 1, 2, 5 and 10 centimes; in silver, 20 centimes and $\frac{1}{2}$, 1, 2, 2$\frac{1}{2}$ and 5 francs; and in

BELGIUM
22 Copper 5 Centimes *of Leopold I.*
23 Zinc 25 Centimes *of the German Occupation.*
24 Aluminium-Bronze 5 Francs *of Baudouin.*

THE NETHERLANDS

FIRST COINS:	second century BC
FIRST DECIMAL COINS:	1815
MAIN MINT:	Utrecht
CURRENCY:	gulden

gold, 10 and 20 francs. Designs featured either the royal portrait or monogram on the front and the Flemish lion, enwreathed mark of value or coat of arms on the back. A continuing characteristic of the coinage of the kingdom of Belgium is the issue of denominations in both French and Flemish versions.

There have been a number of different designs used on the Belgian coinage, but little change in the range of denominations. Smaller ones have ceased to be issued, overtaken by inflation: the 1 centime in 1912, 2 centimes in 1919, 5 centimes in 1942, 10 centimes in 1946 and 20 centimes in 1960. The 2 francs disappeared in 1930, apart from an Allied Occupation issue in 1944. The last gold coins, 20 francs, were struck in 1914.

Under German occupation in the First World War, zinc was used for the denominations below the franc, and, during the Second, for the franc and 2 francs. In the meantime, cupro-nickel, nickel and nickel–brass had replaced copper and silver as the main coining metals, though in 1933 base-silver 20, 50 and 100 franc pieces were revived until the 1950s.

The denominations currently in use range from the 25 centimes in cupro-nickel to the 20 francs in bronze. Designs have been fairly traditional, but the new 5 francs of 1986 has an unusually geometric version of the portrait of King Baudouin. Commemorative coins are sometimes issued, usually silver 50 franc pieces, though a silver 500 francs celebrated the kingdom's 150th anniversary in 1980.

In the second century BC the southern Netherlands were part of the lands of the Celtic Belgae, before being incorporated into the Roman province of Lower Germany (*see* Belgium). In the post-Roman world, Frisia, encompassing the modern Netherlands, north-eastern Belgium and Germany to the mouth of the Elbe, became economically very important. In the sixth century coinage was produced by local rulers and by kings of the Franks. The coins issued were base-gold tremisses (*see* France). Dorestad was a major trading port and mint of the Frankish kingdom. From about 670 until 750 the region produced large quantities of silver deniers, mostly anonymous and with a variety of designs.

Under the Carolingians (*see* France) larger deniers in the name of the ruler were issued at Dorestad until Viking invasions in the mid-ninth century threw the region into chaos. Frisia then came to form part of the German kingdom and imperial mints operated at Deventer, Tiel, Utrecht and Zwolle until the eleventh century, issuing deniers which mostly had a crowned bust design.

Minting rights were then granted to local rulers, most notably the bishops of Utrecht, the counts of Frisia, Zutphen, Gelderland and Holland and the lords of Cuinre, all of whom had mints at a variety of sites. Until the late twelfth century small base-silver deniers alone were produced, but, as in the southern Netherlands, larger fine-silver coinage was revived. The large quantities of English sterling pennies then circulating in the Low Countries encouraged the local rulers to produce imitations of them: the issues of Renaud I of Gelderland (1271–1326) were most common. The bishops of Utrecht began the issue of double sterlings, or baudekins, copied from Flemish issues (*see* Belgium).

Another influence was the French gros tournois, local versions of

NETHERLANDS
1 Silver Denier *of Lothair I, struck at Dorestadt.*
2 Silver Denier *of Herman van Hoorn, Bishop of Utrecht.*
3 Silver Groot *of John of Arkel, Bishop of Utrecht.*
4 Gold Gulden *of William V, Count of Holland.*
5 Gold Gulden *of Floris van Wevelinkhoven, Bishop of Utrecht.*

which were first produced in Holland under Florenz V (1266–96), straightforward copies of the French coin but in the name of the count. The other rulers followed suit, developing local designs: a facing bust of the bishop on groots of Utrecht and designs featuring helmets and lions in Holland and Gelderland.

The coinage of the southern Netherlands, particularly of Flanders, was also influential, affecting the denominations and designs of coins produced. In the fourteenth and fifteenth centuries sequences of silver coins were produced: $\frac{1}{8}$, $\frac{1}{4}$ and $\frac{1}{2}$ groots, groots, double groots (or botdragers) and even quadruple groots. Lesser rulers in the region also joined in the production of larger silver coins: the lords of Asperen, Arkel, Baar, S'Heerenberg, Anholt, Batenburg, Cranenborg, Gennep, Cuinre, the cities of Groningen and Nijmegen and several others.

The fourteenth century saw the revival of gold coinage in the northern Netherlands, as elsewhere in western Europe. The principal gold coinages were those of Utrecht, Gelderland and Holland. Renaud III (1343–71) was the first duke of Gelderland to strike in gold, Florenz van Wevelinkhoven (1379–91) the first bishop of Utrecht, and William V (1346–89) the first count of Holland.

Two main types of gold coins were produced: comparatively small gulden, equivalent to the Florentine florin in size, though with designs showing the local ruler or patron saint (St Martin at Utrecht) under a Gothic canopy and larger coins designed in the style of the French gold issues, particularly moutons and écus like those minted by Kings Philippe VI and Jean II.

BURGUNDY AND THE HABSBURGS

Both northern and southern Netherlands came under the control of the dukes of Burgundy in the fifteenth and early sixteenth centuries, and a common monetary system was established in the area (see Belgium). Their main mints in the north were at Arnhem and Nijmegen in Gelderland and Dordrecht and The Hague in Holland. In the sixteenth century the Habsburgs Charles V and Philip II opened mints at Utrecht, Leeuwarden in Friesland, Middleburg in Zeeland, Campen and Hasselt in Overijssel and Appingedam in the region of Groningen.

The spread of Protestantism and resentment of Spanish rule in the Low Countries produced the great Dutch Revolt in 1572–85. In 1573 the Estates of Holland issued a coinage of copper deniers (= 3 mites), gigots (= 6 mites) and liards (= 12 mites) in the name of Philip II but without his portrait. During the chaos and confusion of the war,

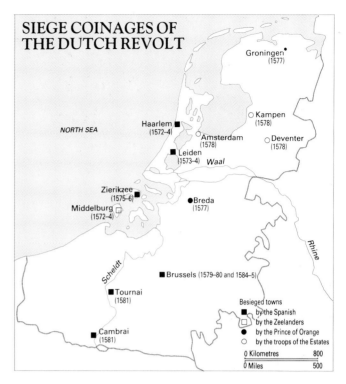

SIEGE COINAGES OF THE DUTCH REVOLT

Groningen (1577)
NORTH SEA
Kampen (1578)
Haarlem (1572–4)
Amsterdam (1578)
Deventer (1578)
Leiden (1573–4) Waal
Zierikzee (1575–6)
Breda (1577)
Middleburg (1572–4)
Scheldt
Rhine
Brussels (1579–80 and 1584–5)
Tournai (1581)

Besieged towns
■ by the Spanish
□ by the Zeelanders
● by the Prince of Orange
○ by the troops of the Estates

Cambrai (1581)

0 Kilometres 800
0 Miles 500

municipal coinages were issued by the town authorities of Ruremonde, Arnhem and Utrecht, and siege coinages, all of different designs but usually square or diamond-shaped silver daalders and gulden, were issued at Haarlem, Middleburg, Leyden, Zierikzee, Groningen, Breda, Amsterdam, Campen and Deventer. Holland produced its own coinage of silver leeuwendaalders or lion daalders (= 38 stuivers) in 1575. An outcome of the Pacification of Ghent (1577) was the issuing of a new coinage throughout the Netherlands, with the exception of Holland, in the name of Philip II.

THE UNITED PROVINCES

In 1579 the seven northern provinces – Holland, Zeeland, Utrecht, Gelderland, Overijssel, Friesland and Groningen – formally set up the Union of Utrecht, declaring themselves independent from Philip II in 1581 as the Republic of the United Provinces. After a period of confusion, when the provinces issued separate coinages, the States General set up a common currency system, with each province issuing the same coins, though distinguished by their own coats of arms.

The basis of the system was large silver daalders: the rijksdaalder (= 40 stuivers) of 1583, which showed a bust of William the Silent, hero of the Dutch revolt, and the Leicester rijksdaalder (= 45 stuivers) of 1586, issued while the Earl of Leicester was commander-general of the United Provinces. Also introduced in 1586 was the gold ducat (= 68 stuivers), which was struck continuously thereafter to the same standards, though its valuation against silver often changed.

In 1606 a monetary ordinance established a new range of principal coins. In gold, the ducat and double ducat were joined by the gouden rijder and its half. Leeuwendaalders and their halves continued to be issued, but the principal silver coin became the Netherlands rijksdaalder (= 47 stuivers), on the front of which was shown a mailed warrior holding a sword and the blazon of the particular province. The

6 SILVER BOTDRAGER *of William V, Count of Holland.*
7 SILVER DAALDER *struck in Leiden under seige.*

7 1574

NETHERLANDS

8 SILVER RIJKSDAALDER of
Holland.
9 GOLD DUCAT of Utrecht.
10 SILVER LEEUWENDAALDER
of Holland.
11 SILVER NETHERLANDS
RIJKSDALER of West
Friesland.
12 SILVER RIJDER of Zeeland.
13 SILVER GULDEN of Gelderland.
14 COPPER DUIT of Overijssel.

9 1597

8 1584

10 1604

11 1623

13 1737

12 1663

14 1767

back displayed a lion holding scales and a sword. Smaller denominations consisted of copper duits ($= \frac{1}{8}$ stuiver) and, in silver, 1, 2 and
10 stuivers. Until 1648 some cities, including Nijmegen, Deventer,
Zwolle and Kampen, remained nominally part of the Holy Roman
Empire and, though they issued coins in line with Dutch issues, they
did so in the name of the emperor.

In the seventeenth century the Dutch republic became a great
commercial and maritime power, though external wars, particularly
against France at the end of the century, undermined her strength. In
1659 a new range of silver coins appeared, based on the ducaton or rijder
($= 60$ stuivers) and $\frac{1}{2}$ ducaton, and the silver ducat ($= 50$ stuivers) and
its half. The lesser silver coins consisted of the 1 and 2 stuivers, the
schelling ($= 5$, later 6, stuivers) and the florijn ($= 28$ stuivers).

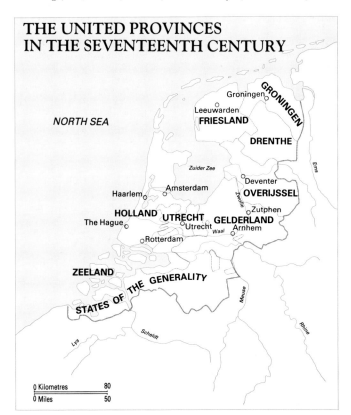

THE UNITED PROVINCES
IN THE SEVENTEENTH CENTURY

Mechanized methods of coin production were established in the
1670s. Much of the coinage produced played an important international role: leeuwendaalders and Dutch rijksdaalders were important
trade currencies, the ducaton was popular in the East Indies, and the
silver ducat in Baltic trade.

The Dutch currency system was further modified in 1680, with the
addition of silver $\frac{1}{4}$, $\frac{1}{2}$, 1, $1\frac{1}{2}$, 2 and 3 gulden pieces (1 gulden $= 20$
stuivers). Most of these had a design on the front of a female figure
personifying Hollandia and on the back the shield of the issuing
province and the value. A new type of duit was created in 1694, with
the provincial arms on the front and the name of the province and the
date on the back. This system remained in being for the remainder of
the eighteenth century, with gold rijders ($= 7$ gulden) and double
rijders ($= 14$ gulden) still providing high-value coins. Ducats ($= 5$
gulden) were primarily trade coins.

The Amsterdam Bourse in the seventeenth century. During the Dutch Golden Age Amsterdam was the centre of a trading and commercial empire without equal, its confidence reflected in the splendour of its civic buildings, of which the Bourse, or Stock Exchange, was a prime example.

THE NAPOLEONIC PERIOD

In 1794 the United Provinces were conquered by the armies of revolutionary France and turned into the Batavian Republic (1795–1806). The coinage was comparatively unaffected, though not all the traditional denominations were produced. In 1806 Napoleon established the Kingdom of Holland, with his brother Louis as king (1806–10). Louis' coins show his portrait on the front and the shield of Holland on the back. He issued 10 stuivers, 1 and 2½ gulden and the rijksdaalder in silver, and 10 and 20 gulden and ducats and double ducats in gold. In 1810 Holland was declared annexed to France, the Utrecht mint producing regular French issues.

THE KINGDOM OF THE NETHERLANDS

In the aftermath of the Napoleonic wars the northern and southern Netherlands were united under the House of Orange until 1830, when Belgium withdrew. A decimal system was introduced, consisting of 100 cents to the gulden and 2½ gulden to the rijksdaalder, a system still in use today. Originally the smallest coins produced were the ½ and 1 cent, struck first in copper and then in bronze. The design on both was a crowned monogram on the front and the coat of arms of the House of Orange on the back until 1878 when, with the change to bronze, the ½ cent was given a new design of the lion of Holland on the front and the mark of value on the back. A similar design was adopted for the 1 cent in 1901 and for the 2½ cent, issued in bronze from 1877 until 1941 and then, under German occupation in 1941–2, issued in zinc, as were most other denominations. These smaller denominations are no longer produced.

The larger denominations issued in 1815 were mostly in silver, base silver for the 5, 10 and 25 cent pieces and fine silver for the ½ gulden (= 50 cents), gulden (= 100 cents), rijksdaalder (= 2½ gulden) and 3 gulden. Gold ducats were still struck for international trade in the nineteenth century and continue to be produced as the Dutch bullion coin. Between 1826 and 1933 gold 5, 10 and 20 gulden pieces were also produced, the 10 gulden being much the most regularly struck.

The Dutch base-silver coins had much the same designs as the

NETHERLANDS

15 Gold Ducat *of Louis Bonaparte.*
16 Base-Silver 10 Cents *of William I.*
17 Bronze 2½ Cents *of William III.*
18 Silver Gulden *of Wilhelmina.*
19 Zinc 25 Cents *of the German Occupation.*
20 Cupro-Nickel Gulden *of Beatrix.*

15 1809
16 1829
17 1884
18 1892
19 1943
20 1987

copper ones until 1848, when they began showing the portrait of the monarch on the front and the mark of value on the back. This design has been retained to the present day, though between 1913 and 1940 the 5 cents was given a distinctive square shape. The 5 cents became a cupro-nickel coin in 1907 and has been bronze since 1984, when the 10 and 25 cents changed from silver to nickel.

The fine-silver coins had the ruler's portrait on the front from the start, with the crowned coat of arms of the kingdom on the back. The 3 gulden was only issued until 1832, and the ½ gulden ceased to be produced in 1930, but the 1 and 2½ gulden are still issued, though in nickel since the 1960s. With the accession of Queen Beatrix in 1980 a new version of the royal portrait has been used on all coins, and the coat of arms has been replaced by the mark of value on a geometric background. This adventurous design sense is also evident on the commemorative pieces produced during her reign.

LUXEMBURG

FIRST COINS:	late tenth century
FIRST DECIMAL COINS:	1854
MAIN MINT:	Brussels
CURRENCY:	franc

Like the other medieval principalities of the Low Countries, Luxemburg emerged in the mid-tenth century, its ruler a vassal of the German emperor. Early counts, Sigefroid II (984–98) and Henry II (1026–47), issued a small number of deniers in the Carolingian style in their own names, but a more substantial coinage began under Henry IV (1136–96). His issues were deniers showing a crowned lion. The deniers of Ermesinde (1196–1247) show the countess on one side and the lion shield of Luxemburg on the other. Henry V's (1247–81) deniers show a knight on horseback, but the design favoured by subsequent rulers was the shield of Luxemburg.

Larger silver coins appeared under Henry VII (1238–1309): esterlins imitating English pennies, baudekins (= 2 esterlins) with the cavalier design, and ½ gros and gros on the French model, though the crowned lion was soon added to the design. John the Blind (1309–46) had a large coinage as king of Bohemia, but his issues in Luxemburg consisted of huge quantities of imitation English pennies, with some doubles tournois and parisis in the French style. Under Charles IV (1346–53) silver placks were introduced with the arms of the imperial house of Luxemburg as their design.

Wenceslas I (1353–83), the first duke, was also the first ruler to mint gold in Luxemburg, issuing gulden showing the ruler under a Gothic canopy. In the later Middle Ages the issue of gulden continued, with esterlins, gros and double gros providing silver and base silver 1/12 gros, deniers and oboles to serve as small change. At times lesser rulers under the dukes issued their own coinage: the abbey of Echternach, the counts of Chiny and Salm, and the lords of Moiry, Schönecken and Orchimont.

In 1444 the duchy passed to Philip the Good of Burgundy. Henceforth, when the mint at Luxemburg was operating, it produced

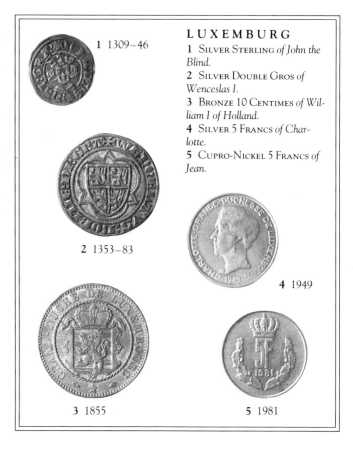

LUXEMBURG
1 SILVER STERLING of John the Blind.
2 SILVER DOUBLE GROS of Wenceslas I.
3 BRONZE 10 CENTIMES of William I of Holland.
4 SILVER 5 FRANCS of Charlotte.
5 CUPRO-NICKEL 5 FRANCS of Jean.

1 1309–46
2 1353–83
3 1855
4 1949
5 1981

coins in line with the other states of the Low Countries ruled by the Burgundian and Habsburg dynasties (see Belgium), differentiated only by the title used on them.

THE NINETEENTH CENTURY
French coinage was current in Luxemburg during the Napoleonic period. In 1815 the region passed to the ruler of the new kingdom of the Netherlands as a nominally autonomous grand duchy. Copper 2½, 5 and 10 centimes were produced under King William III (1849–90), with the old shield of Luxemburg on the front.

INDEPENDENCE
Luxemburg became independent once more in 1890 with the accession to the Dutch throne of Wilhemina who, as a woman, could not inherit the Grand Duchy due to a family compact. However, this did not prevent the succession of Marie-Adélaide (1912–19) and Charlotte (1919–64) as ruling grand duchesses. Local coinage resumed in 1901 with cupro-nickel 5 and 10 centimes and only gradually expanded. Zinc and iron were issued under German occupation after 1915.

Between the world wars 25 and 50 centimes, and 1, 2, 5 and 10 franc coins appeared, the last two in base silver until 1971. Nowadays the franc is the smallest coin issued; a bronze 20 francs was added to the currency in 1980. Designs are relatively simple: the head of the grand duke on the front and the crowned mark of value on the back. Special issues in precious metal commemorated the 600th anniversary of John the Blind in 1946 and the millennium of Luxemburg in 1963.

SPAIN

FIRST COINS:	fifth century BC
FIRST DECIMAL COINS:	1848
MAIN MINT:	Madrid
CURRENCY:	peseta

SILVER coins produced by Greek colonies in Sicily, southern Italy and southern France were circulating in parts of Spain by the fifth century BC and before long Greek settlers in the north-east (modern Catalonia) produced Spain's first coins: small silver pieces imitating the imported coins. These were probably minted at the city of Emporion (Ampurias); the earliest inscribed pieces, dating from the fourth century BC, being marked EM.

During the third century BC the use of coinage spread to other parts of Spain, and issues in gold and bronze also appeared. The different ethnic origins of the peoples inhabiting Spain at this time are reflected in the wide variety of designs, languages, scripts and weight standards used. Greeks in the north-east issued coins in the cities of Emporion and Rhode (Rosas). Native Spanish (Iberian) tribes in the same area produced imitations of these coins. People of Phoenician origin minted in Gadir (Cadiz) in the south, Saita (Jativa) and Arse (Sagunto) on the east coast, and on the island of Ebusus (Ibiza). Saita, Arse and Ebusus may not have begun issuing coinage until after the arrival in Spain in 237 BC of the Carthaginians from North Africa, led by Hamilcar Barcas, father of the famous Hannibal. These invaders issued coinages in Spain which are usually referred to as Hispano-Punic. Many of the designs were borrowed from other Carthaginian coins, with heads of the goddess Tanit and horses prominent. Their capital and principal mint city was Carthagonova (Cartagena).

THE ROMAN PERIOD

Spain was one of the principal battlegrounds in the Second Punic War fought between Rome and Carthage in 218–200 BC. During the war Roman coins began to arrive in Spain, though the Romans also seem to have used local coinage, particularly that of Emporion. Following the defeat of the Carthaginians, Spain was divided into two provinces by the Romans: Hispania Citerior (Nearer Spain) in the north and Hispania Ulterior (Further Spain) in the south. For the next 600 years Spain and its currency were under the domination of Rome, although after the Roman victory large quantities of coinage continued to be issued at Emporion.

In the second century BC the Iberians began to produce a coinage which is usually referred to as the Iberian denarius coinage because it was based on the Roman monetary system, the principal denomination of which was the silver denarius. Iberian issues in both silver and bronze were produced well into the first century BC. Regional differences are marked. In Catalonia and on the east coast both silver and bronze Iberian issues were produced, but bronze seems to have been the more common. Roman silver coins are also found in these areas. Further inland in northern Spain the Celtiberian people also issued Iberian coinage: along the Ebro valley most of the mints produced only bronze, whereas in the interior production was concentrated almost exclusively on silver denarii. Roman coinage did not circulate in these

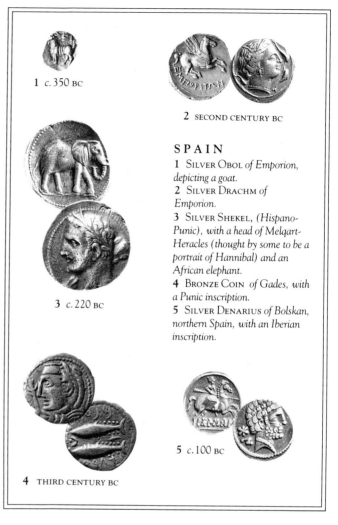

1 c.350 BC

2 SECOND CENTURY BC

3 c.220 BC

4 THIRD CENTURY BC

5 c.100 BC

SPAIN

1 SILVER OBOL of Emporion, depicting a goat.
2 SILVER DRACHM of Emporion.
3 SILVER SHEKEL, (Hispano-Punic), with a head of Melqart-Heracles (thought by some to be a portrait of Hannibal) and an African elephant.
4 BRONZE COIN of Gades, with a Punic inscription.
5 SILVER DENARIUS of Bolskan, northern Spain, with an Iberian inscription.

ROMAN SPAIN

areas. All the local coinages of northern and eastern Spain have Iberian lettering; it is difficult to identify mints because we often know only the Latin names given to the cities by the Romans. The commonest designs on the coins are a male head and a horseman.

In southern Spain, where coinage production centred on the coast and in the Guadalquivir valley, only bronze local coinage was issued, though Roman silver and bronze circulated. Here there was much more variation in lettering on the local coinages and again there are problems in mint attributions. An Iberian script was used in the south-east, Latin in the lower Guadilquivir valley area, and Phoenician scripts in the south-coast region and also in Ebusus.

Very few Roman coins were minted in Spain before the first century BC, but a number of issues were produced during the war between the Romans and the rebel Sertorius (80–72 BC), and again during the civil wars of 49–45 BC, when Julius Caesar was campaigning against Pompey and his sons in Spain. During the early Roman period local coinage continued to be produced, but the increasing influence of Rome is seen in the appearance of bilingual coin inscriptions, with Latin joining Iberian, and it was not long before local scripts disappeared.

The establishment of the Roman Empire under Augustus (31 BC–AD 14) signalled many dramatic changes, not least to the coinage of the provinces, which subsequently came to show the head of the ruling emperor. In Spain under Augustus numerous issues of coinage were produced. Roman gold aurei and silver denarii were minted at various cities, one of which, Emerita (Merida), is named on the coins. Bronze coins for local circulation were produced extensively in the cities of the north and the south.

PRINCIPAL MINTING CITIES IN SPAIN FROM THE REIGN OF AUGUSTUS TO TIBERIUS

City	Roman name	Iberian/other name
Ampurias	Emporiae	Untikesken
Tarragona	Tarraco	Cese
Gelsa or Velilla	Celsa	
Zaragoza	Caesaraugusta	
Calatayud	Bilbilis	
Tarazona	Turiaso	
Huesca	Osca	
Calahorra	Calagurris	
Sagunto	Saguntum	Arse
Ibiza	Insula Augusta	Ebusus
Elche	Ilici	
Cartagena	Carthagonova	
Guadix	Acci	
Cordoba	Patricia	
Seville	Romula	
Santiponce	Italica	
	Carteia	
Algeciras	Iulia Traducta	
Cadiz	Gades	Gadir
Merida	Emerita	

represented. No coinage was produced in Spain under Nero (54–68). Clearly, local coin production came to a sudden halt: from then on it was intended that Spain, in line with the other western provinces of the empire, should use Roman currency.

Civil war afflicted Rome in the years 68–9 and the general in command of the Spanish legions, Galba, briefly became emperor (68–9). Coinage was again issued in Spain – Roman denarii, needed to pay soldiers in the Spanish provinces – and for a short while Roman coins continued to be minted. These were the last official Roman coins from Spain, although the Spanish mines continued to be an important source of metal for Roman coinage. Even when the Roman authorities decentralized coinage production in the third and fourth centuries, setting up branch mints throughout the empire, Spain was left without a mint. During this long period the only coins produced in Spain were locally-made copies of Roman coinage.

The Roman aqueduct in Segovia, dating from the reign of Emperor Trajan, AD 98–117. The mint of Segovia used symbolic representations of the aqueduct as a mint mark on its coins from the sixteenth to eighteenth centuries.

Under Tiberius (AD 14–37) production of local bronze coinage in Spain was still widespread, and in the short reign of Caligula (37–41) a number of cities, notably Caesaraugusta and Carthagonova, continued to mint, but under Claudius (41–54) only one mint, Ebusus, is

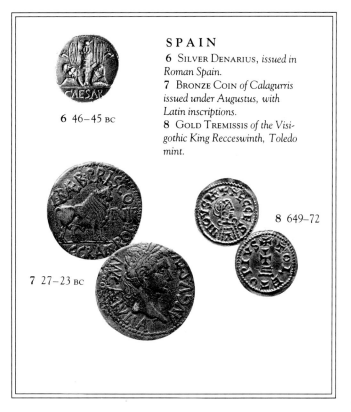

SPAIN

6 SILVER DENARIUS, *issued in Roman Spain.*
7 BRONZE COIN *of Calagurris issued under Augustus, with Latin inscriptions.*
8 GOLD TREMISSIS *of the Visigothic King Recceswinth, Toledo mint.*

6 46–45 BC

8 649–72

7 27–23 BC

KINGS OF VISIGOTHIC SPAIN, 567–714

Liuva I	567–572
Leovigild	568–586
Hermenegild (usurper)	579–584
Reccared I	586–601
Liuva II	601–603
Witteric	603–609
Gundemar	609–612
Sisebut	612–621
Reccared II	621
Swinthila	621–631
Judila (pretender)	631
Sisenand	631–636
Chintila	636–639
Tulga	639–642
Chindaswinth	642–653
Recceswinth	649–672
Wamba	672–680
Erwig	680–687
Egica	687–702
Sunifred (pretender)	692–693
Wittiza	695–710
Roderick	710–711
Achila II (in Septimania)	711–714

THE VISIGOTHIC PERIOD

Following the collapse of Roman authority in the western half of the empire early in the fifth century, Spain was subjected to a series of invasions by tribes who had migrated from eastern Europe. Hordes of Vandals, Alans, Suevi and Visigoths all arrived in the fifth century. Two kingdoms were formed, by the Suevi in north-western Spain and the Visigoths in the rest of the peninsula. An attempted reconquest of the western provinces by the Emperor Justinian (527–65) brought southern Spain back under imperial rule for a while, but the lost territories were mostly recovered by the Visigoths before the end of the sixth century and, following their conquest of the Suevic kingdom, the Visigoths became virtual masters of the peninsula. Their kingdom, with its capital at Toledo, lasted until the Islamic invaders arrived in 711.

In the fifth and sixth centuries the coinages of the Gothic tribes in Spain copied contemporary issues of the Roman emperors. There were wide variations in style: some were close copies, difficult to distinguish from Roman coins, others were crude and easily recognizable. The first king to be named on a coin was King Rechiar of the Suevi (438–48). Mainly gold coins were issued, in two denominations: the solidus and the tremissis. From about 580 the Visigothic kings issued a coinage. They produced only one denomination, the small tremissis, made of gold, but of steadily declining quality. The coins, which were always crude in design, were inscribed in Latin with the name of the king and the mint. Each king issued coinage, and more than 80 mints operated at one time or another, though only a few had a significant output. The commonest design is a facing bust on both sides of the coin. The only other coins produced in Spain at this time were a few Byzantine issues of gold tremisses in the south from the period of imperial reconquest.

THE ISLAMIC PERIOD

In 711–12 the Arabs invaded Spain, destroying the Visigothic kingdom. Until 763–4 Islamic Spain was part of the Umayyad Empire, ruled by governors in the name of the caliph of Damascus. Copper fals, silver dirhems and gold dinars were struck in the Spanish emirate with only the name of the mint, al-Andalus, distinguishing them from other Umayyad coins. Al-Andalus was the name given to the whole Spanish province, but at this time the coins were struck in the capital, Cordoba.

When the 'Abbasids seized the caliphate, Spain broke away under a member of the deposed Umayyad Dynasty. The Umayyad style of coinage was retained, though output was confined to silver. Emir 'Abd al-Raman III (928/9–961/2) took the title caliph in opposition to the eastern dynasties, reformed the coinage in 929 to incorporate his new titles and revived the minting of gold. New mints, notably at his new city of Medinat al-Zahra, came into production.

The coinage kept this form until the disintegration of Umayyad power in 1031, when the Spanish caliphate was declared abolished and split up into about 30 small states. Most of these petty dynasties, the Muluk al-tawa'if or Party Kings, issued coinage, though none in very great quantities. There were some gold issues, mainly of fractions of dinars, but most coins were of base silver.

ISLAMIC SPAIN

9 GOLD DINAR *of 'Abd al-Rahman III, struck at Medinat al-Zahra.*
10 BASE-SILVER DIRHEM *of Ahmad II al-Musta'in, Hudid emir of Saragossa.*

9 912–61

10 1085–1110

11 1248-66

12 FOURTEENTH CENTURY

ISLAMIC SPAIN
11 GOLD DOUBLE DINAR
of the Almohade el-Murteda.
12 SILVER COIN of the
Nasrids of Granada.

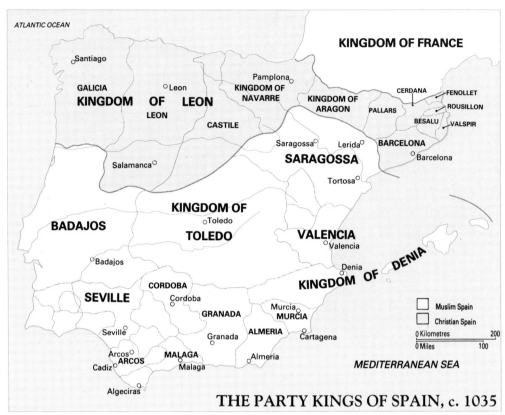

THE PARTY KINGS OF SPAIN, c. 1035

PARTY KINGS WHO ISSUED COINS

Hammudids of Cordoba (1009–55)
Zirids of Granada (1038–74)
Bergawatah Governor of Ceuta (1061–78)
Almirids of Valencia (1021–65)
Almirids of Almeria (1037–44)
Slave kings of Tortosa (1035–54)
Slave kings of Denia (1014–76)
Kings of Majorca (1076–1115)
Tujibids and Hudids of Saragossa (1023–1110)
Hudids of Lerida (1046–67)
Hudids of Denia and Tortosa (1081–99)
Dhunnunids of Toledo (1032–86)
Banu'l-Aflas of Badajoz (1064–94)
Abbadids of Seville (1042–91)

The coinages of the Party Kings had largely ceased by 1106. The petty states could not resist the revived Christian kingdoms of the north led by Alfonso VI of Castile-Leon and the Cid and were forced to submit to the Almoravid rulers of North Africa to prevent a Christian reconquest. From 1096 mints in Spain were issuing Almoravid coinage: gold dinars in the style of Fatimid Egypt and a new silver coinage based on the qirat. The Almoravids also issued a base-silver dirhem solely from their Spanish mints.

Almoravid rule was brief. They were overthrown by the Almohads in North Africa, who then moved into Spain in 1147, ruling from their capital at Seville until 1212, when forced out by the resurgent

Christians. Almohad coinage was distinctive. Their anonymous silver dirhems were square and the gold dinars and double dinars, though round, also had a square as a dominant design feature.

From 1212 until 1492 Islamic power in Spain was confined to Granada, where the Nasrids ruled as tributaries of the king of Castile. They struck a sparse coinage of gold double dinars as well as anonymous square coins in silver.

THE MEDIEVAL CHRISTIAN PERIOD
The small kingdom of the Asturias had held out against the Muslims in north-western Spain, but issued no coinage of its own, its currency consisting of Visigothic survivals and Carolingian and Islamic imports. In the Carolingian-controlled north-east there were mints at Barcelona and Ampurias in the ninth century. By the eleventh century the local rulers in this region had taken over minting and were producing dineros in the French feudal style. The only plentiful issues were those of the counts of Barcelona, but the counts of Ampurias, Besalu, Urgel and Rousillon and the bishops of Gerona and Vich are also known to have issued coinage. Gradually the coinage of Barcelona became dominant throughout Catalonia.

By the later eleventh century the kingdoms of Navarre, Aragon, Leon and Castile had been created and were beginning to issue coinages of their own. These were mostly of base-silver dineros and halves, or obols, and remained a royal monopoly. The first kingdoms to issue coinage were Navarre under Sancho III the Great (1000–35) and Aragon under Sancho-Ramirez (1063–74). Both coinages showed a royal bust on the front and a cross and the name of the kingdom on the back. Shortly afterwards, coinage was also begun in Castile-Leon,

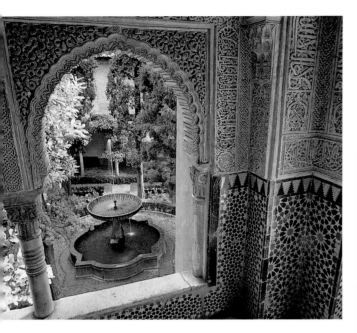

The Alhambra, Granada, built mainly from 1250 to 1350, was the alcazar (palace) of the Nasrid emirs of Granada, the only Islamic dynasty to survive in Spain up to the late middle ages. The palace, with its superb gardens, has been frequently restored.

13 1063–94
14 1158–1214
15 1291–1327
16 1350–69
18 1410–58
17 1369–79
19 1458–79
20 1474–1504

SPAIN

13 BASE-SILVER DINERO of Sancho Ramirez, King of Aragon.
14 GOLD ALFONSINO of Alfonso VIII, King of Castile.
15 SILVER CROAT of Jaime II of Aragon, as Count of Barcelona.
16 GOLD DOBLA of Pedro the Cruel, King of Castile.
17 SILVER REAL of Enrique II, King of Castile.
18 SILVER REAL of Alfonso V of Aragon as King of Valencia.
19 GOLD DUCAT of Juan II, King of Aragon.
20 GOLD DOUBLE EXCELENTE of Ferdinand and Isabella.

united under Alfonso VI (1073–1109). He began to issue dineros following his conquest of Toledo in 1085, minting them in the cities of Leon and Toledo.

In the twelfth century issues of base-silver dineros continued in the Spanish kingdoms. They usually had a cross on the back and on the front a facing or profile bust or some other symbol, such as the lion of Leon and the castle of Castile. In Castile and Leon, separated from 1157, gold coins began to be produced. At Toledo Alfonso VIII of Castile (1158–1214) struck gold maravedis or alfonsini which copied Almoravid double dinars. Their legends were in Arabic script but they affirmed the Christian faith; the design also included a cross. The gold coins of Leon were in western style, with a profile bust and Latin inscription.

Castile and Leon were reunited in 1230 and henceforth had a single coinage, usually showing the lion and castle emblems of the two constituent kingdoms. In 1162 the counts of Barcelona inherited the kingdom of Aragon and their coinage became dominant in eastern Spain. By 1300 a new type of coin had been introduced: the croat of Barcelona, a large fine-silver coin which began to play an important part in the currency of the western Mediterranean. In Aragon itself an extensive gold coinage consisting of imitations of the Florentine florin began under Pedro IV (1335–87). In the new kingdoms of Majorca (conquered in 1228) and Valencia (conquered in 1238), both ruled by the house of Aragon, silver reales and $\frac{1}{2}$ reales were produced. In Castile Pedro the Cruel (1350–68) also issued silver reales with a design which was to survive for a long time on Spanish coins: a crowned initial. He was also able to use Islamic gold captured by his father, Alfonso XI, to issue a substantial coinage of gold doblas with a fine profile bust of a king. Navarre was at this time ruled by kings of French origin and its coinage therefore showed French influence.

In the fifteenth century gold coinage flourished in Castile. Juan II (1404–54) issued the dobla de la banda and Enrique IV (1454–74) the enriques. Enormous multiples were struck for ceremonial purposes. However, the silver and base-silver coinages of Castile were mostly of poor quality. In the eastern kingdoms good-quality silver was still issued in Barcelona, Majorca and Valencia and was introduced into Aragon itself by Juan II (1458–79), who also replaced the gold florins, discredited by debasement, with a new gold coin based on the standards of the Venetian ducat. It had a design showing a facing bust on the front and the arms of Aragon on the back.

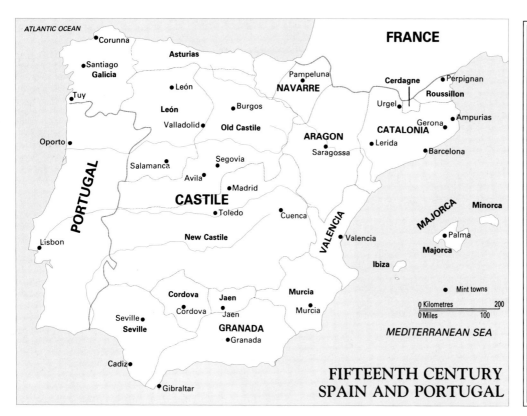

SPAIN

21 1590

FIFTEENTH CENTURY
SPAIN AND PORTUGAL

SPAIN UNITED

The territory of modern Spain was created when the marriage of Isabella of Castile and Fernando II of Aragon in 1479 united virtually all the medieval kingdoms of the peninsula except Portugal. Granada was captured in 1492 and Spanish Navarre acquired in 1512. Castilian coinage was established as the national coinage of united Spain, although coinages of the constituent kingdoms continued to be issued for provincial circulation until the late seventeenth century.

The Castilian coinage was reformed in 1497 when a new monetary system was established. The gold coinage was based on the excelente, which showed facing profile portraits of the joint sovereigns. Multiples of 2, 3, 4, 10 and 20 excelentes were issued. The back of these coins showed the increasingly elaborate coat of arms of the dynasty. Silver coins from the ½ to the 8 reales were issued (1 real = 34 maravedis) and base-silver 2 and 4 maravedis and blancas provided small change. Seven mints issued the national coinage in the early sixteenth century: Burgos, Cuenca, Granada, Seville, Toledo, Segovia and Corunna. Madrid and Valladolid were added later in the century.

THE HABSBURG EMPIRE

This coinage was issued until 1537 when, under Charles I (the Habsburg Emperor Charles V), a new coinage was introduced. The design of the new gold coin, the escudo (= 16 reales), showing the ever more complicated arms of Spain on the front, was retained until the mid-eighteenth century. The new silver coinage also had the arms of Spain on the front. Under Philip II (1556–98) 2 and 4 escudo coins were added to the gold issues, and the real and its multiples up to the famous piece of eight or 'pillar dollar' were issued, their value indicated in Roman numerals.

Even larger multiples were produced under Philip III (1598–1621), including the 8 escudos, known as the onza or doubloon, and a 50 reales silver piece. However, the impression of prosperity these coins gave was illusory. The treasures of Mexico and Peru, once produced either crudely in South America in the form of 'cob' coins or else back in Spain, were exported, mostly to pay the massive debts incurred by the foreign policy of the Habsburg kings.

The manufacture of American silver into coins had begun in Mexico City by 1536. The mint of Santo Domingo on the island of Hispaniola in the Caribbean operated in the 1540s, and under Philip II mints were set up at Potosí in Bolivia and Lima in Peru near the greatest of the silver mines. Eventually other South American mints were opened in the overseas Spanish Empire: Sante Fe de Bogotá (1620s), Guatemala (1731), Popayan (1729) and Santiago (1749). In the sixteenth and seventeenth centuries the designs of the South American products often diverged from coins struck in Spanish mints, but in the eighteenth century the introduction of machinery ensured the production of finely made coins which fell into line with the issues of the Spanish mints.

Shortage of currency and inflation occurred in the seventeenth century. The silver content of the base-silver coinage was reduced and older coins revalued upwards and countermarked to keep them in circulation. Eventually, a petty coinage of pure copper – 1, 2, 4 and 8 maravedis – was initiated under Philip III and the fine-silver coins were reduced in size by a quarter under Charles II (1665–1700).

BOURBON RULE

The only immediate effect on the coinage of the succession of the Bourbons to the Spanish throne in 1700 was the addition of the French

SPAIN
21 SILVER 8 REALES *of Philip II.*
22 SILVER 50 REALES *of Philip III.*
23 COPPER 8 MARAVEDIS *of Phillip III, countermarked under Philip IV to be worth 12 maravedis.*
24 GOLD 8 ESCUDOS *of Philip V.*
25 COPPER 8 MARAVEDIS *of Ferdinand VII, issued during the Peninsula War.*
26 GOLD 80 REALES *of Joseph Bonaparte.*

'The Action between the Centurion and the Nuestra Senora de Covadonga, 20th June, 1743' by Samuel Scott (1701/2–72). This painting depicts the capture of a Spanish treasure ship bound from Mexico to the Philippines with a cargo of silver coin and other goods.

to the Spanish arms on the gold coins. During the War of the Spanish Succession the Archduke Charles, Austrian Habsburg rival to the Bourbon Philip V (1700–46), issued coinage in Catalonia, as King Charles III, from 1707 to 1717. In 1729 a major change was made to the gold issues when a portrait bust of Philip V replaced the traditional coat of arms design. From 1772 the royal portrait was used on all coins and Arabic numerals replaced Roman ones to indicate the multiple denominations: 1, 2, 4 and 8 maravedis in copper; $\frac{1}{2}$, 1, 2, 4 and 8 reales in silver; and $\frac{1}{2}$, 1, 2, 4 and 8 escudos in gold.

THE NAPOLEONIC PERIOD

The nineteenth century was marked by revolution and turmoil in Spain, and this was often reflected in its coinage. In 1808 Napoleon engineered the acquisition of the kingdom for his empire. His brother Joseph Bonaparte issued a coinage as king of Spain. Silver coins from the 1 real, or peseta, to the 8 reales and gold 2 and 8 escudos were issued with his portrait on the front and the Spanish arms, with the French imperial eagle added, on the back. However, coins were still struck in parts of Spain in the name of the imprisoned Bourbon King Ferdinand VII following the style of previous royal issues, often in cities under siege during the Peninsula War. The mints included Cadiz, Gerona, Lerida, Palma de Mallorca, Reus, Tarragona, Tortosa and Valencia. Copper 'Peninsula pennies' were produced for the use of the British forces engaged in the war. Most showed the portrait of the Duke of Wellington and a list of his victories.

DECIMAL COINAGE

The reign of Ferdinand VII's daughter, Isabel II (1833–68), was stormy. Her uncle disputed the succession and issued copper maravedis and silver pesetas as Charles V from the mint at Segovia until 1840. In

1848 the first of a series of decimal coinages replaced the old-style monetary system, though the appearance of the actual coins was little changed, still showing a royal portrait and the arms of Spain. This first decimal system was based on 100 centimos to the real; the second decimal coinage of 1864 on 100 centimos to the escudo (now a silver coin).

In 1868 a revolution drove Isabel into exile. Small coinages were put out by the brief regimes of the Provisional Government (1869–70), the Italian King Amadeus I (1870–3) and the First Republic (1873–4). A lasting innovation from 1868 was the use of two dates on Spanish coins, the most prominent being the date the issue was authorized, and the smaller (usually superimposed on a star shape) denoting the actual year of issue. This practice persists on Spanish coinage in modern times. In 1874 the Bourbons were restored under Isabel's son, Alfonso XII (1874–85). He and his son, Alfonso XIII (1885–1931), mostly retained the traditional design of the coinage with a denomination system based on 100 centimos to the peseta. By the late nineteenth century Madrid was the only mint operating within Spain and the American mints had been lost with the independence of the South American colonies in the 1820s.

MODERN COINAGE

The Bourbons were again ousted in 1931. Little coinage was issued by the government of the Second Republic (1931–7). The outbreak of the Spanish Civil War (1936–9) saw the appearance of a number of small mints issuing low-denomination coins in base metal for particular provinces and regions.

Meanwhile, the regime of General Franco established control of Madrid and the main mint. The issues from 1937 onwards ceased to be in precious metal, instead being nickel, copper–nickel, aluminium–

SPAIN

27 SILVER ESCUDO of Isabella II.
28 SILVER 2 PESETAS of the First Republic.
29 SILVER 2 PESETAS of Alfonso XIII.
30 SILVER 25 CENTIMOS of the Second Republic.
31 CUPRO-NICKEL 25 PESETAS of Franco.
32 CUPRO-NICKEL 5 PESETAS of Juan Carlos I.
33 ALUMINIUM-BRONZE 500 PESETAS of Juan Carlos I.

27 1864

28 1870

29 1889

30 1934

31 1957

32 1981

33 1988

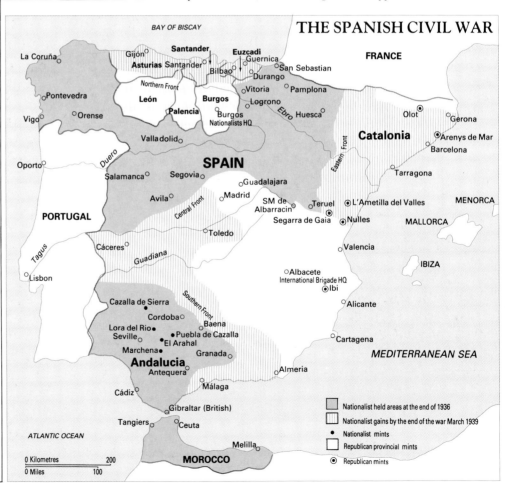

THE SPANISH CIVIL WAR

Nationalist held areas at the end of 1936

Nationalist gains by the end of the war March 1939

• Nationalist mints

□ Republican provincial mints

⊙ Republican mints

bronze and aluminium. From 1947 to 1975 the design of the coinage reverted to the old style of the ruler's head (Franco) on the front and the arms of Spain on the back.

Under Juan Carlos I this was continued until 1980, when the current range of designs was introduced. A feature of modern Spanish currency has been the issue of currency coins commemorating specific events: the coins authorized in 1957 have a design referring to the 1958 Barcelona Exposition and the coins ordered in 1980 refer to the soccer World Cup. In recent years low-value coins, the fractions of the peseta, have ceased to be issued, and new higher denominations have been introduced: the 100 pesetas and, in 1986, the 200 pesetas.

PORTUGAL

FIRST COINS:	second century BC
FIRST DECIMAL COINS:	1836
MAIN MINT:	Lisbon
CURRENCY:	escudo

COINAGE was not produced in Portugal until the second century BC, though coins from Spain probably reached the region in earlier times. Portugal's first coins were issued when most of the Iberian peninsula was under Roman domination. Production was concentrated in the south, where the cities issued bronze coins with inscriptions in Latin, as in neighbouring parts of southern Spain. The main mints were Myrtilis (Mertola), Dipo and Salacia (Alcacer-do-Sal). The designs on the coins also resemble issues from southern Spain, with corn-ears and fish among the subjects depicted.

In 27 BC the Roman emperor Augustus reorganized the administration of Hispania so that Portugal became part of the new province of Lusitania. Only two cities now produced coinage: Pax Julia (Beja) and Ebora (Evora). Their coins have the head of the emperor on the front and local designs, together with the city's name, on the back. These issues were short-lived, with both mints closing before the accession of Tiberius in AD 14.

1 SECOND TO FIRST CENTURIES BC   2 27 BC – AD 14

PORTUGAL
1 BRONZE COIN of Salacia.   2 BRONZE COIN of Ebora, issued under Augustus.

No more coins were produced in Portugal under the Romans. Instead, Roman coins from the city of Rome and the other imperial mints provided all the official coinage circulating in Portugal for the rest of the Roman period. After the collapse of the Roman Empire in the west in the fifth century AD, Portugal became part of the Visigothic kingdom (see Spain), and provided several mints for Visigothic coinage, including Evora, Coimbra and Braga.

MEDIEVAL PORTUGAL
Under Islamic rule Portugal formed part of the caliphate of Cordoba and, in the early eleventh century, the Emirate of Badajoz (see Spain). The territory of the modern state was created as the land was reconquered from the Moors in the late eleventh century. Under Henry of Burgundy the region was a county under the king of Castile-Leon, whose coinage circulated. Henry's son, Alfonso I Henriques (1112–85), became the first king of Portugal in 1128 and began the issue of local coinage by producing base-silver dinheiros and mealhas (= $\frac{1}{2}$ dinheiro), mostly with a cross design. Alfonso's son, Sancho I (1185–1211), introduced the impressive gold morabitino, based on Arabic double dinars but with a design of the king on horseback on the front and, on the back, a cross made up of five shields, the distinctive badge of Portugal.

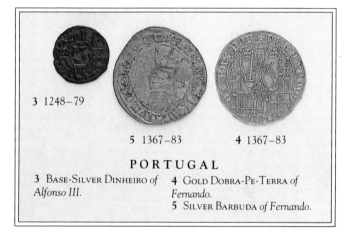

3 1248–79

5 1367–83   4 1367–83

PORTUGAL
3 BASE-SILVER DINHEIRO of Alfonso III.   4 GOLD DOBRA-PE-TERRA of Fernando.
5 SILVER BARBUDA of Fernando.

The coinage of medieval Portugal remained confined to dinheiros, mealhas, and the very occasional issue of morabitinos until the later fourteenth century. Dinis (1279–1325) may have been the issuer of a rare tornes, a large silver coin based on the French gros tournois, and Pedro I (1357–67) is recorded as issuing gold coins, none of which survive. The real expansion of the Portuguese coinage occurred under Fernando I (1367–83), who was spurred to coinage manipulation and debasement by a major war against Castile. He produced a range of coins: in gold (the dobra-pe-terra and dobra-gentil, both copied from current French coins); in silver (the barbuda, with its design of a crowned closed helmet, the $\frac{1}{2}$ real and real, featuring the shield of Portugal and a crowned monogram); and several lesser denominations in base-silver, notably the tornes de busto, with its profile bust of the king. He was the last monarch to issue the dinheiro, by now heavily debased and almost worthless. Lisbon and Oporto were the most active mints at this time.

Portuguese coinage in the fifteenth century was initially confined to new silver leals as the highest-value coins, supported by a petty coinage of base-silver reals branco and, for the first time in medieval Europe, pure copper, in the shape of the ceitil, introduced under Joao I (1385–1433). From the late fifteenth century the real (plural: reis) became the main unit of reckoning, replacing the old libra, which the effects of debasement had made virtually worthless.

THE AGE OF DISCOVERY

Under Alfonso V (1438–81) and with the leadership of Prince Henry the Navigator (1394–1460), Portuguese currency was transformed: the country's leading role in the Age of Discovery gave her a virtual monopoly of the gold of the Guinea coast of Africa. Prosperity was reflected in the appearance of an extensive coinage of gold cruzados (= 400 reis), the name deriving from the prominent cross of St George on the back of the coin. The real grosso, or vintem (= 20 reis), and ½ real, or chinfrao, provided fine-silver issues, base-silver ceased to be struck and copper ceitils served as small change.

Joao II (1481–95) recognized the source of his country's wealth by taking the title 'King of Portugal and Guinea' on his issues. It was a wealth which was reflected in the production of ever larger gold coins: the justo (= 800 reis) of Joao II, the portugues of Manuel I (1495–

Portugal's exploration of the Guinea coast of Africa under Prince Henry the Navigator (above) and their trade with the Far East set the age of discovery underway.

1521) and the beautiful San Vicente (= 1000 reis) of Joao III (1521–57), which showed the patron saint of Portugal on the front. It was on the portugues that the cross of Christ first became a prominent feature on Portuguese coins. The larger gold coins required larger silver ones as appropriate fractions: the silver portugues and the 40 reis, ½ tostao (= 50 reis), 80 reis and tostao (= 100 reis). Copper issues included the real and 3 and 10 reis.

In 1580 Philip II of Spain inherited the throne of Portugal. A rival claimant, Antonio I, issued a coinage until 1583, also countermarking older issues with a goshawk stamp. Spanish rule continued until 1640, with the kings issuing coins in the native tradition: copper 4, 8 and 10 reis (under Philip II only); silver 20, 40, 50, 80 reis and tostaos; and gold 1, 2 and 4 cruzados and 500 reis.

HOUSE OF BRAGANZA

After a brief war Portugal regained its independence under Joao IV (1640–56), first king of the House of Braganza. As a distinct Portuguese coinage had been retained during the rule of Spain, no great transformation was required under the new regime. Joao preserved traditional designs and denominations, issuing 1, 3 and 5 reis in copper; ½, 1, 2 and 4 vintens and ½ and 1 tostao in silver; and 1, 2 and 4 cruzados in gold. However, during Joao's reign the cruzado ceased to be issued as a gold coin, becoming a silver one from 1643, though still with a face value of 400 reis, indicated on the coin in Arabic numerals. The new cruzado was a product of the war of independence, during which the Portuguese currency had to be revalued to prevent it leaving the country. Revaluation was usually indicated by countermarking the older coins with stamps. The gold coinage was heavily upvalued, the 4 cruzados, or moeda, now being worth 4000 reis. Counterstamped Spanish and other European coins were also permitted to circulate.

The reign of Pedro II, regent and king from 1667 to 1706, witnessed the introduction of mechanized coin production to the Portuguese mint at Lisbon in 1678, greatly improving the appearance of the coinage. This reign also saw the beginning of systematic dating on Portuguese coins. An oddity of the time was the continued issue of coins marked with their traditional values when they had in fact been revalued upwards by 20 per cent. Portuguese coinage was also being struck at the mints of Rio de Janeiro and Bahia in Brazil, where new discoveries of gold once again boosted Portuguese wealth (see Brazil).

Under Joao V (1706–50) this increased wealth became evident in the gold denominations: the cruzado again became a gold coin, also called the pinto, valued at 480 reis. A range of higher-value gold coins joined the currency: the escudo (= 1600 reis), meia peca (= 2 escudos), peca (= 4 escudos) and dobra (= 8 escudos). These new coins were further distinguished by the use for the first time of a portrait of the king on the front, the Portuguese coat of arms being shifted to the back of the coin, though it still held its place on the front of the silver coinage (vintem, ½ and 1 tostao, 3 and 6 vintens and silver cruzado, now known as the cruzado novo). This coinage system survived for the rest of the eighteenth century with little change. The gold issues of Maria I (1777–99) are notable for the joint portraits of the queen and her husband and uncle, Pedro III (1777–86). From 1750 Jose I (1750–77) had issued coinage in the Portuguese colony of the Azores: copper 5, 10 and 20 reis and silver 75, 150 and 300 reis.

During the Peninsula War (1807–20) the currency of Portugal was thrown into confusion. The Brazilian gold mines had already ceased to be productive, hitting the country's finances. French, Spanish and

6 1438–81
7 1481–95
8 1521–57
9 1640–56
10 1706–50
11 1777–86
12 1813
13 1829–53
14 1843
15 1924
16 1972

PORTUGAL

6 COPPER CEITIL *of Alfonso V.*
7 GOLD CRUZADO *of Joao II.*
8 GOLD SAN VICENTE *of Joao III.*
9 SILVER CRUZADO *of Joao IV, countermarked with the value 500 reis.*
10 SILVER CRUZADO NOVO *of Joao V.*
11 GOLD PECA *of Maria I and Pedro III.*
12 COPPER PATACO *of Joao, Prince Regent.*
13 SILVER COROA *of Maria II.*
14 COPPER 10 REIS *of Maria II, issued for the Azores.*
15 BRONZE ESCUDO.
16 CUPRO-NICKEL 10 ESCUDOS.

English coins circulated widely, sometimes countermarked with official valuations, and the hard-pressed Portuguese government issued large quantities of a bronze token coin, the pataco (= 40 reis), with the inscription UTILITATE PUBLICAE: 'for the public good'. In 1826 the gold coinage was revalued, the standard coin, the peca, being raised from 6400 to 7500 reis. Between 1828 and 1834 rival rulers issued their own coinages: Pedro IV (1826–8) and his daughter Maria II (1834–53) on one side, and Pedro's brother, Dom Miguel, as their opponent.

During the civil war of 1826–34 the supporters of Pedro IV and Maria II set up their government in the Portuguese possession of the Azores before successfully invading Portugal itself. They issued a coinage there: 20, 40 and 80 reis made of cast gun- or bell-metal. Later in the nineteenth century a variety of Portuguese, Brazilian and other coins were countermarked for use in the Azores and there were also occasionally brief issues of copper 5, 10 and 20 reis specifically for the Azores and Madeira.

Maria II's reign saw many changes to the coinage in Portugal: the introduction of steam-powered presses in about 1835; the disappearance of the cross of Christ as a coin design; the removal from circulation of most foreign coins by 1846; and the replacement of the traditional monetary system by a decimal one in 1838. The new coinage consisted of: 5, 10 and 20 reis in copper or bronze (from 1882); 50, 100 (the tostao), 200, 500 and 1000 (the coroa) reis in silver; and 2000, 2500, 5000 and (from 1878) 10,000 reis in gold. The designs on the high-value coins had usually the head of the ruler on the front and the coat of arms on the back. The low-value coins had the coat of arms on the front and the value on the back.

MODERN PORTUGAL

In the late nineteenth century little gold coinage was produced and in 1900 cupro-nickel replaced silver on the 50 and 100 reis. With the declaration of the republic in 1910 the modern monetary system was introduced, based on the escudo of 100 centavos. Coins of 1, 2, 4 and 5 centavos were issued only briefly, but the 10 centavos, in bronze and, from 1969, aluminium, survived until 1979. The 20 and 50 centavos, issued briefly in silver, then in cupro-nickel or bronze, have also ceased to be issued.

The escudo is now the lowest-value coin, and it has been reduced from a large silver coin through stages – in aluminium–bronze (1924–6), cupro-nickel (1927–68), bronze (1969–80) and brass (1981–5) – to its current insignificant status as a tiny piece in nickel–brass. The 2½, 5 and 10 escudos survived in silver until 1951, when they became cupro-nickel, the 5 and 10 escudos changing to nickel–brass in 1986. From 1977 new coin denominations: 20, 25 and 50 escudos in cupro-nickel, have compensated for the disappearance of the lesser ones.

Designs on modern Portuguese coins have usually featured three main images: the shield of Portugal, a female head in a cap of liberty and an ocean-going sailing ship. There have also been a large number of commemorative designs issued both on precious-metal coins and on currency pieces, usually depicting national figures and international causes, such as campaigns on behalf of the United Nations Food and Agriculture Organization. In 1980 autonomous issues of 25 and 100 escudos in cupro-nickel were produced for the Azores and Madeira.

GIBRALTAR

FIRST COINS:	1842
FIRST DECIMAL COINS:	1971
MAIN MINTS:	Royal Mint, Llantrisant
CURRENCY:	pound

GIBRALTAR, the southernmost point of the Iberian peninsula, has always been of major strategic importance at the entrance to the Mediterranean Sea, but it had no monetary history separate from that of Spain before its capture by Britain in 1704 during the War of the Spanish Succession. Spanish and then British coinage provided the currency in use until 1842, when a special copper coinage was issued for local business. It was Spanish in nomenclature, with 24 quarts or quartos to the real, but the coins produced, ½, 1 and 2 quarts, were British in appearance, showing the head of Queen Victoria on the front and the old fortress of Gibraltar on the back.

British coinage has continued to be current in Gibraltar. The only coins with local reference to be produced are various commemorative pieces: silver and cupro-nickel versions of the crown in 1967–70 and 25 pence pieces since decimalization (1971). The 25 pence of 1971 showed the Barbary ape on the back. Gold 25, 50 and 100 pound coins commemorate royal and local anniversaries.

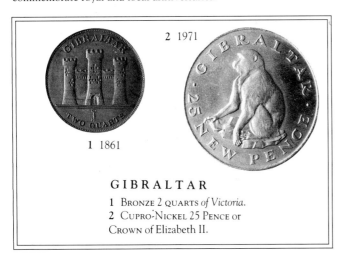

GIBRALTAR
1 BRONZE 2 QUARTS of Victoria.
2 CUPRO-NICKEL 25 PENCE or CROWN of Elizabeth II.

ANDORRA

FIRST COINS:	1982
FIRST DECIMAL COINS:	1982
MAIN MINT:	Franklin Mint
CURRENCY:	diner

THE tiny state of Andorra began to issue its own coinage in 1982, primarily for the tourist and collectors' market. Sovereignty of the state is vested jointly in the French president and the Spanish bishop of Seo de Urgel, and it is usually Spanish currency that is used. The new coinage is issued in the name of the incumbent bishop and is a decimal system of 100 centims to the diner.

The first coins produced were gold sovereigns in 1982 and 1983 with both Latin and Catalan inscriptions. They included the head of the bishop and the coats of arms of the co-sovereigns. In 1983 a nickel 1 diner was produced, in 1984 cast-copper 1 and 5 diners and cast-silver 10 diners, and in 1986 a bronze 25 centims. The other coins issued have had commemorative designs: 2 diners in cupro-nickel with a bronze centre and 10, 20 and 25 diners in silver, mostly illustrating wildlife and Olympic scenes.

1984   **ANDORRA**
2 CAST SILVER 10 DINERS.

ITALY

FIRST COINS:	sixth century BC
FIRST DECIMAL COINS:	1804
MAIN MINT:	Rome
CURRENCY:	lira

THE earliest phase of coinage in Italy comprises the period from the sixth to the third century BC, before the region fell under the domination of Rome. The first and main producers of coinage were the cities of coastal southern Italy and Sicily that had earlier been founded by Greek colonists. From here coinage spread further, to the non-Greek peoples of Italy and Sicily, until a wide variety of coinage was being produced by a great number of different issuing authorities, cities and tribes.

In southern Italy an unusual technique of manufacture was adopted by most of the Greek cities striking silver coins. Called 'incuse', it involved the striking of a similar design on both sides of the coin, in relief on the front and in intaglio on the back. The incuse technique

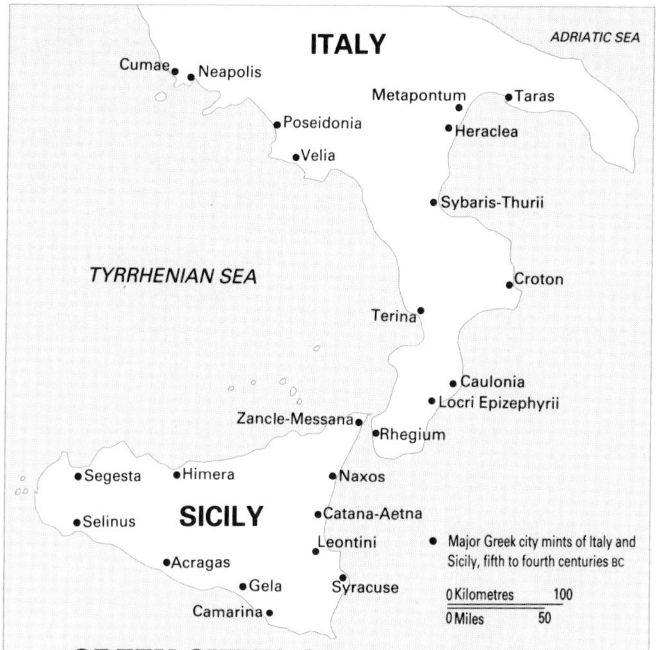
ITALY
ADRIATIC SEA
Cumae
Neapolis
Metapontum
Taras
Poseidonia
Heraclea
Velia
Sybaris-Thurii
TYRRHENIAN SEA
Croton
Terina
Caulonia
Locri Epizephyrii
Zancle-Messana
Rhegium
Segesta
Himera
Naxos
Selinus
SICILY
Catana-Aetna
Leontini
Acragas
Gela
Syracuse
Camarina
Major Greek city mints of Italy and Sicily, fifth to fourth centuries BC
0 Kilometres 100
0 Miles 50

GREEK CITIES OF SOUTHERN ITALY

had its heyday in the period 530–500 BC, though it continued in some cities into the fifth century and did not finally die out until around 440 BC. The chief producers of incuse coinage were the cities of Sybaris, Metapontum, Croton, Caulonia and Poseidonia.

The minting of coins in Sicily also began in the later sixth century BC, in the Greek cities of Naxus, Zancle, Himera, Selinus and Syracuse. None of them used the incuse technique favoured in southern Italy; their early coins, which again were silver, are more akin to the issues of mainland Greece.

The coins of the Greek cities in Sicily and southern Italy in the fifth century BC are especially noted for their designs. Indeed, it is widely believed that the craftsmanship displayed in these coins has never been surpassed. Many different subjects were depicted because each city selected its own designs, and the finest artists were engaged to prepare the dies.

In southern Italy some of the incuse coin issuers, notably Croton and Metapontum, continued to be major coin producers in the fifth century, but they were also joined by other cities, such as Tarentum, Cumae, Velia, and later Thurium and Neapolis. In Sicily, the dominant city was Syracuse, which led the defence of Greek Sicily against Carthaginian invasions in 480 and again at the end of the century. The designs on the Syracusan coinage, of a chariot and the head of the nymph Arethusa, were widely copied throughout the island. Other major issuers of coinage in fifth-century Sicily included Acragas, Catana, Camarina, Himera and Messana (formerly Zancle).

The increasing artistic excellence of Sicilian coinage climaxed with the silver 4 and 10 drachma pieces issued by Syracuse towards the end of the fifth century. Sometimes signed by the artists who engraved them, the dies for these coins were made by such masters as Kimon, Euainetos and Eukleidas, who also worked for other Greek cities in Sicily, and they were copied throughout the Greek world, even by the Carthaginians, who began issuing their first coins at this time.

From the later fifth century the Greek cities of coastal southern Italy came under increasing pressure from the native tribes of the interior, and in Sicily Syracuse was fighting to hold off the Carthaginians. Mercenaries from the Greek homelands were frequently recruited to help in these struggles and thus the need to pay armies was a major influence on coin production. Similarly, the coinage of the Carthaginians, minted at their Sicilian bases of Lilybaeum, Motya and Panormus, was issued largely for military purposes.

Until the middle of the fifth century all the coinage issued by the Greek cities of southern Italy and Sicily was silver, but from about 440 BC bronze coins began to be minted in several cities, and, during the Carthaginian invasions towards the end of the fifth century, gold coins were produced in Sicily. In the fourth century many of the Greek cities of southern Italy and Syracuse in Sicily issued silver, gold and bronze coinage.

In 344 BC the Greek cities of Sicily were freed from Carthaginian domination by Timoleon, a Corinthian general invited to Sicily by Syracuse. As a result of Timoleon's expedition, Corinthian silver staters became the principal circulating currency in Sicily, and some issues were minted locally. Later, under the tyrant Agathocles (317–289 BC), there was a revival of Sicilian-style coinage with the production of 4 drachma coins with chariot designs. Agathocles also introduced new issues with designs clearly based on the coinage of the Macedonians, Philip II and Alexander the Great (*see* Greece). The Carthaginians retained power in western Sicily and also in Sardinia and produced regular issues of coinage in both areas.

1 *c.*530 BC

ITALY

1 SILVER 'INCUSE' STATER *of Sybaris.*
2 SILVER DECADRACHM *of Syracuse, signed by the artist Kimon.*
3 SILVER STATER *of Tarentum.*

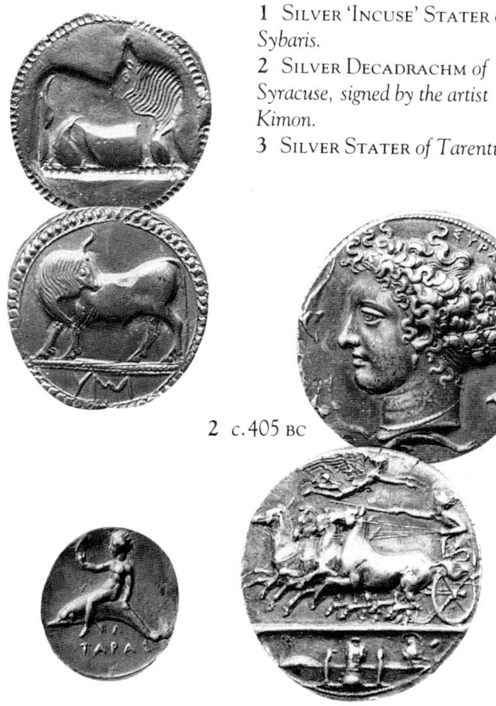

2 *c.*405 BC

3 LATE FOURTH CENTURY BC

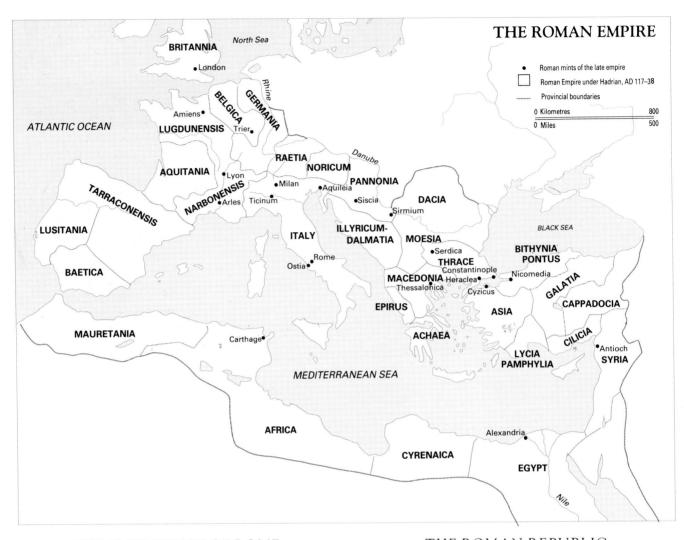

THE EMERGENCE OF ROME

The native Italian and Sicilian peoples had a tradition of measuring values in bronze. Their earliest metallic currency was lumps of cast bronze, referred to as *aes rude* by the Romans, and bronze currency bars (*ramo secco*) were being made in Etruria as early as the sixth century BC. The Romans began issuing cast bronze coinage bars in the later fourth century and heavy round cast coins (*aes grave*) a little later, by which time they were also issuing Greek-style struck coinage in silver and bronze. Other non-Greek peoples also issued struck coinage that was Greek in style, but often with inscriptions in the local scripts.

In the third century BC the Romans fought a series of major wars against Pyrrhus of Epirus (282–274 BC) (*see* Greece) and the Carthaginians (in the Punic Wars of 265–241 BC and 218–201 BC). These wars were the occasions for many important coinages, including the issues of Pyrrhus and of his sponsor, Tarentum; the Carthaginian issues in Sicily; and the coins minted in Italy for Hannibal during the Second Punic War. By 200 BC the Carthaginians had been defeated and expelled from Italy, and the Greek city states of southern Italy and Sicily were no longer producing their own silver coins. Rome was now the major power and the Roman coinage, produced at various mints in Italy, Sicily and Sardinia, was dominant.

THE ROMAN REPUBLIC

The denarius, a silver coin weighing at first about 4.5 g, was introduced around 212 BC. It was the principal coin of the Roman monetary system for the last two centuries of the Roman Republic. The early denarius was valued at 10 bronze asses and so was marked with the Roman numeral x. Similarly, the silver fractions of the denarius were marked v (1 quinarius = $\frac{1}{2}$ denarius = 5 asses) and IIS (1 sestertius = $\frac{1}{4}$ denarius = $2\frac{1}{2}$ asses). The bronze as (marked I) was divided into 12 ounces (unciae) and its fractions were marked with pellets representing ounces. Thus the triens ($\frac{1}{3}$ as) was marked with 4 pellets (= 4 ounces) and the sextans ($\frac{1}{6}$ as) had two pellets (= 2 ounces). Another silver coin, called the victoriate because of the figure of Victory in its design, was also introduced and it was issued in large quantities from 212 BC to about 170 BC.

After 200 BC production of Roman coinage was concentrated at the mint of Rome. At first there were massive issues of bronze coinage, but from about 150 BC there was a shift to much greater production of the silver denarius, probably because this coin was henceforth used for military pay. In 141 BC the denarius was revalued at 16 asses; this equivalence survived as long as both coins were issued.

Early denarii always bore the head of Roma on the front and

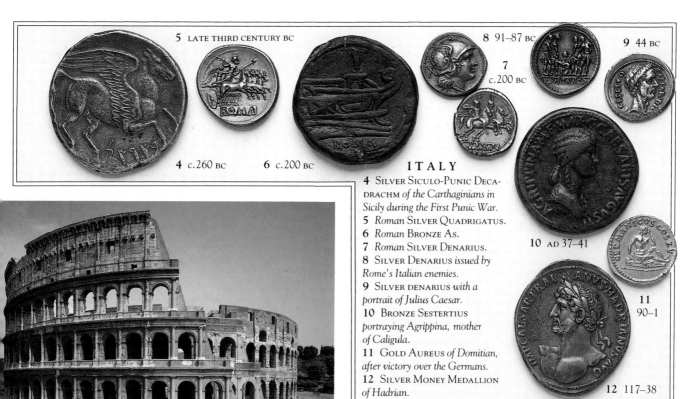

ITALY

4 SILVER SICULO-PUNIC DECA-DRACHM *of the Carthaginians in Sicily during the First Punic War.*
5 *Roman* SILVER QUADRIGATUS.
6 *Roman* BRONZE AS.
7 *Roman* SILVER DENARIUS.
8 SILVER DENARIUS *issued by Rome's Italian enemies.*
9 SILVER DENARIUS *with a portrait of Julius Caesar.*
10 BRONZE SESTERTIUS *portraying Agrippina, mother of Caligula.*
11 GOLD AUREUS *of Domitian, after victory over the Germans.*
12 SILVER MONEY MEDALLION *of Hadrian.*

The Flavian amphitheatre or Colosseum in Rome, opened AD 81 for gladiatorial combat and other entertainments.

equestrian figures of the heavenly twins, Castor and Pollux, on the back. Later, they carried the signature of the officials responsible for production, and designs became much more varied and imaginative. The characteristic designs on the bronze coinage of the Roman Republic were the head of a god on the front and the prow of a ship on the back.

Roman coinage, especially the silver denarius, circulated throughout Italy, but local issues of bronze coinage were still produced by certain cities, notably in Sicily and at Velia and Paestum (Poseidonia) in southern Italy. Non-Roman silver coins were also issued: in the north of Italy, where the local people produced coins imitating the issues of the Greek city of Massalia (Marseilles) until the late second century BC, and in central Italy in the period 91–87 BC, when Rome's Italian allies, in revolt against Rome, produced denarius-style coins with their own designs and script.

Gold coinage did not become a regular part of the Roman monetary system until the mid-first century BC, when, during the civil wars, the various contending generals and their supporters, including Julius Caesar, the Pompeians, Mark Antony and Octavian, issued gold aurei as well as large quantities of silver denarii. Rome continued to be the principal mint, but Roman coins were now produced for the armies wherever they were fighting, in Italy or abroad. Another feature of the coinage in this period was the introduction of portraiture. The earliest portraits on Roman Republican coins were of ancestors of mint officials, but Julius Caesar's head appeared on coins in 44 BC, shortly before his assassination, and after his death portraits of leading figures became commonplace.

THE EARLY ROMAN EMPIRE

The civil wars finally came to an end when Octavian defeated Mark Antony and Cleopatra at the battle of Actium in 31 BC, to become sole ruler of the Roman world and then, under the name Augustus, the first Emperor of Rome.

Augustus reformed the Roman coinage, establishing a system with denominations in gold, silver and bronze that was to survive for more than 200 years.

GOLD, SILVER AND BRONZE COINS OF AUGUSTUS

Denomination	Metal	Value
aureus	gold	= 25 denarii
denarius	silver	= 16 asses
quinarius	silver	= 8 asses
sestertius	brass	= 4 asses
dupondius	brass	= 2 asses
as	copper	= 4 quadrantes
semis	brass	= 2 quadrantes
quadrans	copper	= $\frac{1}{4}$ as

Under Augustus Roman coins were at first minted in various parts of the empire, including Spain, France, Turkey and Egypt, as well as in Rome, but after his reign only two major mints, Rome and Lugdunum (Lyon) in France, survived. Other mints were occasionally opened, notably during periods of civil war in AD 68–9 and 193–7, but otherwise the production of Roman coinage remained centralized and, after the closure of the Lugdunum mint in the reign of Vespasian, Rome was usually the only official mint.

The Roman coinage of the first two centuries AD is probably most remarkable for its superb portraits of the ruling emperors and for the wide variety of designs that accompany the portraits. These often advertised the emperor's achievements and proclaimed the qualities and benefits of his administration.

ROMANS EMPERORS 31 BC – AD 476

31 BC–AD 14	Augustus	270–5	Aurelian
14–37	Tiberius	275–6	Tacitus
37–41	Caligula	276–82	Probus
41–54	Claudius	282–3	Carus
54–68	Nero	283–5	Carinus
68–9	*civil war*	284–305	Diocletian
69–79	Vespasian	286–305	Maximian
79–81	Titus	305–13	Maximinus Daza
81–96	Domitian	306–12	Maxentius
96–8	Nerva	306–37	Constantine I
98–117	Trajan	337–40	Constantine II
117–38	Hadrian	337–50	Constans
138–61	Antoninus Pius	337–61	Constantius II
161–80	Marcus Aurelius	361–3	Julian
180–92	Commodus	363–4	Jovian
193–7	*civil war*	364–75	Valentinian I
193–211	Septimus Severus	364–78	Valens
211–17	Caracalla	367–83	Gratian
217–18	Macrinus	379–95	Theodosius I
218–22	Elagabalus	395–423	Honorius
222–35	Severus Alexander	423–5	Johannes
235–8	Maximinus	425–55	Valentinian III
238–44	Gordian III	455–6	Avitus
244–9	Philip	457–61	Majorian
249–51	Trajan Decius	461–5	Libius Severus
251–3	Trebonianus Gallus	467–72	Anthemius
253–60	Valerian	473–4	Glycerius
253–68	Gallienus	474–5	Julius Nepos
268–70	Claudius II	475–6	Romulus

THE THIRD-CENTURY CRISIS

A gradual decline in the fineness of the denarius reduced its value until, in the early third century, a new silver coin of higher value, the double denarius or antoninianus, had to be introduced. Characterized by its use of a portrait of the emperor with a crown of rays, the antoninianus first appeared briefly in the reign of Caracalla. It reappeared in 238 and quickly took over from the denarius as the principal silver coin.

In the early third century the sestertius was the most abundant Roman bronze coin. Falling values in the later second century had much reduced the usefulness of the dupondius and as (previously the commonest of the larger bronze coins), and the lower-denomination semis and quadrans had disappeared altogether. In the third century all the base-metal coins were made of leaded bronze, rather than brass or pure copper.

The mid-third century was a period of deep crisis for the Roman Empire. There were wars on the northern and eastern frontiers, and a breakaway empire was declared in Gaul. At the same time the coinage suffered a severe decline. The antoninianus, now the only coin being issued regularly, but minted in huge quantities at Rome and, from about 250, Milan and at various other mints throughout the empire, fell drastically in fineness until it became virtually worthless.

Under Aurelian, Rome enjoyed a military recovery, the empire was re-unified and in 274 the coinage was reformed. The reforms included an improvement in the size and fineness of the antoninianus, which now had its silver content fixed at 5 per cent. Also under Aurelian the mint of Milan was closed and another mint at nearby Ticinum (Pavia) was opened.

THE LATER EMPIRE

Aurelian's reformed coinage lasted until Diocletian brought more changes to the Roman coinage system. Diocletian introduced new gold and pure silver coins and, to replace the antoninianus, a new and larger base-silver coin. This new coin, today usually referred to as a follis, at first weighed 10 g and contained 5 per cent silver, but later its size and silver content declined.

No local coinage was now produced anywhere in the Roman Empire. Diocletian's new coinage was issued from mints distributed throughout the provinces. The coins all had the same designs, with an imperial portrait on the front and designs symbolizing Roman rule on the back. The individual mints were distinguished by the mint city's initial letters appearing on the back.

In the first half of the fourth century base-silver and bronze coins were issued in by far the largest quantities of any Roman coins. There was also an increase in production of special large-denomination gold and silver coins for imperial presentations. The most significant development in coin design was the introduction of Christian symbols from the time of Constantine I. In Italy, the main changes in mint organization during the fourth century were the founding of new mints at Aquileia, Ostia and Ravenna.

From the middle of the fourth century bronze coins of varying sizes continued to be issued in abundance. Base-silver issues were rare, but in the period 350–400 there was regular production of pure silver coins, especially of the siliqua. Gold coinage, which circulated at bullion value, was produced steadily throughout the fourth century, but from the late 360s onwards it could be issued only from the mint where the emperor resided.

In the fifth century the most important Roman coins were the gold solidus and its third, the tremissis. These coins were minted in Italy at the imperial residence of Ravenna and in Milan. Little silver coinage was issued, and only the smallest denominations of bronze coinage were minted, but these were still produced in large quantities.

THE OSTROGOTHS

Romulus (475–6) proved to be the last Roman emperor to rule in Italy. After he was deposed, Italy was ruled first by an army officer, Odovacar, and then, from 493, by the Ostrogoths, who had invaded in 488 under their king Theodoric and founded a kingdom. The gold and silver coins issued by the Ostrogoths were imitations of Roman coins, issued in the name of the reigning Roman (Byzantine) emperor in the east. The silver coins often included the name of the Ostrogothic king, sometimes in the form of a monogram. Ostrogothic bronze coins, on the other hand, sometimes displayed the head of the king on the front, or a female head representing the mint city. Under the Ostrogoths Rome once again became the principal mint to serve Italy.

ITALY
13 Base Silver Antoninianus *of the emperor Probus.*
14 Bronze Follis *of the emperor Diocletian, minted in Ticinum.*
15 Gold Aureus *of Maxentius, minted in Ostia.*
16 Gold Solidus *of the emperor Romulus, minted in Milan.*
17 Gold Solidus and Silver ¼ Siliqua *of Theodoric, King of the Ostrogoths, both minted in Rome.*

BYZANTINE RULE

In 552 the Byzantine emperor Justinian I (527–65) embarked on the reconquest of Italy from the Ostrogoths. He eventually achieved his aim, and opened mints at Rome, Ravenna and in Sicily which produced the entire range of current imperial issues in gold and copper (*see* Turkey). Lesser mints also operated, one perhaps at Perugia, just to issue copper coins. Full Byzantine control was short-lived: under Justin II (565–78) the Germanic Lombards invaded northern Italy and gradually conquered much of the peninsula.

However, Emperor Maurice Tiberius (582–602) established the exarchate of Ravenna, while Rome, Naples and Sicily never fell to the Lombards. Imperial mints at Rome, Ravenna, in other parts of Italy and in Sicily continued to be productive. A usurper, Mezezius, briefly seized power in Sicily (668–9) and minted very small quantities of gold solidi at Syracuse. Justinian II (685–95, 705–11) opened a new mint on Sardinia.

The minting of Byzantine coins in mainland Italy ended when the exarchate fell in 751. In Rome the pope turned to the Franks for help and Byzantine coinage there and in Naples petered out, leaving only Sicily in the empire. Minting at Syracuse continued until it fell to the Arabs in 878. However, Byzantine coinage continued to be used in Sicily and southern and central Italy during the early Middle Ages.

THE LOMBARD PERIOD

The Lombards established three main states: the Kingdom of the Lombards in the north, with its capital at Pavia, and the duchies of Spoleto, north east of Rome (which did not issue coinage), and Benevento, in southern Italy. Lombard coinage was largely confined to the gold tremissis, at first imitating official Byzantine coins, but then, in 690–774, it was issued in the name of the Lombard kings. Over a dozen mints are known to have operated in the later Lombard period. Thin silver denarii, probably inspired by the Frankish deniers (*see* France) of the time, were also produced. Coinages of a similar type were issued in Benevento (where imitations of Byzantine solidi were also struck), in Salerno and by municipalities in Tuscany.

After the fall of the Lombard kingdom, Benevento remained independent, though its gold coinage became very debased and was supplemented by silver denarii until local coinage ended in the late ninth century. In Rome the papacy began to strike an autonomous coinage of silver denarii under Hadrian I (772–95).

EARLY MEDIEVAL PERIOD: NORTHERN ITALY

Charlemagne conquered the Kingdom of the Lombards in 774, and thereafter nominal authority in the north rested with the current emperor as King of the Lombards. In 781 the denier was established, distinct only in its mint names from its Frankish original. Milan and Pavia were the most important Carolingian mints from 793–4, with Treviso, Tuscany and Lucca also significant. Treviso was supplanted by Venice under Louis the Pious (814–40). There was also a joint papal–imperial coinage at Rome in the ninth century.

The mints of northern Italy continued to operate through the early tenth century and were little affected by the restoration of strong imperial power under Otto I the Great (936–73). Verona, Milan, Pavia and Lucca provided the imperial denarii, most of which had a monogram of the emperor's name on the front. Venice increasingly went its own way, with denarii issued in the name of Christ, while the papal coinage came to a halt in the 980s with the continuing imperial revival.

In the eleventh century coinage in the name of the German emperors continued to be produced by the four imperial mints of northern Italy. Whatever the name of the current ruler, all imperial coinage bore the name Henry (HENRICUS) from 1039 until the reign of Frederick I Barbarossa (1152–90). However, the fineness of the denarial coinage was beginning to decline, inspiring Frederick I to launch a new finer denaro, the imperialis, around 1160. Meanwhile, civic coinages of local denarii were becoming important, in particular at Venice and Genoa but also at Susa and Asti in Piedmont, Aquileia in the north east, Bologna and Emilia Reggio further south, and Pisa and Siena in Tuscany.

SOUTHERN ITALY

The weakness of Benevento and the remaining Byzantine enclaves in the south laid the region open to invasion, and the Muslims of North Africa conquered Sicily in the later ninth century, producing their own coinage of gold tari, the quarter of a dirhem. On the mainland Byzantine and Beneventan coinage mixed in circulation with Islamic coins and northern denarii. The use of gold and copper marked out the region from the rest of western Europe. Copper follari, which were based on Byzantine folles, were produced by the rulers of Salerno, Gaeta and Capua.

In the late eleventh century the Normans, arriving first as mercenaries, began to establish their own principalities in southern Italy. Robert Guiscard (about 1015–85) seized control in Apulia and at Salerno, and Roger I (1072–1101) ruled Calabria. Both continued the production of follari. In the twelfth century the Norman rulers also struck gold tari in the Islamic style at Amalfi and Salerno in southern Italy and at Palermo and Messina on Sicily, conquered by Roger I from

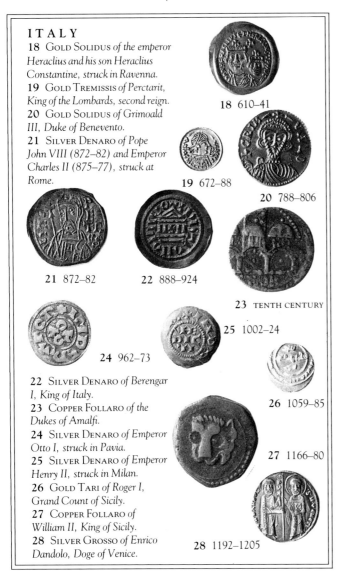

ITALY
18 GOLD SOLIDUS *of the emperor Heraclius and his son Heraclius Constantine, struck in Ravenna.*
19 GOLD TREMISSIS *of Perctarit, King of the Lombards, second reign.*
20 GOLD SOLIDUS *of Grimoald III, Duke of Benevento.*
21 SILVER DENARO *of Pope John VIII (872–82) and Emperor Charles II (875–77), struck at Rome.*

18 610–41

19 672–88

20 788–806

21 872–82

22 888–924

23 TENTH CENTURY

25 1002–24

24 962–73

26 1059–85

27 1166–80

22 SILVER DENARO *of Berengar I, King of Italy.*
23 COPPER FOLLARO *of the Dukes of Amalfi.*
24 SILVER DENARO *of Emperor Otto I, struck in Pavia.*
25 SILVER DENARO *of Emperor Henry II, struck in Milan.*
26 GOLD TARI *of Roger I, Grand Count of Sicily.*
27 COPPER FOLLARO *of William II, King of Sicily.*
28 SILVER GROSSO *of Enrico Dandolo, Doge of Venice.*

28 1192–1205

(1197–1250), the gold coinage being augmented by a spectacular new coin, the augustalis, with its Roman-style bust of the emperor on the front and imperial eagle on the back.

LATER MEDIEVAL ITALY

The twelfth century had seen great commercial expansion in medieval Europe, with the cities of northern Italy in the vanguard, and base-silver denarii were inadequate for the new conditions, though they still formed the basis of the system of reckoning: 12 denarii = 1 soldo, 20 soldi = 1 lira. A new type of fine-silver coin appeared: the grosso denaro, a multiple of the old denaro.

The first grosso, equal to 6 Milanese denarii, was struck at Milan by Emperor Henry VI around 1190, but the most influential version was the Venetian grosso, issued by Doge Enrico Dandolo (1192–1205) to pay the workmen constructing ships for the Fourth Crusade. The Venetian grosso was initially worth 24 Venetian denarii. Its design showed Christ on the front and St Mark presenting a banner to the doge on the back.

By the 1230s many other Italian cities had begun to produce their own grossi: Bologna, Verona and Reggio in the east; Parma and Pavia in Lombardy; Genoa in Liguria; and Florence, Pisa, Siena and Lucca in Tuscany. Civic emblems appeared on these new larger pieces: the holy face of Lucca, the lily of Florence and the virgin and child of Pisa. The Roman Senate struck grossi in 1253 and there was a somewhat larger version at Milan showing St Ambrose.

A further development in the mid-thirteenth century was the revival of gold coinage. In 1252 both Florence and Genoa produced similar-sized gold coins, the florin and genovino, marked with the main local emblems: the lily and St John the Baptist for Florence and a stylized gateway for Genoa. The Florentine coin was highly successful and it became hugely important internationally, in use all over western Europe. Other Italian cities, including Pisa and Siena, issued similar coins, but the only one of comparable influence was the Venetian ducat, introduced in 1284, which became a major trading coin throughout the eastern Mediterranean. Its design, like the Venetian grosso, showed Christ on the front and St Mark presenting a banner to the doge on the back.

In southern Italy and Sicily Charles I of Anjou ousted the Hohenstaufens and reformed the coinage of the region, keeping the base-silver denari, but replacing the gold tari with new coins: the gold saluto or carlino and the silver carlino (= $\frac{1}{20}$ of the gold coin), both of which had an exquisite design depicting the annunciation of the Virgin Mary. After 1282 Sicily was again independent under kings of the Spanish house of Aragon, who struck gold reali and silver pierreali with designs which featured both the Hohenstaufen eagle and the arms of Aragon.

In the late Middle Ages there were dozens of local coinages in central and northern Italy, issued both by communes, which preferred to use patron saints, monograms and names for designs, and by local princes or *signori*, who used heraldic shields and devices. Confusion was mitigated by most cities producing a gold coinage closely based on the florin. The florin, ducat, genovino and Roman ducat were the most plentiful gold issues. In the late fourteenth century florins of Bologna, with images of a lion and saint, and Milan, showing the serpent crest of the Visconti family, became important.

Silver coinages were plentiful and complex. French gros tournois were imitated in Piedmont and Savoy. Venetian coinage grew in

1060 to 1101. Base-silver deniers from Normandy, known as romesini, seem also to have been in use among the Normans.

In 1140 Roger II of Sicily (1130–54), first king of the island and also ruler of Apulia, forbade the use of romesini, replacing them with a new silver piece, the ducalis: a concave coin with an image of himself and his son on the front and Christ on the back. A $\frac{1}{3}$ ducalis was also issued. When Emperor Henry VI of Hohenstaufen became king in right of his wife in 1194, he replaced the copper follaro with a base-silver denaro, though he retained the gold tari. The coinage of tari and denari continued throughout the reign of his son, Emperor Frederick II

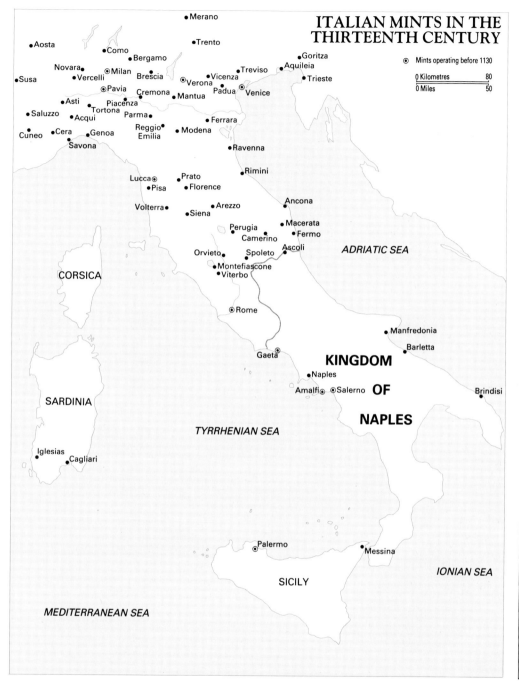

ITALIAN MINTS IN THE
THIRTEENTH CENTURY

◎ Mints operating before 1130

0 Kilometres — 80
0 Miles — 50

Merano
Aosta
Como
Bergamo
Trento
Novara
Vercelli
Milan
Brescia
Treviso
Goritza
Aquileia
Susa
Pavia
Verona
Vicenza
Trieste
Asti
Cremona
Mantua
Padua
Venice
Tortona
Piacenza
Saluzzo
Acqui
Parma
Ferrara
Cuneo
Cera
Genoa
Reggio
Emilia
Modena
Savona
Ravenna
Lucca
Prato
Rimini
Pisa
Florence
Volterra
Arezzo
Ancona
Siena
Macerata
Perugia
Fermo
Camerino
Ascoli
Orvieto
Spoleto
ADRIATIC SEA
Montefiascone
Viterbo
CORSICA
Rome
Manfredonia
Barletta
Gaeta
KINGDOM
Naples
Amalfi
Salerno
OF
Brindisi
SARDINIA
NAPLES
TYRRHENIAN SEA
Iglesias
Cagliari
Palermo
Messina
IONIAN SEA
SICILY
MEDITERRANEAN SEA

29 1220–50

ITALY

29 GOLD AUGUSTALIS of the
emperor Frederick II as King of
Sicily.
30 GOLD SALUTO of Charles I
of Anjou, King of Sicily.
31 SILVER GROSSO of the
Republic of Lucca.
32 SILVER MEZZO GROSSO of
Pisa.
33 GOLD GENOVINO of Genoa.

30 1266–85

31 LATE
THIRTEENTH
CENTURY

32 LATE
THIRTEENTH
CENTURY

33 LATE THIRTEENTH CENTURY

importance in the north as the republic acquired more territory in the early fifteenth century. The coinage of Bologna dominated Emilia and the Marches, and the cities of Tuscany struck coinage to a commonly agreed standard. In Rome grossi and florins were struck in the name of the senate until the early fifteenth century and the return of the popes from Avignon. Thereafter the popes issued coinage of their own, in particular gold ducats with papal insignia: the papal keys and Saints Peter and Paul.

In the Kingdoms of Naples and Sicily gold coinage was rare, the most important coin being the silver gigliato, issued in huge quantities under Charles II (1285–1309) and Robert I (1309–43) of Naples. This coin became immensely significant in Mediterranean trade and was much imitated. Its design of an enthroned king on the front and a highly decorated cross on the back was unusually ornate for a silver piece. The Sicilian equivalent of the gigliato was the pierreale, issued unchanged until 1370. The royal house of Aragon also ruled Sardinia from the early fourteenth century, where silver reali were issued using metal mined on the island at Iglesias. The issue of gold in the south revived in Naples under Alfonso I the Magnanimous (1442–58), who struck ducatones ($=1\frac{1}{2}$ ducats).

RENAISSANCE ITALY

Artistic and political change affected the Italian coinage in the course of the fifteenth century. In the 1450s the Sforza rulers of Milan introduced realistic portraits on their gold ducats, a development rapidly adopted by the other princely families of northern Italy: the Dukes of Savoy, the Este of Ferrara, the Gonzaga of Mantua and the Montefeltro of Urbino. In Naples Ferrante I (1458–94) used portraiture on his ducat and gigliato, known now as the coronato after the crowned bust of the king and equal to $\frac{1}{10}$ ducat.

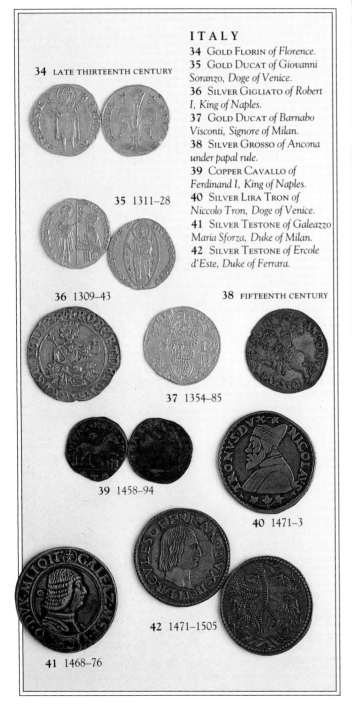

ITALY

34 GOLD FLORIN of Florence.
35 GOLD DUCAT of Giovanni Soranzo, Doge of Venice.
36 SILVER GIGLIATO of Robert I, King of Naples.
37 GOLD DUCAT of Barnabo Visconti, Signore of Milan.
38 SILVER GROSSO of Ancona under papal rule.
39 COPPER CAVALLO of Ferdinand I, King of Naples.
40 SILVER LIRA TRON of Niccolo Tron, Doge of Venice.
41 SILVER TESTONE of Galeazzo Maria Sforza, Duke of Milan.
42 SILVER TESTONE of Ercole d'Este, Duke of Ferrara.

34 LATE THIRTEENTH CENTURY
35 1311–28
36 1309–43
38 FIFTEENTH CENTURY
37 1354–85
39 1458–94
40 1471–3
42 1471–1505
41 1468–76

Italian Bankers: *manuscript illumination, late fourteenth century. The first large-scale banking network across Europe appeared at this time.*

Portraiture was particularly suited to the new types of coin which began to appear, principally larger silver pieces, known appropriately as testones (*testa* = head). Venice produced the first such coin under Doge Niccolo Tron (1471–3). It was the first piece equivalent to a lira in value. Later Venetian lire dispensed with the doge's portrait, deeming it unsuited to a republic. The most influential testone was from Milan under Galeazzo Maria Sforza, produced in 1474, which became the model for other Italian versions. The smaller papal giulio, introduced in 1508 under Julius II, was another influential silver coin.

With larger silver pieces in circulation, higher-value gold coins became useful and several states issued double ducats or gold scudos, among them Milan, Asti, Mantua and Naples. Most states issued a range of silver and base-silver coins of lesser value, and low-value coins in pure copper were considered or introduced: in Venice in 1464 with the piccolo and in Naples in 1472 with the cavallo.

In the late fifteenth and early sixteenth centuries Italy was the scene of major conflicts inspired by the ambitions of France and Spain. Both powers claimed Milan in the north and Naples and Sicily in the south. The Spanish Habsburgs were victorious, though Louis XII and François I of France were able to issue coinage in the peninsula. Power in Italy became consolidated in fewer states. The Habsburgs ruled Lombardy from Milan and the south as Kings of Naples and Sicily; the popes reinforced their authority in central Italy; the Medici of Florence established themselves as rulers of Tuscany; the Republic of Venice dominated the north east and the dukes of Savoy the north west. These, with a few smaller states, remained the political groupings until the nineteenth century.

In the second half of the sixteenth century enormous silver coins, based on the talers of Germany, were adopted in the majority of Italian states. Typically, most states had a petty coinage in base-silver and copper; a silver coinage ranging from the grosso, giulio, lira and testone, up to silver scudi or piastres and very large silver ducats (ducatone); and a gold coinage of scudi or ducats.

NAPLES AND SICILY

In Naples and Sicily the monetary system was based on 20 grana to the tari. The gold scudo was established under Emperor Charles V (1516–54) and it remained the standard gold coin. Copper coins consisted of 1, 2 and 3 cavalli, to which the tornese of 4 (later 6) cavalli was added in 1599. From the later sixteenth century the silver coinage consisted of the cinquina, the $\frac{1}{2}$ carlin, the carlin (= 10 grana), the testone (= 2 carlins), $\frac{1}{2}$ ducatone and ducatone (= 100 grana). The front of the coins usually displayed splendid portraits of the Habsburg kings. New silver coins were introduced in 1684 under Charles II: the $\frac{1}{2}$ and 1 piastre (= 132, later 120, grana), with its design of two hemispheres on the back.

From 1707 until 1734 Naples was ruled by Charles VI of Austria,

A fifth century BC *Greek temple at Segasta, Sicily.*

then Victor Amadeus II of Savoy, both of whom issued coinage, notably Charles's huge silver oncia (= 30 tari). Then rule passed to a branch of the Spanish Bourbons. Traditional denominations were maintained with the addition of larger gold coins under Charles III (1734–59): the doppia (= 4 ducats) and oncia (= 6 ducats).

During the revolutionary and Napoleonic period Naples became first the Parthenopean Republic (1799), issuing copper 4 and 6 tornesi and silver 6 carlini and, after a brief Bourbon restoration, a kingdom ruled by Joseph Bonaparte (1806–8) and Joachim Murat (1808–15). Ferdinand IV of Bourbon retained power in Sicily. Under Murat a decimal system was briefly introduced, and was based on 100 centesimi to the lira.

After the fall of Napoleon and his family, Ferdinand IV returned to Naples in 1816 as Ferdinand I of the Two Sicilies. He and his successors restored the traditional currency: copper tornese and multiples as small change, silver 5, 10, 20, 60 and 120 grana, and gold 3, 6, 15 and 30 ducats.

PIEDMONT-SAVOY

The Dukes of Savoy introduced the tallero, equivalent to the taler, under Emmanuel Philibert (1553–80), along with the testone and lira in silver. Ducatones soon followed. Gold 1, 2 and 4 scudi provided serviceable money for commerce, while prestige pieces were struck for presentation. The seventeenth century saw the expansion of Savoy as it added Montferrat and Sardinia to its territories and became a kingdom under Victor Amadeus II (1675–1730). Sardinia had a different coinage from the mainland until 1816. Charles Emmanuel III (1730–73) reformed the mainland coinage in 1754, basing it on the new gold doppia (= 12 lire), with its $\frac{1}{2}$ and $\frac{1}{4}$ pieces, and with a silver scudo (= 6 lire) and its fractions and base-silver and copper coins providing smaller denominations. On Sardinia the gold 1 (= 5 lire), $2\frac{1}{2}$ and 5 doppietta were struck, supported by silver $\frac{1}{2}$ and 1 reale (= $\frac{1}{4}$ lira) and $\frac{1}{4}$, $\frac{1}{2}$ and 1 (= $2\frac{1}{2}$ lire) scudi.

Piedmont became a republic under French influence in 1798–9 and 1800–1, before being annexed to France (1806–13). French coinage

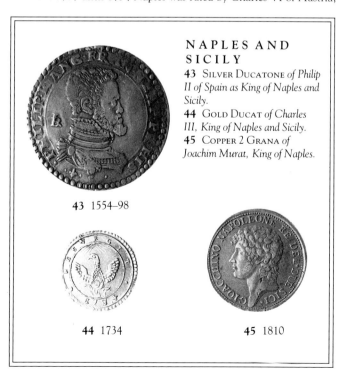

NAPLES AND SICILY

43 SILVER DUCATONE *of Philip II of Spain as King of Naples and Sicily.*

44 GOLD DUCAT *of Charles III, King of Naples and Sicily.*

45 COPPER 2 GRANA *of Joachim Murat, King of Naples.*

43 1554–98

44 1734

45 1810

SAVOY

46 SILVER SCUDO of *Charles Emmanuel I, Duke of Savoy.*
47 GOLD DOPPIA of *Charles Emmanuel III, Duke of Savoy.*
48 BASE-SILVER 7 SOLDI of *Charles Emmanuel V, King of Sardinia.*

46 1581

48 1800

47 1757

was struck for northern Italy at the mint in Turin. Sardinia remained under the house of Savoy and local coinage continued there. However, with their territories restored, the kings of Sardinia issued a common coinage for all their lands from 1816, based on a system of 100 centesimi to the lira.

Genoa survived as an independent republic, issuing coinage for Corsica as well as its own territory. In 1798–1805 Genoa also issued coinage as the Ligurian Republic. After the Napoleonic period it was incorporated into the Kingdom of Sardinia.

VENICE

In the Republic of Venice the ducat or zecchino and the slightly lighter scudo remained the main gold coins, with base-silver quattrini ($= \frac{1}{4}$ soldo) and soldi as small change, and silver issues being the marcello ($= 12$ soldi) and mocenigo ($= 24$ soldi). In 1562 the silver ducat ($= 124$ soldi) was introduced. Pieces of 10, 20 and 40 soldi followed, and in 1578 the silver scudo ($= 160$, then 140 soldi), with fractions down to $\frac{1}{16}$ scudo. Most Venetian coins from the late sixteenth century featured the lion of St Mark or the figure of St Justina in their design. The silver zecchino of the early seventeenth century showed the image of Christ, like the old gold zecchini. This period also saw the first multiple zecchini in gold, up to 20 zecchini pieces.

Later in the century 50 and 100 zecchini coins appeared. Large silver scudi, ducatones and the new ducatello were issued in large quantities, testifying to the republic's commercial power. Special coinages for Venice's Levantine trade and possessions were also produced, and Venice eventually issued the silver tallero to compete with the Spanish 8 reales and Austrian taler in the Turkish Empire.

Independence ended in 1797 when Venice passed to Austrian control. Coinage in the name of Emperor Francis II was struck in 1798–1806; base-silver $\frac{1}{2}$, 1, $1\frac{1}{2}$ and 2 lire and gold zecchini were produced. In 1806–14 Venice was annexed to France by Napoleon before being returned to Austrian control in 1814 (*see* Milan).

MILAN

The Spanish Habsburgs ruled the state of Milan directly as dukes. They issued gold 1, 2 and 4 scudi and a range of silver and base-silver coins:

the denaro ($= \frac{1}{12}$ soldo), trillina ($= \frac{1}{4}$ soldo), sesino ($= \frac{1}{2}$ soldo), 1, $2\frac{1}{2}$, 5, 8 and 10 soldi, testone ($= 25$ soldi) and gradually higher-value silver pieces. Charles V (1535–56) introduced the ducatone ($= 100$ soldi) and later the $\frac{1}{2}$ ducatone, which were designed with magnificent portraits by Leone Leoni, who was also responsible for those of Philip II (1556–98).

Philip added the silver lira ($= 20$ soldi) and 2 lire. New large silver pieces appeared under Philip III and IV: the 80 soldi, and the $\frac{1}{4}$, $\frac{1}{2}$ and 1 filippo ($= 100$ soldi), with the ducatone now worth 112 soldi. From 1712, after the War of the Spanish Succession, the Austrian Habsburgs gained Milan; they maintained the traditional denominations. Under Maria Theresa (1740–80), as well as the doppia ($= 24$ lire) and double doppia, the gold coinage included a zecchino ($14\frac{1}{2}$ lire). Her copper consisted of the sestino, quattrino and soldo, and her silver of the 5, 10 and 20 soldi and the $\frac{1}{2}$ scudo and scudo (6 lire). From 1786 until 1800 versions of coinage in use in the Austrian Netherlands were struck at Milan as trade coins (*see* Belgium).

After the Napoleonic period the territories of Venice and Milan were united in the new Kingdom of Lombardy-Venetia in 1814, with the Habsburg emperor as king. It was given a decimal system of 100 centesimi to the lira, with coinage in copper (1, 3, 5, 10 and 15 centesimi), silver ($\frac{1}{4}$, $\frac{1}{2}$, 1, 3 and 6 lire) and gold (zecchino, 20 and 40 lire). The denominations were equivalent to current Austrian pieces. The revolutionary Government of 1848 issued a little coinage before

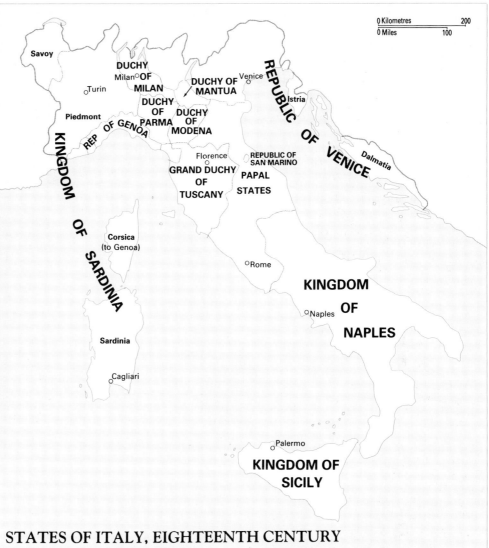

STATES OF ITALY, EIGHTEENTH CENTURY

The Miracle of the Relic of the True Cross *by Vittore Carpaccio (1460/5–1523/6). The painting shows the Rialto, the heart of Venice at the height of her commercial power.*

VENICE AND MILAN

49 SILVER ⅛ SCUDO *of Pasquale Cicogna, Doge of Venice.*
50 GOLD 15 DUCATS *of Silvestro Valier, Doge of Venice.*
51 SILVER DUCATONE *of the Emperor Charles V as Duke of Milan, engraved by Leone Leoni.*
52 COPPER SOLDO *of Empress Maria Theresa as Duchess of Milan.*
53 GOLD 40 LIRE *of Francis I, Emperor of Austria, as King of Lombardy-Venetia.*

49 1585–95
51 1535–56
52 1779
50 1694–1700
53 1831

being crushed. After 1857 the restored Austrian regime produced almost no new coinage, trying instead to establish Austrian issues. Lombardy passed to the new Kingdom of Italy in 1859 and Venetia in 1866.

TUSCANY, PARMA AND MODENA

The smaller states of central Italy used much the same coinage systems as their neighbours. The Tuscan system was based on 20 soldi or 1½ paoli to the lira. A notable series of piastres of Cosimo I de Medici (1537–64) and his son Francesco I (1564–87), Grand Dukes of Tuscany, illustrated scenes from the life of St John the Baptist, patron saint of Florence. Ferdinand I (1587–1608) revived the gold florin, as well as issuing 2 and 4 scudi. Coinage was struck at Pisa and Livorno as well as Florence. Tuscany passed to the Austrian Habsburgs in 1737: subsequent new coins included the silver francescone (= 10 paoli) and gold ruspone (= 3 florins).

Tuscany was briefly elevated as the Kingdom of Etruria by Napoleon, before it was annexed to France in 1807. The restored Austrian grand dukes introduced a new monetary system in 1824 of 100 quattrini to the fiorino (florin). The new coinage of copper 1, 2, 3 and 5 quattrini, base-silver 10 quattrini, silver 20 quattrini and ¼, ½, 1, 2 and 4 fiorini and gold 80 fiorini was retained until union with Italy in 1859. Mantua, Lucca, Parma and Modena also at times maintained local coinages before Italian unification.

54 1555–69

55 1731

TUSCANY
54 Silver Lira *of Cosimo I de Medici, Duke of Florence.*
55 Gold Ruspone *of Giovanni Gaston de Medici, Grand Duke of Tuscany.*
56 Silver 2 Florins *of Leopold II, Grand Duke of Tuscany.*

56 1827

THE PAPAL STATES

Rome, Bologna and Ancona were the most important mints in the Papal States, though a number of lesser provincial mints still operated. The monetary system was based on 10 baiocchi = 1 giulio and 10 giulii = 1 scudo. Base-silver quattrini (= ⅕ baiocco), large silver issues of baiocchi, 1 (= 5 baiocchi) and 2 grossi and testones (= 3 giulii) supporting gold scudi and ducats were the main coins in use until the introduction of the silver scudo or piastre in 1588 under Sixtus IV. Events such as the victory over the Turks at Lepanto, the Holy Year of 1575 and the Papal Jubilee of 1600 were commemorated on special issues. Portraits of the popes were sometimes used on the coinage, engraved by Benvenuto Cellini and Leone Leoni among others, and images from classical literature and the Bible were also depicted.

57 1653

59 1798

58 1759

THE PAPAL STATES
57 Silver Piastre *of Pope Innocent X.*
58 Gold 2 Zecchini *of Pope Clement XIII.*
59 Copper 2 Baiocchi *of Ancona under the Roman Republic.*

In 1600 the first pure copper coin, the ½ baiocchi, was issued. Paul VI (1605–21) introduced the gold 4 scudi. Frequent changes of design continued in the seventeenth century, often the work of leading artists, though the papal tiara, keys and coats of arms were often in evidence. Benedict XIII (1724–30) replaced the old gold scudo with the Roman zecchino (= 20 giulii). A new series of base-silver coins was added under Benedict XIV (1740–58) – 2, 4 and 7½ baiocchi – and the fine-silver 2 giulii. A shortage of coins afflicted the Papal States in the late eighteenth century, leading to large issues of paper money.

In 1798–9 a short-lived Roman Republic replaced papal government, issuing copper ½, 1 and 2 baiocchi and silver scudi, before the Neapolitans restored the Papacy. However, the Papal States were incorporated directly into Napoleon's empire from 1809 to 1814, a mint at Rome issuing French coinage. After 1814 papal government resumed, with traditional forms of coinage, interrupted only by the Roman Republic of 1848, which issued its own copper and base silver. Under Pius IX (1846–78) the Marches and Umbria were lost to the new Kingdom of Italy in 1860, with the Patrimony of St Peter following in 1870. Already in 1866 a new decimal coinage of 100 centesimi to the lira had been introduced in line with Italian issues.

THE KINGDOM OF ITALY

With the unification of Italy in 1860, the coinage of the house of Savoy became that of the whole country. Denominations struck were: in copper 1, 2, 5 and 10 centesimi; in silver 20, 25 and 50 centesimi and 1, 2 and 5 lire; and in gold 10, 20, 50 and 100 lire. Italy was a founder-member of the Latin Monetary Union (*see* France). Coins had the king's head on the front, and on the back either the value and date enwreathed or around the royal coat of arms.

In the twentieth century there have been several changes in design and also materials. The 1 and 2 centesimi disappeared in 1917–18; the 5 and 10 became aluminium-bronze in 1939; the silver coinage up to the 5 lire became first nickel, then, in 1939, stainless steel; and the 10 and 20 lire became silver coins (1926–7).

MODERN ITALY
60 SILVER 2 LIRE *of Victor Emmanuel III, King of Italy.*
61 STAINLESS STEEL 100 LIRE *of the Republic.*

60 1912

61 1971

MODERN ITALY

After the Second World War Italy became a republic. Its coinage since then has been relatively simple and elegant in design. The 1, 2, 5 and 10 lire were struck in aluminium with designs mostly relating to agriculture. The 1 and 2 lire ceased to be issued in 1984, no longer having any useful role in the inflated Italian currency. The larger coins have a head of personified Italy on the front and consist of the 20 lire in aluminium-bronze, 50 and 100 in stainless steel and, since 1977, 200 lire in bronze. The 500 lire was issued in silver until 1982, when it was changed to an unusual piece: aluminium-bronze surrounded by an outer ring of stainless steel. Silver 500 and 1000 lire coins are also issued as commemoratives.

1984

SAN MARINO
ALUMINIUM-BRONZE 500 LIRE.

SAN MARINO

FIRST COINS:	1864
FIRST DECIMAL COINS:	1864
MAIN MINT:	Rome
CURRENCY:	lira

THE tiny republic of San Marino, despite maintaining its independence throughout its history, began to issue coinage of its own only after Italian unification in 1860. The coinage of its neighbours has always been current, but in 1864, after putting itself under

the protection of Italy, it produced the occasional issue of its own, though in line with Italian coins: copper and in 1935 bronze 5 and 10 centesimi; silver 50 centesimi, 1, 2 and 5 lira; and in 1925 gold 10 and 20 lire, which were issued in silver in 1931–8.

From 1938 until 1972 no San Marinian coinage was produced. Since then aluminium 1, 2, 5 and 10 lire, aluminium-bronze 20 and 200 lire and steel 50 and 100 lire have been issued, along with commemorative silver 500 lire and gold 1, 2 and 5 scudi. New designs are used for each denomination every year.

THE VATICAN CITY

FIRST COINS:	1929
FIRST DECIMAL COINS:	1929
MAIN MINT:	Vatican City
CURRENCY:	lira

AFTER the Kingdom of Italy took over the last remaining part of the Papal States in 1870, the Papacy ceased to issue coinage until 1929, when the relationship between it and the government of Italy was finally defined and the sovereign state of the Vatican City was established.

Coinage of the Vatican City follows Italian denominations, though designs are distinct and often changed. The 5, 10, 20 and 50 centesimi and 1 and 2 lire were base metal from the start and until the 1940s all had the papal arms and tiara on the front and religious motifs on the back. The 5 and 10 lire were silver until 1947, when they were changed to aluminium, and have always had the portrait of the pope on the front. The gold 100 lire became stainless steel in 1959 and this was the material used for the new 50 lire (1955), whereas the 20 lire (1957) was in aluminium-bronze. Coins smaller than the 10 lire have not been struck since 1979.

Coins of 200 lire in aluminium-bronze, 500 lire in silver or stainless steel/aluminium-bronze and 1000 lire in silver are also regularly issued, sometimes to commemorate some special event, such as the Second Vatican Council in 1962. Sede Vacante issues, between the death of one pope and the election of the next, are also produced.

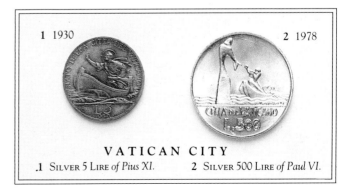

1 1930   **2** 1978

VATICAN CITY
.1 SILVER 5 LIRE *of Pius XI.*   **2** SILVER 500 LIRE *of Paul VI.*

MALTA

FIRST COINS:	third century BC
FIRST DECIMAL COINS:	1972
MAIN MINT:	Franklin Mint, USA
CURRENCY:	pound

Melita (ancient Malta), Gaulos (Gozo) nearby, and Cossura (Pantalleria), between Sicily and Tunisia, were in ancient times colonized by people of Phoenician origin. The earliest coins of these islands were not issued until after the Romans won them from the Carthaginians during the Second Punic War, late in the third century BC, but the coin designs are noticeably Phoenician or oriental. Phoenician inscriptions were also used on the early coins of Melita and Cossura, though Greek was used on the coins of Gaulos and later Melita, and Latin eventually at Melita and Cossura.

These local coinages, which were always bronze, came to an end late in the first century BC. For the rest of the Roman period the official coinage of the islands was Roman imperial.

THE KNIGHTS OF ST JOHN

Medieval Malta had no independent tradition of coinage, the coins in use being those of Sicily (see Italy). However, in 1530, the island was granted to the military Order of the Knights of St John by the Holy Roman Emperor Charles V, as king of Sicily. The order had minted its own coinage on Rhodes for centuries (see Greece) and was determined to retain this right. The site of the order's early mint on Malta is unknown, but from about 1573 it operated in Valletta.

At first coinage brought by the Knights from Rhodes circulated, but the Grand Master Philippe Villiers de L'Isle Adam (1530–4) introduced a new currency system, based on the Sicilian reckoning, of 20 grani to the tari and 12 tari to the scudo. The main gold coin of the

The harbour at Valetta, Malta. The city of Valetta was built by the Knights of St John to be their capital and was also the site of their mint for most of the three centuries of their rule on the island.

knights was the zecchino (= 4 scudi 3 tari), a coin based in standard and design on the Venetian ducat. The zecchino and sometimes multiples of 2, 4, 10 and 12 zecchini were issued by most grand masters until the magistracy of Emmanuel Pinto (1741–73). The coinage had been debased in the mid-eighteenth century and reform was called for, so Pinto introduced a new range of gold coins: 5, 10 and 20 scudi pieces, with new designs of the arms of the grand master or his portrait

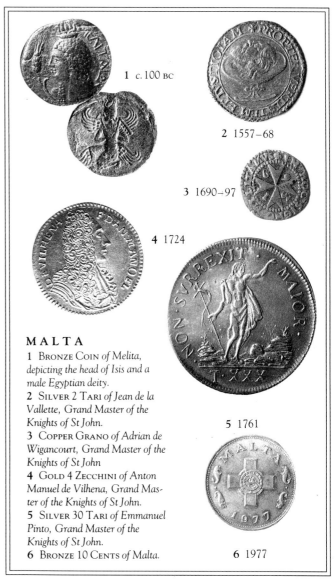

MALTA

1 BRONZE COIN of Melita, depicting the head of Isis and a male Egyptian deity.
2 SILVER 2 TARI of Jean de la Vallette, Grand Master of the Knights of St John.
3 COPPER GRANO of Adrian de Wigancourt, Grand Master of the Knights of St John
4 GOLD 4 ZECCHINI of Anton Manuel de Vilhena, Grand Master of the Knights of St John.
5 SILVER 30 TARI of Emmanuel Pinto, Grand Master of the Knights of St John.
6 BRONZE 10 CENTS of Malta.

on the front and St John the Baptist with the banner of the order on the back. However, debasement soon became necessary again.

A variety of silver coins were issued by the knights, most common being the carlino (= $\frac{1}{2}$ tari) and the 1, 2, 3 and 4 tari. Designs usually featured the arms of the grand master on the front and, on the back, the head of the Baptist on a charger (2 and 4 tari); the eight-pointed star of the order (3 tari); or the paschal lamb (1 tari). In the eighteenth century, denominations smaller than the 2 tari ceased to be issued in silver while larger-value silver coins came into existence, namely the 6 and 8 tari, the 1 scudo, 15 and 16 tari, 2 scudi and 20 tari. It became usual to display a portrait bust of the grand master on the new silver coins.

The order issued a range of copper coins to provide small change, mostly the grano and its fractions and multiples. In the eighteenth century the formerly silver denominations of the carlino and 1 tari became copper. The usual design for the copper coinage was the arms of the grand master on the front and a pair of clasped hands or the eight-pointed cross of Malta on the back. There was an unusually large issue of token copper coins under Grand Master John de la Vallete (1557–68), including copper versions of the 1, 2 and 4 tari, struck to pay workmen engaged on the building of Valletta, a remedy occasionally resorted to at other times.

BRITISH RULE

In 1798 the moribund Order of St John was dispossessed by Napoleon, heading east on his Egyptian expedition. French control was maintained until 1814, when the Maltese rose in revolt. British rule was accepted by plebiscite in that year. Under British control, which lasted until 1964, British coinage became the only legal tender on the island. From 1827 until 1913 the ⅓ farthing was provided as equivalent to the local grano. Its design was identical to British copper issues.

INDEPENDENCE

Independent local coinage began in 1972 with a decimal coinage of 100 mils to the cent and 100 cents to the pound. Coins issued were 2, 3 and 5 mils in aluminium; 1 cent in bronze; 2, 5, 10, 25 and 50 cents in cupro-nickel; and commemorative 1, 2, 4 and 5 pounds in silver. Designs featured a local image or symbol on the front, such as the Cross

of Malta, the George Cross or a fishing boat, with the value on the back. In 1986 the coinage was changed, leaving the 1 cent as the lowest denomination, in copper–zinc, and introducing the pound in cupro-nickel as a currency coin. New designs illustrate local plant and animal life. The silver 5 pounds and higher denominations in gold provide commemorative and bullion pieces.

GREECE

FIRST COINS:	mid-sixth century BC
FIRST DECIMAL COINS:	1831
MAIN MINT:	Athens
CURRENCY:	drachma

BEFORE the invention of coinage, the ancient Greeks used to measure values in terms of livestock, and for money in more portable forms they used objects such as weapons, axes, cooking utensils and iron spits, as well as ingots of precious metal. Greeks in western Turkey produced some of the earliest of all coinage issues in the late seventh century BC (see Turkey). The use of coinage then spread westwards, and the first issues of mainland Greece and the Aegean islands date from the mid-sixth century.

Apart from a few isolated issues of white-gold coins from Athens and northern Greece, all of the early coinage of Greece was silver. The

GREEK AND PHOENICIAN COLONIZATION

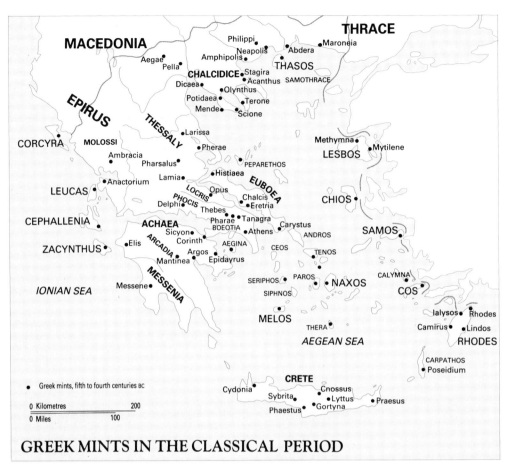

GREEK MINTS IN THE CLASSICAL PERIOD

Greek mints, fifth to fourth centuries BC

0 Kilometres 200
0 Miles 100

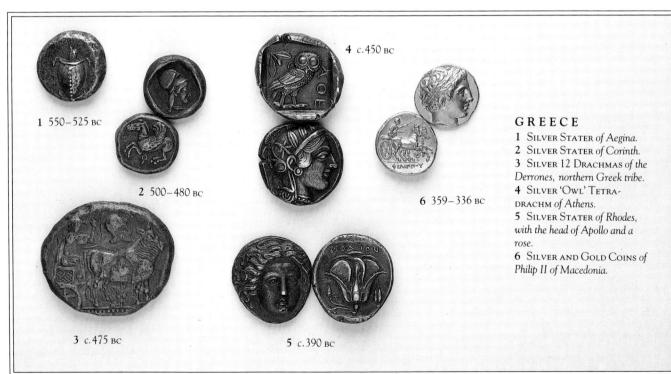

1 550–525 BC

2 500–480 BC

3 c.475 BC

4 c.450 BC

5 c.390 BC

6 359–336 BC

GREECE

1 SILVER STATER of Aegina.
2 SILVER STATER of Corinth.
3 SILVER 12 DRACHMAS of the Derrones, northern Greek tribe.
4 SILVER 'OWL' TETRA-DRACHM of Athens.
5 SILVER STATER of Rhodes, with the head of Apollo and a rose.
6 SILVER AND GOLD COINS of Philip II of Macedonia.

This view of Athens from the Acropolis shows the agora, marketplace and centre of the ancient city with the remains of its many public buildings, stoas and shops.

6 359–336 BC

7 336–323 BC

7 336–323 BC

GREECE

7 SILVER AND GOLD COINS *of Alexander the Great struck in Macedonia. Alexander, and his predecessor, Phillip II, produced great quantities of silver and, for the first time, gold coins.*

main producers of the earliest period (550–480 BC) were the three rival city states of Aegina, Corinth and Athens. Aegina at this time dominated Greek trade in the Aegean and the eastern Mediterranean, and its early coins, known as 'turtles' because of the turtle design on the front, circulated widely in these areas. In the Aegean islands the weight standard of the Aeginetan coinage was widely copied when the first local coinages were made, before 500 BC. The trading interests of Corinth were directed westwards, and the silver 'colts' of Corinth, named after the Pegasus design on the front, were influential in the development of coinage in north-western Greece and also in southern Italy and Sicily. The famous 'owls' of Athens, named after the bird that appears on the back of the coins (the head of Athena appears on the front), began to be issued towards the end of the sixth century BC, when the silver mines of Laurion in Attica came into full production. Earlier coin issues came in a variety of designs.

From these major centres of production coinage spread throughout Greece. The cities of Euboea: Carystus, Chalcis and Eretria; Boeotia and Phocis in central Greece; Corcyra in the west; and various cities and tribes in Macedonia and Thrace in the north all produced significant issues of coinage before 480 BC. Northern Greece contained rich deposits of silver, and this region produced some especially large silver coins, mainly minted for export east to the heartlands of the Persian Empire, where silver was more highly valued: parts of northern Greece were under Persian rule during the reigns of the Persian Kings Darius I (521–486 BC) and Xerxes (486–465 BC).

THE CLASSICAL PERIOD

In 480 and 479 BC the Greeks defeated the invading forces of Xerxes in the sea battle of Salamis and the land battle of Plataea. These victories heralded an era of supreme cultural achievement. Monuments such as the temples of the Athenian acropolis and many works of art and literature survive still, and the Greeks of the Aegean area and Greek settlers elsewhere in the Mediterranean and Black Sea regions produced some of the finest coins ever issued.

The major power in Greece after 480 BC was Athens, leader of the newly formed Delian League, a confederation of Greek states united in opposition against Persia. The silver owl coinage of Athens, now produced from the proceeds of tribute exacted from the league members as well as the mines of Laurion, was issued in massive quantities, particularly in the second half of the fifth century BC. However, Athenian dominance came to an end when the Peloponnesian War (431–404 BC) between Athens and a confederacy of Greek states led by Sparta ended in defeat for Athens.

Other Greek city states which produced substantial coinages in the period 480–400 BC included Corinth and later Sicyon and Elis in the south and Thebes in central Greece. The output of coinage from Aegina and the Aegean islands, on the other hand, declined, and in the north production of large-denomination silver coins by various tribes and cities came to an end towards the middle of the century, though the minting of normal-size silver pieces continued at many cities, notably Abdera, Acanthus, Mende and Thasos.

The first issues of gold coinage were produced by Athens at a time of emergency towards the end of the Peloponnesian War, and the first bronze coins also began to appear in the late fifth century BC, in Macedonia and Thrace in the north. However, silver coinage remained dominant into the fourth century BC. Many more city states and leagues of cities in Greece were now striking coinage so there was great variety in coin designs and the level of artistry was high. Notable coinages include the issues of Thebes, Corinth, the Chalcidian League in the north, islands such as Chios and Rhodes, and Crete. Some of the most attractive coins were produced by various cities in the Peloponnese, including Elis, Argos, Messene and the Arcadian League, by Larissa and the Locrians of Opus in central Greece and by Amphipolis in Macedonia. A notable feature of Greek coinage in the fourth century BC was the more frequent recording of the names of civic officials in coin inscriptions. There was also a marked increase in the production of lower-value coinage, now often struck in bronze.

PHILIP II AND ALEXANDER THE GREAT

Coinage was issued in the name of the kings of Macedonia in northern Greece from the reign of Alexander I (about 498–451 BC), but it was Philip II (359–336 BC) and his son Alexander the Great (336–323 BC) who had the greatest influence on the development of coinage.

Under Philip the Macedonian kingdom became the dominant power in Greece and he prepared an expedition to liberate the Greeks of Asia Minor from Persian rule. He also reorganized the Macedonian coinage, producing great quantities of both silver and, for the first time, gold coinage. After Philip's death his plans for the conquest of the Persians were pursued by his son, who continued to issue identical gold coinage, but he also introduced new coinages with his own designs: the head of Heracles and a seated Zeus on the silver, and the head of Athena and a figure of Victory on the gold. These coinages, needed to finance Alexander's campaigns, were issued in massive quantities from mints established throughout the vast areas eventually conquered, and because of their popularity they continued to be minted long after Alexander's death.

THE HELLENISTIC PERIOD

The empire established by Alexander the Great did not survive intact for long. Various generals fought for the succession and began helping

8 178–168 BC

9 164–163 BC

10 c.100 BC

11 32–31 BC

12 AD 37–41

13 253–268

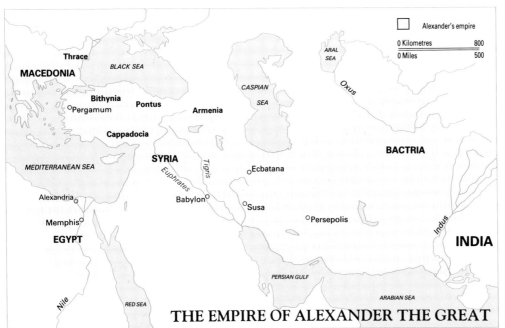

THE EMPIRE OF ALEXANDER THE GREAT

GREECE

8 SILVER TETRADRACHM, *portraying Perseus, last king of Macedonia.*
9 SILVER 'NEW STYLE' TETRADRACHM *of Athens.*
10 SILVER TETRADRACHM *of Thasos.*
11 SILVER DENARIUS *of Mark Antony, minted in Greece just before the battle of Actium.*
12 BRONZE COIN *of Corinth, minted under the Roman emperor Caligula.*
13 BRONZE COIN *of Lacedaemon (Sparta), issued under the Roman emperor Gallienus.*

themselves to portions of the empire. Cassander gained control of Greece and accepted the title of king in 306 BC, issuing his own bronze coinage but continuing to strike silver coins with the designs and in the names of Philip II and Alexander. Demetrius Poliorcetes (the 'besieger'), who replaced Cassander, was another leader to issue posthumous Alexander coins, but he also introduced coins with his own portrait. His descendants, Philip V (221–179 BC) and Perseus (179–165 BC), who were later kings of Macedon, continued the tradition of royal portraiture on coinage.

In addition to the kings of Macedon, various other rulers, such as Lysimachus of Thrace (323–281 BC), Pyrrhus of Epirus (295–272 BC) and the later kings of Sparta, issued their own coinages. Issues of silver coinage by the city states were less frequent, but issues of bronze coinage were still produced by numerous cities. Another feature of the Hellenistic period was the growth of leagues of cities; coinages in silver and bronze were issued, for example, by the Acarnanian, Achaean, Boeotian and Thessalian leagues.

ROMAN DOMINATION

The defeat of the last Macedonian king, Perseus, at the battle of Pydna in 168 BC brought Macedonia under Roman control, and following the destruction of Corinth in 146 BC southern Greece also fell under the domination of Rome. New coinages were introduced for Macedonia, replacing the earlier regal issues. Thasos and Maronea in the north continued to issue their own silver coins, but elsewhere in Greece there was a great reduction in the production of all but bronze local coinage. The only important silver coinage still produced in southern Greece was the new-style owl coinage of Athens, featuring the owl standing on an amphora and surrounded by a wreath.

Roman coins were not introduced into Greece until the mid-first century BC, when the region became involved in the civil wars between Roman generals, and gold Roman aurei and silver denarii (*see* Italy), as well as issues of bronze coinage, were minted locally to pay Roman soldiers. At the same time the production of silver coinage by the Greek city states came to an end. Bronze coins for local use were still produced in the Greek cities, some of which, including Corinth, had been refounded as Roman colonies.

THE ROMAN EMPIRE

The battle of Actium (31 BC), which ended republican Rome's civil wars and brought the Roman world under the rule of one man, Octavian, was fought off the coast of western Greece. Under the Roman Empire Greece was divided into several administrative units. Most of northern Greece formed the province of Macedonia, but the eastern extension was part of Thrace. Southern Greece formed the province of Achaea, but Crete was administered jointly with Cyrenaica (Libya) in North Africa and some of the islands of the eastern Aegean belonged to the province of Asia. Roman gold and silver coins were the standard currency, and Roman imperial bronze coins – sestertii, dupondii and asses – also circulated, but these were outnumbered by the locally produced bronze coins of the Greek cities. Local silver coins were no longer issued, except for a few rare pieces from Crete.

Most of the bronze coins issued by the cities of Greece under the Roman Empire had imperial portraits on the front, coupled with designs of more local significance on the back. Inscriptions on the coins were usually in Greek, except at the cities which were Roman colonies, such as Corinth and Patrae in Achaea, and Dium, Pella and Philippi in Macedonia, which used Latin. Some coins – including all the issues of Athens, those issued by Corcyra before the time of Antoninus Pius (138–61 BC), and most of the third-century AD issues of the province of Macedonia – did not have imperial portraits, but concentrated on figures of local mythology or history.

Output of local bronze coinage under the Roman Empire varied from period to period. Numerous issues under Nero (AD 54–68), who decreed Greeks need pay no taxes, were followed by virtually no issues under Vespasian (69–79), who reversed the order. The peak period was the reign of Septimius Severus (193–211), when many cities in the Peloponnese were added to the list of minting centres. The principal issuers in the Roman period were the province of Macedonia, Thessaly, Crete, and the cities of Amphipolis and Thessalonica in Macedonia, and Athens, Corinth and Patrae in Achaea.

The last local bronze coins were issued under Gallienus (253–68) in Thessaly, Nicopolis and Lacedaemon (Sparta). By this time Greece was relying almost entirely on Roman coins, particularly base-silver antoniniani (*see* Italy), and when the minting of imperial coinage was systematically devolved under Diocletian at the end of the third century a mint was established at Thessalonica. This operated for most of the fourth and fifth centuries, producing standard Roman imperial coinage, regularly in bronze and occasionally in gold or silver, for circulation in the region.

GREECE
14 BRONZE ½ FOLLIS *of Justin II and Sophia, struck at Thessalonica.*
15 GOLD HYPERPERON *of Manuel I Comnenus, struck at Thessalonica.*
16 BASE-SILVER ASPRON TRACHY *of Theodore Ducas-Comnenus, Emperor of Thessalonica.*

THE BYZANTINE EMPIRE

Throughout the early Middle Ages Greece remained under Byzantine control, ruled from Constantinople by the eastern emperors (*see* Turkey). The only coinage in use in Greece until the end of the twelfth century was that of Byzantium. At various times there were mints in Greece producing official Byzantine coins. Most important was that at Thessalonica, one of the greatest cities of the empire and, after the Arab conquests, second only to Constantinople. The mint there was active in the sixth and early seventh centuries, producing the full range of Byzantine coins: petty coinage in copper and the gold solidus or nomisma, semissis and tremissis (*see* Turkey).

Minting at Thessalonica ceased under Constans II (641–68) and was not revived during the Byzantine 'dark ages', when the Balkans

GREECE
17 BASE-SILVER DENIER TOURNOIS *of William de Villhardouin.*
18 BASE-SILVER TORNESELLO *of Andreas Contarini, Doge of Venice.*
19 SILVER GIGLIATO *of Elion de Villeneuve, Grand Master of the Knights of St John of Rhodes.*
20 GOLD DUCAT *of Filippo Maria Visconti, Lord of Chios.*
21 COPPER 10 LEPTA *of John Capodistras.*

17 1246–78   18 1368–83

19 1319–46

20 1421–36   21 1830

BYZANTINE RULERS MINTING IN THESSALONICA

Anastasius (491–518)
Justin I (518–27)
Justinian I (527–65)
Justin II (565–78)
Tiberius II Constantine (578–82)
Maurice Tiberius (582–602)
Phocas (602–10)
Heraclius (610–41)
Constans II (641–68)
Alexius I Comnenus (1081–1118)
John II Comnenus (1118–43)
Manuel I Comnenus (1143–80)
Andronicus I Comnenus (1183–5)
Isaac I Angelus (1185–95)
Alexius III Angelus-Comnenus (1195–1203)
Theodore Ducas-Comnenus (1224–42), emperor of Thessalonica
John III Ducas-Vatatzes (1222–54), emperor of Nicaea
Theodore II Ducas-Lascaris (1254–8), emperor of Nicaea
Michael VII Palaeologus (1261–82)
Andronicus II Palaeologus (1284–1328)
Andronicus III Palaeologus (1328–41)
John V Palaeologus (1341–91)
Anna of Savoy (1451–4)
Manuel II Palaeologus (1391–1423)

and Greece were subjected to invasion and settlement by Slavs and Bulgars. Nevertheless, central Greece remained under Byzantine control and continued to maintain an economy based on the circulation of money throughout the eighth and ninth centuries. Crete, however, was lost to the Arabs from 827 until 961. These gave it its own currency of gold dinars and copper fals, with occasional issues of silver dirhems.

In mainland Greece there was a great expansion in the use of coinage when Byzantine power revived in the tenth and eleventh centuries. Corinth, Thebes and Athens were prosperous centres and mints may have operated, perhaps at Corinth and Thessalonica. Large-scale minting was revived at Thessalonica under Alexius I Comnenus in about 1081–2 and continued until the Fourth Crusade (1204), though in the late twelfth century copper tetartera alone were being issued.

The Latin conquest of Byzantium by the Fourth Crusade in 1204 ended the uniform currency of Greece. Byzantine power revived in the rival empires of Thessalonica and Nicaea (in Asia Minor). Base-silver trachea were minted at Byzantine Thessalonica in the 1230s and 1240s and after the capture of the city by John III Ducas Vatatzes, the Emperor of Nicaea, a full range of gold, electrum, base-silver and copper denominations were produced there. In addition, the Byzantine despots of Epirus struck silver and base-silver trachea at Arta from 1204 to 1271.

Minting at Thessalonica continued under the restored Byzantine Empire from 1262 until the capture of Greece by the Turks; it was the only mint to operate apart from Constantinople itself. Often its issues had distinct designs, featuring in particular the image of St Demetrius, patron of Thessalonica. However, from the late thirteenth century its issues were confined largely to copper. The use of Byzantine coinage was increasingly confined to the enclaves of direct Byzantine control: Macedonia and Thrace and the despotate of the Morea in the Peloponnese.

FRANKISH RULE

In the aftermath of the Fourth Crusade in 1204 the Byzantine Empire became fragmented, divided between Franks, Italians and Byzantines (*see* Turkey). Mainland and Aegean Greece were divided into several states. In the years immediately following the Latin conquest, debased trachea of the type issued at Constantinople became widely used in central Greece and versions were produced in the Frankish kingdom of Thessalonica until its fall in 1224. The Franks also produced copper coins in the 1240s and 1250s in mints at Thebes and Corinth, but an important part of the currency was made up of Venetian grossi, English sterling pennies and deniers tournois imported from France.

In time the principal Frankish rulers came to mint their own deniers tournois, preserving the stylized castle design of the French original but putting their own names on the coins. This began in the principality of Achaea under William de Villehardouin (1246–78) in about 1262, the mint being at Clarentza. The princes of Achaea continued the issue of deniers until the reign of Robert of Taranto (1333–64). The other main issuers of deniers tournois were the dukes of Athens from the time of William de la Roche (1280–7). Their mint was at Thebes. Lesser rulers, Frankish and Byzantine, produced deniers at Lepanto, Corfu, Salona, Karitaina, Neopatras, Arta, Damala and Leucas. The production of counterfeit deniers, often blundered and crude, was also widespread.

ITALIAN RULE

The islands of the Aegean mostly fell under Venetian control, though only a few of the families which established themselves in the archipelago issued coins. There are rare issues from Naxos and Tinos in the early fourteenth century. On Chios the Genoese Zaccaria family

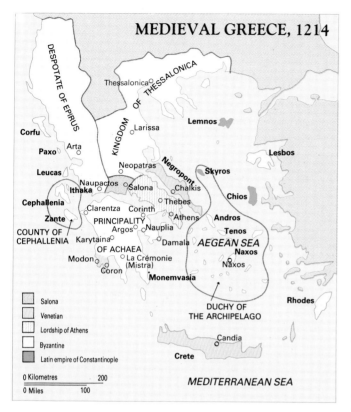

MEDIEVAL GREECE, 1214

DESPOTATE OF EPIRUS

KINGDOM OF THESSALONICA

Thessalonica
Larissa
Lemnos
Corfu
Paxo
Arta
Leucas
Neopatras
Lesbos
Naupactos
Skyros
Ithaka
Salona
Chalkis
Negropont
Cephallenia
Thebes
Chios
Clarentza
Corinth
Zante
Athens
Andros
PRINCIPALITY
Nauplia
COUNTY OF
Argos
Tenos
CEPHALLENIA
Karytaina
Damala
AEGEAN SEA
OF ACHAEA
Naxos
Modon
La Crémonie
Naxos
(Mistra)
Coron
Monemvasia
Rhodes

Salona
Venetian
Lordship of Athens
Byzantine
Latin empire of Constantinople

DUCHY OF
THE ARCHIPELAGO

0 Kilometres   200
0 Miles   100

Candia

Crete

MEDITERRANEAN SEA

(1307–29), ruling by grant from the Byzantine emperor, issued Venetian-style ¼ ducats and grossi as well as deniers tournois. Later Genoese rulers of Chios minted silver gigliati and gold ducats in the fifteenth and sixteenth centuries until the Turkish conquest. On Lesbos the Gattilusio family, also ruling by Byzantine grant, minted versions of Venetian gold ducats and silver soldini in the fourteenth and fifteenth centuries.

The most extensive and important coinage produced on the Greek islands was that of Rhodes under the Knights of St John. The Grand Master Elion de Villeneuve (1319–46) began the issue of silver gigliati, based on the coin issued by the kings of Naples which was in common use in the eastern Mediterranean. The Rhodian gigliati showed on the front the grand master kneeling in prayer before a cross. The issue of gigliati, and sometimes thirds, continued until the Great Siege of Rhodes and the island's surrender to the Sultan Suleyman the Magnificent in 1522. Gold coinage, imitations of the Venetian ducat, became common in the fifteenth century.

In mainland Greece the issue of deniers tournois by Frankish rulers declined in the early fourteenth century, but they remained in use, joined by Venetian soldini, first manufactured in 1332. From about 1350 a new coin became dominant in Greece: the tornesello, a base-silver coin derived from the denier tournois and intended to take its place. It was minted by the Venetians, but intended for use in their colonies at Coron, Modon, Negroponte and Crete. In fact it functioned as the principal low-denomination coin in Greece until the Turkish conquest. The main higher-value coin in use was the gold Venetian ducat. Throughout the centuries of Turkish rule the currency of Greece was that of the Ottoman sultans, struck at Constantinople (*see* Turkey).

INDEPENDENCE

Revolt against Turkish rule broke out in 1821 and independence was effectively achieved in 1827. Independent coinage was begun almost immediately under President John Capodistras (1827–31). The disused minting presses of the Order of St John on Malta were purchased and shipped to Aegina, where the first Greek coinage was struck. Copper coins of 1 lepton and 5, 10 and 20 lepta and a silver phoenix (= 100 lepta) were struck, all with a similar design of a phoenix rising from the ashes, to symbolize the rebirth of the nation, and the date of the Greek Revolt (1821).

THE KINGDOM OF GREECE

The first King of Greece, Otho, was chosen in 1832. He introduced the long-standing Greek monetary system of the drachma of 100 lepta. Denominations were: in copper, 1, 2, 5 and 10 lepta; in silver, ¼, ½, 1 and 5 drachmai; and in gold, 20 drachmai. Designs were straightforward: the head of the king on the front and the coat of arms on the back of the gold and silver, and on the copper the coat of arms on the front and the value on the back. The coinage was struck at Munich, Paris and Vienna, as well as Athens.

For part of the nineteenth century the Ionian Islands were ruled by Britain, which had acquired them from Turkey in 1809–14. Two local coinages were issued. The first was based on a system of 4 lepta to the obol, and the copper lepton, obol and 2 obol were issued in 1819–21. The second, introduced in 1835, had 5 lepta to the obol and the coins issued were the lepton in copper and the 30 lepta in silver. The designs of all these coins showed the lion of Venice on the front and Britannia on the back. In 1864 the islands were handed over to Greece.

In 1862 Otho was forced to abdicate and in his place was chosen George of Holstein, who ruled as George I until 1913. There were no new coins issued until 1868 and in the meantime Greece had joined the Latin Monetary Union (*see* France). Subsequent gold and silver issues were aligned to the equivalent French coins and were minted at French mints (Paris, Bordeaux and Strasbourg). Denominations issued were: in silver, 20 and 50 lepta and 1, 2 and 5 drachmai; and in gold, 5, 10, 20, 50 and 100 drachmai. The lepton and 2, 5 and 10 lepta were in copper. From 1893 base-metal (cupro-nickel, then nickel) was used for the 20 lepta and lesser denominations.

GREECE
22 Silver Drachma *of George I.*
23 Cupro-Nickel 5 Drachmai *of Constantine II.*
24 Cupro-Nickel 50 Drachmai *of the Republic of Greece.*

22 1910

23 1968

24 1984

The issues of 1910–11 featured innovatory designs, with scenes from classical mythology replacing the national coat of arms on the backs of the coins. The silver used a scene from the *Iliad*, copying a coin of King Pyrrhus of Epirus (295–272 BC), and the holed base-metal coins showed either Athena or the Athenian owl.

Until 1897 Crete remained under Turkish rule. In that year it was given virtual independence under a Greek prince, George, who issued a coinage aligned to that of Greece in 1900–1. Full union with Greece came about in 1908.

Under Constantine I (1913–23) little current coinage was issued: only cupro-nickel 50 lepta in 1921 (minted at private mints in Britain) and aluminium 10 lepta (minted at Poissy in France) in 1922. The stormy political events of the time were not reflected in the coinage, but because so little new currency had been issued there was an acute shortage of money in the country.

THE FIRST REPUBLIC

Under the Republic of Greece (1924–35) steps were taken to remedy the situation and a new coinage was introduced, removing the royal portrait and using classical prototypes for the designs, mostly the heads of deities. The coinage was struck at the Royal Mint in London and consisted of cupro-nickel (20 and 50 lepta and 1 and 2 drachmai), nickel (5 drachmai) and silver (10 and 20 drachmai).

RESTORATION OF MONARCHY

The monarchy was restored in 1935 but the only coins produced under George II (1935–47) were commemorative pieces celebrating the restoration. The republican coinage circulated until 1954, when there was an issue in the name of King Paul (1947–64), with designs in the old style of the king's head on the front and the Greek arms on the back. The aluminium coins (5, 10 and 20 lepta) and the nickel 10 drachmai were struck at Berne; the silver 20 drachmai at London; and the cupro-nickel coins (50 lepta and 1, 2 and 5 drachmai) at Paris. Under Constantine II (1964–73) all the high-value coins were of cupro-nickel, struck at Prague. Coinage was issued in his name even after his failure to unseat the military regime in 1968 and his subsequent exile.

SECOND REPUBLIC

In 1973, with democracy restored to Greece, the Hellenic Republic was declared. The republican coinage initially displayed classical images, such as the phoenix and Athenian owl, but from 1976 most denominations show portraits of notable figures of Greek history. The smallest denominations (50 lepta and 1 and 2 drachmai in nickel–brass) show individuals from recent Greek history whereas the larger ones (5, 10, 20 and 50 drachmai in cupro-nickel) show figures from the classical past: Aristotle, Democritus, Pericles and Solon. As in most modern countries, precious-metal coins are produced to commemorate sporting events and national anniversaries.

CYPRUS

FIRST COINS:	late sixth century BC
FIRST DECIMAL COINS:	1955
MAIN MINT:	Royal Mint
CURRENCY:	pound

BEFORE the invention of coinage, precious-metal rings, nuggets and bars, as well as implements such as axes, were used as money in Cyprus. The first coins issued on the island date from the late sixth century BC, when Cyprus was governed by a number of small city kingdoms whose rulers all owed allegiance to the Persian Great King. Situated in the busy waters of the eastern Mediterranean, Cyprus was on the trade route between the Aegean to the west and the important Persian provinces of Phoenicia and Egypt to the east and south, and silver coins travelling east from Greek territory provided models for many of the designs on the early coins of Cyprus.

In the fifth and fourth centuries BC most of the major cities in Cyprus were issuing their own coins, and the wide variety of designs and scripts (Cypriot, Greek and Phoenician) illustrate the cultural diversity of ancient Cyprus. The main centre of Greek civilization on

3 c. 300 BC

4 142–141 BC

1 c. 465 BC

2 c. 425–400 BC

5 76–7

6 76–7

CYPRUS

1 SILVER COIN *of King Nicodamos of Salamis, with Cypriot inscriptions.*
2 SILVER COIN *of King Baalmalek II of Citium, with Phoenician inscriptions.*
2 SILVER TETRADRACHM *of Demetrius Poliorcetes ('Besieger'), with a design commemorating his victory in the naval battle of Salamis.*
4 SILVER TETRADRACHM *of King Ptolemy VIII of Egypt, minted at Paphos in year 29 of his reign.*
5 SILVER TETRADRACHM *of the Roman Emperor Vespasian.*
6 BRONZE COIN *of Vespasian, depicting the cult figure of Zeus Salaminios.*

CITY MINTS OF ANCIENT CYPRUS

MEDITERRANEAN SEA

Lapethus

Salamis

Soli

Idalium

Citium

Marium

• City mints: Fifth to fourth centuries BC

Paphos • Curium • Amathus

0 Kilometres 1000
0 Miles 500

the island was Salamis. Its coins usually had Greek-style designs and Cypriot lettering, whereas the coins of the principal Phoenician city, Citium, used Phoenician script.

When the Persian Empire was conquered by Alexander the Great, Cyprus became part of Alexander's empire and its cities issued coins in his name and with his designs. After his death the island was disputed between his successors but eventually it became a possession of the Ptolemaic Kingdom of Egypt.

THE PTOLEMIES

Under the Ptolemies Cyprus produced coinage very similar to contemporary Egyptian issues. The principal coin was the silver tetradrachm, which bore standard designs that changed very little. The head of Ptolemy I was placed on the front; on the back was the eagle of Zeus, an inscription which invariably provided the date of issue since a Greek numeral recorded the year of the king's reign, and, lastly, the initial of the minting city, usually Citium, Paphos or Salamis. Cyprus also produced issues of bronze Ptolemaic coinage, some of which have Cypriot, as opposed to Ptolemaic, designs.

Cyprus first became a Roman province in 58 BC, but from 47 to 30 BC, during Rome's civil wars, the island was restored to Ptolemaic rule. Cleopatra VII issued bronze coins in Cyprus which portrayed her with her baby son, the child of Julius Caesar.

THE ROMAN PERIOD

The coinage of Roman Cyprus began to be issued in the reign of the first emperor, Augustus (31 BC–AD 14), and appeared quite frequently under his successors in the first century AD. Initially only bronze coins were produced, possibly from two mints at Paphos and Salamis, though no city's name or initial ever appeared on the coinage of Roman Cyprus. The emperor's head always appeared on the front of the coins: other imperial portraits of one of two standard Cypriot designs, the statue of Zeus of Salamis or a view of the Temple of Aphrodite at Paphos, usually appeared on the back. At first Latin inscriptions were used and the name of the Roman governor of the island was sometimes included but from the reign of Claudius (41–54) Greek became the standard script on Cypriot coins and inscriptions usually identified the provincial council of the island as the issuing authority.

Under Vespasian (69–79) and Titus (79–81) a series of silver 2 and 4 drachma coins were issued over a period of about four years. These

coins, which have the usual combination of designs for Cyprus – imperial head on the front, Zeus of Salamis or Temple of Paphian Aphrodite on the back – were the only silver pieces issued by the Romans in Cyprus. The Roman denarius was the standard silver coin circulating in the island.

The issuing of bronze coins continued, though only intermittently, until the early third century, after which the island had to rely completely on imported coinage. From the late third century production of local coinage in the eastern provinces of the Roman Empire ceased altogether. All the new coinage circulating in Cyprus in the fourth and fifth centuries was Roman, produced at the nearest imperial mints, particularly Antioch-on-the-Orontes in Turkey.

THE BYZANTINE PERIOD

From the fifth to the late twelfth century Cyprus remained part of the East Roman or Byzantine Empire and Byzantine coinage alone was in use (see Turkey). Only briefly and in exceptional circumstances were coins minted on the island itself. The first such occasion was in 608–10, during the revolt of Heraclius against the usurping Emperor Phocas. As Heraclius and his supporters advanced from Egypt, mints were opened along their route to Constantinople. There was one such mint opened on Cyprus, though it is not known precisely where. It produced bronze folles in the name of Heraclius and his father, the Exarch of North Africa.

Heraclius's revolt was successful and during his reign (610–41) a mint continued to operate on Cyprus, probably at Constantia, the Byzantine capital. The existence of this and other unusual mints operating at this time probably reflects the political and military crises faced by Heraclius in the east, where he was confronted successively by the Persians and the Arabs. His mint on Cyprus produced only the bronze follis, not the imperial gold coinage, in the names of the emperor, his son Heraclius Constantine and the Empress Martina. They bore the mint mark KYPR in Greek script. Bronze coins of Heraclius and his successor, Constans II, were countermarked on Cyprus with a large K during the reign of Constantine IV Pogonatus (668–85) to signify that they were still current.

The only other Byzantine coins manufactured on Cyprus indicate

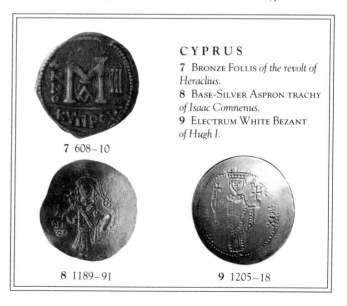

CYPRUS

7 BRONZE FOLLIS *of the revolt of Heraclius.*
8 BASE-SILVER ASPRON TRACHY *of Isaac Comnenus.*
9 ELECTRUM WHITE BEZANT *of Hugh I.*

7 608–10

8 1189–91

9 1205–18

the end of direct Byzantine rule. In 1184 Isaac Comnenus, a minor member of the imperial family, set himself up on Cyprus as emperor. He ruled until 1191, issuing in his own name electrum and base-silver trachea and copper tetartera which otherwise resembled official imperial issues. His mint was probably at Nicosia.

FRANKISH RULE

In 1191 Richard I of England, on crusade to the Holy Land, put in at Cyprus, where he was attacked by Isaac Comnenus. Richard emerged victorious and sold the island firstly to the Templars and then to Guy de Lusignan, former king of Jerusalem. The Frankish Lusignan Dynasty ruled Cyprus until 1489, issuing a substantial coinage. From 1268 they also used the title 'King of Jerusalem', which they claimed by inheritance.

For most of the thirteenth century the kings of Cyprus issued three types of coins. The standard coin was the white bezant, a coin of gold adulterated with silver. It was entirely Byzantine in shape and design, showing the king enthroned on the front and Christ on the back.

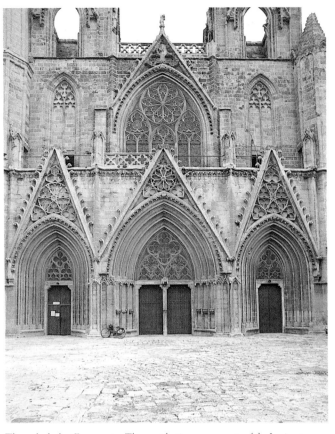

The cathedral at Famagusta. The most lasting monuments of the Lusignan kings of Cyprus, other than their coinage, are the splendid Gothic cathedrals built under their patronage, notably at Famagusta and Nicosia.

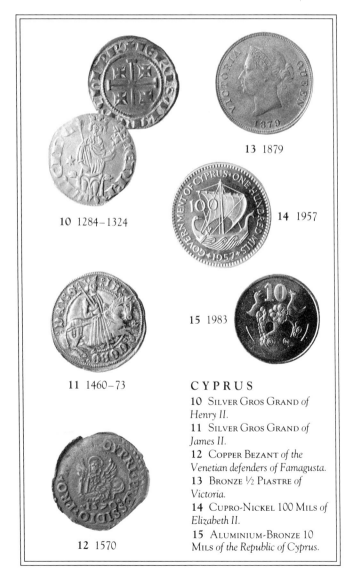

13 1879

14 1957

15 1983

10 1284–1324

11 1460–73

12 1570

CYPRUS

10 Silver Gros Grand *of Henry II.*
11 Silver Gros Grand *of James II.*
12 Copper Bezant *of the Venetian defenders of Famagusta.*
13 Bronze ½ Piastre *of Victoria.*
14 Cupro-Nickel 100 Mils *of Elizabeth II.*
15 Aluminium-Bronze 10 Mils *of the Republic of Cyprus.*

Small change was provided by base-silver deniers and some copper coins which may have been obols ($= \frac{1}{2}$ denier).

The Cypriot coinage was changed dramatically under Henry II (1285–1324). The white bezant was replaced by a fine-silver coin, the gros grand and its half, the gros petit. The bezant remained as a unit of account ($= 4$ gros). The first, rarer version of the gros showed the king enthroned on the front and the lion of Cyprus on the back. The much more common, lighter version had the cross of Jerusalem on the back. Henry's gros coinage was interrupted by that of his usurping brother, Amaury, in 1308–10.

The silver gros, supplemented by $\frac{1}{2}$ gros and deniers, remained the standard Cypriot coin throughout the fourteenth century and the issues of Henry II and Hugh IV (1324–59) always predominated. There was a slight change to the design under Peter I (1359–69), when a drawn sword was added to the image of the king. Coins of the later Lusignans are rare. Janus (1398–1432) introduced a new denomination, the sixain ($= 6$ deniers), and on the gros of Queen Charlotte (1458–9) the traditional enthroned figure was replaced by a crowned shield. James II (1460–73) struck new-style coins showing himself on horseback on the gros grand and in a profile portrait on the gros petit. His Venetian wife and successor, Catherine Cornaro (1473–89), restored the old design, showing herself enthroned and veiled on the gros grand.

VENETIAN RULE

In the fourteenth century Italian influence developed on Cyprus. In 1373 the Genoese seized Famagusta, holding it until 1464. They minted copper coins with a gateway design for use as small change. Venetian power expanded even more and the republic became the formal ruler of Cyprus in 1389, inducing Catherine Cornaro to abdicate. The currency of Venetian Cyprus still consisted largely of Lusignan issues, sometimes countermarked to indicate its current value. Foreign coins were also in use, particularly Venetian and Spanish silver issues. The only coins produced for Cyprus by Venice were low denominations in copper and base silver, notably copper carzias issued in the mid-sixteenth century. In 1570 Cyprus was taken by the Turks. The Venetians, besieged in Famagusta, produced a copper siege piece called a bezant and inscribed in Latin 'on behalf of the garrison of the kingdom of Cyprus'. Under Ottoman rule Turkish currency alone was in use on Cyprus (*see* Turkey).

BRITISH RULE

In 1878 Cyprus passed to British rule. A coinage for Cyprus was minted in England incorporating the old Turkish denomination, the piastre, into a new British-style system of 9 piastres to the shilling and 20 shillings to the pound. Denominations issued were the $\frac{1}{4}$, $\frac{1}{2}$ and 1 piastre in bronze, and 3, $4\frac{1}{2}$, 9 and 18 piastres in silver. Coinage of British Cyprus always had the monarch's head on the front. The smaller denominations had the mark of value on the back, the larger ones a coat of arms or the lions of Cyprus.

The $\frac{1}{4}$ piastre ceased to be issued in 1926 and in 1934 the $\frac{1}{2}$ and 1 piastre became cupro-nickel coins with a wavy edge, though the 1 piastre reverted to bronze in 1942. In 1928 a silver 45 piastres commemorated the 50th anniversary of British rule. In 1955 a new decimal system of 50 mils to the shilling was introduced. The denominations mostly had designs of local plant and animal life on the back with the queen's head on the front.

THE REPUBLIC OF CYPRUS

Cyprus was established as an independent republic in 1960, and its new decimal system survived the transition, but the design on the front of the coins became a shield bearing a dove of peace with, on the back, images of local significance: on different coins, an ancient Greek sailing ship, an ibex and a bunch of grapes. The smallest denominations, below 25 mils, were in bronze, then aluminium; the larger ones, 25, 50, 100 and 500 mils, in cupro-nickel. Silver and cupro-nickel versions of the 500 mils have commemorated refugees and human rights. In 1977 a gold pound was issued in honour of President Archbishop Makarios.

MODERN COINAGE

Since 1974 the island has been divided into Greek and Turkish sections. Currency has been issued only by the Greek Cypriot government. In 1983 a new monetary system was established, of 100 cents to the pound. The design on the front of the coins remained virtually unchanged but a new range of images has been introduced for the backs, mostly of plant and animal life. Denominations issued are the $\frac{1}{2}$ cent in aluminium; 1, 2, 5, 10 and 20 cents in nickel–brass; and 50 cents and 1 pound in cupro-nickel. The 50 cents is a United Nations Food and Agriculture Organization issue promoting forestry and the 1 pound commemorates the World Wildlife Fund.

AUSTRIA

FIRST COINS:	*c.* 100 BC
FIRST DECIMAL COINS:	1857
MAIN MINT:	Vienna
CURRENCY:	schilling

THE first coins to arrive in the territory that is modern Austria were Greek issues paid to Celtic warriors from the region employed as mercenaries, and central European Celtic issues of the third and second centuries BC, particularly imitations of gold staters of Philip II and Alexander III of Macedon (*see* Greece). Production of silver Celtic coins in the Danubian tradition of Philip II imitations eventually reached Austria, but probably not much earlier than about 100 BC. The issues of the first century BC included small silver fractions with

AUSTRIA
1 SILVER CELTIC COIN.
2 SILVER ROMAN ANTONI-NIANUS *of the usurper Regalian, minted in Carnuntum.*

1 FIRST CENTURY BC

2 AD 261

horse designs, as well as silver tetradrachms. The northeastern part of Austria was also within the circulation area of the large silver coins of the mid- and late first century BC known as the Bratislava group (*see* Czechoslovakia). Celtic coinage in Austria came to an end with the Roman conquest of the region around 15 BC.

THE ROMAN PERIOD

Most of present-day Austria was included within the Roman province of Noricum. This was frontier territory, defending the empire against the German tribes to the north, and much of the Roman coinage which arrived there was sent to pay for military expenses. For over 400 years Roman imperial coinage circulated in Noricum. Until the mid-third century most of it came from the mint of Rome: in the later imperial period mints in northern Italy and Yugoslavia became the chief suppliers.

Although the province had no official Roman mint, at least one issue of coinage produced by the many military usurpers of the mid-third century can be identified as Austrian. This is the coinage of Regalian, minted at Carnuntum in about 261. There was also doubtless widespread local production of imitation Roman coinage during the late imperial period, when supplies of official coinage to all the provinces were dwindling. After the barbarian invasions of the fifth century, coinage ceased to circulate in the region.

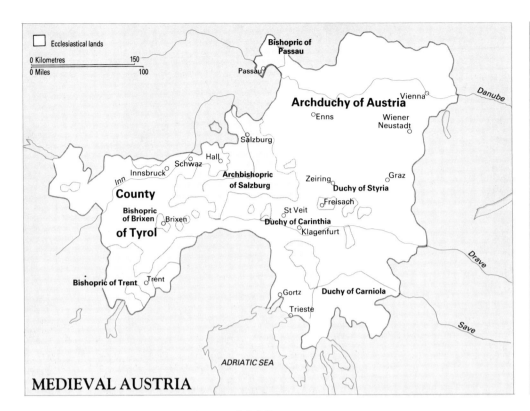

3 1183–1200   **4** 1194–1230

AUSTRIA

3 SILVER PFENNIG of *Adalbert of Bohemia, Archbishop of Salzburg, struck in Freisach.*
4 SILVER PFENNIG of *Leopold II, Duke of Styria, struck in Graz.*
5 SILVER PFENNIG of *Bernhard, Duke of Carinthia, struck in St Veit.*
6 SILVER PFENNIG of *Friedrich II, Duke of Austria, struck in Vienna.*
7 SILVER PFENNIG of *Ottokar II, Duke of Austria, struck in Vienna.*
8 SILVER ADLERGROSCHEN of *Meinhard II, Count of Tyrol.*

THE MEDIEVAL PERIOD

With the barbarian invasions coinage ceased to be manufactured or used in Austria for several centuries. With the expansion of the Carolingian Empire in the ninth century, Austria became its eastern marchland. Coinage in the region consisted of the denars or pfennigs of the German kings until the eleventh century, when minting rights throughout the empire were granted to lesser rulers. In Austria the main states to produce coins were the Duchies of Austria, Carinthia and Styria and the Archbishopric of Salzburg.

In the late twelfth and early thirteenth centuries silver mines in Carinthia provided the metal for the influential Freisacher pfennigs, struck at the Archbishop of Salzburg's mint at Freisach and the Duke of Carinthia's mint at St Veit. These coins circulated widely in southeastern Europe and were copied in many neighbouring states.

Designs were varied, changing regularly, but on the Freisachers included a building with towers, the bust or figure of the archbishop and an angel; and at St Veit the figure or bust of the duke, a winged lion and six-rayed star. In Austria the Viennese pfennig was equally influential, with mints at Vienna, Wiener Neustadt and Enns featuring a great variety of designs, some of which identified a specific mint: the double-headed eagle (Vienna), griffin (Wiener Neustadt) and panther, deer or duck (Enns). In Styria, Graz and Zeiring were the main mints, with the shield of Austria featuring among the many designs. In Tyrol a different coinage tradition was influential, with Italian-style gros struck in the mid-thirteenth century.

THE HABSBURG EMPIRE

Austria passed to the Habsburgs in 1276 and Rudolf of Habsburg (1289–91) was the first ruler to include his name or initial on the local pfennigs. Gold coinage was introduced under Albert II (1339–58) with the production of Florentine-style florins, distinctive designs appearing only under Albert V (1404–39). His gold gulden had the Madonna on the front and an orb on the back. Large silver coins made their appearance only under Frederick III (1458–93) in the shape of groschen and ½ groschen. These almost invariably featured the double-headed eagle on the front.

By the late fifteenth century Styria, Carinthia and Tyrol had all passed to the Habsburgs (who now ruled Austria as archdukes), though local coinages continued, sometimes under cadet members of the family, until the mid-seventeenth century. It was at the mint of Hall in Tyrol that a new type of coin appeared. Large silver guldiners or talers, equal in value to the old gold gulden, were struck in 1486 by Sigismund the Wealthy (1439–90), taking advantage of the silver mines at Schwaz and inaugurating a new age of coinage.

Maximilian (1493–1519) organized coinage reforms throughout his domains as Holy Roman Emperor. Under his rule the taler was issued as part of the Austrian coinage and was also taken up by the Archbishops of Salzburg. Most Austrian examples featured profile portraits of the emperor.

The coinage system of Austria from the early sixteenth century was based on the kreuzer of 4 pfennigs or 8 heller. Initially the taler was equal to the gulden or florin of 60 kreuzer, though its value increased with time, stabilizing at 120 kreuzer in 1692. The weight and fineness of the Habsburg taler was reduced in 1750–3, though the new 'Conventionstaler' retained the old value in kreuzer. The talers of Maria Theresa (1740–80) became extremely important in international trade, particularly in Turkey, the Levant and Ethiopia, and continued to be struck for centuries.

The main coins issued were: in gold, mainly the ducat (= approximately 2 talers) with multiples of 2, 3, 4, 5 and 10 known, and its

1205–56
6 1230–46
7 1261–76
8 1257–95
11 1493–1519
9 1339–58
10 1486
12 1509
13 1628

9 GOLD GULDEN of Albrecht II, Archduke of Austria.
10 SILVER GULDINER of Sigismund of Tyrol, struck in Hall.
11 SILVER TALER of Maximilian I.
12 SILVER 2 GULDINER of Maximilian I.
13 SILVER TALER of Paris, Archbishop of Salzburg.
14 GOLD DUCAT of Ferdinand II.
15 SILVER TALER of Maria Theresa.

14 1636
15 1780

fractions, sometimes down to $\frac{1}{12}$; in silver, $\frac{1}{4}$, $\frac{1}{2}$, 1 and, sometimes, multiple talers; and lesser denominations in silver or base silver – usually $\frac{1}{4}$, $\frac{1}{2}$, 1, 2, $2\frac{1}{2}$ or 3, 5 or 6, 10 and 30 kreuzer. The main mints of the Habsburgs were Vienna in Austria, Hall in Tyrol, Graz in Styria and Klagenfurt in Carinthia, the provinces depicted in the coats of arms on the breast of the Austrian eagle. Portrait busts featured on the front of the large silver coins and, in the eighteenth century, on the gold denominations. Copper coinage of $\frac{1}{4}$, $\frac{1}{2}$ and 1 kreuzer provided the smallest denominations from the mid-eighteenth century.

A number of lesser princes exercised coining rights in the Habsburg Empire. The coinage of the Archbishops of Salzburg continued to be issued, distinguished by splendid baroque versions of Saints Rupert and Virgilius and the Madonna and Child, until the archbishopric was secularized in 1803. Directly subordinate to the Habsburgs were those great nobles who received minting rights in the seventeenth and eighteenth centuries. Their issues usually consisted simply of talers and ducats produced for prestige. They included the Princes of Auersperg, Khevenhüller, Liechtenstein, Orsini-Rosenburg and Paar, the Hungarian families of Batthyani and Esterhazy, the Counts of Montfort and Windischgrätz, the Bishops of Brixen in Tyrol and Gurk in Carinthia, and the Archbishop of Vienna.

THE AUSTRIAN EMPIRE
In 1804, during the Napoleonic Wars, Francis II (1792–1835) renounced the title Holy Roman Emperor, retaining the designation Emperor of Austria. The coinage reflected the change of titles, but otherwise altered little until the monetary convention of 1857 established a new system of 100 kreuzer to the gulden (or florin) and $1\frac{1}{2}$ gulden to the Vereinsthaler. The denominations issued consisted of the $\frac{5}{10}$, 1 and 4 kreuzer in copper; 5, 10 and 20 kreuzer and $\frac{1}{4}$, 1 and 2

gulden and Vereinsthaler in silver; and the $\frac{1}{2}$ and 1 krone in gold. Designs showed the head of Emperor Franz Josef or the Austrian eagle on the front and the Austrian eagle or value on the back. A further new coinage was introduced in 1892, based on 100 hellers to the corona, and consisting of bronze 1 and 2 heller, nickel 10 and 20 heller, silver 1, 2 and 5 corona, and gold 10 and 20 corona.

Throughout the nineteenth century a range of coins was struck for international trade: silver Maria Theresa talers; gold 1, 2 and 4 ducats; and gold 4 and 8 gulden, equivalent to the 10 and 20 francs of the Latin Monetary Union (see France). The only coins to be struck under the last Habsburg emperor, Karl (1916–18), were iron 2, 10 and 20 heller.

REPUBLIC OF AUSTRIA
In the aftermath of the First World War the Habsburg Empire was dismantled and the Republic of Austria created. It experienced massive inflation in these years, producing a monetary system of 10,000 kronen to the schilling. New coinage only appeared in 1923, with bronze 100 and 200 kronen and cupro-nickel 1000 kronen. The currency was revised in 1925 to a system of 100 groschen to the

16 1810

17 1868

18 1894

19 1924

20 1956

21 1978   22 1978

Austrian Silesia
Prague
Bohemia   Kutna Hora
Cracow
Galicia and Lodomeria
Olmütz
Moravia
Zips
Brno
Kremnitza
Danube
Passau
Austria Vienna   Pressburg   **Hungary**   Nagybanya   **Bukovina**
Salzburg   Budapest
Hall
Innsbruck   **Salzburg**   **Styria**
Tyrol   Graz   Klausenburg
Liechtenstein   Brixen   **Carinthia**   **Transylvania**
Klagenfurt
Trent   Hermannstadt
Lombardy   **Venetia**   **Carniola**
Milan   Trieste   Banat
Venice   Slavonia
Istria
Croatia
Danube
ADRIATIC
SEA   Dalmatia

Boundary of Austria–Hungary

0 Kilometres   300
0 Miles   200

THE AUSTRO-HUNGARIAN EMPIRE

AUSTRIA

16 GOLD DUCAT of Franz I.
17 SILVER GULDEN of Franz Josef I.
18 BRONZE 2 HELLER of Franz Josef I.
19 CUPRO-NICKEL 1,000 GROSCHEN.

20 SILVER 25 SCHILLING commemorating the 200th anniversary of the birth of Mozart.
21 CUPRO-NICKEL 5 SCHILLING.
22 ALUMINIUM-BRONZE SCHILLING.

schilling. Denominations in bronze (1 and 2 groschen) and cupronickel (5, 10 and 50 groschen) supported the silver 1 and 5 schilling, though the 1 schilling also became cupro-nickel in 1934. Most denominations featured the Austrian eagle as part of their designs, though the silver schilling displayed the parliament building on the front. After the Anschluss of 1938, German coinage became current in Austria at a rate of 150 schillings to 100 reichsmark.

MODERN COINAGE

Independent Austrian coinage was restored after the Second World War, retaining the system of 100 groschen to the schilling. The smallest denominations – 1, 2, 5 and 10 groschen – were issued in zinc or aluminium. The 50 groschen and 1, 2 and 5 schilling were issued in aluminium until 1957, after which aluminium-bronze took over for the 50 groschen and schilling, the 2 schilling was discontinued and silver 5 and 10 schillings were produced. The latter became cupro-nickel in

1974 and a copper-aluminium-nickel 20 schilling was added to the currency in 1980.

Modern designs have mostly included the Austrian shield on the front, sometimes on the breast of the Austrian eagle. The 1 schilling has edelweiss on the back, the 5 schilling a Lippizaner horse and rider on the front and the 10 schilling a female head in traditional headdress on the back. Modern Austrian coinage includes many commemoratives, mostly silver 25 and 50 schillings, which mark every conceivable national anniversary and celebration.

SWITZERLAND

FIRST COINS:	third century BC
FIRST DECIMAL COINS:	1798
MAIN MINT:	Bern
CURRENCY:	franc

THE first coins of Switzerland were Celtic issues of gold staters and fractions in the Gallic tradition (see France) of imitations of the coinage of Philip II of Macedon. The Swiss series began early, in the third century BC. Initially characterized by their quite faithful copying of the Apollo head and chariot designs of the original Macedonian gold coin (see Greece), the later issues, of the second century BC, developed more individual styles and often bore little resemblance to the prototype. In the first century BC the Celtic tribes of Switzerland issued small silver coins with designs imitating Roman and Danubian Celtic issues. The rainbow-cup gold coinage of southern Germany also circulated!

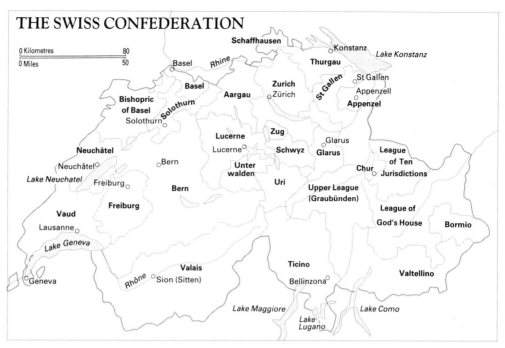

THE SWISS CONFEDERATION

0 Kilometres 80
0 Miles 50

SWITZERLAND

1 GOLD CELTIC COIN of the Helvetii, north Switzerland.
2 SILVER DENAR of Hermann I, Duke of Swabia, struck in Zurich.
3 SILVER OBOL of Conrad, Bishop of Geneva.

1 SECOND CENTURY BC
3 1019–31
2 AD 926–48

THE ROMAN PERIOD

The Roman conquest of the Alpine regions late in the first century BC brought Switzerland into the Roman Empire as the province of Rhaetia, and the local Celtic coinages came to an end. For the next 400 years Roman coinage dominated the region, but no official issues were minted locally. The Roman coinage in circulation in Rhaetia came from Rome and, particularly in the late imperial period, from other mints in Gaul and northern Italy. The supply of coinage ceased with the barbarian invasions of the fifth century AD.

Judas receives the thirty pieces of silver. *Twelfth-century painting in the church at Zwillis, Switzerland.*

EARLY MEDIEVAL COINS

In the Dark Ages the territory of modern Switzerland was occupied by the Ostrogoths and Burgundians, but in the sixth and seventh centuries the region was brought within the Frankish Kingdom (*see France*) and Merovingian gold tremisses were produced at Basel, Geneva, Sitten and Zürich. Basel, Chur and Zürich issued silver deniers under the Carolingians and Chur and Zürich under the early German emperors in the ninth and tenth centuries. From about 926 the Dukes of Swabia struck denars at Zürich with a cross on both sides.

LOCAL COINAGES

However, various local rulers were granted coining rights in the tenth and eleventh centuries. The Bishops of Constance (now in southern Germany) had a very important mint in the region, the first to issue coins being Salomon II (890–919), and the Bishops of Chur, Lucerne, Geneva, Sitten and Basel began to issue significant coinages, as did the Abbeys of Zürich, Rheinau, St Ursus-Solothurn and St Gallen.

In the late eleventh century the denars of southern Germany, including Switzerland, became very thin, semi-bracteates, until in the thirteenth century genuine bracteate pfennigs were made. The Constance coins had the bishop with crozier or book as the single design, the St Gallen coins showed the Paschal Lamb, those of Chur an ibex and those of Rheinau a fish motif.

Further south, Zürich and Basel had important mints, issuing distinctive, almost square bracteates, with lesser coinages produced at Bern, Solothurn and Laufenburg. In the later Middle Ages various cities acquired coining rights of their own, notably Basel (1373), Solothurn (1381), St Gallen and Lucerne (1415), Freiburg (1422) and Zürich (1425).

THE SWISS CONFEDERATION

From the late thirteenth century the Swiss Confederation began to take shape with the gradual association of the constituent cantons. But

4 LATE THIRTEENTH CENTURY

5 1250–62

6 1438–9

7 1497–1514

8 1482–96

10 1610

9 1494

12 1680

11 1641

13 1799

14 1820

15 1871

SWITZERLAND

4 SILVER BRACTEATE DENAR of the Abbey of St Gallen.
5 SILVER BRACTEATE DENAR of Berchtold II, Bishop of Basel.
6 GOLD GULDEN of the Emperor Albrecht II, struck in Basel.
7 SILVER GROSCHEN of Aymon de Montfalcon, Bishop of Lausanne.
8 SILVER DICKEN of Ioducos von Silinen, Bishop of Sitten.
9 SILVER TALER of Bern.
10 SILVER DICKEN of Zug.
11 GOLD DOUBLE PISTOLE of Geneva.
12 GOLD DUCAT of Zürich.
13 SILVER 10 BATZEN of the Helvetian Republic.
14 BASE-SILVER BATZEN of Graubünden.
15 GOLD 20 FRANCS.

distinct local coinages were still provided. In the late fourteenth century biface pfennigs or hellers replaced the bracteates, and were joined by larger silver pieces, varieties of groschen. Local city arms or patron saints were the main designs on all these coins, for instance St Vincent at Bern.

Gold coinage was also begun, first at Basel in 1411 with gold gulden in the name of the Holy Roman Emperor with the Madonna on the front and *Reichsapfel* (imperial orb) on the back. The first cities to strike gold, mostly ducats, in their own names were Freiburg and Lucerne in the late fifteenth century. Lesser coinages in base silver were struck at most places, such as the plapparts (= 15 heller) issued from 1421 at Bern, Lucerne, Freiburg and Zürich.

Separate coinages continued through the early modern period, with each authority issuing a variety of denominations with local designs and often to its own local monetary system, though most featured the batzen of 4 kreuzer, introduced in the late fifteenth century, as the basis of the system. Many produced gold coins, usually florins or ducats and fractions and multiples thereof, the most prolific issuers being Basel, Bern, Lucerne and Zürich. Geneva produced gold pistoles on the line of French écus. Almost all struck silver talers (= 40 batzen in several cantons), $\frac{1}{2}$ talers and testons or dickens (= 6 batzen).

Bern struck the first Swiss taler in 1490. Coats of arms and local patron saints remained the most commonly-used designs, though the effects of the Reformation reduced the representation of saints. For instance, at Bern the town's founder replaced St Vincent on its talers, and at Basel the imperial eagle replaced the Madonna. In addition, the Catholic bishops of Basel were forced to move their seat and mint from Basel to Porrentruy.

Smaller denominations were provided by the batzen and kreuzer in various multiples struck in base-silver, and a variety of local pieces: rappen, heller, angster and stäbler. On the borders of Italy, Bellinzona (later the canton of Ticino) followed the Italian system of 12 denari to the soldo, while Geneva worked to 12 deniers to the sol on French lines, and in Zürich and Chur there were 12 heller or pfennigs to the schilling, following German practice. The principality of Neuchâtel passed from a French family to the Kings of Prussia in 1707, who issued a coinage based on 4 kreuzer to the batzen.

THE HELVETIAN REPUBLIC
In 1798 revolutionary France overran Switzerland and established the Helvetian Republic, with a unified coinage of 10 rappen to the batzen and 10 batzen to the frank. The remaining ecclesiastical mints were closed permanently. All denominations (the rappen, $\frac{1}{2}$ and 1 batzen in base-silver, 5, 10, 20 and 40 batzen in silver, and 16 and 32 franks in gold) showed a mailed figure holding a banner. In 1803 the 19 cantons had their minting rights restored, though they had to conform to the established system.

THE CONFEDERATION RESTORED
The Confederation, now with 22 cantons, was restored in 1815, though the denominational system of the Helvetian Republic was largely preserved. The lesser cantons issued only small denominations infrequently and a few cantons – Geneva, Lucerne, Solothurn and Zürich – issued gold (ducats or franks).

In 1848 with the reorganization of the Swiss Confederation, the local coinages disappeared. They were replaced by a national currency based on the French system (100 centimes or rappen = 1 franc). The designs of that time have continued to the present day and feature a personification of Helvetia (either a figure or a head) or the Swiss arms on the front and the arms and value or just the value on the back.

MODERN COINAGE

The coinage has remained remarkably stable. Pieces of 1 and 2 rappen in bronze have been issued since 1850, with only a brief use of zinc in the Second World War. Cupro-nickel replaced base silver for the 5 and 10 rappen in 1879, though the 5 rappen became aluminium-brass in 1981. Nickel replaced base silver for the 20 rappen in 1881, giving way to cupro-nickel in 1939. The Swiss maintained a silver coinage much later than other European countries, replacing it with cupro-nickel for the ½, 1, 2 and 5 francs only in 1968. The silver 5 francs is now the standard commemorative piece. Gold 10 and 20 francs were struck for currency until 1935.

SWITZERLAND
16 Cupro-Nickel Franc.

16 1981

PRINCIPAL SWISS COINAGES

Name of mint	Period of minting rights (few mints operated continuously)
Aargau (canton)	1803–48
Appenzel (canton)	1737–1848
Basel (bishopric)	c. 1000–1801
Basel (city and canton)	1373–1848
Bern (city and canton)	1218–1848
Chur (bishopric)	959–c. 1789
Chur (city)	1529–1766
Freiburg (city and canton)	1422–1848
Geneva (city and canton)	1535–1848
Glarus (canton)	1798–1848
Graubünden (canton)	c. 1600–1848
Haldenstein (lordship)	1612–1798
Laufenburg (lordship)	1363–1623
Lucerne (city and canton)	1415–1848
Neuchâtel (principality)	1342–1848
St Gallen (abbey)	947–1798
St Gallen (city)	1415–1798
St Gallen (canton)	1798–1848
Schaffhausen (city)	late 12th cent.–1658
Schwyz (canton)	1624–1848
Sitten (bishopric)	999–1798
Solothurn (city and canton)	14th cent.–1848
Thurgau (canton)	1803–48
Ticino (canton)	1803–48
Unterwalden (canton)	16th cent.–1848
Uri (canton)	17th cent.–1848
Vaud (canton)	1803–48
Zug (city and canton)	1564–1848
Zürich (city and canton)	1425–1848

LIECHTENSTEIN

FIRST COINS:	1758
FIRST DECIMAL COINS:	1900
MAIN MINT:	Bern
CURRENCY:	Swiss frank

THE currency used in the territory of Liechtenstein has mostly been that of Austria. The princes received coinage rights in the eighteenth century from the Holy Roman Emperor and a little coinage was struck by Josef Wenzel (1748–72) and Franz Josef I (1772–81): silver ½ and 1 talers and gold ducats unlikely to have been used as currency. Austrian currency still provided money for daily use. In the nineteenth century some coinage was still struck in the prince's name at the Vienna mint: Vereinstalers in 1862, and silver 1 and 5 and gold 10 and 20 kronen between 1898 and 1915.

MODERN COINAGE

The link with Austria was broken with the First World War, and in 1921 Liechtenstein turned to its other neighbour, Switzerland. Since that year Swiss coinage has been current in the principality. A small issue of silver ½, 1, 2 and 5 franks was issued in 1924 in the name of Prince John II (1858–1929), and gold 10, 20, 25, 50 and 100 franks have been produced as bullion pieces or commemoratives. The small amount of coinage issued has had the prince's head on the front and his coat of arms on the back.

LIECHTENSTEIN
1 Silver ½ Taler of Josef Wenzel.
2 Gold 20 Franken of Franz.

1 1758   2 1930

FED. REPUBLIC OF GERMANY

FIRST COINS:	third century BC
FIRST DECIMAL COINS:	1871
MAIN MINTS:	Stuttgart, Hamburg, Munich and Karlsruhe
CURRENCY:	mark

THE first German coins were issued by local tribes, probably in the late third century BC. They belong to the Celtic tradition of imitations of Mediterranean, particularly Macedonian (*see* Greece),

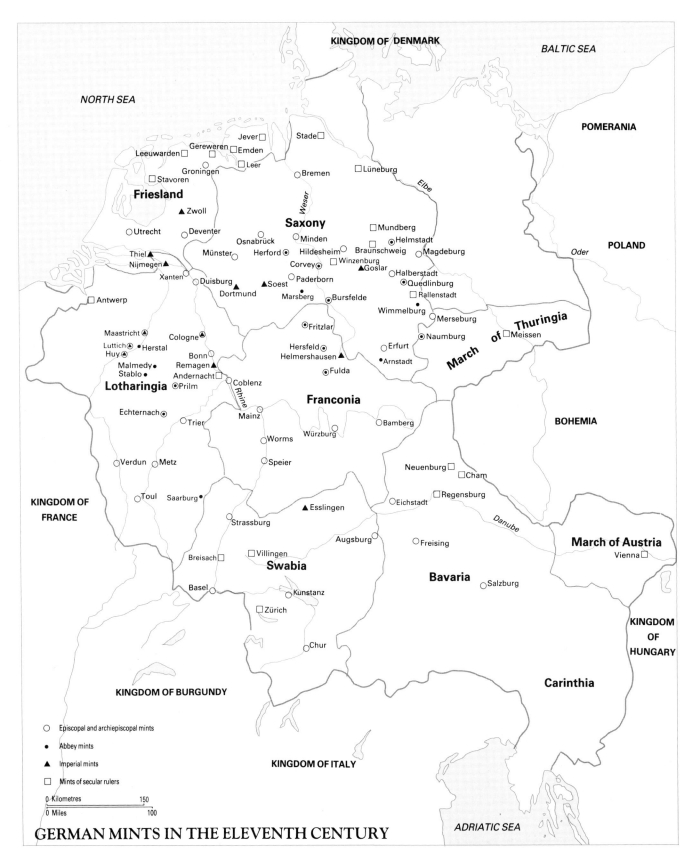

KINGDOM OF DENMARK

BALTIC SEA

NORTH SEA

POMERANIA

POLAND

BOHEMIA

MARCH OF AUSTRIA

KINGDOM OF FRANCE

KINGDOM OF BURGUNDY

KINGDOM OF ITALY

KINGDOM OF HUNGARY

Carinthia

ADRIATIC SEA

□ Jever
Stade □
Gereweren
Leeuwarden □ ☐ Emden
Groningen ☐ Leer
□ Stavoren
Friesland
▲ Zwoll
○ Utrecht ○ Deventer
Thiel ▲
Nijmegen ▲
Xanten ○
□ Antwerp
Maastricht ▲
Cologne ▲
Luttich ● ● Herstal
Huy ▲
Malmedy ●
Stablo ● Remagen ▲
Lotharingia Andernacht □
Echternach ◉ ◉ Prüm
○ Trier

Osnabrück ○
Münster ○
Herford ◉
Corvey ◉
○ Duisburg
Dortmund ▲
▲ Soest
Marsberg ●
Bonn ○
Coblenz
Mainz ○
○ Worms
○ Speier

Bremen ○
□ Lüneburg
Saxony
□ Mundberg
Minden ○ ◉ Helmstadt
Hildesheim ○ □ Braunschweig
Winzenburg □ ○ Magdeburg
Paderborn ● ▲ Goslar
○ Halberstadt
◉ Quedlinburg
Bursfelde ○ □ Rallenstadt
Wimmelburg ●
◉ Fritzlar ○ Merseburg
March of Thuringia
□ Meissen
Hersfeld ◉ ○ Naumburg
Helmershausen ▲ ○ Erfurt
◉ Fulda ● Arnstadt
Franconia
○ Bamberg
○ Würzburg

Verdun ○ ○ Metz
Toul ○ Saarburg ●
Strassburg ○
Breisach □
□ Villingen
Swabia
Basel ○
Kunstanz ○
□ Zürich
Chur ○

Neuenburg □
□ Cham
□ Regensburg
Eichstadt ○
▲ Esslingen
Augsburg ○
○ Freising
Bavaria
● Salzburg
Vienna □

Weser
Elbe
Oder
Rhine
Danube

GERMAN MINTS IN THE ELEVENTH CENTURY

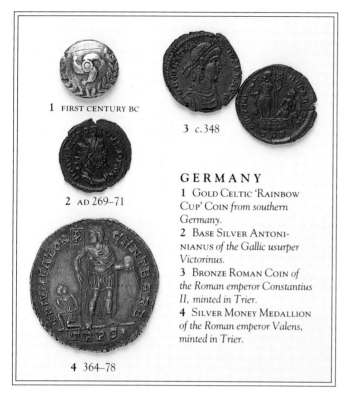

1 FIRST CENTURY BC

3 *c.*348

2 AD 269–71

GERMANY
1 GOLD CELTIC 'RAINBOW CUP' COIN *from southern Germany.*
2 BASE SILVER ANTONINIANUS *of the Gallic usurper Victorinus.*
3 BRONZE ROMAN COIN *of the Roman emperor Constantius II, minted in Trier.*
4 SILVER MONEY MEDALLION *of the Roman emperor Valens, minted in Trier.*

4 364–78

coinage. In the Rhineland, imitations of Philip II's gold staters were dominant; in the Elbe region and Bavaria, Alexander III's gold staters were the usual models. Small fractional gold pieces with a wide variety of animal and human-figure designs were also issued.

In the first century BC there was a shift to production of small silver coins with designs influenced by both Danubian Celtic and Roman coinage. However, a distinctive local gold coinage with abstract designs struck on saucer-shaped flans of metal continued to be produced, principally in Bavaria. Known as 'rainbow-cup' coinage, it suddenly came to an end in the mid-first century BC, apparently following an invasion by Germanic tribes from the north. Bronze coins with designs clearly based on Roman republican issues were produced in the later first century BC in the Rhineland and cast potin (tin-bronze) coins from Gaul also circulated in Germany at this time.

THE ROMAN FRONTIER

Julius Caesar's conquest of Gaul in 49 BC brought all the lands to the west of the Rhine under Roman domination, and, although an attempt was made under Augustus (31 BC–AD 14) to extend the frontier eastward to the Elbe, the Rhine–Danube remained the effective border between the Roman Empire and the German tribes for several centuries. The Rhine frontier became a heavily fortified military zone with garrisons of Roman legionaries and auxiliary troops. These were paid with Roman coinage and it was through the military camps that much of the Roman coinage of the region entered into circulation. Beyond the frontier the German tribes also obtained Roman coinage.

Until the mid-third century the majority of the Roman imperial coins circulating in Germany came from the mint of Rome, but in the period 259–73 the breakaway Gallic empire of Postumus and his successors, which included the German provinces, produced its own

Roman coinage from mints in Cologne and Trier. This consisted largely of base-silver antoniniani (*see* Italy) which were issued in massive quantities.

After the restoration of central imperial control under Aurelian (270–5), the Rhineland mints were closed, but Trier was later reopened as an official Roman mint under Diocletian (284–305). In the fifth century the city of Trier grew in importance when one of the imperial residences was based there, and its mint was among the most prolific in the empire, supplying much of the coinage that was required for the western provinces.

The barbarian invasions of the fifth century brought about the fall of the western half of the Roman Empire. The mint of Trier closed about 430, and by the end of the century coinage had largely ceased to be used.

THE EARLY MIDDLE AGES

The Franks were a West German people from the lower Rhineland and during the sixth century they made most of the Rhineland part of their kingdom. By the mid-seventh century this territory was included in the sub-kingdom of Austrasia. Frisia, Alamannia (Swabia) and Bavaria also came to recognize Merovingian overlordship, though the Saxons remained consistently independent and hostile. Merovingian and Carolingian coinage (*see* France) circulated in these regions, particularly after Charlemagne conquered the lands between the Rhine and the Elbe. By 802 he had incorporated all of Germany into his empire. Merovingian moneyers operated at Cologne, Bonn, Zülpich, perhaps Mainz and probably other Rhineland sites.

Under Charlemagne (768–814) and Louis the Pious (814–40), Carolingian mints in Germany operated at Aachen, Bonn, Cologne, Mainz, Worms, Frankfurt and Trier. The only mint to open away from the Rhineland was Regensburg, capital of Bavaria. The silver denar

GERMANY
5 SILVER DENAR *of Charlemagne, struck in Mainz.*
6 SILVER DENAR *of Charles the Simple, struck in Cologne.*

5 768–814   6 898–929

was the only coin produced. After Louis the Pious's death, Germany west of the Rhine formed part of the Middle Kingdom (*see* Belgium) while the east became East Frankia, by then known as Germany. The German kings took over the German part of the Middle Kingdom in 870 as well as the title of emperor. Comparatively little coinage was in use in Germany under the Carolingians. Only under Arnulf (887–99) and Louis the Child (899–911), last of the German Carolingians, did the number of mints begin to increase as coins were produced at Mainz, Würzburg, Cologne, Trier, Constance and Strasbourg.

THE SAXON EMPERORS

The Carolingian monetary system survived in Germany from the early tenth to the early twelfth centuries and was used in Lorraine, the Low Countries, Switzerland and Austria as well as Germany proper. Minting rights spread in the later tenth century as the dukes, margraves and counts of the empire took over the profits and control of

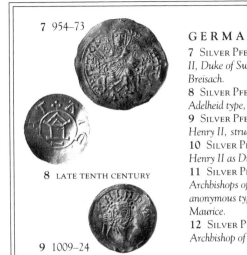

7 954–73

8 LATE TENTH CENTURY

9 1009–24

GERMANY

7 SILVER PFENNIG *of Burkhardt II, Duke of Swabia, struck in Breisach.*
8 SILVER PFENNIG, *Otto-Adelheid type, struck in Goslar.*
9 SILVER PFENNIG *of Emperor Henry II, struck in Mainz.*
10 SILVER PFENNIG *of Emperor Henry II as Duke of Bavaria.*
11 SILVER PFENNIG *of the Archbishops of Magdeburg, anonymous type showing St Maurice.*
12 SILVER PFENNIG *of Philip I, Archbishop of Cologne.*

11 ELEVENTH CENTURY

10 1009–24

12 1167–91

14 1138–60

13 1152–90

16 1160–

mints in the areas under their authority, while many ecclesiastics received imperial grants of the profits of minting and gradually adopted minting rights.

The great dukes of Germany began to issue their own coins under Henry the Fowler of Saxony (918–36), the first being Arnulf of Bavaria (911–14 and 919–37) at Regensburg and Salzburg. The first bishop to issue coins without the imperial name was Ulrich of Augsburg (923–73). Eventually lesser feudal lords and con.munities and cities also received minting rights. Sometimes imperial and local mints existed in the same city, but usually the local ruler was the dominant power and the number of imperial mints dwindled.

Although designs differed widely, the silver denar or pfennig and the obole, or ½ denar, varied little. Carolingian designs continued to be widely used in the tenth century, particularly the temple design. Also popular was the use of the mint name across the coin, favoured at Cologne and then imitated throughout the Rhineland, Westphalia and Lower Lorraine. Anglo-Saxon and Byzantine designs were also sometimes copied. A newer design was the profile bust, common in Swabia under Otto I (936–73) and spreading into Lower Lorraine, Bavaria and Westphalia in the early eleventh century. Invariably a cross formed the design on the back of all these coins.

THE OTTONIAN EMPERORS

The output of the imperial mints was considerable in the eleventh century, as Otto I the Great (936–73) and his successors, Otto II (973–83) and Otto III (983–1002), opened new mints, such as Dortmund, Quedlinburg, Bonn and Hildesheim. Among the most prominent and extensive imperial issues were the Otto–Adelheid pfennigs of Goslar, coins bearing the names of the Emperor Otto III and the Empress Adelheid, struck in silver from the Rammelsberg mines of the Harz mountains from 991 until 1040.

However, many ecclesiastical coinages also began at this time, as did the coinages of lesser feudal rulers. The first such ruler to issue his own coinage was Ekhard, Margrave of Meissen (985–1002). Images of archbishops and bishops, usually with crozier or book, began to replace the imperial bust on coinages from the 1020s, and other popular designs included the representation of saints or towers and domes.

Emperor Otto III, portrayed in Aachen cathedral. Ottonian emperors in tenth-century Germany sought to revive the imperial power of their Roman forebears. They retained control over the coinage, despite the increasing role of local ecclesiastical and feudal coinages.

13 SILVER BRACTEATE
PFENNIG *of Emperor Frederick I
Barbarossa, struck in
Gelnhausen, showing the Emperor
and Empress.*
14 SILVER BRACTEATE
PFENNIG *of Beatrix II von
Schwaben, Abbess of Quedlinburg.*
15 SILVER BRACTEATE
PFENNIG *of Hermann I,
Landgrave of Thuringia.*
16 SILVER BRACTEATE
PFENNIG *of Gero, Bishop of
Halberstadt.*
17 SILVER HOHLPFENNIG *of
Hamburg.*

15 1190–1217

17 LATE THIRTEENTH CENTURY

THE AGE OF BRACTEATES

In the mid-eleventh century weakening imperial control further encouraged the spread of minting rights and the weight standard of the pfennig dropped considerably. In Lower Saxony and Bavaria the coins became so thin that the design on one side was virtually obliterated by that on the other. This paved the way for a drastic change in the form of the pfennig in parts of Germany from the 1130s. In Saxony, Thuringia, Pomerania, Brandenburg and parts of Franconia and Swabia, the pfennig became a larger, extremely thin and fragile sheet of silver with only one design, which was usually visible in reverse on the back of the coin.

The large flan and thinness of these so-called 'bracteate' coins permitted the use of more elaborate and detailed designs, such as the portrayal of the issuing ruler on horseback as on coins of Meissen; the bishop, abbot, abbess or patron saint enthroned as at Halberstadt and Quedlinburg; heraldic beasts like the lion of Brunswick; and architectural features. The great age of bracteate design was in the north in the late twelfth and early thirteenth centuries. The bracteates of the south never attained such size and magnificence. Single-sided coins continued to be produced throughout the later Middle Ages but the pfennig was then shrinking in size and uninscribed, less elaborate images being preferred. These later single-sided pfennigs were known as hohlpfennigs.

In some areas biface pfennigs were struck alongside bracteates, but in western Germany, particularly the Rhineland, Lorraine and Westphalia, biface coins alone were struck. Discoveries of silver at Freiberg in Meissen stimulated increased supplies of the most important coinages: the pfennigs of the Archbishops of Cologne were particularly significant because of their relatively high silver content and weight. English pennies were also widely used in Germany in the early thirteenth century, inspiring a substantial imitative coinage produced above all by the counts of Lippe. In southern Germany the hellers of Schwäbisch Hall began to be struck in large numbers, circulating widely and being commonly used as ½ pfennigs. From the late thirteenth century increasing numbers of cities bought or leased minting rights from their imperial or feudal lords, for instance Ham-

burg and Lüneburg (1293), Rostock (1325), Göttingen (1351) and Mainz (1420).

GROSCHEN AND GULDEN

The fourteenth century witnessed the arrival in Germany of new types of coin. First to arrive was a larger silver piece, the groschen, which was initially usually equivalent to 12 pfennigs and served as a multiple of the old pfennig. In the south west the main model for the groschen was the French gros tournois, the basic design of which was followed in the earliest German versions struck in the principal mints of the Rhineland and Westphalia. The Rhenish mints came to issue a lighter, less fine type of groschen known as the albus, with the design of St Peter on the front and the arms of the issuing authority on the back.

The groschen of Saxony and Meissen took as their model the Praguergroschen of Bohemia (*see* Czechoslovakia) and became nearly as influential in the north east, being much copied. A number of mints in southern Germany allied to produce a common type of groschen (= 6 rappen), and similar arrangements occurred in Franconia, where the burgrave of Nuremburg and Bishops of Bamberg and Würzburg coordinated their coinages. In the north the common version was the smaller witten (= 4 pfennigs) of Lübeck, Hamburg, Rostock, Lüneburg and Wismar, struck from 1379. Larger schillings were added in these cities from 1432. Witten were also used in Pomerania. Most groschen had on the front either a patron saint or, in the case of both ecclesiastical and secular rulers, the bust, enthroned figure or heraldic device of the ruler.

19 FOURTEENTH CENTURY

18 1323–49

21 *c.*1350–81

20 FOURTEENTH CENTURY

22 1370–1414

GERMANY
18 SILVER GROSCHEN *of Friedrich II, Margrave of Meissen.*
19 SILVER HELLER *of
Schwabisch Hall.*
20 GOLD GULDEN *of Lübeck.*
21 SILVER WITTEN *of Rostock.*
22 GOLD GULDEN *of Friedrich
II, Archbishop of Cologne.*
23 SILVER ALBUS *of Werner
von Falkenstein, Archbishop of Trier.*

23 1388–1418

The fourteenth century also saw the introduction of gold coinage into some parts of Germany. Emperor Ludwig IV, the Bavarian, (1314–47) struck copies of French écus, but these did not prove influential. It was the example of the Florentine florin which instead proved popular. From the mid-fourteenth century the major Rhineland princes began to issue imitations of the florin in their own names, and from the 1360s local designs replaced the Florentine ones to produce the typical Rhenish gulden of the later Middle Ages.

The principal issuers of gulden were the four Rhineland imperial electors: the Archbishops of Trier, Mainz and Cologne and the Count Palatine of the Rhine. They founded a monetary union in 1385 which lasted until 1515 and usually issued gulden to an agreed standard. The Rhenish gulden was initially equal to 20 albus or groschen. The gulden commonly had St Peter or Christ on the front and the arms of the partners in the union arranged on the back. Other neighbouring princes, such as the Dukes of Cleves and Jülich and the Bishops of Münster and Osnabrück in Westphalia, sometimes participated in the Rhenish monetary conventions.

The example of the Rhenish gulden was followed elsewhere in Germany: for the imperial gold coinage of the fifteenth century, known as apfelgulden because the back of the coin showed the imperial Reichsapfel, or orb, and struck principally at Dortmund, Augsburg, Frankfurt and Nördlingen; and for the gulden of Lübeck from the 1340s, for which the Florentine design was appropriate as St John the Baptist was also its patron. Lübeck was the only substantial issuer of gold in the north and its gulden were important in the Baltic trade of the Hanseatic League. In the fifteenth century the emperors granted permission to issue gold to a number of imperial cities and secular rulers, who issued versions of the gulden.

24 1410–37   **25** 1410–36   **26** 1443–55

GERMANY

27 1461–75

24 GOLD APFELGULDEN *of Emperor Sigismund.*
25 GOLD GULDEN *of Ludwig II, Count Palatine of the Rhine.*
26 SILVER SCHILLING *of Gottfried IV von Limburg, Bishop of Würzburg.*
27 GOLD GULDEN *of Adolf II, Archbishop of Mainz.*
28 SILVER HOHLPFENNIG *of Berthold von Hennesberg, Archbishop of Mainz.*

28 1484–1504

However, in some parts of Germany the groschen and gulden were not used until the very end of the Middle Ages. In Swabia and Bavaria small silver denominations, versions of pfennigs known as heller, batzen, kreuzer and schilling (the schilling in this region was equal to 1 or 2 kreuzer), were the only currency until the late fifteenth century, when gulden began to be issued by local rulers, such as the Counts of Württemburg, Dukes of Bavaria and Bishops of Regensburg.

THE AGE OF THE TALER

Major new discoveries of silver were made within the Holy Roman Empire in the mid-fifteenth century: in the Tyrol and at Schneeburg in

Illustration from Georgius Agricola's De Re Metallica, *which included a treatise on the mining of metals. Production of silver from German mines greatly increased in the later fifteenth and sixteenth centuries.*

Saxony. This made possible the widespread appearance of new types of coins. The Italian testone inspired similar German coins from 1478, called dicken or pfundner, and equal to 12 kreuzer or $\frac{1}{4}$ gold gulden. But the most important new coin was the taler, a large silver coin initially equal to the gold gulden in value and thus also known as the guldiner or guldengroschen. Frederick III of Saxony began the production of talers in Germany in 1500 with a coin portraying the prince and his two brothers, and the mints of Saxony moved from the capital, Dresden, to be near the mines of Annaberg, Freiberg and Schneeberg. The name dicken was soon used to refer to the $\frac{1}{4}$ taler.

The size of the taler offered great scope for engravers to produce fine portraits and elaborate versions of dynastic emblems for German princes, like the 'wildman' of the house of Brunswick, and especially magnificent talers and multiple talers to celebrate or commemorate notable events. Cities often chose to portray patron saints on their issues, such as the Three Magi and St Ursula at Cologne.

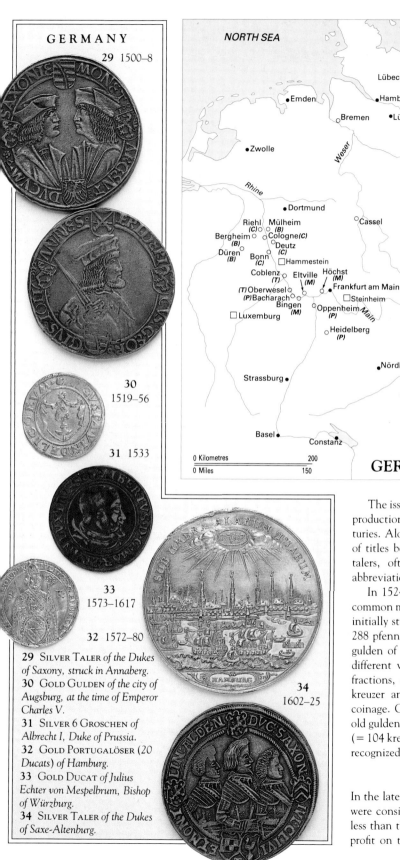

GERMANY

29 1500–8

30
1519–56

31 1533

33
1573–1617

32 1572–80

34
1602–25

29 SILVER TALER of the Dukes of Saxony, struck in Annaberg.
30 GOLD GULDEN of the city of Augsburg, at the time of Emperor Charles V.
31 SILVER 6 GROSCHEN of Albrecht I, Duke of Prussia.
32 GOLD PORTUGALÖSER (20 Ducats) of Hamburg.
33 GOLD DUCAT of Julius Echter von Mespelbrum, Bishop of Würzburg.
34 SILVER TALER of the Dukes of Saxe-Altenburg.

NORTH SEA · BALTIC SEA

Lübeck · Emden · Hamburg · Stettin · Bremen · Lüneburg · Zwolle · Oder · Dortmund · Cassel · Leipzig · Liegnitz · Riehl *(C)* · Mülheim *(B)* · Bergheim *(B)* · Cologne*(C)* · Schweidnitz · Düren *(B)* · Deutz *(C)* · Bonn *(C)* · Hammestein · Coblenz *(T)* · Eltville *(M)* · Höchst *(M)* · Frankfurt am Main · *(T)* Oberwesel · Steinheim · *(P)*Bacharach · Bingen *(M)* · Oppenheim *(P)* · Luxemburg · Heidelberg *(P)* · Nuremburg · Danube · Strassburg · Nördlingen · Augsburg · Munich · Basel · Salzburg · Constanz

0 Kilometres 200 / 0 Miles 150

Mints issuing imperial apfelgulden
Mints issuing gulden of the Rhenish Monetary Union and related issues
(C) Mints of the archbishop of Cologne
(T) Mints of the archbishop of Trier
(M) Mints of the archbishop of Mainz
(P) Mints of the Count Palatine
(B) Mints of the duke of Jülich-Berg
☐ Other gold issues

GERMAN MINTS ISSUING GOLD COINS

The issuing of talers coincided with the spread of mechanized coin-production through Germany in the sixteenth and seventeenth centuries. Alongside magnificent portraits often went an immense chain of titles belonging to the issuing prince, which, even on the large talers, often had to be represented by a string of initials and abbreviations.

In 1524 the Emperor Charles V (1519–58) sought to establish a common monetary standard for his domains. The guldiner or taler was initially struck in silver and equivalent to 24 groschen, 72 kreuzer or 288 pfennigs, though in Austria and southern Germany the smaller gulden of 60 kreuzer was preferred, and Saxony also had a slightly different version, tariffed at 68 kreuzer. In most states a range of fractions, often $\frac{1}{16}$, $\frac{1}{8}$, $\frac{1}{4}$ and $\frac{1}{2}$ taler, were provided, with pfennigs, kreuzer and groschen, usually in base-silver, providing the petty coinage. Gold coinage continued to be struck widely, with both the old gulden (= 75 kreuzer in the mid-sixteenth century) and the ducat (= 104 kreuzer), following the standards of the Venetian ducat, being recognized as money of the empire.

THE THIRTY YEARS' WAR

In the later sixteenth century the lesser coins of many German states were considerably overvalued, their silver content being very much less than their face value indicated, as local rulers sought to make a profit on their coinage. Major states operated dozens of mints and

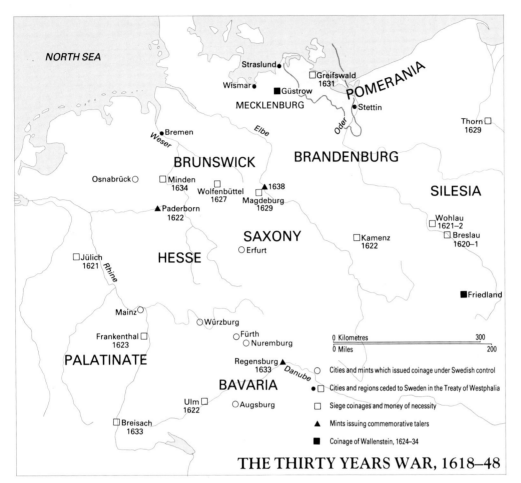

THE THIRTY YEARS WAR, 1618–48

35 1622

36 1739

39 167

many lesser rulers who did not have minting rights nevertheless began to issue coinage to profit in this way. The situation was exacerbated by the Thirty Years' War (1618–48), when the need for money to pay troops further encouraged the debasement of coinage, and compounded by widespread clipping and counterfeiting. The result was economic crisis and far-reaching inflation during the *Kipper-und-Wipper* period (1618–23); the term referring to the swaying of a balance while dubious coin was weighed.

During the Thirty Years' War a number of siege and necessity coinages were produced, for instance at Jülich (1621), Frankenthal (1623), Breisach (1633), Magdeburg (1629) and Minden (1634), and the intervention of Gustav II Adolf of Sweden resulted in coinage in his name being struck in various cities in 1632–5 as well as in his inherited Duchy of Pomerania.

By 1623 the need to restore good coinage was recognized and the base coin was devalued and replaced. However, the number of states legally entitled to issue coinage was further increased as a number of ecclesiastical states were secularized and followers of the emperor were rewarded for their service in the war. After the Thirty Years' War the taler, now valued at 90 kreuzer, became less important as a currency coin, its place being largely taken by the silver gulden or $\frac{2}{3}$ taler (= 60 kreuzer).

Most rulers still continued to produce impressive medallic talers – Schautalers or 'show talers' – for prestige and to commemorate

particular events, for instance a taler was struck at Magdeburg to commemorate its restoration after the terrible sack of the city in 1631. Often the death of a ruler would be marked by the issue of a memorial Sterbetaler. It was popular to hollow out the coin to create Schraubtalers – box talers – in which sets of miniature paintings were kept. Silver-rich rulers like the dukes of Brunswick-Lüneburg issued 'mining talers' with views of mine-workings, and city issues sometimes displayed panoramas of the city, Nuremberg providing one particularly striking example.

THE EIGHTEENTH CENTURY

In 1701 the lands of the Hohenzollern margraves of Brandenburg were unified as the Kingdom of Prussia. The new regal coinage mostly featured the king's portrait on the front and the Hohenzollern eagle or shield of arms on the back. The Prussian gold coinage featured the frederick d'or, a 5 taler piece. Under Frederick II the Great (1740–86) the eagle was shown with military accoutrements of banners, drums and cannon. Frederick the Great's wars, during which he acquired Silesia from Austria, encouraged another wave of debasement in Germany. The Prussian coinage took a new standard for the taler in 1750, which was followed by a number of neighbouring states.

In 1753 a convention between Austria and Bavaria reduced the weight of the taler and in the next few years most German states came to base their coinages on the new Conventionstaler, issuing fractions

GERMANY

35 BASE-SILVER 6 ALBUS *of Lothar von Metternich, Archbishop of Trier, struck at a kipper-mint.*
36 SILVER KLIPPE-TALER *of the siege of Münster.*
37 SILVER 4 TALERS *of Johan Friedrich, Duke of Brunswick-Lüneburg.*
38 SILVER STERBETALER *of Sibylla Ursula, Duchess of Holstein-Sonderburg-Glücksburg, struck on her death.*
39 SILVER GULDEN *of Lothar Friedrich, Archbishop of Mainz.*
40 COPPER 2 HELLER *of Friedrich I, Duke of Hesse-Cassel.*
41 SILVER CONVENTION-STALER *of the Imperial City of Nuremburg.*
42 SILVER GULDEN *of Maximilian Josef I, Elector of Bavaria.*
43 GOLD FREDERICK D'OR *of Frederick II the Great, King of Prussia.*
44 SILVER TALER *of Friedrich Wilhelm II, King of Prussia.*

THE EARLY NINETEENTH CENTURY

The victories of Napoleon transformed the German scene. The Holy Roman Empire was declared abolished in 1806 and all the ecclesiastical states secularized, their coinages coming to a sudden end. Many other lesser states and free cities were also absorbed into their neighbours and renounced their coinage rights.

The number of coin-issuing authorities fell from over 300 to under 50. Westphalia was created from various states to form a kingdom, ruled over by Napoleon's brother, Jerome Bonaparte in 1807–13. It produced a French-style coinage in his name, but the territory was redistributed after Napoleon's fall. However, nineteenth-century Germany still consisted of many fewer states: 32, including Prussia and four other kingdoms, Bavaria, Hanover, Württemberg and Saxony; five grand duchies; 13 duchies and principalities; and three free cities. Each state maintained its own coinage.

The monetary unification of Germany advanced in the nineteenth century. In 1837 two new monetary systems were agreed. One for the north, where Prussia and Saxony were dominant, consisted of 12 pfennigs to the groschen and 30 groschen to the taler (with only 10 pfennigs to the groschen in Saxony), and the other for the south (the states around Bavaria, Würtemburg and Hesse) consisted of 8 heller or 4 pfennigs to the kreuzer and 60 kreuzer to the gulden. Two northern talers equalled $3\frac{1}{2}$ southern gulden and these denominations, each the major silver piece of its system, linked the systems.

from the $\frac{1}{48}$ to $\frac{2}{3}$ taler. Prussia and Hanover, however, remained aloof. German gold coinages were all based on the ducat, with both fractions and multiples commonplace, though such huge pieces as the 10 ducat portugalösers of Hamburg can be regarded only as presentation pieces. Some Rhineland states used gold panned from the Rhine for some of their ducats. The use of copper for the lowest denominations became widespread in the mid-eighteenth century.

In 1857 all the states agreed on a uniform Vereinstaler, though they continued to use their regional lesser denominations. In most states the smallest denominations were in copper and their design usually featured a coat of arms, local emblem or monogram of the ruler's name on the front and the value in pfennigs or heller on the back. The smaller fractions of the taler were of base-silver and the ½ taler and taler of silver; these larger coins typically had the ruler's head on the front and coat of arms on the back. Gold coinage consisted of the ½, 1 and 2 krone, expressed as multiples of the taler or gulden. The traditional ducat continued to be struck as a trade coin in several states, with gold gulden similarly struck in Bavaria and fredericks d'or in Prussia.

THE GERMAN EMPIRE

In 1871 Germany was formally united and the King of Prussia became Emperor Wilhelm I. A uniform coinage system was established, based on 100 pfennigs to the mark. The lesser denominations were struck in one form for the whole empire and comprised: in copper, 1 and 2 pfennigs; in cupro-nickel, 5, 10 and (after 1887) 20 pfennigs; in silver,

20 and 50 pfennigs and the mark. A nickel 25 pfennigs was added in 1909. All had the value on the front and the imperial eagle on the back. From 1915 iron and zinc were used for the 5 and 10 pfennigs. The higher-value denominations had the head and titles of the local ruler on the front, with the imperial eagle on the back. The denominations issued were 2, 3 and 5 marks in silver and 10 and 20 marks in gold, the latter being virtually identical to the earlier 1 and 2 krone. The collapse of the German Empire and the unseating of the traditional dynasties in 1918 put an end to these coinages.

THE FIRST WORLD WAR

During the First World War there was a great increase in the hoarding of coins and an inevitable shortage of currency. To remedy this and make daily business possible, hundreds of cities, towns and businesses began to issue their own token coinage from about 1917. Most was paper money, known as *Notgeld*, but soon low-denomination coins, known as *Notgeld* or *Kriegsgeld* (war money) were also being produced. About 7000 varieties are known from 1500 places. The highest

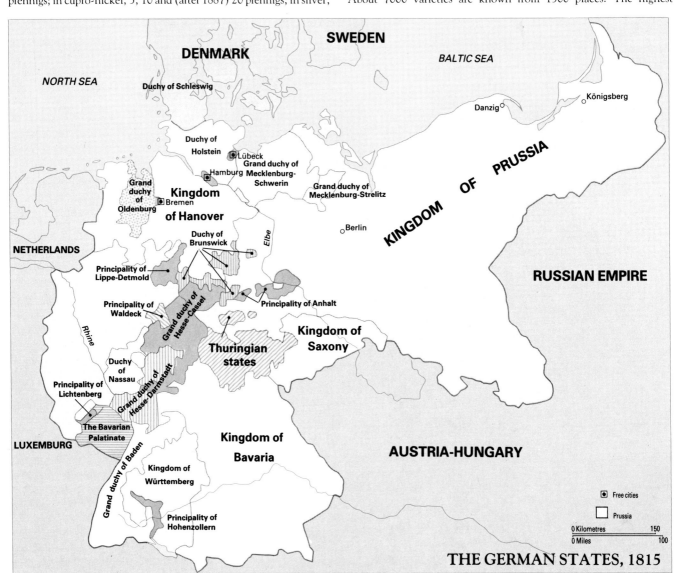

THE GERMAN STATES, 1815

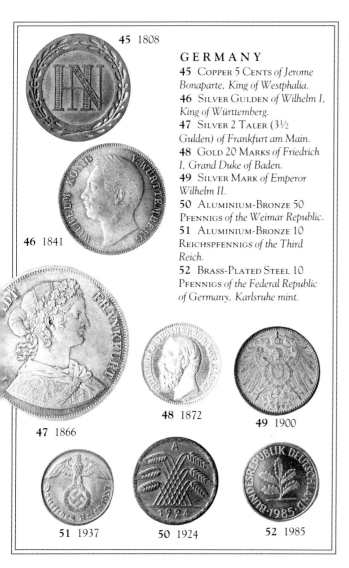

GERMANY
45 Copper 5 Cents *of Jerome Bonaparte, King of Westphalia.*
46 Silver Gulden *of Wilhelm I, King of Württemberg.*
47 Silver 2 Taler (3½ Gulden) *of Frankfurt am Main.*
48 Gold 20 Marks *of Friedrich I, Grand Duke of Baden.*
49 Silver Mark *of Emperor Wilhelm II.*
50 Aluminium-Bronze 50 Pfennigs *of the Weimar Republic.*
51 Aluminium-Bronze 10 Reichspfennigs *of the Third Reich.*
52 Brass-Plated Steel 10 Pfennigs *of the Federal Republic of Germany, Karlsruhe mint.*

45 1808
46 1841
47 1866
48 1872
49 1900
51 1937
50 1924
52 1985

monetary system, although new designs were introduced, showing an eagle perched on a wreath enclosing a swastika on the front and the value on the back. Exceptions were the 5 and 10 reichpfennigs, which in 1940 became pierced coins, the hole passing through the centre of a swastika. These coins, and the 1 pfennig, were made of zinc from 1940, whereas the 2 pfennigs ceased to be issued. The 50 pfennigs became aluminium in 1939 and the reichsmark was made in nickel from 1933. The silver 2 and 5 marks had commemorative designs which were changed each year. In 1944 a zinc coinage of 1, 5 and 10 reichspfennigs was provided for Germany under Allied occupation.

THE FEDERAL REPUBLIC OF GERMANY
Those parts of Germany occupied by the Western Allies were restored to self-rule in 1949. A new coinage system was installed, of 100 pfennigs to the deutschemark. Four mints have produced the West German coinage since then: Munich, Stuttgart, Karlsruhe and Hamburg. The smaller denominations are made of copper-plated steel (1 pfennig), bronze (2 pfennigs) and brass-plated steel (5 and 10 pfennigs) and have a simple design of an oak frond on the front and the value under wheatears on the back. The cupro-nickel 50 pfennigs shows a female figure planting an oak-sapling. The 1 mark has an eagle on the front and the value on the back, but the back of the 2 mark (which was changed from cupro-nickel to cupro-nickel clad nickel in 1969) has carried the heads of prominent national figures: Max Planck, Konrad Adenauer, Theodor Heuss and Kurt Schumacher. The 5 mark was struck in silver until 1975 when, though preserving the design of the value on the front and eagle on the back, its composition was also changed to cupro-nickel clad nickel. Silver 5 and 10 mark pieces are frequently produced as commemoratives.

GERMAN DEMOCRATIC REPUBLIC

FIRST COINS:	1949
FIRST DECIMAL COINS:	1949
MAIN MINT:	Berlin
CURRENCY:	mark

The German Democratic Republic was formed in 1949 out of the provinces occupied by the Soviet Union at the end of the Second World War: Mecklenburg, Brandenburg, Lusatia, Saxony and

denomination issued as a coin was the 50 pfennigs and the materials used were mostly iron and zinc, though tin and even pressed coal were also known. Porcelain was used for coins made for a number of towns at the Meissen factory in 1921–2, but these rapidly became souvenir items as much as currency. The issue of metallic Notgeld continued until 1921.

WEIMAR AND NAZI GERMANY
After the First World War Germany was re-established as the Weimar Republic. A coinage was provided in 1923–4 of 100 rentenpfennigs to the rentenmark, the inflation of the time requiring the introduction of coins of 20, 100, 200 and 500 marks, mostly in aluminium. The currency system was revalued in 1924, changing to 100 reichspfennigs to the reichsmark. Denominations were: in bronze, 1, 2 and 4 pfennigs; aluminium-bronze, 5, 10 and 50 pfennigs; nickel, 50 pfennigs from 1927; and silver, 1, 2, 3 and 5 marks. Designs consisted of the value on the front and wheatears on the back for the lesser coins, and the eagle on the front and value on the back for the silver pieces.
The founding of the Third Reich in 1936 did not change the

GDR
Aluminium-Bronze 50 Pfennigs, *German Democratic Republic.*
1983

Thuringia. Its coinage is based on 100 pfennigs to the mark. Early issues featured the value on the front of its coins and a wheatear superimposed on a cogwheel on the back, but since 1960 most coins have had a hammer and compasses surrounded by wheatears on the front and the value on the back. Denominations consist of 1, 5 and 10 pfennigs in aluminium, 20 pfennigs in brass, and 50 pfennigs and 1 and 2 marks also in aluminium. The only design variation occurs on the cupro-nickel or cupro-nickel-zinc 5 mark and the silver 10 mark, which have new commemorative designs each year.

POLAND

FIRST COINS:	late tenth century
FIRST DECIMAL COINS:	1923
MAIN MINT:	Warsaw
CURRENCY:	zloty

POLAND
1 SILVER DENAR of Vladislav Hermann.
2 SILVER DENAR of Boleslav IV.
3 SILVER BRACTEATE DENAR of Miesko III Stary.
4 SILVER POLGROSZ of Vladislav Jagello.
5 SILVER SCHILLING of Casimir IV, struck in Thorn.
6 SILVER SCHILLING of Johann von Tiefen, Master of the Teutonic Knights.

1 1079–1102   2 1146–73   3 1183–1202   4 1386–1434   5 1444–92   6 1489–97

THE first coins to be produced in Poland were issued by the founder of the country, Mieszko I (960–92). These were silver denars following German and Bohemian models, with the design of a crown on the front and a cross on the back. His successors issued denars in larger quantities but the bulk of the coinage circulating in Poland throughout the late tenth and eleventh centuries were German denars (or pfennigs), primarily pfennigs of Saxony. There were, however, large numbers of imitations of these Sachsenpfennige struck in Poland itself.

The Polish kings continued to issue denars in the eleventh and twelfth centuries, both small, biface coins and uniface bracteates, each type with a great variety of designs. Such issues persisted into the thirteenth century and the monetary situation was further complicated by the existence of a large variety of issuing authorities, exacerbated by civil war and the Mongol invasion of 1241. In 1225 the Teutonic Knights were given sovereignty over eastern Prussia by a Polish duke and began their own coinage of bracteate pfennigs showing a cross or a cross on a shield. Szczezin (Stettin), the capital of the Duchy of Pomerania, and the eastern part of the duchy lay within modern Poland, but its coinage followed German trends.

It was only under Casimir III the Great (1333–70) that anything other than the denar began to be issued in Poland. He introduced the grosz, a Polish version of the Bohemian Praguergroschen, which bore the eagle of Poland in place of the Bohemian lion. The new coin was struck at Cracow. The next king, Louis the Great (1370–82), struck only denars in Poland but in his Russian territories produced silver kwartniks. In 1394 these were adopted in Poland under Ladislas Jagiello (1386–1434) as ½ grosz or polgrosz. This, with its design of a crown on the front (hence the alternative name of 'coronat') and the Polish eagle on the back, became the standard Polish coin of the later Middle Ages.

In the north a mint at Thorn provided coinage for western Prussia, mostly denars and schillings, and the city of Danzig (Gdansk) also issued coinage. In the lands of the Teutonic Knights a groschen-type coin called a 'halbskoter' was struck under Master Winrich de

Kniprode in 1370, but more important was the other denomination he produced: a schilling with the shield and name of the master on the front. This was the main coin of the order until its dissolution in 1525.

Eastern Prussia became a duchy belonging to the Hohenzollern margraves of Brandenburg. It remained a fief of Poland until 1657 and retained a separate coinage until 1701, when the kingdom of Prussia was created and a common coinage struck for all the Hohenzollern lands (see Germany).

SIXTEENTH TO EIGHTEENTH CENTURIES

In the early sixteenth century Sigismund I (1506–48) sought to reform the Polish coinage. He suppressed the kwartnik and introduced a range of new royal coins: the silver denar, ternar (= 3 denars), and 1, 3 and 6 groszy. The system was based on the zloty of 30 groszy. The mints of Danzig and Thorn provided similar coins for western Prussia, but Danzig also issued a gold ducat (= 45 groszy). In Poland itself the ducat and, in 1533, the double ducat were introduced, as was the large silver taler (= 30 groszy), with magnificent portraits of the king and his son, Sigismund Augustus, last of the Jagellon Dynasty. Under the latter the Vilna mint in Lithuania provided most of the coinage for the Polish kingdom, although the Danzig mint was also very active. Silver denars, 1, 2 and 4 groszy and ½ and 1 talers were struck.

Foreign coinage was also important: Sicilian scudos were counter-marked at Vilna for circulation in Poland, and Henri de Valois, elected king in 1573, imported French écus, valued at 50 groszy.

The next king to be elected was Stephen Bathory, Prince of Transylvania (1576–86). He established a unified system of coinage for the entire kingdom, though he had to impress his authority on Danzig in 1577 by force of arms, during which expedition a siege coinage of talers and ducats was issued on which an image of Christ replaced the royal portrait.

Under Sigismund III Vasa (1587–1632) and Ladislas IV (1633–48) there was an extensive gold coinage and ducats and silver talers continued to be struck to a high standard both of fineness and of artistic

POLAND AND THE BALTIC, 1772

□ Polish territory 1618–1772

Mint Cities

representation, although the lesser coinage was weakened through debasement and large-scale counterfeiting, particularly from mints in the Swedish-held cities of Elbing and, in Livonia (modern Estonia and Latvia), Riga. A large number of mints had come into operation in the Polish territories: Cracow, Olkusz, Lublin, Bromberg and Marienburg among others.

Poland came under increasing pressure from Sweden, Russia and the Tatars in the seventeenth century and its currency continued to suffer. The commonest coins produced were 1, 2, 3 and 6 groszy, with talers (now = 80 groszy) and ducats (= 18 zlotych) providing the large denominations. Because of silver shortages, a large number of copper schillings, called 'boratinki' (= $\frac{1}{3}$ grosz), were put into circulation in the 1650s and '60s, driving out good silver coinage. Another token coin, the tympf (= 18 groszy), intended as $\frac{1}{3}$ taler, was introduced in 1662. Little new royal coinage was produced under King Michael Korybut (1669–73), although Danzig, Thorn and Elbing continued to issue ducats and talers.

In most of Poland tympfs and boratinki were still the principal coins in use well into the eighteenth century. Frederick Augustus, king in 1697–1733, was elector of Saxony, and what new coinage was produced for Poland was mostly struck in Leipzig and Dresden. Sweden occupied large parts of the country and its coinage became common.

Late in the eighteenth century Stanislas II Augustus Poniatowski (1764–96) sought to reform the Polish currency with a range of new

POLAND

7 SILVER TALER of Stephen Bathory.
8 SILVER 6 GROSZY of Sigismund III.
9 GOLD DUCAT of Sigismund III, struck at Danzig.
10 SILVER TALER of Thorn.
11 GOLD DOUBLE DUCAT of Ladislas IV.
12 COPPER BORATINKI of John Casimir.

silver coins: 1 silver grosz and 1, 2 and 8 zlotych, mostly featuring splendid portraits of the king. Copper schillings and 1 and 3 grosz provided small change, while the gold ducat was struck to the international standard (initially equal to 16 zlotych). In 1794 a new gold coin, the stanislas (= 3 ducats), was introduced. However, under Stanislas II the political pressures on Poland had become immense and its territory was dismantled in the three Partitions of Poland, Galicia going to Austria, western Prussia to Prussia and the remainder to Russia. The state of Poland disappeared in 1796.

POLAND
13 Gold Stanislas of *Stanislas Augustus.*
14 Copper 3 Grosz of *Frederick Augustus of Saxony as Grand Duke of Warsaw.*
15 Copper 3 Polsgrosz of the *Great Revolt.*
16 Silver 30 Kopek (2 Zloty) *of Tsar Nicholas I of Russia.*
17 Iron 20 Fenigow of Poland *under German and Austrian control.*
18 Silver 5 Zlotych.
19 Nickel-Brass 2 Zlotych.
20 Silver 2 Gulden *of the Free City of Danzig.*

THE NINETEENTH CENTURY

In 1807 Napoleon created the Grand Duchy of Warsaw out of Prussian and Austrian Poland, with Frederick Augustus, King of Saxony, as ruler. Between 1810 and 1814 coinage was issued in his name: copper 1 and 3 groszy; silver of different finenesses for the 5 and 10 groszy and $\frac{1}{6}$, $\frac{1}{3}$ and 1 (= 6 zloty) taler; and a gold ducat.

With the defeat of Napoleon, Austria and Prussia regained their Polish territories, and the remaining Polish lands became a kingdom under the Russian tsar. A coinage system was produced in 1832 aligning the Polish system to that of Russia, with the zloty equal to 15 kopeks. Denominations issued consisted of the 1 and 3 groszy in copper; 5 and 10 groszy and 1 zloty, 40 and 50 groszy, and 2, 5 and 10 zlotych in base silver and silver; and 20, 25 and 50 zlotych in gold. Designs featured either the Russian eagle or the tsar's head on the front and the value or Russian eagle on the back.

In 1815 Cracow had been established as an independent republic and an issue of coins was produced in 1835, comprising 5 and 10 groszy and 1 zloty. However, in 1846 the city reverted to Austrian control. Local issues were struck by the Kings of Prussia for Danzig, Posen and eastern Prussia when they were regained.

During the Polish Revolution of 1830–1 coinage was struck in the name of an independent Poland. No local coinage was struck after 1850 under Russian rule, Russian issues being current until the First World War, when the Germans occupied Poland and issued 1, 2 and 3 kopek coins in 1916. In 1917–18 iron and zinc 1, 2, 10 and 20 fenigow were produced under the German–Austrian regency.

INDEPENDENCE REGAINED

Independent Poland was reconstituted in 1919 and a new decimal coinage of 100 groszy to the zloty instituted in 1923. The small denominations were of bronze or nickel and the zloty and its multiples in base silver. In 1925 commemorative gold 10 and 20 zlotych featured King Boleslaus I. Designs included the Polish eagle and a female head personifying the nation. Small denominations in iron and zinc were struck under German occupation during the Second World War: the 10 groszy, though struck through 1941–4, was always dated 1923. From 1919 till 1939 Danzig survived as a free city, issuing a coinage based on 100 pfennig to the mark until 1923 and thereafter on 100 pfennig to the gulden.

In the post-war period an issue in aluminium and cupro-nickel in 1949 was the only coinage in circulation before the proclamation of a people's republic in 1952. The coinage of communist Poland was introduced in 1957–8 and consisted of the 5, 10, 20 and 50 groszy and 1, 2 and 5 zlotych, all in aluminium, and the 10 zlotych in cupro-nickel. The designs of the coins were mostly simple: featuring the Polish eagle on the front and the value on the back. The 5 groszy has not been struck since 1972 and the 2 and 5 zlotych became brass in 1975. The 10 zlotych coin usually had a commemorative design, but in 1984 a standard design corresponding to that of the other denominations was introduced.

Since 1972 larger denominations, issued both as commemoratives and for circulation, have been added to the coinage: 20 zlotych in cupro-nickel; 50 zlotych in silver and cupro-nickel; and 100 zlotych (of which there had been 34 versions up to 1986) and 200 zlotych in silver. Gold 1000, 2000, 10,000 and 20,000 zlotych have also been issued, particularly to commemorate the visit to Poland of Pope John Paul II.

CZECHOSLOVAKIA

FIRST COINS:	third century BC
FIRST DECIMAL COINS:	1921
MAIN MINT:	Kremnitza
CURRENCY:	koruna

CZECHOSLOVAKIA's first coins were issued by Celtic tribes in the third and second centuries BC. In Bohemia in the west and in Moravia (central Czechoslovakia) the earliest coins were gold pieces imitating the staters of Alexander III of Macedon (*see* Greece). From about the end of the third century smaller gold coins were also produced in these regions with a design of a standing goddess Athena on the back, copying coins of Philip V of Macedon. These later developed into the series known as 'mussels' because the designs degenerated to such an extent that they resembled sea shells. In the second century there also developed in Bohemia and southern Germany gold 'rainbow-cup' coinage (*see* Germany) and issues of small silver coins with designs derived from various Mediterranean coinages.

In Slovakia (eastern Czechoslovakia) the earliest coinage, also dating from the third and second centuries BC, belonged to the Danubian tradition of Celtic imitations based on the silver coinage of Philip II of Macedon. The most distinctive Slovakian Celtic coinage was, however, issued later, in the first century BC. This coinage, of large silver pieces with lettering in Latin, is known as the 'Biatec', after the commonest inscription, or the 'Bratislava series', because of the concentration of finds in southern Slovakia. Many of the designs on these coins copy Roman republican issues. They were produced around the mid-first century, ending apparently before the Roman conquest of Pannonia in 12 BC. The Celtic coinage of Bohemia ended somewhat earlier, in the middle of the first century, probably as a result of the advance of German peoples from the north.

From the late first century BC until the fifth century AD the Romans ruled all the lands immediately to the south of Czechoslovakia. After the end of the local Celtic coinages, no coins were issued by the German tribes inhabiting Czechoslovakia, but it is known that the Romans regularly paid 'protection money' in the form of Roman coinage to tribes across the northern frontiers, and discoveries of hoards, particularly of silver Roman denarii, demonstrate that Roman coinage continued to reach the region.

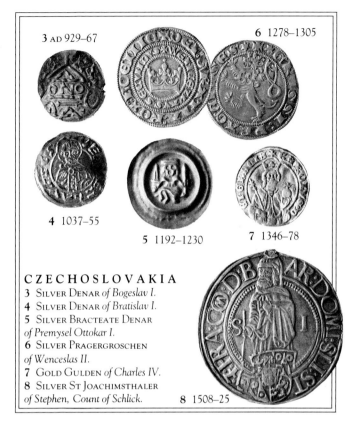

CZECHOSLOVAKIA

3 SILVER DENAR *of Bogeslav I.*
4 SILVER DENAR *of Bratislav I.*
5 SILVER BRACTEATE DENAR *of Premysel Ottokar I.*
6 SILVER PRAGERGROSCHEN *of Wenceslas II.*
7 GOLD GULDEN *of Charles IV.*
8 SILVER ST JOACHIMSTHALER *of Stephen, Count of Schlick.*

THE MIDDLE AGES

Between the late Roman period and the tenth century, little if any coinage was in use in Czechoslovakia, and what there was, imports from Byzantium or the West, would not have functioned as currency. Things began to change in the tenth century when, under the Ottonian emperors of Germany, the striking and use of coinage began to spread east of the Rhine. Duke Bogeslav I (929–67) of Bohemia and his successors issued denars copied from Bavarian coins, with a temple design. In the late tenth century coins of Ethelred II of England were also copied. Prague was the site of the Bohemian mint.

From the early Middle Ages Bohemian mines were an important source of European silver and the early coinages of Bohemia are relatively plentiful. Denars of Jaromir (1004–12) and Oldrich (1012–37) used a variety of designs, mostly showing Byzantine influence. Under Bratislav I (1037–55) reference to St Wenceslas began to dominate the coinage. In 1085 Bratislav II (1061–92) was granted the title of king by the German Emperor Henry IV and the new title appeared on the coinage. Denars of a variety of designs remained the sole coinage of Bohemia throughout the twelfth century. In Moravia, ruled directly by the Duke or King of Bohemia or by one of his family, local denars with designs resembling those of Bohemia were produced.

In 1210 King Przemyl Ottokar I transformed Bohemian coinage, replacing the biface denars with large, uniface bracteates of poor style. Bracteates were also struck in Moravia. This phase of Bohemian coinage was short-lived, however, as in 1294 the huge silver deposits at Kutna Hora were discovered.

King Wenceslas II (1278–1305) took advantage of his country's asset to launch a new coinage, comprised of biface denars and the

CZECHOSLOVAKIA

1 GOLD 'MUSSEL' STATER *of the Celtic Boii tribe.*
2 SILVER 'BIATEC' COIN *from the Bratislava region, issued by the Boii.*

famous Pragergroschen (= 12 denars). This piece, with its design of a crown on the front and the double-tailed Bohemian lion on the back, became the standard silver coin of eastern Europe in the later Middle Ages. It was much more important than the small Bohemian gold coinage, florins imitating the Florentine coin and, under Charles IV (1346–78), showing the figure of the king.

The Bohemian coinage declined in the early fifteenth century, at the time of the Hussite wars, until the Pragergroschen was revived in 1469. Medieval Slovakia formed part of the Kingdom of Hungary, whose rulers were able to exploit its gold mines.

BOHEMIA UNDER THE HABSBURGS

Under Habsburg rule from 1526, coinage continued to be produced specifically for Bohemia until the death of Empress Maria Theresa in 1780. It came mostly from the mint at Prague, though Kutna Hora was active until 1726 and Joachimsthal until 1670. In general the denominations and designs used were the same as those current throughout the Habsburg dominions (see Austria), though the Bohemian lion usually featured. Local names were used, such as the haler for the pfennig, krejcaru for groschen and zlaty for gulden. Also the greshl (= 3 haler) was issued as a copper coin for use just in Bohemia.

In 1618–21, during the revolt of Bohemia and Moravia against Emperor Matthias II, coinage in the name of the Count Palatine Frederick V, the Winter King, was issued. Other local novelties included an issue of 3, 10 and 20 kreuzer and ½ taler struck in pewter in 1757 during the Turkish siege of Prague. The prince-bishops of Olmutz, capital of Moravia, held coining rights under the Habsburgs, but exercised them only occasionally in the eighteenth century. The princes of Paar and counts of Schlick also retained minting rights. In the early sixteenth century it was the large silver gulden of the counts of Schlick which, using metal from their new mine and mint at St Joachimsthal, gave rise to the name 'taler' (dollar) for this type of coin. Under the Habsburgs Slovakia remained part of the Kingdom of Hungary (see Hungary).

The Parliament building at Budapest, on the Danube. As the ancient capital of Hungary, Budapest has usually been its main mint also, though in this role it has been challenged in the past by Kremnitz, near the gold mines of Slovakia and Nagybanya.

REPUBLIC OF CZECHOSLOVAKIA

With the dissolution of the Austro-Hungarian Empire in 1918, Bohemia, Moravia and Slovakia became united as the Republic of Czechoslovakia. The new state set up its own monetary system consisting of 100 haleru to the koruna. Denominations most regularly issued since then have been the 1, 5, 10, 20 and 50 haleru, and 1, 2 and 5 korun. Coins of 2, 3 and 25 haleru and 3 korun have been issued for short periods. All these denominations have always been base-metal: bronze, aluminium or cupro-nickel.

Base-silver 10 and 20 korun were produced in the 1930s, but post-war precious-metal issues – 10, 20, 50, 100 and 500 korun in silver – have all been commemoratives. The Republic of Czechoslovakia issued a substantial gold coinage in the late 1920s and 1930s: dukats and multiples up to 10 dukats, often with commemorative designs, intended as trade coins. These were produced at the Kremnitza mint.

During the Second World War Czechoslovakia was divided into two provinces under a German protectorate: Bohemia-Moravia and Slovakia. Zinc coinages were provided for the two regions: 10, 20 and 50 haleru and 1 koruna for the former; and 5, 10, 20 and 50 halierov and 1 koruna for the latter, which also had higher-value coins in nickel and base silver.

After liberation Czechoslovakia was restored to its pre-war territories, but in 1948 the communists seized control and established a people's republic. The pre-war coinage system was restored, with small denominations in aluminium and the 50 haleru and larger pieces in cupro-nickel or aluminium-bronze. The 5 haleru is the smallest coin now produced. The designs on Czech currency coins have remained fairly standard, usually depicting the lion of Bohemia on the front and the value, sometimes with some other feature, on the back.

12 1743

9 1575

11 1674

10 1620

13 1815

CZECHOSLOVAKIA
9 SILVER TALER of Maximilian II.
10 SILVER 24 KREUZER of Frederick V, Elector Palatine, as King of Bohemia.
11 GOLD 10 DUCATS of Carl II of Liechtenstein, Bishop of Olmutz.
12 GOLD DUCAT of Maria Theresa.
13 SILVER TALER of Franz I.
14 SILVER 5 KORUNA.
15 ALUMINIUM-BRONZE KORUNA.

HUNGARY
1 SILVER CELTIC COIN *from southwestern Hungary, with designs derived from the silver coins of Philip II of Macedonia.*
2 SILVER COIN *imitating Roman denarii, issued by the Celtic Eravisci tribe.*

1 SECOND CENTURY BC

2 MID-FIRST CENTURY BC

HUNGARY

FIRST COINS:	third century BC
FIRST DECIMAL COINS:	1857
MAIN MINT:	Budapest
CURRENCY:	forint

Hungary's first coins were issued in the third and second centuries BC by Celtic tribes in the region. The earliest coins were all of silver and they had designs imitating Greek coins from the Balkan region. They copied in particular the silver 4 drachma coins of Philip II of Macedon (*see* Greece) and of the kings of Paeonia, Patraus (335–315 BC) and Audoleon (315–286 BC) (*see* Yugoslavia). In the second

century BC bronze coins were also produced. These coinages apparently ceased in the first century BC, when they were replaced by Roman republican denarii and locally produced imitations. The imitation denarii were issued until almost the end of the first century BC. The last issues included coins inscribed by the Eravisci, a Celtic tribe from the Budapest area.

THE ROMAN PERIOD

Under the Roman Empire, western Hungary was within the province of Pannonia, annexed by the Romans under Augustus (31 BC–AD 14). Roman imperial coinage circulated within the province and beyond, much of the money arriving to pay troops since Pannonia was a frontier territory. Until the mid-third century AD most of the Roman coinage in the region was from the mint of Rome, but in the later imperial period mints in Yugoslavia, notably Siscia and Sirmium, were the major suppliers. Early coinage came to an end in the fifth century, when Pannonia was overrun by barbarians from the north and east.

14 1925

15 1970

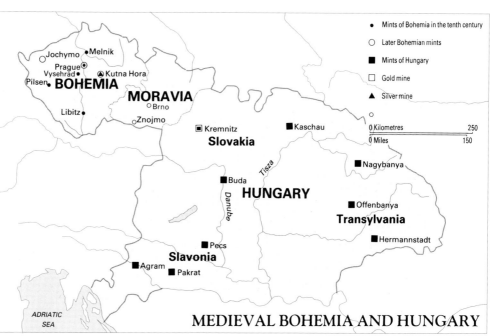

- • Mints of Bohemia in the tenth century
- ○ Later Bohemian mints
- ■ Mints of Hungary
- □ Gold mine
- ▲ Silver mine

MEDIEVAL BOHEMIA AND HUNGARY

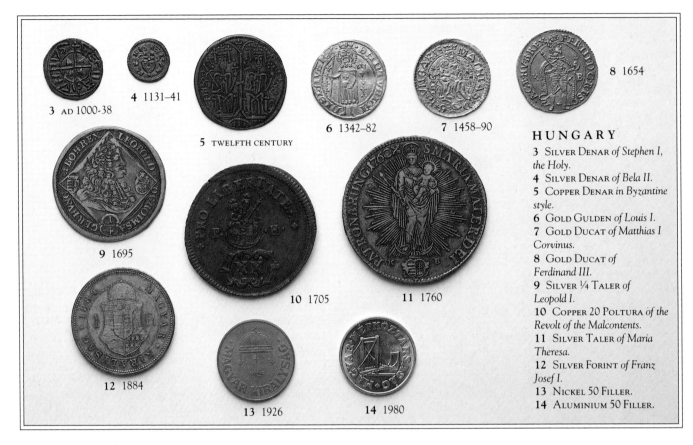

3 AD 1000-38

4 1131–41

5 TWELFTH CENTURY

6 1342–82

7 1458–90

8 1654

9 1695

10 1705

11 1760

12 1884

13 1926

14 1980

HUNGARY

3 SILVER DENAR of Stephen I, the Holy.
4 SILVER DENAR of Bela II.
5 COPPER DENAR in Byzantine style.
6 GOLD GULDEN of Louis I.
7 GOLD DUCAT of Matthias I Corvinus.
8 GOLD DUCAT of Ferdinand III.
9 SILVER ¼ TALER of Leopold I.
10 COPPER 20 POLTURA of the Revolt of the Malcontents.
11 SILVER TALER of Maria Theresa.
12 SILVER FORINT of Franz Josef I.
13 NICKEL 50 FILLER.
14 ALUMINIUM 50 FILLER.

THE MIDDLE AGES

The Avars, who occupied the Hungarian plain in the Dark Ages, issued no coinage. They and the Magyars amassed coin only as treasure and booty. However, in the tenth century the Hungarian state began to take shape, particularly after 955, when the German Emperor Otto the Great defeated the Magyars at the Battle of Lechfeld.

As was often the case, the issue of coinage virtually coincided with the introduction to the area of Christianity. In 1000 the Hungarian king, Stephen, converted to Christianity and soon afterwards began the issue of denars, coins similar though lighter than those of Germany and Bohemia, and with a simple design of a cross on each side. Subsequently other designs came into use: a crowned head, a half-length royal figure or three sceptres. Half denars, or obols, were also quite common in the region.

In the twelfth century geometric designs were frequently used on denars, though anomalous bronze denars in Byzantine and Islamic style appeared in the mid-century and there was also a small issue of bracteate denars. In the thirteenth century well-made figurative designs became popular, featuring crowned heads, enthroned and equestrian figures and the Paschal Lamb, influenced by the Freisach pfennigs (see Austria) which came into Hungary and circulated in large numbers. The Hungarian coins were mostly issued anonymously or with just the royal initial.

Hungarian coinage grew under King Charles Robert (1308–42), who introduced large silver groszy and gold gulden, with a substantial coinage of silver denars and oboles. The first gold coins were imitations of the florin, but under Louis I (1342–83) national emblems – the

shield of the dynasty of Anjou-Hungary and the image of St Ladislas – replaced those of the Florentine rulers.

The extensive Hungarian gold coinage was supported by the gold mines of Slovakia, above all at Kremnitza, then ruled by Hungary. It complemented the Bohemian Praguergroschen in Eastern Europe and circulated throughout eastern and northern Europe. The design of the Hungarian gulden was not changed until 1470, when Matthias Corvino (1458–90) replaced St Ladislas with the Virgin Mary, patron of Hungary. Ladislas II (1490–1516) struck the first Hungarian talers, with a shield on the front and St Ladislas on horseback on the back.

HABSBURG HUNGARY

In 1525 Ferdinand I of Austria inherited the Hungarian throne, though much of the territory was held by a rival, John Zapoly of Transylvania, who struck a regal coinage until his death in 1540. The coinage of Habsburg Hungary was gradually assimilated until the denominations produced matched those issued in Austria, though local designs, in particular those showing the Hungarian arms, the Virgin and St Ladislas, were maintained, apart from a period in the late eighteenth century. The mints of Hungary were at Kremnitza, Nagybanya, Hermannstadt and Pressburg.

The principal coins in use were the gold ducat, with multiples up to 10 and fractions down to $\frac{1}{16}$ ducat sometimes issued; and in silver the $\frac{1}{4}$, $\frac{1}{2}$ and 1 taler. For small change obols, denars and groschen sufficed until the reign of Leopold I, when coins of 2, 6 and 15 krajczar (kreuzer) were added (5 denars = 3 krajczar). Pieces of 10, 17, 20 and 30 krajczar appeared in the eighteenth century.

During the Revolt of the Malcontents in 1704–8, the rebels issued bronze 1 (= 1½ krajczar), 4, 10 and 20 poltura, silver ½ talers and gold ducats, replacing the royal bust with the Hungarian arms and having the inscription PRO LIBERTATE (For Liberty). The Hungarian coinage in the name of the Habsburg emperors was interrupted again by the revolt of 1848, when a range of coins was produced with Magyar inscriptions, comprising copper 1 and 3 krajczar, base-silver 6 krajczar, silver 10 and 20 krajczar and gold ducats.

MODERN HUNGARY

With the dissolution of the Habsburg Empire in 1918, Hungary became a separate state (formally a kingdom, though without a king), while losing much of its earlier territory to Czechoslovakia, Romania and Yugoslavia. Hit by devastating inflation, most of its currency was provided by paper money, the only coins being iron 10 and 20 filler pieces resembling the Austrian wartime issues.

In 1925 a new coinage system was introduced, consisting of 100 filler to the pengo. Small denominations were in cupro-nickel and bronze, with the 1, 2 and 5 pengo in silver. Designs featured a crown, the Hungarian arms or the Virgin Mary on the front and the value or coat of arms on the back. During the Second World War, when Hungary was a German ally, steel fillers and aluminium pengos were issued. Hungary was declared a republic in 1946 and received a new monetary system of 100 filler to the forint, which remained unchanged with the organization of the country as a people's republic in 1949. Modern denominations consist of the 2, 5, 10, 20 and 50 filler and 1 forint in aluminium and the 2 forint in cupro-nickel, then brass; the 5 forint in cupro-nickel, and the 10 forint in nickel, then aluminium-bronze.

All denominations have the value on the back and on the front a variety of designs, including wheatears, the country's coat of arms, a dove, a bridge and the head of the nineteenth-century patriot, Kossuth. A large range of high-value commemoratives are also issued, often with unusually innovative and distinctive designs.

YUGOSLAVIA

FIRST COINS:	fifth century BC
FIRST DECIMAL COINS:	1920
MAIN MINT:	Belgrade
CURRENCY:	dinar

THE first coins from what is now Yugoslavia may have been issued by the Derrones, a tribe whose coins circulated in the southern corner of the country and in northern Greece in the early fifth century BC. Other coins issued in Macedonia and Thrace and by Greek cities and colonies on both sides of the Adriatic Sea arrived in parts of Yugoslavia in this early period. By the mid-fourth century BC there were two areas of coin production in Yugoslavia: the islands of Pharos, issuing silver and bronze coins, and Issa (bronze coins only) off the Dalmatian coast, and in the south the city of Damastium (location uncertain) and the kingdom of Paeonia, bordering Greece and Bulgaria. The most important issues of the Paeonian kings were the

silver coins of Lycceius (about 359–340 BC), Patraus (about 340–315 BC) and Audoleon (about 315–286 BC).

From the third to the first centuries BC coinage in the islands and coastal cities of Dalmatia was restricted to bronze issues, but inland the Celtic and other tribes produced silver coins imitating northern Greek issues.

CELTIC COINAGE

The earliest 'Celtic' issues of Yugoslavia, dating from the late fourth century BC, imitated the silver coins of the Paeonian kingdom and the city of Damastium, but for the more abundant issues of the third and second centuries BC the usual model was the silver tetradrachm of Philip II of Macedon, with designs of a head of Zeus on the front and a rider on the back. In the first century BC there was a shift in the circulation pattern, as smaller silver coins began to dominate, notably the issues of Apollonia and Dyrrhachium (see Albania) and Roman republican denarii. Local imitations of these coinages were also issued in the Yugoslavian region.

THE ROMAN PERIOD

Parts of southern Yugoslavia came under Roman control following the annexation of Macedonia in the mid-second century BC. Under Augustus (31 BC–AD 14) the rest of Yugoslavia (Illyricum) was incorporated into the Roman Empire, eventually to form the province of Dalmatia and parts of Pannonia and Moesia. Large quantities of Roman silver denarii arrived with the armies of conquest, and they continued to be imported to finance the garrisons that were stationed in this predominantly military region.

2 SECOND CENTURY BC

1 c.340–315 BC

3 AD 198–217

4 270–5

5 364–75

YUGOSLAVIA

1 SILVER STATER of King Patraus of Paeonia.
2 SILVER CELTIC COIN from Croatia, with designs derived from the coins of Philip II of Macedonia.
3 BRONZE COIN of the city of Stobi, issued under the Roman emperor Caracalla.
4 BASE-SILVER ANTONINIANUS of the Roman emperor Aurelian, minted in Siscia.
5 BRONZE COIN of the Roman emperor Valentinian I, minted in Sirmium.

For the first 300 years of Roman imperial rule much of the coinage circulating in Yugoslavia, in gold, silver and bronze, was minted in Rome, but in the mid-third century AD a mint for production of Roman coinage was opened at Viminacium, and under Aurelian (270–5) another Roman mint began operating at Siscia (Sisak). In the fourth century mints at Sirmium (Sremska Mitrovica), Siscia and Aquileia in southern Italy supplied the region with most of its Roman coinage.

In addition to the Roman imperial coins, local issues of bronze coinage intended for much more limited circulation were produced in Yugoslavia at Stobi in Macedonia from about AD 70 to 200, and at Viminacium in the period 239–57.

THE MIDDLE AGES

In the early medieval period such currency as was in use in the lands comprising modern Yugoslavia was mostly Byzantine (*see* Turkey). This changed in the twelfth century when pfennigs of Freisach (*see* Austria) began to be in common use at the head of the Adriatic and denarii of Venice and Verona were current along the Dalmatian coast. Imitations of Freisacher pfennigs began to be produced in Croatia under Duke Andrew (1196–1204). In the thirteenth century local coinage production increased and denarii of Aquileia, Trieste and Goritza became important.

In Slavonia local rulers, or bans, under the Hungarian king issued denars and halves, known as 'denarii banales', with the design of a wolf between two stars on the front and a patriarchal cross on the back. In the mid-thirteenth century the city of Split (Spalato) produced copper bagattini, known as spalatini, which circulated in Dalmatia.

In the 1260s the Kings of Serbia began to issue imitations of the Venetian grosso, with St Stephen and the king replacing St Mark and the doge. Under Stefan IV Dragutin (1272–5) the enthroned king replaced the derivative design, to be replaced in its turn under Stefan Dusan (1331–55), who took the title emperor, by an ornamental helmet. Under the influence of Serbia, similar grossi began to be produced in the cities of Ragusa (Dubrovnik) and Cattaro (Kotor), with the local patron saints Blasius and Tryphon replacing St Mark, and by the bans of Bosnia from the time of Stefan Kotromanic (1322–53). The Dalmatian cities of Zara (Zadar), Sibenik, Trogir and Hvar also issued local coinage in the late fourteenth and fifteenth centuries.

VENETIAN AND FRENCH INFLUENCE

Serbia fell to Turkish rule in the mid-fifteenth century, Slavonia and the north mostly remained under Hungarian rule, while Montenegro kept its independence. Venetian power was important along the Adriatic coast and the republic's sovereign authority was recognized in coastal Dalmatia until 1797. Venetian coinage, including some made specially for her colonies, made up most of the currency. Ragusa survived as a republic under Turkish protection from 1526 until 1806, with a coinage and monetary system similar to that of Venice: 6 soldi to the grossetto and 40 grossetti to the ducat. Copper soldi, base-silver 1, 6 and 12 grossetti and silver 1 and 2 ducats were issued.

In 1805–13 Dalmatia came under French control until the defeat of Napoleon. The French were besieged in the ports of Zara and Cattaro in 1813 and issued cast-silver siege pieces to pay their troops.

SERBIA AND MONTENEGRO

Serbia regained independence from Turkey in 1887, though its kings had in the 1860s begun to issue coinage in their own name. It adopted a

SERBIA AND THE DALMATIAN COAST, c. 1340

Goritza
Trieste
HUNGARY
Drava
SLAVONIA
Danube
Zara
CROATIA
Sibenik
BOSNIA
Spalato
DALMATIA
Hvar
Belgrade
HUM
Ragusa
ADRIATIC SEA
Cattaro
SERBIA
Bar
Drivasto
Ulcinj
Shkoder
Morava
Durazzo
EPIRUS
THESSALY
Thessalonika
Stroma

☐ Serbia under Stefan Uras II
☐ Byzantine lands
☐ Hungarian lands
☐ Serbian Empire of Stefan Dusan, 1340

AEGAN SEA

0 Kilometres 100
0 Miles 150

currency system of 100 para to the dinar, issuing bronze 1, 2, 5 and (until 1883) 10 para; cupro-nickel 10 and 20 para; silver ½, 1, 2 and 5 dinara; and 10 and 20 gold dinara. Most coins had the king's head on the front and the enwreathed value on the back. Montenegro, though never subjected to Turkey, issued coinage only while it was briefly established as a kingdom in 1910–18 under Nicholas I. It produced coins in bronze, silver and gold in a system of 100 para to the perper.

MODERN YUGOSLAVIA

In 1918 Serbia, Montenegro and the formerly Austrian South Slav territories were united as the Kingdom of the Serbs, Croats and Slovenes under Petar I (1918–21), its name being changed to Yugoslavia in 1929. Coinage was issued intermittently and struck in a variety of foreign mints. Zinc 5 and 10 and nickel-bronze 25 para appeared in 1920 and nickel-bronze 1 and 2 and gold 20 dinara in 1925. Gold 1 and 4 dukats were later issued. Silver 10, 20 and 50 dinara were added in 1931 and a new set of all denominations from 25 para to 50 dinara was issued in 1938 in bronze, aluminium-bronze, nickel and (for the 50 dinara alone) silver. Designs mostly featured the king's head or a crown on the front and the value or Yugoslavian eagle on the back. Cyrillic lettering was used on most coins.

During the Second World War Yugoslavia was occupied by Germany and dismantled, Croatia and Serbia being established as separate puppet states with coinages in zinc. After the war Yugoslavia was restored as a people's republic in 1946 under Marshal Tito. A stop-gap coinage of 50 para and 1, 2 and 5 dinara in zinc was provided in 1945, but modern Yugoslavian coinage began in 1953 with the formation of the Federated People's Republic.

Since 1953 a regular coinage has appeared consisting of 5, 10, 20 and 50 para in copper-zinc and 1, 2, 5 and 10 dinara in copper-nickel-zinc. Since 1981 the new 25 para has been the smallest denomination issued and new materials have been introduced: bronze for the 25 and 50 para; nickel-brass for the 1, 2 and 5 dinara; cupro-nickel for the 10

dinara and copper-zinc-nickel for the new 20, 50 and 100 dinara. The designs of all currency coins are the same: five blazing torches surrounded by wheatears on the front and the value flanked by wheatears on the back. The large number of modern Yugoslavian commemorative coins which have been issued in silver and gold depict national and sporting events.

ROMANIA

FIRST COINS:	late fifth century BC
FIRST DECIMAL COINS:	1867
MAIN MINT:	Bucharest
CURRENCY:	leu

Ancient Romania produced a richly varied coinage, with contributions from several different peoples, including Greeks, Celts and the native Getae and Dacian tribes. The first coins produced in the country were issued by Greek settlers in the city of Istrus (Histria) on the Black Sea coast in the late fifth and fourth centuries BC. The silver coins of Istrus have one of the most bizarre designs in the ancient Greek series: a pair of human faces joined together, but with one upside down. The design on the back is also interesting, showing a sea eagle apparently clutching a dolphin.

The other Greek colonies in Romania which issued coinages, Callatis (Mangalia) and Tomi (Constanta), were also on the Black Sea coast. Callatis began to issue coinage in the late fourth century, Tomi around 200 BC. Istrus and Callatis produced posthumous 'Alexander' gold and silver coins (*see* Greece) in the third century BC, and later

---

ROMANIA

1 SILVER COIN of Istrus.
2 SILVER COIN of Callatis.
3 SILVER CELTIC COINS with designs derived from the coinage of Philip II of Macedonia.
4 BRONZE COIN of Tomi issued under the Roman emperor Hadrian

1 FOURTH CENTURY BC
2 FOURTH CENTURY BC
3 THIRD-FIRST CENTURY BC
4 AD 117–38

posthumous 'Lysimachus' coins (see Turkey), as also did Tomi. All three cities also issued bronze coins in their own names down to the first century BC.

Inland, coinage in the Danubian Celtic tradition of imitations of Greek coins were produced by various tribes from the third to the early first century BC. Many issues were produced by non-Celtic Thracian tribes, so the term 'Geto-Dacian' is often used to describe these native coinages. The earliest were imitations of silver tetradrachms of Philip II of Macedon, with the head of Zeus on the front and a horseman on the back. Other coins copied were the issues of Alexander III and Lysimachus of Thrace, and a facing-head design copied coins of Larissa or Amphipolis in northern Greece. Later influences included the silver tetradrachms of the Macedonian republics (after 168 BC) and of Thasos (after 146 BC). There were wide variations in style, from close copies of the prototypes in the earliest issues to barely recognizable abstractions in some of the later versions. In the lands of the Dacians in central and western Romania the silver tetradrachms tended to become scyphate (saucer-shaped) and of poor-quality metal.

In the late second and early first centuries BC there was increasing circulation of smaller silver coins in the region: firstly the drachms of Apollonia and Dyrrhachium from Illyria (see Albania), and later, from about 70 BC, Roman republican denarii (see Italy). Local production of Geto-Dacian tetradrachms ended; instead, imitations of Roman denarii were made.

THE ROMAN PERIOD

Roman denarii continued to be the principal coins circulating in Romania in the first century AD, and after 107 when most of the country was incorporated into the Roman Empire following Trajan's conquest of Dacia. Roman imperial coins in all metals were used in Romania, but the Greek cities in the east of the country also issued their own bronze coins with the emperor's head on the front and a local design, together with the city's name, on the back. Tomi began issuing these coins under Nero (54–68); Istrus and Callatis did not start until

the second century. Bronze coins were also issued in the name of the province of Dacia within the period 238–53. These local issues all ended in the mid-third century, when production of the increasingly debased Roman imperial coinage began to be devolved throughout the empire. But no city in Romania was used for an official mint; the lands north of the Danube had recently been lost to barbarian invaders, and the parts of Romania remaining in the empire could be supplied with official Roman coinage from mints elsewhere in the Balkans, such as Serdica in Bulgaria and Heraclea and Constantinople in Turkey.

THE MIDDLE AGES

Byzantium's direct political control over the Romanian region was broken during the Slavic invasion of the sixth and seventh centuries and the rise of the first Bulgarian Empire in the ninth and tenth centuries. The use of coinage dwindled, but what did circulate in the territory of modern Romania was Byzantine in origin.

In the twelfth century the influence and coinage of Hungary and Slavonia (see Yugoslavia) became dominant until the emergence of the principalities of Moldavia and Wallachia in the wake of the defeat of the Hungarians in the Carpathian mountains in 1330. Coinage in the region was a mixture of many types: Hungarian, Bohemian (see Czechoslovakia), Serbian (see Yugoslavia), Bulgarian, Venetian and Genoese and, originating at the mouth of the Danube, silver aspers of the Golden Horde (see USSR). The earliest native coinage began under the voivode Vladislav I of Wallachia (1364–77), with designs of a shield on the front and a helmet on the back. Three denominations were produced in the fourteenth century: silver ducats and dinars and base-silver bani.

Coinage in Moldavia began at much the same time under the voivode Bogdan I (1348–55). His issues copied the Polish kwartnik or $\frac{1}{2}$ groszy, with the badge of Moldavia as their main design: a facing bull's head with a star between the horns. Wallachian coinage came to an end in the mid-fifteenth century with the establishment of Ottoman power in the Balkans. The Voivodes of Moldavia continued to rule under Turkish protection and still issued their own groschen, though Poland increasingly provided the lesser coinage and Hungarian ducats were used for larger transactions. The adventurer John Jacob Heraclides issued ducats and talers during his brief rule (1561–3).

5 1364–74
6 1374–91
7 1612
8 1672
9 1772
10 1867

EUROPE

114

TRANSYLVANIA

Transylvania did not fall to Turkish control but was forced to submit to Hungary to preserve itself. When Hungarian power collapsed in 1526, Transylvania survived as an independent principality until 1699, when it fell under Habsburg control. The abundance of gold and silver in the mines of Transylvania ensured a plentiful coinage. Gold ducats were struck under all voivodes and multiples up to 10 ducats were common. Silver ½, 1 and 2 talers were also issued and for small denominations oboles, denars, and 1, 3 and 6 groschen were occasionally produced.

The Transylvanian coinage mostly used heraldic emblems for its designs, notably the arms of the House of Bathory, until the reign of Sigismund Bathory (1581–1602), who began a magnificent series of portraits. Turkish pressure continued in the seventeenth century, but after the defeat of the Turks at Vienna in 1683 the last independent voivode, Michael Apafi, nominated the Habsburg emperor as his heir. The last years of Transylvanian independence saw the issue of huge gold prestige pieces, including 100 ducat coins.

ROMANIA UNDER AUSTRIA AND TURKEY

Habsburg coinage was struck for Transylvania with the local arms and titles included, but otherwise identical to that of Hungary. Moldavia and Wallachia remained under Turkish control, providing a buffer against the expanding Russian Empire. They were occupied by Russia in 1768–74 and a special coinage equivalent to both Russian and Turkish denominations was briefly issued, comprising bronze 1 para/3 dengi and 2 para/3 kopeks. In 1866 the provinces became the principality of Romania under Turkish authority.

INDEPENDENCE

Romania declared itself fully independent in 1877 and became a kingdom in 1881, issuing coinage under Carol I (1866–1914), first prince and king. In 1918 Transylvania was acquired after the break-up of the Habsburg Empire.

Romanian coinage is based on the leu of 100 bani. It first appeared in an issue of 1867, consisting of copper 1, 2, 5 and 10 bani, with gold 20 lei added in 1868 and silver 50 bani and 1, 2 and 5 lei appearing in the 1870s. Most of these coins had the arms of the country on the front and the enwreathed value on the back. A new coinage followed the proclamation of the kingdom in 1881. The same denominations and materials were kept, but the king's head was introduced as the main design. In 1900 cupro-nickel replaced copper for the 5 and 10 bani, which also featured a central hole as part of their design, and the 20 bani in cupro-nickel was introduced. In 1906 a series of special gold issues commemorated the 40th anniversary of Carol I's reign.

No new coinage appeared between 1914 and the 1920s, when a number of new denominations and changes in materials occurred. Romania was badly hit by the great inflation of the time and the small denominations vanished from use while much higher ones were introduced or became commonplace. The aluminium 25 and 50 bani were the smallest coins issued, and the 1 and 2 leu became cupronickel. The 5, new 10 and formerly gold 20 and 50 lei were struck in nickel-brass. The new 100 lei was issued in base silver in 1932, then in nickel (1936–8) and nickel-clad steel (1943–4). Base-silver 200, 250 and 500 lei were issued in 1935–44, but in 1946 they were struck in brass along with coins of 2000 and 10,000 lei, and base-silver 25,000 and 100,000 lei.

REPUBLIC OF ROMANIA

Romania had installed a fascist government and fought alongside Germany in the Second World War, before experiencing Russian occupation. In 1947 Romania became a people's republic and the coinage received much needed reform. In 1947 an issue in brass of 50 bani and 1 and 2 lei and in aluminium of 1, 2, 3, 5 and 20 lei prepared the way for a more thoroughgoing reform in 1952, which involved a major revaluation of the leu.

The new coinage featured the revival of the 1, 3 and 5 bani in aluminium-bronze, and 10, 25 and 50 bani in cupro-nickel, with designs of the communist arms on the front and the value on the back. In 1963 the 1 and 3 lei in nickel-clad steel were added to provide higher-value denomination coins, while new issues of 5, 15 and 25 bani were also produced in the same metals. The backs of most of these coins showed agricultural and industrial scenes. An aluminium 5 lei piece was produced in 1978.

11 1930   12 1947   13 1966

ROMANIA

5 SILVER GROSCH *of Vlad I, Voivode of Wallachia.*
6 SILVER GROSCH *of Peter I Muschat, Voivode of Moldavia.*
7 GOLD DUCAT *of Gabriel Bathori, Prince of Transylvania.*
8 GOLD 10 DUCATS *of Michael Apafi, Prince of Transylvania.*
9 COPPER 3 DENGI *of Catherine II of Russia, issued for Wallachia and Moldavia.*
10 BRONZE 10 BANI *of Carol I as Prince of Romania.*
11 NICKEL-BRASS 20 LEI *of Michael I.*
12 BRASS 10,000 LEI *of Michael I (restored).*
13 NICKEL-CLAD STEEL LEU.

ALBANIA

FIRST COINS:	fifth century BC
FIRST DECIMAL COINS:	1926
MAIN MINT:	Tirana
CURRENCY:	lek

THE earliest coins in the area now known as Albania were made in the fifth century BC by two cities on the coast, Apollonia and Dyrrhachium (Durres), which had been founded by Greek colonists from Corcyra (Corfu). The silver coins of these cities were based on the issues of Corcyra, with designs of a cow and calf on the front and a geometrical pattern on the back. The early series at both cities continued until about 350 BC when they were replaced by issues of

ALBANIA
1 SILVER STATER of Dyrrhachium.
2 SILVER DRACHMA of Apollonia.

Corinthian-style coins (*see* Greece) with designs of the winged horse Pegasus on the front and head of the goddess Athena on the back.

Production of civic issues with the cow and calf design resumed late in the third century and ran until about 50 BC. During this period Apollonia and Dyrrhachium were on friendly terms with the rising power of the region, Rome, and the weights of the city coins were changed to link them with the Roman republican monetary system. These coins were produced in large quantities and their circulation extended into Yugoslavia, Romania and Bulgaria.

In addition to the issues of Dyrrhachium and Apollonia, various other cities in Albania produced bronze coins in the third to first centuries BC, notably Phoenice, Lissus and Scodra (Scutari).

THE ROMAN PERIOD

Roman coinage became the main currency of the region in the late first century BC, when Albania was absorbed into the Roman Empire, and continued to be so throughout the Roman imperial period, though bronze coins for local circulation were issued by a few cities, notably Apollonia and Buthrotum.

THE MEDIEVAL PERIOD

In the early Middle Ages Albania remained under Byzantine authority, with no local coinage produced in the region. From the twelfth century Italian coinage, specifically the denarii of Venice and Verona, and pfennigs of Freisach (*see* Austria) began to play a part in the currency of the Dalmatian and Albanian areas. The Venetian grosso became extremely important in the thirteenth and early fourteenth centuries, though from the 1260s Serbian silver coinage was also significant and deniers tournois from Frankish Greece circulated as well.

In the late fourteenth century a number of northern Albanian towns, Shkoder (Scutari), Drivasto, Sas and, in modern Yugoslavia, Bar (Antivari) and Ulcinj, produced small local coinages in silver and copper. Other parts of Albania remained under Venetian control, with Venetian coinage dominant, until the region was captured by the Turks in the sixteenth century (*see* Turkey).

INDEPENDENCE

Albanian independence from Turkey was achieved in the revolt of 1912, but its political organization took some time to become established. A republic was set up in 1925 with Ahmed Zogu as president, but in 1928 he proclaimed himself King Zog I. Coinage was begun in 1926, in a system of 100 quindar leku to the lek and 5 lek to the franga ar. The denominations produced were 5 and 10 quindar leku in bronze (issued only in 1926); ¼, ½ and 1 lek in nickel; 1, 2, 5 and 10

THE BALKANS IN THE GRECO-ROMAN PERIOD

POLAND

CZECHOSLOVAKIA

USSR

AUSTRIA

HUNGARY

ROMANIA

ITALY

YUGOSLAVIA

Sirmium
Viminacium

Danube

Istrus
Tomi
Callatis

BLACK SEA

ADRIATIC SEA

BULGARIA

Mesembria

Deultum
Apollonia
Pontica

Philippopolis

Nicopolis

Celtic coinage zones:-
☐ Silver tetradrachms based on Philip II of Macedon
☐ Silver tetradrachms based on Alexander III of Macedon, and Thasos
☐ Gold staters based on Alexander III of Macedon
• Ancient Greek or Roman mint cities
— Modern Boundaries

Stobi
Dyrrhachium PAEONIA
ALBANIA MACEDONIA
Apollonia

Thasas

0 Kilometres 300
0 Miles 200

Buthrotum GREECE
AEGEAN SEA

TURKEY

3 AD 1428

4 1926

5 1926

franga ar in silver and 20 franga ar in gold, of which versions commemorated the national hero Skanderbeg and the 25th anniversary of independence in 1937. The system was slightly altered in 1935 when new small denominations were introduced: 1 and 2 quindar ar (100 quindar ar = 5 lek = 1 franga ar). The new coins had a two-headed eagle on the front, but from 1935 the other denominations issued had the king's head on the front and coat of arms on the back. Gold 50 and 100 franga ar were added, principally to commemorate royal events.

During the Second World War King Zog was sent into exile when the Italians occupied and annexed Albania. A coinage was produced in the name of Victor Emmanuel III, aligning the Albanian system to the Italian one (100 lek = 1 lira). Aluminium-bronze 0.05 and 0.1 lek, stainless steel 0.2, 0.5, 1 and 2 lek and silver 5 and 10 lek were issued.

PEOPLE'S SOCIALIST REPUBLIC OF ALBANIA

Communist partisans took power in 1944, with Enver Hoxha as president of the People's Republic of Albania, changed in 1976 to the People's Socialist Republic of Albania. Coinage for the new state has been produced only intermittently, to a system of 100 qindarka to the lek. In 1947 zinc ½, 1, 2 and 5 lek were struck. In 1964 an issue of 5, 10, 20 qindarka, and ½ and 1 lek in aluminium was provided, to be followed by a repeat issue in 1969, commemorating the 25th anniversary of liberation.

Designs have been simple: the arms of Socialist Albania on the front and on the back the coin's value on the 1947 and 1964 issues, and in 1969 on the ½ and 1 lek images reflecting the communist triumph.

Commemoratives have also been produced in silver (5, 10, and 25 lek) and gold (20, 50, 100, 200 and 500 lek).

BULGARIA

FIRST COINS:	fifth century BC
FIRST DECIMAL COINS:	1901
MAIN MINT:	Sofia
CURRENCY:	lev

THE first coins to arrive in what is now Bulgaria were the northern Greek silver coins issued by Thracian and Macedonian tribes and cities around 500 BC. Coins of the island of Thasos (see Greece) are particularly common in finds from this early period.

Some of these tribal coinages of Thrace may have originated in Bulgaria, but the earliest that can definitely be attributed to this region were not produced until the Greek colonies of Apollonia Pontica (Sozopol) and Mesembria (Nesebar) on the Black Sea coast issued series of silver and bronze coins in the later fifth and fourth centuries BC. Some issues of the various dynasties of Thracian kings may also have been minted in Bulgaria in this period. In the Hellenistic period (third to first centuries BC), the city of Odessus (Varna) began minting,

6 1939

7 1969

ALBANIA
3 SILVER SOLDINO of Scutari (Sköder), issued under Venetian rule by Doge Paolo Morosini.
4 CUPRO-NICKEL LEK of the Republic.
5 SILVER 5 FRANGA AR of Zog I.
6 STAINLESS STEEL 2 LEK of Victor Emmanuel III, issued under Italian occupation.
7 ALUMINIUM 50 QINDARKA.

1 FIFTH CENTURY BC

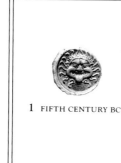

2 FIFTH CENTURY BC

3 386–385 BC

4 c.100 BC

BULGARIA
1 SILVER DRACHMA of Apollonia Pontica depicting the head of Gorgon.
2 SILVER OBOL of Mesembria.
3 BRONZE COIN of the Thracian king Hebryzelmis.
4 SILVER THRACIAN IMITATION of a coin of Thasos.
5 BRONZE COIN of Philippopolis, issued under the Roman emperor Septimius Severus.
6 BRONZE COIN minted in Serdica under the Roman emperor Maximinus Daza.

5 AD 193–211

6 308

and Bulgarian mints also produced some of the many posthumous Alexander (*see* Greece) and Lysimachus (*see* Turkey) coins.

CELTIC COINAGE

In addition to the Greek issues, and contemporary with them from about the third century BC, were numerous issues of coins produced by the native Thracian tribes of Bulgaria, which are usually listed under the general classification 'Celtic'. In the third and second centuries BC these tribes issued silver tetradrachms and drachmae mostly imitating the coins of Alexander III of Macedon, with Heracles-head and Zeus designs. In the first century BC the principal coin imitated was the silver tetradrachm of Thasos with designs of a head of Dionysus and a standing Heracles.

THE ROMAN PERIOD

In the mid-first century BC Roman denarii became a major circulating currency in Bulgaria. Neighbouring Macedonia had been annexed by the Romans in 146 BC, and in the reign of Augustus (31 BC–AD 14) northern Bulgaria was incorporated into the Roman Empire as part of the province of Moesia, while the rest of Bulgaria was left under the rule of a local dynasty approved by Rome. Later, in AD 46, this region was also annexed, becoming the Roman province of Thrace.

Roman imperial coinage in gold, silver and bronze provided the main currency in circulation for the first five centuries AD. However, from the late first century AD to the mid-third century, many of the cities of Bulgaria also issued their own bronze coins. The main mints, which included a number of Roman foundations, were at Anchialus, Dionysopolis, Deultum (Develt), Hadrianopolis, Marcianopolis, Nicopolis (Nikopol), Pautalia and Philippopolis (Plovdiv).

Most of the cities stopped minting their own coins in the 240s: the debased Roman antoninianus was virtually the only coin in circulation over much of the empire. In the later third century production of imperial coinage was devolved to the provinces, and for a brief period in the early fourth century Serdica (Sofia) operated as one of the Roman mints in the Balkans, but otherwise Bulgaria did not have a mint in the late imperial period. Instead, it was supplied with Roman coinage from mints in neighbouring Yugoslavia, Greece and Turkey.

THE MIDDLE AGES

Bulgaria continued to form part of the Byzantine Empire until the incursions of the Slavs and Bulgars into the Balkans in the sixth and

seventh centuries. A separate Bulgarian Empire was established in the late seventh century and survived until its conquest by the Byzantine emperor Basil II in 1019. Bulgaria remained under Byzantine control until the late twelfth century. The rulers of the First Bulgarian Empire issued no regular coinage and throughout the early Middle Ages such coinage as was in use in Bulgaria was mostly Byzantine.

The tsars of the Second Bulgarian Empire began to strike coinage in the early thirteenth century, probably under Boril (1207–18) and Ivan Asen II (1218–44). The coins produced were copper trachea in the Byzantine style, silver groshove imitating Venetian grossi, and a small ceremonial gold coinage. The silver grosh showed the figures of the king and St Demetrius on the front and Christ on the back. The copper trachea were most plentiful under Constantine Asen (1257–77) and showed the tsar on horseback on the front and Christ on the back, but in the fourteenth century, particularly under Ivan Aleksandur (1331–55), enormous issues of silver grosh were produced.

The empire began to break up later in the century, with separate coinages produced by Ivan Stratsimir (1360–96), ruling from Vidim, and Ivan Shishman (1371–93) from Turnovo. Pressure from the Ottoman Turks was responsible for the weakening of Bulgaria and in 1393 they annexed the empire, which remained part of the Turkish Empire until the late nineteenth century.

BULGARIA

7 SILVER GROSCHOVE *of Ivan Asen II.*
8 SILVER GROSCHOVE *of Mikhail III.*
9 SILVER GROSCHOVE *of John Stracimir.*
10 BRONZE 10 STOTINKI *of Prince Alexander.*
11 SILVER LEVA *of King Ferdinand I.*
12 NICKEL-BRASS 50 STOTINKI.
13 SILVER 50 LEVA.

7 1218–41
9 c.1360–96
11 1913
12 1974
13 1981
8 1323–30
10 1881

THE KINGDOM OF BULGARIA

In 1878 Bulgaria became a principality under Turkish suzerainty, being united with eastern Rumelia in 1884 to form what was approximately the territory of modern Bulgaria. Coinage was begun only in 1881 under Prince Alexander I (1879–86), with a monetary system which has survived unchanged: 100 stotinki = 1 lev. Bronze 5 and 10 stotinki were struck in 1881 at Heaton's of Birmingham in England. Other denominations were gradually added: the silver 1 and 2 leva in 1882; 50 stotinki in 1883; 5 leva in 1884; and a range of small denominations in 1888: bronze 2 stotinki, and cupro-nickel 2½, 5, 10 and 20 stotinki. Gold 10, 20 and 100 leva appeared in 1894 and the bronze 1 stotinka in 1901. Designs featured the Bulgarian coat of arms or the head of the prince on the front and the enwreathed value on the back.

Bulgaria became a kingdom in 1908 under Ferdinand I (1887–1918). New coinage was issued infrequently, particularly after the wartime zinc issues of 1917. Under Boris III (1918–43) precious-metal coinage was replaced by aluminium-bronze 50 stotinki, aluminium and then cupro-nickel 1 and 2 leva and cupro-nickel 5 leva. During the Second World War iron 1, 2 and 5 leva were issued.

REPUBLIC OF BULGARIA

The monarchy was abolished in 1946, to be replaced by a people's republic on the Soviet pattern. A new style of coinage was inaugurated from 1951: brass 1, 2, 3 and 5 stotinki, cupro-nickel 10, 20, and 25 stotinki, cupro-nickel then nickel-brass 50 stotinki and 1 lev, and 2 and 5 leva in silver or base alloys. Most coins, even the smallest denominations, feature the commemoration of national anniversaries and events and there are larger and more elaborate commemoratives in precious metal.

USSR

FIRST COINS:	fifth century BC
FIRST DECIMAL COINS:	1704
MAIN MINT:	Leningrad
CURRENCY:	ruble

THE earliest coins produced in the USSR were minted by Greek colonies around the coasts of the Black Sea. On the north-west coast there were the cities of Tyra and Olbia (Parutino), both originally founded by Greek settlers from Miletus in western Turkey; in the Crimea and the region of the Cimmerian Bosporus the most important settlement was another Milesian colony, Panticapaeum (Kerch); and in the east were the cities of the Colchis (Georgia) region.

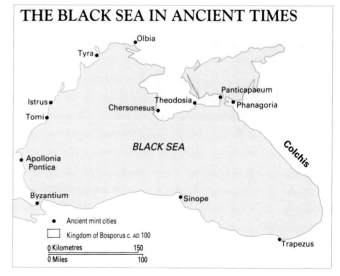

Olbia was a prolific producer of coinage. The earliest issues, around the fifth century BC, consisted of bronze pieces of varying sizes cast in the shape of dolphins, followed by cast coin-shaped pieces. Conventional struck coins, in gold, silver and bronze, were issued from the fourth century BC. Most of Olbia's coinage was issued in the name of the city, but some coins were issued for local Scythian kings. The city of Tyra began producing silver coins in the fourth century BC and issued bronze coins from the fourth to the first century BC.

In the Crimea, Panticapaeum was another prolific coin-issuing city from the fifth to the first century BC. Its most remarkable coins were

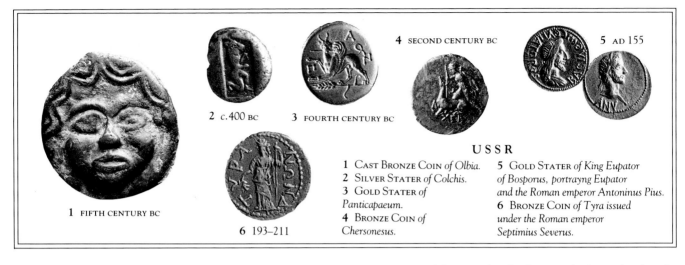

4 SECOND CENTURY BC

5 AD 155

2 *c.*400 BC

3 FOURTH CENTURY BC

1 FIFTH CENTURY BC

6 193–211

USSR

1 CAST BRONZE COIN *of Olbia.*
2 SILVER STATER *of Colchis.*
3 GOLD STATER *of Panticapaeum.*
4 BRONZE COIN *of Chersonesus.*
5 GOLD STATER *of King Eupator of Bosporus, portrayng Eupator and the Roman emperor Antoninus Pius.*
6 BRONZE COIN *of Tyra issued under the Roman emperor Septimius Severus.*

gold staters of the fourth century BC depicting the head of Pan on the front and a griffin, legendary guardian of southern Russia's gold mines, on the back. Other cities issuing coins in this region included Chersonesus (near Sebastopol), Theodosia and Phanagoria, situated across the straits of the Cimmerian Bosporus opposite Panticapaeum. There was also a dynasty of Kings of the Cimmerian Bosporus who issued coins from the third or second century BC. This kingdom was united with the Kingdom of Pontus under the Pontic king Mithradates VI (120–63 BC), and bronze coins were issued for Mithradates in Bosporus.

In the region of Colchis an issue of silver coins dates from perhaps as early as the fifth century BC, and in the first century BC silver coins were issued in the name of Aristarchus, a local ruler installed by the Roman general Pompey.

Further east, beyond the Caspian Sea in the regions known as Chorasmia and Sogdiana (Russian Turkestan), the first coins to appear were Seleucid pieces (*see* Turkey and Syria), and in the third and second centuries BC local imitations of these and of Bactrian Greek coins (*see* Afghanistan) were made in the region.

THE ROMAN PERIOD

The influence of the Romans is clearly visible on the later coinages of Russia's Black Sea cities and kingdoms, even though this region was outside the Roman Empire. Tyra and Olbia produced civic bronze coins which bore the portraits of ruling Roman emperors. The cities of Panticapaeum and Phanagoria were renamed Caesareia and Agrippia and issued bronze coins in the time of Augustus (31 BC–AD 14). The kingdom of Bosporus, now the main coin-issuer in the northern Black Sea region, was a client kingdom of the Roman Empire throughout the imperial period and had a coinage system linked to that of Rome; many of its coins, notably the gold staters, bore the portrait of the ruling Roman emperor as well as the king's portrait and the year of issue, calculated from the date of foundation of the Kingdom of Pontus. An extensive bronze coinage was also issued by the Bosporan kings, and the gold coins were gradually debased with silver, and later copper, until eventually they also became bronze. The last issues of Bosporan coinage were produced by King Rhescuporis VI (AD 304–42).

In the course of the first four centuries AD Chorasmia and Sogdiana developed local coinages with designs derived from Kushan (*see* Afghanistan) and Sasanian (*see* Iran) coins which circulated in the region. Parthian and Sasanian coins from Iran also penetrated into southern Russian territories west of the Caspian Sea.

KIEVAN RUSSIA

In the early medieval period, the eighth to the eleventh centuries, large quantities of Islamic silver dirhems entered Russia through the land of the Volga Bulgars, circulating as far north as Kiev, Pereyaslavl and Chernigov and eventually reaching the Baltic region. The Volga Bulgars themselves issued copies of tenth-century dirhems and another area where such imitations were produced was the Khazarian steppes. The extensive use of dirhems seems to have occurred in the Upper Volga, the Ukraine, Byelorussia, the Ladoga region and the Baltic coast. In the eleventh century the influx of dirhems largely ceased as production in the Islamic world tailed off.

KIEVAN COINAGE

In the meantime, the rulers of Kiev had begun to issue their own coinage, copying the standards and, to an extent, the designs of Byzantine coins (*see* Turkey), by mostly showing the figure of Christ on the front. The first of these coins may have appeared under Vladimir I (978–1015), at about the time that Christianity was officially adopted in Kiev; other names on them include Svyatopolk (1015–19) and Jaroslav (1019–1054). The gold zlatnik (equivalent to the Byzantine nomisma) appeared first, followed by the silver srebrenik. The rulers of Novgorod and Tmutarakan issued similar coins in the late tenth century. North of the Kievan state, however, the Islamic dirhems were replaced in circulation by western European coins, particularly German and Anglo-Saxon pieces.

THE 'COINLESS' PERIOD

Monetary currency was not firmly established in the Russian lands, and silver ingots, broken jewellery, fragments and clippings of coins all seem to have been used as means of payment. From the twelfth to the early fourteenth centuries Russia ceased to use coins almost completely.

Silver ingots, known as grivnas, became the principal form of precious-metal circulation. The Kievan grivnas of the eleventh to the thirteenth centuries were cast hexagonal bars and were used in

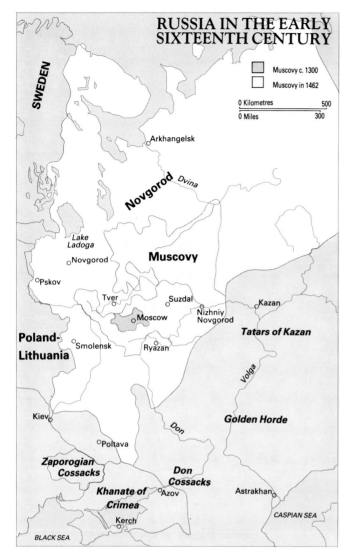

RUSSIA IN THE EARLY SIXTEENTH CENTURY

Muscovy c. 1300
Muscovy in 1462

0 Kilometres 500
0 Miles 300

7 c. THIRTEENTH CENTURY

8 1456–64

9 1420–78 **10** 1462–1505

11 1495–1515

USSR
7 SILVER GRIVNA of Novgorod.
8 SILVER DENGA of Ivan Vasili of Ryazan.
9 SILVER DENGA of Novgorod.
10 SILVER DENGA of Ivan III, Prince of Moscow.
11 SILVER GROSSUS of Walter von Plettenberg, Master of the Livonian Knights, struck at Reval.
12 SILVER GROSSUS of John von Blankenfeld, Bishop of Dorpat.
13 SILVER KOPEK of Ivan IV as Tsar Ivan I.

12 1515–26

13 1547–84

southern Russia. In the north the heavier Novgorod grivnas were initially long straight bars, later becoming slightly curved. So-called 'Lithuanian' grivnas were longer and thinner and marked with incisions. Furs and cowrie shells may have functioned as small change. In the mid-thirteenth century the Mongols invaded and conquered southern Russia. The so-called 'boat-shaped' ingots produced in the Lower and Middle Volga regions may have been produced by them.

INDEPENDENT COINAGES

The Khans of the Golden Horde in the late fourteenth and early fifteenth centuries issued silver dirhems which circulated in the west and south west, mingling with Bohemian Praguergroschen (*see* Czechoslovakia). In Livonia (modern Estonia and Latvia) western-style coinage was introduced as German settlers penetrated and conquered the region. The only local issuers of coinage in the later Middle Ages were the Archbishop of Riga, the Bishop of Dorpat and the military Livonian Order. These struck bracteates in the fourteenth century and, in the fifteenth, versions of Swedish ortugs and 3 pfennig pieces of Lübeck.

LATE MEDIEVAL RUSSIA

In the late fourteenth century the word 'ruble' began to replace grivna to describe a set weight of silver, an ingot of about 200 g. The fractions of the ruble were its half, the poltina, and quarter, the chetvert. It was at this time that the Russian principalities revived the use of coinage in the shape of the silver denga (originally $\frac{1}{200}$ of a ruble) and $\frac{1}{4}$ denga (the chetveretsa), with copper puls for local circulation in some areas.

The main principalities to issue dengi were Moscow under Prince Dmitri Donskoi (1359–89), Suzdal-Nizhny Novgorod (annexed to Moscow in 1451), Ryazan (ceased coinage in 1461 and annexed to Moscow in 1520) and Tver (annexed to Moscow in 1486). A variety of cities, such as Novgorod and Pskov, and subordinate rulers also issued coinage in the fifteenth century, until the growing power of Moscow reduced local autonomy. Coinage in the Grand Duchy of Lithuania (which included Kiev and most of the Ukraine) was provided by the Kings of Poland from their mint at Vilna after the two states were united in the late fourteenth century.

The earliest dengi of Moscow had Mongol inscriptions, though as the importance of the denga coinage grew it became purely Russian in appearance, usually bearing Russian inscriptions, giving the name and title of the prince, and one of a great variety of designs depicting subjects such as fabulous beasts, hunting scenes and patron saints.

By the time of Ivan III (1462–1505) the coinage of the Princes of Moscow, who had assumed the title 'Monarch of all Russia', was much the most important and widely circulating in Russia. Four mints alone remained in use: Moscow, Tver, Novgorod and Pskov. The heavier dengi of Pskov and Novgorod were equivalent to two Muscovite dengi. The most commonly-used design was the representation of the prince on horseback. Ivan III also produced a very small issue of gold ugorsky, based on the Hungarian ducat. Gold coins, however, did not yet become current, but were used as rewards and marks of favour.

EARLY TSARIST RUSSIA

Ivan IV the Terrible (1534–84) took the title 'tsar' in 1547. A unified coinage system for Russia had been established in 1534, based on a new coin, the silver kopek (= 2 dengi). The denga and polushka (= $\frac{1}{2}$ denga) were also produced, though intermittently and in smaller quantities. The design of a horseman with a spear remained in use. Minting ceased at Tver with this reform. Novgorod and Pskov survived as mints until the 1630s.

The earliest Russian coins to carry the date of issue were the kopeks of Tsar Feodor Ivanovich (1584–98). Polish and Swedish interventions in Russia in the early seventeenth century produced issues of kopeks under the auspices of these invaders and in the 1620s–30s Danish imitation kopeks, called 'korelkas' and struck for use by Danish traders in Lapland, entered Russian currency. Lithuania and the Ukraine were at this time part of the Polish–Lithuanian kingdom and Polish and other European coins circulated there (see Poland).

In the seventeenth century the weights of the kopek and denga were gradually reduced until by the time of Peter the Great (1682–1725) they were half their original weight. German talers entered the country in some quantity and in 1654 Peter's father, Tsar Alexei Mikhailovich, issued talers restruck as silver rubles (= 100 kopeks). Some talers were cut into quarters and issued as polupoltinas (= 25 kopeks). Large copper poltinas (= 50 kopeks) and smaller grosh (= 2 kopeks) and altyn (= 3 kopeks) were also struck. The new copper money was used in European Russia only, payments in Siberia still being made in the old silver issues.

In 1655 the government authorized the minting of copper kopeks. This soon drove the silver coinage out of circulation and caused financial hardship and general unrest which culminated in the 'copper riot' of 1662 in Moscow. A coinage of silver was restored in 1663. The silver kopek was by now tiny, though still of relatively high value.

14 1655
18 1721
15 1682–9
17 1706
16 1694

Smaller-denomination coins were extremely rare and some local tokens were produced to help cope with the shortage of small change.

Much foreign coin still circulated in Byelorussia, including Kiev and Smolensk, which was under Polish control; around Ladoga, where Swedish coins were common; and in the Ukraine. In 1686 a mint was set up at Sevsk to produce chekhs, western-style coins with Latin inscriptions intended to compete with foreign coins circulating in the Ukraine region.

THE RUSSIAN EMPIRE, 1914

19 1738

21 1780

20 1762

22 1808

USSR

14 SILVER TALER *of the city of Rostock, 1639, countermarked under Alexis in 1655.*
15 GOLD UGORSKY *of Ivan II.*

16 BASE-SILVER 6 GROSZY *of Frederick Casimir, Duke of Courland.*
17 COPPER KOPEK *of Peter I the Great.*
18 GOLD 2 RUBLES *of Peter the Great.*
19 SILVER RUBLE *of Anna.*
20 GOLD 10 RUBLES *of Catherine II the Great.*
21 COPPER 5 KOPEKS *of Catherine II the Great, issued for Siberia.*
22 SILVER RUBLE *of Alexander I.*

THE EIGHTEENTH AND NINETEENTH CENTURIES

Peter I the Great transformed the Russian monetary scene, expelling foreign coins and introducing machine-manufactured coinage. By 1705 his new issues had been established, based on a decimal system of 100 kopeks to the ruble and comprising: in copper the poluposhka (= $\frac{1}{8}$ kopek), polushka (= $\frac{1}{4}$ kopek), denga (= $\frac{1}{2}$ kopek) and kopek; in silver the 10 dengi (= $\frac{1}{20}$ ruble), grivennik (= $\frac{1}{10}$ ruble), polupoltinnik (= $\frac{1}{4}$ ruble), poltina (= $\frac{1}{2}$ ruble) and ruble; and in gold the chervonets, a ducat coin, and, later, the 2 ruble piece. Most coins had the tsar's portrait on the front and the double-headed eagle on the back.

The structure of the Russian coinage remained little changed throughout the eighteenth and nineteenth centuries, though the size and alloy of coins varied. Other denominations were added: 2 kopeks in copper from 1757 and 3 kopeks from 1840; and 5 and 10 kopek pieces were issued both as large copper and small silver coins through much of the nineteenth century, sometimes concurrently, though from different mints. From 1764 silver 15 and 20 kopeks were produced, but the polupoltinnik ceased to be issued in 1810.

In the early nineteenth century high-value coinage in platinum, of which Russia was a main producer, was issued in 3, 6 and 12 ruble pieces. These existed alongside gold 5 and 10 ruble coins, first introduced under Empress Elizabeth (1741–62).

Mints operated in Moscow and St Petersburg, though silver coinage was produced only at the latter from 1775. A new mint at Ekaterinburg operated consistently from 1762 until it was closed down in 1877. The Moscow mint had closed in the previous year. Also, in the late eighteenth and early nineteenth centuries temporary mints, such as Sestroretsk (1763–7), Anninsk (1789–99) and Ichora (1811–21), opened to produce just copper issues during large-scale recoinages. Copper coinage was also struck in remote Siberia in 1764–81 at a mint in the mining region of the Altai Mountains.

Portraiture remained in use on the high-value coins throughout the 'age of the empresses' – the representation of Empress Anna (1730–40) in particular was often altered – but ceased under Paul I (1796–1801). The standard design in the nineteenth century consisted of a monogram or the Russian eagle on the front and the date and value within a wreath on the back. Portraiture was restored to the silver and gold coinage under Alexander III (1881–94).

The Russian Empire was expanding greatly in both east and west. The dukes of Courland, now part of Latvia, intermittently issued coinage in the eighteenth century: the solidus and grosz in copper, 3, 6 and 18 groszy in base silver, taler in silver and ducat in gold, before the duchy was absorbed into Russia. Livonia and Estonia had passed to Russia from Polish control in 1721, and the Empress Elizabeth produced a local coinage in 1756–7. Lithuania passed to Russia in the third partition of Poland in 1795.

The Mint at St Petersburg (Leningrad) in the late nineteenth century. When Peter the Great built his new westernised city and capital, he also created a new, highly-mechanized mint there.

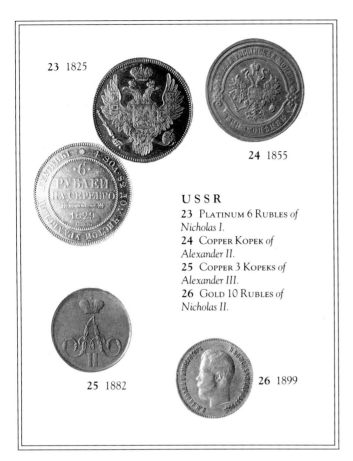

USSR
23 PLATINUM 6 RUBLES *of Nicholas I.*
24 COPPER KOPEK *of Alexander II.*
25 COPPER 3 KOPEKS *of Alexander III.*
26 GOLD 10 RUBLES *of Nicholas II.*

23 1825

24 1855

25 1882

26 1899

(692–8) were in the style of the Iranian Sasanian silver coins in circulation there before the Islamic conquest. At Bukhara the first 'Abbasid issues (late eighth century) also had Sasanian designs (*see* Iran). In eastern Sogdiana, around the city of Pendishkent, the forces of Islam were resisted by an independent Sogdian Kingdom which issued cast bronze coins with central square holes based on contemporary Chinese issues but with Sogdian inscriptions.

'Abbasid-style coins were issued in the area by the local successors of the 'Abbasids: the Tahirids of Nishapur (821–73), the Samanids of Bukhara (819–1005) and the Saffarids (867–963) and Buyids (932–1062) of Iran (*see* Iran and Afghanistan).

From 992 a new phase in the coinage of Central Asia began with the arrival in Bukhara of Turkish nomads ruled by the Qarakhanids (992–1211). The Qarakhanids issued coins at several mints in the Bukhara–Samarkand area and also in Chinese Turkestan. Their early issues imitated the coins of the Samanids, who previously ruled the area, but they also created a series of new ornamental designs, in which the Arabic inscriptions were made into star and square patterns. As an extension of this, they also enclosed the inscriptions in a variety of frames, a decorative device rarely used before on Islamic coins.

The designs introduced by the Qarakhanids were also adopted by the Khwarezm Shahs (1077–1231), who succeeded them, and by the next wave of Central Asian nomad invaders, the Mongols.

Although a few coins were issued within what is now Soviet territory by the Great Mongols and their Ilkhanid successors in Iran, the main Mongol coinages of Central Asia were issued by two other Mongol groups, the Chagatayids (1227–1370), east of the Caspian, and the Golden Horde (1226–1502), to its north and west. The Chagatayids issued broad silver coins with inscriptional designs derived from Khwarezm Shah and Ilkhanid issues (*see* Iran). The Golden Horde coins have Ilkhanid designs. A splinter group of the Golden Horde, known as the Girai khans, eventually settled in the Crimea, where they continued to issue coins with designs influenced by the Turkish coins of the Ottoman sultans until the eighteenth century.

In the south the Crimean khans shifted their allegiance from Turkey to Russia in 1777 before the region was fully annexed by Catherine II the Great (1764–96) in 1783. An issue of 2, 5, 10 and 20 kopeks in silver was struck at Feodosia on the orders of Prince Potemkin to commemorate the empress's visit to the Crimea in 1787. In Caucasia Georgia shifted from Persian to Russian control in 1783, coming under direct rule in 1801. A local coinage using Georgian script was struck at Tbilisi under Alexander I (1801–25) and Nicholas I (1825–55) to a system of 4 puli to the bisti and 50 bisti to the abaze. Coins issued were 1 and 2 puli and 1 bisti in copper and ½, 1 and 2 abazi in silver. The rest of Caucasia, including Armenia and the Khanates of Azerbaijan, was also taken over in the mid-nineteenth century. The main states of Turkestan – Bukhara, Khiva and Khoqand – were annexed in the late nineteenth century and their coinages brought to an end.

CENTRAL ASIA

During the late seventh century the southern borders of what is now Soviet Central Asia, from the Black Sea to the Tian Shan Mountains of Chinese Turkestan, became part of the Islamic Empire of the Umayyad caliphs. During the following centuries the grip of Islamic rule tightened as more and more of the local peoples were converted or conquered. Silver Islamic coins with inscriptional designs of the Umayyad caliphs of Damascus (661–750) and the 'Abbasid caliphs of Baghdad (749–1258) were issued at mints to the east and west of the Caspian Sea (*see* Syria and Iraq). At Merv, the first Umayyad issues

27 770–85

29 1154–84

28 1000

RUSSIAN CENTRAL ASIA
27 SILVER DIRHEM *of al-Mahdi, 'Abbasid caliph, struck in Bukhara.*
28 BRONZE DIRHEM *of Mu'ayyad al-Din Nasir, Qarakhanid khan, struck in Khujindah.*
29 COPPER COIN *of George III, King of Georgia.*

The Qarakhanids were overthrown by their vassal Timur (Tamberlane, 1370–1405). Timur issued coins with decorative designs derived from his overlords and the Jalayrids of Iran (1336–1432). In the east his descendants and their governors elaborated his designs by using an elegant cursive script. The Timurid coins of Samarkand and Bukhara provided the inspiration for the beautiful coins of their successors, the Shaybanids (1500–98) of Bukhara, and their neighbours, the Safavids of Iran (1501–1732) and the Mughals of India (1526–1858).

Although the territory west of the Caspian was gradually absorbed into the Russian Empire during the eighteenth century and into the Iranian and Afghan empires to the east, local Islamic states survived in Bukhara, Khiva and Khoqand until the late nineteenth century. They all produced coins in the style of the contemporary issues of Iran, but developed an elegant decorative frame design which makes their coinage easily distinguishable. The last Islamic issues of the area were struck by Sayyid and Junaid, the last Khans of Khiva (1918–20), and the Khwarezm Soviet People's Republic which replaced them in 1920. The khanate coins were denominated as copper falus and silver 1, 2½ and 5 tenga, but the Soviet issues later adopted the Russian system and were denominated in rubles.

GEORGIA

Since the seventh century Georgia, between the Black and Caspian seas, has remained a Christian enclave within the Islamic world. The Georgian capital, Tblisi, was the site of an Islamic mint of the rulers of Iran in the mid-seventh century. From the tenth century the power of native princes grew and members of the Bagratid Dynasty were recognized as kings, issuing coins in the eleventh, twelfth and thirteenth centuries. These were mostly copper and had either Arabic or Georgian inscriptions, or both. The Bagratids remained as vassal kings after Georgia fell to the Mongols in the 1230s and there was a joint Bagratid–Mongol coinage in the later thirteenth century.

Georgia continued under Persian and then Mongol control, with a brief Ottoman occupation in 1723–35 (during which silver 10 para

were issued). Local coinage recommenced under Theimuraz II (1744–1801), who produced copper pulis and silver abazi (40 pulis = 1 abazi) with Persian inscriptions.

THE SOVIET UNION

During the struggles which followed the Bolshevik Revolution (1917), much local currency was produced, but it was mostly paper money, apart from a White Russian coinage at Armavir in 1918. In 1921–3 a silver coinage of 10, 15, 20 and 50 kopeks and 1 ruble was issued in the name of the Russian Socialist Federated Soviet Republic. In 1925 the first coinage of the Union of Soviet Socialist Republics appeared, still based on 100 kopeks to the ruble.

The designs used since then have been relatively simple for currency coins: an enwreathed globe with hammer and sickle superimposed on it on the front and the value surrounded by wheatears on the back. The issues of 1967 celebrated the 50th anniversary of the 1917 Revolution by having a set of different designs for the higher denominations.

The earliest issues (1924–6) were in bronze and base-silver, but in 1926 bronze was replaced by aluminium-bronze for the 1, 2, 3, and 5 kopeks. In 1961 this was replaced by brass for all but the 5 kopeks. The silver coinage consisted of 10, 15, 20 and 50 kopek and 1 ruble pieces. In 1931 cupro-nickel replaced silver, except for the ½ and 1 ruble, which ceased to be issued as coins. They were revived in 1961, when cupro-nickel was replaced by copper-nickel-zinc for all denominations above the 5 kopeks.

As well as the ordinary currency ruble a large number of commemorative rubles in copper-nickel-zinc have been issued, alongside the following precious-metal commemoratives with nominal values: 5 and 10 rubles in silver, the chernovetz (a bullion coin) and 100 rubles, in gold, and 150 rubles in platinum.

Between 1919 and 1939 Latvia, Lithuania and Estonia were independent republics with their own distinctive coinages. The Estonians went through two monetary systems: one of 100 marka to the kroon (1922–6) and one of 100 senti to the kroon. All denominations

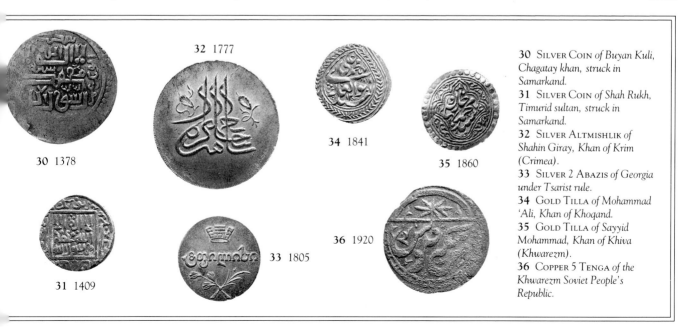

30 1378

32 1777

34 1841

35 1860

31 1409

33 1805

36 1920

30 SILVER COIN of Buyan Kuli, Chagatay khan, struck in Samarkand.
31 SILVER COIN of Shah Rukh, Timurid sultan, struck in Samarkand.
32 SILVER ALTMISHLIK of Shahin Giray, Khan of Krim (Crimea).
33 SILVER 2 ABAZIS of Georgia under Tsarist rule.
34 GOLD TILLA of Mohammad 'Ali, Khan of Khoqand.
35 GOLD TILLA of Sayyid Mohammad, Khan of Khiva (Khwarezm).
36 COPPER 5 TENGA of the Khwarezm Soviet People's Republic.

featured the national emblem of three lions on the front. The Latvian system consisted of 100 santimu to the lats and the coins had the national coat of arms on the front. In Lithuania there was another decimal system, 100 centu to the litas, with a knight on horseback as the main design. The Baltic republics lost their independence during the Second World War.

In the east Tannu Tuva, which was formerly part of Outer Mongolia, existed as a people's republic from 1921 until 1944, when it became an autonomous region of the USSR. A coinage in aluminium-bronze and cupro-nickel was produced in 1934 in a system of 100 kopejek to the aksha.

Left: *Banknotes of 250 and 500 rubles of the Russian Socialist Federated Soviet Republic, 1919. These notes are sometimes known as 'Babylonian' notes because they carry the phrase 'Workers of the world unite' in seven languages.*
Above: *Soviet cartoon depicting the personification of Capital, a porcine figure in evening dress at the centre of a spider's web and thigh-deep in gold coins.*

38 1924

39 1936

37 1922

USSR
37 SILVER RUBLE *of the Russian Socialist Federated Soviet Republic.*
38 SILVER LATS *of Latvia.*
39 NICKEL-BRONZE 50 SENTI *of Estonia.*
40 CUPRO-NICKEL-ZINC RUBLE *of the USSR, commemorating the 30th anniversary of the Second World War.*
41 CUPRO-NICKEL-ZINC 50 KOPEKS.

40 1975

41 1980

ASIA

CORPER DOUBLE PAISA *of Tipu Sultan, the ruler of Mysore, India, from the Patan mint, 1782–99.*

I T WAS in Asia that coinage began. In the late seventh century BC the Lydian kingdom in western Turkey was the provider of the first coins. From this beginning coinage spread into Europe and to North Africa and the Indian subcontinent. The western tradition established by the Lydians and developed by the Greeks, Phoenicians and Romans remained strong in western Asia until adapted by the Arabs for the Islamic coinage at the end of the seventh century AD. In south and central Asia the western idea was shaped into a new Indian tradition which, later absorbing many Islamic features, flourished until the opening years of the present century.

Further east a separate invention of coinage took place in northern China during the sixth century BC and a distinctive system was established which also survived, throughout the Far East, until this century. The coinages of South East Asia represent a mingling of the three Asiatic traditions of Islam, India and China.

Although Asia's coins still exhibit some local features, the independent traditions have now largely disappeared under western influence.

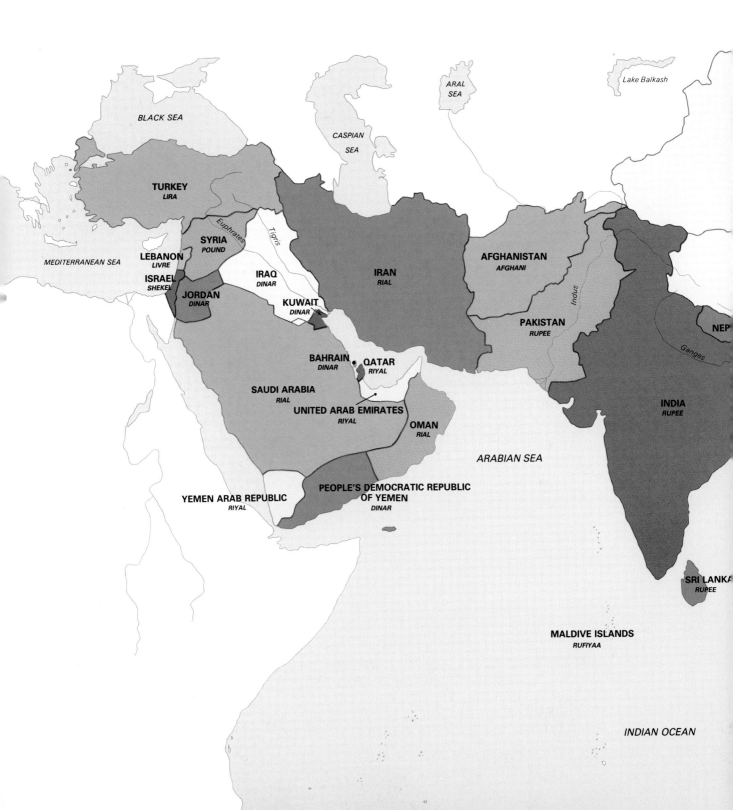

USSR
RUBLE

Lake Balkash

ARAL SEA

BLACK SEA

CASPIAN SEA

TURKEY
LIRA

Euphrates

Tigris

SYRIA
POUND

AFGHANISTAN
AFGHANI

LEBANON
LIVRE

MEDITERRANEAN SEA

IRAQ
DINAR

IRAN
RIAL

ISRAEL
SHEKEL

JORDAN
DINAR

KUWAIT
DINAR

Indus

PAKISTAN
RUPEE

NEP

Ganges

BAHRAIN
DINAR

QATAR
RIYAL

INDIA
RUPEE

SAUDI ARABIA
RIAL

UNITED ARAB EMIRATES
RIYAL

OMAN
RIAL

ARABIAN SEA

YEMEN ARAB REPUBLIC
RIYAL

PEOPLE'S DEMOCRATIC REPUBLIC
OF YEMEN
DINAR

SRI LANKA
RUPEE

MALDIVE ISLANDS
RUFIYAA

INDIAN OCEAN

Lake Baikal

Amur

MONGOLIA
TUKHRIK

NORTH KOREA
WON

JAPAN
YEN

SOUTH KOREA
WON

Hwang Ho

CHINA
YUAN

Yangtse-Kiang

AN
RUM

LADESH
A

BURMA
KYAT

LAOS
KIP

Mekong

TAIWAN
YUAN

MACAO
PATACA • **HONG KONG**
DOLLAR

SOUTH CHINA SEA

PACIFIC OCEAN

THAILAND
BAHT

VIETNAM
DONG

KAMPUCHEA
RIEL

PHILIPPINES
PISO

BRUNEI
RINGGIT

MALAYSIA
RINGGIT

SINGAPORE
DOLLAR

INDONESIA
RUPIAH

TURKEY

FIRST COINS:	late seventh century BC
FIRST DECIMAL COINS:	1844
MAIN MINT:	Istanbul
CURRENCY:	lira

IT was in western Turkey in the late seventh century BC that coinage was invented. The exact origins of the earliest coins are uncertain, but examples of the first issues have been discovered in coastal cities, notably Ephesus. The coastal areas of what is now western Turkey had been colonized by Greek settlers in earlier centuries, and it may have been these Greeks, or possibly the Lydians who ruled over most of the region at the time, who invented coinage.

The earliest coins were all made of electrum, an alloy of gold and silver which occurs naturally in some of the rivers of western Turkey, including the Pactolus, which ran through Sardes, the capital city of the ancient Lydian kingdom. They were just blobs of metal distinguished by a simple punchmark on one side and a basic pattern, often consisting of little more than scratched lines, on the other. The earliest identifiable designs are animal shapes, including a lion's head, which became the standard badge of the Lydian kingdom, and a seal, known to be the badge of the city of Phocaea. Coins bearing these designs were produced in the first half of the sixth century BC. The earliest inscriptions on coins also date from this period.

EARLY SILVER COINAGE

The most famous Lydian king was Croesus (c. 560–547 BC), a man of legendary wealth, who is also generally believed to have issued the earliest pure gold and silver coinages. To him were attributed coins in both metals with designs combining the foreparts of a lion and bull, though it is now believed that many of these so-called 'Croeseid' coins were in fact issued after the Persian conquest of Lydia in 547 BC. Once silver began to be used for coinage it was quickly adopted throughout western Turkey, and across the Aegean Sea in Greece and beyond. In western Turkey most of the cities of the coastal areas which had earlier issued electrum coinage were producing silver coins by the end of the sixth century. Inland, the Persians issued silver sigloi and gold darics (20 sigloi = 1 daric) depicting a crowned figure, usually referred to as the royal archer, at Sardes, the former Lydian capital. Further north, various silver coinages were produced in northwestern Turkey and across the Hellespont in the European part of Turkey. However, electrum coinage retained its popularity in certain areas, notably in the cities of Cyzicus and Phocaea, which continued to produce electrum coins until the fourth century BC.

In the course of the fifth century BC the use of silver coinage spread along the coastal areas of both northern and southern Turkey, reaching cities such as Sinope (Sinub) and Trapezus (Trebizond) in the north and Aspendus (Balkyzi), Side (Eski-Adalia), Celenderis (Tchelindre) and Tarsus in the south. Contemporary developments included the first attempts at portraiture on coinage, by Persian satraps (governors) in western Turkey and local rulers in Lycia (in the south west), and at the end of the fifth century the first appearance in Turkey of bronze coinage. In the fourth century BC the spread of coinage continued. Although most of Turkey was still under the rule of the Persians, extensive coinages, usually making no reference to their Persian overlords, were issued by numerous cities, and also by the dynasties of vassal kings, such as the Hecatomnids of Caria (also in the south west).

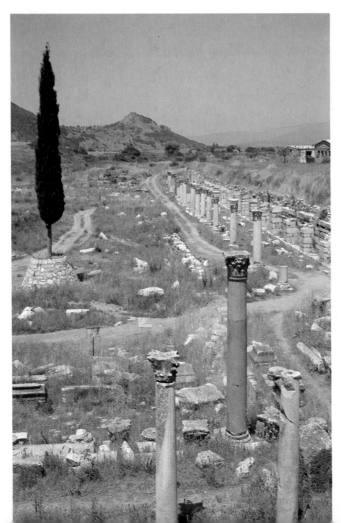

A view of the agora (marketplace) of Ephesus, western Turkey, an important city of the Greco-Roman period.

TURKEY

1 ELECTRUM STATER *from western Turkey.*
2 SILVER STATER *attributed to Croesus, King of Lydia.*
3 GOLD PERSIAN DARIC.
4 SILVER TETRADRACHM *of L... machus, King of Thrace 306–... BC, minted in Alexandria Tro...*

1 LATE SEVENTH CENTURY BC

2 561–547 BC

3 FOURTH CENTURY BC

4 c. 300 BC

ANCIENT TURKEY

THE HELLENISTIC KINGDOMS

The conquest of the Persian Empire by the Macedonian Alexander the Great (336–323 BC) brought Persian rule in Turkey to an end; it also completely transformed the coinage of the region. His gold and silver coinage (*see* Greece) was produced at mints all over the empire, including many in Turkey. After Alexander's death the leading generals of his armies, known as the *diadochi* (successors), fought for control of the empire and continued to use the minting cities of Turkey for production of their own coins. At first these were dominated by issues of 'posthumous Alexanders', but new coin designs were also introduced. The term 'Hellenistic' is used to describe the period from the death of Alexander to the late first century BC, when the Mediterranean world, including Turkey, was dominated by the kingdoms which emerged during the wars of the successors (323–281 BC) and in the century that followed. In this period the spread of coinage in

Turkey continued, with many more cities and regions producing their first issues.

The most prominent coinages in Turkey soon after Alexander were the issues of Lysimachus and of Seleucus. Lysimachus was king of Thrace, and from 301 BC until his death in 281 BC he also controlled much of western and northwestern Turkey. His coinage had designs which featured a portrait of Alexander on the front and a seated goddess Athena on the back. These coins were issued in gold and silver in vast numbers from many mints, and long after his death they retained their popularity with the cities and with the Celtic tribes hired as mercenaries by these cities. Byzantium (Istanbul) was still striking posthumous Lysimachi as late as the first century BC.

When Seleucus defeated Lysimachus in 281 BC, he became ruler of virtually all the eastern provinces of Alexander's empire, and he founded the Seleucid Dynasty, which was to survive until 64 BC. Seleucus and his successors issued coins from mints widely scattered in Turkey, from the western seaboard, through Cilicia in the south, to the Levant coast, where their most important city, Antioch (Antakya), was founded, and to the borders of Iraq in the south east. From the reign of Antiochus I (280–261 BC) the Seleucid coinage was dominated by portraits of the ruling king. The principal Seleucid mints operating in Turkey were Antioch and Tarsus; until the reign of Antiochus III (223–187 BC) Sardes was also a significant producer of Seleucid coinage.

Several smaller kingdoms came into existence in Turkey as the Seleucid Empire gradually declined from the mid-third century BC. The Attalid kings, who ruled Pergamum and later much of western Turkey in the period 264–133 BC, were major coin producers. Early issues of silver coinage were dominated by the portrait of their founder, Philetaerus, but from about 170 BC new designs were introduced, featuring the sacred chest of Dionysus (*cista mystica*) on the front, which gave the coins their name, 'cistophori', and two coiled serpents and a bow case on the back.

5 SILVER TETRADRACHM *of Seleucid king Antiochus II.*
6 SILVER CISTOPHORIC TETRADRACHM *of Pergamum.*
7 SILVER TETRADRACHM *portraying Mithradates VI, King of Pontus.*

5 261–246 BC

6 SECOND CENTURY BC

7 120–63 BC

Other lesser kingdoms issuing coins in Turkey in the Hellenistic period included Bithynia, Pontus, whose most significant ruler was Mithradates VI (126–63 BC), a passionate adversary of the Romans, Cappadocia and Armenia, whose Artaxiad Dynasty produced another famous opponent of Rome, Tigranes the Great (97–56 BC). The coins of all these kingdoms were dominated by portraits of their rulers.

CITY COINAGES

In the Hellenistic period silver remained the most important metal for coinage in Turkey, but there was also a great increase in production of bronze coinage. Many cities whose mints produced regal silver coins for the kingdoms also issued bronze coins in their own names. There were in addition cities which at times governed their own territories and issued their own coinages in silver, and sometimes even gold, as well as bronze. The free cities of Turkey often chose to issue posthumous Alexander silver coins, presumably because these were most widely acceptable. From about 170 BC many cities issued 'wreathed coinages', with the main design on the back surrounded by a wreath, in the fashion of the new-style silver tetradrachms of Athens and the cistophori of the kingdom of Pergamum.

Although the Romans had much influence in western Turkey from the early second century BC, they tended not to interfere with the existing coinages. Thus the cistophoric coinage of the Attalids continued to be issued after the kingdom of Pergamum became the Roman province of Asia in 133 BC.

The giant statues of Nemrut Dag, mountain top sanctuary of the Kings of Commagene in eastern Turkey, first century BC.

THE EARLY ROMAN PERIOD

The Romans extended their control over Turkey in the first century BC, gaining Bithynia and Pontus in the north and Cilicia and the Antioch region in the south. Under the Roman emperors, Galatia, Lycia, Cappadocia and Commagene were added, and finally, in the reign of Trajan (AD 98–117), the eastern provinces of Armenia and Mesopotamia.

The Roman policy of non-interference continued during the first century BC so that after the overthrow of the last Seleucid kings the Antioch mint continued to issue regal Seleucid coinage in the name of an earlier king, Philip Philadelphus (89–94 BC), until as late as the reign of Augustus (31 BC–AD 14). However, Roman coins, especially silver denarii, were arriving in Turkey with the Roman armies, and issues of denarii began to be struck locally in 49 BC.

In western Turkey the cistophoric tetradrachm remained the standard silver coin, though under the emperors the designs were changed to include portraits of the imperial family. A similar transformation affected the other surviving Greek silver issues of Turkey, notably the drachms of the Lycian League, the issues of Caesarea in Cappadocia, and the silver tetradrachms of Antioch, which became under Nero (AD 54–68) the principal silver coins of the eastern provinces of the empire.

Greek silver coinage thus continued in Turkey under the Roman Empire, but from the end of the first century BC the number of mints involved was small and some struck silver only occasionally. However, production of local bronze coinage actually increased under the empire, until the number of mints which at some time issued the so-called 'Greek imperial' bronze coins, with imperial portraits on the front and local designs on the back, exceeded 400. These mints were scattered throughout Turkey, but there was a concentration in the coastal areas and in the west. The coins they produced were intended only for local circulation, but their designs, being expressions of civic pride, were often imaginative and varied, featuring local mythological themes, cult figures, temples and other public buildings.

In addition to the Roman and Greek imperial issues, there were also some eastern coinages circulating in parts of Turkey in the Roman period. The issues of the client kingdoms of Armenia in the north east

TURKEY

8 SILVER TETRADRACHM *of Antioch issued by the Roman emperor Nero.*
9 BRONZE COIN *of the city of Laodiceia in Phrygia, western Turkey, minted under the Roman emperor Caracalla.*
10 SILVER ROMAN IMPERIAL ANTONINIANUS *of Philip I, minted in Antioch.*
11 BRONZE ROMAN IMPERIAL COIN *of Constantius II, minted in Cyzicus.*

8 AD 64–5

9 198–217

10 244–9

11 c.348

and of Commagene came to an end in the first century AD, when these regions were fully incorporated into the Roman Empire. The coinages of the powerful Parthian kingdom and its successor, the Sasanian Empire, based further east in Iran, circulated in the far eastern parts of Turkey. The kingdom of Osrhoene in northern Mesopotamia, whose rulers were vassals of the Parthians, and later of the Romans, issued coins in the second and third centuries AD from its capital, Edessa, in south east Turkey.

THE LATE ROMAN PERIOD

In the second half of the third century AD the Greek imperial issues of Turkey came to an end as Roman coinage, now in the form of debased silver antoniniani (*see* Italy), gradually dominated the currency. Roman silver denarii and gold aurei and Roman-style bronze coins had occasionally been minted in Turkey during the early empire. However, it was not until the third century that regular production of Roman coinage in Turkey began, first in issues of denarii from Antioch, and later in issues of antoniniani from the mints of Antioch and, from the reign of Aurelian (270–5), Cyzicus. In the 290s two more Roman mints were established in Turkey, at Heraclea and Nicomedia in the north west, and in 326 another opened at the new city of Constantinople. All these mints supplied Turkey with Roman coinage in the fourth and fifth centuries.

EARLY BYZANTINE COINAGE

Byzantium was the predominant power in Turkey until the eleventh century providing virtually all of its coinage, and it retained some power there until 1453. Constantinople was throughout most of that period the capital of the East Roman or Byzantine Empire and its main mint, normally providing the bulk of coinage circulating in Turkey. Mints at Nicomedia, Antioch and Cyzicus were in operation from the fifth to the seventh centuries, as were mints in other parts of the empire, but thereafter Constantinople and Thessalonica (*see* Greece) were usually its only mints.

The basis of Byzantine coinage was the gold solidus or nomisma,

TURKEY

12 COPPER FOLLIS of Justinian I, mint of Constantinople.
13 SILVER MILARESION of Leo III the Isaurian, minted in Constantinople.

14 GOLD SOLIDUS of Basil I the Macedonian and his son Constantine (867–86), mint of Constantinople.

which continued to be struck to the same standards of weight and fineness from the fourth to the mid-eleventh century, and was during that time the dominant coin of the whole Mediterranean world. The $\frac{1}{3}$ and $\frac{1}{2}$ solidus coins – the tremissis and semissis – ceased to be produced under Basil I (867–86).

The design of the solidus featured the bust of the emperor or empress on the front; under Justinian I (527–65) the typically Byzantine facing bust replaced the Roman profile. Sometimes other members of the imperial family would be depicted alongside the emperor, as were the associate or co-emperors who at times shared power. The back of the solidus normally displayed one of a variety of crosses or a member of the imperial family. From the time of Michael III (842–67), the image of Christ or sometimes the Virgin appeared on the front, that of the emperor being relegated to the back.

Silver coinage was only occasionally important in the Byzantine world. Siliquae and milarenses (24 siliquae = 12 milarenses = 1

MINTS OF THE BYZANTINE EMPIRE

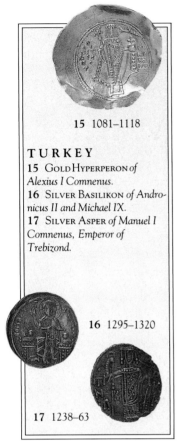

15 1081–1118

TURKEY

15 Gold Hyperperon *of Alexius I Comnenus.*
16 Silver Basilikon *of Andronicus II and Michael IX.*
17 Silver Asper *of Manuel I Comnenus, Emperor of Trebizond.*

16 1295–1320

17 1238–63

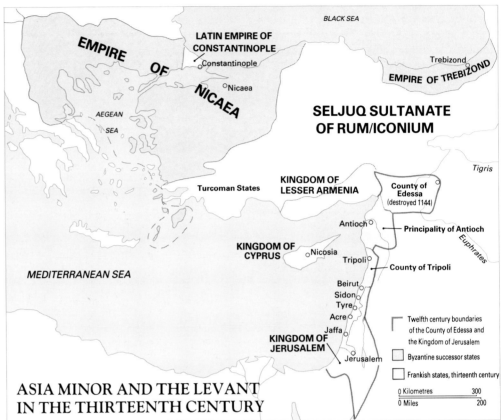

ASIA MINOR AND THE LEVANT IN THE THIRTEENTH CENTURY

Map legend:
Twelfth century boundaries of the County of Edessa and the Kingdom of Jerusalem
Byzantine successor states
Frankish states, thirteenth century

0 Kilometres 300
0 Miles 200

solidus) were sometimes issued in the sixth century, but more important was the hexagram (= 2 milarenses) of Heraclius (610–41). Longer-lasting was the milaresion, another version of the milarense, introduced under Leo III (717–41) and intermittently issued until the late eleventh century. It showed a cross on steps on the front and a Greek inscription on the back.

The reforms of Anastasius I (491–518) introduced large copper multiples of the late Roman nummus: the 5, 10, 20 and 40 nummi, the latter equalling 1 follis. The imperial bust appeared on the front and a letter indicating the value in nummi on the back. From the eighth century the follis alone provided petty coinage, being much reduced in size, and a four-line inscription giving the names and titles of the emperors became the design on the back. There were initially 180 folles to the solidus, but by the ninth century the rate was 288. From the reign of John Tzimisces (969–76), the copper coinage became anonymous, and the image of Christ replaced the imperial bust on the front.

BYZANTINE DECLINE

Many changes affected the Byzantine coinage in the mid-eleventh century. Political and economic disasters encouraged the first debasement of the nomisma. It also changed from a small, flat, thick coin to a larger, spread, cup-shaped or scyphate piece. Under Basil II (976–1025) the two versions of the nomisma were issued concurrently.

Imperial decline was halted by Alexius I Comnenus (1081–1118), and part of his success was due to his reform of the coinage. He introduced a new set of denominations, all scyphate in design: the base-silver aspron trachy (= $\frac{1}{48}$ hyperperon), the electrum aspron

trachy (= $\frac{1}{3}$ hyperperon) and the gold hyperperon. Also produced was a flat copper coin, the tetarteron. Full-length figures normally appeared on these pieces: Christ or the Virgin on the front and on the back the emperor often accompanied by the Virgin or a saint.

This reformed coinage was continued throughout the twelfth century and survived the Fourth Crusade of 1204, when Constantinople was captured. The Byzantines set up an empire in exile, its capital at Nicaea in northwestern Turkey, which continued the traditional coinage, replacing the electrum trachy with one of pure silver. Another breakaway empire was set up on the Black Sea coast around Trebizond. This survived independently until 1461, its coinage consisting of silver aspers mostly showing St Eugenius, patron of Trebizond, on the front and the emperor on the back.

In 1261 Michael VIII Palaeologus, Emperor of Nicaea, recaptured Constantinople. His dynasty ruled the shrinking empire until its end. A new silver coin, the basilikon, based in size and design on the Venetian grosso, was introduced under Andronicus II (1282–1328), supplemented by flat copper assaria. In the fourteenth century the hyperperon was gradually debased and no gold coinage was produced after the 1350s. Its place was taken by a new large silver piece, the stavraton (= $\frac{1}{2}$ hyperperon). By this time the territory of the empire hardly stretched beyond the environs of Constantinople, which was finally captured by the Ottomans in 1453.

ISLAMIC INVASIONS

Although both naval and land assaults were made by Arab fleets and armies on the central domain of the Byzantine Empire during the seventh and eighth centuries, Islam failed to make any deep inroads into Turkey. Only the eastern border areas, adjacent to Syria, Iraq and Iran, fell under the rule of the early Umayyad caliphs, who issued coins with a picture of the Caliph 'Abd al-Malik (685–705) at al-Ruha, Manbij and Kurus and also with Arabic inscriptional designs at Antakia, Tarsus, al-Masisa, Harran, Ras al-'Ain, Amid, Mardin, Nisibin, Saruj and Ma'dan Bajunais (see Syria and Iraq).

As the power of the caliphate was weakened from the late ninth century, similar inscriptional coins were issued in the same area by the Tulunids of Egypt (868–905), the Hamdanids (905–1004) and 'Uqaylids (990–1096) of Iraq and the locally based Marwanids of Diyabakr (990–1085). The Hamdanids opened a new mint at Mayyafarqin and the Marwanids one at Khilat.

THE ARRIVAL OF THE TURKS
The Seljuq victory over a Byzantine army at Malzgird in 1071 signalled the arrival of the Turkish peoples, who have since dominated the history of Turkey. The Seljuqs, based in Iran, did not rule directly, but local Turkish chieftains, the Seljuqs of Rum at Qunya (1077–1307), the Danishmendids at Siwas (1071–1174) and the Saltukids at Erzerum (eleventh century), established control over the area and the Seljuqs issued coins only at Dunaisir near the Syrian border.

These Turkish rulers issued copper coins with designs borrowed from the Byzantine coinage already circulating. They also countermarked Byzantine coins with short Arabic inscriptions. The early Rum Seljuq and Saltukid coins were inscribed with the name and titles of the ruler in Arabic, but the Danishmendid coins bore a curious mixture of Greek and Arabic written in Greek script.

CRUSADER COINAGE
The establishment of Islamic Turkish principalities in central Turkey shook the Byzantine Empire and prompted a Christian response in the form of the First Crusade in 1096. In opposition to the Turkish states, the Crusaders founded their own states at Edessa and Antioch. In the early twelfth century the rulers of both issued a copper coinage based on contemporary Byzantine issues. The Edessene coppers mostly show the count standing in armour with sword or shield. The Antiochene coppers had a variety of designs, several showing Christ or St Peter, first Bishop of Antioch. One issue, of Roger of Apulia, shows St George

slaying the dragon. Edessa was conquered by Zengi in 1144 and issued no more coinage, but between the mid-twelfth century and about 1268 the Princes of Antioch made a large issue of base-silver deniers with a cross on the back. Their front initially showed the prince bareheaded, but this was changed to show him wearing chain-mail and a helmet. A variety of copper coins provided fractional money.

CILICIAN ARMENIA
On the southern coast of Turkey, part of Cilicia, many Armenians had been settled by the Byzantines, and the members of the aggressive and capable Roupenid Dynasty carved out a principality there in the early twelfth century. Levon I (1187–99) received the title of king in 1199 by grant of the pope and German emperor. The Armenian kingdom survived until 1375 and a considerable coinage was issued.

This was mostly in the form of silver trams, which displayed the ruler on the front and one or two lions holding a cross on the back. The trams of Hetoum I (1226–71), the first Hetoumid king, show the king and his queen, Zabel (the Roupenid heiress), with a cross between them. A series of bilingual trams, with an Armenian design, the king on horseback, on one side and an Arabic inscription on the other reflected the overlordship of the Seljuqs of Rum. Copper coins were also struck in quantities for the Armenian kings.

THE SELJUQS OF RUM
The Crusader attacks on Constantinople and the subsequent fragmentation of the Byzantine state gave the Seljuqs of Rum, who already controlled the other Turkish principalities, the opportunity to establish a powerful state in central Turkey. From their main mints at Qunya, Qaisaria and Siwas and from 15 other mints they issued a massive silver coinage, some copper, but rarely gold coins.

They introduced pictorial designs and ornamental frames around the Arabic inscriptions, naming the Seljuq ruler and his titles and proclaiming the Islamic religion. The pictorial coins used lion and sun or horseman designs inspired by the issues of their southern neighbours, the Artuqids in Diyabakr (1098–1232). The ornamental frames were derived from the Ayyubid and Mamluk coins in use in Syria.

THE ARTUQIDS AND ZENGIDS
After the Seljuqs had established control in central Turkey, they

19 LATE TWELFTH CENTURY

18 1187–1218

20 1152–76

21 c.1190

TURKEY
18 SILVER TRAM of Levon I, King of Armenia.
19 BASE-SILVER 'HELMET' DENIER of the Princes of Antioch.
20 COPPER COIN of Najm al-Din, Artuqid ruler of Mardin.
21 COPPER COIN of Suleyman Shah Seljuq king of Tokat.
22 SILVER COIN of Kaikhusru II, Seljuq Sultan of Rum, struck in Qonyah.
23 SILVER COIN of Suleyman Khan, Mongol Ilkhanid khan, struck in Hisn Keyfa.
24 SILVER COIN of Orkhan ibn 'Uthman, Ottoman sultan.

22 1242

23 1344

24 1326–60

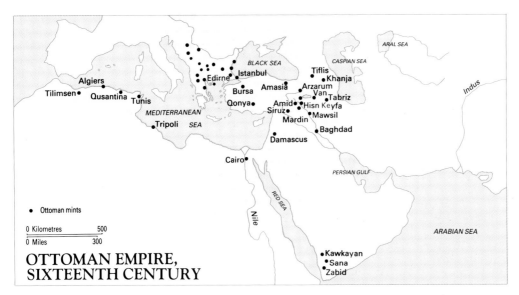

OTTOMAN EMPIRE, SIXTEENTH CENTURY

• Ottoman mints

0 Kilometres 500
0 Miles 300

25 1520

26 1765

founded two more Turkish statelets on the northern edge of the Iranian Seljuq Empire: the Artuqids in Diyabakr (1098–1232) and the Zengids in northern Iraq (1127–1222). Like the early Seljuqs of Rum, their coinage fell under the influence of Byzantium and was decorated with pictorial devices.

As well as directly copying contemporary Byzantine designs, the Artuqids and Zengids made use of ancient coin designs on Greek, Roman, early Byzantine and Iranian coins found in their region, including coins of the Seleucid kings of Syria, of the Roman emperors Augustus, Constantine the Great and Julian the Apostate, of the Byzantine emperor Heraclius and the Sasanian emperor Shapur I (see Iran). There are also many original designs, which seem to refer to astrological subjects or attempt to depict the Turkish ruler.

When the Ayyubids of Syria briefly held this area in the late twelfth and early thirteenth centuries they also issued their own versions of the Turkish picture coins, copying Artuqid originals.

EASTERN INVASIONS

During the thirteenth century the Seljuq sultans were forced by a military defeat in 1243 to become vassals of the Mongols. The Christian kingdom of Trebizond also acknowledged them as overlords. As Seljuq power dwindled, so did the issue of Seljuq coinage until it had virtually ceased by about 1300. During the reign of the Mongol Khan Abu Sa'id (1317–35), Iranian Ilkhanid administrations took over most of the Seljuq mints and issued coins in his name (see Iran).

In 1277 an attack by Baybars, the Mamluk ruler of Syria, also hastened the end of the Christian kingdom of Cilician Armenia, which had issued coins which were inscribed in Armenian and decorated with pictorial designs, such as horsemen, lions and crosses, since the twelfth century.

THE OTTOMANS

The Mongol push into Turkey forced some Turkish tribes to migrate further west towards the vestiges of the Byzantine Empire around Constantinople. The most powerful of these were the Ottomans, descendants of 'Uthman, a vassal of the Seljuqs of Rum during the thirteenth century. As the Seljuqs went into decline, the Ottomans

built themselves an empire in western Turkey and in eastern Europe. Although their progress was halted by the sudden invasion of Timur (Tamberlane, see Afghanistan and Iran) in 1402, the Ottomans soon recovered and continued to expand their empire until, by the early sixteenth century, they had established control over not only Turkey and southeastern Europe (as far as Hungary), but had also added North Africa (except Morocco) and Syria, Lebanon, Israel, Iraq, Kuwait, Bahrain, Arabia and Yemen to their possessions.

The early coins of the Ottomans and their eastern neighbours, the Qarmanids (1256–1483) were modelled on Ilkhanid issues. From 1388 Ottoman coins used numerals to express the date of issue according to the Islamic era. In the far east of Turkey coins were issued by the last of the Artuqids and by the White Sheep of Iran and other smaller Turkmen groups until the invasion of Turkey by Timur in 1402. Timur also briefly issued coins in eastern Turkey.

During the re-establishment of the Ottoman state in the wake of Timur's invasion Suleyman, the Ottoman amir in Edirne in European Turkey, introduced coins with a new design, the *tughra*, the ruler's ornate official signature. The *tughra*, which would characterize Ottoman coins until the present century, was formed by writing the ruler's

The Mosque of the Sea, Istanbul. Istanbul was the centre of the Ottoman Empire and the site of its main mint.

25 GOLD ASHRAFI of Suleyman I the Magnificent, Ottoman sultan, struck in Constantinople.
26 GOLD PRESENTATION COIN of Mustafa III, Ottoman sultan, struck in Islambul (Constantinople).
27 SILVER KURUS (PIASTRE) of Mustafa III, Ottoman sultan, struck at Islambul.
28 SILVER 2 KURUS of Mustafa IV, Ottoman sultan, struck in Constantinople.
29 COPPER 40 PARA of Abdul Aziz, Ottoman sultan, struck in Constantinople.
30 SILVER 100 KURUS, of Turkish Republic, with portrait of Kemal Ataturk.
31 STEEL 2½ LIRA, of the Republic.

name and titles in an elaborate cursive type of Arabic script so that they formed a single compact unit, with the curved strokes making a rounded base and the upright strokes protruding like a crest from the top. It was used on official documents as well as on coins.

Once the Ottomans had captured Byzantium (Constantinople, now Istanbul) in 1453, they were able to concentrate on expanding their empire. Ottoman coinage entered a new phase during the reigns of Sultan Mehmet the Conqueror (1444–6 and 1451–81) who took Istanbul, Selim the Grim (1512–20) who conquered Syria, Egypt, Arabia and Yemen, and Suleyman the Magnificent (1520–66), during whose reign Iraq, Algeria and Tunisia were also integrated into the Ottoman Empire.

The growing empire brought wealth and increasing trade to Turkey. Trade brought Italian gold ducats, florins and sequins into Turkey and in 1473 a new gold coin called the ashrafi altin, the same size and weight as all the Italian coins, was struck at Qustantiniya (Istanbul). By 1566 the ashrafi altin was also being struck at Amasya, Amid, Bursa, Cezayir, Edirne, al-Ruha and Siruz in Turkey, and at mints in the territories now known as Bulgaria, Greece, Yugoslavia, the USSR, Iran, Syria, Iraq, Egypt, Libya and Tunisia.

The ashrafi altin was inscribed in Turkish with the sultan's name and titles and the mint and date. The words 'Sultan Selim Khan, son of Bayazid Khan, may his victory be glorious: striker of bright coins and lord of might and victory by land and sea, struck at Amid in year 918', appeared on a coin of Selim the Grim issued in 1512. The other denominations had a brief or modified version of this legend. Alongside the altin small silver and copper coins called akce and mangir were issued.

The *tughra* and decorative ornaments were only used on silver and copper coins until the reign of Mustafa II (1695–1703) who introduced the gold ashrafi altin bearing the *tughra*. From 1687 new larger silver coins called kurus had also been introduced. The kurus initially weighed about 19.5g, but after 1730 its weight was increased to 25.5 g to make it closer in size to the Austrian thalers, Venetian ducatoons, Dutch rijksdaalders and Spanish 8 reales which were being traded into Turkey.

Multiple ashrafis and other gold denominations and fractions of the

kurus were issued in abundance during the next 150 years, but the Ottoman coinage remained essentially the same until the end of the empire in 1923. Even the introduction of a decimal system, with 100 kurus = 1 Turkish pound (lira), in 1844 had only a limited effect on the designs used on the coins. In fact, this system was not completely decimalized as the kurus was divided into 40 para, a small copper coin. The new coins were all made on Western machinery at the Qustantiniya mint. Copper 1 and 5 para, silver 20 para and 1, 2, 5, 10 and 20 kurus and gold 25, 50, 100, 250 and 500 kurus coins were made. From 1855 copper 10, 20 and 40 para coins were also struck.

The last Ottoman issues (1918–22) were of cupro-nickel 40 para, silver 2, 5, 10 and 20 kurus and gold 25, 50, 100, 250 and 500 kurus in the name of Muhammad VI (1918–23).

REPUBLIC OF TURKEY

In 1924, Mustafa Kemal, the Turkish revolutionary, established the Republic of Turkey, and in the same year republican coins were issued. The star and crescent emblem of the republic appeared on the new coins, which were denominated according to the traditional Ottoman system as para and kurus.

From 1934 a completely new coinage was initiated. The inscriptions were no longer in Arabic script, but were written in Turkish using the western alphabet, and dated according to the western calendar. The star and crescent remained the main design, but foliage was also used to decorate the lower denominations, and the portrait of Kemal appeared on the 50 and 100 kurus coins. Kemal's bust has remained a frequently used design, but since the issue of stainless steel 25 and 50 kurus coins, featuring agricultural workers, in 1959–60, many other pictorial designs have appeared, particularly on United Nations Food and Agricultural Organization and other commemorative issues.

The current issue, minted since 1981, has no kurus denominations, but consists of aluminium 1, 5, 10, 20, 25, cupro-nickel 50 and 100 lira coins, all portraying Kemal on the front, and the denomination and date within a wreath of wheat and olives below the star and crescent emblem on the back.

SYRIA

FIRST COINS:	fifth century BC
FIRST DECIMAL COINS:	1921
MAIN MINT:	Damascus
CURRENCY:	pound

The first coins to arrive in Syria were Greek issues of silver coinage from the Aegean area, which were exported in quantity to the Levantine coastal region in the fifth century BC. At that time Syria was part of the Persian Empire, but Persian silver sigloi and gold darics were issued further west in Asia Minor (Turkey) and barely circulated in Syria. The island city of Aradus, off the Phoenician coast (see Lebanon), issued Syria's first coins in the second half of the fifth century BC. The early silver staters and fractions have maritime designs of a Phoenician fish god on the front and a galley on the back. They were inscribed with Phoenician letters and used the same (Persic) weight standard as nearby Cyprus. Bronze coins were added to the city's output in the fourth century.

When Syria became part of the empire of Alexander the Great (336–323 BC), Aradus was one of the more important minting cities for production of Alexander's coinage of gold staters and silver tetradrachms (see Greece). New mints were also established to issue Alexanders, including Damascus. Another mint, in the city of Bambyce-Hierapolis (Membij), issued coins in Alexander's name but struck to the Persic weight system and with local designs and inscriptions in Phoenician.

THE SELEUCID KINGS

Following the break-up of Alexander's empire, Syria became part of the Kingdom of Seleucus I (321–280 BC), whose descendants, the Seleucid kings of Syria, ruled the region until the Romans arrived in the first century BC. A number of mints in Syria, including Damascus, Hierapolis, Apamea and Laodiceia (Latakia), issued Seleucid coinage (see Turkey), which was dominated by portraits of the ruling kings, and consisted largely of silver tetradrachms and fractions, as well as various denominations of low-value bronze coinage. Issues of gold coins were rarely produced. From 83 to 69 BC Tigranes the Great, King of Armenia, ruled the Seleucid kingdom and issued a regal Seleucid coinage bearing his portrait. Following Tigranes's defeat by the Romans, the Seleucid Dynasty was briefly restored, but in 64 BC the Romans formally annexed Syria.

Under Seleucid rule, some of the cities of Syria issued increasing numbers of coins in their own names. Towards the end of the period the issues included silver as well as bronze. The most important city coinages were the silver tetradrachms of Aradus from 137 to 46 BC and of Laodiceia from 77 to 16 BC.

THE EARLY ROMAN PERIOD

Immediately following the Roman annexation of Syria, both Seleucid regal coinage and Syrian civic coinage in silver continued. The Seleucid coins struck under Roman authority were straight imitations of the issues of an earlier king, Philip Philadelphus (92–83 BC), but some also bore the initials of Roman governors.

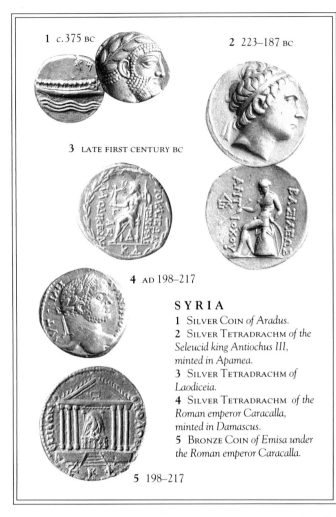

SYRIA

1 SILVER COIN of Aradus.
2 SILVER TETRADRACHM of the Seleucid king Antiochus III, minted in Apamea.
3 SILVER TETRADRACHM of Laodiceia.
4 SILVER TETRADRACHM of the Roman emperor Caracalla, minted in Damascus.
5 BRONZE COIN of Emisa under the Roman emperor Caracalla.

By the end of the first century BC these issues were being replaced by the new silver tetradrachms of Roman Syria, for which Antioch (Antakya in Turkey) soon became the principal mint, though issues were also produced at Laodiceia in Syria. Also circulating in the region were Roman silver denarii, shekels from the mint of Tyre (see Lebanon), and, in the south, silver and bronze coins of the Nabataean Kingdom, which was centred in Jordan but at this time also controlled Damascus and its mint.

Under the Roman emperors there was an increase in production of bronze city coinages, especially after the incorporation into the empire under Trajan (AD 98–117) of Arabia Petraea in the south and Mesopotamia in the north east. The long-established mints of cities such as Aradus, Laodiceia and Damascus continued, but these were now joined by many others throughout the length and breadth of the country. Most of the so-called 'Greek imperial' bronze coins had portraits of the imperial family on the front accompanied by local designs on the back.

In the early third century silver coins were once more minted in Syria, when cities such as Hieropolis, Damascus and Emisa produced Antioch-style silver tetradrachms. Production of bronze Greek imperial issues reached a peak in this period, but then steadily declined until it ceased altogether in the reign of Gallienus (253–268), by which time the Roman base-silver antoninianus had become the most common coin in circulation in the region.

THE LATE ROMAN AND BYZANTINE PERIODS

In 259–60 the Sasanian king of Persia, Shapur I, overran the eastern provinces and captured the Roman emperor Valerian. The defence of Syria was left in the hands of the King of Palmyra, Odenathus, who successfully led the Roman forces against the Sasanians. Under the successors of Odenathus, Zenobia and Vabalathus, the Kingdom of Palmyra, which now controlled most of the eastern Roman Empire, attempted to win full independence from Rome, but was defeated by Aurelian (270–5). The rulers of Palmyra issued Roman-style coinage.

From the late third century until the arrival of Islam in the seventh century, the Roman imperial coinage, and, from the late fifth century, the coinage of the Byzantine emperors (*see* Turkey), was the official currency. None of this coinage was minted in Syria, the nearest mint being at Antioch. However, for most of this period, the eastern parts of the country were held by the Sasanians, and there the Sasanian coinage circulated (*see* Iran).

ISLAMIC CONQUEST

An Arab army brought the Islamic faith to Syria within a few years of the death of its founder, Mohammad, in 632. When his second successor, the caliph 'Umar, captured Damascus in 635, Byzantine copper and gold from Turkey and Sasanian silver coins from Iran were in use, but by the 680s a need for additional coins was felt, and copper and gold coins with designs copied from the current Byzantine coins were struck at Damascus.

The first Arab copper coins were inscribed with their mint name in Greek and Arabic. Similar coins were also struck at Hims and Tartus. The first gold coin retained the Byzantine inscriptions, but removed the crosses from the designs.

CALIPH 'ABD AL-MALIK

From about 691 changes were made to the designs to remove the Byzantine influence. An image of the Umayyad caliph 'Abd al-Malik, whose capital was Damascus, replaced the image of the Byzantine emperor on the gold and copper coins. An issue of silver coins with Sasanian designs, but Arabic inscriptions, like those produced by local

Monumental archway, dating from AD 220, in Roman Palmyra, centre of the ancient caravan trade route across the Syrian desert.

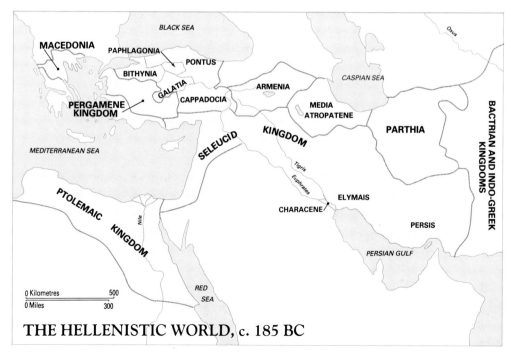

THE HELLENISTIC WORLD, c. 185 BC

SYRIA

6 c.680

6 COPPER FALS *of the Umayyad Caliphate, struck in Hims (Emisa), with Byzantine designs.*

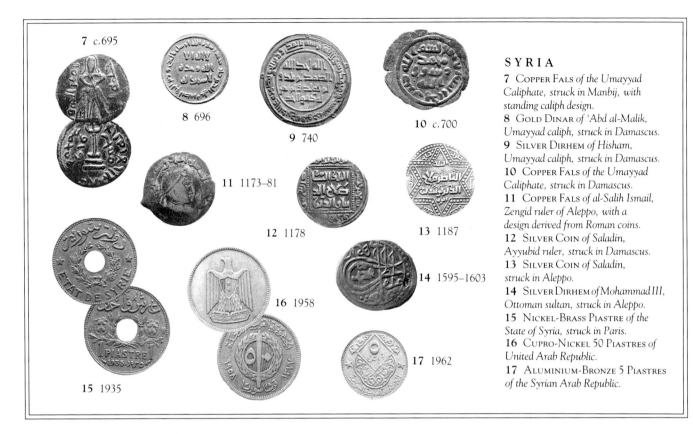

Arab governors in Iraq and Iran, was also issued at Damascus. Arabic inscriptions proclaiming the Islamic faith, 'There is no god but God alone, Mohammad is the prophet of God', were placed on all the new coins. Copper coins with the caliph's image were also struck at Hims, Aleppo, Qinnasrin and Ma'arrat Misrin.

From 696 the pictorial designs were removed and purely inscriptional designs were introduced in response to the Islamic distaste for pictorial images. This was a gradual process and, after experimental silver issues, removing the Zoroastrian fire altar design from the back, in 694, the first inscriptional silver coins were issued from 698. Some copper coins still used non-Byzantine pictorial designs over the following decades, such as an elephant at the Hims mint and a branch or a rat at Damascus.

THE 'ABBASID CALIPHATE

The fall of the Umayyad Caliphate in 750 led to the transfer of the Arab capital to Baghdad in Iraq. The mints in Syria now began to issue coins with the modified inscriptional designs introduced from 749 by the first 'Abbasid caliph, al-Saffah.

'Abbasid rule over Syria became nominal as the area came under the control of the Tulunid (868–905) and Ikshidid (935–69) governors of Egypt and the Hamdanid (905–1004) governors of Mosul (northern Iraq) and Aleppo. Although taking power as 'Abbasid governors, all these dynasties ruled Syria in their own right and struck 'Abbasid-style coins with their own names.

THE FATIMID CALIPHATE

From 1004 most of Syria fell to the Fatimid rulers of Egypt. Parts of northern and eastern Syria remained under the control of northern Iraq, which was now ruled by the 'Uqaylids (990–1096). The Fatimids and their Iraqi neighbours were followers of the non-orthodox Shi'a sect of Islam and modified their coin inscriptions to reflect their beliefs (*see* Tunisia and Egypt). The Fatimids introduced into Syria new decorative designs which presented the inscriptions in concentric circles. Fatimid-style gold coins were also struck by the rulers of Aleppo, the Mirdasids (1023–79) who were also Shi'ites.

Certain areas of Syria formed part of the Kingdom of Jerusalem (*see* Israel) at the beginning of the twelfth century and the coinage of European Crusaders circulated.

SALADIN

Crusader control over Syria ended in 1183 as Salah al-Din (1169–93), the Ayyubid ruler of Egypt, known in Europe as Saladin, re-established Islamic rule. Saladin's uncle and father had been generals of the Turkish Zengid rulers of northern Iraq and eastern Syria when they established the kingdom later inherited by Saladin. The Zengids in Syria had a mint at Aleppo, which, during the mid-twelfth century, struck copper coins with pictorial designs like those issued at Zengid mints in Iraq and Turkey. The Aleppo coins used designs copied from contemporary Byzantine coins.

Saladin opened a new mint at Damascus and issued silver coins of a new type, with inscriptional designs enclosed within a square frame, copied from the gold coins of his western neighbours, the Muwahhid rulers of North Africa. He also established mints at Aleppo and Hamah, both striking his new silver coins. At Aleppo a star-shaped frame was used instead of the square one. The inscription on one side of

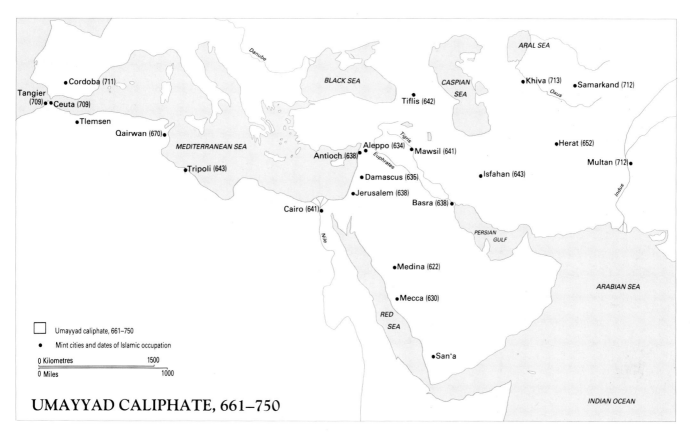

UMAYYAD CALIPHATE, 661–750

the coin was the traditional proclamation of the Islamic faith first used on coins by the Umayyads, but on the other side it gave only Saladin's name and titles.

THE MAMLUKS

Saladin's new silver coins were very successful and were soon copied in Iraq, Turkey and Iran. Their designs were also adopted in Syria and Egypt by the Mamluks, who succeeded to the Ayyubid kingdom in 1250 and held Syria until its conquest by the Ottoman Turks. During the Ayyubid and Mamluk period copper coins with both framed and pictorial designs became more widely used. These coppers are often badly made on misshapen blanks, but have interesting designs, such as a fleur-de-lis, chalice or lion.

THE OTTOMAN EMPIRE

From the time of Selim I's conquest in 1517, Ottoman gold, silver and copper coins were struck at both Damascus and Aleppo, but not in great quantity. The gold and silver have the usual Ottoman designs (*see* Turkey and Egypt), but the coppers have local designs featuring decorative patterns. Ottoman coins from Turkey and Egypt also circulated in Syria, and in the coastal region imported European silver and gold coins were in use. From the mid-seventeenth century imported coins formed the only currency because the Ottoman mints in Syria were closed during the reign of Muhammad IV (1648–87) and were not reopened during the remainder of the Ottoman period.

FRENCH RULE

After the defeat of the Ottoman Empire in the First World War, Syria

came under French control and from 1921 coins were minted in Paris for Syria. The first issue was only of cupro-nickel ½ piastre pieces with a wreath design like that on French Tunisian issues. They were inscribed with the name of the Bank of Syria and their denomination and date in both French and Arabic. The denomination system (100 piastres = 1 Syrian pound) was of Ottoman origin (*see* Turkey).

From 1926 new aluminium-bronze 2 and 5 piastre coins were issued in the name of the State of Syria, still with wreath designs. A further issue of brass and silver 1, 10 and 50 piastre pieces with ornamental frame designs followed in 1929. New brass ½ and aluminium-bronze 2½ piastre coins were added in 1935 and 1940 respectively. The 1935 coin was issued in the name of the Syrian Republic. During the Second World War the Paris mint could no longer supply coins, and crude brass 1 and aluminium 2 piastre pieces with purely inscriptional designs were made locally.

INDEPENDENCE

In 1944 Syria gained full independence and from 1947 issued its own coins with entirely Arabic inscriptions and decorated with an Islamic eagle design (*see* Egypt). The piastre–pound denomination system was retained and by 1950 cupro-nickel 2½, 5 and 10 and silver 25 and 50 piastre and 1 pound coins had been issued. In 1958, the establishment of the United Arab Republic, linking Syria with Egypt and Yemen, prompted a new issue retaining a version of the eagle design, but with a new inscription. The pound denomination was omitted from the issue. The dissolution of the republic in 1961 led to a further modified issue in 1962. The pound denomination was reintroduced in 1968 and has since been used for several commemorative issues.

LEBANON

FIRST COINS:	fifth century BC
FIRST DECIMAL COINS:	1924
MAIN MINT:	Royal Mint
CURRENCY:	livre

THE sites of most of the coastal cities of ancient Phoenicia are in modern Lebanon. Despite their reputation as the great traders of the Mediterranean, the Phoenicians were not among the first producers of coinage. Their earliest coins, issued in silver by the cities of Aradus (*see* Syria), Sidon, Tyre and Byblus date from the second half of the fifth century BC, by which time the region was already familiar with Greek silver coinage, particularly the tetradrachms of Athens, which had been acquired through trade with the Aegean area since about 500 BC.

When the first coins were minted in Lebanon, local vassal kings were named on the coins of Sidon and Byblus, although the whole region recognized the rule of the Persian king. The Phoenician script and Phoenician designs were used, but images borrowed from Persian art were also prominent, particularly on the coinage of Sidon, which frequently depicted the Persian king or other symbols of Persian rule. The coinage of the cities continued in the fourth century BC when bronze coins were also produced.

SELEUCID AND PTOLEMAIC RULE

When the region became part of the empire of Alexander the Great (336–323 BC), the mints of Lebanon joined in the production of

1 372–362 BC

2 114 BC

3 AD 98

The cedars of Lebanon. Solomon used their timbers for the Temple in Jerusalem, and they now feature on Lebanese coins.

Alexander's coinage of silver tetradrachms and gold staters (*see* Greece), continuing after his death because Alexander coinage had become the most widely acceptable currency in the eastern Mediterranean. In the Hellenistic period (*see* Turkey) Lebanon was disputed territory, ruled by the Seleucid kings of Syria in the early third century and again in the second and first centuries BC and by the Ptolemaic kings of Egypt from the 270s BC until the end of the third century BC. Regal Seleucid and Ptolemaic coinages were issued by the mints in Lebanon, as well as coins produced in the name of the cities, some of which gained their independence as Seleucid power weakened. Many more mints were operating, compared with the period before Alexander. New mints included those at coastal cities such as Berytus (Beirut) and Tripolis, and inland the city of Chalcis sub Libano, which issued coins for a dynasty of local kings in the first century BC. By far the most important coins in the region were the silver shekels struck in the name of the city of Tyre, which were issued regularly from 126 BC and continued well into the Roman period. The designs on these coins were a head of Melqart (the Phoenician Heracles) on the front and an eagle on the back.

THE ROMAN PERIOD

Phoenicia was formally annexed by the Romans in 64 BC. From this date Roman coinage, particularly silver denarii, began to circulate in the region, though not at first to the exclusion of the local coinages. The silver shekels of Tyre continued to be issued until the reign of Nero (AD 54–68), after which they were replaced by the tetradrachms of Roman Syria, which served as the staple silver coins of the region until the mid-third century. Most of the Syrian tetradrachms were struck at Antioch in Turkey, but other mints, including Tyre and Tripolis in Lebanon, were also used occasionally. Tyre's bronze coinage continued until the reign of Gallienus (253–68), and many other cities in Lebanon also produced regular issues of bronze coin until the mid-third century. New mints included those at Botrys on the coast and Heliopolis (Ba'albek) inland, which also issued silver Syrian

UMAYYAD MINTS IN THE LEVANT

TURKEY

0 Kilometres 200
0 Miles 100

- Aleppo (Halab)
- Qinnasrin
- Ma'arat

Latakia

SYRIA

Tartus

MEDITERRANEAN SEA

Homs

LEBANON ⊡ Ba'albek

Tyre

Damascus

Acre

Tiberias

Saffariyah

Baisan

ISRAEL

Gerash

Yubna
Ascalon

Lydda
Ramla

Amman

Jerusalem

Gaza

EGYPT

⊡ Jabrin JORDAN

SAUDI ARABIA

- Umayyad mint city
- ○ Issued coins with Byzantine designs
- □ Issued coins with caliph designs
- ------ Modern Boundaries

LEBANON

1 SILVER 2 SHEKELS *of King Abdashtart of Sidon.*
2 SILVER SHEKEL *of Tyre.*
3 BRONZE COIN *of the Roman colony of Berytus under Emperor Trajan.*
4 COPPER FALS *of the Umayyad Caliphate, struck in Ba'albek.*
5 GOLD DINAR *of al-Hakim, Fatimid caliph, struck in Tyre.*
6 COPPER COIN *of John d'Ibelin, Lord of Beirut.*
7 GOLD BEZANT *of the Counts of Tripoli.*
8 SILVER GROS *of Bohemond VI, Count of Tripoli.*
9 COPPER COIN *of al-Nasir Nasir al-Din Hasan, Mamluk sultan.*

tetradrachms in the early third century.

In the mid-third century the surviving city mints closed, and the Roman imperial coinage became the only official currency in circulation. At first the dominant coin was the base-silver antoninianus, but in the fourth and fifth centuries the commonest coins were the various bronze denominations. Antioch was the principal mint supplying Roman coinage to the region in the late imperial period, and it continued to be the main mint under the Byzantine emperors, who ruled Phoenicia from the late fifth century until the arrival of the forces of Islam in the seventh century.

ISLAMIC COINAGE

Byzantine coins continued to circulate in Lebanon after the Arab conquest during the 630s, but under the Umayyad caliphs of Damascus (*see* Syria) a new Islamic coinage was gradually introduced. From this period until the end of Ottoman rule in 1917, Islamic coins from Syria circulated in Lebanon. Coins from Egypt, Israel, Turkey and Europe also entered the area. Local coin production was virtually non-existent. The only recorded minting was at Ba'albek during the Umayyad period (661–750), at Tyre and Tripoli during the Fatimid period (909–1171), and at Tripoli during the Mamluk period (1250–1517) (*see* Egypt and Syria). The coins issued had the standard designs of these dynasties.

CRUSADER COINAGE

In the twelfth and thirteenth centuries most of modern Lebanon was included in two of the states founded by European Crusaders after the First Crusade. The cities of Tyre, Sidon and Beirut and their hinterlands belonged to the Kingdom of Jerusalem and its coinage circulated there (*see* Israel). Among the baronial coinages of the kingdom were copper or base-silver issues of Raynald of Sidon, produced in about 1170–87; an anonymous coinage of deniers of Sidon from the 1230s; copper pieces of Beirut under Raymond of Tripoli, issued in 1184–6; base-silver deniers and copper obols (= ½ denier) of John I of Ibelin,

Lord of Beirut (*c.* 1200–36); and copper coins of the Lords of Tyre, Philip (1246–70) and John (1270–83) of Montfort.

North of Beirut as far as Latakia and inland to the Orontes lay the second Crusader state of Lebanon, the county of Tripoli. The coinage of the counts was issued from about 1150 until the 1280s. It included gold bezants, which until about 1250 were copies of dinars of the Fatimid caliph al-Mustansir (*see* Egypt). At some point the letters B and T, presumably standing for Bohemond (the name of all thirteenth-century counts), and Tripoli were added to the design, and, probably in 1251, a cross. There was a plentiful series of base-silver deniers with either a star and crescent or simple star design on the front and a cross on the back. Copper coins with a star and crescent and a gateway design were also struck. In the 1260s or 1270s under Bohemond VI (1251–75) or VII (1275–87), Tripoli became the only mainland Crusader state to introduce the new European-style gros and ½ gros (*see* France). Two versions are known, both with a cross on the front. One has the star of Tripoli on the back, the other a gateway. The county fell to the Mamluks in 1289.

FRENCH MANDATE

After the First World War Lebanon passed from Turkish into French control. From 1924 the Paris mint struck 1, 2 and 5 piastre coins with French and Arabic inscriptions naming the State of Greater Lebanon. The piastre denomination was based on the Turkish kurus and 100 kurus equalled a Lebanon pound (livre). The 1 piastre had a central hole and bore two lion faces on its back and a wreath on the front; the other denominations had a cedar tree design.

In 1926 Lebanon became a republic, still under French control, and, from 1929, 10, 25 and 50 piastre silver coins were struck in the name of the republic. The new coins also bore the cedar tree design. In 1940, ½ and 2½ piastre coins with wreath designs were introduced. During the Second World War, while the Paris mint was unable to supply coins, crude ½, 1 and 2½ piastre coins were made locally.

INDEPENDENCE

In 1941 France granted independence to Lebanon, but new republican coins did not appear until 1952. By 1961, 1, 2½, 5, 10 and 25 piastre coins with cedar tree, lion head, galley or wreath designs were in use. From 1968 a new series of coins in the name of the Bank of Lebanon was initiated. Coins denominated 5, 10, 25 and 50 piastres, all with the cedar tree designs, were issued. In 1975 a 1 livre coin was added to the set. Higher denominations only appear as commemoratives.

LEBANON

10 ALUMINIUM-BRONZE 5 PIASTRES *of the State of Greater Lebanon, struck in Paris.*
11 ALUMINIUM 2½ PIASTRES *of the Republic of Lebanon.*
12 NICKEL LIVRE *of the Bank of Lebanon.*

ISRAEL

FIRST COINS:	fourth century BC
FIRST DECIMAL COINS:	1927
MAIN MINT:	Jerusalem
CURRENCY:	sheqel

ISRAEL's first coins date from the period when the country was under Persian rule. Issued in 400–330 BC and usually referred to as 'Philisto-Arabian', these small silver coins had designs either drawn from Persian art or imitating coins already circulating in the region, notably those of Athens. The place of origin of many Philisto-Arabian coins cannot be determined, but some were certainly struck at Gaza, and one particular piece inscribed with the word YEHUD (Judaea) in Aramaic script is believed to be from Jerusalem.

THE HELLENISTIC PERIOD

When Alexander the Great (336–323 BC) conquered the Persian Empire, Israel came under his rule and a mint was opened at Ake (Acre) for production of his coinage of silver tetradrachms and gold staters (see Greece). An unusual feature of most of Alexander's issues from Ake is that the coins were dated, with Aramaic numerals indicating the number of years since his arrival in Phoenicia. The issues continued after Alexander's death, until 304 BC.

In the Hellenistic (see Turkey) period both the Ptolemaic kings of Egypt and the Seleucid kings of Syria at some time ruled Israel, and coins were struck for both at mints in Ake (renamed Ptolemais by Ptolemy II, 285–246 BC), Ascalon and Gaza. Some bronze issues of Antiochus VII (138–129 BC) were also minted in Jerusalem.

THE HASMONAEAN AND HERODIAN RULERS

By the late second century BC the local Hasmonaean kings had secured Judaean independence from the Seleucids, and starting in the reign of Alexander Jannaeus (103–76 BC) the Hasmonaeans issued small bronze coins, minted in Jerusalem, with inscriptions in Hebrew and Greek. In 37 BC the Hasmonaeans were overthrown by another local dynasty, the Herodians, whose first king, Herod the Great (37–4 BC), extended the Judaean kingdom with the support of the Romans. Again, only bronze coins were issued by Herod and his successors, who ruled Judaea or the neighbouring kingdoms (Samaria, Galilee and Trachonitis) as vassal Kings of Rome until the death of the last Herodian king, Agrippa II (c. AD 95). Silver coins used in the region included Roman denarii, shekels of Tyre in Lebanon, and later the silver tetradrachms of Roman Syria.

After the death of Herod the Great, the Romans exercised direct rule over parts of Israel, notably Judaea, for most of the Herodian period and the Roman governors, including the infamous Pontius Pilate (AD 26–36), issued small bronze Jewish-style coins, minted in Jerusalem, in the name of the ruling Roman emperor. In 66 the Jews rebelled against Roman rule, and until the revolt was crushed in 70, a Jewish nationalist coinage in silver and bronze was issued, with inscriptions in Hebrew. In the aftermath of this revolt the Romans assumed firmer control over Judaea, and the emperors issued Greek

ANCIENT MINT CITIES OF THE NEAR EAST

ISRAEL

1 SILVER PHILISTO-ARABIAN DRACHM *of ancient Palestine.*
2 SILVER TETRADRACHM *with the designs of Alexander the Great minted in Ake after his death.*
3 BRONZE COIN *of King Herod the Great.*
4 BRONZE COIN *of the Roman procurator of Judaea, Pontius Pilate.*
5 SILVER SHEKEL *of the First Jewish Revolt, year 3.*
6 SILVER COIN *of the Bar Kochba Revolt, overstruck on a denarius of the Roman emperor Trajan.*
7 BRONZE COIN *of Gaza issued under the Roman emperor Septimius Severus.*

imperial-style bronze coinage, at first with inscriptions in Greek celebrating their victory over the Jews. A second Jewish revolt, led by Simon Bar Cochba between the years 132 and 135, provided the occasion for another series of nationalist Jewish issues of coinage, again in silver and bronze. Most of the coinage of this revolt was overstruck on existing Roman or Greek imperial coinage in circulation in Judaea.

THE ROMAN AND BYZANTINE EMPIRES

After the suppression of the Bar Cochba revolt, no further Jewish coinage was produced in ancient Israel. The Greek cities of the region, some of which had issued their own civic bronze coins since before the Romans arrived, continued to issue Greek imperial bronzes; among them were Gaza, Ascalon, Caesarea and Ptolemais on the coast, and inland Gaba, Tiberias, Eleutheropolis, and Neapolis (Nablus) and Sebaste in the West Bank territory. Jerusalem had been refounded as a pagan city by the emperor Hadrian (117–138). It became a Roman colony with the name Aelia Capitolina, and from Hadrian's reign it also issued coins with the emperor's portrait. For silver coinage both Roman denarii and the tetradrachms of Roman Syria were available in the region. In the third century these were replaced by base-silver Roman antoniniani, and at the same time production of civic bronze coinage began to tail off, ceasing altogether in the 250s.

From the mid-third century Roman coinage, and, from the late fifth century, Byzantine coinage, mostly struck at the nearest imperial mints of Antioch in Turkey and Alexandria in Egypt, were the only official currency circulating in Israel.

ISLAMIC CONQUEST

Byzantine gold and copper coins continued to circulate when the Sasanian emperor Khusru II of Iran (590–628) occupied the territory now known as Israel during his western campaign against the Byzantine Empire during 613–627, and also when the Arab leader Caliph 'Omar captured Damascus (635) and Jerusalem (638) and made Israel part of the Islamic province of Filistin (Palestine).

By the 680s the supply of Byzantine coins could no longer match local needs, so the Arab rulers issued their own imitations. Gold copies were made only in Syria, but in Palestine several mints were employed to make coppers. Baisan mint copied coins of Justin II (565–78) and Lydda and Tiberias mints coins of Heraclius (610–41). The copies were inscribed in Greek and Arabic with the mint name. The names of the Byzantine emperors were omitted.

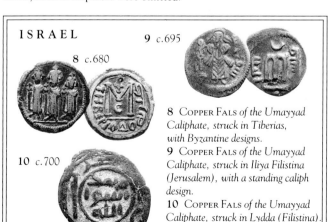

ISRAEL

9 *c.695*

8 *c.680*

10 *c.700*

8 COPPER FALS *of the Umayyad Caliphate, struck in Tiberias, with Byzantine designs.*
9 COPPER FALS *of the Umayyad Caliphate, struck in Iliya Filistina (Jerusalem), with a standing caliph design.*
10 COPPER FALS *of the Umayyad Caliphate, struck in Lydda (Filistina).*

Once the rule of the Umayyad Caliphate had been established at Damascus, the Palestine mints of Iliya Filistina (Jerusalem) and Jabrin followed the lead of the Damascus mint and from the 680s began to issue copper coins with the standing figure of the caliph holding a sword. The new Islamic design was accompanied by an Arabic inscription proclaiming the Islamic faith. The mint name was also written in Arabic.

The caliph issue was short-lived and replaced from c. 796 by a new coinage without pictorial designs, inscribed on both sides in Arabic with the proclamation of the Islamic faith and sometimes the mint and date. Within Israel these coins were issued at Iliya Filistina, Akka (Acre), Lydda, Ramla, Yubna, Saffariya, Ascalon, Gaza and Tiberias (with the mint name al-Urdunn, that is 'the Jordan').

FROM THE 'ABBASIDS TO THE FATIMIDS

Once the Islamic inscriptional design coins had been initiated by the Umayyad caliphs at Damascus, the coinage of Israel remained the same as that of its eastern and southern neighbours, Syria and Egypt. Under the 'Abassid caliphs (*see* Iraq), Islamic coins were made in Israel at Akka (Acre), Ramla and Tiberias. During the late ninth and tenth centuries their issue was continued by the Tulunid (868–905) and Ikshidid (935–69) rulers of Egypt at Lydda and Tiberias. A new coinage was, however, introduced before the end of the tenth century by the Fatimid caliphs (909–1171). Fatimid coins with unorthodox Shi'ite inscriptions, arranged in concentric circles, were struck at Ascalon, Akka, Lydda and Tiberias (*see* Egypt).

THE KINGDOM OF JERUSALEM

Fatimid control of Israel was ended by the arrival of the First Crusade in 1094. The Crusaders set up the kingdom of Jerusalem, stretching from Beirut down to Gaza, Darum and into Sinai, bounded by the River Jordan and the Dead Sea in the east. After the conquests of Saladin in 1187, the kingdom was reconstructed to survive in the thirteenth century as a coastal strip of territory ruled from Akka.

11 LATE TWELFTH CENTURY

12 1162–74

ISRAEL
11 GOLD BEZANT *of the kings of Jerusalem.*
12 BASE-SILVER DENIER *of King Amalric of Jerusalem, showing the dome of the holy sepulchre.*

The Kings of Jerusalem issued a coinage of gold bezants, imitating dinars of the Fatimid caliph al-Amir (*see* Egypt), from the mid-twelfth century until c. 1251, when, in response to pressure from the pope, they changed the design to incorporate a cross and Christian proclamations, though still written in correct Arabic. In the thirteenth century Jerusalem also produced imitations of Ayyubid silver dirhems.

The main coinage of the kingdom consisted of base-silver deniers. Initially western deniers were imported, particularly from Lucca in Tuscany and Valence in southern France, but probably from the 1140s local issues were struck. Two main series were produced. One, in the name of King Baldwin, probably Baldwin III (1143–63), had a cross on the front and the Tower of David (the citadel of medieval Jerusalem) on the back. The second, in the name of King Amalric (1163–74), had the dome of the Holy Sepulchre on the back. This type continued to be produced until the 1220s. Obols or ½ deniers accompanied both series of deniers. A number of small and anomalous issues can be ascribed to the time of the temporary collapse, before reconstruction, of the kingdom in 1187.

Royal control of the coinage broke down somewhat in the early thirteenth century, as leading barons began to produce local issues of their own, though not in great quantities. One such was Walter of Brienne (c. 1235/6–44) at Jaffa (see also Lebanon). Deniers in the name of King John of Brienne (1210–25) were issued in reasonable quantities, distinguished by their reference to Damietta in Egypt, held by the king in 1219–21 during the Fifth Crusade, but the later thirteenth century seems to have seen a return to the use of imported coins, until the destruction of the kingdom by the Mamluks in 1291.

REINTRODUCTION OF ISLAMIC COINAGE

In 1187, following the battle of Hattin, Saladin (al-Nasir Salah al-Din Yusuf ibn Ayyub, founder of the Ayyubid Dynasty) (1169–1260), the new ruler of Egypt, captured Jerusalem from the Crusaders and reintroduced Islamic coinage of the same kind as he issued in Egypt and Syria. During Ayyubid rule the only mint in action in Israel was Gaza. The coins in circulation mostly came from the Damascus and Aleppo mints in Syria or from Egypt. The same situation applied during the period of Mamluk (1250–1517) and Ottoman (1517–1917) rule.

BRITISH MANDATED TERRITORY

After the First World War the British took control of Palestine and in 1922 it became a British mandated territory. From 1927 the British authorities supplied the region with a coinage of bronze 1 and 2, cupro-nickel 5, 10 and 20 and silver 50 and 100 mil pieces, struck at the Royal Mint in London. The mil represented a thousandth of a Palestine pound. The bronze and silver coins were decorated with an olive branch design on the back, but the cupro-nickel coins had a central hole and the only pictorial design appeared on the front, a wreath around the hole. The coins were inscribed in English, Arabic and Hebrew.

INDEPENDENCE

The British coinage stopped in 1946, although a 1947 coinage was prepared and then destroyed before issue. In 1948, after a protracted armed conflict between the native Palestinians and Jewish settlers,

Palestine became the state of Israel. Coins for the new state, dated 5708 (1948) and 5709 (1949) according to the Jewish era, were issued from 1949. The new coins were inscribed entirely in Hebrew and were decorated with designs copied from ancient Judaean coins: grapes, anchor, lyre, ewer, vine leaf, palm tree, wheatears and poppy-seed heads.

It was planned to denominate the coins according to the British Palestine system, but, after only a 25 mil coin had been issued, a new system with 1000 pruta to the lira was introduced. This was changed in 1960 so that the lira contained 100 agora. New coins with slightly modified designs, including, from 1963, ½ and 1 lira coins bearing a Jewish candelabra, were introduced.

A fourth system was introduced in 1980. A new sheqel denomination worth 100 new agora, each worth 10 old agora, was adopted. Smaller coins with similar designs to the previous issues were put into circulation. The new coins had additional Arabic and English inscriptions and on the ½ sheqel a new design featuring a roaring lion. In 1982 5 and 10 sheqel coins with cornucopia and galley designs, derived from ancient Jewish coins, were added.

MODERN COINAGE

Inflation led to the issue of 50 and 100 sheqel coins in 1984, before the denomination system was again revised in 1985 with a new sheqel worth 1000 old sheqel. The new coins – 1, 5 and 10 agorat and ½ and 1 sheqel – continue the tradition of using ancient Jewish designs. Since 1958 Israel has also been a very active producer of commemorative and collector coins.

JORDAN

FIRST COINS:	first century BC
FIRST DECIMAL COINS:	1949
MAIN MINT:	Royal Mint
CURRENCY:	dinar

THE first coins to reach Jordan were Greek issues of silver, especially from Athens, which circulated in the Levantine region in the fifth century BC, and later the coinages of Alexander the Great and of the

ISRAEL
13 BRONZE 20 MILS of the British Mandated Territory of Palestine.
14 CUPRO-NICKEL 250 PRUTOT.
15 SILVER LIRA (POUND), commemorating the Jewish Law.
16 CUPRO-NICKEL LIRA.
17 CUPRO-NICKEL 10 SHEKELIM.

14 1949
15 1958
13 1942
16 1969
17 1982

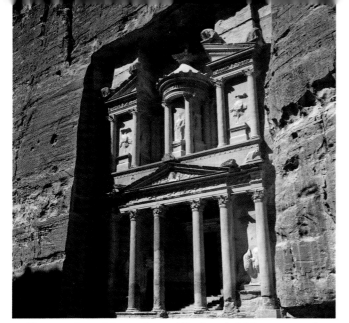

Building carved out of the standstone cliff-side in the Nabataean city of Petra, first century BC–first century AD.

Seleucid kings of Syria. Some imitation Athenian owl coins may have been minted in Jordan, but the first definitely Jordanian coins were not made until the first century BC, when the kings of Nabataea, whose capital was the city of Petra in Jordan, began to issue silver and bronze coins. Starting with Aretas III (87–62 BC), Nabataean coinage was issued for nearly 200 years, until AD 106, when the Roman emperor Trajan annexed the kingdom. The Nabataean king who issued the most coinage was Aretas IV (9 BC–AD 40).

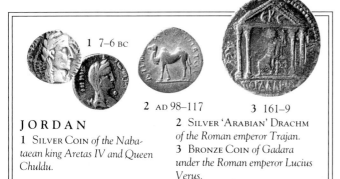

JORDAN
1 SILVER COIN *of the Nabataean king Aretas IV and Queen Chuldu.*
2 SILVER 'ARABIAN' DRACHM *of the Roman emperor Trajan.*
3 BRONZE COIN *of Gadara under the Roman emperor Lucius Verus.*

THE ROMAN AND BYZANTINE EMPERORS

The northeastern part of Jordan had been under Roman control since the annexation of Syria in 64 BC. Here were located most of the cities of the Decapolis (a Roman buffer zone of ten cities separating Roman Syria from Judaea and Nabataea), including Gadara, Gerasa (Jerash), Pella and Philadelphia (Amman), which produced regular issues of Greek imperial bronze coins until the mid-third century AD. The cities of the province of Arabia Petraea, formed after the annexation of the Nabataean kingdom, also issued Greek imperial bronze coins. These included Esbus (Heshbon), Medaba, Charach-Moba (al-Karak), Rabbath-Moba and Petra.

For silver coinage the whole region used either Roman denarii or the tetradrachms of Roman Syria. For a brief period under Caracalla (AD 212–17) Gadara was used as one of the mints for production of

JORDAN ──────

Syrian tetradrachms. The only other occasion when silver coins were produced specially for Jordan by the Romans was at the time of Trajan's annexation of Nabataea, when silver drachmae were issued with his head on the front and a camel on the back.

In the mid-third century the local city mints were closed. The base-silver Roman antoninianus was the commonest coin in circulation, and in the following centuries Roman, and, from the late fifth century, Byzantine, coinage in gold, silver and bronze were dominant. None of this coinage was minted in Jordan; most came from the nearest imperial mints, Antioch in Turkey and Alexandria in Egypt.

ISLAMIC COINAGE
Throughout most of its history since Jordan came under Islamic rule it has been without a specific coinage of its own. During the Umayyad Caliphate of Damascus (*see* Syria) copper coins with Umayyad designs were made at 'Amman and Gerash. The mint of Tiberias in Israel also made Umayyad coppers issued in the name of al-'Urdunn (the Jordan). From the Umayyad period (661–750) until the present century Jordan has used the coinages produced by its Islamic rulers in neighbouring Syria and Iraq and those imported through Israel from Egypt.

THE HASHEMITE KINGDOM
After the First World War, Jordan, formerly part of the Turkish Ottoman Empire, came under British control as Transjordan. From 1927 the coins produced by Britain for Palestine circulated in the region, though it was officially ruled by a local emir (*see* Israel).

In 1946 the British Mandate for Transjordan ceased and the Emir 'Abdullah became King of the Hashemite Kingdom of Transjordan, which was renamed Jordan in 1950. The first coins for the new kingdom, dated 1949, were struck at the Royal Mint in London and issued in 1950. They were denominated according to a decimalized version of the traditional Arabic system as 1000 fils = 10 dirhems = 1 dinar. Bronze 1, 5 and 10 fils and cupro-nickel 20, 25, 50 and 100 fils coins were made, all decorated with the Hashemite royal crown and a wreath of wheatears. Their inscriptions named the state, denomination and date in Arabic and English.

The portrait of King Hussein appears on the current issue of coins, which began in 1968 and has included a $\frac{1}{4}$ dinar since 1970. It also appears on the commemorative coins produced since a United Nations' Food and Agriculture Organization issue in 1969.

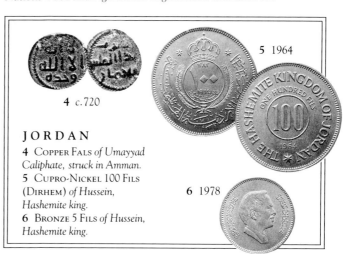

JORDAN
4 COPPER FALS *of Umayyad Caliphate, struck in Amman.*
5 CUPRO-NICKEL 100 FILS (DIRHEM) *of Hussein, Hashemite king.*
6 BRONZE 5 FILS *of Hussein, Hashemite king.*

147

IRAQ

FIRST COINS:	fourth century BC
FIRST DECIMAL COINS:	1931
MAIN MINT:	Royal Mint
CURRENCY:	dinar

THE land of ancient Mesopotamia (modern Iraq) between the Rivers Tigris and Euphrates was the site of some of the ancient world's great civilizations, but coinage was not produced in the region until relatively late, in the fourth century BC, when it was part of the Persian Empire. Greek silver coins had been arriving in the region through trade since the early fifth century BC, and the first coins made in Mesopotamia were imitations of the most abundant and widely circulating Greek issues, the owl tetradrachms of Athens. Some of the imitation owls bore the name of the local Persian satrap (governor) in Aramaic script.

ALEXANDER THE GREAT

Alexander the Great became Great King of the Persian Empire when he defeated Darius III at the battle of Gaugamela in Iraq in 331 BC. Alexander's army brought with it his coinage of silver tetradrachms and gold staters (*see* Greece), and mints were opened to convert into this coinage the massive wealth which Alexander discovered in the

1 331–328 BC

2 281–261 BC

IRAQ

1 SILVER LION STATER *of Babylon, issued by the governor Mazaeus.*
2 SILVER TETRADRACHM *of the Seleucid king Antiochus I, minted in Seleuceia.*

3 SILVER TETRADRACHM *of the Parthian king Artabanus II, minted in Seleuceia.*
4 SILVER TETRADRACHM *of Attambelos I, King of Characene.*

3 88–77 BC

4 41–40 BC

captured Persian treasuries. Special large-denomination silver coins were issued, some with designs illustrating Alexander's victories, as well as standard silver tetradrachms and gold staters of Alexander. A mint at Babylon also produced a coinage of Persic-weight gold double darics and silver staters for local circulation in Babylonia. The silver

staters, which copied earlier issues from the Syrian region, had designs of a seated figure of the god Baal on the front and a lion on the back. The double darics had the same royal-archer design as the earlier Persian darics and sigloi of Asia Minor (Turkey).

THE SELEUCID AND PARTHIAN EMPIRES

The two separate coinages produced in Babylonia under Alexander continued under his successors, until Seleucus I (321–280 BC) replaced them with his own regal coinages late in his reign. Seleucus founded a new city on the River Tigris, which he named Seleuceia, and this became the principal mint for the Seleucid (*see* Syria) and later Parthian (*see* Iran) coinages issued in Iraq.

The Seleucids ruled Mesopotamia from about 171 BC to 138 BC, when the region was conquered by the Parthian king Mithradates I. Henceforth, production of Parthian silver tetradrachms was concentrated almost exclusively at the mint of Seleuceia. From the late second century BC to the first century AD Seleuceia also issued bronze coins in its own name. The last Parthian coins from Seleuceia date from the reign of Vologases VI (*c.* AD 208–28). Meanwhile, the Kings of Characene ruled in southern Iraq as vassals of the Parthians. They issued an independent coinage from the 120s BC until the second century AD. The coinages of Parthia and Characene belong to the Hellenistic Greek tradition, since both were originally derived from the Seleucid coinages (*see* Turkey and Syria), but they gradually developed their own characters, more oriental in design.

In the long history of conflict between the Parthian and Roman empires, Iraq suffered several invasions from Roman armies, notably under Trajan (AD 98–117) and Septimius Severus (193–211). Most of the Roman province of Mesopotamia, whose cities issued coinage in the second and third centuries, was to the north, in southeastern Turkey, but the city of Singara (Sinjar) in Iraq issued coins for Gordian III (238–44) with the emperor's head on the front and local designs on the back. Roman influence is also evident in the second-century coinage of the city of Hatra (al-Hadr), which imitated the bronze coinage of Roman Syria.

Parthian rule in Iraq was finally ended not by the Romans but by the Sasanians, who seized power in Persia in the 220s and then went on to capture Mesopotamia and the rest of the Parthian Empire.

THE SASANIAN EMPIRE

During the 220s to 230s Iraq's Parthian coinage was quickly replaced by the new issues of Ardashir I (*c.* 224–42), founder of the Sasanian Empire of Iran. Ardashir's coins were mostly silver and were decorated with his portrait on the front and a Zoroastrian fire altar on the back (*see* Iran). Sasanian silver coins with designs based on Ardashir's issue continued to be used and occasionally made in Iraq until the collapse of Iranian rule in the face of Arab invasion.

ISLAMIC CONQUEST

Arab armies brought the Islamic faith to northern Iraq in the 620s and southern Iraq in the 630s. At first the Arabs made use of the Sasanian coins already in circulation. In Iran the Arabs also made their own copies of the Sasanian coins, but in Iraq this happened only at Basra and Dasht-i-Maisan, in southern Iraq, after 671.

From 698 the Iraq mints followed the practice established at Damascus (*see* Syria) of issuing coins with inscriptional designs. Several other mints were established by the Umayyad caliphs to strike their new purely Islamic coins. The most active was the mint at Wasit, the governor's residence established in 703. Copper coins were rarely made in Iraq, except at the al-Mawsil (Mosul) mint in the north.

THE 'ABBASID CALIPHATE

In 749 an uprising against the Umayyads brought to power a new caliphate, based in Iraq. In 750 the first 'Abbasid caliph, al-Saffah, defeated the last Umayyad and established control over the whole of the Islamic Empire except in the far west (*see* Spain), where Umayyad rule was preserved. The 'Abbasids founded a new capital at Baghdad, which they called Madinat al-Salam (the City of Peace). The Umayyad coin inscriptions were modified by the new regime, but the overall design was retained at the 11 mints used by the 'Abbasids. The transfer of the capital from Damascus to Baghdad meant that Islamic gold coins were now struck in Iraq in the latter city.

The inscriptional formula adopted by the 'Abbasid mints in Iraq remained the standard throughout most of the Islamic world for the next four centuries and persisted in some regions long after that. It proclaimed the Islamic faith in the centre of the front of the coin, 'There is no god but God alone' and continued the theme in the centre and around the margin on the back: centre, 'Muhammad is the prophet of God'; margin, 'Muhammad is the prophet of God who sent him with guidance and the faith of truth to make it supreme over all other faiths, even though the polytheists may despise it'. The inscription round the margin on the front stated that the coin was made in the name of God and in which mint and which year it was struck. The inscriptions

named the gold coins dinar, the copper fals and the silver dirhem. These denominations were derived respectively from the Latin coin names denarius and follis and the Greek drachma.

From the period of the Caliph al-Mamun (813–33), an additional religious margin was added to the front of the coin, outside the first margin: 'The Command is from God, both past and future, and on that day the faithful will rejoice in the victory given by God'. By then it had become increasingly common for the names of the caliph or his heir and high-ranking governors to appear on the coins.

An 'Abbasid caliph remained in power in Baghdad and continued to issue coins there until the thirteenth century, but from the late ninth century the rest of Iraq was gradually lost to independent rulers, some of whom gave nominal allegiance to the 'Abbasids. 'Abbasid-style coins were issued for Iraq in their own names by the Arab Hamdanids (905–1004) from Syria, the Buyid amirs (936–1055) from Iran, the Kurdish Marwanids (990–1085) from eastern Turkey and the Arab 'Uqaylids (c. 990–1096) of al-Mawsil.

TURKISH CONQUEST

In 1055 the Turkish Seljuq sultan Tughril Beg from Iran entered Baghdad and with the support of the 'Abbasid caliph al-Qa'im established control over Iraq. The Seljuqs continued to issue coins in the name and style of the 'Abbasids, but added small symbols to the coins, such as the bow and club emblems on some of their Iranian issues. They also made use of decorative forms of the Arabic script.

During the twelfth century the 'Abbasid caliphs staged a revival, regaining some control over southern Iraq, and issued gold and silver coins at Baghdad. Their gold coins retained the traditional inscriptions, but under Turkish influence used decorative Arabic and on the later (from the 1220s) issues the square and other decorative frames recently introduced in Syria by the Ayyubids.

The 'Abbasid revival weakened Seljuq control and the local Atabegs, the military leaders of the Seljuqs, gained independence in northern Iraq and eastern Turkey. In both areas the Atabegs issued

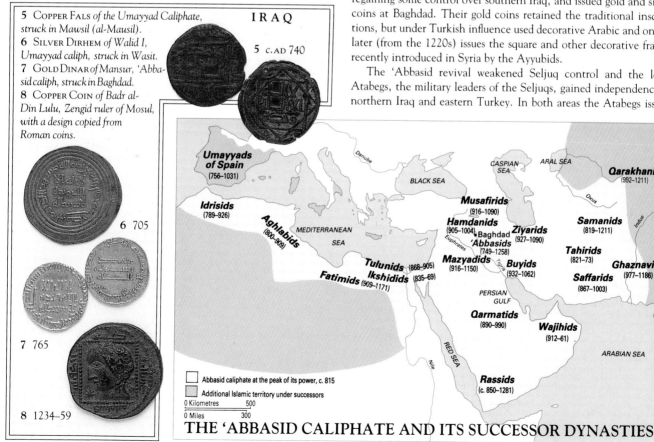

5 COPPER FALS *of the Umayyad Caliphate, struck in Mawsil (al-Mausil).*

6 SILVER DIRHEM *of Walid I, Umayyad caliph, struck in Wasit.*

7 GOLD DINAR *of Mansur, 'Abbasid caliph, struck in Baghdad.*

8 COPPER COIN *of Badr al-Din Lulu, Zengid ruler of Mosul, with a design copied from Roman coins.*

IRAQ

5 C. AD 740

6 705

7 765

8 1234–59

THE 'ABBASID CALIPHATE AND ITS SUCCESSOR DYNASTIES

Umayyads of Spain (756–1031)

Idrisids (789–926)

Aghlabids (800–909)

Tulunids (868–905)

Ikshidids (835–69)

Fatimids (909–1171)

Musafirids (916–1090)

Hamdanids (905–1004)

Baghdad 'Abbasids (749–1258)

Ziyarids (927–1090)

Mazyadids (916–1150)

Buyids (932–1062)

Qarmatids (890–990)

Wajihids (912–61)

Rassids (c. 850–1281)

Qarakhanids (992–1211)

Samanids (819–1211)

Tahirids (821–73)

Ghaznavids (977–1186)

Saffarids (867–1003)

Abbasid caliphate at the peak of its power, c. 815

Additional Islamic territory under successors

0 Kilometres 500

0 Miles 300

'Abbasid-style gold coins, but introduced a new series of copper coins with pictorial designs under Byzantine and Crusader influence. The Zengid Atabegs issued a copper coin with a facing-head design copied from an ancient Greek coin during the 1160s in al-Mawsil, and a variety of coins with Roman-inspired designs at Sinjar in the early 1200s. Similar coins with a seated-figure design were also issued by the Ayyubids while they occupied Sinjar in 1218–20.

MONGOL INVASION

Hulagu, son of Genghis Khan, Ilkhanid ruler of Iran (1256–65), defeated an 'Abbasid army in 1256 and executed the last 'Abbasid caliph, al-Musta'sim, when in 1258 his army took Baghdad. The Atabeg kingdoms in northern Iraq and Turkey also fell to the Mongols. Initially the Ilkhanid Mongols issued coins like the 'Abbasid and Zengid coins already in circulation, but by the 1270s the general Mongol issues, with decorative frames and scripts designed in Iran, were also being made in Iraq.

The Mongol coinage was continued until the late fourteenth century by the Jalayrid Mongols (1336–1432), governors and then successors of the Ilkhanids in Baghdad. Like the Ilkhanids, they occasionally used Mongolian script alongside Arabic on their coins (see Iran).

BLACK AND WHITE SHEEP

During the late fourteenth century northern Iraq fell under Turkish control again. The Qara Qoyunlu (Black Sheep Turkmens) issued coins with decorative frames and inscriptional designs, like the

Mongols. Jalayrid Mongol rule in southern Iraq was broken by the invasion of Timur (also known as Tamberlane, see Afghanistan and Iran) in 1400. Timur and his successors issued coins at Baghdad until the whole of Iraq again fell under Turkish control, as the White Sheep Turkmens (Aq Qoyunlu) drove back the Timurid Abu-Sa'id (1451–69) and established a brief empire reaching east to Afghanistan and south to Oman on the Persian Gulf. Aq Qoyunlu coins (see Turkey) were not issued in Iraq, but circulated in the area. In 1504 Turkish rule in Iraq was briefly interrupted by an Iranian invasion. Isma'il, founder of the Iranian Safavid Dynasty, held Baghdad for ten years until it was captured by Selim I, the Ottoman ruler of Turkey in 1514.

THE OTTOMAN EMPIRE

Iraq was part of the Ottoman Empire until the end of the First World War. Ottoman mints operated at Baghdad and Mosul. The Mosul mint began to issue gold and silver coins with regular Ottoman designs (see Turkey) from 1518. Baghdad began also to issue gold and silver coins soon after. From 1526 the silver coins for Iraq and the other eastern Ottoman provinces were larger than the regular Turkish issues. During the seventeenth century the Ottoman official signature mark or tughra also began to appear on Baghdad coins and remained the standard design until the end of Ottoman minting in the area.

During the early nineteenth century copper coins with either the tughra design or a star (sometimes with crescent) motif began to be struck at Baghdad, but were abandoned before the middle of the century. Base-silver coins, like the issues made in Turkey, continued to be struck until the reign of Abdul Mejid (1839–61), but after that Ottoman coinage in Iraq was imported from Turkey and Egypt.

THE HASHEMITE KINGDOM OF IRAQ

The defeat of the Ottoman Empire in the First World War brought Iraq independence and in 1921, after a brief period of British rule, a kingdom was established. The first king, Faisal I (1921–33), issued coins bearing his portrait from 1931. They were denominated according to a decimal system based on the Iraqi pound, known as a dinar. The dinar was divided into 1000 fils. Bronze 1 and 2, nickel 4 and 10 and silver 20 and 50 fils coins were made at the British Royal Mint. In 1932 a silver 200 fils coin called a riyal was also issued. The coins were inscribed entirely in Arabic.

Further issues with the portraits of Faisal's successors, Ghazi (1933–39) and Faisal II (1939–58), were made from 1936 and 1943 respectively. The 200 fils coin was not included in these issues, but a 100 fils coin appeared from 1953.

THE REPUBLIC OF IRAQ

Following a military coup in 1958, the royal coinage was replaced with a new issue of 1, 5, 10, 25, 50 and 100 fils pieces, introduced in 1959. Still made in Britain, the new coins featured the national emblem, an ear of wheat within a star. From 1967 a new series of coins, with three date palms replacing the star design, was gradually introduced. The 1 fils denomination was not included, but from 1970 a 250 fils coin was produced for commemorative issues. In 1980 octagonal 250 fils and square 500 fils coins for circulation were also adopted.

The currency issue introduced in 1982 included a decagonal 1 dinar coin and featured historical designs referring to Iraq's Babylonian heritage. The denominations above 100 fils are normally only used for commemorative issues.

9 1242–58

10 1258–65

11 1782

12 1932

IRAQ

9 GOLD COIN of al-Must'asim, 'Abbasid caliph, struck in Madinat al-Salam (Baghdad).
10 GOLD DINAR of Hulagu, Mongol khan, struck in Baghdad.
11 SILVER COIN of Abdul Hamid I, Ottoman sultan, struck in Baghdad.
12 SILVER RIYAL of Faisal I, Hashemite king.

IRAN

FIRST COINS:	c. 330 BC
FIRST DECIMAL COINS:	1931
MAIN MINT:	Tehran
CURRENCY:	rial

THE earliest Persian coins were issued under the authority of the Achaemenid kings of the sixth century BC, but the gold and silver pieces they produced, first with lion and bull designs and later with a crowned figure usually referred to as the 'royal archer', were minted not in Iran but in the distant provinces of western Turkey. These coins did circulate as far east as Iran, but so also did other issues from the Aegean area, notably the ubiquitous silver owls of Athens.

ALEXANDER THE GREAT

The first coins minted in Iran were silver tetradrachms and gold staters (see Greece) of Alexander the Great (336–323 BC), produced during his campaigns in the region and after his death. A brief issue of Greek-style coins was also produced in northern Iran in the name of a governor, Andragoras, probably appointed by Alexander. Two mints in Iran, at Susa and Ecbatana, made Alexander coins, and both later became major mints for the Seleucid kings of Syria, who ruled over most of the eastern provinces of Alexander's empire, including much of Iran, in the third and second centuries BC.

THE PARTHIANS

In the 230s BC the Parthians, an Iranian people from the region to the south east of the Caspian Sea, emerged as a major force in the region. They eventually gained control over most of the eastern provinces of the Seleucid kingdom, which they ruled until the third century AD. The founder of the ruling Parthian Dynasty was Arsaces, and his name was used officially by all the kings, which makes the attribution of the Parthian coins to individual rulers difficult. The coins they produced were modelled on those of the Seleucids, with a portrait of the king on the front, a seated figure (though Iranian, not Greek) on the back, and inscriptions, including dates, in Greek (and occasionally Aramaic). Unlike Mesopotamia (Iraq), where silver tetradrachms were struck, in Iran the silver drachm was by far the most important coin. Lower-denomination bronze coins were also issued. The principal Iranian mints for Parthian coinage were the former Seleucid mints of Susa and Ecbatana, and also Rhagae (Tehran). Many lesser mints in Iran have also been identified.

Co-existing with the Parthians for much of their history were two kingdoms in southern Iran, Persis and Elymais, which produced extensive coinages of their own. Both kingdoms were at first independent, but later they became vassals of the Parthians. The coinage of Persis began just before the rise of Parthia, in the mid-third century BC, and continued through to the early third century AD. Only

silver coins were issued, at first tetradrachms and drachms, later just drachms and fractions. Inscriptions were always in Aramaic, and the standard designs for most of the series were the portrait of the ruler on the front and a scene depicting the Zoroastrian fire-altar (later adopted by the Sasanians) on the back. The coinage of Elymais was issued from the second century BC to the second century AD. It was broadly similar to Parthian coinage. At first silver and bronze coins were struck, but later issues were confined to small bronze coins with crudely drawn designs.

IRAN
1 SILVER TETRADRACHM *with the designs of Alexander the Great minted at Ecbatana after his death.*
2 SILVER TETRADRACHM *of King Bagadat of Persis.*
3 SILVER DRACHM *of the Parthian king Mithradates II.*
4 SILVER TETRADRACHM *of Elymais depicting King Kamnaskires and Queen Anzaze.*
5 SILVER DRACHM *of the Parthian king Vologases IV.*

1 c.300 BC   2 c.220 BC   3 123–88 BC   4 82–1 BC   5 AD 191–208

The Parthian coinage continued in a virtually unbroken series, from the late third century BC until the reigns of Vologases VI (c. AD 208–28) and Artabanus IV (c. 216–24). On the later Parthian coinage the Greek inscriptions became increasingly garbled and at the Iranian mints Parthian (Pahlavi) script was frequently used.

THE SASANIAN EMPIRE

In c. 224 Ardashir I, the local ruler of Persis (Fars, the region around modern Shiraz) set out on a campaign of conquest which, within a decade, had made him master of Iran, Iraq, Afghanistan and most of Soviet Central Asia. He introduced a new coinage with his own portrait on the front and his throne with a Zoroastrian fire-altar on the back. Inscriptions in Pahlavi on back and front identified the portrait and the altar. Most of Ardashir I's coins were silver, but some gold and copper were also struck.

Modified versions of the designs adopted by Ardashir were used throughout Iran and the neighbouring territories for the next 450 years. With each new reign the portrait was changed, even though it became increasingly stylized from the fifth century onwards.

The first significant change to the design on the back took place during the reign of Ardashir I's son, Shapur I (241–70), when the throne was dropped and the fire-altar was shown flanked by two divine or royal figures. During Shapur's reign mint marks also began to appear but did not come into regular use until the reign of Varharan IV (388–99). The mint names were always abbreviated and are difficult to identify. Regnal dates were also used on the coins from 498, the twelfth year of Kavad I's reign.

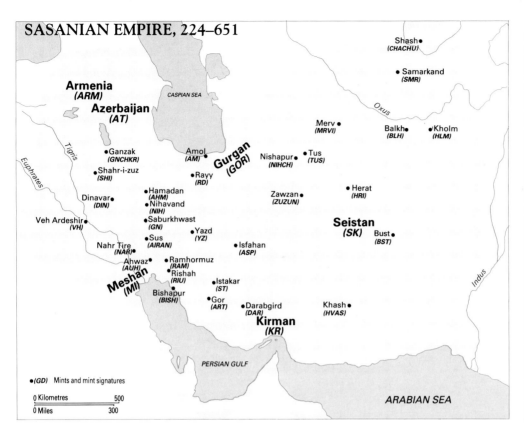

SASANIAN EMPIRE, 224–651

•(GD) Mints and mint signatures

0 Kilometres   500
0 Miles   300

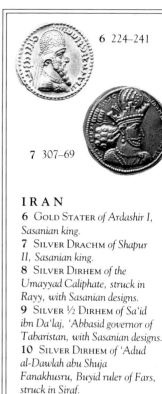

6 224–241

7 307–69

IRAN

6 GOLD STATER of Ardashir I, Sasanian king.
7 SILVER DRACHM of Shapur II, Sasanian king.
8 SILVER DIRHEM of the Umayyad Caliphate, struck in Rayy, with Sasanian designs.
9 SILVER ½ DIRHEM of Sa'id ibn Da'laj, 'Abbasid governor of Tabaristan, with Sasanian designs.
10 SILVER DIRHEM of 'Adud al-Dawlah abu Shuja Fanakhusru, Buyid ruler of Fars, struck in Siraf.

ISLAMIC CONQUEST

In 651 the last Sasanian emperor, Yazdigird III, was assassinated. Iran was already under the control of the Arab army of the Caliph 'Uthman, who had begun his campaign of conquest in 638. The Arabs initially retained the Sasanian coinage system and from 651 began to copy the coins themselves.

Early copies simply added a word or words in Arabic, such as 'good' or 'in the name of God' to the margin of the coin, but after 661 the name of the caliph or of the local governor also appeared in Pahlavi or Arabic. Arab rebels of the Khajirite sect also put their names and titles on the coins. The dating on the coins either continued the regnal years of the dead Sasanian king, or adopted new systems, based on the Islamic era or on the death of the Sasanian king.

In Tabaristan, the Iranian province along the southern shore of the Caspian Sea, local Ispahbad princes held out against Arab rule. They issued their own versions of the Sasanian coinage until Tabaristan finally fell to the 'Abbasid Caliphate in 761. The new governors continued to issue Ispabhad-style Sasanian coins until about 812.

UMAYYAD REFORM

The use of Sasanian designs in Iran had been abandoned (apart from Tabaristan) by 702, in favour of the new reformed Umayyad coins with inscriptional designs, invented in Damascus around 696 (see Syria). Traces of the original Sasanian coin design can, however, still be identified in the enclosing circles, three on one side and two on the other, which the Umayyad coins derived from their Sasanian predecessors. The size and weight of the new silver coins also makes it clear that they were originally modelled on the Sasanian coinage.

The inscriptional designs first appeared in Iran at the mints of Mah al-Kufah, Mah al-Basra, Suk al-Ahwaz, Biramkubadh, Jayy (Isfahan), Shakk al-Taimara and Fasa. Initially only silver coins with the new designs were issued. Some Iranian copper coins attributable to this period retained Sasanian designs.

THE 'ABBASID CALIPHATE

From 750 the content and style of the inscriptional designs of the Islamic silver coins issued in Iran were slightly modified, following the establishment of the 'Abbasid Caliphate (see Iraq). The issue of Islamic copper coins, with designs based on the new silver coins, also became more widespread.

'Abbasid coin designs were used in Iran for the next 500 years, until the establishment of Mongol Ilkhanid rule in 1256. From the early ninth century many of the 'Abbasid-style coins were not issued by the 'Abbasid caliphs, but by independent rulers, many of whom came to power as local governors of the 'Abbasids. These coins often retained the 'Abbasid caliph's name, but were also inscribed with the local rulers' names and titles.

Eastern Iran was the first area to have coins issued by independent rulers: the Samanids of Bukhara (819–1005), the Tahirids of Nishapur (821–73) and the Saffarids of Seistan (867–1003). In northern Iran the Ziyarids in Tabaristan (927–1090) and the Musafirids in Azerbaijan (941–c.1000) also broke away from 'Abbasid rule. The main coinage for Iran during this period, however, were the 'Abbasid-style issues of the Buyids (932–1062), an Iranian Shi'ite dynasty originating in Daylam, the territory between Azerbaijan and Tabaristan. The Buyid amirs controlled not only most of Iran, but also Baghdad and the

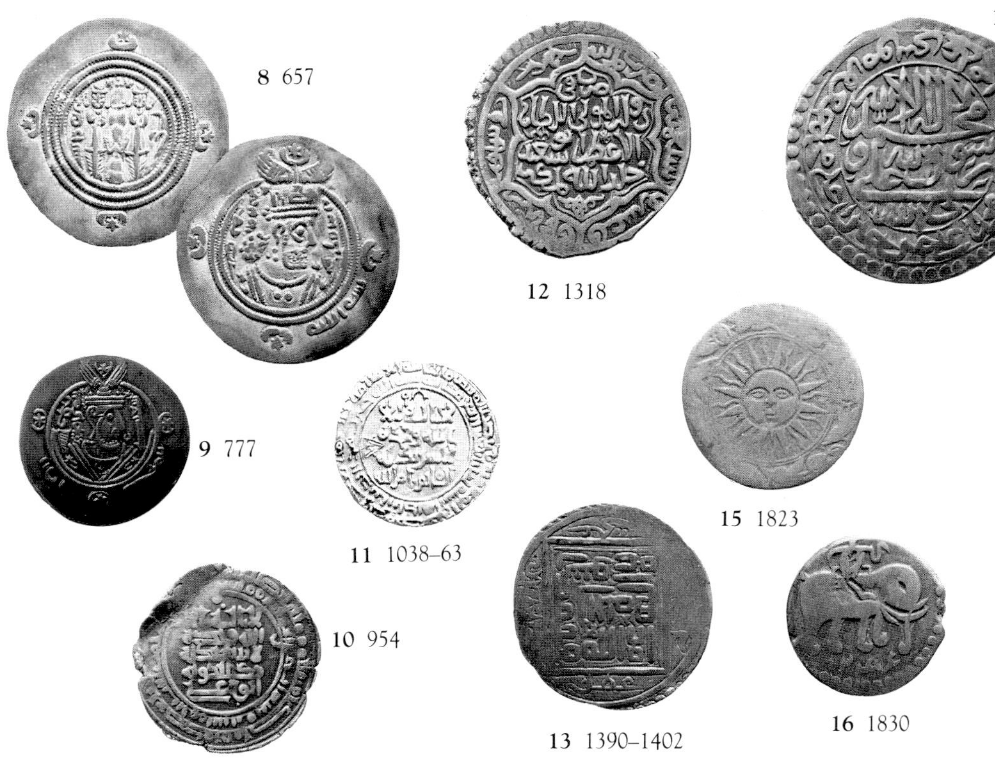

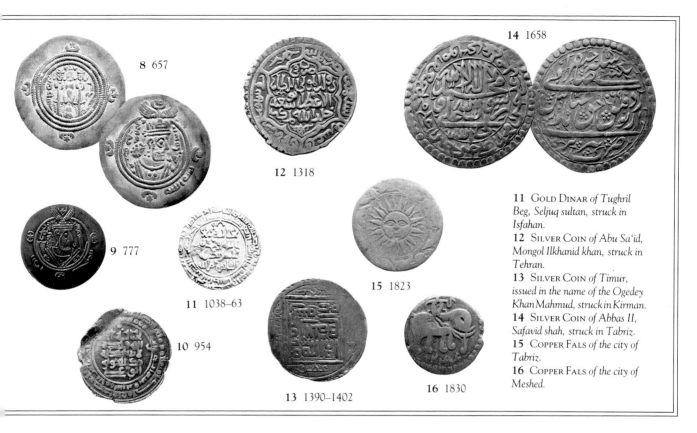

11 Gold Dinar *of Tughril Beg, Seljuq sultan, struck in Isfahan.*
12 Silver Coin *of Abu Sa'id, Mongol Ilkhanid khan, struck in Tehran.*
13 Silver Coin *of Timur, issued in the name of the Ogedey Khan Mahmud, struck in Kirman.*
14 Silver Coin *of Abbas II, Safavid shah, struck in Tabriz.*
15 Copper Fals *of the city of Tabriz.*
16 Copper Fals *of the city of Meshed.*

'Abassid caliphs who lived there. They issued coins at more than 30 mints, mostly in Iran.

The 'Abbasid-style coinage continued to be issued in Iran even after the Buyids had been overcome during the early eleventh century, first by the Ghaznavids of Afghanistan and then by their former Turkish supporters, the Seljuqs. Both the Ghaznavids and the Seljuqs added small symbols – a sword and a bow and club respectively – to the 'Abbasid-style coins they issued. The symbols were added as a statement of their right to issue coins in their own names. Seljuq and Ghaznavid rule in Iran eventually succumbed to the brief expansion of the Khwarezm shahs, based in Khurasan. Although the Ghaznavids and the Khwarezm shahs were beginning to issue coins with new designs in their central Asian mints, they preserved the 'Abbasid coining tradition within Iran.

THE MONGOLS

The wave of destruction that Genghis Khan's Mongol hordes inflicted as they swept across Iran during the 1220s put an end to the Islamic coinage tradition established almost 600 years before. From 1251, Hulagu, one of the sons of Genghis, subsequently began to consolidate Mongol control over Iran. After a brief period in which coins closely imitating Seljuq, Khwarezm shahs and Ghaznavid issues were struck, Hulagu's successors, the Ilkhanids, began to produce coins, mostly in silver, with new designs. Abaqa, the second Ilkhanid ruler of Iran (1265–82), introduced the use of Mongolian inscriptions. Later Ilkhanid coins also featured inscriptions in a Tibetan script called Phagsba, the official script used throughout the Mongol Empire from China to Iran.

Apart from the introduction of non-Arabic scripts, the new designs adopted for Mongol issues were not original. Instead they were derived from the coinages of their eastern neighbours, the Ayyubids and Mamluks in Syria and the Seljuqs in Turkey. The designs on the coins were still essentially inscriptional, but elaborate frames and decorative scripts were normally used. The most distinctive decorative script that can be found on Mongol coins is square Kufic, a rectangular form of early Arabic script in which the words are arranged around the sides of a square. The inscriptions continued to proclaim the Islamic faith, but they now gave more prominence to the name and titles of the ruler.

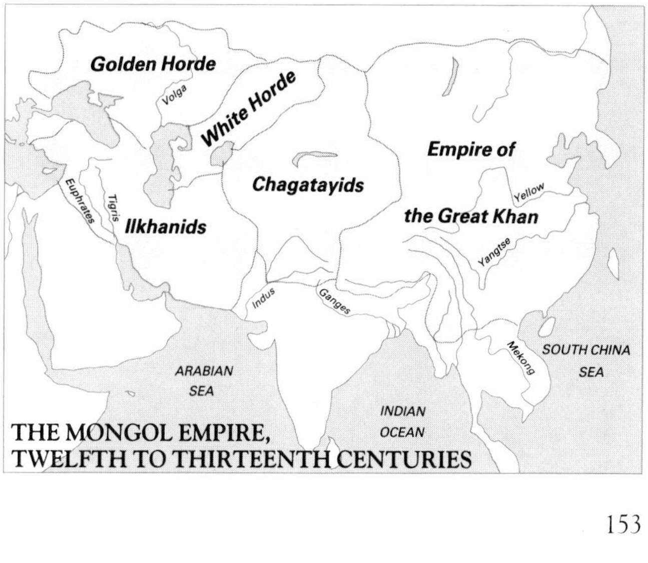

THE MONGOL EMPIRE, TWELFTH TO THIRTEENTH CENTURIES

TAMBERLANE

In the early fourteenth century Ilkhanid control of Iran collapsed as former governors, the Muzaffarids in the south and the Jalayrids in the north, seized power in their own right. Iran was briefly united again by Timur, known in Europe as Tamberlane, the ruler of Samarkand (1370–1405), as he campaigned as far westward as Turkey, adding Iran to his empire.

The coin designs established by the Mongols continued to be used in Iran, but Mongolian inscriptions were used only by the Jalayrids, who were also of Mongol origin. The use of decorative scripts became an increasingly important part of coin design, with the adoption on the coins of Timur's successors of an elegant cursive script with long uprights and interwoven strokes.

The same calligraphic designs were adopted by the Mongol Shaybanids, who took over the eastern part of the Timurid Empire. In western Iran the Timurids were overrun by the Black Sheep and White Sheep Turkmens (see Iraq), who also issued coins with Mongol designs, but less elegant, more compact inscriptions.

THE SHAHS OF IRAN

In 1501 a new force arose in Iran, as Isma'il, the Kurdish leader of a Shi'ite faction, seized Azerbaijan. Isma'il raised an army of Turks and within ten years had used it to establish so firm a control over the whole of Iran that his successors, the Safavid shahs, continued to rule for more than two centuries.

Isma'il I's religious beliefs had an immediate impact on the coinage issued in Iran. Shi'ite acclamations appeared on his coins, which used the calligraphy and decorative frames favoured by the Timurids and Shaybanids. References to the Caliph 'Ali, the founder of the Shi'ite sect, abounded on Safavid coins, but the name and elaborate titles of the ruler were an equally important part of the designs. The inscriptions were often in the form of verses in Persian. Under Iranian influence this practice also spread to Mughal India.

The Safavid coinage was mostly in silver, but an abundant local copper coinage also circulated during this period. It was, however, not issued in the name of the shah, but in the name of the city where it was

made. These local coppers often had pictorial designs, featuring animals and plants. Their issue appears to have begun during the Timurid period and to have continued after the fall of the Safavid shahs until the late nineteenth century, when the issue of copper coinage was reformed and placed under central control by the Qajar Shah Nasir al-Din (1848–96).

The style of coinage issued by the Safavids was continued by their successors, the Afshari shahs (1736–50), the Zand shahs (1750–79) and the Qajar shahs (1779–1924). A more compact, but equally beautiful, script was developed on Afshari coins, but the content and arrangement of the inscriptions followed a similar pattern to that established by the Safavids.

The excellence of the calligraphy used on Iranian coins from the sixteenth to the nineteenth century was enhanced by the large size of many of the coins issued. The massive presentation coins made by both the Safavids and the early Qajar shahs are particularly splendid examples. The quality of the designs used by the shahs of Iran is also apparent in the influence their coinage exercised on that of their eastern neighbours.

MODERNIZATION

During the reign of the Qajar Shah Fath 'Ali (1797–1834) standardization of the Iranian coinage system began. In the early Qajar period more than 40 mints operated throughout Iran: Fath 'Ali standardized the designs and denominations for all mints. Under European influence he also allowed his portrait, both on horseback and on a throne, to appear on his coins.

Portraits also appeared on the coins of Nasir al-Din Shah (1848–96), who in 1876 began issuing Iran's first machine-made coins. These copper and later cupro-nickel pieces were decorated first with a crowned sunburst in wreath design and then from 1900 with a lion and sun design, the emblem of Iran.

The machine-struck coinage system set up by Nasir al-Din continued in use until 1931, when a new coinage was instituted by Reza Shah (1925–41), the founder of the Pahlavi Dynasty, who overthrew Sultan Ahmad, the last Qajar shah. A decimal-based denomination

IRAN
17 Gold Toman of Fath 'Ali Shah, Qajar shah, struck in Isfahan.
18 Gold 5 Pahlavis of Reza Shah, Pahlavi shah, struck in Tehran.
19 Cupro-Nickel 10 Rials of Mohammad Reza Shah, Pahlavi shah, struck in Tehran.
20 Aluminium Bronze 50 Rials of the Islamic Republic.

system was introduced (100 dinars = 1 rial). The new coins, which retained the lion and sun design, were the 1, 2, 5, 10, 25 and 50 dinars and 1, 2, 5 and 10 rials. At first the earlier shahi denomination was retained for the 5 dinar coin, but from 1935 this was discontinued. From 1927 gold coins with Reza's portrait were also issued for collectors. The coins were denominated as ½, 1, 2 and 5 pahlavis (1 pahlavi = 100 rials).

ISLAMIC REPUBLIC OF IRAN

Portrait and lion and sun designs continued to be used on Iran's coins until 1979, when Muhammad Reza, the second Pahlavi shah was overthrown. The ousting of Muhammad Reza led to the establishment of an Islamic republic, in which an imageless coinage was immediately introduced. Cupro-nickel 1, 2, 5, 10 and 20 rial coins were issued with a new inscriptional design, enclosed on both sides in a wreath. Architectural and floral designs, however, have since appeared on commemorative coins of the Islamic Republic, but the coins for currency continue to be from the issue introduced in 1979.

KUWAIT

FIRST COINS:	1887
FIRST DECIMAL COINS:	1961
MAIN MINT:	Royal Mint
CURRENCY:	dinar

EXCAVATIONS in Kuwait have shown that coins have circulated there since the third century BC. Archaeologists have found Greek silver coins of this period and early Islamic coins of the eighth century. All of these coins were imported into the region from Iran and Iraq.

LOCAL COINAGE

Although Iranian and Iraqi coins have been imported and used in Kuwait since the early Islamic period (eighth century), it was the trade

An oil well in Kuwait. Oil wells appear on the coins of the United Arab Emirates, Algeria, Nigeria and Brazil.

1 142   **2** 1987   **3** 1987
KUWAIT
1 COPPER 4 DRACHMAS *of* Meredates, *king of Characene.*
2 CUPRO-NICKEL 100 FILS *of* the State of Kuwait.
3 CUPRO-NICKEL 50 FILS *of the* State of Kuwait.

with India which determined the nature of the first coinage to be issued for Kuwait. In 1776 Basra, Ottoman Iraq's main port, was seized by Iran and its trade had to be diverted through Kuwait, which caused Indian merchants to resettle in the port. They introduced their own monetary system, silver rupees and copper paisa, for local use, alongside the Iranian and Ottoman coins already in circulation. As elsewhere in the Gulf, Austrian silver dollars were also in use.

In 1886–7 the local governor of Kuwait, Sheikh Abdullah al-Sabah II, ordered the issue of copper paisas. They were inscribed in Arabic on both sides, bearing the sheikh's name in an ornamental pattern on the front and the mint and date on the back. The Ottoman authorities were not pleased by this breach of their coinage laws and ordered the immediate withdrawal of the issue. To defend itself from Ottoman oppression, from 1899 Kuwait placed itself under British protection, but no further coin issues were attempted until 1961.

MODERN COINAGE

The current coinage of Kuwait, introduced in 1961, is denominated in fils, 1000 of which equal 1 dinar, and consists of brass 1, 5 and 10 and cupro-nickel 20, 50 and 100 fils, inscribed in Arabic and English with the name of the state and decorated with an Arab ship. Denominations of 2, 5 and 100 dinars have also been struck, but only as commemoratives.

BAHRAIN

FIRST COINS:	eighth century
FIRST DECIMAL COINS:	1965
MAIN MINT:	Royal Mint
CURRENCY:	dinar

RECENT excavations at al-Qatif on the Saudi Arabian coast close to Bahrain have produced examples of the early eighth-century coins issued in this area; lead and copper coins with Umayyad-style inscriptional designs (*see* Syria). These coins appear to have been struck by the Umayyad governors of al-Bahrain, the province which included the present island and the adjacent coastal region, al-Hasa. Similar coins, particularly of lead, continued to be issued in this area until the thirteenth century. Their use was described by an Iranian

BAHRAIN
1 Lead Fals *of the Umayyad Caliphate, struck for use in Bahrain.*
2 Copper Fals *of 'Abdu Rabbihi, 'Abbasid governor of al Bahrain.*
3 Cupro-Nickel 100 Fils *of the State of Bahrain, struck at the Royal Mint, Llantrisant, in 1987.*

traveller, Nasir-i-Khusru, who visited Bahrain in 1051: 'Commercial transactions are made by means of lead (coins) contained in baskets, each weighing 6,000 dirhems. When a bargain is concluded, they count a number of baskets and carry them away; this money is not allowed to be exported'.

Although the earliest coins were issued by local governors appointed by the Umayyad and 'Abbasid caliphs (*see* Syria and Iraq) during the eighth and early ninth centuries, the later examples were mostly issued by the local Qarmatid religious sect. This sect, based in Bahrain, briefly, during the tenth century, ruled an empire reaching west to Mecca and north into Palestine, but later was restricted to Bahrain. They were ruled by a religious council and its title 'the elders, the chiefs' appeared on their early lead coins as the issuing authority. On later coins they recognized the Ilkhanid (1256–1353) and Muzaffarid (1314–93) rulers of Iran as their overlords. From 1236 to 1253 Bahrain was occupied by the Salghurids, Turkish Atabegs of Fars in Iran, who issued large copper coins for local use.

IMPORTED COINS

As elsewhere in the Persian Gulf, international trade brought many other coins into Bahrain. Chinese and Iranian copper coins of the thirteenth century have been excavated on the island. In the sixteenth century it was occupied by a Portuguese garrison and recent finds show that they brought silver coins from Portuguese India with them.

In 1622 the Portuguese were driven out and the island again came under Iranian rule until 1718, when the Omanis occupied Bahrain. During the seventeenth century silver wire coins, known as larins, were issued at the Bahrain mint in the name of the Safavid shahs of Iran (1501–1732).

During the eighteenth and nineteenth centuries the local rulers of Bahrain maintained a delicate balance between the Omani, Iranian, Ottoman and British forces in the Gulf, but eventually placed Bahrain under British protection. During the nineteenth century Bahrain's currency was like that of the other Gulf states (*see* Oman and Kuwait), and under British influence Indian coins dominated.

INDEPENDENCE

A coinage specifically for Bahrain did not re-emerge until 1965, when Britain was preparing to relinquish its control in the Gulf. The 1965 coinage was denominated in fils, 1000 of which equalled a dinar. Bronze 1, 5 and 10 and cupro-nickel 25, 50 and 100 fil coins were issued. Higher denominations have since been produced, but only as commemoratives. The current coins, struck in 1987 at the Royal Mint in Britain, retain the 1965 date.

QATAR

FIRST COINS:	third century BC
FIRST DECIMAL COINS:	1966
MAIN MINT:	Royal Mint
CURRENCY:	riyal

ALTHOUGH Alexander the Great, according to the Greek historian Strabo, contemplated conquering Arabia and prepared a fleet in Iraq, he died before putting his plan into action. Nevertheless, his coins (*see* Iraq) became symbolic agents of his intention as the first coins to arrive in the Gulf states of Qatar, Kuwait and the United Arab Emirates.

In the lower Gulf, silver and copper imitations of Alexander's coins were also made for local circulation. They have been found in Qatar and in Umm al-Qaiwain (in what is now the United Arab Emirates). The original design of the Alexander coins was modified on the imitations, particularly that on the back, where the seated figure of Zeus was shown holding a horse on his arm in place of the usual eagle. Later Greek coins of Iran and Iraq, particularly from the Parthian kingdom of Iran and its successors, are also found locally.

LOCAL COINAGE

Since the advent of Islam during the seventh century the coinage history of Qatar has been the same as that of the other Gulf states (*see* Bahrain, Kuwait and Oman), but it seems never to have been a minting centre. The first coins minted specifically for the emirate were struck by the British Royal Mint in 1966. Qatar had been a full British protectorate since 1916 and the coins were made during the preparation for full independence.

The 1966 coins were a joint issue struck for Qatar and Dubai. Dubai, a sheikhdom on the Trucial Coast, east of Qatar, had entered into a monetary union with Qatar, but this was soon dissolved in 1971, when Dubai became one of the members of the United Arab Emirates. The joint coins were inscribed in English and Arabic with the names of the two states and the denomination and date, and decorated on the front with a gazelle.

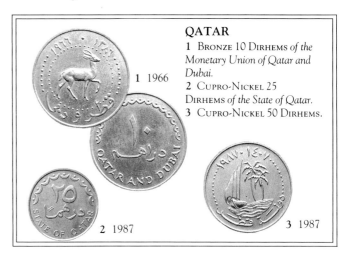

QATAR
1 Bronze 10 Dirhems *of the Monetary Union of Qatar and Dubai.*
2 Cupro-Nickel 25 Dirhems *of the State of Qatar.*
3 Cupro-Nickel 50 Dirhems.

INDEPENDENCE

After independence, which was gained in 1971, a new coinage was prepared by the Royal Mint for Qatar alone. The designs were similar to the 1966 issue, but the gazelle was replaced by a boat and two palm trees, and the necessary changes to the inscriptions were made. For both the 1966 and the 1973 issues bronze 1, 5 and 10 and cupro-nickel 25 and 50 dirhem coins were made. The dirhem = $\frac{1}{100}$ riyal.

UNITED ARAB EMIRATES

FIRST COINS:	third century BC
FIRST DECIMAL COINS:	1966
MAIN MINT:	Royal Mint
CURRENCY:	riyal

During excavations in the ancient fort site of al-Dour in the Emirate of Umm al-Qaiwain in 1974, five copper coins of the third or second century BC were found. Four of them were imitations of silver coins of Alexander the Great (336–323 BC) (*see* Greece) and the fifth was a second-century BC coin of Characene (southern Iraq). The Alexander imitations were either made locally or in Qatar. Coins from the ancient kingdom of Elymais in eastern Iran have also been found in the area.

THE TRUCIAL STATES

During the nineteenth century British influence in the southern Gulf brought the pirate sheikhdoms of Abu Dhabi, Ajman, Dubai, Fujairah, Ras al-Khaimah, Sharjah and Umm al-Qaiwain into a loose grouping of statelets known as the Trucial States, which agreed to respect international, and particularly British, shipping passing

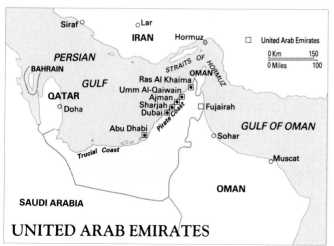

UNITED ARAB EMIRATES

through the Gulf. In 1892 this was formalized as a British protectorate over the sheikhdoms in return for freedom from piracy.

There was little need for currency in the ports along this coast until very recently because the population has always been small and there was little trading activity, but, as elsewhere in the Gulf (*see* Kuwait, Qatar and Bahrain), imported coinage has been found locally, particularly Iranian, Indian and Austrian coins.

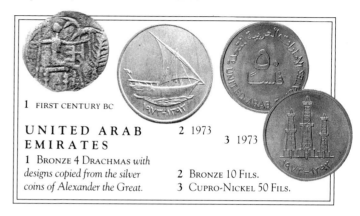

1 FIRST CENTURY BC

UNITED ARAB EMIRATES 2 1973 3 1973
1 BRONZE 4 DRACHMAS *with designs copied from the silver coins of Alexander the Great.*
2 BRONZE 10 FILS.
3 CUPRO-NICKEL 50 FILS.

INDEPENDENCE

In 1971 Britain returned these territories to independence as the United Arab Emirates, and in 1973 a coinage was struck for them in the British Royal Mint. The Arab denomination system, with 1000 fils = 10 dirhems = 1 dinar (common in one form or another to most of the smaller Gulf states), was used, and bronze 1, 5 and 10 and cupro-nickel 25 and 50 fils and 1 dirhem were issued. All denominations were inscribed in Arabic and English with the name of the Emirates, the denomination and date, and decorated with designs reflecting Arab culture: palm trees, fish, a boat, a gazelle, oil wells and a metal ewer. This series is still in use.

During the preparations for independence, there was a plan for Dubai to have a distinct coinage, jointly issued in 1966 with Qatar, but this was abandoned once the United Arab Emirates was formed.

Separate coinages have been struck for Ajman (1970–1), Fujairah (1969–70), Ras al-Khaima (1969–70), Sharja (1964, 1970) and Umm al-Qaiwain (1970), but these were all commemorative issues. Commemoratives have also been issued in the name of the United Arab Emirates since the 1980 silver 50 dirhem and the gold 750 dirhem coins struck to celebrate UNESCO in the International Year of the Child.

OMAN

FIRST COINS:	708
FIRST DECIMAL COINS:	1945
MAIN MINT:	Royal Mint
CURRENCY:	rial

Because of Oman's position as an important trading centre at the mouth of the Iranian Gulf, many imported coins from Iraq and Iran and from India have been found there. The earliest coins are ancient Iranian and Iraqi issues of the Hellenistic kingdoms of the third to first centuries BC. Sasanian coins from the same areas were also traded through Oman. The earliest coin issued in Oman was, however, produced in AD 708 by the local Umayyad governor. It is a typical Umayyad silver coin bearing the mint name 'Uman (see Syria).

Imported coins of the Umayyad and 'Abbasid caliphs (see Iraq) have been found in Oman, together with small silver coins thought to have been issued during the ninth century by the local Ibadi imams.

In the tenth century coins were struck at Oman by the Saffarids of Iran (901–7), the local Wahijids (912–61) and the Buyids of Iraq and Iran (970–c. 1040).

MUSCAT AND OMAN
Coins were not issued again in Oman until 1893, when Sultan Faisal ibn Turki (Feisal bin Turkee), the imam of Muscat and Oman, struck copper coins with Indian denominations. The first issue was of copper ¼ and ½ anna pieces with a depiction of the Muscat fort and an English inscription, naming the issuer and denomination, on the front and on the back an Arabic inscription in a wreath, also naming the issuer and giving the date.

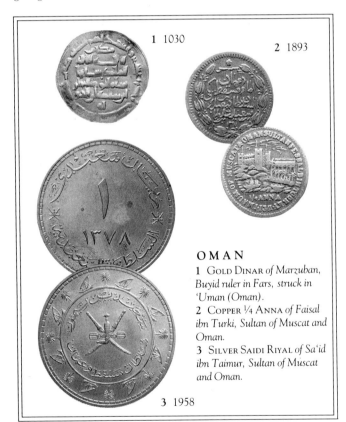

OMAN
1 GOLD DINAR of Marzuban, Buyid ruler in Fars, struck in 'Uman (Oman).
2 COPPER ¼ ANNA of Faisal ibn Turki, Sultan of Muscat and Oman.
3 SILVER SAIDI RIYAL of Sa'id ibn Taimur, Sultan of Muscat and Oman.

An Indian denomination system was adopted because Indian copper coins had circulated in Oman since the sixteenth century, when from 1508 to 1650 the port of Muscat was occupied by the Portuguese as part of their trading empire in the Indian Ocean. During the late seventeenth and early eighteenth centuries Muscat had been controlled by the Safavids of Iran, and Iranian copper coins also came in quantity into Oman until the late nineteenth century.

At the time of the 1893 issue, however, Faisal had just concluded a trade treaty with Britain, and imported British Indian coins had already become an important part of the local currency system.

Copper ¼ annas, known locally as baisa (i.e. paisa), continued to be issued by Faisal for the next five years, but after the first year the Muscat fort design was dropped. One consignment of ¼ annas was made in Birmingham, England, in 1898.

In 1940 the baisa denomination was incorporated into a formal coinage system issued by Sultan Sa'id ibn Timur (1932–70). The new system was based on the riyal, the Arabic name for the Austrian thaler, which was divided into 200 baisa. Two separate series were issued, one for circulation in Oman itself, the other for Dhofar, the southwestern half of the sultanate. All the coins had a crossed swords and dagger motif on the front, but different inscriptions on the back. Initially only cupro-nickel 10, 20 and 50 baisa and ½ riyal coins for Dhofar were issued, but, in 1946, 2, 5 and 20 baisa coins for Oman appeared. By 1970, 3, 25 and 100 baisa and 1 riyal coins were also being made.

SULTANATE OF OMAN
In 1970 after Sultan Qabus ibn Sa'id had seized the throne from his father, the name of the sultanate was changed from Muscat and Oman to simply Oman. New coins were issued by Qabus from 1975. The crossed swords and dagger motif was used on all denominations, which comprised bronze 5 and 10, cupro-nickel 25, 50 and 100 baiza and aluminium-bronze ¼ and ½ rial. The rial was now equal to 1000 baiza. Presentation and commemorative coins of these and higher denominations have also been made.

PEOPLE'S DEMOCRATIC REPUBLIC OF YEMEN

FIRST COINS:	fourth century BC
FIRST DECIMAL COINS:	1964
MAIN MINT:	Royal Mint
CURRENCY:	dinar

UNTIL captured by the British East India Company in 1839, the western part of the territory now known as the People's Democratic Republic of Yemen was part of the coinage area now mostly contained within the Yemen Arab Republic. Many of the coins made for the Yemen in both the pre-Islamic and Islamic period were minted at 'Adan (Aden) (see Yemen Arab Republic). The eastern part of the republic had little experience of coinage until the British made it a series of protectorates during the late nineteenth century.

When Britain established control over Aden and its hinterland, the main currency, apart from the coins of the imams of San'a, was of

PEOPLE'S DEMOCRATIC REPUBLIC OF YEMEN

1 BRONZE COIN *of Hadramaut.*
2 SILVER COIN *of the Himyarites, with designs copied from the coins of Athens and Rome.*
3 GOLD COIN *of al-Mu'ayyad Hizabr-al-Din Da'ud, Rasulid king, struck in Aden.*
4 SILVER COIN *of al-Afdal Dirgham-al-Din al-'Abbas, Rasulid king, struck in Aden.*
5 BRONZE CHOMSIH *of the port of Mukalla.*
6 BRONZE 5 FILS *of South Arabia.*
7 CUPRO-NICKEL 250 FILS *of the Bank of Yemen.*
8 CUPRO-NICKEL 100 FILS *of the Bank of Yemen.*

(coin labels)
1 FIRST CENTURY BC
2 FIRST CENTURY AD
3 1319
4 1372
5 1859
6 1964
7 1981
8 1981

BRITISH PROTECTORATES

When Britain took Aden in 1839, the area to the north and east of the port was controlled by a number of independent sultans. One of them, the Sultan of Lahej, to the north east of Aden, had briefly held the port before the British arrived, but thereafter none of them wielded real power. Throughout the territory Maria-Theresa thalers and Indian rupees were the main currency. For small change, bronze and silver coins were issued by the sultanates of Khurfar, Lahej, Mukalla and Tarim. They were denominated in chomsih, 120 of which equalled a Maria-Theresa thaler, known locally as a riyal. Most of the coins were struck in Britain, but some were local or Indian products. The designs were inscriptional or copied from Indian copper coins. The final issue was made in 1925. Locally countermarked Indian coins and Austrian dollars also circulated.

INDEPENDENCE

In 1967, after a protracted period of conflict with local freedom fighters, Britain yielded independence to Aden and the protectorates. One issue of coins was made by the British Royal Mint for the new state of South Yemen, before the National Liberation Front overthrew the new government and established the People's Democratic Republic of Yemen in 1970. The South Yemen issue was made in 1964 in preparation for the British departure, which had been planned since 1959. The coins all had an eight-pointed star design on the front and a crossed dagger or boat design on the back, and were denominated in fils (1000 = 1 dinar). Aluminium 1, bronze 5 and cupro-nickel 25 and 50 fils were struck.

THE DEMOCRATIC REPUBLIC OF YEMEN

The Democratic Yemen coins first appeared in 1971, with the same design and denomination system, but only the bronze 5 fils was made. In 1973 aluminium $2\frac{1}{2}$ and 5 fils with new designs featuring local wildlife were introduced. These have been replaced since 1976 by a new set of coins issued by the Bank of Yemen, all depicting the Aden fort. Aluminium 10 and cupro-nickel 25, 50, 100 and 250 fils coins were produced. Higher denominations exist only as commemoratives.

YEMEN ARAB REPUBLIC

FIRST COINS:	fourth century BC
FIRST DECIMAL COINS:	1974
MAIN MINT:	Royal Mint
CURRENCY:	riyal

Austrian dollars, the famous Maria-Theresa thaler, first struck at Vienna in 1780. Demand for this dollar led the British Royal Mint to participate in its production. However, Aden was placed under the control of the Bombay Presidency of the British East India Company, and British Indian rupees and pice soon began to flow into the port.

From 1839 to 1951 British Indian currency was the official legal tender, but in practice many different coins were in use, including British sterling and Iranian coins. Occasional shortages of small change were resolved by the cutting up of the current coins, particularly Indian rupees. After 1951 the coinage of British East Africa (*see* Kenya) was made the official currency of the area, as India was no longer under British rule.

THE earliest coins to reach the Yemen were fifth-century BC Athenian silver 4 drachma pieces, with their distinctive owl design (*see* Greece). They must have been imported in exchange for incense, which was ancient southern Arabia's main export. The first locally made coins were imitations of these Athenian 'owls' with local symbols and inscriptions replacing the Greek inscription. Some of the

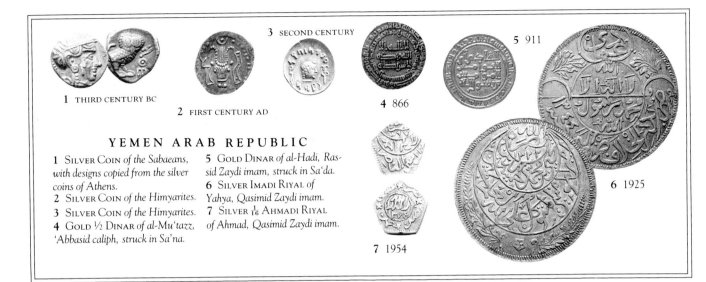

YEMEN ARAB REPUBLIC

1 SILVER COIN *of the Sabaeans, with designs copied from the silver coins of Athens.*
2 SILVER COIN *of the Himyarites.*
3 SILVER COIN *of the Himyarites.*
4 GOLD ½ DINAR *of al-Mu'tazz, 'Abbasid caliph, struck in Sa'na.*
5 GOLD DINAR *of al-Hadi, Rassid Zaydi imam, struck in Sa'da.*
6 SILVER IMADI RIYAL *of Yahya, Qasimid Zaydi imam.*
7 SILVER $\frac{1}{16}$ AHMADI RIYAL *of Ahmad, Qasimid Zaydi imam.*

designs which were imitated did not appear in Athens until the early fourth century BC; it is presumed that the Yemen imitations began later in the same century. During the third century some of the local owls were designed with a male head in place of the Greek goddess Athena. Imitations of Alexander the Great silver coins have also been reported from the area.

The tradition of copying imported Athenian coins continued into the second century BC, when local versions of Athenian new-style owls were introduced. Although these retained the original head and owl on amphora designs of the Athenian issues, considerable changes were made to suit local taste. Instead of a helmeted Athena, the Yemen imitations had a long-haired male bust enclosed in a wreath on the front. The wreath was copied from the back of the Athenian coin.

In the late first century BC, under the influence of imported Roman silver coins, the head on the front was modified again, this time to resemble the bust of Augustus (31 BC–AD 14). It is thought that these imitations of Athenian and Roman coins were issued by the rulers of the Sabaean, Minaean and Himyarite peoples of southern Arabia. The Minaeans lived on the northern border of the Yemen, in southwestern Saudi Arabia. The Sabaeans, who controlled central Yemen from their capital at Marib, were the most powerful group during the period of the new-style owls and Augustus-head coins. The Himyarites came to power in southern Yemen during the first century and were possibly responsible for some of the Augustus-head issue.

During the first and second centuries a series of small silver coins with a head on both sides was developed by the Himyarites and issued in large quantities in the Yemen and in modern South Yemen, the People's Democratic Republic of Yemen. These coins normally bore the names of Himyarite kings.

A group of large cast-bronze coins with a head on the front and an eagle on the back have also been attributed to the Himyarites, but could be issues of the rulers of Hadhramaut in South Yemen. Their date of issue is between the first century BC and third century AD.

It is not known how long the Himyarite coins continued in use, but it was possibly until the sixth century, when the Yemen fell under Ethiopian Axumite and then Iranian Sasanian rule. During this period coins of both these states entered the Yemen.

ISLAMIC RULE

The Yemen became an Islamic province in 628 during the life of Muhammad. The first Islamic coins of the area were coppers of the 'Abbasid caliphs with inscriptional designs, struck from 772 to 774 bearing the name of the al-Yaman mint. In 788 the 'Abbasid governor in the Yemen began the issue of silver coins from the San'a mint. These had the standard 'Abbasid inscriptional designs, but were smaller than regular 'Abbasid issues. From 835 'Abbasid gold coins were also struck at San'a. After 916 the weight standard of the gold coins was halved. Coppers were rarely issued. The Arabic inscription on the later 'Abbasid coins are written in a very crude uneven style.

'Abbasid coins continued to be issued from San'a by the local governor until 955, even though the rule of the 'Abbasid caliphs in the area was severely limited, both by local governors exercising their own authority and by the rise to power of local independent dynasties. The Ziyadids (818–1018) and the Yu'furids (847–997), who periodically controlled San'a and its governor, allowed the San'a mint to continue issuing in the name of the 'Abbasid caliphs, and did not indicate their own authority beyond placing their title AL-AMIR in the margin of the coins after 937. Mints at Dhamar, Sa'dah and Surdad, and at 'Adan in South Yemen and 'Aththar, Baysh and Bishah in Saudi Arabia were also involved in issuing 'Abbasid gold coins until c. 970.

From 905 the San'a mint also began on occasions to issue coins in the name of the Zaydi imams, Shi'ite religious leaders (from c. 806 to 1962), based in Sa'dah in northern Yemen. The Zaydi imams (also known as the Rassids) issued their own 'Abbasid-style gold and silver coins at Sa'dah during the same period. At Zabid the Ziyadids and the Najahid slave usurpers also issued coins in their own name during the late tenth century.

The last known 'Abbasid-style gold coins issued in the Yemen were struck at San'a by the city ruler Yahya bin Abi-Hashid (1030–48).

EGYPTIAN INFLUENCE

During the second half of the eleventh century the coinage of the Yemen took on a new appearance as the Sulayhid rulers (1047–1138) began to issue coins in the Fatimid style. Their gold coins, struck at Dhu Jiblah and 'Adan (Aden, in South Yemen), bore the name of the

Fatimid caliph and adopted a decorative script-style from Egyptian coins of the Fatimids (*see* Egypt). Similar coins were issued by the Zuray'id amirs, vassals of the Sulayhids.

Another new form of coin design was introduced in 1174, when Turanshah, the brother of Saladin, the Ayyubid ruler of Egypt and Syria, conquered the Yemen. From 1196 Ayyubid-style silver coins (*see* Egypt and Syria) were being issued by his successors in the Yemen, at San'a, Ta'izz, Raydah, al-Dumluwah and Zabid, and 'Adan in South Yemen. The ornamental style introduced by the Ayyubids continued into the following centuries and was used on coins issued by their successors, the Rasulids (1229–1454) of Zabid, and by their rivals, the Zaydi imams of northern Yemen.

During the early fourteenth century the Rasulids introduced, at the mint of 'Adan, a new broad gold coin which had a square-framed design copied from the Hafsid and Marinid coins of North Africa (*see* Tunisia).

The Rasulids also carried the ornamental designs of the Ayyubids a step further by introducing pictorial elements on their coins. In the centre of the back of their fifteenth-century silver coins, they placed an animal motif, such as a fish, lion or peacock, as a mint mark.

The rare coins of the Tahirids (1454–1517), who succeeded the Rasulids in southern Yemen, have inscriptional designs only.

OTTOMAN RULE

By 1538 the army of Suleyman the Magnificent, Ottoman emperor of Turkey, had completed its conquest of the Yemen. The Ottoman governor issued Turkish-style gold coins at Zabid, coppers at San'a, Sa'dah and Kawkaban and silver at San'a and 'Adan. In the 1620s silver coins were again struck by the Ottomans at San'a, just before they were expelled from the Yemen by the Zaydi imams (Qasimid line). During the Turkish occupation Ottoman coins from Egypt and Syria and European silver dollars and gold ducats were imported into the Yemen.

THE IMAMS OF SAN'A

After independence was restored, the Zaydi imams reassumed the issue of coins. At first a number of small mints were in use, but from the mid-eighteenth century San'a became the only mint. The main issue was of silver coins with Ottoman-style inscriptional designs. In the late eighteenth century the imams followed the Ottoman innovation of issuing large silver coins (*see* Turkey) to match the European dollars circulating in the Middle East. In the Yemen the favourite dollar coinage was that of the Austrian issues. During the eighteenth century Iranian coins must also have been current in the Yemen because the inscriptions and decorations on the imams' silver coins were in the same style as those on Iranian Safavid coins.

The coinage of the imams continued until the 1830s and was then not resumed until 1900. From 1872 to 1918 the Ottoman Turks again occupied the Yemen, but issued no coins there. Throughout the nineteenth century, foreign coins continued to be imported, particularly British sovereigns, European dollars, Ottoman coins from Egypt and rupees and pice from British India.

The re-emergence of imam coins marked a change in Yemen coinage. After a brief issue in 1900, the new coins were all made with British minting machinery, smuggled to Imam Yahya (1904–48) past the Turkish authorities from the British port at 'Adan. The use of Iranian-style designs was retained, but a new crescent-shaped frame

was also added and became a distinctive feature of the coinage until the last imam was overthrown in 1962.

The coins of the imams were denominated in terms of the dollar, called riyal (from the Spanish real), with 1 riyal = 40 buqshah = 80 hilalah = 160 zalat. Bronze 1 zalat, 1 hilalah and 1 buqshah and silver 2, 2½, 4, 5, 10 and 20 buqshah and 1 riyal pieces have been issued. The 2½ and 5 buqshah coins of 1947 were pentagonal. The crescent frame was used on all issues except the zalat (1921–7) and also the 1 hilalah and 1 buqshah of 1947, which were struck in Lebanon with a cedar-tree design.

YEMEN ARAB REPUBLIC

In 1962 the National Liberation Front ousted Imam al-Badr from power during his first year of rule. The first coinage of the Yemen Arab Republic was issued in 1963 and retained the denomination system of the imams. The crescent motif was replaced by a hand holding a torch or by an olive branch.

The second republican issue began in 1974, when a decimal coinage was introduced. The decimal system divided the riyal into 100 fils, and aluminium 1, brass 5 and 10 and cupro-nickel 25 and 50 fils and 1 riyal coins were issued. All denominations were decorated with an eagle design based on the Egyptian and Syrian coins issued from 1958 to 1961 while these two countries were linked to the Yemen in the United Arab States. Only Arabic inscriptions appear on the coins, which are inscribed in an ornate version of the early Arabic script used on coins of the Sulayhid period. Numerous commemorative issues have been made, including a set for the United Nations Food and Agriculture Organization in 1974.

SAUDI ARABIA

FIRST COINS:	fourth century BC
FIRST DECIMAL COINS:	1962
MAIN MINT:	Royal Mint
CURRENCY:	rial

ALTHOUGH Saudi Arabia was the birthplace and remains the spiritual centre of Islam, one of the world's great religions, it has played little part in the history of the coins issued in the name of that religion. Until very recently Saudi Arabia experienced coinage only through its neighbours. The ancient coins of the Gulf states, Iran, Iraq, Yemen, Jordan, Israel and Egypt have all been found in Saudi

SAUDI ARABIA
1 BRONZE 4 DRACHMAS *of the Minaeans, with designs copied from the silver coins of Athens.*

1 THIRD CENTURY BC

Arabia, and some of the ancient Yemenite coins must have been made within what is now its territory. Islamic coins from most parts of the Islamic world have also found their way into Saudi Arabia, in the hands of pilgrims on the road to Mecca.

Some of the mints which were run by the medieval rulers of Yemen are situated across the border within what is at the present time Saudi Arabian territory.

CALIPHATE COINAGE

No coins were issued by the early caliphs who ruled Islam after the death of Muhammad, until the caliphate had firmly established itself in Damascus, which is far from Saudi Arabia. The earliest coin of the caliphate to be recorded from a mint in Arabia was struck in 723, during the reign of the Umayyad caliph Yazid II, at the mint of the 'mine of the Commander of the Faithful in the Hijaz', which is thought to have been located somewhere in the mountains west of Mecca and Medina. The next Arabian issue was struck at Medina, with the mint name Madinat Rusulallah ('City of the Messenger of God', i.e. Muhammad), in 805 during the reign of the 'Abbasid caliph Harun al-Rashid. During the early Islamic period, lead and copper coins were also issued by the local governors of al-Hasa in eastern Arabia (*see* Bahrain).

Mecca's first Islamic coins were not issued until later in the 'Abbasid period. Several 'Abbasid gold coins with the mint name 'Makka' have been recorded between 873 and 936. During 781–6 'Abbasid silver coins were also issued at the mint of al-Yamamah, at Hajr, near the present capital, Riyad, in eastern Saudi Arabia. The Ikshidid governors of Egypt also minted gold at Mecca in 968.

During the tenth century Mecca was briefly controlled by the Qarmatid sect of Bahrain, who in 971 struck gold coins in the Holy City. In 976 the rival Shi'ite Fatimid caliphs of Egypt also issued gold coins at Mecca, and struck a gold coin for Medina in 1061. Both the 'Abbasid and the Fatimid coins for Mecca and Medina are likely to have been made for ceremonial rather than currency purposes, as was the gold coin with the mint name 'Makka' issued by the Zengids of Aleppo in 1160.

THE SHARIFS OF MECCA

After the 'Abbasid Caliphate, Saudi Arabia was ruled in part or whole by the Fatimids of Egypt, Qarmatids of Bahrain, the Seljuqs of Iran and Iraq, the Ayyubids and the Mamluks of Egypt and the Ottoman Turks, but the local Sharifs also issued coins. Their earliest recorded issue is a silver coin of the Mecca mint dated 1253. Their only substantial issue made for local use in Arabia, however, did not appear until much later, during the period of Ottoman rule, when copper and silver coins were issued in the first three decades of the nineteenth century by the Sharif governors of Mecca. Their coins have very simple designs, naming the mint 'Makka' and the date, and decorated with bird and fish motifs.

HEJAZ AND NEJD

During the First World War Lawrence of Arabia fought alongside the local Arab chieftains to free Arabia from Turkish Ottoman rule. By the end of the war the regions of both Hejaz and Nejd had been established as separate kingdoms under Arab rule. In 1925 'Abd al-'Aziz ibn Sa'ud (1905–53) of Nejd incorporated Hejaz into his kingdom, which became the Kingdom of Saudi Arabia in 1926. In both Hejaz and Nejd, during the struggle against Turkey and before the kingdoms were

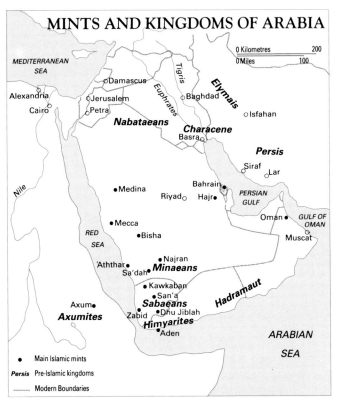

MINTS AND KINGDOMS OF ARABIA

- Main Islamic mints
Persis Pre-Islamic kingdoms
——— Modern Boundaries

SAUDI ARABIA

2 GOLD DINAR *of al-'Aziz, Fatimid Caliph, struck in Mecca.*
3 COPPER MAHMUDI *of Ghalib ibn Ma'sud, Sharif ruler of Mecca.*
4 GOLD DINAR (POUND) *of al-Husain ibn 'Ali, King of Hejaz, struck at Mecca.*
5 SILVER RIYAL *of 'Abd al-'Aziz ibn Sa'ud, King of Saudi Arabia.*
6 CUPRO-NICKEL 2 GHIRSH *of Sa'ud ibn 'Abd al-'Aziz, King of Saudi Arabia.*

united, locally countermarked Turkish coins and Austrian thalers circulated. Between 1919 and 1921, al-Husain ibn 'Ali, the King of Hejaz, had coins with inscriptional designs struck in his own name in Britain. Bronze $\frac{1}{8}$, $\frac{1}{4}$, $\frac{1}{2}$ and 1 and silver 5, 10 and 20 ghirsh (piastres) and a gold dinar were issued. 'Abd al-'Aziz also produced copper $\frac{1}{4}$ and $\frac{1}{2}$ ghirsh pieces for Nejd before he expanded his kingdom to include Hejaz. His coins, struck at Mecca, used a *tughra* design copied from current Turkish coins.

KINGDOM OF SAUDI ARABIA

Once Arabia had been united by 'Abd al-'Aziz ibn Sa'ud, a new coinage was prepared. In 1926 cupro-nickel $\frac{1}{4}$, $\frac{1}{2}$ and 1 ghirsh coins with inscriptional designs were made at Mecca in the name of the Kingdom of Saudi Arabia, and two years later a further set with additional silver coins denominated $\frac{1}{4}$, $\frac{1}{2}$ and 1 rial were struck in Birmingham, England. Some later consignments were also made at the British Royal Mint, the US mint and the Bombay mint. The silver coins had a palm tree and crossed swords emblem on both sides. The same emblem also appeared in the centre of the front of cupro-nickel 1, 2 and 4 ghirsh coins introduced in 1956.

MODERN COINAGE

In 1972 these coins were all replaced by issues in the name of King Faisal, made to a decimal system with 1 rial divided into 100 hilalah. Cupro-nickel 5, 10, 25, 50 and 100 hilalah coins were issued. The 1 hilalah denomination had already been issued in 1963. The new coins all had inscriptional designs and the palm tree and crossed swords.

AFGHANISTAN

FIRST COINS:	fourth century BC
FIRST DECIMAL COINS:	1925
MAIN MINT:	Kabul
CURRENCY:	afghani

THE FIRST COINS

This central Asian state, astride the Hindu-Kush Mountains, has occupied an important place in the history of Asian coinage, providing a meeting point for the coinage traditions of India, Islam and the West. Afghanistan has rarely been under local control, ruled in turn by Iranians, Greeks, Indians, Scythians, Huns, Turks, Arabs, Mongols, Britons and Russians, and virtually every period of foreign rule has been marked by issues of new coins reflecting the origins of the invaders.

Coins first reached Afghanistan during the fifth century BC, while it was a province of the Achaemenid Empire of Iran. Silver coins made in the Greek and Persian cities of the eastern Mediterranean circulated as bullion in Iran and, by the beginning of the fourth century, had reached as far as Afghanistan. By the time Alexander the Great had overthrown the Achaemenid Empire and, during 329 BC, captured Afghanistan, locally made imitations of these Greek coins were being produced there. The imitations were struck in the same way as the Greek coins, but with local stylized animal and geometrical designs.

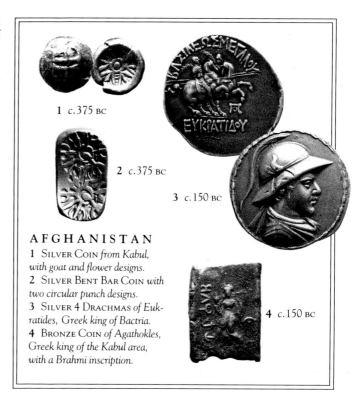

AFGHANISTAN
1 SILVER COIN *from Kabul, with goat and flower designs.*
2 SILVER BENT BAR COIN *with two circular punch designs.*
3 SILVER 4 DRACHMAS *of Eukratides, Greek king of Bactria.*
4 BRONZE COIN *of Agathokles, Greek king of the Kabul area, with a Brahmi inscription.*

1 *c.*375 BC
2 *c.*375 BC
3 *c.*150 BC
4 *c.*150 BC

A local coinage, consisting of silver bars with two similar geometrical designs stamped on one side only, was developed during the late Achaemenid period. These bar coins were also made in Pakistan and exported into India, where they provided the model for punch-marked coins (*see* India).

THE GREEK KINGDOM OF BACTRIA

Alexander's conquest was short-lived, but it opened up the territory to Greek influence. Soon after his death Afghanistan was invaded by the Indian ruler Chandragupta Maurya (*c.* 321–297 BC) and silver punch-marked coins were introduced into the area. By about 270 BC Greek rule, under the Seleucid kingdom of Syria, had been re-established in Bactria (northern Afghanistan) and mints coining Greek copper coins were in operation. In about 250 BC Diodotos, the Seleucid governor of Bactria, declared independence and made himself king. He issued gold and silver coins with his portrait on the front and a standing image of the Greek god Zeus on the back, and copper coins decorated with other Greek deities. For the next century the Greek successors of Diodotos continued to issue Greek-style silver and copper coins.

Some of the copper coins of the Bactrian Greeks are a silver colour because they were made from a local supply of natural cupro-nickel ore. These issues were, therefore, unintentionally the world's first cupro-nickel coins.

The Greek kingdom of Bactria was overthrown by a nomad invasion in about 140 BC, but imitations of Greek silver coins continued to be made by the nomads who settled in northern Afghanistan.

THE INDO-GREEK KINGDOM OF KABUL

During the early second century BC a separate Greek kingdom had been established around Kabul in eastern Afghanistan. Greek silver and

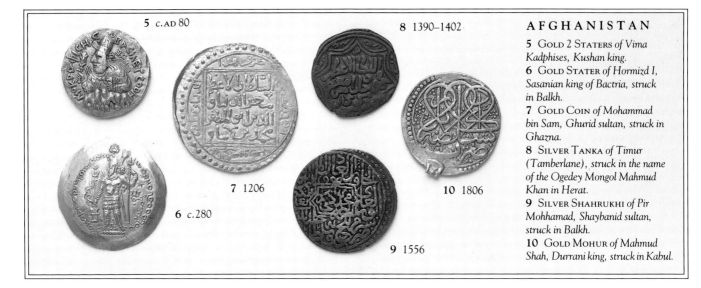

5 c.AD 80

8 1390–1402

7 1206

10 1806

6 c.280

9 1556

AFGHANISTAN

5 GOLD 2 STATERS of Vima Kadphises, Kushan king.
6 GOLD STATER of Hormizd I, Sasanian king of Bactria, struck in Balkh.
7 GOLD COIN of Mohammad bin Sam, Ghurid sultan, struck in Ghazna.
8 SILVER TANKA of Timur (Tamberlane), struck in the name of the Ogedey Mongol Mahmud Khan in Herat.
9 SILVER SHAHRUKHI of Pir Mohhamad, Shaybanid sultan, struck in Balkh.
10 GOLD MOHUR of Mahmud Shah, Durrani king, struck in Kabul.

copper coins were also issued here, but with Indian Brahmi and Kharosthi inscriptions and sometimes with Indian designs. Although briefly under Bactrian control during the middle of the century, the Kabul kingdom outlasted Bactria, and Greek kings continued to issue coins there until the mid-first century BC. These coins were often square, like contemporary Indian coins, and had both Greek and Indian (Kharosthi script) inscriptions.

During the mid-second century BC the Kabul kingdom expanded its territory into Pakistan and northwestern India, and when the nomad conquerors of Bactria pushed further south into the Kabul valley during the early first century BC, the Greek kingdom transferred its base to Pakistan.

SCYTHIANS, PARTHIANS AND KUSHANS

Three different groups of central Asian peoples, Scythians, Parthians and Kushans succeeded the Greeks. During the first century BC Scythians, previously employed as troops by the Greeks in eastern Afghanistan, overthrew their masters and issued coins as kings of the former Greek kingdom. They continued to issue Greek-style coins with Greek and Indian Kharosthi inscriptions, but the royal portrait was replaced by a depiction of the Scythian king on horseback. In the early first century AD the Scythians were themselves overthrown by Parthian rulers from Iran, who also issued Greek-style coins with a horseman design. However, in southern Afghanistan these Parthian kings issued coins with royal portrait designs, derived from contemporary Iranian coins.

The Kushans, a nomad people originally from northwestern China, are thought to have been one of the groups responsible for the destruction of the Greek kingdom of Bactria. During the first century BC they again moved southwards and took territory from the Greek kingdom in eastern Afghanistan. At first they made coins directly copying Greek issues, but during the early first century AD, they began to strike coins in the name of their chieftain, Kujula Kadphises. These coins used designs copied from the earlier Greek and contemporary Scythian and Parthian issues. One issue, however, copied a contemporary gold coin of the Roman Emperor Augustus. Finds in

Afghanistan show that Roman gold and silver coins were being imported into the area during the first and second centuries AD.

The Kushans defeated the Scythian and Parthian rulers and established a vast empire based on Afghanistan, but reaching from Russian Turkestan to North India. Their coins are found throughout this empire. Until the early second century they retained Greek inscriptions, but from around AD 110 these were replaced with inscriptions in their own language, known as Bactrian, but still written in Greek script. Some issues retained a royal portrait design, but most were decorated with a full-length image of the Kushan king, normally standing making a sacrifice, although on some coins the king was shown seated or riding an elephant. They issued both gold and copper coins, but almost no silver. Although the Greek practice of depicting a deity on the back of the coins was retained, they often used Roman coin designs as their models.

THE SASANIAN CONQUEST

The Kushans maintained their control over Afghanistan until the mid-third century, but they never managed completely to oust the Parthians from Qandahar, where they continued to issue Parthian-style coins until the area was incorporated into the Sasanian Empire of Iran soon after its establishment in AD 224.

Kushan territory in northern and eastern Afghanistan also fell into Sasanian hands during the third century. A Sasanian principality was established and its rulers issued coinage imitating and adapting Kushan designs. Their large dish-shaped gold coins depicted a standing image of the king on the front and a Kushan god on the back; smaller copper coins used the Sasanian Zoroastrian fire-altar design, together with a royal portrait bust. The Sasanian princes each wore a distinctive crown.

THE HUN CONQUEST

A further wave of central Asian nomads brought an end to Sasanian rule when Hun invaders swept into Afghanistan and Pakistan. At first they issued coins copying the Sasanian and Kushan gold and copper issues, but by the end of the fourth century they were also issuing silver coins with designs derived from the Sasanian issues of Iran. These retained the bust and fire-altar design, but the Hun ruler was depicted with a diadem instead of a crown.

Although the Huns issued their own coinage, large quantities of Sasanian silver coins also circulated. These entered Afghanistan as booty captured from Iran or as bribes to keep the Huns out of Iran. Changes were made to Hun coin designs in response to changes in the contemporary Iranian coins. During the fifth century the Huns also issued a silver coin with a horseman design copied from Indian gold coins produced by the Guptas.

The Hun coin designs were also adopted by the next nomad invaders to overrun Afghanistan, the Turks. During the seventh century bust and fire-altar designs were used, but in the eighth century silver coins with a horseman on the front and a reclining bull on the back were issued for eastern Afghanistan by the Turkish rulers of Gandhara (see Pakistan). The rest of Afghanistan was already by this period under Islamic control.

ISLAMIC RULERS

Northern and southwestern Afghanistan were first conquered by the forces of Islam during the 650s, but were ruled by converted local governors. Under the Umayyad caliphs mints were established at Balkh, Herat and Zaranj. The first Islamic issues, struck at Zaranj, were silver coins with Sasanian designs retaining the bust of the last Sasanian king and the traditional fire-altar design, plus Islamic inscriptions and dates. From 708 the purely inscriptional designs proclaiming the Islamic faith, introduced by Caliph 'Abd al-Malik in 698 (see Syria and Iran), were adopted and soon used at the other Afghan mints for both silver and copper issues. After the establishment of the 'Abbasid Caliphate in 754, these mints, and a new one at Panjhir, continued to strike silver and copper coins, but with a new version of the purely inscriptional designs. A Sasanian design was, however, still used for a copper coinage struck at Bust in 824.

During the ninth century the power of the 'Abbasid Caliphate in Afghanistan declined as local governors made themselves independent. Coins with 'Abbasid designs, but including the governors' names in the inscriptions, were issued at Zaranj, Bust and Herat by the Tahirids (821–73), ruling the western region from Nishapur in Iran. From 867 the southern half of Afghanistan fell under the control of the Saffarids, who also issued 'Abbasid-style coins at Zaranj and Panjhir. In 900 Isma'il, the Samanid ruler of Bukhara, defeated the Saffarids and was made governor of the 'Abbasid province of Khurasan, which included Afghanistan.

The Samanids ruled, but issued 'Abbasid-style coins in the name of the 'Abbasid caliphs. Under Samanid rule rich silver deposits were exploited in central Afghanistan, and silver coins were issued from at least 12 mints in Afghanistan and exported, both westward into the Islamic world and northward into Russia, from where they were carried into northern Europe by Viking traders. Hoards containing coins of Afghanistan are found as far west as the British Isles.

Towards the end of the Samanid period curious large silver coins were also issued. These had the usual Islamic inscriptional designs, but were more than twice the normal diameter and often weighed more than five times the normal weight.

TURKISH RULE

The Samanids eventually lost control of Afghanistan to one of their vassals, Sebuktegin, the Turkish governor of Ghazna in southern Afghanistan. Sebuktegin and his Ghaznavid successors divided the Samanid realm with another Turkish dynasty, the Qarakhanids (see USSR and China). The Qarakhanids ruled north of the River Oxus (Amu-Darya). Under Mahmud (998–1030), Sebuktegin's son, the Ghaznavids expanded their realm east and west of Afghanistan to include northern India and Iran. The Ghaznavid coinage used inscriptions like those on the coins of the Samanids, but a more decorative form of Arabic script was introduced. A scarcity of precious metals led to the issue of debased gold and silver coins.

During the late tenth century the use of square, triangular and star-shaped decorative frames around part of the inscription was introduced on both Ghaznavid and Qarakhanid coins. Such frames, first used on a Samanid coin from Bukhara in Russian Turkestan, were unusual on Islamic coins until popularized by their use on Muwahhid coins in Morocco and Ayyubid coins in Syria during the second half of the twelfth century.

The most active Ghaznavid mint was at Ghazna, but Balkh, Herat and several other small mints were also in operation. Ghaznavid coins, some with the local horseman and bull designs, were also issued in Pakistan.

After the reign of Mahmud, the Ghaznavid Empire declined and western and northern Afghanistan fell into the hands of the Seljuq rulers of Iran, who issued coins only at Herat and Balkh in Afghanistan.

As Seljuk interests became more focused on their western territories the local Ghurid rulers, who succeeded the Ghaznavids in southern and eastern Afghanistan (1168–1215), and the Khwarezm shahs (1077–1231), who controlled the north and eventually the whole of Afghanistan, asserted their independence and began to issue coins using horseman, bull and elephant designs from Pakistan and decorative frame designs like those used by the Ghaznavids.

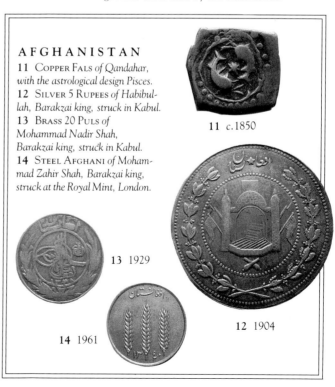

AFGHANISTAN
11 Copper Fals of Qandahar, with the astrological design Pisces.
12 Silver 5 Rupees of Habibullah, Barakzai king, struck in Kabul.
13 Brass 20 Puls of Mohammad Nadir Shah, Barakzai king, struck in Kabul.
14 Steel Afghani of Mohammad Zahir Shah, Barakzai king, struck at the Royal Mint, London.

11 c.1850

13 1929

14 1961

12 1904

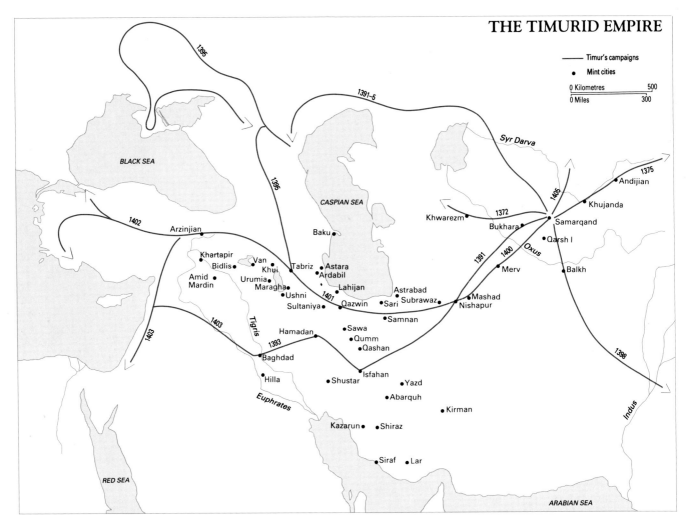

THE TIMURID EMPIRE

THE MONGOLS

In 1221 Genghis Khan and his Mongol horde invaded Afghanistan and drove out the last Khwarezm shah. The Mongols issued no coins in the region until after 1236, when an administration was re-established at Herat. Once they were secure in Iran, Genghis Khan's successors ignored Afghanistan, but lesser Mongol princes continued to control the area until the end of the thirteenth century, when it came under the sway of the Chagatai Mongols of Samarkand, who issued some of their large silver coins with decorative inscriptional designs at the mint of Badakshan in northeastern Afghanistan. During the Mongol period the name and titles of the ruler began to be the most prominently placed part of the inscription and the proclamations of the Islamic faith were subordinate.

The rise to power of Timur, known in the West as Tamberlane, put an end to Chagatai rule in Afghanistan. Timur, from his base in Samarkand, established a vast empire from India to Turkey, but it did not survive him (see USSR and Iran). After his death his descendants continued to rule Afghanistan and Russian Turkestan, but family conflicts kept even this area of the Timurid Empire fragmented. Many of Timur's coins were marked with his personal three-circles badge and used elaborate decorative frames around the inscriptions, which gave his name and titles and the usual religious proclamations. His suc-

cessors, and the Shaybanid Mongols who succeeded them during the fifteenth century, perfected this use of decorative frames by adopting an elegant cursive form of Arabic script on broad silver coins. Unfortunately, the mint workers often obscured the beautifully engraved designs by their poor workmanship.

The coin designs which were developed by the Timurids and Shaybanids were also adopted by the Savafid rulers of Iran and the Mughal emperors of India, who during the sixteenth century divided Afghanistan between them.

Under Iranian rule a system of local copper coinage like that in Iran was established, with city authorities responsible for issuing coppers for local circulation. Many of these local coins had pictorial designs featuring animals and weapons.

THE KINGDOM OF AFGHANISTAN

In 1747 Afghanistan once again achieved independence when the Afghan troops of Iran elected as shah their commander Ahmad (1747–72). Ahmad established control over eastern Iran and invaded Mughal India. He established a silver coinage with inscriptional designs modelled on the Mughal rupee (see India), but often with decorative motifs derived from Iranian coins. He and his Durrani successors struck coins at Balkh, Herat, Kabul and Qandahar, as well as several mints in

Pakistan and India. A similar coinage was continued when the Durranis were overthrown by Dost Muhammad (1824–39, 1842–63), founder of the Barakzai Dynasty which ruled Afghanistan until the 1973 revolution.

During the Durrani and Barakzai periods the issue of local city copper coins continued, with swords and flower motifs as the commonest designs. When the British invaded and occupied the city of Qandahar in 1878–9, they had local coppers made there with a British imperial crown design.

In 1891, during the reign of the Barakzai king Abdur Rahman (1880–1901), a machine mint employing British equipment was established at Kabul, and a new coinage was produced. Copper, silver and gold coins were struck, all featuring the Afghan national emblem, a stylized view of the shrine of the 'Ali Mosque at Mazar-i-Sharif in northern Afghanistan. On the higher denominations the design also featured the ornate official signature (tughra) of the king, a motif copied from contemporary Ottoman coins (see Turkey). The only other inscriptions were the denomination, date and mint name. Some crudely made copper coins with the mosque design were also made at Herat and Qandahar until the 1920s.

A decimal system based on the afghani (rupee) divided into 100 pul was introduced in 1925. The mosque and tughra designs were still used, but not on all denominations until 1961, when a new nickel-clad steel issue of three denominations – 1, 2 and 5 afghanis – was produced, all decorated with wheatear motifs. The 5 afghani also had the portrait of King Muhammad Zahir Shah on the front. On this and all the issues since 1925 the denomination numeral has also been an important part of the design.

MODERN COINAGE

A new national emblem, the Islamic eagle (see Egypt) in a wheatear wreath, dominated the new coins of the Republic of Afghanistan, established after a coup in 1973, but the design survived only until the founding of the Democratic Republic following a further coup in 1978. The coins of the present regime have a typical socialist national emblem design. The latest issue of aluminium-bronze 25 and 50 pul and cupro-nickel 1, 2 and 5 afghani coins have their denominations within a border of stars on the back and the national emblem featuring a shrine, the Quran, the rising sun, and a star and cog within a wreath of wheatears on the front.

PAKISTAN

FIRST COINS:	fourth century BC
FIRST DECIMAL COINS:	1961
MAIN MINT:	Lahore
CURRENCY:	rupee

THROUGHOUT its history the monetary systems in use in Pakistan have been closely linked to those of its neighbours, Afghanistan and India. The earliest coins found in Pakistan are the silver bent-bar coins issued in eastern Afghanistan during the early fourth century BC.

It seems likely that these coins were also made in Pakistan. Greek silver coins of the same period have also been found.

During the early second century BC copper coins made on the model of the contemporary Indian punch-marked silver and cast-copper coins were issued by local authorities for use in the cities of the Upper Indus. Silver punch-marked coins made in India were also in use in the area.

GREEK RULE

By the end of the second century BC the Upper Indus area and the Punjab were under the control of the Greek kings of eastern Afghanistan. At several, as yet unidentified, mints in Pakistan, Greek coins were issued by these kings. Like their eastern Afghan issues, the silver coins were decorated with the royal portrait, name and titles in Greek on the front and the image of a deity and an Indian Kharosthi inscription translating the Greek name and titles on the back. Their bronze coins bore these designs as well as divine portraits, animals and ritual objects (see Afghanistan).

2 c.175 BC

1 c.200 BC

3 c.150 BC

PAKISTAN
1 COPPER COIN cast in Taxila.
2 COPPER COIN minted in Taxila.

3 SILVER 4 DRACHMAS of Menander, Greek king, with a Kharosthi inscription.

MAIN GREEK KINGS AND COIN DESIGNS

Greek King	Indian name	Usual deity
Amyntas	Amita	Athena
Antialkidas	Amtialikida	Zeus
Antimachos	Amtimakha	Nike (Victory)
Apollodotos I	Apaladata	Apollo
Apollodotos II	Apaladata	Athena
Archebios	Arkhebiya	Zeus
Artemidoros	Artemidora	Artemis
Epander	Epadra	Athena
Heliokles	Heliyakreya	Zeus
Hermaios	Heramaya	Zeus
Hippostratos	Hipastrata	Tyche (Fortune)
Lysias	Lisika	Herakles
Menander	Menadra	Athena
Philoxenos	Philasina	Tyche
Straton	Strata	Athena
Theophilos	Theuphila	Herakles
Zoilos	Jhoilasa	Herakles

THE SCYTHIANS AND PARTHIANS

During the first century BC Scythians seized control of the Greek kingdom in Pakistan. A Scythian usurper, Maues (c. 80–60 BC), overthrew the Greek king, Hippostratos, and issued a new style of coin, without the king's head, but retaining Greek and Indian Kharosthi inscriptions. Although Maues was ousted by another Greek king, Apollodotos II, a new Scythian dynasty under King Azes I from southern Afghanistan restored Scythian rule in 57 BC. Azes and his successors continued to issue silver and bronze coins with Greek and Kharosthi inscriptions and designs, but replaced the royal portrait with a mounted figure of the king.

Coins with the mounted-king design and Greek and Kharosthi inscriptions were also issued by the Parthian Dynasty, founded by King Gondophares who, from AD 26, ousted the Scythians. Gondophares is reputed to have met St Thomas the Apostle when he visited this part of the Indian sub-continent in the AD 40s. His successors issued small silver coins with Iranian designs, bearing a royal portrait on the front and Nike, the Greek goddess of victory, with a Greek inscription on the back, in the far south of Pakistan, before that area came under the control of the Scythian rulers of Gujerat at the end of the first century AD (see India).

THE KUSHANS

During the late first century the Parthian kingdom in Pakistan was gradually absorbed into the empire of the Kushans, a nomad people who ruled Afghanistan. At first the Kushans issued coins imitating the Scythian and Parthian coinage already circulating in Pakistan. By the end of the first century, however, they had established a new coinage system, consisting of gold and copper coins, with new designs featuring a portrait or a standing or seated image of the king appearing on the front and a deity on the back. The inscriptions in Greek script, but in the Kushan language, gave the king's name and titles on the front, and the name of the deity on the back. The Greek, Iranian and Indian gods and goddesses depicted on the back of Kushan coins indicate the wide range of beliefs existing in their kingdom. The location of the Kushan mints is not known, but it is generally thought that the main mint was located in or near the Peshawar region.

During the third century the northern parts of the Kushan Empire was conquered by the Sasanian rulers of Iran. The Kushans continued to hold their territory in the Punjab, but the land west of the Indus was ruled by Sasanian princes, who issued bronze coins like the Kushans, but with Sasanian designs. Under the Sasanian king Shapur II (307–79) some territory to the east of the Indus was also lost. Weakened by Sasanian attacks the Kushan state declined and by the end of the fourth century had disappeared. During the decline the bronze coins issued became smaller and smaller, and the gold coinage was debased.

THE HUNS AND TURKS

The end of Kushan rule did not mean the end of foreign rule for Pakistan. After the Sasanian invasion, Hun nomads from Afghanistan pushed down into Pakistan to fill the power vacuum. The Huns imitated both Kushan and Sasanian coins. They also used imported Sasanian silver coins from Iran. The Hun versions of Sasanian coins normally retained the basic design, with a royal bust on the front and a fire-altar on the back, but the portraits were of distinctive nomad types with central Asian facial features. A religious symbol – a wheel, conch or altar – was frequently placed before the Hun chieftain's face on the front, and the fire-altar design on the back was often so badly struck that it was almost unidentifiable. On a few rare issues a new horseman design replaced the portrait. This design is thought to have been copied from Indian Gupta gold coins.

During the sixth and seventh century Turkish nomads also began to enter Pakistan from Afghanistan. By the seventh century they had seized control from the Huns. There is still uncertainty about the precise identity of the issuers of many of the coins of this area during the Hun and early Turkish period, but it seems likely that some of the later Sasanian-style coins that were issued in the area were made by Turkish rulers.

The earliest coins that were clearly Turkish were issued in the Peshawar area by the Turkish kings of Gandhara from the eighth century. These reused the Hun horseman design and linked it with a reclining bull design of Indian origin. The horseman is thought to depict the Turkish ruler and the bull to represent the Indian god Siva, identified by his trident symbol on the rump of the bull.

The Turkish horseman and bull design was imitated widely in India. It was also used by the Turkish Ghaznavid rulers of Afghanistan when they established control over northern Pakistan.

ISLAMIC RULE

Islam arrived in Pakistan by sea. Muslim traders from the Red Sea region settled in the Sind area of Pakistan during the eighth century. Tiny silver coins with Arabic inscriptions were struck in the name of the local rulers, and later in the name of the Fatimid caliph (see Egypt).

Northern Pakistan came under Islamic rule during the reign of Mahmud of Ghazna (997–1030). In 1028 Mahmud issued a curious silver coin at Lahore. On one side it had the usual Arabic inscription, proclaiming the Islamic faith and naming Qadir, the Abbasid caliph (991–1031), but the other side is written in Indian Nagari script with a Sanskrit translation of the Islamic proclamation, the date and mint name, Mahmudpur (Lahore). During its final phase the Ghaznavid

4 c. AD 100

6 c. 350

5 c. 130

7 c. 800

8 953–78

PAKISTAN

4 COPPER 2 DRACHMAS of Kaniska, Kushan king, with an image of the Buddha.
5 GOLD STATER of Huviska, Kushan king.
6 COPPER COIN of Shapur II, Sasanian king of Iran.
7 SILVER COIN of Spalapatideva, Turkish shah.
8 SILVER COIN of the Fatimids in Sind, in the name of the Fatimid caliph al-Muizz.

9 SILVER DIRHEM of Mahmud, Ghaznavid sultan, with an Islamic inscription in Sanskrit, struck at Mahmudpur (Lahore).

9 1028

Dynasty ruled only in the Lahore area and issued base-silver horseman and bull coins there.

Ghaznavid rule in Pakistan was eventually overthrown in 1150 by another Afghan dynasty, the Ghorids, who issued Ghaznavid-style Islamic coins bearing both inscriptional and bull and horseman designs. By the end of the twelfth century the Ghorids, under the joint rule of the brothers Ghiyath al-Din Mohammad (1163–1203) and Mu'izz al-Din Mohammad (also known as Mohammad bin Sam), (1173–1206), had extended their territory to include northern India. Although Afghanistan was soon lost to the Khwarezm shahs and then the Mongols in 1221, the Ghorids had established a firm base of Islamic rule in Pakistan and northern India. This was inherited by their Turkish commander in India, Qutb al-Din Aybak.

THE SULTANS OF DELHI

After the death of the Ghorid ruler Mohammad bin Sam, his military commander established a new sultanate, based on Dehli, to rule the Ghorids' eastern conquests. The Dehli sultans continued the issue of Islamic inscriptional coins in Pakistan, soon abandoning the use of the horseman and bull design. Both Ghorid and Delhli Sultanate coins were distinguished from the earlier Ghaznavid issues by their increased size and the predominant use of square frames around the central inscription, a motif borrowed from the Ayyubid coins of Syria. Dehli Sultanate coins continued to be issued and used in Pakistan until the sixteenth century, when the Mughals seized power. During the later Delhi period independent sultanate coins were also issued in Kashmir, Multan and the Sind. Timurid and Shaybanid coins from Afghanistan also entered the region.

THE MUGHALS

Like the Ghorids, the Mughals conquered Pakistan and India from a base in Afghanistan. In 1526, Babur, the ruler of Kabul and a man of both Mongol and Timurid descent, defeated the Sultan of Delhi and established control over Pakistan and a large part of northern India. From his mint at Lahore Babur issued silver coins with Arabic inscriptions, copied from the Shaybanid Afghan issues. Babur's successors, the Mughal Emperors of India, continued to issue coins like those they issued in India until the mid-eighteenth century, at the following mints in Pakistan: Attock, Bakkhar, Dera, Derajat, Dewal, Jalalpur, Kalanpur, Khairpur, Lahore, Lahri Bandar, Multan, Peshawar, Rohtas and Tatta.

AFGHAN AND SIKH RULE

During the 1750s Pakistan was seized from the Mughals by an Afghan invasion led by the first Durrani king, Ahmad Shah (1747–73). Ahmad retained the Mughal coinage system in Pakistan and issued coins with inscriptional designs similar to the Mughal coins, but in his own name, at several of the Mughal mints listed above. His successors also issued coins in Pakistan. In southern Pakistan the coins were issued in the name of the Durrani kings by the local rulers, the Amirs of Sind and Khairpur. In 1843, when the British occupied Bakkhar, the capital of Khairpur, they issued Afghan-style coins with a lion motif on the back. The local rulers of Bahawalpur, further up the Indus, at first issued coins in the name of the Afghan king, but from the 1830s, issued coins in their own right, under British protection. The Khans of Kelat in Beluchistan also issued their own copper coins with Afghan inscriptional designs.

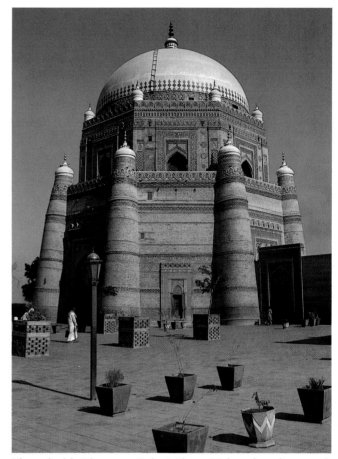

The tomb of the Islamic saint Rukn-I-Alam in Multan, the earliest part of South Asia to use Islamic coins.

In northern Pakistan Afghan control was short-lived as the Punjab was captured in 1763–4 by the Sikhs, who issued Mughal-style coins. A silver issue from Lahore, struck in 1836, shows a portrait of Guru Nanak, the founder of the Sikh religion. During the early nineteenth century Sikh coins were also issued at Multan, Peshawar, Dera and Derajat and in Kashmir.

BRITISH RULE

Some local Sikh and Afghan coinages continued to be used after Pakistan had come under direct British rule during the second half of the nineteenth century, but the coinage of British India became the standard money of the area until the end of British rule in partition and independence in 1947.

INDEPENDENCE

The new state of Pakistan, established in 1947, consisted of British India's two predominantly Islamic regions: present-day Pakistan in the north west and eastern Bengal, present-day Bangladesh. New coins, with a denomination system derived from the British India issues current before independence (1 rupee = 16 anna = 32 pice) were issued from 1948 (two years before independent India's first issue).

In keeping with the Islamic identity of Pakistan, the new coins had predominantly Islamic designs, a star and crescent emblem on the

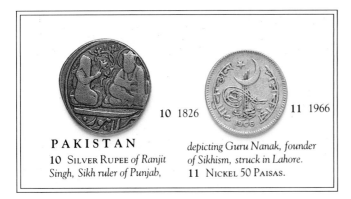

PAKISTAN
10 SILVER RUPEE of Ranjit Singh, Sikh ruler of Punjab,

10 1826   11 1966

depicting Guru Nanak, founder of Sikhism, struck in Lahore.
11 NICKEL 50 PAISAS.

front and an ornamental official signature (*tughra*) on the back. The only other decorations were borders or wreaths of plants.

The coins had the same shapes as the British coins they replaced. The 1948 issue consisted of bronze 1 pice, cupro-nickel $\frac{1}{2}$, 1 and 2 anna and nickel $\frac{1}{4}$, $\frac{1}{2}$ and 1 rupee pieces. In 1951 a bronze 1 pie, equal to $\frac{1}{3}$ pice was also issued. Minor changes in the designs of some denominations were made in 1950 and 1953.

DECIMAL COINAGE

A decimal system (1 rupee = 100 pice) was adopted in 1961 and new coins denominated 1, 5 and 10 pice were issued. The star and crescent designs were retained, but the back of the 5 pice was decorated with a traditional sailing boat. Before the end of 1961 a decision was made to change the name of the small denomination from 'pice' to 'paisa', and new coins with the altered name were issued. In 1963, 25 and 50 paisa coins were also issued, and in the following year a 2 paisa was added. When a set of currency coins to promote the United Nations' Food and Agriculture Organization was issued in 1974, a minaret replaced the *tughra* on the front of the coins.

Although a commemorative rupee was issued in 1977 to celebrate the centenary of the birth of Pakistani poet Mohammad Iqbal, 1 rupee coins were not issued for circulation from 1949 until a new design was introduced in 1979. The new rupee was decorated simply with the star and crescent and a floral wreath. Lower denominations with simple decorative designs were issued to match it from 1981.

INDIA

FIRST COINS:	early fourth century BC
FIRST DECIMAL COINS:	1957
MAIN MINT:	Bombay
CURRENCY:	rupee

INDIA has an independent coinage tradition which adopted and adapted many features from both the European and Islamic traditions, but has always retained a separate identity. The coinages of many East Asian countries have been influenced by the Indian tradition, particularly of its closest neighbours, Pakistan, Bangladesh,

Nepal, Bhutan, Tibet (*see* China) and Sri Lanka. This influence has also been felt further afield – in South East Asia: Thailand, Kampuchea, Malaysia, Indonesia and the Philippines; in the Indian Ocean: the Maldives, Mauritius, Réunion and the Seychelles; in East Africa: Somalia, Kenya, and Tanzania; and in South Arabia: Oman and Yemen.

PUNCH-MARKED COINS

The precise date of the first appearance of coins in India is not known, but archaeological evidence suggests that coins were already being made and used in northern India by the mid-fourth century BC. The oldest coins so far discovered in India were made of weighed pieces of silver, stamped on only one side with between one and five punches. Such coins are now known as 'punch-marked' coins. The earliest of these seem to be oval and stamped by four round punches with symbolic designs. The force of the punches curved the metal so that these coins are dish-shaped. Smaller examples have also been reported with one or two punches only.

These dish-shaped punch-marked coins are found around the city of Varanasi on the River Ganges in Uttar Pradesh Province. It seems likely that the idea of making the dish-shaped coins came into northern India from Afghanistan through Pakistan, as they appear to derive their shape and method of manufacture from the bent-bar punch-marked coins made there in the early fourth century BC.

THE MAURYAN EMPIRE

The use of coins spread quickly in northern India. By the end of the fourth century BC, many centres of coin issue had come into being from the Punjab and Bombay in the west to Bengal and Orissa in the east.

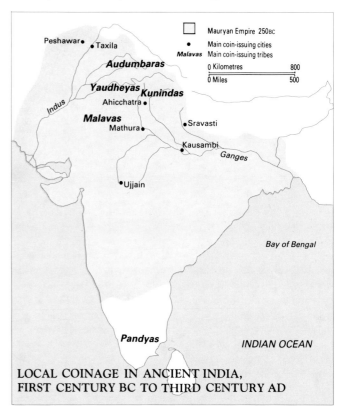

LOCAL COINAGE IN ANCIENT INDIA, FIRST CENTURY BC TO THIRD CENTURY AD

INDIA
1 SILVER PUNCHMARKED COIN *of Varanasi (Benares).*
2 SILVER PUNCHMARKED COIN *of the Mauryan kings.*
3 COPPER CAST COIN *of the Mauryan kings.*
4 COPPER CAST COIN *of the Mauryan kings.*
5 COPPER COIN *of Dionysios, Greek king in northern Punjab, with a Kharosthi inscription.*

2 *c.250* BC

6 *c.100* BC

3 *c.200* BC

1 *c.350* AD

6 COPPER COIN *of Ramadatta, king of Surasena (Mathura).*

4 *c.200* BC

5 *c.50* BC

The identity of the authorities who issued the early punch-marked coins is not known, but there is evidence that by about 300 BC some of the coins in use were being issued by the Mauryan emperors, who had gradually assumed control over northern and central India during the late fourth century BC, overthrowing the local kings and tribal leaders. Ignorance of the identity of the issuers results from the absence of inscriptions on the early coins. The stamped designs were all symbolic, representing, for example, animals, plants, the sun, the moon and the planets, and their purpose can no longer be understood. Mauryan coins are also found in Pakistan, Afghanistan and Bangladesh, which were all part of the Mauryan Empire.

The Mauryan silver coins are distinguished by having five punches, always including a sun symbol and a six-branched symbol. They were mostly smaller than the dish-shaped coins and were made from flat, square or round pieces of silver. They are also found in southern India and Sri Lanka.

During the period of the early coins some copper punch-marked coins were also issued for local use, but in the Mauryan period a new kind of copper coinage appeared. Square copper coins with four symbols on both sides were made by being cast in moulds. These were soon joined by round cast-copper coins with fewer symbols, sometimes just one on each side. In northern India these are found wherever the Mauryan silver coins were used.

GREEK INFLUENCE IN NORTHERN INDIA

The north-west corner of the Indian sub-continent, particularly eastern Afghanistan and northern Pakistan, was an area of great influence on the coinage of India. During the second century BC this area and the neighbouring part of India, particularly the Punjab, came under the control of Greek kings. Their silver coins, with Greek designs and inscriptions, circulated in India and provided inspiration for Indian coin makers. The coins showed little sign of Indian influence, apart from the occasional square coin and a few designs representing Indian deities, but they were normally inscribed with an Indian Prakrit translation of the Greek inscription on the back.

When the Greek kingdoms were overthrown by Scythians in the mid-first century BC, one group of Greeks took refuge in Kashmir–Jammu and the northern Punjab and issued silver, bronze and lead coins there. The silver coins of these kings all depict the Greek goddess Athena on the back and the king's head on the front. The issues of one of these kings, Apollodotos II, were still circulating in India, particularly in Gujerat, during the early first century AD.

By the end of the first century BC the Greek kings in Kashmir–

Jammu had been overthrown by a Scythian ruler, Rajuvula, who was in turn overthrown by a Parthian (Iranian) king, Gondophares (*see* Pakistan). Both Scythian and Parthian rulers continued to issue Greek-style coins with Athena on the back until about AD 60.

TRIBES, KINGS AND CITIES

At about the same time as Greek coins began to enter India, another change was taking place. The collapse of the Mauryan Empire in the early second century BC led to decentralization of power in northern India and many new coin-issuing authorities grew up.

By the first century coins were being issued by tribal states, such as the Audumbaras, Kunindas and Yaudheyas in the Punjab, and by kingdoms, including Surasena (Mathura), Panchala (Ahichhatra), Vatsa (Kausambi) and Kosala (Ayodhya) in the Ganges plain. Some cities, such as Ujjain and Eran in Madhya Pradesh, were also producing coins, but their political status is not clear. The Satavahana kings, who ruled most of southern India, and the Pandyas, who ruled the far south, also began to issue coins.

The new tribal, regal and civic issues were mostly in copper, although a few silver tribal coins were made in the Punjab. Their designs combined the symbols found on Mauryan coins with designs and inscriptions derived from Greek coins. The inscriptions were all Indian, but were often arranged around the edge of the design as on Greek coins. They were mostly written in Brahmi script, but some Punjab coins were also inscribed in the Kharosthi script used in the north west to write the Indian inscriptions on Greek coins.

Greek influence is seen most clearly in the widespread adoption of the technique of striking coins between two engraved dies and in the disappearance of both punch-marking and casting techniques. The issue of square coins, however, continued. A good example of the combination of Indian and Greek influences is the coinage of the Kuninda tribe, which features a deer and goddess, surrounded by a Brahmi inscription on the front, and six symbols surrounded by a Kharosthi inscription on the back.

Greek influence was slower to reach some areas, and the early coins of the city of Ujjain and of the Satavahanas and Pandyas show little evidence of it. Although struck between two dies, they normally have designs featuring groups of symbols, similar to those that appeared on the punch-marked and cast coins.

SOUTH INDIAN KINGDOMS

The Satavahana coinages issued for southern India established a distinct coinage region which remained into the nineteenth century.

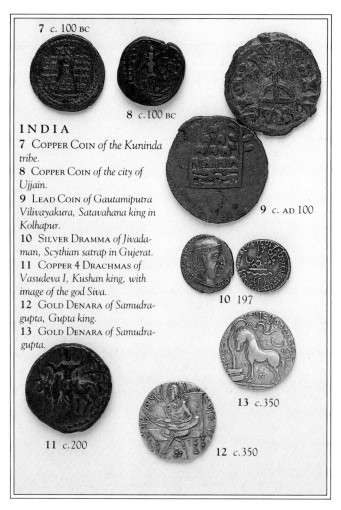

INDIA

7 COPPER COIN of the Kuninda tribe.

8 COPPER COIN of the city of Ujjain.

9 LEAD COIN of Gautamiputra Vilivayakura, Satavahana king in Kolhapur.

10 SILVER DRAMMA of Jivadaman, Scythian satrap in Gujerat.

11 COPPER 4 DRACHMAS of Vasudeva I, Kushan king, with image of the god Siva.

12 GOLD DENARA of Samudragupta, Gupta king.

13 GOLD DENARA of Samudragupta.

Apart from their Greek-influenced silver coins, the Satavahana kings issued many lead coins with symbolic designs. The centre piece was normally an animal, most commonly the elephant, lion or bull, all of which had religious significance. Animal designs, still featuring other symbols, continued to be issued by the Iksvaku, Salankaya, Visnukundin and Pallava kingdoms which succeeded the Satavahanas. The most commonly used symbols were the conch shell, wheel, fish, lamp, tree and bow, all of which were used as emblems of particular Hindu gods.

The precise dates of many southern Indian coins and their attributions to individual rulers and kingdoms are very uncertain. Where inscriptions occur, they do not refer to the names of the kingdoms, their locality or particular kings, but give instead the religious titles used by the issuing kings. Since these titles were commonly used by many kings in different kingdoms they are of limited use in attribution. This uncertainty means that it is difficult to outline the development of coinage in southern India during the period from the third to the ninth century.

ROMAN TRADE

During the first century AD direct trade links were established between India and Roman Egypt. Ships regularly sailed from the Red Sea across the Indian Ocean, carrying large quantities of Roman gold and silver coins to buy Indian gems, spices, cotton and Chinese silk at ports on India's western coast. In the Gujerat area imported Roman silver coins were melted down to make new silver coins in the names of the local Scythian satraps and Satavahana kings, but further south the Roman coins seem to have circulated as money. The Scythian and Satavahana coins used designs based on Greek coins, with a portrait of the ruler on the front, but also bore Indian symbolic designs on the back.

Further north, in Pakistan and Afghanistan, Roman coins influenced the coin designs of the Kushans, a new group of invaders who overthrew the Parthian rulers of the area (*see* Pakistan). Some of the Roman-influenced Kushan coins circulated into northwestern India.

THE KUSHANS

The Kushans, a Central Asian people who had settled in Afghanistan during the second century BC, extended their empire into India during the late first century AD. By the end of the second century AD their coinage was well established in northern India and had a considerable influence on local coins.

The Kushan coins depicted the portrait of the Kushan king on the front, normally as a full-length figure sacrificing at an altar, but on some issues riding on an elephant or seated on a throne. The back always showed a god or goddess. Both sides were inscribed in the Kushan language written in Greek script. Coins were struck in both copper and gold, the first time gold coinage had been issued in India. The copper coins were imitated in many areas, both unofficially, as in Orissa, and officially by local tribal groups, such as the Yaudheyas and Kotas in the Punjab.

THE GUPTAS

By the mid-fourth century the Kushan Empire was in decline and had lost most of its territory to the Sasanians and the Kidarite Huns in Afghanistan and Pakistan and to the rising power of the Gupta kings in India. The first Gupta king to issue coins, Samudragupta (about 350–70), followed the Kushan practice and issued gold coins with a

THE KUSHAN EMPIRE,
SECOND CENTURY AD

depiction on the front of the king making a sacrifice at an altar and a seated goddess, Lakshmi, on the back. The inscriptions on both sides were written in Brahmi script.

The Guptas, originally the rulers of a small state in eastern India, quickly built an empire which extended throughout northern India, reaching its greatest extent under Samudragupta's grandson, Kumaragupta I (about 415–50). The Guptas were great patrons of the arts and literature, and this is evident on their coins. Already under Samudragupta, the Kushan designs were modified with great elegance. On his most famous coins Samudragupta is shown seated on a couch playing a harp, and the inscriptions in Sanskrit poetry describe him as 'The king of kings of irresistible prowess, the protector of the earth who wins heaven'. The coin inscriptions of his son Chandragupta II (376–414) are equally eloquent; on a coin showing him slaying a lion with bow and arrow Chandragupta is called 'Moon among kings, brave as a lion, whose fame is far-spread, unconquered on earth, wins heaven'.

Copper coins were rarely issued by the Guptas, who left their issue to the tribal authorities over whom they ruled, but from the reign of Chandragupta II silver coins began to be issued. These followed the Greek-derived design used on the coins of the Scythian satraps of Gujerat and Malwa, whose kingdom Chandragupta conquered. Like the Scythian issues, Chandragupta's coins had the royal head on the front and a symbol surrounded by an Indian inscription on the back. The Gupta issue used an image of the bird-god, Garuda in place of the hill symbol of the satraps.

THE HUNS
Following the collapse of Kushan rule in the north west, several waves of Hun invaders entered India during the fifth and sixth centuries and captured territory from the Guptas. When the Huns left their Central Asian homeland, they were unused to coins, so they tended to imitate the coins of the peoples they conquered. In India they decorated their coins with designs derived from Kushan coins or from the coins of Sasanian Iran. They also imitated a king on horseback design used by Chandragupta II. One Hun ruler called Mihiragula (early sixth century) issued silver coins in the Sasanian style and copper coins in the Kushan and Gupta style. On other copper issues he matched a Sasanian-style portrait with a bull design copied from a local Indian tribal coinage.

During the same period another group of invaders from the north west, probably of Hun origin, brought with them into India a huge treasure of Iranian silver coins of the Sasanian Emperor Peroz I (457–83). These coins, with a head on the front and a fire altar on the back, were circulated in the Gujerat area, but the supply soon ran out and the coins were imitated by local coin makers. These imitations, known as *gadhya paisa*, established a model which survived in a gradually modified form until the twelfth century.

In Kashmir in the north west, Kushan designs survived long after the end of the Kushan period. The Kashmir kings issued coins featuring a standing king on the front and a seated goddess on the back, derived from Kidarite Hun copies of Kushan gold coins. These designs, in a modified style, were still being used on Kashmir copper coins until the thirteenth century.

DECLINE OF COINAGE
The use of coins declined in southern and eastern India during the sixth century. A few small kingdoms, the Abhiras, Kalachuris and

Traikutakas, in the region around Bombay issued coins based on the silver coins of the Guptas. This model was also adopted in the east by the Vardhanas and Maukharis. Gupta-style gold coins were issued in Bengal by an early seventh-century king, Sasanka, ruler of Gauda, with an image of the Indian god Siva riding a bull (*see* Bangladesh). But after this gold coins were scarce until the eighth century.

Contemporary inscriptions suggest that cowrie shells were used for small change during this period. In Bengal these shells, mostly imported from the Maldive Islands, were still being used as money until the eighteenth century.

TURKISH INFLUENCE
During the eighth century a new phase in India's coinage history began with the Turkish invasion from Central Asia of northwestern India. In the ninth century the invaders issued silver coins in Pakistan with a horseman design derived from the Hun version of the Gupta king on horseback design. On the back of these horseman coins was a reclining bull, with an Indian inscription naming the Turkish rulers Spalapatideva and Samantadeva.

These coins circulated widely into India and during the eleventh and twelfth centuries were copied by many local Indian rulers: the Tomaras of Delhi, the Gahadavalas, the Chahamana of Sakambhari and Ranathambhora, the Jajapellas of Narwar and the Pratiharas of Gwalior. Many of the Indian issues were of such base silver that the coins look like they are made of copper.

During the ninth century, before the bull and horseman coins became popular in India, a series of coins developed out of the Sasanian-derived *gadhya paisa* series. The Pratihara kings of Kanauj, ruling the Ganges plain region, issued silver coins with an abstract version of the Sasanian fire altar design on the back and a boar-headed image of the Indian god Vishnu on the front.

REVIVAL OF GOLD COINAGE
Contemporary with the bull and horseman coins, gold coinage was revived in northern India by the Kalachuri kings of Tripuri and Ratnapura, in a form apparently derived, but much modified, from the Gupta coinage. On the front of the coins was a seated figure of the goddess Lakshmi, based on the design used on the back of many Gupta gold coins. Filling the back was the name of the ruler in Nagari script.

The same design was adopted by the Chandellas of Jejakabhukti, the Paramas of Malwa, the Kachchhapaghatas of Gwalior, the Chaulukyas of Gujerat and the Gahadavalas of Kanauj, but on some issues Lakshmi was replaced by a different divine image. Although the Lakshmi coins were originally only gold, versions in silver and copper were also later issued.

INDIA
14 Silver Dramma *of Bhoja I, Pratihara king, with the image of the Hindu god Vishnu.*
15 Gold Coin *of Gangeyadeva, Kalachuri king, with the image of the goddess Sri.*
16 Gold Coin *of Mohammad bin Sam, Ghurid sultan, struck in Delhi.*

15 1005–35

14 *c.*850–80

16 1192–1206

During the tenth century punch-marked coins began to be issued again: gold coins made by the Chalukya kings of Kalyana (near Bombay), they were all broad thin discs stamped with as many as seven punches on one side. The central punch depicted a boar, a symbol for Vishnu and the emblem of the Chalukyas. The other punches were engraved with letters in southern Indian script and spelt out the Chalukya king's name. Similar coins with different symbols and inscriptions were also issued by the Kalachuris, who succeeded the Chalukyas as kings of Kalyana, the Kabdambas and the Cholas.

The emergence of a southern Indian gold coinage during the tenth and eleventh centuries coincided with the issue of the Lakshmi gold coins further north and, during the period of the Chola kings (ninth to thirteenth century), the northern designs began to have an influence on southern gold coinage. Gold, silver and copper coins, struck between two dies, and inscribed with the name of the king on the back were issued by the Cholas. The main issue, in the name of Uttamachola (about 973–85), was decorated on the front with the Chola symbols, a tiger and two fish. Later issues in the name of Rajaraja (about 985–1016) have a standing deity on the front and a seated deity and the royal name on the back. Rajaraja's coins were extensively copied by the later kings of southern India and in Sri Lanka during the twelfth and thirteenth centuries.

ISLAMIC INVASION

From the late seventh century Muslim traders and missionaries began to visit India, and Islamic coins from the Umayyad (661–750) and early 'Abbasid (750–1258) caliphates are frequently found in India. The first locally made Islamic coins appeared during the eighth century: tiny silver coins with Arabic inscriptions issued by a small Islamic settlement on the India–Pakistan border, near the mouth of the Indus River.

A large-scale occupation of Indian territory by Muslims did not occur, however, until the eleventh century, when Mahmud (998–1030), the Ghaznavid ruler of Afghanistan, invaded northwestern India. Mahmud struck Islamic coins in India of the type he already issued in Afghanistan, but on one of them he specified that it was struck for use in the cities captured during his *jihad* (holy war) against India. On some issues he took the opportunity of promoting Islam to his Indian subjects by inscribing the proclamation of Islamic faith in Nagari on the back of the coins (*see* Pakistan).

SULTANATE OF DELHI

Mahmud of Ghazna's invasion was soon followed by the full conquest of northern India by another Afghan prince, Mohammad bin Sam (1187–1206) of Ghor (southern Afghanistan). Mohammad's army advanced as far as Bengal, and gold and base-silver coins were issued in his name. Although the coins of his Afghanistan and Pakistan territories were inscribed in Arabic, most of his Indian issues bore Nagari inscriptions and used the gold Lakshmi and base-silver bull and horseman designs from the coins of the peoples he conquered. The exception was in Bengal, where his general issued gold coins inscribed in Arabic, but with a horseman design.

The horseman on the Bengal coins was not copied from the bull and horseman coins, but was a novel design modelled after the reclining bull on earlier Bengal silver coins of the kingdom of Harikela (*see* Bangladesh and Burma).

Muhammad's successors established themselves as sultans of northern India with Delhi as their capital and gradually introduced Islamic designs for their coins. The Lakshmi design was not reused after Mohammad bin Sam's issue, but Sultan Iltutmish (1211–36) reused the Bengal horseman design on large silver coins issued at Gaur in Bengal, and the bull and horseman issues continued until the time of Sultan Balban (1266–87).

Although the coinage of the Delhi sultanate from the late thirteenth century was an Islamic coinage with Arabic inscriptions as designs, some elements of Indian origin remained. Square coins were still occasionally issued, and many round coins had square frames around the inscription, recalling the popularity of the square shape in earlier Indian coinages. Indian inscriptions and symbols were also occasionally used as part of the Islamic design.

The proclamation of the Islamic faith: 'There is no God except God, Muhammad is the messenger of God' remained the main part of the design on many Dehli coins; otherwise the inscriptions named the sultan and his titles. The Delhi sultans often called themselves the 'Glory of the World and of the Faith' and the 'Father of the Victorious'. The date of issue, mint name and denomination also occasionally appeared. Some of the inscriptions are not Arabic, but Persian written in the Arabic script.

Gold, silver and copper coins were issued by the mints of the Delhi sultanate. In 1329 Sultan Mohammad ibn Tughlaq (1325–51) experimented with an issue of copper tokens representing silver and

17 1192–1206 20 1468–1500 21 1509–30 23 1605

18 1326

24 1669–72

22 1568

19 1511–26

19 GOLD COIN of Muzaffar II, Sultan of Gujerat.
20 COPPER COIN of Ghiyath Shah, Sultan of Malwa.
21 COPPER COIN of Krishna Raya, Vijayanagar king, with an image of the god Garuda.
22 GOLD MOHUR of Akbar, Mughal emperor, struck at Delhi.
23 GOLD MOHUR of Jahangir, Mughal emperor, with portrait of his father Akbar, struck in Agra.
24 GOLD MOHUR of Sunyatpha Udayaditya Simha, King of Assam.

INDIA

17 BASE-SILVER COIN of Mohammad bin Sam, Ghurid sultan, struck in Delhi.
18 GOLD COIN of Mohammad ibn Tughlaq, Delhi sultan, struck in Delhi.

base-silver denominations, inscribed with the words 'I hope this coin will be used in all payments'. Inevitably the production of unofficial copies of these tokens soon caused this experiment to fail.

THE INDEPENDENT SULTANATES

Under the later Delhi sultans the Muslim state expanded to include almost the whole of modern India, as well as Pakistan and Bangladesh. But from 1335 control began to disintegrate as local provincial rulers declared their independence from Delhi, local sultanates were established and southern India again came under Hindu rule.

Delhi sultan-style coins were issued by the independent sultanates of Madura (1334–71), Bengal (1339–1538), the Bahamani shahs of the Deccan (1346–1538), Kashmir (1346–1588), Sind (1390–1591), Jaunpur (1394–1476), Malwa (1401–1530), Gujerat (1403–1572), Berar (1487–1574), Bidar (1490–1619), Ahmadnagar (1491–1600), Bijapur (1499–1686) and Golconda (1518–1687).

The coin inscriptions and designs used by the local sultans normally reflected those in use by the Delhi sultans when they became independent, but in some sultanates particular adaptations were made. The Bengal sultans made large silver coins with decoratively arranged inscriptions; the Malwa sultans' coins were mostly square. On the coins of the Qutb Shahi sultans of Golconda was the threatening inscription 'God curse anyone who doubts the King's coin'.

KINGDOM OF VIJAYANAGAR

As the independent sultanates were throwing off the rule of Delhi, the far south of India gradually came under the control of a new Hindu kingdom based on Vijayanagar (City of Victory). The kingdom of Vijayanagar had been founded in 1336 by an Indian Muslim, Harihara, who converted to Hinduism.

The coins of the Vijayanagar kings were very different to contemporary Islamic issues. Like some earlier southern Indian coins, their gold and copper pieces had an animal or deity on the front and an Indian inscription naming the issuing king filling the back. The inscription was normally written in Nagari script, but some coins bore southern scripts, such as Kannada and Telegu. Harihara's coins depicted the monkey-god, Hanuman; later Vijayanagar coins used images of Garuda, the eagle-god, on whose back the god Vishnu rode, and of Rama and Varaha, both incarnations of Vishnu.

In 1565 Vijayanagar's northern Muslim neighbours inflicted a massive defeat on its army and the kingdom was fragmented. The Vijayanagar kings continued to issue coins in the territory they retained, but local rulers also issued coins in the Vijayanagar style without royal names. Gold and copper coins with gods or animals on the front and inscriptions on the back were issued by local rulers in the far south of India until the present century.

THE MUGHALS

The disintegration of the Delhi sultanate not only created the independent sultanates, but also left India open to external conquest. By the early sixteenth century the Delhi sultanate had been reduced to a strip across northern India from the Punjab to Bihar. In 1525 the army of the Central Asian prince Babur, who claimed both Mongol and Turkish descent, invaded India from Babur's base in Kabul (*see* Afghanistan). In 1526 he and his son Humayun overthrew the Delhi sultan Ibrahim and ruled northern India until Humayun was driven out in 1542 by the forces of the new sultan Sher Shah. During the

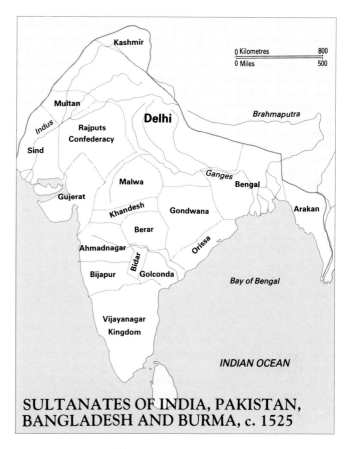

SULTANATES OF INDIA, PAKISTAN, BANGLADESH AND BURMA, c. 1525

A European traveller in India. This sixteenth-century Mughal miniature portrays the Indian view of the European traders who were establishing trading settlements around India's coast during the early Mughal period.

occupation of northern India both Babur and Humayun issued silver coins at Delhi, of the type they had already issued in Afghanistan to pay the Afghan troops.

A second invasion followed in 1556, when the army of Humayun's son Akbar (1556–1605) overthrew the Delhi sultanate. Akbar's conquest achieved what his grandfather and father had failed to do and he established a new Muslim dynasty to rule India. This new dynasty was known as the Mughal dynasty (a reference to Babur's claim to

Mongol descent). By his death Akbar had conquered the remaining independent sultanates of northern India and laid the foundation for his successors to bring the whole of India, Pakistan and Bangladesh under Mughal rule. Although his first coins were, like Humayun's, in the Afghan style, Akbar soon began to issue coins on which the Afghan designs were adapted to fit the coinage system that had been used by the Delhi sultanate.

Akbar's coins were often inscribed in Persian in Arabic script. He retained the religious inscriptions, but modified them to his own taste, issuing from 1584 coins inscribed with the acclamation ALLAH AKBAR (meaning 'God is the greatest'), a word play on his own name. He established a monetary system for his empire, with a gold, silver and copper coinage, which was to last until the nineteenth century. His gold and silver coins, called mohurs and rupees, were occasionally square.

MUGHAL PICTURE AND POEM COINS

Apart from one or two exceptions, Muslim rulers in India kept to the Islamic tradition of avoiding pictorial images on coins. The second Mughal emperor, Jahangir (1605–27), departed from this tradition in the first year of his reign with the issue of a gold coin portraying his father Akbar. He followed this with several issues bearing his own portrait on the front and his personal badge, the lion and sun, on the back. From 1619 Jahangir also issued a series of coins decorated on the front with zodiac symbols, indicating the month of issue.

The Mughals paid close attention to the designs of their coins and ensured that the inscriptions were written in an elegant style. From the time of Akbar they also used verse: 'By Akbar's seal this gold becomes bright; / His name on this gold is light upon light.' (on a gold mohur of Akbar); 'The face of this gold was decorated at Agrah / By Akbar's son, Jahangir Shah.' (on a gold mohur of Jahangir); 'While the heavens still turn, let this current be; / In the name of Jahangir Shah, this Lahore money.' (on a silver rupee of Jahangir).

MUGHAL CEREMONIAL COINS

For ceremonial purposes the Mughals also made both tiny and giant coins. The tiny coins, known as nisar (meaning 'scattering'), were thrown into crowds as largesse on official occasions. The giant coins were given to local princes and foreign guests at court. Contemporary records of the reign of Akbar speak of 100 mohur coins (weighing about 1 kg), but an immense gold 1000 mohur coin dated 1613 from the reign of Jahangir has recently been discovered. It is the world's largest and most valuable coin.

LATER MUGHALS

By the end of the seventeenth century the remarkable large coins and pictorial designs were no longer being used. From the reign of Aurangzib (1659–1707) religious inscriptions were also abandoned: the emperor thought that the sacred words would be defiled because the coins were used by his unbelieving Hindu subjects. Until the last Mughal issue, silver rupees struck at Delhi in 1842 by Emperor Muhammad Bahadur Shah II (1837–57), the coin design settled into a standard formula, with inscriptions naming the emperor and his titles, and a florid statement indicating the mint and date of issue. At some mints small symbols were added to the design to distinguish issues. However, on some occasions the formula was modified to include a verse like those used by Akbar and Jahangir.

MUGHAL MINTS

The Mughals issued coins from a large number of mints. While the empire was expanding and the emperor was based in his military camp, coins were struck with the mint name Urdu (meaning 'camp').

LOCAL MINT NAMES

City	Descriptive name
Agrah	City of the caliphate
Ahmadabad	Beauty among cities
Akbarabad	Royal abode
Aurangabad	Auspicious foundation
Delhi	Venerable
Hyderabad	City of the holy war
Jodhpur	City of the victor
Surat	Harbour of blessings

PORTUGUESE SETTLEMENTS

Coins have provided evidence of European trade with India since Roman times. During the Middle Ages Italian coins, in the form of Venetian gold ducats, again appeared on the southern Indian coast. A new phase of trade began in 1498, when an Indian navigator led the Portuguese explorer Vasco da Gama from East Africa across the Indian Ocean into the port of Calicut on the Kerala coast, the centrepoint of the spice trade. The Portuguese who followed Vasco da Gama soon established trading settlements along the Indian coast under the Portuguese crown, and issued their own coins for local use.

The first and most important of the Portuguese settlements was at the port of Goa, captured from the Sultanate of Bijapur in 1510. Copper coins were being issued in Goa before 1521. They were the same size as contemporary Bijapur coins, but were decorated with Portuguese designs: the royal arms and a globe on the smaller coins and a cross and globe on the larger denominations. Apart from the occasional use of the GA mint mark of Goa, the coins were uninscribed. Two gold coins, $\frac{1}{2}$ and 1 cruzado, are also attributed to the same period; both have the globe design, but the smaller coin also has the initial of Portugal's King Manuel (1495–1521).

The Portuguese mint in Goa continued to produce coins for local use until it was closed by the British in 1869. Of consistently bad workmanship, they were made by Indian craftsmen, but always with European designs. The arms of Portugal was the usual design, but other images were also used. The early gold issues often featured the standing figure of St Thomas the Apostle, the Christian patron saint of India. Other saints appeared on the silver denominations until 1726, when the royal portrait began to be used. Inscriptions were variable, and normally named only the denomination, date and mint until the royal portrait coins appeared, when the royal name and title also became regular features.

The Portuguese also issued coins at their settlements in Bacaim, Chaul, Diu and Damao, taken during the mid-sixteenth century from the sultanate of Gujerat. Similar designs to the Goa coins were used on these issues, but during the eighteenth century distinctive large tin coins were cast, similar to those issued by the British in Bombay. The Portuguese Gujerat coins were often cruder in design than the Goan issues, and never adopted the royal portrait design. An issue of copper coins was also made at the Portuguese southern Indian port of Cochin, before it fell into Dutch hands in 1669.

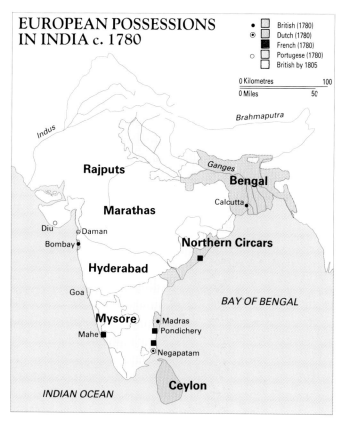

EUROPEAN POSSESSIONS IN INDIA c. 1780

British (1780)
Dutch (1780)
French (1780)
Portugese (1780)
British by 1805

0 Kilometres 100
0 Miles 50

Brahmaputra

Indus

Rajputs

Ganges

Bengal

Calcutta

Marathas

Diu
Daman
Bombay

Northern Circars

Hyderabad

Goa

BAY OF BENGAL

Mysore

Mahe

Madras
Pondichery
Negapatam

Ceylon

INDIAN OCEAN

areas further north, where Mughal coins were in use, from 1738 Pondichery made silver rupees in the name of the Mughal emperor, with a distinctive crescent mint mark.

THE BRITISH EAST INDIA COMPANY

Like the French, the British East India Company struck different series of coins to match local trading conditions. Three main minting centres were operated by the company in Madras, Bombay and Calcutta.

The earliest British Indian mint was at Madras, and it began issuing Vijayanagar-style coins during the 1640s. By the end of the century some of its copper issues were being struck with the company's orb trade mark. From about 1750 it also began striking silver rupees in the name of the Mughal emperor, distinguished by a lotus-flower mint

25 1687
26 1801

INDIA
25 SILVER RUPEE of the British East India Company, struck in Bombay.

26 SILVER 2 RUPEES of Tipu Sultan, ruler of Mysore, struck at Patan.

After the Goa mint had been closed, the coins for Portugal's Indian colonies were all made in Lisbon, the first being issued in 1871 and inscribed INDIA PORTUGUEZA for use in all the colonies still under Portuguese rule: Goa, Damao and Diu. They continued to be issued until 1962, when these territories were annexed by India.

DUTCH, DANISH AND FRENCH SETTLEMENTS

Portuguese ships were soon followed by other European merchantmen in search of spices, jewels and gold. The Dutch East India Company captured Cochin from the Portuguese but also opened trading posts at Pulikat (1610) and Negapatam (1690) on southern India's east coast. France, with its settlement at Pondichery, and Denmark, at Tranquebar, also established bases on the same coast. All three settlements issued gold, silver and copper coins based on Vijayanagar coinage; the Dutch and Danish also issued some lead coins.

The Dutch coins were mostly decorated with the VOC monogram of the Dutch East India Company, but all had designs on the back loosely copied from local southern Indian coins.

A few Danish coins were decorated with local animal designs, but most had the Danish king's monogram on their front, and inscriptions giving the date and denomination on the back. Some Danish coins also used the DAS monogram of the Danish Asiatic Company, which controlled the Tranquebar settlement.

The Pondichery mint issued two kinds of coin. For trade with southern India from 1700, it made gold coins, copied from a Vijayanagar issue, and silver and copper coins with local denominations but French designs, such as the fleur-de-lis and the cockerel. For trade with

mark. In 1807 the designs and denomination system of the mint's southern Indian coins was reformed, to make use of a new machine mint. Copper coins denominated as 5, 10, 20 and 40 cash; silver 1, 2 and 5 fanam and $\frac{1}{4}$ and $\frac{1}{2}$ pagoda, and gold 1 and 2 pagoda coins were issued. The copper and smaller silver coins were inscribed in English, Persian and Telegu; the larger silver and gold coins were also so inscribed, but had, in addition, pictorial designs: a tall temple (pagoda) on the front and a stylized Indian deity on the back. The machinery was also used to strike Mughal-style coins with the lotus mint mark.

Bombay also struck coins for the company during the eighteenth century. Its earliest coins followed the lead of local Portuguese issues, using the company arms or the British crown as the main design. For gold, silver and copper the Mughal denomination system was adopted, but later some tin coins, like the Portuguese issues for Diu, were also cast. In the second half of the eighteenth century the company trade mark was also used as a design.

Mughal designs predominated on the British coins struck at Calcutta and its subsidiary mints at Benares (Varanasi) and Farukhabad. Original designs did not appear until the late eighteenth century, when a series of copper coins with an added Nagari script began to be issued.

In the late eighteenth century another new British coinage began to appear in India. The development of steam-driven minting machinery in Britain meant that it was cheaper to make copper coins in Britain and ship them out to India. The first consignment was of copper $\frac{1}{2}$, 1, $1\frac{1}{2}$ and 2 pice coins with a pan-balance design for Bombay (64 pice = 16 anna = 1 rupee). Later issues of the 1 pice were

27 1828

28 1892

29 1862

30 1974

INDIA

27 SILVER RUPEE *of Akbar II, Mughal emperor, struck in Shah-jahanabad (Delhi).*
28 COPPER 2 PAISAS *of Sāyaji Rao, ruler of the State of Baroda.*
29 COPPER ½ ANNA *of Queen Victoria, struck in Bombay.*
30 CUPRO-NICKEL 10 RUPEES *of the Republic, a commemorative coin issued for the United Nations Food and Agriculture Organization to promote family planning.*

denominated ¼ anna. Two sets of coins were sent to Madras: coins denominated as fractions of a rupee decorated with the company arms arrived in 1794; coins denominated in the southern Indian cash with an inscriptional design arrived in 1803. Bengal's first consignment did not arrive until 1831.

From 1835 the three main mints of the company united to produce a unified coinage for the whole of British India, based on the Mughal standard, but with British designs; the company arms on the copper $\frac{1}{12}$ anna, ½ pice, ¼ and ½ anna, and a portrait of the British king, William IV, on the silver ¼, ½ and 1 rupee and the gold 1 and 2 mohur.

THE PRINCELY STATES

The impact of European mercantile and military intervention in India gradually undermined Mughal control. This had two effects on the coinage. The first, the introduction of European-style coinages, has been described above; the second was the end of the right to make coins by independent local princes who had thrown off Mughal rule.

A few areas continued to issue independent coins throughout the period of Mughal rule. Among them were the southern India successors to the Vijayanagars, who continued to issue Vijayanagar-style coins. The other areas of independent coinage were in the far west and north east.

In the west the Rajput rulers of Kutch, Nawanagar and Porbandar struck silver and copper coins in the style of the former Gujerat sultans, some with added Nagari inscriptions giving the issuers' name. In the north west the mountain kingdoms of Cooch Bihar, Assam, Tripura, Manipur and Cachar issued coins with Bengali or other local Indian inscriptions. Of these only the coins of Tripura had pictorial designs, featuring mythical animals of deities. Most of these coinages were large, round silver coins derived from the issues of the Bengal sultanate (*see* Bangladesh), but in Assam and Manipur other shapes were preferred: octagonal in Assam and square in Manipur. These states were still issuing coins during the nineteenth century, when the Kingdom of Sikkim also issued coins, and Cooch Bihar and Tripura continued to strike presentation coins until 1923 and 1934 respectively.

The first serious internal threat to Mughal supremacy was the uprising led by the Marathas, who, from their base in Bijapur, gained control of central India. At mints throughout the territory they and their supporters controlled, silver and copper coins imitating Mughal issues were struck. In the southern parts of their territory at Satara some coins with Nagari inscriptions naming Sivaji, the Maratha leader

(1664–80), were also issued. The Marathas came close to taking power from the Mughals, but an Afghan invasion of northwestern India, taking advantage of the Maratha uprising, destroyed the Maratha army in 1761. The Afghan invaders also issued Mughal-style coins at mints in India, in the name of the Afghan ruler Ahmad Shah (1747–72).

From the time of the Maratha uprising Mughal India gradually disintegrated into a myriad of small independent states and foreign enclaves. Most issued their own coins, normally modelled on the Mughal coinage, but now often with Indian inscriptions and pictorial designs. The Mughals had often used small symbols to distinguish different mints and issues, and local states used these symbols as their distinctive pictorial coin designs: fish (Awadh), sword (Baroda), dagger (Bharatpur), bow and arrow or trident (Gwalior), sun face (Indore), branch (Jaipur), sword (Jodhpur) and leaf (Kashmir).

In the late eighteenth and early nineteenth centuries the largest independent coin-issuers were the Sikh kings of the Punjab, the Nizams of Hyderabad and the Rajas of Mysore.

Although many of the smaller states remained under the nominal rule of the Mughal emperor, they gradually came under British control, either by force or to protect themselves from stronger neighbours.

Tipu's tiger: This macabre mechanical toy belonged to Tipu Sultan of Mysore, opponent to the British East India Company's imperial ambitions.

Some British influence was noticeable on the coins of the princely states. European-style coats of arms appeared on the coins of Awadh from 1819 and Tripura from 1869; the British lion decorated the coins of Mysore from 1833. Queen Victoria's portrait was featured on the coins of Bharatpur and Bindraban from 1858, and her name appeared in Persian on the coins of Jaipur, Jodhpur and Kutch from 1857, and in English on Bundi coins from 1858.

The introduction of British imperial coins in 1862 did not put an end to the coinages of the princely states, some of which were still being issued until independence in 1948. Some states did, however, modify their issues to match the 1862 coins: Alwar in 1877, Bikanir in 1892, Dewas in 1888, Dhar in 1887 and Sailana in 1908, all of which issued machine-made coins with the British monarch's face.

BRITISH RULE

The 1862 coinage was issued in the name of Queen Victoria as sovereign ruler of India. Full control of India was taken by the British government from the British East India Company following the Indian Mutiny of 1857. The new coins were struck at the former company mints in Calcutta, Bombay and Madras. All denominations had the crowned portrait of Victoria on the front and a decorative border containing an inscription naming India and giving the denomination and date on the back.

Copper $\frac{1}{12}$ anna, $\frac{1}{2}$ pice, $\frac{1}{4}$ and $\frac{1}{2}$ anna, silver 2 anna, $\frac{1}{4}$, $\frac{1}{2}$ and 1 rupee and gold 1 mohur coins were struck, according to the Mughal system of 64 pice = 16 anna = 1 rupee and 15 rupee = 1 mohur. The British authorities also considered issuing gold 5 and 10 rupee coins, but only the 5 rupee was issued, briefly in 1870 and soon withdrawn.

Apart from the change in Victoria's title (from Queen to Empress from 1877), the imperial coinage continued unchanged until the end of her reign in 1901. Under Edward VII (1901–10) a new design for the back, a floral wreath around the inscription and a crown above, was introduced for the silver coins. The inscription also included the denomination in Urdu. In 1911 the design for the silver coins reverted to the Victorian border-pattern, but the Urdu was retained.

In 1906 a new denomination in a new metal was introduced: a scallop-edged cupro-nickel 1 anna. The reverse inscription of this coin included the denomination written in English and in four Indian scripts: Nagari, Urdu, Tamil and Bengali. In 1918, during the reign of George V (1910–36), another new cupro-nickel coin was introduced: a square 2 anna in place of the earlier silver issue. In the following year cupro-nickel 4 and 8 anna were also issued instead of the silver $\frac{1}{4}$ and $\frac{1}{2}$, but the silver issues were resumed in 1925.

George V also issued a gold 15 rupee coin, of the same weight as the British sovereign, in 1918. In the same year the Bombay mint struck British sovereigns of the usual design, distinguished from Royal Mint strikings by an I for India mint mark below the hooves of St George's horse on the back. Gold did not circulate widely in India, as the silver rupee was the main coin. The Bombay mint did, however, occasionally also issue gold 1 tola (the Indian ounce) bullion pieces for the Indian gold trade.

The economic effects of the Second World War caused silver to be removed from the Indian coinage system. During the war the shortage of nickel had led to the use of brass for the cupro-nickel denominations, but after the war the use of cupro-nickel was resumed. Before the war bronze $\frac{1}{2}$ pice and $\frac{1}{4}$ anna, cupro-nickel 1 and 2 anna and silver $\frac{1}{4}$, $\frac{1}{2}$ and 1 rupee coins were issued.

Buddhist lion emblem from the Asokan pillar at Sarnath. The extent of the Indian empire of the Mauryan king Asoka is marked by the widespread finds of Mauryan silver punch-marked coins.

During 1945–7, as coinage recommenced, new denominations were issued: bronze 1 pice (a holed coin without the king's portrait, first issued in 1943), cupro-nickel 1 and 2 anna and nickel $\frac{1}{4}$, $\frac{1}{2}$ and 1 rupee. To distinguish the nickel coins from their silver predecessors they were given a new design on the back, featuring a tiger. The denomination on the new rupee was written in English, Nagari and Urdu. These changes were short lived because India gained full independence in 1948.

INDEPENDENCE

Coins in the name of the Republic of India were not issued until 1950, when a series with the same denominations as the last British issues was struck at the Bombay and Calcutta mints. The new coins all had the emblem of the republic on the front: the three lions device from the top of the ancient Asoka column at Sarnath, made for the Mauryan king Asoka (third century BC). Mauryan horse and bull designs appeared on the back of the lower denominations, but the nickel coins were decorated on the back with two ears of wheat.

In 1957 a decimal coinage was introduced with 100 paisa = 1 rupee. The Asokan lions design was retained, but the backs of all denominations were purely inscriptional, naming the denomination and date. Bronze 1, cupro-nickel 2, 3, 5 and 10 and nickel 25 paisa were issued, distinguished by size and shape: 1 and 25 paisa round, 2 and 10 paisa scallop edged, 3 paisa hexagonal and 5 paisa square. From 1960 a round nickel 50 paisa was introduced, and in 1962 a round nickel rupee with the same wheatear design as the pre-decimal issue.

Until 1964 the coin inscriptions called the paisa a *naye paisa* (new paisa). From 1965 a new set of paisa coins without the *naye* inscription commenced. The new coins were made of aluminium and 1, 2, 3 and 5 pieces were issued. In 1967 the 10 paisa denomination was changed from cupro-nickel to brass and again in 1971 to aluminium. From 1972 the nickel ¼, ½ and 1 rupee denominations were converted to cupronickel. As part of these changes, a new denomination, 20 paisa, was tried from 1968, but abandoned in 1971. This brass coin had a lotus blossom on the back, the only pictorial design used on a paisa denomination.

Since 1976 the Indian government has also issued for circulation special coins promoting the UN Food and Agriculture Organization. These 5, 10, 20, 25 and 50 paisa coins have pictorial designs referring to agricultural development. Collectors' commemoratives have also been issued since 1969.

BANGLADESH

FIRST COINS:	*c.* second century BC
FIRST DECIMAL COINS:	1961
MAIN MINT:	Bombay
CURRENCY:	taka

THROUGHOUT most of its history the region now known as Bangladesh has used the coinages of neighbouring India. The earliest coins recorded from Bangladesh are silver punch-marked coins and cast-copper coins of the kinds used throughout the third and second centuries BC. It is very likely that some of the cast-copper coins were made within Bangladesh, but no varieties specific to the area have yet been identified.

There is no firm evidence of coins being made locally until the late Gupta period, when Sasanka, king of Gauda (*c.* AD 600–25), issued Gupta-style gold coins with religious designs. On the front of the coin was the Hindu god Siva riding on his bull companion, Nandi, and on the back was Siva's wife Parvati in the form of the mother goddess Sri, seated on a lotus and being bathed by elephants. During the later seventh and early eighth centuries, Gupta-style gold coins, with a standing king on the front and a standing goddess on the back, were issued by the Chandra Dynasty, which succeeded Sasanka in the southeastern corner of Bangladesh.

The unidentified successors of the Chandras replaced the gold coinage copied from the Gupta Dynasty of India with a silver coinage copied from their eastern neighbours, the Chandra Dynasty of Arakan in Burma. These silver issues, with a reclining bull on the front and a symbolic representation of the mother goddess Sri on the back, were inscribed with the name of the city of Harikela, in south east Bengal. Versions of the Harikela coins continued to be issued through the eighth and ninth centuries. Archaeological finds suggest that Indian, Burmese and Middle Eastern Islamic coins also came into the region during the same period, and contemporary inscriptions indicate that

cowrie shells circulated as money in Bengal during the medieval period.

ISLAMIC RULE

During the 1190s Muhammad Bakhtyar Khilji, leading the army of Mohammad bin Sam, the Ghorid ruler of Afghanistan, invaded Bengal as part of his master's conquest of northern India. Bakhtyar issued gold coins in the name of his master in Bengal. They had Arabic inscriptions, but depicted a charging horseman on the front in a design which was closely based on the reclining bull design previously circulating in Bangladesh. The Sultans of Delhi, who inherited Mohammad bin Sam's conquests, continued to strike Islamic coins for Bengal. Most of these had purely inscriptional designs, but one issue of Sultan Iltutmish (1211–36) reused the horseman design. The Delhi Sultanate coins for Bengal were large silver pieces known as 'tankas'. Many of them were issued in the name of the local governor.

In 1339 the local governors established their independence as sultans in their own right and continued to issue the large silver tankas in their own name until the Delhi Sultanate re-established control in 1538. Like the Delhi issues, the Bengal Sultanate coins had inscriptional designs which proclaimed the Islamic faith, but they also gave the sultan's full name and his elaborate titles, such as 'Father of the victorious, Glory of the world and the faith, Fighter of infidels, may Allah perpetuate his kingdom'. Occasionally short Bengali inscriptions were included in the designs.

Apart from Chittagong, the mints for these coins were either unidentifiable or not in Bangladesh but across the Indian border in western Bengal. Towards the end of the sultanate period Chittagong fell into the hands of the Kings of Arakan, who issued silver tankas and ¼ tankas with Arabic, Bengali and Burmese inscriptions there.

THE MUGHALS

In 1576 Bengal was absorbed into the newly-established Mughal Empire by Akbar, its first emperor (1556–1605), and the Mughal

BANGLADESH
1 GOLD SUVARNA of Sasanka, King of Gauda, with an image of the god Siva.
2 SILVER TANKA of the city of Harikela.
3 SILVER TANKA of Firuz Shah, Sultan of Bengal.
4 SILVER TANKA of Nara Narayana, King of Cooch Bihar.
5 SILVER TANKA of Ratna Manikya, King of Tripura.
6 SILVER RUPEE of the British East India Company, Bengal Presidency.
7 STEEL 50 POISHAS of the Republic.

coinage system, based on the gold mohur and silver rupee, was soon esablished in Bengal (*see* India). During the reign of Akbar's son, Jahangir (1605–26), a mint to coin gold and silver was opened at Dacca (renamed Jahangirnagar). It continued to produce coins occasionally for the next century.

BRITISH RULE
Bengal, because of its position at the mouth of the Ganges, acquired many European trading settlements during the seventeenth century. Few European coins entered the area, but the Mughal-style coins made by the Europeans in their other Indian territories were freely imported. By 1772 the British had wrested control of the whole of the Bengal area, both from the Mughals and from their European competitors. At Calcutta the British East India Company opened a mint to issue silver rupees in the name of the Mughal emperor to circulate throughout Bengal. Company coins and, from 1862, British coins made at Calcutta, Bombay and Madras circulated in Bangladesh until the end of British rule in southern Asia in 1947, when eastern Bengal, known as East Pakistan, became part of the Islamic state of Pakistan.

INDEPENDENCE
Until 1971, when East Pakistan declared its independence from Pakistan as Bangladesh (i.e. the State of Bengal), Pakistani coins circulated in eastern Bengal in place of the earlier British issues. Coins for the People's Republic of Bangladesh were first issued in 1973, and the Pakistani paisa and rupee were renamed poisha and taka (after the earlier tanka coinage). The 1973 issue consisted of aluminium 5 and 10, steel 25 and cupro-nickel 50 poisha coins, with the same shapes as their Pakistani predecessors. All denominations had the state emblem on the front, a lotus rising from water, between two wheatears, but various designs representing Bengali agriculture and wildlife appeared on the back. The inscriptions were in Bengali.

In 1974 a 1 poisha was added to the series, as part of a United Nations' Food and Agriculture Organization set for general circulation. A second FAO set was introduced in 1977 and is still in use. The taka denomination was added to the series in 1975, during the first FAO issue, but has not been issued since 1977.

NEPAL

FIRST COINS:	sixth century AD
FIRST DECIMAL COINS:	1932
MAIN MINT:	Katmandu
CURRENCY:	rupee

ALTHOUGH Indian second-century BC Punch-marked silver and second-century AD Kushan copper coins have been reported from Nepal, the earliest coins issued in the country appeared during the late sixth century AD. These copper coins were issued by the Licchavi kingdom of Nepal and bear religious designs of Indian origin, including the Hindu goddess Sri and the god Vaishravana; animals: the lion, bull, cow and calf, elephant and winged horse; and religious symbols: the sun, trident, vase and srivatsa (Sri's symbolic representation). The Indian inscriptions mostly refer to deities, but some name rulers. This coinage seems to have continued until the early eighth century.

THE MALLA KINGDOMS
From the eighth until the seventeenth century only a handful of Nepalese coins has so far been identified. Small gold, silver and copper coins with winged-lion or trident designs have been attributed to Nepalese rulers of the twelfth to sixteenth centuries.

Substantial issuing of coinage for Nepal did not recommence until the mid-seventeenth century, when large issues of silver coins were made by the three Malla kingdoms of Kathmandu, Patan and Bhatgaon. All these issues followed the model of the sixteenth-century coins of Kathmandu and Dholakar, which consisted of silver tankas with designs and denominations modified from the coins of the Bengal Sultanate (*see* India and Bangladesh). Until the second half of the seventeenth century garbled Arabic inscriptions formed an important part of the coin designs used by all three kingdoms.

During the 1650s and 1660s distinctive designs were gradually introduced, a 'star' on the Patan coins, a triangle on the Bhatgaon coins

NEPAL

1 COPPER COIN of *Jishnugupta, Licchavi king.*
2 SILVER MOHUR of *Pratapa Malla, King of Katmandu.*
3 SILVER MOHUR of *Jagatprakash Malla, King of Bhatgaon.*
4 SILVER MOHUR of *Yoga Narendra Malla, King of Patan, issued in the name of his queen, Narendra Lakshmi.*
5 GOLD PRESENTATION COIN of *Rana Bahadur, Gorkha king.*
6 COPPER 2 PAISAS of *Prithvi Vira Vikrama, Gorkha king.*
7 ALUMINIUM 10 PAISAS of *Mahendra Vira Vikrama, Gorkha king.*

1 652–70
2 1641–7
3 1644–73
4 1685–1705
5 1777–99
6 1893
7 1967

MINTS OF NEPAL, SIXTEENTH TO EIGHTEENTH CENTURIES

- Mint towns

0 Kilometres 300
0 Miles 200

TIBET

NEPAL

Gorkha • Bhatgaon
Katmandu • • Patan • Dolakha
○Lucknow Gogra Gandak Bagmati Darjeeling○

INDIA Mount Everest SIKKIM

BENGAL

THE GORKHAS

The three kingdoms issued coins until they were all overthrown in 1768–9 by Prithvi Narayan, the Shah ruler of the Kingdom of Gorkha, west of Kathmandu. The Gorkhas continued the mohar coinage, using square- and lotus-frame designs. They also issued gold mohars and copper paisa. The copper coins imitated contemporary Indian paisa until the late nineteenth century, when copper coins with designs like the silver, but often featuring two crossed Gorkha knives, were made.

In 1932 a new denomination system was introduced, based on the Indian rupee divided into 100 paisa. Silver 20 and 50 paisa and 1 rupee coins were issued, all with the traditional design, with a trident in the centre of the square and a sword in the centre of the lotus. Between 1933 and 1947 copper 1, 2 and 5 paisa coins with the crossed-knife design were also introduced.

Although the traditional designs still play an important part in the coinage, a variety of other motifs have appeared in recent decades. A sunrise over the mountains was used on an issue of 1, 2, 5, 10, 20, 25 and 50 paisa coins in 1953 and a royal portrait on the higher-denomination 50 paisa and rupee of the same issue. Since 1956 the royal crown has been the most commonly featured emblem of the Gorkha king of Nepal. After coronation and United Nations' Food and Agriculture Organization issues in 1974, commemorative coins have also been produced for general circulation. The current coins are aluminium 1, 5, 10 and 25 paisa and cupro-nickel 50 paisa and 1, 2 and 5 rupee coins, although denominations of rupee and above are rarely seen in circulation. The 1984 issue of cupro-nickel coins all had designs promoting family planning.

and curved lines on the Kathmandu coins, all separating or framing inscriptional designs naming and titling the issuing king in Nepali. Many other decorative elements, including religious symbols, were also occasionally featured. The curved lines on the Kathmandu issues were borrowed from the design of the silver coins of Mughal India.

By the 1640s the denomination system of the Bengal coins had been abandoned in favour of a local system with a smaller silver coin, the mohar, weighing about 5.5 g as the main denomination. Some very small fractions of the mohar were issued, and during the mid-eighteenth century Nepal produced the smallest coins ever used: gold $\frac{1}{2048}$ mohar, weighing 0.002 g, cut quarters of official $\frac{1}{512}$ mohar coins.

Both during the Malla period and later, Nepal exported silver coins, often debased, in quantity to Tibet (*see* China). The exports continued until a regular issue began in Tibet in the late 1700s.

1 *c.*1920
2 1974

BHUTAN

1 SILVER ½ RUPEE of *King Ugyen Wangchuck.*
2 CUPRO-NICKEL NGULTRUM of *King Jigme Singye Wangchuck.*

BHUTAN

FIRST COINS:	c. 1790
FIRST DECIMAL COINS:	1966
MAIN MINT:	Royal Mint
CURRENCY:	ngultrum

Bhutan, alone of all the coin-issuing mountain statelets of India's northeastern border, has survived with its sovereignty intact to the present day. It maintains the coinage tradition established in the north east by the Hindu kingdoms created after the demise of the Bengal Sultanate (see India and Bangladesh).

Silver coins with Indian Nagari inscriptions, replacing the Arabic inscriptions used on the tankas of the sultanate, were issued from the sixteenth century by the kingdoms of Cooch Bihar, Assam, Jaintipur, Kachar, Manipur and Tripura. Until the end of the eighteenth century the coins of Cooch Bihar circulated in Bhutan. From around 1790 the Bhutanese made their own crude debased copies of the Cooch Bihar silver coins, with inscriptional designs.

BRITISH PROTECTORATE

In the mid-nineteenth century, when Bhutan became a British protectorate, British Indian coins also circulated in the area, but the issue of bronze versions of the Cooch Bihar coins with additional religious symbols continued until the 1920s.

INDEPENDENCE

The rupee and paisa coinages of British, and then republican India, provided Bhutan with most of its coinage until 1974, when a decimal coinage (100 chetrum [paisa] = 1 ngultrum [rupee]) with the portrait of the Bhutanese king Jigme Singye Wangchuck on the front and religious symbols on the back was introduced. Aluminium 5 and 10 and cupro-nickel 25 chetrum and 1 ngultrum pieces were issued.

Coins with similar designs had been made for use as royal gifts from 1928 to 1986. The 1966 issue used the contemporary decimal system of India (1 rupee = 100 naya paisa). Gold presentation coins were also struck for the 1966 issue and were denominated in sertums (1 sertum = 100 rupees).

In 1979 the currency coins acquired a new design when the royal portrait was replaced with religious symbols, such as the conch and wheel.

SRI LANKA

FIRST COINS:	first century BC
FIRST DECIMAL COINS:	1870
MAIN MINT:	Royal Mint
CURRENCY:	rupee

The earliest coins recorded in Sri Lanka were imported Indian punch-marked silver coins. Although issued during the late third and second centuries BC, their appearance on the island seems to date from the first century BC. Excavations at various sites suggest that, alongside the Indian silver coins, two groups of large copper coins were used. These seem to have been made in Sri Lanka, but derived their designs from contemporary Indian copper coins, which have also been found there.

The earliest Sri Lankan copper coins appear to have been round coins with a variety of Indian symbols, copied from Indian cast-copper coins, on both sides. The second group were rectangular and are now known as 'Lakshmi plaques', because of the standing image of the Hindu goddess Lakshmi on the front. The back of the Lakshmi coins was decorated by a symbolic tree design with its foliage in the form of a swastika. The same swastika-tree motif also appeared on the earlier coins. Both issues, like most contemporary Indian coins were without inscriptions. Although these coins had designs apparently of Hindu origin, they seem to have been issued during the period when Buddhism began to be an important force in Sri Lanka.

ROMAN COINS

The subsequent early history of Sri Lanka's coinage is still unclear. The earliest fixed point is the arrival on the island during the fourth century AD of large quantities of Roman bronze coins. There is considerable archaeological and literary evidence of Roman trade with southern India and Sri Lanka during the early centuries of the Christian era, and it seems likely that these coins arrived as part of that trade, perhaps as scrap metal. People living on the island readily adopted them as money and, when the supply ran out, made their own copies for local use. Large hoards of these Roman and imitation Roman coins are still found in Sri Lanka.

SRI LANKAN KINGDOM

Apart from the imitations, there seems to have been no local coin

1 FIRST CENTURY   **2** 1197–1200   **3** FOURTEENTH CENTURY   **4** 1645   **5** 1645

SRI LANKA
1 COPPER COIN *with an image of the goddess Lakshmi.*
2 COPPER COIN *of Queen Lilavati.*
3 COPPER COIN *of the Kingdom of Jaffna.*
4 SILVER 2 TANGAS *of the Portuguese colony, struck in Goa, later countermarked by the Dutch in Jaffna.*
5 SILVER TANGA *of the Portuguese colony, struck in Goa, later countermarked by the Dutch in Galle.*

production until the ninth or tenth century, when copper coins with Hindu designs, copied from contemporary southern Indian issues, began to appear. The commonest designs recorded are a bull, a vase, fish and a lion. The appearance of coin designs from southern India in Sri Lanka seems to reflect the migration of the Tamil and other southern Indian peoples onto the island.

During the eleventh century a new series of gold coins, also with designs of southern Indian origin, were issued. This series adopted the Chola Dynasty standing king and seated goddess designs (ultimately of northern Indian, Kushan origin), but added the inscription *Sri Lankesvara* (Lord of Sri Lanka). It has been suggested by historians that these coins were issued by a Chola king, Rajaraja (985–1016), following his conquest of the island.

King and goddess designs and inscriptions were a successful innovation and appeared on a long series of coins until the late thirteenth century. After Rajaraja's issue, various religious inscriptions were adopted until the reign of the Sri Lankan king Vijaya Bahu (1055–1111), who introduced a series of king and goddess gold, silver and copper coins, inscribed with the royal name. In the fourteenth century the seated goddess was replaced on a Tamil issue by a reclining bull design, but the standing king on the front was retained.

During the Middle Ages Islamic coins from Iran and Egypt arrived on the island with the Arab and Persian merchants who used it as a base for their trade with eastern India and south east Asia. There is no evidence to indicate whether these coins circulated beyond the trading settlements.

PORTUGUESE AND DUTCH RULE

The voyage of discovery by the Portuguese navigator Vasco da Gama (1498) brought Sir Lanka within direct reach of Europe. A Portuguese presence was established on the island during the first decades of the sixteenth century, but without any substantial settlement. The Portuguese traders brought their own coins from Portugal and from their settlements in India.

By the middle of the century Portuguese control had extended to most of the island, even though the local rulers retained some autonomy. The Portuguese did not, however, issue any coins in Sri Lanka until the beginning of the seventeenth century, when silver and copper coins like those made by the Portuguese in Goa (*see* India) were struck at Colombo, distinguished from their Indian issues by their mint marks. In 1640 the Colombo mint was closed and the Goa mint made coins specifically for Sri Lanka until 1649, when their issue ceased.

The Portuguese stopped making coins for Sri Lanka because they were gradually losing control of the island to the Dutch, who, between 1612 and 1658, united with the local king of Kandy to expel the Portuguese. During the same period, the Dutch East India Company established trading settlements to exploit the island trade. At first they did not issue coinage, but countermarked the coins in local use with the company's voc monogram.

Surviving pieces provide clear evidence of the coins in circulation during the mid-seventeenth century. As well as the Portuguese local and Indian issues, coins from Spanish Mexico, Portuguese Malacca (*see* Malaysia), Mughal India, Saffavid Iran and China have been recorded with the countermark.

Many of the Iranian coins are of the type known as 'larins', made from bent wire stamped between coin dies (*see* Maldive Islands). Seventeenth-century travellers' reports make it clear that larins were widely used as trade coins along the eastern coast of the Arabian Sea, from Iran to Sri Lanka. The Dutch also imported copper coins from their settlements in Indonesia, silver and gold coins from the Netherlands and gold coins from Venice in Italy.

From 1660 the Dutch East India Company began to strike copper coins for local use in Sri Lanka. At first the coins were simply stamped on both sides with their denomination, but from 1782 the voc monogram and date were added. Both issues included curious bar-shaped coins, known as 'bonks'. These were made from chopped-up bars of Japanese copper, stamped at each end with coin dies (*see also* Indonesia and St Helena). In 1784 a silver coin, denominated as a rupee, like the contemporary Mughal coinage in India, was also introduced. Its designs were crudely copied from Mughal issues.

BRITISH RULE

During the Napoleonic Wars Britain seized control of Sri Lanka, and in 1798 a formal British government, under the British East India Company, was established. British coinage for the island commenced in 1801 with issues of copper coins inscribed CEYLON GOVERNMENT. They were denominated according to the Dutch stuiver and rixdollar (= 48 stuiver). Silver coins were also issued from 1803. Some of the

SRI LANKA

6 Copper Stuiver *of the Dutch East India Company, struck in Colombo.*
7 Copper 4¾ Stuiver *of the Dutch East India Company, struck in Colombo from Japanese bar copper.*
8 Copper ¹⁄₂₄ Rupee *of the British Government of Ceylon.*
9 Copper 5 cents *of Queen Victoria, struck at the Royal Mint, London.*
10 Cupro-Nickel 10 Rupees, *struck at the Royal Mint, Llantrisant.*

6 1783
8 1803
7 1785
9 1870
10 1987

coins were hand-made on the island and some were made by machine in England, but all had the same design: an elephant on the front and the denomination, expressed as a fraction of the rixdollar, on the back.

The local issues were replaced in 1816 because in the previous year a new design with the British king's portrait had been adopted for the English-made coins. Copper ½, 1 and 2 stuiver coins with the portrait of George III were struck, and then the issue ceased, except for a silver rixdollar with the portrait of George IV struck in 1821.

No more coins bearing the name Ceylon were struck until a new issue, produced at the British mint in Calcutta and denominated according to the Indian rupee, was introduced in 1872. Between 1821 and 1872 coinage was supplied to the Ceylon government in the form of British sterling coins, struck at the Royal Mint, but in denominations suited to the island's rixdollar system. From 1828 copper ½ farthings and, from 1839, ¼ farthings were struck specifically for use in Sri Lanka. A silver 1½ pence coin was also introduced in 1834 (*see* Jamaica).

The 1872 issue was of copper ¼, ½, 1 and 5 cents, with Queen Victoria's portrait (copied from the 1866 Hong Kong coinage) on the front and a palm tree on the back. The inscription on the back named the colony and denomination, the latter being written in Singhalese and Tamil as well as English. From 1892 silver 10, 25 and 50 cent coins were also produced. The rupee, equal to 100 cents, was not issued, but Indian issues were officially in use on the island from the 1820s.

The British rupee and cent coinage system remained in use until 1951, four years after full independence was granted. Some changes were made to the design and form of the coinage, such as the introduction of a cupro-nickel square 5 cent in 1909 and of scallop-edged 2 and 10 cent pieces in 1944.

INDEPENDENCE

The introduction of a non-British coinage took place in 1963. The British denomination system was retained, but with an aluminium 1 cent and a cupro-nickel rupee. All denominations were decorated with the national emblem, a lion within the Buddhist Wheel of the Law.

The island became the Republic of Sri Lanka in 1972 and a new issue was made the following year, with the same designs and denominations, but including the new name instead of Ceylon. In 1984 new 2 and 5 rupee coins were added to the series. Commemorative coins of these denominations and the 1 rupee have also been issued since 1957.

MALDIVE ISLANDS

FIRST COINS:	seventeenth century
FIRST DECIMAL COINS:	1960
MAIN MINT:	Royal Mint
CURRENCY:	rufiyaa

THE earliest coins recorded from the Maldive Islands are some first-century BC Roman republican silver pieces found buried in a Buddhist monument. They had probably arrived in the East during

that century, but the date of their burial is not known. The earliest evidence of coins actually in use in the islands is from the seventeenth century, when a French traveller noticed Iranian silver larins, coins of silver wire, in use. Some locally made larins have also been found.

The first coins so far known to have been made in the Maldives are silver coins, denominated as larins but circular in shape, issued on the island of Mali by the local sultans. The earliest recorded examples are of Sultan Ibrahim Sikandar I (1648–87); they are inscribed in Arabic with the name and title of the sultan, the date of issue and the name of the mint. The normal title used on these coins by the Mali sultans was Sultan of Land and Sea.

MALDIVE ISLANDS

1 SILVER LARIN, *from the Persian Gulf.*
2 SILVER LARIN *of Sultan Mohammad Muhi al-Din.*
3 COPPER 4 LARINS *of Sultan Mohammad Imad al-Din V Iskandar.*
4 NICKEL-BRASS 50 LAARIS *of Sultan Mohammad Farid Didi.*

BRITISH PROTECTORATE

Although the islands were a British protectorate from 1887, and had during earlier periods been under both Portuguese and Dutch economic and political influence, round larins inscribed in Arabic were issued by the sultanate of the Maldives until 1913, when the last set of bronze 1 and 4 larin coins with the traditional inscriptional designs were struck for the islands in Birmingham, England. Alongside these and earlier bronze coins, British Indian and Sri Lankan silver and bronze coins were also used.

From the 1913 issue until a decimal issue began in 1960, India and Sri Lanka provided the islands with all the coins needed for local circulation. The 1960 issue of the sultanate borrowed the decimal system of contemporary Sri Lanka, but with a rupee, called a rufiyaa, divided into cents, called laari, after the traditional larins. Bronze 1 and 2 and brass 5, 10, 25 and 50 laari coins were issued, all decorated with the national emblem, a crescent and star before a palm tree, flanked by flags. Apart from the denomination and date numerals, the coins were still inscribed in Arabic. The Maldives became independent in 1965 and a republic in 1968. Since 1970 the coins have been issued in the name of the Republic of the Maldives (in English only), and since 1984 with designs illustrating local wildlife and history. The national emblem was, however, retained for the 1 rufiyaa coin introduced in 1982. Higher denominations have been issued only as commemoratives.

BURMA

FIRST COINS:	seventh–eighth century
FIRST DECIMAL COINS:	1952
MAIN MINT:	Berlin
CURRENCY:	kyat

C OINAGE was adopted in the country now known as Burma a few centuries before it was invaded by the Burmese people. The first coins were issued in the kingdom of Arakan on Burma's western coast by kings of the Chandra Dynasty. Silver coins with a reclining bull or a conch-shell design on the front were issued by the Arakanese king Devachandra in the late seventh or early eighth century AD. These designs were of Indian origin and were accompanied by inscriptions naming the king in Indian Brahmi script. The backs of the coins were all decorated with the Indian Srivatsa symbol representing the mother-goddess Sri. For the next 200 years his successors continued to issue silver coins with the reclining bull and mother-goddess designs, in several denominations. The same design was also copied in neighbouring Bengal (see Bangladesh).

PYU AND MON PEOPLES

To the east and south of Arakan, Burma was ruled by the Pyu and Mon peoples respectively. During the eighth and ninth centuries both these peoples issued silver coins derived from those of Arakan. The Pyu used a throne or rising-sun symbol on the front of their coins, and the Mon used a conch or wheel symbol, but all these issues bore a version of the Srivatsa on their backs.

THE KINGDOMS OF ARAKAN AND BURMA

The invasion of the Burmese people from the north during the ninth century brought an end to local coinages until the sixteenth century, when coins were issued again in the Arakan area. From the fourteenth century the silver coins of the Islamic sultans of neighbouring Bengal (see Bangladesh) had circulated in Arakan. From the end of the sixteenth century until 1784, when Arakan was conquered by the Burmese king Bodawpaya (1782–1819), regular issues of Bengal-style silver coins were struck by the Arakanese, inscribed in the local script, and at first also in Persian and Bengali. The coins often bore the honorary titles of the Arakanese kings: Lord of the White Elephant, Lord of the Golden Palace or King of Righteousness.

After his conquest of Arakan, Bodawpaya issued his own rupees in the Arakanese style and inscribed them with his title, Lord of Many White Elephants. He also attempted to restore the coinage of the Pyu and had rupees struck with the Pyu throne and the Srivatsa designs. These were made at his request at the Calcutta mint of the British East India Company in 1796. At the same time an issue was also prepared of copper coins with a Burmese inscription dated 1782 (the first year of his reign) on one side and two fish on the other. The coins were delivered to Bodawpaya in 1797, along with minting machinery to produce more. However, the coins were not a success because the Burmese, outside Arakan, were unfamiliar with coinage.

TENASSERIM

In Tenasserim, the southern coastal strip of Burma from Rangoon to the Isthmus of Kra, an independent coinage was developed during the Burmese period. This appears to have been influenced by the tin coins of the Malay peninsula. The Tenasserim coins were large tin or lead pieces with symbolic religious designs, featuring lions, birds, wheels

BURMA

3 1782

1 EIGHTH CENTURY

2 1761

1 SILVER TANGKA of the Pyu kingdom of Srikshetra.
2 SILVER TANGKA of Sanda Parama, King of Arakan, 'Lord of the Golden Palace'.
3 COPPER ¼ PE of Bodawpaya, King of Burma, 'Lord of the Many White Elephants'.

4 LEAD MONEY of Tenasserim, southern Burma, showing the mythical Hamsa bird.
5 SILVER KYAT (RUPEE) of King Mindon.
6 ALUMINIUM 10 PYA of the Royal Union of Burma State People's Bank, with a portrait of Aung San.

5 1865

6 1966

4 EIGHTEENTH CENTURY

The Buddhist Kuthodaw Temple in Mandalay. Mandalay was home of the first machine mint in Burma in 1865.

and lotus plants, and inscribed in Burmese. Most are round, but some are octagonal. The largest pieces have a diameter of about 80 mm. Their date of issue is uncertain, but they were reported as early as the mid-seventeenth century and seem to have continued to circulate into the early nineteenth century.

THE MANDALAY MINT AND BRITISH RULE

From 1852 British troops occupied coastal Burma. In 1857 the Burmese king Mindon Min (1853–78) built a new capital at Mandalay. Mindon had silver coins decorated with a peacock, his personal emblem, made for use as royal gifts at his court. An issue of coins for general circulation was not considered until 1862, when Mindon made arrangements to obtain the modern machinery needed. It eventually arrived from Birmingham, England, in 1865 and silver coins were issued from early 1866.

The new coins also used the peacock design and were inscribed in Burmese with their denominations and the Burmese era date 1214 (= 1853, the first year of Mindon's reign). The denominations were based on the Burmese weight system, but in reality the coins were equal in size and weight to the contemporary coins of British India which circulated in the part of Burma under British occupation (1 kyat = 1 rupee). Other issues also appeared once the Mandalay mint was in operation: copper $\frac{1}{4}$ pe (20 pe = 1 kyat) with the peacock design, dated 1227 (= 1866); gold $\frac{1}{20}$, $\frac{1}{4}$ and 1 kyat coins with a lion design, dated 1228 (= 1867); and lead $\frac{1}{16}$ and $\frac{1}{32}$ pe with a rabbit design, dated 1231 (= 1870).

Mindon's silver coins continued to be issued after his death, but new bronze and gold coins, with a lion design, were issued by his successor, Thibaw, dated 1240 (= 1879). The Mandalay mint produced coins until the British capture of Thibaw in 1885. This gave Britain complete control of Burma, but the Mandalay mint coins were allowed to circulate alongside the British India coins, which now became the official currency.

INDEPENDENCE

A separate coinage for Burma was not issued again until it gained independence from Britain in 1948. During 1949 a new coinage was prepared for Burma at the British Royal Mint. The denomination system, 64 pya = 16 pe = 1 kyat, was based on the Indian system, 64 pice = 16 anna = 1 rupee. Cupro-nickel 2 pya and 1 and 2 pe and nickel 4 and 8 pe coins were struck, all with a traditional Burmese lion design. The cupro-nickel coins were square or scallop-edged like their Indian counterparts. In 1952 this issue was replaced by a new series with decimal denominations (100 pya = 1 kyat). Bronze 1, cupro-nickel 5, 10, 25 and 50 pya and 1 kyat coins were issued, all still using the lion design.

SOCIALIST REPUBLIC

In 1962 a military coup led to the establishment of the Socialist Republic of the Union of Burma. A new set of aluminium 1, 5, 10, 25 and 50 pya coins, dated 1966, were struck in the name of the Burmese People's Bank at the Berlin mint. All denominations were decorated with the portrait of Aung San, Burma's first president (1948). These issues are still current.

THAILAND

FIRST COINS:	ninth century
FIRST DECIMAL COINS:	1908
MAIN MINT:	Bangkok
CURRENCY:	baht

THE earliest coins issued in the territory now known as Thailand were made by the Mon people during the ninth century AD. Silver coins decorated with a conch on the front and a mother-goddess Srivatsa symbol on the back have been found at several Mon sites in central Thailand to the north of Bangkok. These designs were of Indian origin, copied from the issues of the Mon people in southern Burma (see Burma). Silver coins, similar but with original designs, were issued at the Mon cities of Dvaravati and Lopburi. These also had Indian symbolic religious designs, such as the cow and calf, the vase of plenty, the wheel or deer, and on a few rare issues there are Indian inscriptions naming the mint city. Burmese silver coins of the same period have also been found in Thailand.

By the eleventh century the Mon peoples of Thailand had been conquered by the Khmer rulers of Cambodia, and there is no evidence to suggest that their coinages continued to be used under Khmer rule. The Khmers themselves had no coinage until the sixteenth century (see Kampuchea).

RING AND BULLET COINS

During the thirteenth century the Thai people, who had been gradually moving from southern China into south-east Asia since the tenth century, completed their conquest of Thailand and coinage re-emerged in a curious form. The Thai people were unfamiliar with coins and used silver rings as money. From the thirteenth century they developed a new form of coinage based on the silver ring. In the northern kingdom of Chiengmai the rings were made from silver bars with a square section; in the southern kingdoms of Sukhotai and Ayuthia they were made from rounded bars.

The coins of Chiengmai were stamped with the name of the city of issue and with their weight '4 [baht]' in Thai script. After stamping, each bar was bent into a ring which was then cut half-way through with a chisel and bent again to open the cut in order to show that it was solid silver.

The coins of the kingdoms of Sukhotai and of Ayuthia were first bent into a ring and then cut and stamped. The stamps bore small symbols, such as wheels, flowers, conch shells and elephants. During the fourteenth and fifteenth centuries these coins continued to look

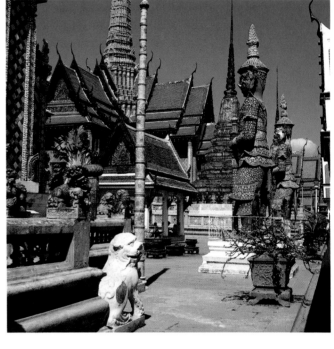

The Emerald Buddha Temple, Bangkok. Bangkok became the capital of Thailand in 1782 with the foundation of the Bangkok Dynasty by General Chakri whose chakra (wheel) appeared on the coins of his successors.

like rings, but later they were bent and hammered into a tight ball, from which is derived the description 'bullet coins' often given them by Western collectors. The Thai name for the coins is *pot duang*, meaning 'curled-up worm'.

THE BANGKOK DYNASTY

In the late eighteenth century the Ayuthian kingdom was overthrown from within by General Chakri, who had repelled successfully a

1 SEVENTEENTH CENTURY

ANCIENT INDIANIZED KINGDOMS

☐ Indian style coins found

Kediri Ancient Indianized kingdoms in South East Asia c. AD 700–1200

0 Kilometres 1500
0 Miles 1000

Pyu **Arakan** **Mon** **Dvaravati** **Champa** **Khmer** **Luzon** **Srivijaya** SOUTH CHINA SEA BORNEO SUMATRA CELEBES INDIAN OCEAN **Kediri** JAVA

2 1809–24

3 c.1850

4 1860

5 1890

6 1979

THAILAND

1 SILVER 4 BAHT *of Chiengmai, northern Thailand.*
2 SILVER BAHT *of King Rama II, Bangkok mint, with chakra and garuda marks.*
3 PORCELAIN SALUNG TOKEN, *the Jade Hare gambling house, Bangkok.*
4 SILVER 2 BAHT *of King Rama IV Mongkut.*
5 BRONZE 2 ATT *of King Rama V Chulalongkorn.*
6 CUPRO-NICKEL 5 BAHT *of King Rama IX Bhumipol.*

Burmese attack. Chakri moved the capital from Ayuthia to Bangkok and made himself king as Rama I of the Bangkok Dynasty (1782–1809). He and his successors continued the Ayuthian-style coinage, marking all their coins with a *chakra* or bladed disk symbol, as a reference to Rama I's personal name. Each ruler added his own mark or marks to the *chakra*.

MINT MARKS OF THE BANGKOK DYNASTY

King	Royal name	Date	Marks
Rama I	Pra Buddha Yot Fa	1782–1809	conch shell
Rama II	Pra Buddha Lot La	1809–24	Garuda (eagle-god)
Rama III	Pra Nang Klao	1824–51	Garuda holding snake, star, palace, flower, fruit, beehive
Rama IV	Pra Chom Klao	1851–68	arrowhead, water pot, crown

Both gold and silver bullet coins were issued by the Bangkok kings until the reign of Rama IV, popularly known as Mongkut. After Mongkut, they were only made for ceremonial use as largesse at royal funerals.

Base-metal bullet coins do exist, but it is not known if they were produced for use as money or as weights. They were mostly made from copper–tin alloys, but some zinc pieces are also known. During the Ayuthian and Bangkok period official small change took the form of cowrie shells. There were, however, various unofficial token coins in circulation during both periods. During a shortage of cowries under the Ayuthian kingdom, it is recorded that clay tokens were used.

Most of the tokens of the Bangkok period were made of porcelain, but some in brass and glass have also been recorded. They were originally issued as gambling tokens by Chinese gambling houses in Bangkok, but their usefulness quickly led them to be used throughout the capital and they were still in use until the 1870s. These porcelain tokens bore Chinese inscriptions naming the issuing house or wishing the users good fortune, and pictorial designs, mostly of Chinese origin. They were often glazed with bright colours. Examples copying Chinese, Japanese, Burmese, Indian and Hong Kong coins have also been found.

Base-metal small change was also issued during the nineteenth century in the southern Thai districts of Songkhla, Patalung, Ligor, Jaring, Patani, Reman and Saiburi. These districts were all close to the border with Malaya and issued round-holed coins with Chinese or Malay inscriptions, like their Malayan neighbours. In Songkhla, Patalung and Ligor, coins with Chinese and Thai inscriptions were also produced, some without a central hole. Malay gold coins, decorated with a bull and a Malay inscription, were also issued in Patani during the eighteenth century.

WESTERN-STYLE COINAGE

In 1835 a British trader called Hunter made machine-struck copper tokens decorated with an elephant or lotus design and inscribed with the name of Thailand in the Thai language. He tried to persuade the Thai authorities to adopt them, but without success. Western-style coinage was not adopted by Thailand until the reign of Rama IV. In

1859 the British Queen Victoria sent him a small coining-press as a gift. With the press there were dies for striking silver $\frac{1}{8}$, $\frac{1}{4}$ and 1 baht coins, with the royal Thai elephant within a *chakra* on the front and the royal Thai crown between two umbrellas on the back. Further machinery, ordered by the king from England, arrived in the following year, making possible the striking of silver 2 and 4 baht pieces. The 2 baht had the same designs as the smaller coins but on the 4 baht the elephant and *chakra* were replaced by inscriptions in Chinese and Thai naming the Thai kingdom. The 4 baht denomination was abandoned after the first issue.

In 1862 Mongkut issued bronze coins as small change for the silver coinage, and in the following year gold coins were also minted. All had the elephant–*chakra* and crown–umbrellas designs.

Rama V, Chulalongkorn (1868–1910), issued coins like those of his father, Mongkut, until 1874, when he introduced a new bronze coinage with the royal monogram as its main design. In 1887 he replaced these and his silver elephant coins with a new issue of coins made in England. Their designs were based on contemporary British coins and had a portrait of the king on the front and either a Britannia-like figure representing Thailand or the Thai coat of arms on the back. Bronze 1 and 2 att (64 att = 1 baht) and silver $\frac{1}{8}$, $\frac{1}{4}$ and 1 baht coins were issued.

DECIMAL COINAGE

An attempt to introduce a decimal system was made in 1898 with the issue of nickel $2\frac{1}{2}$, 5, 10 and 20 satang coins with a three-elephant design (100 satang = 1 baht). The earlier coins continued to circulate.

In 1908 the Thai coinage was converted to a completely decimal system. Bronze $\frac{1}{2}$ and 1 and nickel 5 and 10 satang, all with a central hole and a *chakra* design, and silver 1 baht, with the royal portrait and a three-elephants motif, were issued. Royal portraits, *chakras* and elephants continued to be the main designs used on Thai coins until the last year of the reign of Rama VIII, Ananda (1935–46), when the Garuda, eagle-god, design was reused. During the Second World War Garuda had also been used on a set of tin 1, 5 and 10 sen coins prepared in 1943 for Thailand by the Japanese Occupation force.

The coins of Rama IX, King Bhumipol, depict the royal portrait and the royal arms or Garuda and other Thai motifs. Thailand is also a very active issuer of commemorative coins, particularly to record important royal events, such as birthdays, weddings and graduation ceremonies.

KAMPUCHEA

FIRST COINS:	sixteenth century
FIRST DECIMAL COINS:	1875
MAIN MINT:	Berlin
CURRENCY:	riel

Dᴜʀɪɴɢ the ninth and tenth centuries ᴀᴅ Cambodia (Kampuchea) became familiar with coins in the form of imported Pyu and Mon coins from Burma and Thailand. The earliest evidence of a locally-made coinage is a European report of silver coins circulating in the Khmer capital of Angkor during the sixteenth century. Examples of the coins described survive. They are small round pieces with a variety of designs on one side only. Although struck on round pieces of metal like contemporary European coins, they were stamped with only one die onto a flat blank surface. The designs were of real and mythical animals or plants, but had no inscriptions. Coins of this type, particularly with a stylized cockerel design, were still in use in the nineteenth century.

During the nineteenth century the Thai authorities occupying the Cambodian province of Battembang issued a modified version of the traditional coins, with a Chinese character above the cock design. In the 1880s a machine mint of French origin was used at Battembang to strike coins like the traditional one-sided designs, but with an inscription in Khmer naming Battembang on the back. After a few years minting was abandoned.

MACHINE MINTING

In the 1850s Ang Duong, king of Cambodia (1841–59), established the country's first machine mint, purchasing from England the machinery and dies needed to strike silver and copper coins. He chose to decorate the coins with the mythical Hamsa bird and the Khmer monument at Angkor. His coins were inscribed in Khmer with the date of his coronation, 1847, and the name of his kingdom. He issued a copper 1 att and silver $\frac{1}{8}$, $\frac{1}{4}$, 1 and 4 baht coins on the Thai standard, but he also minted copper coins of the traditional one-sided design. Ang Duong's coinage was not a success. Most of his subjects preferred to use imported Vietnamese and Siamese coins.

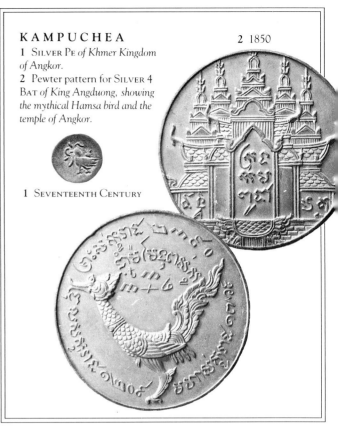

KAMPUCHEA   2 1850
1 SILVER PE of Khmer Kingdom of Angkor.
2 Pewter pattern for SILVER 4 BAT of King Angduong, showing the mythical Hamsa bird and the temple of Angkor.

1 SEVENTEENTH CENTURY

The Angkor Wat was the main religious establishment of the Khmer people (Kampuchea). A representation of it appears on the back of the coins issued by Ang Duong, King of Cambodia, in 1847.

COLONIAL PERIOD

Ang Duong was succeeded by King Norodom (1859–1905), during whose reign Cambodia became a French protectorate. In 1875 an independent coinage for Cambodia was struck in Belgium in the name of Norodom. The coins were all dated 1860, the year of Norodom's coronation, and had his portrait on the front and the Cambodian arms on the back. Bronze 5 and 10 centimes and silver 25 and 50 centimes and 1, 2 and 4 franc coins were struck. A silver piastre (dollar) was also made. In 1885 all were replaced by the French Indo-China coinage (*see* Vietnam).

INDEPENDENCE

In 1949 Cambodia became a nominally independent kingdom, and in 1953 the Paris mint struck aluminium 10, 20 and 50 centime coins for King Sihanouk (1941–70). The coins were inscribed in both Khmer and French and had Cambodian designs, such as the Hamsa bird on the 10 centimes. The same designs and denominations were retained for the next issue in 1959, when the denominations were renamed as 10, 20 and 50 sen. 'Sen' was the Khmer name for the centime and 100 sen equalled 1 riel, the renamed piastre.

THE FIRST AND SECOND REPUBLICS

Following a coup in 1970, Sihanouk was ousted and a republic was established. Cupro-nickel 1 riel coins were prepared for the republic, but not issued. The republic was overthrown in 1975 by the Khmer Rouge, who abolished all money. Coinage was again issued in 1979 after Vietnam invaded and installed a new government in the name of the Democratic Republic of Kampuchea. The new coins were aluminium 5 sen pieces with a design, based on Vietnamese issues, featuring the national emblem, the Angkor monument within a wreath.

LAOS

FIRST COINS:	before seventeenth century
FIRST DECIMAL COINS:	1952
MAIN MINT:	Berlin
CURRENCY:	kip

THE people of Laos were of Thai origin and established an independent Thai state in Laos during the fourteenth century. From then until the nineteenth century, Laos, with its rival kingdoms of Luang Prabang and Vien Chang (Vientiane), was under constant pressure from its neighbours, Thailand and Vietnam.

The early history of coins in Laos is obscure. European visitors to Laos during the seventeenth to nineteenth centuries found stamped metal bars being used as currency. The earliest form of bar was made of silver and looked like that from which Thai bullet coins were made (*see* Thailand). Like the Thai coins, they were stamped with symbols such as elephants and wheels. It is not known when bar coins were first issued, but by the nineteenth century they were in decline, and by that date most pieces were made of brass and bore no stamps. Cowrie shells, Vietnamese, Thai and British Indian coins also circulated.

FRENCH PROTECTORATE

In 1893 Laos became part of French Indo-China and the French coinage issued since 1885 for its South East Asian territories came into use in Laos. A separate coinage for Laos was not issued until after it had gained nominal independence in 1949.

1 EIGHTEENTH CENTURY   2 1952

LAOS

1 BASE-SILVER BAR *with elephant, boat and chakra marks.*
2 ALUMINIUM 10 CENTS *of King Sisavang Vong.*

THE KINGDOM OF LAOS

Aluminium 10, 20 and 50 cent coins, inscribed in Laotian and French with the name of the Kingdom of Laos, were struck in Paris in 1952. The denomination system was derived from the French Indo-China 1 piastre = 100 cents system. All had a round central hole, with a lotus design on the back and a female head, triple-elephant symbol or book of Buddhist scripture on the front. In 1971 commemoratives of

the coronation of King Savang Vatthana denominated in kip were issued. The kip (= 100 att) replaced the piastre.

DEMOCRATIC REPUBLIC

In 1975 after two decades of civil war the kingdom was abolished and the People's Democratic Republic of Laos was established. Coins in the name of the new republic were not issued until 1980, when aluminium 10, 20 and 50 att coins were struck in Berlin. They were without a hole and inscribed only in Laotian, all bearing the national emblem, a wreath encircling a hammer and sickle above paddy fields on the front and a design referring to local food on the back. Silver 50 kip commemoratives celebrating 10 years of the republic were issued in 1985.

MALAYSIA

FIRST COINS:	1450
FIRST DECIMAL COINS:	1787
MAIN MINT:	Kuala Lumpur
CURRENCY:	ringgit

THE earliest coins to be issued in Malaysia were small tin pieces struck by Muzaffar Shah, Sultan of Malacca (1446–59). These pieces were inscribed in Arabic with the sultan's name and titles. The style of the inscriptions shows that Malacca was already familiar with silver coins of the Indian sultanate of Bengal (*see* Bangladesh). Chinese coins were also exported into Malaya from the tenth century.

1 1446–59

2 1685–99

3 1741

4 EIGHTEENTH CENTURY

MALAYSIA

1 TIN PITIS *of Muzaffar Shah, Sultan of Malacca.*
2 GOLD KUPANG *of Muhammad Shah II, Sultan of Johore.*
3 SILVER REAL *of Zainal 'Ala-al-Din Shah, Sultan of Kedah.*
4 TIN PITIS *of the Trengganu Sultanate.*
5 TIN HAT MONEY *of the Pahang Sultanate.*

5 NINETEENTH CENTURY

The capture of Malacca by the Portuguese in 1511 put an end to its Islamic tin coins, but also soon led to the issue of South East Asia's first European coins. D'Albuquerque, the first Portuguese governor of Malacca, issued tin coins with a cross and globe design in the name of Manuel I (1495–1521), King of Portugal. In 1517 a further issue with the arms of Portugal on the front was made. Tin coins, and from 1615 silver coins, both with similar designs, continued until 1641, when Malacca was seized by the Dutch East India Company. The Dutch used the same coins as they circulated in Java (see Indonesia).

GOLD AND TIN

Following the lead of the Sultanate of Malacca, the Sultanate of Johore issued Islamic coins from the reign of Ala'al-din (1527–64). Only gold issues were made at first, with designs copied from the coins of the sultanates of northern Sumatra. Most of the Johore gold issues, which continued until the mid-eighteenth century, were octagonal, a local feature copied by several other Malayan sultanates. Johore also issued tin and silver coins during the eighteenth century, with similar designs.

Gold and tin coins were issued by the sultans of Kedah, Patani, Kelantan and Trengganu during the seventeenth to nineteenth centuries. Silver coins were less usual and the only other issue was from eighteenth-century Kedah. The role of silver money was played, as elsewhere in East Asia, by Spanish silver dollars (8 real pieces).

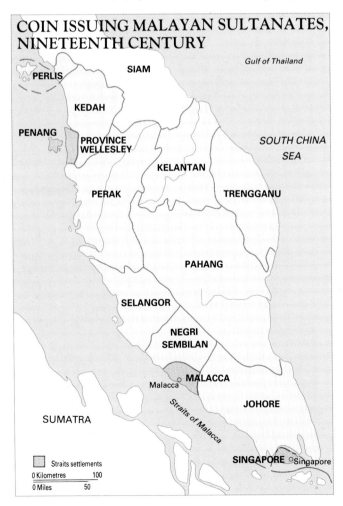

COIN ISSUING MALAYAN SULTANATES, NINETEENTH CENTURY

SIAM
PERLIS
Gulf of Thailand
KEDAH
PENANG
PROVINCE WELLESLEY
SOUTH CHINA SEA
KELANTAN
PERAK
TRENGGANU
PAHANG
SELANGOR
NEGRI SEMBILAN
MALACCA
Malacca
JOHORE
SUMATRA
Straits of Malacca
SINGAPORE
Singapore

Straits settlements
0 Kilometres 100
0 Miles 50

From the eighteenth century some districts began to issue a different kind of tin coin, based on the traditional coins of China. Although inscribed in Arabic, these coins had a central square or round hole. Issues are known from Kelantan, Trengganu, Perak and the Malay districts in southern Thailand. During the nineteenth century tin and lead holed coins with Chinese inscriptions were also issued in several sultanates by Chinese merchants for use as local small change. Some are also inscribed in Malay, Thai or English. The inscriptions mostly name the Chinese issuer.

Another form of tin money circulated in some parts of Malaya. In Pahang and Perak tin ingots were used from as early as the fifteenth century. During the nineteenth century stylized square hat-shaped ingots with Arabic and Chinese inscriptions were issued in Pahang.

BRITISH MALAYA

European interest in Malaya was at first centred around the ports which provided a staging post in the long-range trade with the spice islands of Indonesia and with Japan and China. Malacca was passed from Portuguese to Dutch and finally, in 1824, to British hands. Britain also opened up bases on Penang and Singapore. The British East India Company relied on Spanish silver dollars for the area, but also imported silver rupees from India. From 1787 the company introduced a copper coinage struck in Calcutta as decimal fractions of the silver dollar, producing $\frac{1}{2}$, 1 and 2 cent pieces, with the company seal and an Arabic inscription naming Penang as Prince of Wales Island. In the following year 10, 25 and 50 cent silver coins with the same designs were also made. A second series of bronze coins was struck at the British Royal Mint and issued in 1810, 1825 and 1828, all bearing the company arms. During the period 1800–9 large tin tokens inscribed with the governor's initials were made on Penang for local use.

STRAITS SETTLEMENTS

In 1826 the British settlements in Malaya were unified under a single governor as the Straits Settlements. Coins were issued by the British East India Company for the Straits in 1845: bronze $\frac{1}{4}$, $\frac{1}{2}$ and 1 cent pieces with a portrait of Queen Victoria in the name of the company. After the abolition of the company a second issue was made, inscribed INDIA–STRAITS, in 1862. The name STRAITS SETTLEMENTS finally appeared on the coins in 1871, when silver 5, 10 and 20 cent pieces were issued. Bronze $\frac{1}{4}$, $\frac{1}{2}$ and 1 cent coins with the same inscription appeared from 1872. Silver 50 cent coins were issued from 1886.

The dollar in use in the Straits during the nineteenth century continued to be the silver dollar of Spanish and later republican Mexico. During the 1870s Japanese and US silver dollars also began circulating in the area. The first British-made dollar appeared in 1895 (see Hong Kong), and was issued in the Straits until 1903, when a dollar was struck specifically for the territory, with the portrait of King Edward VII and the denomination in English, Chinese and Malay.

SARAWAK AND BORNEO

Straits coins circulated beyond Malaya into the other British territories of East Asia. In Sarawak they provided the denomination system and design for the issues of the local British rajah, James Brooke (1841–68). In 1863 Brooke issued bronze $\frac{1}{4}$, $\frac{1}{2}$ and 1 cent coins, struck in Birmingham, with his own portrait in place of Queen Victoria's. From 1892 to 1897 the 1 cent coin was issued with a central hole. The rajah's head was reduced to fit the space above the hole and crossed

MALAYAN CURRENCY COMMISSION

In 1938 the Board of Commissioners of Currency of Malaya was established to issue coins for both the British Straits Settlements and the Malayan sultanates. Bronze ½ and 1 cent and silver 5, 10 and 20 cent coins with the portrait of King George VI were issued both before and after the Japanese occupation.

After the Second World War the decision was taken to form a unified Malay state. In 1948 Perak, Selangor, Pahang, Negri Sembilan, Perlis, Kedah, Kelantan, Trengganu, Johore, Penang and Malacca joined to become the Federation of Malaya. From 1956 a joint coinage with British Borneo was issued by the commission. In 1957 the federation gained independence, but Queen Elizabeth II's portrait continued to be used on the coins until 1961. The last issue of the commission was a 1 cent coin dated 1962 with crossed kris (Malay daggers) in place of the royal portrait.

MALAYSIA

The next coinage for Malaya was issued in the name of the newly founded state of Malaysia, formed in 1963 by the union of the Federation with Sarawak, Singapore and British Borneo (Sabah). From 1967 bronze 1 sen and cupro-nickel 5, 10, 20 and 50 sen coins (100 sen = 1 ringgit) were struck for Malaysia. All denominations depict the Malaysian parliament building with a star and crescent, symbolizing democracy and Islam. Cupro-nickel 1 ringgit coins have been issued since 1971. With this issue coin production (apart from some commemoratives) passed from the British Royal Mint to the mint of the Malaysian National Bank at Shah Alam in Selangor. Higher-denomination coins have been issued only as commemoratives.

SINGAPORE

FIRST COINS:	1845
FIRST DECIMAL COINS:	1845
MAIN MINT:	Singapore
CURRENCY:	dollar

MALAYSIA

6 SILVER 50 CENTS *of the British East India Company, Prince of Wales Island (Penang).*
7 COPPER CENT *of the Straits Settlements.*
8 SILVER BRITISH DOLLAR, *also for use in Hong Kong.*
9 SILVER DOLLAR *of the Straits Settlements.*
10 BRONZE CENT *of the Commissioners of Currency, Malaya.*
11 CUPRO-NICKEL 50 SEN.

6 1788

7 1862

8 1895

9 1903

10 1945

11 1973

FROM its foundation as a British trading settlement in 1819 until it became an independent republic in 1965, the official coinage of Singapore was that of British Malaya (*see* Malaysia). Although a pattern ⅓ cent coin for Singapore was made at the Calcutta mint in 1824, its first official coins were those struck in 1845 by the British East India Company for the Straits Settlements. Singapore was one of the Straits Settlements from their establishment in 1826 until they were dissolved in 1946 and from 1836 Singapore became their administrative centre.

However, an unofficial coinage system developed in Singapore soon after it became a Straits Settlement. During its early years small change was brought in from the British settlement in Sumatra, and in 1828 the British merchants in Singapore began to issue bronze tokens with designs copied from the Sumatran coins and the copper duits of the Dutch East Indies (*see* Indonesia). These tokens found easy

flags filled the space beneath. Silver 5, 10, 20 and 50 cent coins were also issued from 1900.

British Borneo, comprising lands leased from the Sultanate of Brunei, acquired its own coinage in 1882, when the British North Borneo Company issued bronze 1 cent pieces. The front was decorated with the company arms and on the back the denomination was written in English, Chinese and Malay. Later ½, 2½, 5 and 25 cent coins were also issued. The Chinese and Malay inscriptions were not used after 1907 and the coinage was last issued in 1941.

acceptance, so in 1831 the merchants began to issue more tokens for export to all the parts of Malaysia and Indonesia with which Singapore traded.

Many had a cockerel and a Malay inscription meaning 'Land of the Malays' on the front and the denomination 1 keping on the back (about 400 keping = 1 dollar). Some had an additional inscription naming the place where the Singapore merchants intended to trade them: Trengganu, Selangor and Perak in Malaya, Siak, Dilli, Menengkabau, Percha, Tarumon and Acheh in Sumatra and the Land of the Bugi (Sulawesi in eastern Indonesia). These tokens continued to be used in Singapore, Malaysia and Indonesia until the 1850s.

INDEPENDENCE

The first coins for the Republic of Singapore were struck in 1967. Bronze 1 and cupro-nickel 5, 10, 20 and 50 cent and 1 dollar coins were issued. The 1 cent coin was decorated with a stylized representation of a housing development, the 1 dollar depicted the lion emblem of

SINGAPORE
1 COPPER 1 KEPING MERCHANT'S TOKEN, *inscribed 'Land of the Malays'.*
2 CUPRO-NICKEL 5 DOLLAR, *commemorating the opening of Changi Airport.*

Singapore while the other denominations featured local wildlife. From 1976 the 1 cent was struck in copper-clad steel instead of bronze.

New coins were introduced in 1985. The same denominations were retained, but the coins featured new designs: the arms of Singapore on the front and a local plant on the back. The name of Singapore is written in English, Malay, Chinese and Tamil to reflect the multi-cultural nature of Singapore's population.

BRUNEI

FIRST COINS:	sixteenth century
FIRST DECIMAL COINS:	1887
MAIN MINT:	Singapore
CURRENCY:	ringgit

Coinage first came to Brunei during the medieval period in the form of Chinese cast-bronze coins. From the sixteenth century European coins, particularly Spanish silver dollars (8 real pieces), were also brought into the area in trade. The earliest record of coins being

made in the Sultanate of Brunei is also from the sixteenth century, by a Portuguese visitor who described the casting of base-metal coinage. Cast-tin coins have been found in Brunei which are thought to represent the coins described.

They are inscribed in decorative Arabic with the titles of the sultan – 'The Just Sultan and The Acknowledged King' – on one side and a floral pattern or animal design on the other. The form of the Arabic titles suggests that they were adopted from the sultanates in northern Sumatra (*see Indonesia*). The floral and animal designs are local, but elements in them seem to be of Chinese origin. Most of the coins are round, but a few use the octagonal shape peculiar to the coins of Malaya (*see Malaysia*).

BRUNEI
TIN COIN *of the Brunei Sultanate, depicting a camel.*

SEVENTEENTH CENTURY

The earliest datable Brunei coins are in the same style as the sixteenth-century issues but are inscribed with the names of sultans: Nasir al-Din (1690–1710) and Kamal al-Din (1710–30, 1737–40). Decorative animal designs, thought to represent a tiger and a camel, also appear on these issues. Apart from the coins of these two sultans, the other cast-tin coins are without names.

During the eighteenth and early nineteenth centuries a large number of tin coins from Trengganu in Malaya were imported into Brunei and some local imitations are also thought to have been made.

Brunei's first European-style coins were issued in 1868 by Sultan Abdul Mumin. Tin ½ and 1 pitis (the denomination used for Chinese coins) were made with the royal umbrella emblem on one side and a Malay inscription on the other which stated that they were issued by the Finance Ministry of the State of Brunei. Brunei's first decimal coin, a bronze 1 cent dated AH 1304 (= 1887), intended to serve as $\frac{1}{100}$ of a silver dollar, was struck for Sultan Hashim Jelal in Birmingham, England. It was inscribed in English, SULTANATE OF BRUNEI, and in Malay with its denomination, 1 sen, and issuer, the Finance Ministry of Brunei.

BRITISH RULE

Brunei became a British protectorate in 1888 and in 1905 a dependency, adopting the currency systems of British Malaya, but Sarawak and British Borneo coins were also used. Independence was gained in 1959 but British Malaya coins continued to be used into the 1960s.

INDEPENDENCE

Sultan Omar Ali Saifuddin III began to issue his own coins in 1967. Bronze 1 sen and cupro-nickel 5, 10, 20 and 50 sen pieces, with his portrait on the front, were struck at the British Royal Mint. The 50 sen had the royal umbrella emblem, like the 1868 tin coins, but the lower denominations had traditional decorative designs. In the following year new coins were issued in the name of Sultan Hassanal Bolkiah, Saifuddin's successor: the same designs were used, with a new portrait. From 1970 a 1 ringgit coin has also been issued, but only for inclusion in specimen sets for sale to collectors.

Until 1984 the coins were struck in Britain, but from 1985 the Singapore mint has been used by the Brunei Currency Board, which is responsible for their issue. In 1977 a silver 10 ringgit commemorative coin, depicting the Brunei Mosque, was struck to celebrate the Currency Board's 10th anniversary.

INDONESIA

FIRST COINS:	before twelfth century
FIRST DECIMAL COINS:	1833
MAIN MINT:	Djakarta
CURRENCY:	rupiah

THE earliest recorded coin from Indonesia is a fourth-century AD Indian gold coin of the Gupta Dynasty, found in Java. The first locally-made coins, however, seem to have been produced during the medieval period. The earliest record of their use is in a Chinese report of the thirteenth century, but archaeological finds suggest that they may have been in use a few centuries earlier. The surviving coins are gold and silver lumps crudely stamped with Indian letters and religious designs. Found on both Java and Sumatra, similar coins are known from the Philippines. They are thought to have been issued by Indianized kingdoms such as the Sailendras of Java and the Srivijaya of Sumatra.

CHINESE AND ISLAMIC INFLUENCE

In Java the gold and silver coins went out of use before the late thirteenth century, when imported Chinese bronze coins were adopted as the official currency. In Sumatra the arrival of Islam brought about a different development. From the fourteenth century the local sultanates of northern Sumatra began to issue gold and tin coins with Arabic inscriptions. The content of the inscriptions suggests that their issuers were influenced by Egyptian coin designs. Similar coins were also issued in Sulawesi (Celebes). The use of Chinese coins and Islamic gold and tin became well established and continued until the nineteenth century in some areas.

EUROPEAN INFLUENCE

From the late fifteenth century European traders began to arrive in

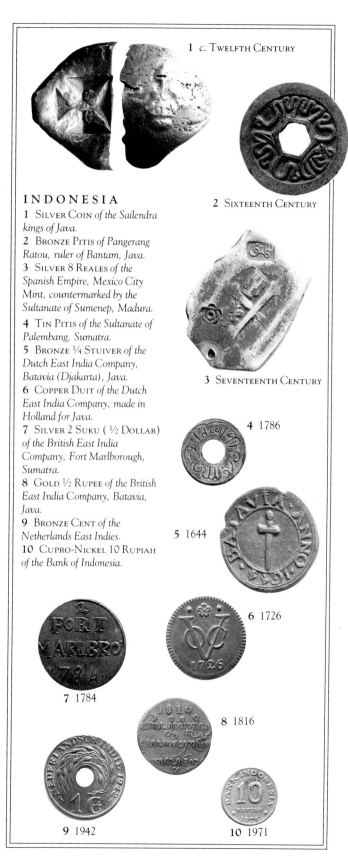

1 c. TWELFTH CENTURY

2 SIXTEENTH CENTURY

3 SEVENTEENTH CENTURY

4 1786

5 1644

6 1726

7 1784

8 1816

9 1942

10 1971

INDONESIA
1 SILVER COIN of the Sailendra kings of Java.
2 BRONZE PITIS of Pangerang Ratou, ruler of Bantam, Java.
3 SILVER 8 REALES of the Spanish Empire, Mexico City Mint, countermarked by the Sultanate of Sumenep, Madura.
4 TIN PITIS of the Sultanate of Palembang, Sumatra.
5 BRONZE ¼ STUIVER of the Dutch East India Company, Batavia (Djakarta), Java.
6 COPPER DUIT of the Dutch East India Company, made in Holland for Java.
7 SILVER 2 SUKU (½ DOLLAR) of the British East India Company, Fort Marlborough, Sumatra.
8 GOLD ½ RUPEE of the British East India Company, Batavia, Java.
9 BRONZE CENT of the Netherlands East Indies.
10 CUPRO-NICKEL 10 RUPIAH of the Bank of Indonesia.

South East Asia, bringing with them gold coins from Portugal and Venice and Spanish silver dollars (8 real pieces) from Mexico, Peru and Bolivia. The silver dollars had already become accepted as money in Indonesia by the seventeenth century. During the early seventeenth century Portuguese, Dutch and British trading settlements were founded in Java and Sumatra, and Dutch coins joined the Spanish coins in local use.

The Dutch became the dominant force in the area and gradually established control over the whole of the territory now known as Indonesia, except for a small British settlement (Fort Marlborough) in Sumatra, ceded to the Dutch in 1824, and the eastern half of the island of Timor, which remained under Portuguese rule until incorporated into Indonesia in 1975.

The British East India Company made coins, like those it issued in India, for its Sumatran settlement from 1786 until 1804. Portuguese colonial coins were issued for Timor, using the same denomination system as Macau, from 1945 until 1970.

THE DUTCH EAST INDIES

During the seventeenth century most of the money introduced by the Dutch, other than silver dollars, was in the form of Chinese and Japanese bronze coins. But Japanese gold coins were imported and stamped with the Dutch lion for use in Java in 1673, and Indian rupees were imported in 1693 and stamped with a horseman design like that used on Dutch dollars. In 1644 a brief issue of cast-bronze coins denominated as $\frac{1}{4}$ and $\frac{1}{2}$ stuiver pieces was made by the Dutch settlement in Batavia (Djakarta). Silver 12, 24 and 48 stuiver coins ($\frac{1}{4}$, $\frac{1}{2}$ and 1 dollar) were also made the following year, but both bronze and silver coins were soon withdrawn.

The local sultanates of Java and Sumatra were also importing Chinese coins, often contemporary forgeries made specially for the Indonesian market. The Sultanates of Jambi, Palembang and Siak in Sumatra and Bantam in Java made their own cast holed coins in place of the imported Chinese coins. These were inscribed in Javanese or Arabic, and some issues were made of lead. Tin cast holed coins with Chinese inscriptions were also issued by Chinese merchants in Borneo.

Eventually, the Dutch East India Company began to issue its own coins for use in Indonesia. Copper duits and silver dollars were struck in the Netherlands for use in Java from 1726. The duits were the same size as the Chinese and Japanese coins, but without a central hole. They had the voc monogram of the company on one side and the arms of the Dutch province in which they were made on the other. These coins were used until the early nineteenth century.

Gold ducats and silver rupees with Arabic inscriptions were struck in Java and issued from 1744. Shortages of duits during the Napoleonic Wars prompted the company to make copper coins locally. Some of these were crude copies of the duit, but most were large rectangular 'bonk' coins, made from chopped lengths of Japanese copper bars (see Sri Lanka and St Helena), stamped with the date and denomination.

In 1811 Java was captured by the British East India Company and British duits and rupees were issued. Unlike Dutch rupees, the British ones were inscribed in both Arabic and Javanese. The East Indies were restored to the Netherlands from 1816, and in 1821 copper $\frac{1}{2}$, 1 and 2 duit coins, struck at Surabaya in eastern Java, were issued in the name of the Netherlands Indies. These were $\frac{1}{8}$, $\frac{1}{4}$ and $\frac{1}{2}$ stuiver pieces; 30 stuivers equalled a rupee, and 66 equalled a dollar. New 1 and 2 duit coins were issued from 1833, denominated as 1 and 2 cents. The 1821

and 1833 issues used the same design, derived from the 1726 duit. One side bore the incription NEDERL INDIE and the date, the other the royal arms of the Netherlands and the denomination.

The coinage of the Dutch East Indies continued to be issued in the Netherlands until the Second World War. From 1854 the coins were inscribed in Javanese, Arabic and Dutch. Bronze $\frac{1}{2}$, 1, 2$\frac{1}{2}$ and silver 5, 10 and 25 cent coins were now issued. The silver coins were denominated as fractions of a guilden (100 cents = 1 guilden). From 1913 the 5 cent was struck in cupro-nickel with a central hole. A holed 1 cent also appeared from 1936. During the Second World War coins for the Dutch East Indies were struck in the USA, but after the war no further Dutch coins were issued. The Dutch East Indies were occupied by the Japanese from 1942 to 1945 and the Japanese administration struck coins with Japanese denominations for local use. The 10 sen was decorated with a Javanese shadow-theatre puppet.

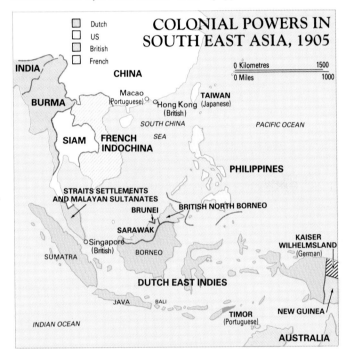

COLONIAL POWERS IN SOUTH EAST ASIA, 1905

INDEPENDENCE

In 1945 Indonesia proclaimed its independence, but only fully ousted Dutch rule from 1949. Aluminium 1, 5, 10 and 25 sen and cupro-nickel 50 sen coins (100 sen = 1 rupiah) were issued for the republic from 1951. After 1970 these were replaced by aluminium 1, 2, 5 and 10 and cupro-nickel 25, 50 and 100 rupiah coins, issued in the name of the Bank of Indonesia. The 1951 coins had a rice or eagle design; the later coins featured local wildlife and art.

Two parts of modern Indonesia, Riau and New Guinea (western Irian), were transferred from Dutch control later, in 1963. In that year aluminium 1, 5, 10, 25 and 50 sen coins were issued by the republic for the use of these newly acquired territories. The coins all had the same design, portraying President Sukarno, but those for Riau were inscribed KEPULAUAN RIAU on the edge.

Since 1970 silver and gold commemorative coins, also featuring local wildlife and art, have been struck for Indonesia at the British Royal Mint.

PHILIPPINES

FIRST COINS:	before thirteenth century
FIRST DECIMAL COINS:	1861
MAIN MINT:	Royal Mint
CURRENCY:	piso

CHINESE reports confirm that small gold coins known as *piloncitos*, stamped with an Indian Brahmi letter, found in the Philippines were already in use by the early thirteenth century. There is no evidence to show when they were introduced, but their design shows that they were derived from the small gold and silver coins of Java and Sumatra (*see* Indonesia). Alongside the gold coins, imported Chinese cast-bronze square-holed coins were also used. By the sixteenth century a large Chinese trading community was well established in the Philippines.

THE SPANISH COLONIAL PERIOD

In 1572 the Spanish founded a settlement at Manila on the Philippine island of Luzon. It expanded quickly, becoming the major port in Spain's trade with eastern Asia. Chinese traders brought silk, porcelain and gold to Manila to sell for Spanish silver dollars (8 real pieces). Most of these coins were forwarded to China, but they also became current in the Philippines.

Imported Spanish coins provided the Philippines with all the currency it needed until the supply was cut in the 1820s by the overthrow of Spanish rule in Central and South America. From 1820 until 1835 the Spanish authorities had to issue their own coins. Copper ½, 1, 2 and 4 quarto pieces (4 quarto = 1 real) were struck in Manila in the name of the Spanish king, Ferdinand VII, with the Spanish royal arms on the front and a lion holding a sword on the back. Silver dollars were also issued in 1827. These were made from repubican dollars from Mexico, Bolivia and Peru by overstamping them with dies bearing the arms of Spain in a wreath on the front and inscribed MANILA and the date on the back. From 1832 to 1837 they were simply countermarked on one side with the crowned initials of the Spanish monarch.

In 1861 the Spanish government began to make official coins for the Philippines at the Madrid mint. The new coins were denominated on a decimal basis with the dollar of 8 reales renamed a peso, divided into 100 centimos. At first only gold 1, 2 and 4 peso coins were struck, but from 1864 silver 10, 20 and 50 centimos also appeared. All denominations had the portrait of Isabella II, queen of Spain, on the front and the arms of Spain between two pillars on the back. Under King Alfonso XII bronze 1 and 2 centimo and silver 1 peso coins were also introduced.

THE US COLONIAL PERIOD

In 1898 revolutionary forces in the Philippines, with the support of the USA, declared a republic. But the USA then assumed control, suppressing the independence movement. The revolutionaries were, however, able to issue copper 1 and 2 centimos at two of their revolutionary bases in Panay and Malolos, before being brutally defeated by the US army of occupation. The country remained under American control until the Japanese invasion of 1941, although limited self-rule was granted in 1934. During the period of American rule a coinage was struck for the Philippines at the US mints in Philadelphia, San Francisco and Denver, but from 1920 some coins were also struck in Manila. The first issue, commencing in 1903, consisted of bronze ½ and 1, cupro-nickel 5 and silver 10, 20 and 50 centavos, and silver 1 peso coins. All denominations have the arms of the USA on the front. After the Philippines became a commonwealth in 1934, the design was modified and the 1 peso coin depicted the portraits of presidents Theodore Roosevelt of the USA and Manuel Luis Quezon of the Philippines.

THE REPUBLIC OF THE PHILIPPINES

After the expulsion of the Japanese, the Philippines gained full independence, becoming a republic in 1946. Apart from an issue in 1947 of commemorative ½ and 1 peso coins portraying General MacArthur, who had ended the Japanese occupation of the Philippines, the Republic of the Philippines did not issue any coins until 1958, when bronze 1 and brass 5, 10, 25 and 50 centavo coins were issued in the name of the Central Bank of the Philippines. The same design was used as before independence, but the national arms replaced the USA arms.

In 1967 the denomination system was revised and the centavo and peso were renamed sentimo and piso. New coins denominated 1, 5, 10, 25 and 50 sentimos and 1 piso were issued, bearing new designs featuring national heroes and the national emblem, a man turning a cog. The new coins were all inscribed in Tagalog, the main language of the Filipino people. From 1975 a change was made to the shape of the 1 and 5 sentimo pieces, which became square and scallop-edged. The round shape was readopted for the 5 sentimo coin in 1983, when a new series of designs was adopted featuring local wildlife. As part of this change a 10-sided 2 piso coin was introduced. Higher denominations have been issued only as commemoratives.

PHILIPPINES
1 SILVER 8 REALES *of the Republic of Peru, overstruck in Manila.*
2 COPPER 2 QUARTO *of Isobella II of Spain.*
3 SILVER PESO *of the US Administration.*
4 CUPRO-NICKEL PISO *of the Republic of the Philippines.*

1 1828
2 1835
3 1907
4 1976

CHINA

FIRST COINS:	sixth century BC
FIRST DECIMAL COINS:	first century AD
MAIN MINT:	Beijing
CURRENCY:	yuan

OINS were first made in China about 100 years after they had been invented in the kingdom of Lydia in ancient Turkey. China's first coins were, however, completely different from the Lydian ones and represented a separate discovery of the idea that money could be used in the form of standardized units of metal. Whereas Lydia's coins, and the European coinages which developed from them, were mainly struck with dies, Chinese coins were cast in moulds. Cast coins continued to be used in China until the first decades of this century, and only began to be replaced by European-style struck coins from 1890.

For 2500 years China's coinage tradition flourished and exerted a strong influence on its neighbouring states. Cast coins with Chinese designs were issued in Japan, Korea, Vietnam, Indonesia, Malaysia and Thailand, and exported Chinese coins were used even further afield; in India, Iran and East Africa.

FIRST COINS

The earliest references to money in China describe sea shells (specifically cowries) being used for payment during the second millennium BC. By about 600 BC cloth and bronze tools, such as hoes and knives, were also reported in use as money. The invention of coins was a standardization of this kind of money. During the sixth century a decision was taken in the kingdom of Zhou in north China to make imitation hoes, the same shape, but smaller than the actual tool, specifically for use as money. These small hoes, inscribed with a serial number or the responsible worker's name as a guarantee of their correct value, were China's first coins.

Other states in northern China soon adopted the same idea. Some made hoe coins, but others made coins imitating knives or cowries. All these imitations were of cast bronze and most bore inscriptions. The hoes and knives of each state were readily distinguishable from each other by variations in their shape and design. The inscriptions normally gave the name of the issuing state or town, and occasionally indicated the weight or value of the coin.

The idea of coinage spread and developed very quickly in China. By the mid-third century BC coins were in use throughout northern China (southern China had not yet been occupied by the Chinese people). Hoe-shaped coins were issued in the central and western regions (modern Henan, Shaanxi and western Shanxi provinces), knife-shaped coins in the north-east (modern eastern Shanxi, Hebei, Manchuria and Shandong provinces) and cowrie-shaped coins in the south-east (modern Anhui and Jiangsu provinces). A new kind of coin had also begun to appear by about the same date. Round coins with central holes were being made at a few mints as a more conveniently shaped substitute for the tool- or shell-shaped coins.

Both the new round coins and the tool coins were issued in different denominations. All the denomination systems used were based on the

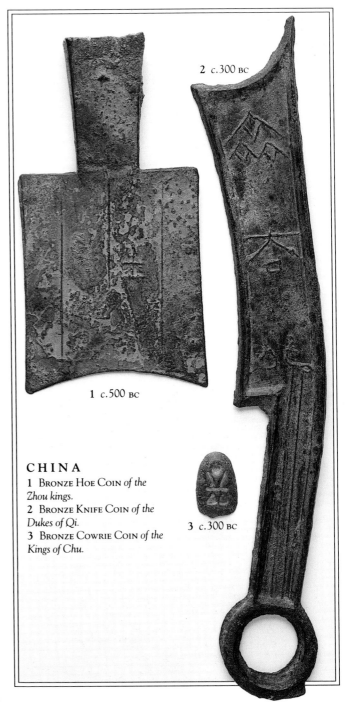

CHINA
1 BRONZE HOE COIN *of the Zhou kings.*
2 BRONZE KNIFE COIN *of the Dukes of Qi.*
3 BRONZE COWRIE COIN *of the Kings of Chu.*

2 c.300 BC

1 c.500 BC

3 c.300 BC

weight of the metal contained in each coin, and the different denominations were mostly expressed using the name of a weight. The word *jin*, used on the coins to mean a hoe, is still used in modern Chinese to mean a pound weight. Hoe coins valued as ½, 1 and 2 hoes were issued at some mints. Knife coins tended to be of only one denomination, but one series were valued as '30 coin' pieces and circulated alongside an issue of round coins denominated as 1, 4 and 6 coin pieces.

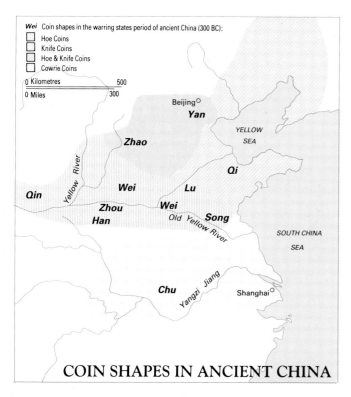

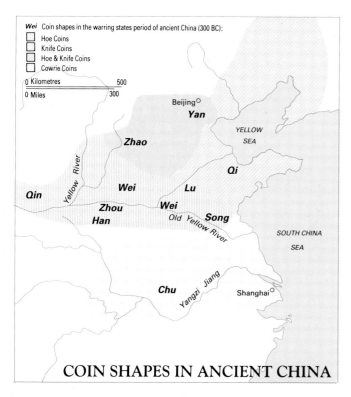

Wei Coin shapes in the warring states period of ancient China (300 BC):
☐ Hoe Coins
☐ Knife Coins
☐ Hoe & Knife Coins
☐ Cowrie Coins

COIN SHAPES IN ANCIENT CHINA

A section of the Great Wall of China, near Beijing. The Great Wall, the largest man-made edifice on earth, was mostly constructed during the reign of the first Emperor of China, Qin Shi Huangdi, who also issued China's first national coinage in 221 BC.

FIRST EMPEROR OF CHINA

During the early third century BC China, divided between numerous feudal states, went through a prolonged civil war which ended when the ruler of the western state of Qin succeeded in defeating all the others and made himself China's first emperor in 255 BC. This remarkable man, Qin Shi Huangdi, was responsible for two extraordinary creations: the Great Wall of China and the recently discovered terracotta army, which was built to guard his tomb at Xian.

Almost equally long lasting was his reorganization of China's coinage system. In 221 BC, as part of a large programme of reforms, the Qin emperor ended the use of hoe-, knife- and cowrie-shaped coins and commenced the issue of a new cast-bronze round coin with a central square hole. Coins of this shape continued to be made in China until 1912, and the same shape was issued in Vietnam until at least 1933.

The Qin emperor's new coins were issued in only one denomination and with one design throughout his empire. The inscription, written with two Chinese characters to right and left of the central hole, merely indicated the weight of the coin: $\frac{1}{2}$ ounce (about 8 g).

THE HAN DYNASTY

In 206 BC the Qin emperor's son was overthrown by the first of the Han emperors, who continued to issue $\frac{1}{2}$-ounce coins with the same inscription for the next 90 years. There was, however, a series of official reductions in the weight of the issued coins, so that by 118 BC the $\frac{1}{2}$-ounce coins in use weighed about $\frac{1}{8}$ ounce.

The Han emperor Wudi (140–87 BC) reformed the coinage and reset its weight at 5 grains (about 3.5 g). His new coin, like its Qin predecessor, was inscribed only with its weight, written with two Chinese characters to right and left of a central square hole. Apart from a brief interlude during the early first century AD, Wudi's new coin continued to be issued until the end of the Han Dynasty in AD 220 and was occasionally reused until the Sui Dynasty (581–618).

During the Han period the Chinese Empire was expanded to include parts of Korea and Vietnam and the Han 5-grain coins circulated there. The Han coins are also found in Chinese Turkestan, which was under Chinese military occupation. Locally made coins with Indian designs but Chinese inscriptions were also used at Khotan, in the most westerly part of this territory.

WANG MANG

From AD 7 to 23, the Han emperors were temporarily ousted by a usurper called Wang Mang, who reformed the coinage and reintroduced knife- and hoe-shaped coins. During his brief period of power Wang Mang issued 21 different kinds of coins. Unlike the Qin and Han coins their value was not based on the amount of metal they contained. Each piece was given a token, decimal value.

THE DECIMAL COINS OF WANG MANG

Round coins	1, 10, 20, 30, 40, 50
Hoe coins	100, 200, 300, 400, 500, 600, 700, 800, 900, 1000
Knife coins	500, 5000

Wang Mang's reform was not a success because the people would not accept the token values fixed for each coin. In AD 14 he again reformed the coinage, simplifying the system so that there were two coins: a round coin with the same weight and value as the Han 5-grain coin and a hoe coin worth 25 of the round coins. His new system was abolished when the Han Dynasty was restored in AD 24. The 5-grain coin was reintroduced from AD 26.

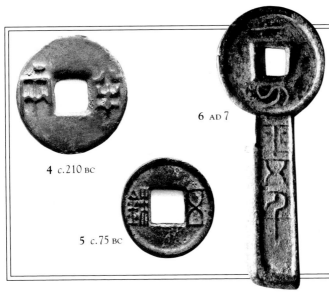

4 Bronze ½ Ounce *of the Qin Dynasty.*
5 Bronze 5 Grain *of the Han Dynasty.*
6 Bronze Knife Coin 'Value 5000', *with a gold inlayed inscription 'one knife'.*
7 Bronze 24 Grain Coin *of King Gurgamoya of Khotan, with a Chinese and Indian (Prakrit) inscription.*
8 Bronze 'Big Worth 100 Coin' *of the Western Jin Dynasty.*

9 Bronze 5 Grain *of the Northern Wei Dynasty.*
10 Bronze 'Everlasting Coin For Ten Thousand Nations' *of the Northern Zhou Dynasty.*
11 Bronze Kai Yuan Coin *of the Tang Dynasty.*
12 Bronze 10 Coin Token *of the Tang Dynasty.*

6 AD 7

4 c.210 BC

5 c.75 BC

CHINA DIVIDED

The 5-grain coin introduced by the Han Dynasty in 118 BC continued to be used and to be considered the standard until the early seventh century AD. The collapse of the Han in 220 left China divided between a succession of rival kingdoms and statelets during the next four centuries. Many of these attempted to issue coins closely modelled on the Han 5-grain coin, but few were able to do so; shortages of copper and other economic problems prompted many states to attempt to adjust the weight, or to use iron or lead as substitutes for bronze in casting coins. Some also reused Wang Mang's idea of token coins.

The coins of this period retained the square-holed round shape, but new inscriptions were introduced, referring to their values, dates of issue and often function.

CHINESE COINS FROM 214 TO 579

Kingdom	Date	Inscription
Shu Han	214	5 grains, worth 100
Western Jin	214	big worth 100 coin
Wu	238	big coin worth 1000
Former Liang	302	new coin made by Liang
Later Zhao	330	abundant coin
Cheng Han	338	Han prosperity
Song	454	Xiaojian period, 4 grains
Northern Wei	529	Yongan period, 5 grains
Northern Qi	553	everlasting peace, 5 grains
Northern Zhou	574	big coin of the five directions
Chen	579	big money, 6 grains

THE SUI AND TANG DYNASTIES

In 581 China became a single nation again under the Sui Dynasty. The Sui emperor restored the Han 5-grain coin and for the next 40 years this was the only coin issued. The Sui Dynasty and its coinage were short-lived.

In 618 Gaozu, the first Tang emperor, became ruler of China, and in 621 he established a new coin with a design that was to last until the end of China's traditional coinage. Like the Han and Sui coins, it was still a round square-holed cast-bronze piece, but its value and size were now fixed on a decimal basis; it weighed $\frac{1}{10}$ ounce and measured $\frac{1}{10}$ foot

across. It was inscribed with four Chinese characters *kai yuan tong bao*, 'circulating money of the opening [of the dynasty]'. Almost all later coins in China, and in the surrounding countries, used a similar four-character inscription naming the dynasty or reign period during which they were issued and identifying the function of the coin.

The new Tang Dynasty (618–907) coin continued to be issued and to be used until the early tenth century. (Brief experiments in 666 and 758–9 with token issues worth 10 and 50 of the regular coins failed.) The last major issue began in 844 when a new series of coins, all with a single character mint name on the back, were cast.

During the Tang period Chinese Turkestan once again came under Chinese rule and Tang coins circulated there. In 769 and 780, however, two special issues were made for local circulation. Their inscriptions named them as coins of the Dali and Jianzhong periods respectively.

Recent archaeological discoveries have shown that during the Tang period foreign gold and silver coins were imported into China, mostly in exchange for Chinese silk. The gold coins were early Byzantine solidi and the silver coins Sasanian drachms from Iran. In some areas the foreign coins seem to have been used as money, but the Chinese did not abandon their traditional cast-bronze coins in favour of the imported struck precious-metal coins. Gold and silver were used widely as money in China at this time, but normally in the form of ingots.

FIVE GENERATIONS AND TEN KINGDOMS

The collapse of Tang rule in 907 left China once again in a period of disunity. The Chinese call this time (907–60) the period of five generations and ten kingdoms. Most of the small rival states issued their own coins using the model of the standard Tang coin. Some states were very short of copper and issued coins made of iron or lead, and token coins. In the kingdom of Southern Tang a beautiful set of coins, inscribed *Tang Guo Tong Bao*, 'coin of the Tang kingdom', were issued in two varieties, distinguished by the style of the Chinese characters. The different styles are thought to indicate that the coins were made at different mints.

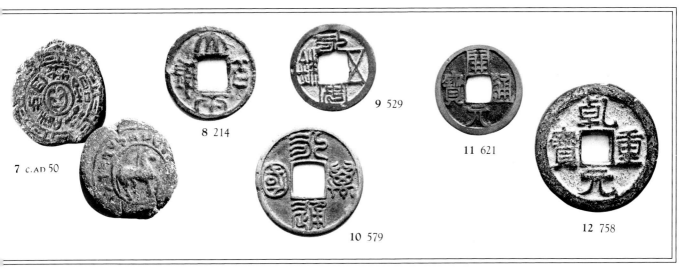

THE SONG DYNASTY

The reunification of China was achieved by the Song Dynasty (960–1279). The new dynasty's coins followed the model of the Tang coinage.

The Song introduced token coins, but in a more restrained way than their predecessors, issuing coins worth only 2 or 3 regular coins at first. Once these were accepted and in use, 5 and 10 coin tokens were also issued. In some regions it was also necessary to issue iron coins. The Song coinage was very successful and was produced in such vast quantities that exported Song coins also provided Japan, Vietnam and Indonesia with the bulk of the coins they needed until the sixteenth century. By the end of the Song period China had also successfully introduced the idea of a paper currency.

In the north of China two small states remained independent of Song rule and issued their own coins also based on the Tang issues. The Western Xia, a Tibetan dynasty, ruled in the north-west (in the modern province of Gansu); the Liao, a Tartar dynasty, ruled in the north-east (in modern Hebei, Inner Mongolia and Manchuria). On a few rare issues of both these dynasties the inscriptions were written in local non-Chinese scripts. In Turkestan Turkish rulers of the Qarakhanid Dynasty issued Islamic-style coins with Arabic inscriptions. The main issues were of the Khans Muhammad and Suleyman, both during the eleventh century.

THE TARTARS AND THE MONGOLS

In 1115 the far north-eastern part of China, in the territory now known as Manchuria, a Tartar state, under the Chinese name of the Jin Dynasty (1115–1234) came into being and quickly grew until the whole of northern China was under its control. The Jin used Song coins and also made occasional issues of their own in the same style.

Within 100 years the Jin were themselves overrun by another group of northern invaders, the Mongols. Under their leader, the renowned

CHINA

13 Bronze 2 Coin Token *of the Song Dynasty.*
14 Bronze 10 Coin Token *of the Song Dynasty.*
15 Bronze 100 Coin Token *of the Song Dynasty.*
16 Bronze Dirhem *of Suleyman Qarakhanid Khan in Kashgar, Chinese Turkestan.*

Genghis Khan, and his son Ogedei, the Mongols quickly conquered the whole of Inner Asia from China to Iran. In 1204 they overthrew the Western Xia, in 1211 the Qarakhanids, and in 1215 the Jin. By 1279 the whole of China was under Mongol control and the Mongol Khan Kubilai made himself Emperor of China, using the Chinese dynastic name Yuan (1279–1368).

The Mongol rulers of China issued few coins because they adopted and expanded the Song invention of paper money. A few issues of coins in the Song style were made in 1295, 1297, 1310 and 1351–5. Part of the 1310 issue was of large 10 coin tokens, inscribed in Chinese, but using a script called Phagspa, normally used to write Mongolian. The inscription states that the coin is an issue of the 'Great Yuan Dynasty'. Phagspa versions of Chinese date-characters are also used on the back of some of the 1351–5 coins to indicate the precise year of issue.

In the 1360s, as inflation began to undermine the Mongol paper-money system, the Yuan made a curious issue of coins with denominations inscribed on their backs. These denominations were expressed in terms of paper money.

THE MING DYNASTY

The power of the Mongols in China was finally broken in 1368 when a former Buddhist monk, Zhu, re-established Chinese rule as the Ming emperor Taizu. Taizu had already begun to issue coins in 1361 during his struggle against the Mongols. His coins were in the traditional form, but those issued by provincial mints also had a mint name inscribed on the back like the Tang coins issued in 844. Apart from his central mint in Nanjing he issued coins from eight named mints in 1361 and 1368. Several denominations were cast: 1, 2, 3, 5 and 10 coin pieces.

The new Ming coinage was not a success and in 1375 was abandoned in favour of a paper money like that issued during the Mongol period. Apart from limited issues in 1408 and 1433, most of which were exported to Japan and Indonesia, the production of coins was suspended until 1503, when an attempt was made to reintroduce coins as a workable substitute for paper money. From 1505 coins made of brass, instead of bronze, began to be cast and this change marks the reintroduction of successful coinage in China after almost three centuries dominated by paper money.

During the last century of the Ming Dynasty (1368–1644) brass coins were regularly produced, with occasional issues of 2, 5 and 10 coin token pieces also made. The inscriptions invariably stated that the coin was the circulating money of the appropriate reign period of issue. Inscription also frequently appeared on the backs of the coins during the last two reign periods of the Ming, stating the name of the mint or the value and weight of the coin.

During the Ming Dynasty Chinese Turkestan was under the control of Islamic dynasties descended from the earlier Turkish and Mongol rulers. A few Islamic coins using Iranian designs were issued in the area; Chinese coins also continued to be imported and used in some areas.

The late Ming Dynasty period saw the introduction into China of foreign silver coins, brought to the ports of southern China by European traders. Most of these were silver 8 real pieces (dollars) from Spain's Central and South American mints, particularly Mexico City and Potosí. Foreign silver dollars continued to flow into China during the following centuries and the Chinese began to use them as money.

CHINA
17 BRONZE 10 COIN TOKEN of the Yuan Dynasty.
18 SILVER DIRHEM of the Mongol Khanate, Kucha.
19 BRONZE COIN of the Ming Dynasty.
20 BRONZE COIN of Nurhachi, ruler of Manchuria.
21 BRASS COIN of the Qing (Manchu) Dynasty, Board of Revenue mint in Beijing.
22 SILVER SHO of the Chinese administration in Tibet.
23 SILVER DOLLAR for military pay, Fujian Province.
24 GOLD TILLA of Yakub Beg of Kashgar, Chinese Turkestan, struck in the name of Abdul Aziz, Ottoman Emperor of Turkey.

THE MANCHUS

Brass coins continued to be issued by the Manchurian invaders who overthrew the Ming in 1644. In 1616 a Manchurian prince, Nurhachi, had declared himself emperor and cast Chinese-style coins, with both Chinese and Manchurian inscriptions. His successor, Abahai, invaded China and quickly defeated the Ming, but died before the claim had become a reality. In 1644 his son Shizu was made the first emperor of the Qing Dynasty, which was to rule China until 1911.

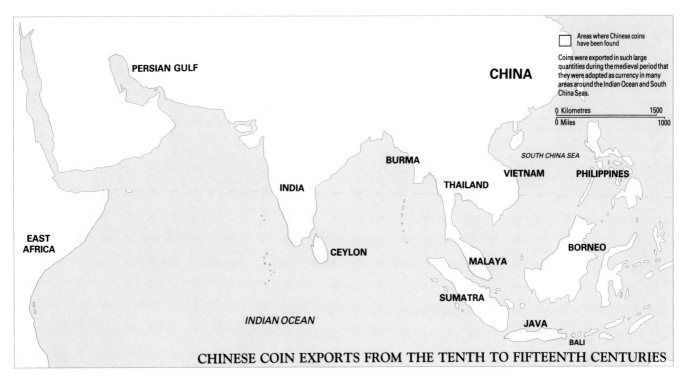

CHINESE COIN EXPORTS FROM THE TENTH TO FIFTEENTH CENTURIES

Under the Qing a large network of mints was soon established throughout China to cast brass coins. For the first two centuries of the Qing only standard coins were issued. They were inscribed normally with the name of the reign period of issue on the front and the mint name on the back. At first the mint name was written in Chinese, in the following years in Chinese and Manchurian, and from 1723 in Manchurian only.

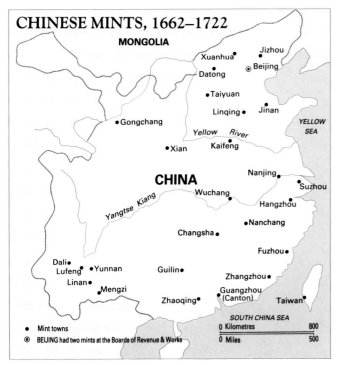

THE MAIN MINTS OF THE QING DYNASTY

Name	Location
Baoquan	Board of Revenue, Beijing
Baoyuan	Board of Works, Beijing
Baozhi	Baoding, Hebei (Zhili) Province
Baoqi	Qinan, Shandong Province
Baojin	Taiyuan, Shaanxi Province
Baoshan	Xian, Shaanxi Province
Baohe	Kaifeng, Henan Province
Baosu	Suzhou, Jiangsu Province
Baojiang	Nanjing, Jiangsu Province
Baozhe	Hangzhou, Zhejiang Province
Baowu	Wuchang, Hubei Province
Baonan	Changsha, Hunan Province
Baochang	Nanchang, Jiangxi Province
Baofu	Fuzhou, Fujian Province
Baotai	Taibei, Taiwan
Baoguang	Guangzhou, Guangdong Province
Baogui	Guilin, Guangxi Province
Baodian	Guiyang, Guizhou Province
Baochuan	Chengdu, Sichuan Province
Baoyun	Kunming, Yunnan Province
Baodong	Dongchuan, Yunnan Province

During the first 35 years of Qing rule coins in the late Ming style continued to be issued in southern China by several Chinese princes who resisted the Manchu invasion.

CHINESE TURKESTAN AND TIBET

During the late eighteenth century Manchu conquest extended China to its present-day borders. New coins were issued by the Qing emperor Gaozong in Chinese Turkestan from 1755. At the mint of Ili he issued brass coins like his regular issues, but at the mints of Aksu, Ushi and Yarkand he issued a new kind of coin, still round with a square central hole and four Chinese characters on the front, but cast in copper with the mint names in Turkish and Manchurian on the back.

His successors also cast similar coins at new mints in Kuche, Kashgar, Khotan and Urumchi. During the late nineteenth century some of the Turkestan mints cast coins inscribed with the name of the reign period of the emperor Gaozong to commemorate his conquest.

In 1792 Gaozong also extended his sovereignty to Tibet and opened a mint in Lhassa. Since the sixteenth century the coins used in Tibet had been imported from Nepal. The imports were in sufficient quantity for the Nepalese to make coins specifically for export to Tibet. These were struck silver coins with Indian inscriptions and religious designs. A local issue of such coins began in Tibet only a few decades before Gaozong's intervention.

His first issue was closely modelled on the Tibetan coins, but in 1793 a different design was introduced, with a Chinese inscription saying 'Tibetan money of the Qianlong period, 58th year' on one side and a Tibetan translation of it on the other. Similar coins were issued by the next two emperors.

During the second half of the nineteenth century Chinese control of both Tibet and Turkestan weakened. The Tibetans began again to make their own silver coins modelled on the earlier imported Nepalese coins. In Chinese Turkestan a series of Islamic revolts led to the issue of various new coins. One rebel, Rashid Khan, cast copper coins like the Chinese issues, but with a purely Turkish inscription on both sides; another, Yakub Beg, issued gold, silver and copper Islamic coins copying the contemporary issues of the Khanates of Bukhara and Khokand in Russian Turkestan.

FOREIGN DOLLARS

During the Qing period the Chinese gradually became familiar with Western-style coins in the form of imported Spanish and Mexican silver dollars. By the mid-nineteenth century these dollars were the

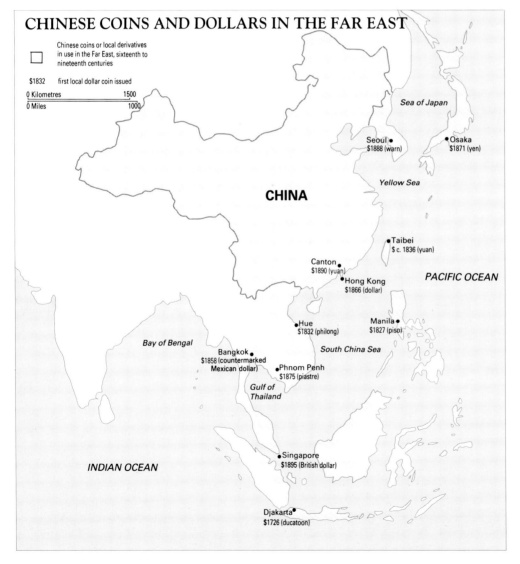

CHINESE COINS AND DOLLARS IN THE FAR EAST

☐ Chinese coins or local derivatives in use in the Far East, sixteenth to nineteenth centuries

$1832 first local dollar coin issued

0 Kilometres 1500
0 Miles 1000

Sea of Japan

Seoul
$1888 (warn)

Osaka
$1871 (yen)

Yellow Sea

CHINA

Taibei
$ c. 1836 (yuan)

Canton
$1890 (yuan)

Hong Kong
$1866 (dollar)

PACIFIC OCEAN

Hue
$1832 (philong)

Manila
$1827 (piso)

Bay of Bengal

South China Sea

Bangkok
$1858 (countermarked Mexican dollar)

Phnom Penh
$1875 (piastre)

Gulf of Thailand

Singapore
$1895 (British dollar)

INDIAN OCEAN

Djakarta
$1726 (ducatoon)

25 1890

26 1897

27 1898

28 c.1905

only coins being used in trade in large parts of southern China. The popularity of the dollar was increased by a rapid decline in the reliability of the traditional coinage. This decline was the consequence of a major revolt against Manchu rule by the Chinese.

The Taiping Rebellion (1851–64) succeeded in disrupting Manchu rule in southern China and forced the Qing emperor Wenzong to allow token coins and paper money to be issued. His token coins were valued as worth 5, 10, 20, 50, 100, 500 and 1000 standard coins, but, because their value in terms of metal was so much lower, the people would not accept them. The traditional system never recovered from this experiment, even though the Taiping Rebellion was soon suppressed with European help. From 1854 until 1861 the Taiping rebels had also issued their own cast brass coins inscribed with six Chinese characters, four on the front and two on the back, stating that the coins were the 'sacred money of the heavenly kingdom of Great Peace'.

In the 1870s silver dollars from the USA and Japan and silver 5, 10 and 20 cent pieces from Hong Kong were also being circulated in China. The Chinese government was put under pressure to abandon the traditional cast copper-alloy coinage in favour of a dollar-based European-style monetary system. From 1877 the Chinese had been issuing struck silver coins in Turkestan, copying the designs of the rebel issues. There had also been some local-government issues of dollars to pay troops in Fujian and Taiwan during the 1840s. It was not until 1890, however, that the Chinese government finally agreed to the official issue of silver dollars at one of its mints.

QING DRAGON COINS

In 1890 the Guangzhou mint in southern China began to strike silver 5, 10, 20 and 50 cent and 1 dollar coins. On the front they were inscribed in Chinese and Manchurian with the reign period of issue and a statement that they were silver coins, and in Chinese with the mint name and their weight. On the back the mint name and weight were repeated in English around a Chinese dragon design. By the end of the century several other provincial mints were issuing these dragon coins. From 1900 copper cents with similar designs also began to be issued from these mints. The cents were mostly denominated as 10 cash pieces ('cash' was the English name for the traditional standard coin). The machinery to make these coins was imported mostly from England.

During the last decade of Manchu rule imported silver dollars and the traditional cast coins continued to circulate alongside the new coins. The imported coins now included French and British dollars. Some of the new machine mints were also striking versions of the traditional holed copper-alloy coins.

THE REPUBLIC OF CHINA

The last cast coins were supposedly made in 1912, in the first year of the republican government which overthrew the Manchu Qing Dynasty. Reports, however, suggest that in rural areas cast coins continued to be used until about 1925.

The new Republic of China began to strike dollars and cents with designs reflecting the change of regime. The dollars depicted the portrait of the president, Sun Yat Sen in 1912 and Yuan Shikai in 1914; the cents were mostly decorated with the flags of the republic and its army. Imported dollars still continued to be used until the 1930s. Some provincial mints used different designs for their coins, such as the motor car featured on the 1928 dollar of the Guizhou Province mint and the star on the 1912 cent of the Guangxi Province mint.

In Turkestan the republican flag design also replaced the dragon used under the Manchus. In Tibet, although machine minting had been introduced, the traditional designs derived from Nepal were used until the 1930s, when a lion emblem was incorporated into some designs. From 1909, copper coins were also issued alongside the regular silver denominations and from 1918 to 1921 a gold denomination was added. The Chinese also made coins for Tibet, but only one issue in Tibet itself, in 1910, when copper and silver dragon-design coins were struck. Larger issues for Tibet were, however, made from 1903 until the 1930s at the Sichuan Province mint, which struck copies of British Indian silver rupees for export to Tibet, where the rupee had become popular.

NATIONAL COINAGE

In 1905, 1911, 1912 and 1914 the Chinese government tried to standardize the dollar coinage on a national basis, but the activities of provincial mints under local government control had frustrated the attempt. In 1936 the Nationalist government (1928–49) under

30 1912

29 c.1910

33 1936

34 1964

31 1928

32 1934

CHINA

25 BRASS COIN of the Qing Dynasty, struck by the machine mint at Guangzhou.
26 SILVER DOLLAR of the Qing Dynasty, Anhui Province mint.
27 SILVER 5 MISCAL of the Qing Dynasty, Kashgar, Chinese Turkestan, with a Turki inscription.
28 COPPER 10 CASH (CENT) of the Qing Dynasty, Sichuan Province mint.
29 BASE SILVER GA-DEN TANKA of Tibet.
30 SILVER DOLLAR of the Republic.
31 SILVER DOLLAR of the Republic of China, Guizhou Province mint.
32 SILVER DOLLAR of the Sichuan-Shaanxi Soviet Base Area.
33 CUPRO-NICKEL 20 FEN of the Nationalist government.
34 ALUMINIUM FEN of the People's Republic.

General Chiang Kai-shek set up a new central mint at Shanghai and struck bronze ½ and 1 cent and nickel 5, 10, 20 and 50 cent coins, all with a design based on an ancient Chinese hoe-coin on the back and with the Nationalist star on the front of the bronze denominations and the portrait of the first president, Sun Yat Sen, on the nickel. This reform, accompanied by the abolition of the use of silver dollars and silver ingots, would have been successful if China had not been involved already in civil war and under attack by Japan.

JAPANESE AND SOVIET ISSUES

In northern China local puppet governments, set up by the Japanese in the territory they conquered, began to issue their own coins with designs influenced by contemporary Japanese issues in particular. Manchuria, Inner Mongolia, Hebei, Beijing and Shanghai are known to have made such issues.

From 1931 local issues were also being made by the Communist base areas. The hammer and sickle design appears on most of these soviet issues, and on two issues of silver dollars the portrait of Lenin also appears. From 1934 most of the small change in use in the Communist-held areas was in the form of paper money. The Nationalist currency during the 1940s was also virtually coinless.

LIBERATION

When the Red Army, under the leadership of Mao Zedong, reunified and stabilized China in 1949 there were no coins in use, except on the island of Taiwan, which was still in the hands of the Nationalists under Chiang Kai-shek. In 1955 preparations were made for the reintroduction of coinage. Large numbers of aluminium 1, 2 and 5 fen (cent) coins dated 1955 were struck and issued in the following year. They all had the same design, with the denomination in a wreath above the date on the back and the national emblem, a wreath encircling the Tiananmen Gate and five stars, above the name of the People's Republic of China, on the front. These three coins, still with the same design, remain the only ones in use to the present day.

Since an issue in 1979 of collectors' coins to commemorate the 30th anniversary of the People's Republic, the China Mint Company in Beijing has remained a prolific issuer of commemorative coins.

Soldiers from the terracotta army guarding the tomb of Emperor Qin Shi Huangdi, recently discovered near Xian.

JAPAN

FIRST COINS:	708
FIRST DECIMAL COINS:	1870
MAIN MINT:	Osaka
CURRENCY:	yen

JAPAN adopted the idea of coinage from China. The first Japanese coins were issued by the Japanese imperial court at Nara in AD 708.

They were silver and copper imitations of Chinese cast-bronze coins of the contemporary Tang Dynasty. The silver coins were not successful and were soon withdrawn, but copper coins were used and issued for the next 250 years, during which time 11 new issues, all with designs derived from Chinese coins, were made. After 958 no copper coins were issued by the Japanese government, and by the end of the tenth century they had gone out of use.

It was not until the thirteenth century, when imported Chinese bronze coins began to circulate, that coins came back into fashion in Japan. The Chinese had begun to use paper money and so exported the coins they no longer needed. For the next few centuries China provided Japan with almost all the bronze coins it needed. The only coins being cast in Japan during this period were unofficially made copies of the imported Chinese coins.

THE TOKUGAWA SHOGUNS

In 1603 Japan entered a new phase of monetary history, with the rise to power of the Tokugawa Shoguns. In 1606 the issue of officially cast copper coins began again. They were still modelled on contemporary Chinese coins. Further issues were made in 1615 and 1626. The shoguns' new coins were inscribed in Chinese characters with the name of the official imperial period during which they were made and the Chinese words for circulating money (this practice was copied from Chinese coins). The 1606 coins were inscribed *Keicho-Tsuho*, meaning 'current money of the Keicho period', and the 1615 coins were inscribed *Genna-Tsuho*, meaning 'current money of the Genna period'. The 1626 coin, inscribed *Kanei-Tsuho*, 'current money of the Kanei period', was such a success that the shogun decided to continue issuing it after the Kanei period had ended in 1643. The Kanei-tsuho coins were issued until the nineteenth century at many mints, often bearing a mint mark on the back.

Alongside the new copper pieces the shoguns' government also issued gold and silver coins. These were very unusual: their designs were based on the shapes of gold and silver ingots which had been used as money in Japan during the Middle Ages. The gold coins were oval or rectangular slabs; the silver coins were bars or round lumps and later also rectangular slabs. These coins were not made in the same way as the copper coinage, but were cast and hammered into the desired shape and then stamped with marks to show that they were official coins.

LOCAL COINS

Besides the shoguns' coins there were also many kinds of local money, mostly issued by clans. From 1661 most of the local money took the form of paper notes denominated in the shoguns' coins or in local produce, such as rice or wine, but, later, there were also many local

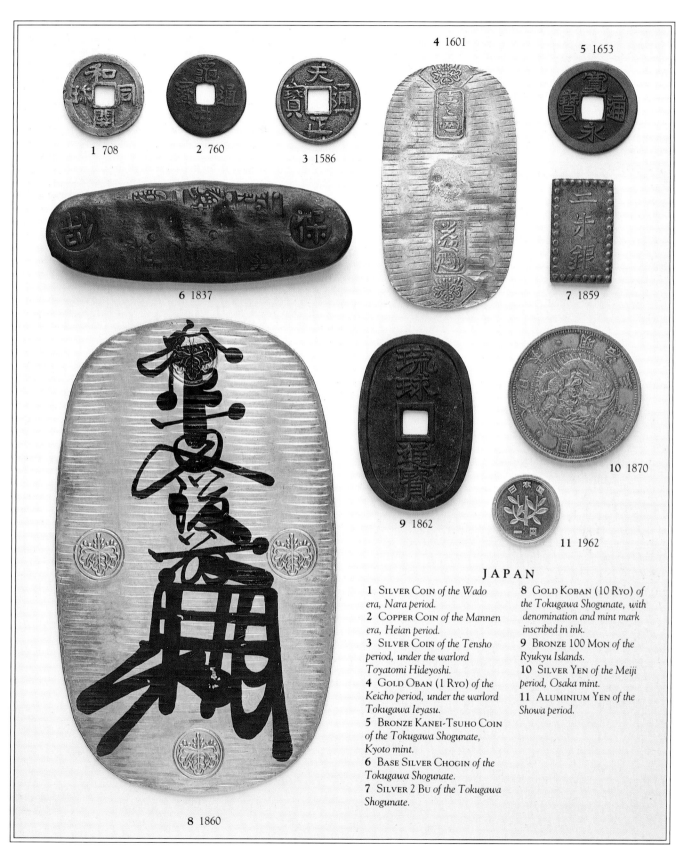

JAPAN

1 Silver Coin of the Wado era, Nara period.
2 Copper Coin of the Mannen era, Heian period.
3 Silver Coin of the Tensho period, under the warlord Toyatomi Hideyoshi.
4 Gold Oban (1 Ryo) of the Keicho period, under the warlord Tokugawa Ieyasu.
5 Bronze Kanei-Tsuho Coin of the Tokugawa Shogunate, Kyoto mint.
6 Base Silver Chogin of the Tokugawa Shogunate.
7 Silver 2 Bu of the Tokugawa Shogunate.
8 Gold Koban (10 Ryo) of the Tokugawa Shogunate, with denomination and mint mark inscribed in ink.
9 Bronze 100 Mon of the Ryukyu Islands.
10 Silver Yen of the Meiji period, Osaka mint.
11 Aluminium Yen of the Showa period.

JAPANESE MINTS OF THE TOKUGAWA PERIOD, 1603–1867

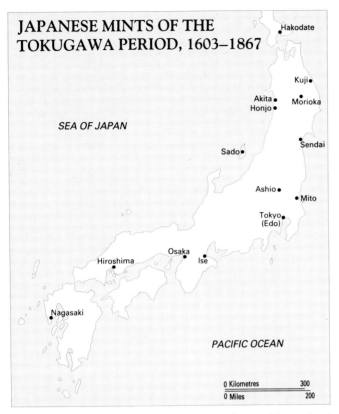

SEA OF JAPAN

Hakodate

Kuji
Akita
Honjo
Morioka

Sado

Sendai

Ashio
Mito

Tokyo
(Edo)

Osaka
Hiroshima
Ise

Nagasaki

PACIFIC OCEAN

0 Kilometres 300
0 Miles 200

coins issued. Unusual metals and shapes were often used for the local coins: for example, square iron coins in Sendai district, oval silver coins in Akita, oval lead coins in Yonezawa and lead bar coins in Kanragori. By 1800 the coinage system of the Shoguns was running into trouble. The copper coins were being replaced by tokens made of brass or iron, and the size and quality of the official gold coins had to be reduced.

The opening of Japan to foreign trade by Commodore Perry in 1853 brought the silver dollar into Japan as an alternative coinage to the Shoguns' deteriorating system. Within a decade the dollar, mostly in the form of imported Mexican issues, was circulating in the trade ports of Yokohama and Kobe.

MEIJI REFORM

In 1868 the last shogun was overthrown and power restored to the emperor. Two years later the Meiji emperor reformed the coinage. He replaced the official and local coins and paper money issued under the shoguns with a new European-style coinage, based on the silver dollar. The Japanese for dollar was yen, meaning a round coin, and for cent sen, meaning a copper coin. A new imperial mint was built at Osaka, using minting machinery from Birmingham, England. Its first coins, dated third year (1870) of the Meiji (Brilliant Rule) period, were issued the following year, 1871. Gold 1, 5, 10 and 20 yen pieces, silver 1 yen and 5, 10, 20 and 50 sen, and copper ½, 1 and 2 sen and 1 rin coins were issued from 1871. The rin coin, representing one-thousandth of a dollar and intended to equal in value the shoguns' traditional copper-alloy coin, the mon, was not popular and soon disappeared from use.

The designs of the Meiji emperor's new coins used Japanese motifs with a Chinese inscription. The silver yen dated 1870 had a dragon on

the front and a sun surrounded by a floral border on the back. The inscription around the dragon named the issuer, date and denomination. From 1873 the sun motif was replaced by an inscription naming the denomination, while the denomination on the dragon side was written in English: ONE YEN.

MODERN COINAGE

Although the Japanese economy has become one of the strongest in the world, the value of the yen coin today is tiny when compared with the silver dollar it originally represented. It has dropped to such an extent that the sen denomination is no longer issued. The denominations now in use are aluminium 1 yen pieces, brass 5 yen, bronze 10 yen and cupro-nickel 50, 100 and 500 yen. Higher denominations are represented by banknotes. The designs used on each denomination include plant motifs. The 10 yen also depicts the Imperial Palace. Since the 1964 Olympic Games when silver 100 and 1000 yen coins were issued, numerous other silver and gold commemorative coins have also been produced.

NORTH KOREA

FIRST COINS:	996
FIRST DECIMAL COINS:	1882
MAIN MINT:	Pyongyang
CURRENCY:	won

THE use of coins in the northern half of Korea, in the territory now known as the Democratic People's Republic of Korea, began during the third century BC, when Chinese knife coins of the state of Yan were brought into the area by Chinese settlers. In 108 BC the Chinese Han Dynasty conquered northern Korea and introduced its 5-grain coins as the official currency. Imported Chinese coins continued to be used in Korea after Chinese rule had been replaced by the native kingdom of Koguryo (37 BC–AD 668). No coins were issued by Koguryo or by the southern Korean kingdom of Silla (57 BC–AD 935), which conquered it in 668. Silla had close links with China and imported Tang Dynasty bronze coins.

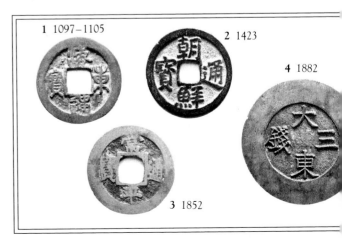

1 1097–1105
2 1423
4 1882
3 1852

THE KINGDOM OF KORYO

Korea's first coins were issued in 996 by the kingdom of Koryo, which had succeeded Silla in 935. They were imitations of Chinese Tang coins, inscribed on the back with the Chinese characters *dong guo* meaning 'Eastern Kingdom', that is Koryo. Coins with an original Korean design were not issued until 1097. Between that year and 1105 three new coin issues were commenced. They were all cast-bronze coins with square holes and inscribed in Chinese, like contemporary Chinese coins, but their inscriptions refer directly to Korea.

KOREAN COINS OF THE KINGDOM OF KORYO

Chinese inscription	Translation
Dong guo tong bao	Current money of the Eastern Kingdom
Hai dong tong bao	Current money of the land east of the sea
San han tong bao	Current money of Sanhan (Korea)

Many versions of these coins were issued, some written in decorative and archaic versions of Chinese, and some replacing the character *tong*, meaning 'circulating', with characters meaning 'heavy' or 'chief'. Korean histories do not record how long these coinages continued.

THE YI DYNASTY

Chinese coins continued to be imported, but no new coins were issued until 1423 when Korea's next coinage was cast by King Sejong of the Yi Dynasty (1392–1910). In 1401 Sejong's predecessor, Taejong, had attempted to issue a Chinese-style paper currency. When it failed, Sejong replaced it with his new coins. They closely resembled contemporary Chinese coins, but were inscribed with a Chinese inscription meaning 'circulating money of Choson [Korea]'. Large coins worth 10 standard ones were also cast. The coinage, like the paper currency, was not considered successful.

In 1625 the Yi Dynasty made a fresh attempt at issuing coins. The 1423 design was reused with different calligraphy. In 1633 a second issue followed with a new inscription. Cast by the mint of the government's Food Supply Stabilization Office, the coins were inscribed in Chinese *chang ping tong bao*, meaning 'circulating money of Stabilization'. The success of this issue led in 1678 to mints being opened at 24 other government offices, all to issue coins with the same Stabilization currency inscription. From 1679 they issued double-weight brass coins, and from 1742 standard coins again. In 1866–7

token coins worth 100 standard coins with the same inscription were issued, but soon withdrawn. The 'Stabilization money' continued until 1888, when an issue of underweight 5 coin tokens led to it being discredited. The different issues of Stabilization currency were distinguished by mint marks, furnace numbers, control marks and denominations, mostly written in Chinese, on their backs.

MODERNIZATION UNDER THE YI DYNASTY

In 1882 the Korean government, under King Kojong, began to reform Korea's coinage system. The first step was to issue a silver coinage. Three denominations, 1, 2 and 3 chon (tenths of an ounce) were cast and then marked with a blue enamel circle before issue. They were without the traditional square hole, but were inscribed on the front, like the brass coins, with four Chinese characters. The inscription stated that the coin was of the Great Eastern Nation [Korea] and its weight. An unexpected change in the price of silver meant that the coins were withdrawn in the following year.

In 1884, a machine-minting section was set up at the central mint in Seoul and in 1888 some struck silver and bronze coins, with a dragon design copied from contemporary Japanese coins, were briefly issued. In 1892 a more substantial issue with modified designs was struck on new machinery, under Japanese supervision. The denomination system for the struck coinage was revised with each new issue. In 1888, 1000 mun = 1 warn; in 1892, 100 fun = 1 yang; in 1893, 500 fun = 1 whan; and finally in 1907, 100 chon = 1 won. The last version was intended to be parallel to the 100 sen = 1 yen currency of the Japanese Empire, which since 1905 had effectively ruled Korea.

In 1910 the last Yi king abdicated and Korea came under direct Japanese rule. Japanese coinage rapidly replaced the Korean coinage.

THE DEMOCRATIC PEOPLE'S REPUBLIC

Korea was freed from Japanese rule by the Allied invasion of 1945 and divided into northern and southern zones at the Potsdam Conference later the same year, but coinage did not recommence in the northern part of Korea until 11 years after the Democratic People's Republic had been established there in 1948. Aluminium 1, 5 and 10 chon pieces inscribed in Korean were struck. Their design was closely based on that used on the aluminium coins of contemporary China, with the national wreath and star emblem on the front and the denomination on the back. In 1978 a 50 chon denomination was added to the aluminium coinage introduced in 1959 and used in North Korea until the present day.

SOUTH KOREA

FIRST COINS:	996
FIRST DECIMAL COINS:	1882
MAIN MINT:	Seoul
CURRENCY:	won

IN THE southern part of Korea now known as the Republic of Korea, imported Chinese coins began to circulate during the kingdom of

---

NORTH KOREA

1 BRONZE COIN of 'the land of the eastern sea', Kingdom of Koryo.

2 BRONZE COIN of 'Choson' (Korea), Yi Dynasty.
3 BRASS 'STABILIZATION MONEY' COIN of the Board of Revenue mint, Seoul
4 SILVER 3 CHON of King Kojong of the Yi dynasty.
5 SILVER ½ WON of the Japanese Protectorate.
6 ALUMINIUM 10 CHON of the Democratic People's Republic.

5 1908

6 1959

Silla (57 BC–AD 935) period. Silla, originally a small state in the south-eastern part of the Korean peninsula, used Chinese support to overrun the kingdoms of Paekche (17 BC–AD 660), its western neighbour, and Koguryo (37 BC–AD 668) in the northern half of Korea. Chinese Han and Tang coins have been found in large numbers in the territory originally ruled by Silla. From the time of Silla's conquests until the Allied invasion of 1945, Korea remained unified and the coinage history of South and North Korea was the same (see North Korea).

During the Yi Dynasty (1392–1910) the capital of Korea was in Seoul and the main mints for casting the Stabilization currency were located at government offices in the capital. The Treasury, Board of Works, Land Tax Office, Transport Office, Charity Ministry, Food Supply Ministry, Defence Ministry, Public Supply Department, Special Military Office, Armament Office, Court Guard Section, Military Academy, Naval Office and Local Defence Office all had mints in Seoul.

THE REPUBLIC OF KOREA
After the Japanese occupation had been ended by the Allied invasion in 1945 and Korea had been divided into two zones at the Potsdam Conference later the same year, southern Korea was without a coinage until an issue in 1959 of 10, 50 and 100 hwan coins by the Republic of Korea (established in 1948). Before that, small change circulated in the form of paper money issued by the Bank of Korea and by the American military authorities. In 1966 the Bank of Korea took over responsibility for the issue of coins and made 1, 5 and 10 won coins (1 won = 10 hwan). Both the 1959 and 1966 coins used designs featuring Korean historical subjects, such as the sixteenth-century ironclad ships of Admiral Yi on the 50 hwan and the 5 won denominations. A new 100 won coin depicting King Sejong (1419–51) was introduced in 1970, and a 500 won coin depicting a flying crane was added in 1983. Since 1970 the Republic of Korea has issued many commemorative coins with varying denominations up to the 50,000 won gold coin struck to mark the Seoul Olympics of 1988.

TAIWAN

FIRST COINS:	1689
FIRST DECIMAL COINS:	1893
MAIN MINT:	Taibei
CURRENCY:	yuan

TAIWAN became a part of the Chinese Empire in 1683, when the Manchu army captured it from a rebel, Koxinga (Geng Jingzhong), who was using it as a base for piracy along the Chinese coast. Imported Chinese coins probably were used by the local Taiwanese long before this event, and certainly were brought to the island by Koxinga. European silver coins were also already known on the island in the form of silver dollar-sized coins brought by the Dutch, who had a settlement on Taiwan from 1624 until driven out by Koxinga in 1661. Soon after the capture of the island the Manchu authorities established a mint and issued brass square-holed coins with a 'Tai', for Taiwan, mint-mark in Chinese and Manchu.

NINETEENTH-CENTURY COINAGE
In the 1840s a new coin began to be issued on the island. Silver dollars, the same size as the Spanish 8 real piece but with Chinese designs and Chinese and Manchu inscriptions, were struck on the island to pay troops. Although these were specifically for local use, they represent China's first attempt to issue European-style coins. These dollars were denominated by their weight and the quality of the silver, as if they were to circulate as bullion, like the contemporary Chinese silver money ingots.

The dragon dollars introduced throughout China in the 1890s were not struck in Taiwan, but from 1893 silver 5, 10 and 20 cent dragon coins were struck at a machine mint in Taibei, in the name of Taiwan

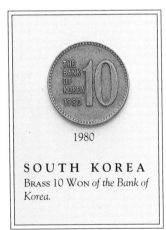

1980

SOUTH KOREA
BRASS 10 WON of the Bank of Korea.

The opening ceremony of the 1988 Olympic Games in Seoul, South Korea. South Korea, along with many other countries, issued coins to commemorate these Games.

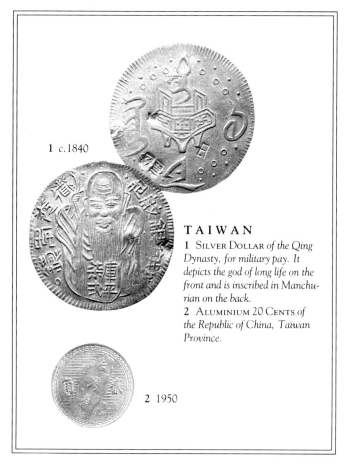

1 *c.1840*

TAIWAN
1 SILVER DOLLAR *of the Qing Dynasty, for military pay. It depicts the god of long life on the front and is inscribed in Manchurian on the back.*
2 ALUMINIUM 20 CENTS *of the Republic of China, Taiwan Province.*

2 *1950*

Province. In 1895 Taiwan was occupied by Japan and Japanese coinage was introduced, particularly the silver 1 yen, which had recently been removed from circulation in Japan itself.

THE REPUBLIC OF CHINA

Soon after Taiwan had been returned to Chinese rule following the defeat of Japan in 1945, it became a refuge for the Nationalist government of Chiang Kai-shek. From 1949 the Nationalist government issued coins specifically for Taiwan Province. The first issue, consisting of bronze 10 cents and silver 50 cents, was decorated by the portrait of Sun Yat Sen, first president of the Republic of China on the front and a map of the island on the back. The same designs were reused from 1950 for an issue of aluminium 10 and 20 and brass 50 cents. Both issues were inscribed only in Chinese.

In 1960 responsibility for coin issue was given to the Bank of Taiwan, which issued cupro-nickel yuan (dollar) pieces with floral designs. From 1967 aluminium 10 and brass 50 cent coins with floral designs were also issued. Cupro-nickel 5 yuan coins with the portrait of Chiang Kai-shek appeared in 1970.

A reorganization of the coinage took place in 1981, when a bronze 50 cent and 1 yuan with a cherry-blossom design and cupro-nickel 5 and 10 yuan, portraying presidents Chiang and Sun respectively, were issued. Each denomination has the Western numeral for its value on the back. Commemorative coins in silver and gold have been made since 1961.

MACAO

FIRST COINS:	1952
FIRST DECIMAL COINS:	1952
MAIN MINT:	Lisbon
CURRENCY:	pataca

ALTHOUGH the port of Macao on the southern coast of China has been under Portuguese control since 1577, a coinage was not produced for the settlement until 1952. Issued in the name of the Republic of Portugal, it was decorated with the crowned arms of Portugal on a globe on the front. The name of the port and the denomination were inscribed on the coin in both Portuguese and Chinese.

Originally, the currency of Macao had been that of China, predominantly brass square-holed coins and imported silver dollars, but from 1863 the cent and dollar currency of nearby Hong Kong was also adopted. The local name for the silver dollar was pataca and for cents, avos (an abbreviation of centavos). Paper-money patacas were issued first in 1905 and paper avos appeared in 1944. The 1952 coin issue consisted of bronze 5 and 10 avos, cupro-nickel 50 avos and silver 1 and 5 patacas. From 1967 the metals were altered and brass 5 and 10 avos and nickel 1 and 5 patacas with similar designs were gradually introduced.

In 1982 a new coinage was issued. The bronze 10, 20 and 50 avos all had a decorative Chinese good-luck character on the back. The cupro-nickel 1 and 5 patacas had Chinese decorative designs on the back, a vase and dragon respectively. A large number of commemorative coins have also been struck for Macao since 1974.

MONGOLIA

FIRST COINS:	1925
FIRST DECIMAL COINS:	1925
MAIN MINT:	Leningrad
CURRENCY:	tukhrik

THE Mongols have been responsible for numerous coin issues throughout central Asia, from Turkey to China, but few coins have been issued in Mongolia itself. The earliest coins in use in Mongolia were Chinese, imported from the Han period (206 BC–AD 220). During the seventeenth century Mongolia came under direct Chinese rule and Chinese brass coins were circulated officially.

It was only after Mongolia had gained independence with Russian support and established itself as a republic that coins were made specifically for it. These were minted in the USSR, using designs like those on contemporary Soviet coins, but inscribed in Mongolian in the Mongolian script. Copper 1, 2 and 5 mongo and silver 10, 15, 20 and 50 mongo and 1 tukhrik (= 100 mongo) coins were struck. A second

MONGOLIA
SILVER TUKHRIK *of the Mongolian People's Republic.*

1925

issue of coins with the same designs and denominations, up to the 20 mongo, but made of aluminium–bronze and cupro-nickel was issued in 1937.

From 1945 a new coin design, featuring on the front the national emblem, a horseman and the rising sun within a wreath, was adopted. The same denominations as the 1937 issue were struck. The new coins were still inscribed in Mongolian, but the inscription was written in the Cyrillic alphabet. An issue of aluminium coins replaced these in 1959, but in 1970–1 the 50 mongo and 1 tukhrik denominations were reintroduced in cupro-nickel. Higher denominations have been struck since, but only as commemoratives.

HONG KONG

FIRST COINS:	1863
FIRST DECIMAL COINS:	1863
MAIN MINT:	Royal Mint
CURRENCY:	dollar

THE first coins in the territory now known as the British colony of Hong Kong arrived during the Chinese Han period (206 BC–AD 220), when the south of China became part of the Chinese Empire.

Its coinage history became distinct from that of China only from 1863, when the British government issued bronze 1 and silver 10 cent coins for Hong Kong (under British control since 1841). These coins had typical British colonial designs, with Queen Victoria's crowned bust on the front and the denomination and name of the colony on the back. A slightly unusual feature was the inclusion on the back of a Chinese translation of the English inscription. As part of the same issue, there was also an unsuccessful attempt to issue a small holed bronze coin as a substitute for the Chinese brass coins which circulated in Hong Kong.

THE HONG KONG MINT

In 1866 the British government opened a branch of the Royal Mint in Hong Kong expressly to issue silver coins for the colony. In addition to the 10 cent, it also made 5 and 20 cent and ½ and 1 dollar pieces with designs similar to the 1863 issue. It was hoped that the new Hong Kong dollar would compete with the Mexican dollar in circulation in China, but this part of the venture failed. In 1868 the mint was closed and

from 1872 the Royal Mint in England recommenced striking coins for the colony, including the 5 and 20 cent coins, but not the ½ and 1 dollar denominations which were abandoned.

THE BRITISH DOLLAR

Larger coins were still needed and in 1890 a silver 50 cent piece, the same size as the earlier ½ dollar, was issued. In 1895 this was joined by a new silver 1 dollar. This coin, known as the 'British Dollar', was struck at the Bombay mint in India and was issued for use throughout the British Far East. On the front of the dollar was the standing figure of Britannia and on the back was the denomination in Chinese and Malay in an ornamental border. It was officially current in Hong Kong until 1935. Silver 5, 10, 20 and 50 cents with the 1863 designs also continued to be used until the same year, but apart from small strikings of 5 cents in 1932–3, were not issued from 1905. The large issues of silver coins in the previous decade, for export to China, served the colony's needs for the next 30 years. Bronze cents continued to be issued and used until the Japanese invasion in 1941.

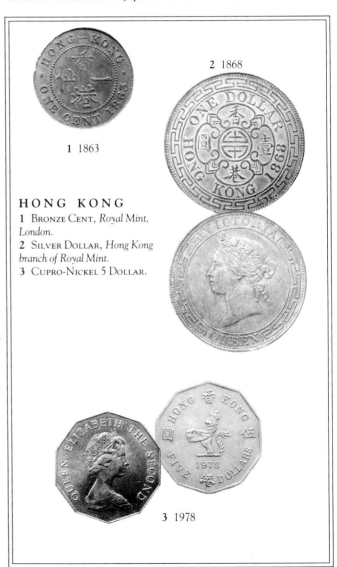

HONG KONG
1 BRONZE CENT, *Royal Mint, London.*
2 SILVER DOLLAR, *Hong Kong branch of Royal Mint.*
3 CUPRO-NICKEL 5 DOLLAR.

1 1863

2 1868

3 1978

A 10 cent small change note, from the government of Hong Kong, 1945. From 1945 until the early 1960s, government paper currency, denominated 1, 5 and 10 cents and 1 dollar, circulated in the place of coins.

PAPER MONEY SMALL CHANGE

In 1935 the silver coinage of Hong Kong was replaced by an issue of cupro-nickel 5 and 10 cent coins. Apart from the change of monarch, the 1935 designs were the same as those originally introduced in the 1860s. These new issues were short-lived as the demand for nickel created by the Sino-Japanese War caused them to be melted down. By 1941 the Hong Kong authorities had replaced them with paper money. After the Second World War coins were not reintroduced until 1949 and then only partially. Paper-money small change continued to be used until the 1960s.

MODERN COINAGE

The new post-war coins retained the traditional designs, but the 5 and 10 cent coins were now brass and the 1 cent denomination was abandoned. A cupro-nickel 50 cent was introduced in 1951 and a 1 dollar in 1960. The 1 dollar had a new design, featuring the lion crest of the colony. Following an official review of the coinage in 1975, a new brass 20 cent coin and a cupro-nickel 2 dollar, both scallop-edged, were introduced and in the following year a 10-sided 5 dollar coin, with the same design as the dollar, was also struck. As part of the same process, the size of the 50 cent was reduced in 1977 and the 10 cent in 1981. The new 50 cent was a brass coin. As the new 5 dollar coin was easy to forge, a smaller round 5 dollar coin with an inscribed edge was introduced in 1980.

Since 1975 a series of gold 1000 dollar collectors' coins have been struck. The 1975 and 1986 issues commemorate royal visits to the colony.

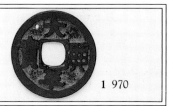

VIETNAM
1 BRONZE COIN of Prince Dinh Bo-linh.

1 970

VIETNAM

FIRST COINS:	970
FIRST DECIMAL COINS:	c. 1830
MAIN MINT:	Hanoi
CURRENCY:	dong

THE first coins to circulate in the territory now known as the Socialist Republic of Vietnam were Chinese. From 111 BC until about AD 968 northern Vietnam was under direct Chinese rule, and Chinese Han and Tang coins were put into circulation. Independence from China was achieved during the period of disorder following the end of the Tang Dynasty (618–907).

In 968 the Vietnamese prince Dinh Bo-linh established himself as independent ruler and in 970 issued Vietnam's first local coinage. His cast round bronze coins, with four Chinese characters on the front around a central square hole, followed the model established by the Chinese Tang Dynasty. The inscription, *tai ping xing bao*, indicated that the coins were the 'abundant money of the Taiping period' (970–80). On the back, where the Tang issue of 845 had a mint name, Dinh placed the Chinese character *ding*, representing Dinh, his family name.

This design was followed by Dinh's successors until the present century. Chinese-style coins with inscriptions referring to their function as money and their period of issue were issued by successive dynasties, but until the eighteenth century they continued to compete with imported Chinese coins.

THE FORMER LE, LI, TRAN AND LATER LE DYNASTIES

Following the Dinh issue, the Former Le and the Li dynasties issued new coins in 980, 1010, 1042 and 1044, but then for 150 years minting

213

ceased. During this period the demand for coin was small and met entirely by imports of Chinese coins. Production began again in 1205, when the Tran Dynasty issued a new coin, copied from an earlier Chinese Song issue. Regular but small issues continued throughout the Tran period (1225–1400) and under the Later Le Dynasty (1428–1527), the Mac usurpers (1527–92) and the restored Later Le (1592–1788).

During the interval between the Tran and Later Le dynasties northern Vietnam was occupied by the Chinese (1406–28) and it is thought that coins were issued by the Chinese Ming emperor specifically for use in Vietnam. Finds in Vietnam suggest that the importation of Chinese coins continued throughout the Tran, Le and Mac periods. During the period of the restored Later Le, locally made imitations of Chinese and official Vietnamese coins were also issued and circulated widely.

SOUTHERN VIETNAM

After the restoration of the Le, the southern part of present-day Vietnam finally came under Vietnamese rule. This area had previously been under the control of the Cambodian Champa and Khmer kingdoms. No coins were issued by these kingdoms, but imported silver and gold coins from the eighth- to tenth-century Pyu and Mon kingdoms, which ruled part of present-day Thailand and Burma, have been found in southern Vietnam and perhaps circulated there.

Chinese and Vietnamese coins entered the area as it was absorbed gradually into the Vietnamese Empire. The kingdom of Champa in central Vietnam was captured by the Le in the late fifteenth century, the rest of the south was taken from the Khmer during the seventeenth and eighteenth centuries. Although formally part of the Le Empire, the south was under the control of the Nguyen clan, relatives, but rivals, of the Trinh clan who ruled in the name of the Le emperors in the north. Although a few Le coins were issued by the Trinh, the Nguyen issued no official coins and relied instead on the private production of small imitation coins, mostly with inscriptions copied or adapted from Chinese coins.

NORTHERN VIETNAM

From the 1750s, when the Trinh recaptured the copper mines of northern Vietnam from the Mac clan and their Chinese supporters, large-scale coin production began in northern Vietnam. Coins inscribed with the name of the Le Dynasty's Canh Hung period (1740–80) were issued. On some issues mint names appear on the back of the coins, while numerous variations in the front inscriptions have also been recorded. These variations are thought to relate to the mints at which they were issued. During this period Vietnamese mints also began to issue large presentation coins with pictures of dragons on the back.

CANH HUNG PERIOD COIN INSCRIPTIONS

Inscription	Translation
Canh hung thong bao	current money of Canh Hung period
Canh hung cu bao	large money of Canh Hung period
Canh hung da bao	big money of Canh Hung period
Canh hung thuan bao	favoured money of Canh Hung period
Canh hung vinh bao	eternal money of Canh Hung period
Canh hung tuyen bao	coin money of Canh Hung period
Canh hung trong bao	heavy money of Canh Hung period
Canh hung trung bao	middle money of Canh Hung period
Canh hung noi bao	private money of Canh Hung period
Canh hung chinh bao	correct money of Canh Hung period
Canh hung chi bao	valuable money of Canh Hung period

THE TAYSON REBELLION AND THE NGUYEN DYNASTY

In 1773 three brothers led the Tayson district in a revolt against the Nguyen rulers of southern Vietnam. By 1788 they had overthrown the Nguyen and the Trinh and the eldest brother, Nguyen Van Hue, had declared himself emperor. Both he and his son, Nguyen Quang Toan, who succeeded him in 1792, cast coins with designs like those of the Canh Hung issue. Most Tayson coins were very light in weight and made of brass. Some large dragon coins were also issued by the son.

VIETNAM
2 ZINC COIN of Emperor Gia Long, Nguyen Dynasty.
3 SILVER OUNCE BAR COIN of Emperor Minh Mang.
4 SILVER DOLLAR of Emperor Minh Mang.
5 SILVER PIASTRE DE COMMERCE of French Indo-China, Paris mint.
6 BRASS SAPEQUE of Emperor Bao Dai, Nguyen Dynasty.

2 1802–20
6 1933
4 1833
3 1820–40
5 1885

The Tayson rebels' hold on Vietnam was short-lived and only served to allow the Nguyen, who previously had ruled only the south in the name of the Le, to take control of the whole of the country and to establish their own dynasty. Nguyen Anh completed his campaign to suppress the Tayson rebels in 1802 and issued coins in the name of the Gia Long period (1802–20) from that date.

The Nguyen opened a new phase in the history of coinage in Vietnam. Although some brass minting continued, a large proportion of the coins now made were cast from zinc and a silver coinage was also introduced. The use of zinc was the consequence of a general shortage of copper. The silver coinage came into being in response to an increase in foreign trade, particularly with France.

Silver coins first appeared during the Gia Long period. They were a modified version of the rectangular bar-shaped silver ingots which were already being used as money in Vietnam. The coins weighed 1 ounce and were stamped on four faces with an inscription in Chinese characters indicating the period of issue, the weight and quality of the silver, and the value in terms of brass and zinc coins.

During the following Minh Mang period (1820–40), silver bar coins with values in tenths of ounces and round coins equal in value to the Spanish dollar (8 real piece) were also issued. Trade with Europeans had familiarized the Vietnamese with the Spanish dollar as a practical form of silver coinage and the Minh Mang dollars were an attempt to adopt their issue locally. The silver dollars had a dragon design and an inscription in Chinese stating that they were the current money of the Minh Mang period. Struck in 1832, they were the first officially issued dollars in East Asia. Half dollars were also minted. However, lack of financial control by the government caused the experiment to fail.

The Nguyen emperors made many coin-shaped award pieces. Struck in silver and gold or cast in brass with inscriptions stating that they were current money, they were shaped either like the traditional square-holed coins or like foreign dollars and bore inscriptions referring to good fortune. The gold and silver pieces also had pictorial designs featuring good-luck symbols, such as dragons.

FRENCH PROTECTORATE

The Nguyen coinage continued until 1933, when the last issue of square-holed coins was made, but it had ceased to be a significant part of Vietnam's coinage long before that. From 1863 the Nguyen emperors gradually yielded power to France, which in 1887 established a protectorate over a large part of South East Asia, including Vietnam, Cambodia and Laos, as French Indo-China.

The earliest French coins for the area were bronze square-holed sapeque and 1 cent and silver 10, 20 and 50 cent pieces, struck in 1879 for part of southern Vietnam in the name of French Cochin China. A further issue in 1884 was followed in 1885 by the striking of a silver piastre (or dollar).

From 1885 the same denominations began to be struck for French Indo-China. These were for use throughout Vietnam, but in 1905 a separate sapeque was struck for northern Vietnam in the name of the Protectorate of Tonkin. All sapeques and cents were inscribed in both French and Vietnamese (in Chinese characters), but the silver coins were inscribed only in French and decorated with a seated woman, representing the French Republic.

The French Indo-China issues continued until after the Second World War. The coinage had gone through various changes, such as the introduction of a cupro-nickel 5 cents in 1923 and the issue of zinc $\frac{1}{4}$ and 1 cent and aluminium 1 and 5 cents by the Vichy government during the Second World War. The last French issues consisted of aluminium 5, 10 and 20 cents and cupro-nickel 50 cents and 1 piastre issued from 1945 to 1947, all decorated on the front with a female bust, representing the French Republic, holding a laurel branch to symbolize victory over Germany in 1945, and, on the back, a design of two stalks of rice.

INDEPENDENCE

In 1949, France made Vietnam independent within the French Union. New aluminium coins, denominated 10, 20 and 50 su, were issued. The su (spelt 'xu' on the largest coin) replaced the cent (100 su = 1 dong). The dong replaced the French piastre. The overthrow of the French by the Vietnamese in 1954 left Vietnam once again divided into northern and southern states.

The Communists, who held the north, had already established a democratic government in 1945, during their struggle against the French. Aluminium and bronze coins, featuring a star design or portraying the revolutionary leader Ho Chi Minh, were issued in the name of the Democratic Republic of Vietnam in 1945–6, using the xu–dong denomination system. Once Ho Chi Minh's government was fully established in the north, a new set of aluminium coins, denominated 1, 2 and 5 xu, with designs based on contemporary Chinese coins was issued. Both the 1945–6 and the 1958 coins were inscribed in Vietnamese, in a phonetic script.

VIETNAM
7 BRASS 2 DONG of the Democratic Republic of Vietnam.
8 ALUMINIUM 5 XU of the Democratic Republic (North Vietnam).
9 CUPRO-NICKEL 5 DONG of the Republic of Vietnam (South Vietnam).
7 1946
8 1958
9 1966

THE REPUBLIC OF VIETNAM

The xu and dong denominations were also used on the coins of the Republic of Vietnam, the state established in southern Vietnam with US support in 1955. Coins issued with rice plants as the main design were the 50 xu and 1, 5, 10 and 20 dong pieces.

THE SOCIALIST REPUBLIC OF VIETNAM

The civil war between north and south ended in 1975, and in the following year Vietnam was reunited as the Socialist Republic of Vietnam. New aluminium 1, 2, 5, 10, 20 and 50 xu and 1 dong pieces were issued from 1976 and featured designs of the star and wreath national emblem.

AFRICA

Gold 500 Shilling *commemorative coin of
Kenya, 1966.*

Coins first appeared in Africa during the late sixth century BC in Libya. Greek, Phoenician and Roman settlements ensured the spread of coinage along the coastal territories of North Africa during the following centuries. Local Numidian and Ethiopian kingdoms also issued their own coins.

Although most medieval and early modern European gold coins were made from African gold exported as coin from the Islamic states of North Africa, most parts of Africa were unaware of the concept of coinage until Islamic and European traders and slavers brought coins further into the continent. By the tenth century, Islamic cities in East Africa were issuing their own coins, although European issues, mainly Portuguese and British, did not appear in quantity until the late eighteenth century. During the nineteenth century the expansion of European imperialism brought coins into use throughout the continent.

The wide variety of coins being issued by the states of modern Africa still reflects in part the systems introduced during the period of European domination.

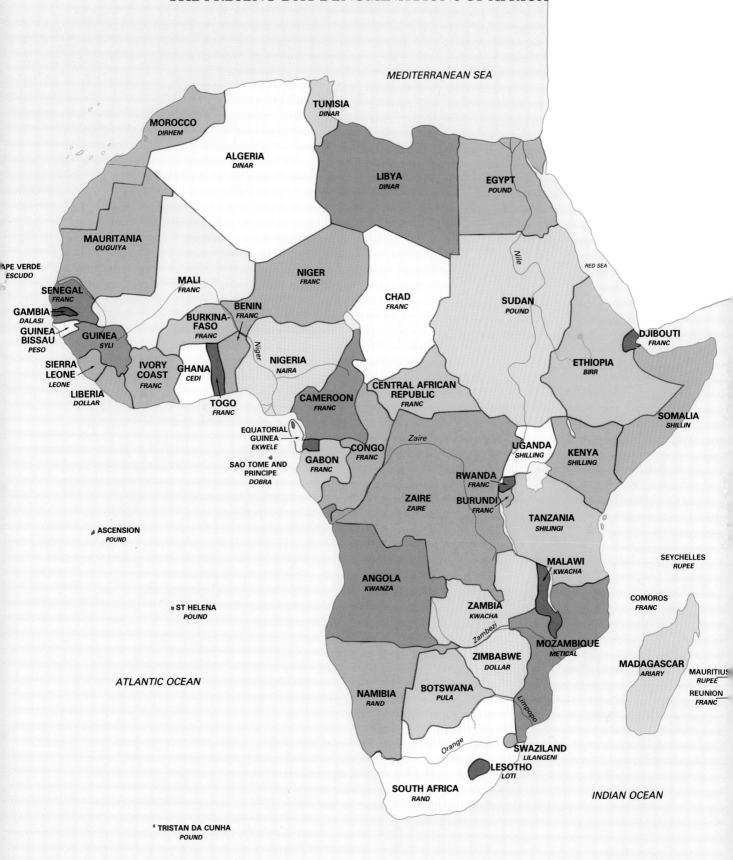

THE PRESENT-DAY DENOMINATIONS OF AFRICA

MEDITERRANEAN SEA

MOROCCO
DIRHEM

TUNISIA
DINAR

ALGERIA
DINAR

LIBYA
DINAR

EGYPT
POUND

MAURITANIA
OUGUIYA

Nile

RED SEA

APE VERDE
ESCUDO

NIGER
FRANC

MALI
FRANC

CHAD
FRANC

SUDAN
POUND

SENEGAL
FRANC

GAMBIA
DALASI

GUINEA
BISSAU
PESO

BENIN
FRANC

BURKINA-
FASO
FRANC

GUINEA
SYLI

DJIBOUTI
FRANC

ETHIOPIA
BIRR

SIERRA
LEONE
LEONE

IVORY
COAST
FRANC

GHANA
CEDI

Niger

NIGERIA
NAIRA

LIBERIA
DOLLAR

TOGO
FRANC

CENTRAL AFRICAN
REPUBLIC
FRANC

SOMALIA
SHILLIN

CAMEROON
FRANC

EQUATORIAL
GUINEA
EKWELE

Zaire

UGANDA
SHILLING

KENYA
SHILLING

CONGO
FRANC

SAO TOME AND
PRINCIPE
DOBRA

GABON
FRANC

RWANDA
FRANC

BURUNDI
FRANC

ZAIRE
ZAIRE

TANZANIA
SHILINGI

ASCENSION
POUND

MALAWI
KWACHA

SEYCHELLES
RUPEE

ANGOLA
KWANZA

COMOROS
FRANC

ST HELENA
POUND

ZAMBIA
KWACHA

Zambezi

MOZAMBIQUE
METICAL

MADAGASCAR
ARIARY

MAURITIUS
RUPEE

ZIMBABWE
DOLLAR

ATLANTIC OCEAN

NAMIBIA
RAND

BOTSWANA
PULA

REUNION
FRANC

Limpopo

Orange

SWAZILAND
LILANGENI

LESOTHO
LOTI

SOUTH AFRICA
RAND

INDIAN OCEAN

TRISTAN DA CUNHA
POUND

EGYPT

FIRST COINS:	fourth century BC
FIRST DECIMAL COINS:	1916
MAIN MINT:	Abbasia since 1954
CURRENCY:	Egyptian pound

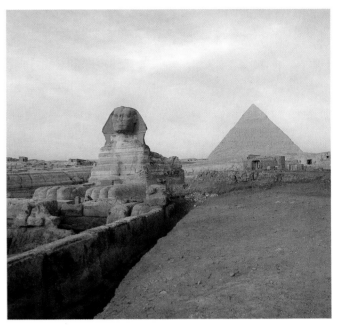

The famous Sphinx at Giza, with the Pyramid of Khephren (Cheops) in the background. Both are featured on Egyptian coins issued since 1953.

THE ancient Egyptians had long been familiar with the use of precious metals as money, valued by weight, when coinage first began to circulate in Egypt around 500 BC. The earliest coins found in Egypt are silver pieces from the Greek mints of the Aegean area and gold coins from Sardes in western Turkey. The Persian governor of Egypt, Aryandes, is said to have been deposed by the Persian King Darius I (521–486 BC), whose empire then included Egypt, because he had dared to issue his own silver coinage in imitation of the king; but no examples of the coinage of Aryandes have yet been identified.

In the fifth century BC by far the most common coins circulating in Egypt were the silver 'owls' of Athens, and the first-known coins minted in Egypt, dating from the fourth century, were imitations of these. Most Egyptian 'owls' (*see* Greece) have no identifying inscription, but some have the name of the ruling Persian king or his governor. Most were probably minted at Memphis. An exceptional Egyptian gold coin from this period has different and unusual designs: on the front it has a prancing horse and on the back Egyptian hieroglyphic characters.

As Alexander the Great (336–323 BC) conquered the Persian Empire he introduced his gold and silver coinage to Egypt and the mint of Memphis joined in the production of these 'Alexanders'. The output of this mint also included small bronze coins bearing the head of Alexander – the first use of Alexander's portrait on coinage.

THE PTOLEMIES

After the death of Alexander and the break-up of his empire, Egypt fell into the hands of one of his former generals, Ptolemy. He founded the Ptolemaic dynasty, which was to rule Egypt until 30 BC, when its last queen, Cleopatra VII, killed herself following defeat by the Romans.

Ptolemy I moved the mint from the ancient capital, Memphis, to the new city of Alexandria, and made important changes to weight standards and coin designs. Ptolemaic Egypt became a closed currency zone, in which only the coinage of the Ptolemies circulated. The silver coins usually carried on the front a portrait of Ptolemy I, and on the back the eagle of Zeus, patron deity of the Ptolemies. The gold coinage, which was issued more frequently by the Ptolemies than was usual elsewhere in the Greek world, had a wider range of regal portraits. The bronze coinage usually depicted the head of Zeus and his eagle. A notable feature of Ptolemaic coinage was the issuing of very large bronze coins. Throughout the Ptolemaic period Alexandria was the only mint for Egypt, though Ptolemaic possessions abroad, such as Cyrenaica (Libya), Cyprus and the Levant coastlands (Israel and Lebanon), also had mints.

EARLY ROMAN PERIOD

When the Romans absorbed Egypt into their empire the individual character of the Egyptian coinage was at first retained. Some Roman coinage inevitably arrived in Egypt, and occasionally issues of Roman coinage were minted there, for example under Vespasian (AD 69–79) and Septimius Severus (193–211), but the bulk of coinage circulating in Egypt in Roman times was the provincial coinage struck at Alexandria to Egypt's own unique weight system.

The principal denomination of Roman Egypt was the tetradrachm. Initially its weight was approximate to four Roman denarii but because of the base-quality silver used it exchanged for only one denarius, or even less. The tetradrachm was at first accompanied by a full range of fractional denominations in bronze but these disappeared in the third century when the weight and fineness, and hence the value, of the tetradrachm plummeted even further.

The coins of Roman Egypt usually have the emperor's head and titles in Greek on the front. In contrast, a wide variety of designs, mostly with Egyptian or Greek themes, appear on the back. The coins are dated by the year of the emperor's reign, which is invariably included in the inscription.

The Alexandria mint also at times produced issues of small denomination coinage for Egypt's many separate administrative districts, known as nomes. These coins again have the emperor's head on one side, and a design symbolic of the individual nome on the other.

LATE ROMAN AND BYZANTINE PERIOD

From AD 296 Egyptian coinage was no longer issued. The province was now converted, as was the rest of the Greek-speaking eastern Roman Empire, to the use of Roman coinage. The Alexandria mint remained in service, but it was now striking Roman coins with Latin inscriptions, distinguishable from the products of the other imperial mints only by the mint mark: ALE. In the period of transfer from local to Roman coinage Egypt was taken over by a usurper, Domitius Domitianus (295–6), who issued both Greek- and Latin-inscribed coinages.

Most of the coinage produced in Egypt after 296 was base billon or bronze, though at first occasional gold and even rarer silver issues also appeared. Bronze coins were produced regularly throughout the fourth century, but early in the fifth century the mint was closed and it did not reopen until the reign of the Byzantine Emperor Justin I (518–27). For over a hundred years, until the Arab conquest, the Alexandria mint issued Byzantine coinage. Gold solidi were minted occasionally, but output was concentrated mostly on bronze coins. The system of denominations at Alexandria differed from that used elsewhere in the Byzantine Empire. The standard 40 nummi bronze piece was provided with fractions marked in Greek numerals; 3, 6, 12 and 33 units, rather than the usual 5, 10 and 20. One unusual issue, which has a star and crescent either side of the emperor's bust, has been attributed to the period of Persian occupation (617–28), following the invasion by the Sasanian King Khusru II.

ISLAM

Byzantine rule in Egypt did not survive for long after the Persian invasion had been repulsed. In 640 Egypt was again invaded from the east, now by the forces of Islam, led by the Caliph 'Umar (634–44). For a long time Byzantine coins continued to circulate and, as during the Persian invasion, imitations of Alexandria mint bronze coins were again made. Byzantine gold coins also continued to be imported for use in Egypt almost to the end of the century.

In the 690s the Islamic rulers of Egypt were forced to put an end to their use after the Byzantine Emperor Justinian II (685–95) had introduced a new design for his gold coins which was offensive to the Islamic religion; the coins were decorated with a portrait of Christ and Christian inscriptions. These are thought to have been aimed directly at the Islamic users of the coins, who were said to be waging a similar campaign of provocation by including their own religious declarations on sheets of paper (papyrus) being exported from Egypt for official use in the Byzantine Empire.

Byzantine gold coins were replaced by imports from Syria, new

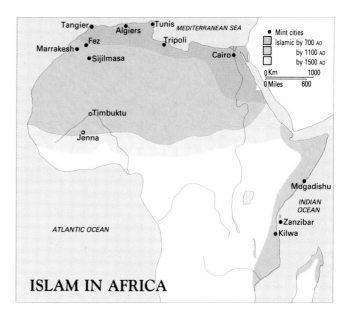

ISLAM IN AFRICA

Islamic gold coins without pictorial designs, inscribed in Arabic, which were first issued in 697 by the Umayyad Caliph 'Abd-al Malik (685–705).

THE FIRST EGYPTIAN ISLAMIC COINS

Egypt's first locally-made Islamic coins were bronze coins issued from 711, struck at al-Fustat (old Cairo), al-Iskandariya (Alexandria), Atrib and al-Fayyum. In 750 a new regime under the rule of the 'Abbasid caliphs was established in Egypt and the al-Fustat mint continued to issue coins. At first these were just bronze, but later gold and silver coins were also made, all with only inscriptional designs, proclaiming 'There is no God except God, he is alone and has no

EGYPT

1 SILVER 'OWL' 4 DRACHMAS *of the Persian king Artaxerxes III.*
2 GOLD COIN *of Pharaoh Nectanebo II.*
3 SILVER 4 DRACHMAS *of Ptolemy I, with the eagle of Zeus.*
4 BRONZE COIN *of Ptolemy III, with the head of Zeus.*
5 GOLD 10 DRACHMAS *of Queen Berenice II, wife of Ptolemy III.*
6 BRONZE COIN *of the Roman emperor Hadrian, showing an eagle and Egyptian deities.*
7 BILLON 4 DRACHMAS *of the Roman emperors Hadrian and Domitius Domitianus.*
8 GOLD SOLIDUS *of Licinius I.*
9 BRONZE COIN *of the Byzantine emperor Justinian I.*

1 342–338 BC
2 359–343 BC
3 305–283 BC
4 246–221 BC
5 246–221 BC
6 AD.134–5
7 126–7
8 311–13
9 527–65

equal; Mohammad is the Messenger of God' and indicating the denomination, mint and date of issue. On some coins an additional inscription gave the name of the 'Abbasid caliph or his heir and the local governor.

When the power of the 'Abbasid caliphs went into decline, the independent Tulunid (868–905) and Ikhshidid (935–69) governors of Egypt put their own names on the coins, mainly gold, of the al-Fustat mint, as well as those issued in Palestine and Syria at mints which they controlled.

THE FATIMIDS

In 969 Egypt was conquered from the west by the rival Fatimid caliphs (907–1171) from Tunisia. The Fatimids were followers of Islam, but belonged to the Shi'a sect claiming descent from Fatima, Mohammad's daughter. They changed the designs of Egypt's coins, adding the name of 'Ali, the husband of Fatima and the founder of the Shi'a sect. Their coins also tend to have elegantly written inscriptions arranged to form decorative patterns, such as concentric circles. A statement of the quality of the gold was also occasionally added to the inscription.

The Fatimids reopened the Alexandria mint, and also struck coins at mints in modern Tunisia, Libya, Italy, Palestine and Syria. During the Fatimid period Egypt became immensely rich. Italian merchants, particularly from Venice, Genoa and Amalfi, came to Egypt to buy spices imported from the Far East. Fatimid coins also played a part in this trade, being exported into Europe and to India. Apart from the spice trade, Egypt's wealth was also based on its trade across the Sahara with West Africa. So much gold came into Egypt from this trade that the Fatimids produced vast quantities of gold coins, but little else. Inscribed glass weights may also have been used as small change in the place of bronze coins.

THE AYYUBIDS

In 1169 Amaury, the crusader king of Jerusalem, invaded Egypt and brought about the end of Fatimid rule there. The invasion was repulsed, but only with the help of a Turkish army from northern Iraq, which then destroyed the Fatimid army, overthrew the Shi'a caliph and restored Egypt to the nominal authority of the orthodox 'Abbasid caliph in Baghdad.

By 1171 new coins were being issued in the names of the 'Abbasid Caliph al-Mustadi (1170–80) and al-Malik al-Nasir Salah-al-din Yusuf bin Ayyub, the Kurdish commander of the Turkish army. This ruler, better known in Europe as Saladin, founded the Ayyubid dynasty and quickly established a large empire which extended to eastern Turkey and Aden.

The Ayyubid sultans' gold coins were similar in design to Fatimid coins, but no longer carried the name of 'Ali. They were made at the mints of al-Fustat, al-Qahira (new Cairo) and Alexandria. Crudely made base-silver coins were also issued for circulation within Egypt, but elsewhere the Ayyubids issued good-quality silver coins which occasionally were imported into Egypt.

THE MAMLUKS

In 1250 Ayyubid rule came to an end as power was seized by their own military commanders, known as Mamluks. Gold continued to be the most important coinage metal, and the first Mamluk gold coins looked very similar to Ayyubid issues. But the Mamluks also began to issue silver coins at the Cairo mint with a new kind of design. These, also copied from Ayyubid coins, used Syrian issues as their models. The main part of their inscription was written in horizontal lines within a decorative frame. Bronze coins were also decorated in the same way.

Like earlier Islamic coins, Mamluk issues were still inscribed with religious statements and indications of the denomination, mint and date, but now the ruler's name and titles were the predominant part of the inscription. The sultan's name was often accompanied by a declaration in his praise. These inscriptions were written in a very elegant form of Arabic script, but the coins were often extremely badly made.

On some Cairo mint coins the Mamluk ruler Baybars (1260–77) placed his personal badge, a small lion, below his name. Other symbols – flowers, wheels, etc. – also appeared on later Mamluk bronze coins.

The prosperity of Egypt began to decline during the Mamluk period (1250–1517) as Italian traders took control of the African gold trade. Gold continued to come into Egypt in exchange for spices from the Far East in the form of Italian gold coins, called ducats, so the Sultan Barsbay (1422–38) introduced a new gold coin, the ashrafi, which was the same size and value. Because the supply of gold was now controlled by Europeans, there were often shortages and by the 1470s gold coins were so scarce that people had to use wheat as money instead.

THE OTTOMANS

In 1517 the Ottoman sultans of Turkey added Egypt to their empire. Their local representative continued to make gold ashrafis and silver and copper coins at the Cairo mint, but with designs copied from Turkish coins. Religious statements were no longer used, but the new inscriptions named and honoured the Ottoman sultan: 'Sultan Selim

A street market by the Bab el-Zueila city gate of Cairo, built during the period of the Fatimid Caliph al-Mustansir (1036–94).

Khan, son of Bayazid Khan, his victory will be glorious, maker of bright coins, lord of power, mighty on land and sea' (on a Cairo coin of 1517). Decorative motifs, such as stars, flowers and knots, often appeared on the coins. The most distinctive feature of Ottoman coins was the tughra, a decorative signature including the sultan's name and titles. It had been used on Ottoman coins since the fifteenth century, but only appeared on Egyptian coins from the eighteenth century. Later coins in contrast were often inscribed with just the tughra, mint name and date.

Twice during the eighteenth century Ottoman control of Egypt was threatened, and on both occasions a small change made to the coin designs reflected the new circumstances. In 1769 'Ali Bey, the governor of Egypt, revolted and declared Egypt to be independent, but he was defeated three years later. During his rebellion coins were still issued in the name of the Ottoman Sultan Mustafa III (1757–74), but with 'Ali's name added. Similarly coins with an Arabic 'B' for Buonaparte were issued during the French invasion of 1798.

In 1835 a substantial reform of Egypt's coinage took place. Western coining machines were installed at the Cairo mint, while large bronze and good silver coins were issued to replace the previous base-silver coinage.

French influence was again felt in Egypt during the construction of the Suez Canal and caused the issue in 1865 of tokens with French denominations to pay the canal workers.

BRITISH OCCUPATION

Ottoman rule was finally overthrown in 1882 when Egypt was occupied by British troops. Nevertheless, Ottoman coins continued to be issued, although they were often made abroad (Berlin 1885–1904, Birmingham 1904–14). Britain put a formal end to Turkish rule in 1914 by making Egypt a British protectorate. From 1916 coins made in Britain were issued in the name of the Egyptian governors Hussein Kamil (1914–17) and Fuad (1917–22). These coins were denominated according to a decimal system, 1000 milliemes = 100 piastres = 1 Egyptian pound. The 1, 2, 5 and 10 milliemes had central holes like the contemporary British-made coins of East Africa (Uganda).

KINGDOM OF EGYPT

Fuad was made king in 1922 and a new series of coins with his portrait was issued. Although most of these were made in England, in 1929 a batch was also made at the Budapest mint. Fuad's coins and those of his successor, Farouk (1936–52), included some unusual pieces: hexagonal, octagonal and scallop-edged coins were all issued.

REPUBLIC OF EGYPT

When a republic was declared in 1953 the royal coins continued in use, but were eventually replaced by republican issues, struck at a new mint at Abbasia and decorated with the sphinx (1954–7), an eagle (1958–80) and most recently the pyramids and a tughra (since 1984). The eagle was copied from the design used on Syrian coins since 1948. It was introduced while Egypt was joined with Syria and Yemen in the United Arab States (1958–61).

Coins are now little used in Egypt, where most small denominations are represented by much used and soon worn-out bank notes.

The Mosque of Muhammad 'Ali, built from 1824–57, in the Ayyubid citadel of Saladin, Cairo. The citadel, founded in 1176, was the home of the Ayyubid mint.

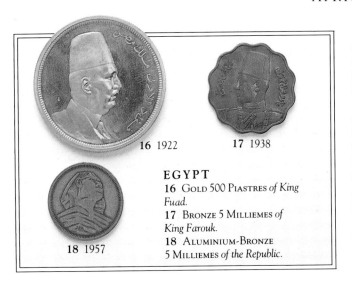

16 1922   **17** 1938

18 1957

EGYPT
16 Gold 500 Piastres of King Fuad.
17 Bronze 5 Milliemes of King Farouk.
18 Aluminium-Bronze 5 Milliemes of the Republic.

EARLY CYRENAICA

Africa's earliest coins were produced in Cyrenaica in the late sixth century BC. When these first coins were issued, Cyrenaica was part of the Persian Empire but was governed by the kings of Cyrene of the Battid dynasty, who remained in power until about 435 BC.

Cyrenaica's early coinage, which consisted of issues of silver staters and fractions, was typically Greek in character. The first coins cannot be ascribed to individual mints, but later issues can be identified to Cyrene (al-Bayda), the principal mint, Barce (al-Marj) and Euhesperides (Benghazi). The now extinct silphium plant, unique to Cyrenaica and possessing famous healing powers, was depicted on the earliest coins. In the early fifth century BC it was joined by the head of Zeus Ammon with the ram's horn.

Following the overthrow of the Battid dynasty the cities of Cyrenaica were governed as republics. Cyrene and Barce continued to be major coin producers, issuing various denominations in silver and also gold. From about 400 BC the names of local officials were included in the coin designs.

CYRENAICA UNDER THE PTOLEMIES

In 331 BC Cyrenaica declared allegiance to Alexander the Great and after his death was absorbed into the Ptolemaic kingdom of Egypt. Under Alexander and Ptolemy I the cities of Cyrenaica at first continued to issue their own autonomous coinages, which now also included issues in bronze. From about 305 BC, however, coinage was struck in the name of the Ptolemies; there was also, about 305 BC, a single 'posthumous' issue of the coinage of Alexander the Great.

The Ptolemies issued coinage in Cyrenaica for 200 years. At first gold, silver and bronze coins were produced, but only bronze coins were issued throughout this period. The principal mint was Cyrene; only occasional issues of bronze coins were produced by Barce, Berenice (Euhesperides) and other minor mints. There were breaks in the production of regal Ptolemaic coinage: between 277 and 261 BC when the governor of Cyrenaica, Magas, was in revolt from Ptolemy II, and in the middle of the third century BC when coinage was issued in the name of the regional *koinon* (council) of Cyrenaica, with designs depicting the silphium plant and Zeus Ammon copied from earlier independent Cyrenaican coinage.

ROMAN CYRENAICA

Cyrenaica was bequeathed to the Romans in 96 BC, but the first coins of Roman Cyrenaica were not issued until after the province was joined to nearby Crete for administration in 67 BC. Issues of provincial bronze coinage, usually signed by the governors, were produced until the reign of Tiberius (AD 14–37). A single issue of Roman silver denarii was minted in Cyrenaica in 31 BC. Finally, an issue of silver drachms and hemidrachms depicting the head of Zeus Ammon was produced for Cyrenaica under the Emperor Trajan in AD 100. After this date no more coinage was issued for Roman Cyrenaica; the province had to rely on imported Roman coinage.

Egypt is, however, still issuing many coins, but most of them are commemoratives made for collectors, for a wide range of occasions.

EGYPTIAN COMMEMORATIVES

1938	Royal Wedding
1955	Revolution 3rd anniversary
1956	Suez Canal Nationalization
1960	Aswan Dam
1964	Diversion of the Nile
1968	Koran 1400th anniversary
1970	President Nasser
	Workers' Congress
1974	October War 1st anniversary
1976	Reopening of the Suez Canal
1979	Muslim Era 1400th anniversary
	Abbasia Mint 25th anniversary
1980	Egypt–Israel Peace Treaty
1982	Sinai Peninsula restored
1985	Moharram Press 100th anniversary
	Tutenkamun
1986	National Census

LIBYA

FIRST COINS:	sixth century BC
FIRST DECIMAL COINS:	1952
MAIN MINT:	Tripoli
CURRENCY:	dinar

THE coastlands of ancient Libya contained two separate regions of settlement: Cyrenaica in the east, bordering Egypt, which was settled by Greeks, and Syrtica in the west, which had been colonized by Phoenicians.

SYRTICA

This coastal area of western Libya was part of the Roman province of Africa, formed following the destruction of Carthage in 146 BC. Until the first century BC the cities of Syrtica used imported coinage, mainly from Carthage. After 146 BC Roman silver coinage was used and some issues of denarii for Roman military use were minted in the region.

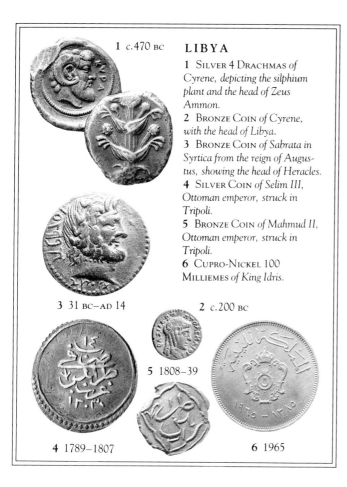

LIBYA

1 SILVER 4 DRACHMAS *of Cyrene, depicting the silphium plant and the head of Zeus Ammon.*
2 BRONZE COIN *of Cyrene, with the head of Libya.*
3 BRONZE COIN *of Sabrata in Syrtica from the reign of Augustus, showing the head of Heracles.*
4 SILVER COIN *of Selim III, Ottoman emperor, struck in Tripoli.*
5 BRONZE COIN *of Mahmud II, Ottoman emperor, struck in Tripoli.*
6 CUPRO-NICKEL 100 MILLIEMES *of King Idris.*

1 c.470 BC

3 31 BC–AD 14

2 c.200 BC

5 1808–39

4 1789–1807

6 1965

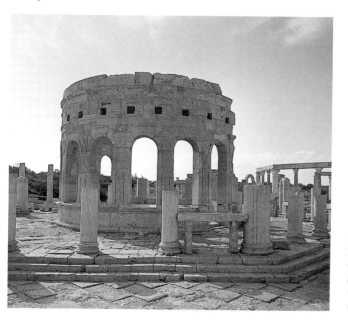

The market place of Lepcis Magna, a Roman city in ancient Libya. Lepcis Magna, in the Roman province of Africa, issued coins during the first century AD.

From about the middle of the first century BC until the reign of Tiberius the major cities of Syrtica, notably Lepcis Magna (Lebda), Oea (Tripoli) and Sabrata, issued their own bronze coins. Lepcis also produced a single issue of silver coins. All used a form of Phoenician script on their coins and their designs tended to combine both native and Roman elements. After the first century AD Syrtica, like Cyrenaica, relied entirely on coinage imported from elsewhere in the Roman Empire.

BYZANTINE PERIOD

Cyrenaica and Syrtica belonged to the Byzantine Empire for most of the sixth and seventh centuries. During this period the coins circulating in the region were Byzantine issues, most of which would have come from the mint of Carthage.

EARLY ISLAMIC COINAGE

During the 640s the Byzantine Empire lost the territory now known as Libya to Arab invaders. As elsewhere in North Africa Byzantine coins continued to be used during the first decades of Islamic rule, but the first Islamic coins definitely known to have been struck in Libya were made at the mint of Tripoli (Atrabulus) during the period AD 699–704. They were small bronze coins in the name of the Umayyad governor Musa, who later brought Tunisia, Algeria, Morocco and Spain under Islamic rule.

Musa's coins are inscribed in Latin, 'In the name of God, Musa, Commander of Africa, ordered this coin made at Tripoli', but the design shows the former Byzantine Emperor Heraclius (AD 610–41) and his son. About 10 years later the Tripoli mint began to make occasional issues of bronze coins with Arabic inscriptions.

Apart from these bronze coins, no coins were made in Islamic Libya until gold and silver coins were struck at Tripoli by the Hafsid rulers of Tunisia (1237–1551). During the medieval period the coins in circulation were imported from the east, from Syria and Egypt, while Libya was ruled by the Tulunids (868–905) and Fatimids (909–72), or from the west, from Tunis, Algeria and Morocco, while it was ruled by the Aghlabids (800–68), Zirids (972–1148), Almohads (1148–1237) and Hafsids. European coins from Italy, France and Spain were also imported and circulated alongside the Islamic coins.

OTTOMAN PROVINCE OF TRIPOLI

The first large-scale, locally made coinage was not produced until the late sixteenth century, once Libya had become a part of the empire of the Ottoman sultans of Turkey. After almost a half century of struggle between Spain, Tunis and Turkey for control of the city of Tripoli, Ottoman rule was sufficiently settled by 1574 for gold coins to be issued in the city in the name of Sultan Selim II (1566–74). The new coins were modelled on the Ottoman issues of the Constantinople mint, but with the name of the mint of Tripoli (Trablus). From 1648 the mint was renamed Tripoli–West (Trablus–Gharb) to distinguish it from Tripoli in Syria, also under Ottoman rule.

In addition to the gold coins which were issued by the Ottoman rulers from the time of Ahmad III (1703–30) bronze coins were produced by the mint based at Tripoli. These coins had various local designs, featuring the name of the sultan, the mint, the date and sometimes a pattern, such as a knot or flower. From 1774 silver coins with Turkish designs, sometimes including the typical Ottoman tughra, were issued in addition.

EUROPEAN RULE

In 1836 the Tripoli mint was closed down and Libya returned to the use of imported coins from Egypt, Tunis and Turkey until the end of Ottoman rule in 1911, when Tripoli was invaded by Italian troops. During the Italian occupation (1911–43) and the following period of Anglo–French administration, no coins were made specifically for local use and once again imported coins circulated. The Italian occupiers did, however, make paper money denominated in Italian lire for use in this and their other African colonies. The British also issued notes denominated in lire BY MILITARY AUTHORITY IN TRIPOLITANIA. The French circulated West African franc notes overprinted FEZZAN, the name of the area in southern Libya under their authority.

INDEPENDENCE

Libya gained independence in 1951 when, following a United Nations declaration, Muhammad Idris el Senussi became King Idris I of Libya. His reign was cut short by a revolution in 1969, but not before he had made two issues of coins: in 1952, decorated with his portrait, and in 1965, with the royal arms. His coins were entirely inscribed in Arabic, except for the denomination, which was in English. Since the establishment of the republic a further two issues struck in Britain have been made. The first, issued in 1975, was based on the coinage of neighbouring Egypt, using the eagle design of its United Arab States coinage; the second, issued in 1979, after the establishment of Libya as a socialist republic, features a bedouin on horseback. During the kingdom the coins were denominated in milliemes and piastres (1000 milliemes = 100 piastres = 1 Libyan pound); since 1975 the same denominations have been used but renamed as dirhems and dinars. The dinar denomination has been used once, for Libya's only issue of commemorative coins: silver 5 dinars and gold 70 dinars to celebrate the International Year of the Disabled in 1981.

TUNISIA

FIRST COINS:	fifth century BC
FIRST DECIMAL COINS:	1891
MAIN MINT:	Paris
CURRENCY:	dinar

THE Tunisian coast was colonized in ancient times by Phoenician traders. Carthage, their most important settlement (founded 814 BC), became the capital of a great maritime empire, which included much of the North African coast and parts of Spain, Sardinia and Sicily.

EARLY CARTHAGINIAN COINAGE

The earliest coinage issued by the Carthaginians dates from the time of their invasion of Sicily, late in the fifth century BC. The silver coins issued were designed to fit into the well-established coinage systems of Sicily's Greek cities and most were actually minted in Sicily. Nevertheless some issues signed 'Carthage' were probably struck in that city. In the fourth century BC much of the silver coinage issued by the Carthaginians was minted in Sicily for use there, and so were the earliest small issues of gold coinage. From about 350 BC Carthage began to mint large issues of gold and later electrum coinage on a regular basis, possibly from stocks of gold acquired from West Africa through trade. The characteristic designs on Carthaginian coins were the head of the goddess Tanit, the horse and the palm tree.

THE PUNIC WARS

It was inevitable that the Carthaginians would clash with Rome as its power increased, and between 265 and 146 BC there were three major periods of conflict. By now Carthaginian coinage in gold, electrum, silver and bronze was produced throughout the empire. Many issues can be linked to military campaigns, such as the large silver and electrum coins struck in Sicily during the First Punic War (265–241 BC) and various issues in Spain, Italy and Sicily from the period of Hannibal's campaigns in the Second Punic War (218–201 BC). A particularly interesting series was minted in Tunisia by Libyan mercenaries in rebellion against their Carthaginian paymasters in the period 241–238 BC. As well as re-issuing Carthaginian coins overstamped with their own designs, the rebels struck new coins made of copper mixed with arsenic to give a silvery appearance.

THE ROMAN PERIOD

Carthage was destroyed by the Romans in 146 BC. From that date the Roman denarius became the official silver coin of the newly formed province of Africa and issues of denarii were struck locally by Roman military commanders during periods of civil war in the first centuries BC and AD. Between the second century BC and the reign of Tiberius (AD 14–37) the cities of Tunisia, including Utica, Hippo Diarrhytus (Bizerta), Hadrumetum (Sousse), Leptis Minor and the rebuilt (in 45 BC) Roman city of Carthage struck their own occasional issues of bronze coinage. The use of Phoenician script on some pieces is a reminder of the eastern origins of these populations.

After the local civic bronzes ceased under Tiberius the province of Africa became entirely dependent on Roman currency, but only briefly, from AD 296–313, was an official Roman mint established in the city of Carthage.

THE VANDAL AND BYZANTINE PERIODS

The Vandals captured Carthage in 439 and established a North African kingdom centred on Tunisia, but extending also into eastern Algeria and western Libya, which lasted until it was conquered by Byzantine forces in 534. The Vandals issued small silver coins which imitated Roman imperial pieces, later marked with the names of their kings, and larger bronze coins struck in the name of Carthage with civic designs (a figure representing the city and a horse's head) in three separate denominations marked 12, 21 and 42.

Byzantine rule lasted from 534 until the fall of Carthage to the Arabs in 698. During this period the Carthage mint was prolific, regularly producing issues of coinage in the name of the Byzantine emperors in gold, silver and, most abundantly, bronze.

ISLAMIC CONQUEST

Parts of Tunisia were under Islamic domination more than 20 years before the final capture of Carthage. By 698 Arab gold and bronze coins were already being made in the town of al-Qairwan, founded in 670, at a mint named after the Arab province of Africa – al-Ifriqiya.

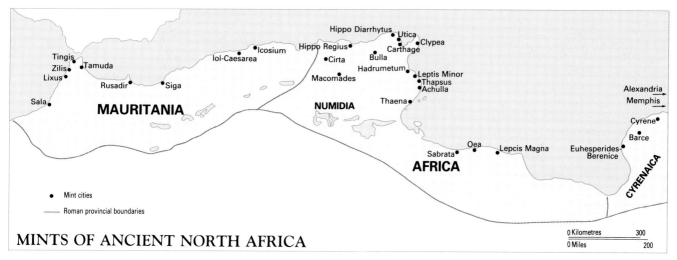

MINTS OF ANCIENT NORTH AFRICA

TUNISIA
1 SILVER 4 DRACHMAS of Carthage with Punic inscription.
2 ELECTRUM COIN of Carthage depicting the goddess Tanit and horse.
3 SILVER SHEKEL of the Libyan revolt with the head of Heracles and a lion. The inscription is in Greek.
4 SILVER COIN of the Vandal king Gelimer.
5 BRONZE 20 NUMMI of the Byzantine emperor Constans II, minted in Carthage.

The Africa coins were copies of earlier Byzantine issues of the Carthage mint. They were struck on small, thick flans and depicted the Byzantine Emperor Heraclius (610–41) and his son on the front and a modified cross without its cross-bar on the back. They were inscribed with a statement of the Islamic faith, 'There is no God, but God who has no equal – God, our Lord, the Great, the Eternal, knowing all things and creating all things', written in abbreviated Latin. The portraits were soon dropped from the design, and from 704 dated gold coins were issued with the mint name added, FRT IN AFRK (feritus in Afrika, 'struck in Africa').

THE FIRST ARABIC COINS

In 715 part of the Latin inscription was replaced by Arabic and in the following year the use of Latin was abandoned completely when the Africa mint began to introduce the standard Arab coins of the Umayyad caliphs, first issued from the Damascus mint in 696. Gold, silver and bronze coins were issued.

THE AGHLABIDS AND FATIMIDS

Ibrahim ibn Aghlab, governor of Tunisia, became independent of the 'Abbasids in 800 and from 805 began to add his title ghaliba, meaning victorious, to his coins. The Aghlabids brought Sicily and Malta under Islamic rule.

Throughout their rule the Aghlabids were troubled by attacks from the local Berber peoples and in 909 al-Qairwan eventually fell to a Berber army under the leadership of a Syrian, 'Ubaydallah. Giving himself the title al-Mahdi, the chosen, 'Ubaydallah then conquered Algeria and made the Idrisid rulers of Morocco his subjects. His successors, known as the Fatimids, also brought Sicily, Egypt, Palestine and Syria under their rule. He issued coins similar to the Aghlabid issues, but with his own name and title as Caliph and with Shi'ite declarations, at al-Qairwan. In 922 al-Mahdi opened a mint at his new capital, al-Mahdiya, on Tunisia's eastern coast. Later another Fatimid capital, al-Mansuriya, was founded by the Caliph al-Mansur at Sabrah and a new mint opened there. Al-Mansur also introduced new coins with a distinctive design: still consisting of inscriptions, but now arranged into concentric circles.

THE ZIRIDS

In 972 the Fatimids handed over control of Tunisia and their other North African territories west of Egypt to Bulukkin ibn Zirid, governor of al-Ifriqiya, a Berber chieftain. His successors, the Zirids, made themselves independent of the Fatimids in 1049 and removed the Fatimid religious statements from their coins, struck at al-Qairwan, al-Mahdiya and Sabrah. They ruled Tunisia until 1148, when it was conquered by the al-Muwahhids, another Berber dynasty from Morocco.

Under Zirid rule Tunisia enjoyed great prosperity and during the eleventh century was the main route by which West African gold reached Europe. They minted it into coins at their two main mints and at smaller mints at Safaqus, Sabrah and Qabis. The Zirids traded with Italy through Sicily, which was under Islamic rule until 1090, when it was captured by the Normans.

THE AL-MUWAHHIDS AND HAFSIDS

The rule of the Moroccan al-Muwahhids brought two new types of coin into circulation in Tunisia – broad, thin gold coins with their main religious inscription within a square frame, and small, square silver coins. The inscriptions reflected the Muwahhids' puritanical religious fervour. Within Tunisia they struck them only at the new regional capital, Tunis. These coins circulated throughout the Muwahhid Empire and the gold ones were frequently exported into Europe. Curiously the silver coins moved the other way, imitations of them being made in Christian Spain, France and Italy for trade with North Africa. The imitations circulated alongside the genuine coins.

The same types of coins continued to be issued at Tunis, from 1252 under the Hafsids, who succeeded the al-Muwahhids in their eastern possessions. Like the Muwahhids they were devout followers of Islam and inscribed their broad gold coins in a very elegant style, with lengthy religious inscriptions, in praise of God, his Prophet and his chosen one, the Mahdi.

THE OTTOMANS

Hafsid rule came to an end at the intervention of Turkey and Europe. The Hafsid capital was vulnerable to attack from the sea and already briefly had fallen into Moroccan hands, when the Marinids had issued coins in the city in 1374. In 1534 the Turkish admiral Barbarossa, Ottoman governor of Algiers, captured Tunis. During the next 35 years Tunisia gradually became a battleground for Turkish and Spanish interests until, in 1574, it was finally made a province of the Ottoman Empire. An Ottoman mint was set up at Tunis and began operations in 1574, issuing gold and silver coins with Turkish designs.

Hafsid coins did not disappear from use immediately, and during the reign of Sultan Ahmad I (1605–17) the Tunis mint made an issue of square silver coins of Hafsid design for local use. Bronze coins were not made at the Tunis mint until 1704 when very crudely struck pieces were issued.

The Ottomans issued gold, base-silver and bronze coins with inscriptional designs naming the sultan, the mint and the date, occasionally with decorative details, such as flowers, leaves and ornamental borders. During the reign of Abdul Mejid (1839–61) British machinery was installed at the Tunis mint and good silver, bronze and later gold coins, decorated on both sides with wreath borders, were introduced. From 1856 the denomination and the name of the local governor were added to the inscription.

FRENCH PROTECTORATE

When in 1881 Ottoman control was yielded to France, the local governor continued to rule the French protectorate of Tunisia and to place his name on the coins. Ten years later a new design with French inscriptions was devised and struck for Tunisia at the Paris mint. The new coins had French denominations, francs and centimes, and were dated using both the Arabic and the Christian eras. In 1918 a modified design was introduced with the lower denominations having a hole in the middle like contemporary French issues. The new coins also indicated the status of Tunisia as a PROTECTORAT FRANÇAIS.

The French coins used a more ornamental range of decorations, replacing the wreath borders on some issues with complex oriental patterns. The last French coins, dated 1950, 1954 and 1957, gave the local ruler Mohammad the title 'king' and were decorated with an Islamic crescent and his tughra-type signature.

INDEPENDENCE

In 1956 Tunisia gained its independence and in the following year the

TUNISIA
6 GOLD DINAR of Walid I, Umayyad caliph, inscribed in abbreviated Latin; 'struck in Africa in the name of the merciful God'.
7 GOLD DINAR of Sulayman, Umayyad caliph, inscribed in Latin and Arabic, struck in al-Qairwan.
8 GOLD DINAR of al-Mahdi struck in al-Qairwan.
9 CUPRO-NICKEL 100 FRANCS of the French Protectorate.
10 ALUMINIUM 5 MILLIMS of the Republic, minted in Czechoslovakia.

monarchy was replaced by a republic. New coins in the name of the Republic of Tunisia were issued from 1960, but always with that date. They were denominated in millim and dinars and decorated with an olive tree and a wreath on the lower denominations – 1, 2 and 5 millim – and decorative borders on the higher ones – 10, 20, 50 and 100 millim. In 1968 a ½ dinar coin, struck in Paris, with the portrait of President Habib Bourguiba was added to the series.

ALGERIA

FIRST COINS:	late third century BC
FIRST DECIMAL COINS:	1949
MAIN MINT:	Paris
CURRENCY:	dinar

Only the northern, coastal regions of Algeria were touched by ancient civilization. Cities were founded on the coast by Phoenician traders and two major kingdoms were established: Numidia in the east and Mauritania in the west. Numidia became part of the Roman province of Africa in 46 BC, while Mauritania became a Roman province in AD 40.

Coins of Carthage and other cities of the Mediterranean world would have arrived in the coastal cities of Algeria in earlier times, but the first coins actually made in Algeria date from not much earlier than

200 BC. These coins were issued in the names of the local kings. The first Mauritanian kings to strike coins were Syphax (213–202 BC) and his son Vermina, minting at the cities of Siga and Cirta (Constantine). The first Numidian king to issue coins was Massinissa (202–148 BC), who extended his kingdom to include eastern Mauritania as well as parts of Libya. A later Numidian king, Juba I (about 60–46 BC), minted large issues of silver denarii on the Roman model to finance his military support for the Pompeian faction against Julius Caesar in the civil wars (*see* Italy). By this time Roman coinage was already well established in this part of North Africa. The coinages of the later Mauritanian kings, Juba II (25 BC–AD 23) and Ptolemy (AD 23–40), also included issues of Roman-style denarii. The principal mint for these was Iol–Caesarea (Cherchell).

The cities of Numidia and Mauritania also struck issues of bronze coinage for local circulation in the second and first centuries BC and some continued into the reign of Augustus (31 BC–AD 14). The minting cities included Cirta, Icosium (Algiers), Hippo Regius and Iol–Caesarea. After Augustus, the only coinage officially circulating in the Roman provinces in Algeria was Roman currency produced in the imperial mints.

After the fall of the Roman Empire coinage issued by the Vandal kingdom in North Africa (*see* Tunisia) and by the Byzantine emperors circulated in Algeria (*see* Turkey).

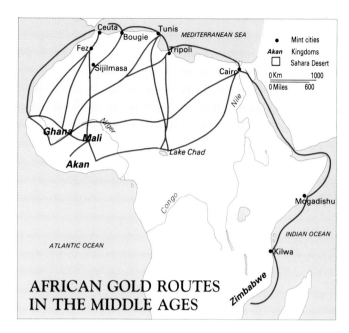

AFRICAN GOLD ROUTES IN THE MIDDLE AGES

EARLY ISLAMIC ISSUES

The region of modern Algeria became part of the Islamic world in about 700, but substantial issues of Islamic coins were not made there until the twelfth century when mints were established at al-Jaza‘ir (Algiers), Bijayah (Bougie) and Tilimsen (Tlemcen) by the al-Muwahhid rulers of Morocco. A few earlier, brief issues have been recorded: bronze coins were struck at Tlemcen under the Umayyad caliphs (early eighth century); the Hammadid Berbers of eastern Algeria are thought to have issued a gold coin at Bougie in 1184; the Idrisids of Morocco issued a few silver coins at Tlemcen during the ninth century and the al-Moravid rulers of Spain and Morocco issued gold coins in the same city just before the Muwahhid conquest.

MUWAHHID COINAGE

The Muwahhid coins made in Algeria were the same broad, thin gold and small, square silver coins they issued in Morocco, Spain and Tunisia. Coins like this continued to be used in Algeria until the area became part of the Ottoman Empire in 1556. Muwahhid-style coins

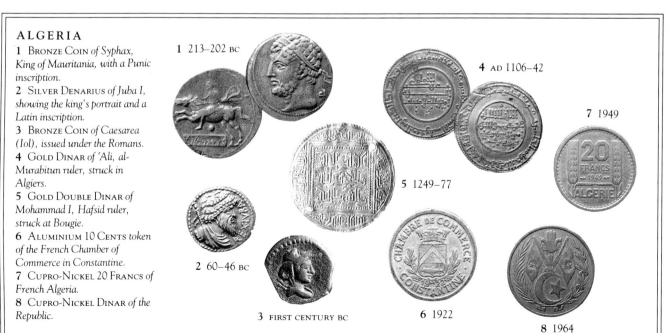

ALGERIA

1 Bronze Coin of Syphax, King of Mauritania, with a Punic inscription.
2 Silver Denarius of Juba I, showing the king's portrait and a Latin inscription.
3 Bronze Coin of Caesarea (Iol), issued under the Romans.
4 Gold Dinar of ʿAli, al-Murabitun ruler, struck in Algiers.
5 Gold Double Dinar of Mohammad I, Hafsid ruler, struck at Bougie.
6 Aluminium 10 Cents token of the French Chamber of Commerce in Constantine.
7 Cupro-Nickel 20 Francs of French Algeria.
8 Cupro-Nickel Dinar of the Republic.

1 213–202 BC
4 AD 1106–42
7 1949
5 1249–77
2 60–46 BC
3 FIRST CENTURY BC
6 1922
8 1964

were issued in Algiers, Bougie and Tlemcen by the Tunisian Hafsids, the western Algerian Ziyannids and the Moroccan Marinids as they vied for control of the region. The Hafsids also used mints at Biskirah, Tanas and Qustantinah.

From the late eleventh to the fifteenth century Algeria was an important part of the route by which West African gold reached Europe. Most of it came through southern Morocco, but then followed a route skirting the Moroccan Atlas Mountains and passing through Tlemcen to reach the ports of Bougie and Oran, which were visited by Italian, French and Spanish merchants trading European silver for African gold. Much of the silver was imported in the form of imitation Islamic coins, which were made in Europe, but freely circulated in North Africa.

OTTOMAN EMPIRE

From the early sixteenth century the ports of Algiers, Bougie and Oran came under attack from Spanish ships. Oran was captured in 1509 and remained under Spanish control until 1790, when the town was destroyed by an earthquake. During the 1590s bronze coins inscribed ORAN were made at the Spanish mint of Toledo for issue in the port. In order to prevent a complete Spanish conquest of the area Turkish help was sought and in 1529 Algeria became a province of the Ottoman Empire of Sultan Suleiman the Magnificent (1520–66), in spite of continued Spanish attacks and the temporary capture of Bougie during the 1530s.

An Ottoman mint at Algiers began to make regular issues of gold coins in the Turkish style from the time of Suleiman. Indeed, this mint often supplied more gold coins for the empire than the main mint at Constantinople. Apart from a single issue from the time of Sultan Murad III (1574–95), silver coins were, however, not issued until the late eighteenth century. Bronze coins, too, did not appear in the provincial coinage until an issue of tiny coins in the reign of Sultan Mahmud II (1808–37).

The Ottoman coins of Algiers were decorated only with ornamental borders or small flower and knot symbols until 1829, when a series of coins was made with an Ottoman tughra and wreath design copied from contemporary Turkish issues.

FRENCH OCCUPATION

In 1830 the French captured Algiers and by 1848 they had gained the whole of Algeria. During the conquest Ottoman mints were opened at Qusantinah (Constantine) and Medea, and from 1834 mints at al-Taqidemt and al-Mascara were also making Ottoman-style coins in the name of an anti-French resistance fighter Abdul Qadir (1834–37).

The French did not issue coins specifically for Algeria except from 1949–52, when the Paris mint made cupro-nickel 20, 50 and 100 franc coins with almost the same design as contemporary French 10 franc coins, but with the name ALGERIE. Before that ordinary French coins had circulated in Algeria, although during the German occupation of France a special-issue 2 franc piece dated 1944 had to be made in the USA for issue in liberated Algeria. Some local Chamber of Commerce tokens with French denominations had also circulated in Algeria during the First World War and shortly afterwards.

INDEPENDENCE

After a bitter struggle Algeria became independent in 1962 and began to issue coins in the name of the Republic of Algeria two years later.

The new coins, inscribed in Arabic, were denominated in centimes and dinars. Since 1971 these have been gradually replaced by issues with designs referring to national agriculture and industry. Commemorative issues, mostly on the anniversaries of independence or UN Food and Agriculture Organization (FAO) sets, have also been issued.

MOROCCO

FIRST COINS:	second century BC
FIRST DECIMAL COINS:	1921
MAIN MINT:	Royal Mint
CURRENCY:	dirhem

THE ancient kingdom of Mauritania extended westward into Morocco and so the regal Mauritanian coinage, beginning late in the third century BC, would have circulated there. The city of Lix (Lareche) on Morocco's Atlantic coast provided one of the mints striking bronze coins in the name of Bocchus II (49–33 BC) and Juba II (25 BC–AD 23). Some of the cities of western Mauritania, notably Tingis (Tangier), Lix and Tamuda, also issued bronze coinage for local circulation in the second to first centuries BC. The later issues of Tingis reveal the growing influence of Rome, with Latin inscriptions replacing the Phoenician script used on earlier issues.

After its incorporation into the Roman Empire, western Mauritania used Roman currency produced by the imperial mints. The only coinage to reach Morocco in the centuries following the collapse of Roman authority would have been issues of the Vandals and the Byzantine emperors (see Tunisia).

EARLY ISLAMIC COINAGE

Tangier again became a mint about 20 years after the conquest of Morocco by the Arab army of the Umayyad Caliph 'Abd al-Malik in 699. Tangier's first Islamic coinage was bronze with a peculiar design derived both from earlier Vandal issues and from the Arab issues of Tunis. The front had a crude, Vandal-style head, surrounded by an Islamic religious statement in Latin, 'Lord God, who is your equal?'; the back was inscribed in Arabic, 'Struck at Tanja in the name of God'. The following issues did not have the head or Latin text, but simply bore an Arabic religious formula and the name of the mint. From 717 they also carried the date in the Islamic era. Plant and star symbols were sometimes included in the design.

INDEPENDENT CALIPHS

Morocco did not stay under central Islamic rule for long. Although one issue of 'Abbasid coins was made from Tugdhah in southern Morocco, by the 750s the far western provinces of Islam, both Morocco and its northern neighbour Spain, had made themselves independent of the 'Abbasid caliphs. Morocco fell under the rule of the Idrisids of Fez, an Arab family descended directly from the Caliph 'Ali, Mohammad's son-in-law. The Idrisids were members of the unorthodox Islamic Shi'a sect and to indicate this they included the name of the Caliph 'Ali on

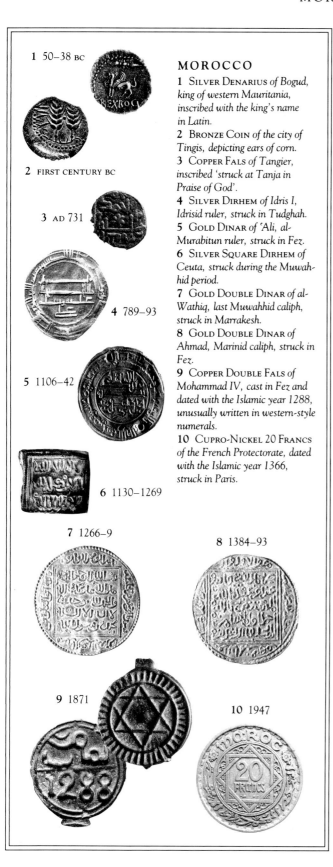

MOROCCO

1 SILVER DENARIUS *of Bogud, king of western Mauritania, inscribed with the king's name in Latin.*
2 BRONZE COIN *of the city of Tingis, depicting ears of corn.*
3 COPPER FALS *of Tangier, inscribed 'struck at Tanja in Praise of God'.*
4 SILVER DIRHEM *of Idris I, Idrisid ruler, struck in Tudghah.*
5 GOLD DINAR *of 'Ali, al-Murabitun ruler, struck in Fez.*
6 SILVER SQUARE DIRHEM *of Ceuta, struck during the Muwahhid period.*
7 GOLD DOUBLE DINAR *of al-Wathiq, last Muwahhid caliph, struck in Marrakesh.*
8 GOLD DOUBLE DINAR *of Ahmad, Marinid caliph, struck in Fez.*
9 COPPER DOUBLE FALS *of Mohammad IV, cast in Fez and dated with the Islamic year 1288, unusually written in western-style numerals.*
10 CUPRO-NICKEL 20 FRANCS *of the French Protectorate, dated with the Islamic year 1366, struck in Paris.*

1 50–38 BC

2 FIRST CENTURY BC

3 AD 731

4 789–93

5 1106–42

6 1130–1269

7 1266–9

8 1384–93

9 1871

10 1947

their coins. They produced silver coins in the style of the 'Abbasid issues of Tunisia at the mints of al-Aliyyah (Fez), Tugdhah, Walila, al-Basrah, Baht, Tanja (Tangier), Wargha, Warziga, Wazaqur, Wajtah, Subu, Tangara and Marira.

Gold coins began to be issued in Morocco when the Fatimid rulers of Tunis overthrew the Idrisids. These were Tunisian-style coins issued at Sijilmasa in southern Morocco during the 920s. After the Fatimid army withdrew, local Midradid rulers also issued gold coins, copying the Fatimid issues.

During the tenth and early eleventh centuries northern Morocco fell under Spanish rule, first by the Umayyads, who minted silver coins at al-Nakur on the coast and briefly at Fez (gold coins were also issued in their name by their vassals in Sijilmasa), and later by the Hammudids of Malaga, who issued coins at the city of Ceuta, on the Straits of Gibraltar.

THE MURABITUN

In the late eleventh century a new force arose in Morocco, bringing for the first time a large-scale gold coinage into use. From a fortified Berber outpost in West Africa, at the mouth of the Senegal River (on the border between modern Senegal and Mauritania), a holy war was mounted to restore to Morocco the fundamentals of the Islamic faith. Through their contacts with West Africa, the al-Murabitun (the outpost people) were able to bring massive amounts of gold into Morocco and they set up mints at their capital Marrakesh and at Fez, Miknash, Nul, Sijilmasa, Tangier, Ceuta, Aghmat, Sala and Bani Tavula to turn it into coin.

The Murabitun carried their holy war into Europe in 1086 and conquered Islamic Spain, where they issued gold coins which were exported in large quantities to Christian Spain, Portugal and beyond. Christian Spain and Portugal subsequently struck their own gold coins, morabitino, in imitation of the al-Murabitun issues.

THE MUWAHHIDS

The extensive gold coinage of Morocco survived the fall of the al-Murabitun to a new fundamentalist Islamic Berber group, the al-Muwahhids (the Divine Unity sect, known in Spain as the Almohades), but the new rulers changed the design and size of the coins. The new Muwahhid gold coins were broad and thin with their central inscription framed in a square. Small, square silver coins were also issued by the Muwahhids.

The Muwahhids extended Morocco's domain along the North African coast to include Libya, and issued their distinctive new coins at mints in Spain, Algeria and Tunisia. In the early thirteenth century Muwahhid control began to disintegrate under pressure from the Hafsids of Tunisia and a new Moroccan Berber dynasty invading from the edge of the Sahara, the Marinids. During the next century Morocco's north coast was contested by the Marinids, Hafsids, the Spanish Hudids of Murcia and Nasrids of Granada and various local rulers, all of whom issued Muwahhid-style coins at the mint of Ceuta. In spite of these disruptions, the flow of African gold into Europe continued at a great rate.

THE SHARIFS

During the fifteenth century Marinid control declined and Portuguese and Spanish attacks left Ceuta, Agadir and Tetuan in Christian hands. On the death of the last Marinid two rival groups, the Wattasids, successors of the Marinids in Fez, and the Sa'di Sharifs in the south fought for control of the rest of Morocco, the latter extending their empire as far south as Timbuktu in modern Mali. Like the Marinids, both issued Muwahhid-style coins.

As they gained the upper hand, the Sa'di Sharifs began to abandon the traditional Muwahhid designs and at their capital Marrakesh issued coins without the square frame for the gold and square shape for the silver. Their successors, the Filali Sharifs, made a further change, eliminating religious inscriptions from their coins and dating them using western-style numerals. Their gold coins were the same weight as the Ottoman ashrafi and the Italian ducat, and they also experimented with issues of large silver coins, the same weight as the Spanish dollar.

MOROCCAN STAR

At the end of the eighteenth century the Sharifs began to issue bronze coins using a new technique, by casting them in batches. Most of the cast coins have a distinctive design with a large star on the front and the date and mint on the back. The cast coinage continued until 1893, when the Fez mint began to make machine-struck coins: small denominations in bronze with a simple design featuring the date and mint within a decorative border. The silver coins of the same issue were struck in Paris and bore the name of the Sharif King al-Hasan, the mint *Bariz* (i.e. Paris) and date, contained in an ornamental frame, based on a star, on the larger coins.

FRENCH PROTECTORATE

In 1921 there was a reform to bring Moroccan issues into line with the French coinage system. Although the coins had continued to be issued in the name of the Sharif kings, Morocco had become a French protectorate in 1912. In 1921 the old denomination system, 500 mazunas = 10 dirhems = 1 rial, was abandoned and the new coins were valued in centimes and francs. Like contemporary French coins, the lower denominations had a central hole, but the traditional Arabic inscriptions and star designs were retained. In addition to these features, the denomination and the name of the kingdom were inscribed on the coins in French, EMPIRE CHERIFIEN, and from 1945 also MAROC. In the same year the western date was also added, but not on all issues.

INDEPENDENCE

Since independence in 1956 there have been two further reforms in the country: the first in 1960 coincided with the French *nouveau franc* reform and for Morocco meant the introduction of a new 1 dirhem coin, struck in Britain, equal to 100 old francs; the second in 1974 was the introduction of a santimat (centime) denomination to replace the old franc. From 1960 the new coins were decorated with the portrait of the king, Mohammad V (1956–62) and al-Hasan II (1962–) and/or the royal arms.

SPANISH MOROCCO

Part of Morocco still belongs to Spain as a consequence of the conquest of Morocco's northern coast by Spain and Portugal in the fifteenth century. Until independence the whole of Morocco's Mediterranean coast was Spanish and used Spanish coins. Tangier was also outside Moroccan control as a free port from 1925, and British, French, US and Moroccan currency was in use there. In 1956 the whole area, except the ports of Ceuta and Mellila, was returned to Morocco.

DJIBOUTI

FIRST COINS:	1948
FIRST DECIMAL COINS:	1948
MAIN MINT:	Paris
CURRENCY:	franc

THIS tiny country on the Red Sea coast is likely to have had its first experience of coinage through trade with Egypt in the Ptolemaic period, but its first official coins were not in fact issued until about 40 years ago.

FRENCH COLONY

In 1884 the port of Djibouti was made a French protectorate in order to provide a secure base for the French naval presence in the area. In 1896 Djibouti became a French colony, known as the French Somali Coast (Côte Française des Somalis). During the early French period the local currency was the same as its neighbours: including the Maria Theresa thalers in Ethiopia and the British Indian rupees in Aden (South Yemen). It is thought to have been during this period that some of these coins were stamped with countermarks in Arabic naming a local Djibouti sheik and the neighbouring city of Obock.

In the early 1920s the Djibouti Chamber of Commerce issued

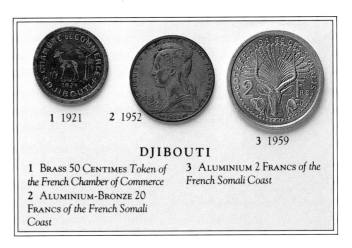

1 1921   2 1952   3 1959

DJIBOUTI

1 BRASS 50 CENTIMES *Token of the French Chamber of Commerce*
2 ALUMINIUM-BRONZE 20 FRANCS *of the French Somali Coast*
3 ALUMINIUM 2 FRANCS *of the French Somali Coast*

centime and franc tokens for local use. The first coins of the colony, struck in Paris, were 1, 2 and 5 franc coins issued from 1948. They all had the same design: a female head symbolizing the French Republic on the front and the head of an antelope, surmounted by a fan palm and flanked by a pair of fish gripped in clam shells, representing the colony on the back. A set of higher denominations added to the series, the 20-franc from 1952 and the 10-franc from 1965, had a new design for the back depicting ships with both eastern and western designs. Two years later the name of the colony was changed to Territoire Français des Afars et des Issas and a new coinage was issued from 1968, using the new name but the same designs. This was followed in 1970 by an issue of two higher denominations, 50 and 100 francs, with a newly-designed female head on the front and a pair of camels on the back.

INDEPENDENCE

In 1977, when the colony gained independence and changed its name to the Republic of Djibouti, new coins were issued retaining the back designs, but replacing the female head with the new national shield and dagger emblem. The new coins were still inscribed in French: REPUBLIQUE DE DJIBOUTI – UNITÉ. ÉGALITÉ. PAIX.

ETHIOPIA

FIRST COINS:	second century AD
FIRST DECIMAL COINS:	1931
MAIN MINT:	Royal Mint
CURRENCY:	birr

THE earliest report of coinage in Ethiopia dates from the mid-first century AD, when traders on the Red Sea coast exchanged Roman coins for local goods. By the second century the Axumite kings of Ethiopia had introduced their own coinage in gold, silver and bronze, bearing the royal portrait, normally within a barley wreath. The earliest coins were inscribed in Greek with the royal name and titles, but later issues were also inscribed in the Ethiopian Ge'ez script. The

coinage is thought to have continued into the seventh century, but the dating of the Axumite kingdom and its coins is still not certain.

Designs on later Axumite issues included the Christian cross, indicating the conversion of the Axumites to Christianity from the fourth century. Accompanying the cross were various inscriptions meaning 'in this sign is victory', 'by the grace of Christ' or 'may this please the nation'.

ISLAMIC COINAGE

Although Byzantine and Islamic coins must have been imported in trade from the Red Sea coast throughout the Middle Ages, no coins were officially issued in Ethiopia from Axumite times until the nineteenth century. During this period, however, some crude copies of late eleventh-century Yemenite coins are thought to have been made in Ethiopia by local traders. Coins again began to be made in Ethiopia in the eastern province of Harar. The Sultanate of al-Harar, founded in 1647, issued coins from 1807. They were small base-silver and brass pieces with Arabic inscriptions, naming the sultan, the mint and the date. The last issue, made from melted-down Egyptian Army brass shell-cases and dated 1885 and 1886, is anonymous, inscribed with the religious title 'the weak slave' [of God].

ABYSSINIA

In 1887 al-Harar was conquered by the Christian kingdom of Abyssinia based on Addis Ababa. Roused by an Egyptian invasion of Ethiopia in 1875, the Abyssinians with Italian help established control over

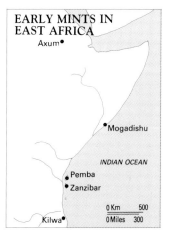

EARLY MINTS IN EAST AFRICA

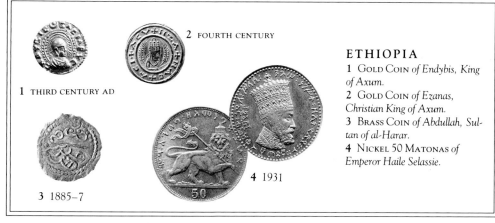

1 THIRD CENTURY AD
2 FOURTH CENTURY
3 1885-7
4 1931

ETHIOPIA
1 GOLD COIN of Endybis, King of Axum.
2 GOLD COIN of Ezanas, Christian King of Axum.
3 BRASS COIN of Abdullah, Sultan of al-Harar.
4 NICKEL 50 MATONAS of Emperor Haile Selassie.

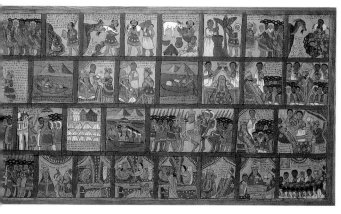

Ethiopia, but at the expense of yielding the coastal province of Eritrea to Italy. Menelik (1889–1913), the new Abyssinian king, after a brief issue in 1892 of silver coins decorated with the royal crown and inscribed in Amharic (the modern form of Ge'ez), minted at al-Harar, ordered from Paris a large consignment of bronze, silver and gold coins bearing his portrait. On the back of the silver and gold pieces there was a representation of the Lion of Judah, a reference to the claim of the Abyssinian kings to have been descendants of King Solomon and the Queen of Sheba.

Ethiopian narrative painting of the Bible story of the Queen of Sheba and King Solomon, eighteenth century. The rulers of Ethiopia were Christian since the fourth century, as can be seen from the Christian designs on the coins of the kings of Axum.

Menelik's coins were denominated in *birr*, the local name for the dollar, because, before the coins were issued, the main currency of Ethiopia, apart from salt, was imported Austrian silver dollars (thalers), struck in the name of the Holy Roman Empress Maria Theresa (1745–80). These coins had become so popular in Ethiopia and Arabia that they were still being issued at the Vienna mint with the fixed date 1780. When the Italians and the British needed money in Ethiopia during the 1930s the Rome and London mints also started to make them. The Vienna mint is still striking these coins, but other mints stopped in the 1960s.

After Menelik's death, portrait and lion coins continued to be issued, some struck in Addis Ababa during the reign of his daughter Zauditu. Her regent, Ras Tafari, subsequently became king, as Haile Selassie, in 1930 and in 1931 new coins, struck in England and Addis Ababa, denominated as matonas (cents) were issued. After the Italian occupation (1937–41) a new coinage, dated 1944, was struck in London and Philadelphia. For this issue the matona was renamed the santeem (centime). Later issues, still dated 1944, were made in Britain in 1947, 1952, 1953 and 1975.

SOCIALIST ETHIOPIA

In 1974 Haile Selassie was deposed by a military committee and a new coinage was ordered from the British Royal Mint. The new coins were still santeems, but depicted a lion's head on the front and people or animals on the back. The inscriptions were still written in Amharic. Gold and silver commemoratives celebrating national and international events and personalities were issued before and after the revolution of 1974.

ERITREA

In 1952 the province of Eritrea, under British military rule since 1941, was returned to Ethiopia as an autonomous region. In 1962 it was formally reintegrated into Ethiopia, resulting in civil war.

While Eritrea was under Italian control (1890–1941), the Rome and Milan mints had struck for the colony a set of coins with the portrait of King Umberto, denominated in centesimi and lire. Three issues were made, dated 1890, 1891 and 1896. In 1918 the Rome mint also struck an issue of thaler (tallero) in the style of the Austrian coins in use in the area. During the British administration, the coins of the British East Africa Currency Board circulated in Eritrea.

SOMALIA

FIRST COINS:	fourteenth century
FIRST DECIMAL COINS:	1906
MAIN MINT:	Royal Mint
CURRENCY:	shilin

Coins first came to Somalia, often known as the Horn of Africa, in the first century AD or earlier. They were brought by traders from Egypt, not for use as coins, but as bullion. Locally made coins first appeared in the fourteenth century, when the local sheikhs of Mogadishu struck base-silver and copper coins inscribed in Arabic. The inscriptions appear to be copied from the contemporary coins of Mamluk Egypt and the Islamic cities then flourishing on the coast of Tanzania. Their later coins, issued in the name of the sultan of Mogadishu, also show influence from the Ottoman coins of Syria.

The Sultanate of Mogadishu survived into the seventeenth century, paying tribute to the Portuguese, who controlled the East African coast. After the Islamic coastal settlements were overrun by the inland Somali people in about 1700, Somalia was without an official coinage until Britain in the north and Italy in the east each took possession of half of the territory in 1888 and 1893 respectively.

BRITISH INDIAN COINAGE

During the early nineteenth century Arab and British traders had been active in the area, which was nominally under the rule of the Sultanate of Zanzibar, and had introduced the British Indian rupee as a trade coin. When the British and Italians authorized coins for their Somali possessions, they were denominated as rupees and pice on the Indian standard, with 64 pice to the rupee. For Italian Somalia silver $\frac{1}{4}$, $\frac{1}{2}$ and 1 rupia and bronze 1, 2 and 4 besa (pice) with the portrait of King Victor Emmanuel III were struck at the Rome mint between 1909 and 1924. In the British Somaliland Protectorate imported Indian coins continued to be used, but a bronze 1 pice coin with a portrait of Queen Victoria, struck in 1897, 1898 and 1899 by the Royal Mint for the British East African Protectorate (Kenya), also circulated.

ITALIAN AND BRITISH INTERESTS

In 1925 the coinage of Italian Somalia was changed to correspond with contemporary Italian issues and silver 5 and 10 lire, with a royal portrait and the arms of Somalia, were issued. British Somalia's coinage had already been changed in 1905, when the rupee was decimalized, divided into 100 cents. The cent coins of the British East African Protectorate and Uganda, issued from 1906, were also used.

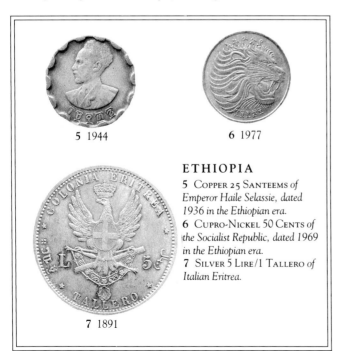

5 1944

6 1977

ETHIOPIA

5 Copper 25 Santeems of *Emperor Haile Selassie, dated 1936 in the Ethiopian era.*
6 Cupro-Nickel 50 Cents of *the Socialist Republic, dated 1969 in the Ethiopian era.*
7 Silver 5 Lire/1 Tallero *of Italian Eritrea.*

7 1891

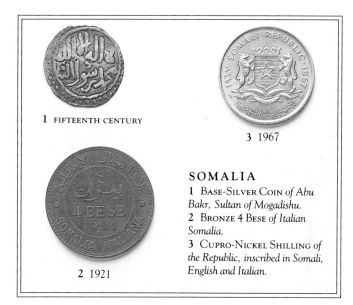

SOMALIA
1 Base-Silver Coin *of Abu Bakr, Sultan of Mogadishu.*
2 Bronze 4 Bese *of Italian Somalia.*
3 Cupro-Nickel Shilling *of the Republic, inscribed in Somali, English and Italian.*

1 FIFTEENTH CENTURY

3 1967

2 1921

During the Second World War Italian troops occupied the British half of Somalia, but after the defeat of Italy the territory was returned and British East Africa coins, which had been issued by the British East Africa Currency Board since 1920, were introduced to the whole of Somalia. In 1920 the rupee had been replaced by the florin worth 100 cents and then in the following year the shilling, originally the name of the 50 cent, became the standard unit worth 100 cents to bring it into line with the British coinage.

In 1950 control of its former colony was restored to Italy and a new issue of coins denominated as centesimi and somalo was made at the Rome mint, decorated with an elephant head or a leopard. The coins were dated and denominated in Italian and Arabic.

INDEPENDENCE

When Somalia achieved independence as a unified territory in 1960, the British shilling and cent system was adopted. The first republican coins struck in England in 1967 were decorated with the national arms and denominated in Arabic, Italian and English. After a second issue dated 1975, the design was changed for a new issue, dated 1976, on which the denominations are spelt SENTI and SHILIN.

SUDAN

FIRST COINS:	1885
FIRST DECIMAL COINS:	1956
MAIN MINTS:	Royal Mint and Khartoum
CURRENCY:	pound

The first Sudanese coinage was issued little more than a century ago, but for over 2000 years Sudan has had experience of coinage through its northern neighbour, Egypt. Ptolemaic, Roman, Byzantine,

Arab and Turkish coins entered the area, both overland following the Nile and through the ports of the Red Sea. It is also likely that in pre-Islamic times Axumite coins from Ethiopia were imported.

The official circulation of coins probably did not pre-date the Egyptian annexation of northern Sudan in 1820 and the building of the city of Khartoum in 1830. No Ottoman coins were issued, but Cairo mint coins circulated and local imitations were also used.

THE FIRST COINS

In 1884 the British General Gordon, who had been made Governor-General of Sudan by the Khedive of Egypt in 1877, was besieged in Khartoum by the army of the Mahdi, Mohammad Ahmad, and in the following year Sudan's first locally made currency was issued. Both Gordon and the Mahdi made an issue of money, but it was the Mahdi who introduced the first coins, Gordon's new currency being paper money. The Mahdi's issue was of silver 10 and 20 piastre pieces, copying contemporary Ottoman coins of the Constantinople mint, but distinguished by the absence of a mint name and the modified tughra saying 'by order of the Mahdi'. They were dated 1885 and struck in Khartoum. The Mahdi is also thought to have been the issuer of crude copies of Cairo mint gold coins.

From 1887 the Mahdi's successor, the Khalifa Abdullah, issued a large series of similar coins from the mint of Omdurman on the other side of the Nile from Khartoum. In 1898, however, an Anglo-Egyptian army occupied the Nile Valley up to Khartoum. By a joint agreement between Britain and Egypt, Sudan became an Anglo-Egyptian condominium, within which the coins issued by the British for Egypt were used.

The next Sudanese coinage was also a rebel issue, struck in 1909 by 'Ali Dinar at the mint of al-Fasher in the western province of Darfur. The coins were bronze piastres, crudely copying coins of the Cairo mint issued in the name of the Ottoman Sultan Mahmud II (1808–39) or of the Khalifa's Omdurman issues.

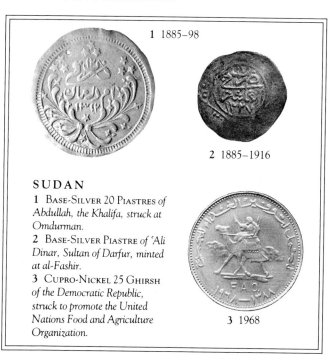

SUDAN
1 Base-Silver 20 Piastres *of Abdullah, the Khalifa, struck at Omdurman.*
2 Base-Silver Piastre *of 'Ali Dinar, Sultan of Darfur, minted at al-Fashir.*
3 Cupro-Nickel 25 Ghirsh *of the Democratic Republic, struck to promote the United Nations Food and Agriculture Organization.*

1 1885–98

2 1885–1916

3 1968

INDEPENDENCE

In 1954 Sudan gained self-government and in 1956, on achieving its independence, issued a series of coins denominated in millim and ghirsh (1000 millim = 100 ghirsh = 1 pound). These coins, made by the British Royal Mint, were inscribed in Arabic and decorated with a picture of an armed camel rider. In 1975 a new series was issued with an eagle design, based on the contemporary Egyptian coinage. This design had already been used on commemorative coins issued in 1971 to celebrate 15 years of independence.

KENYA

FIRST COINS:	eleventh century
FIRST DECIMAL COINS:	1906
MAIN MINT:	Royal Mint
CURRENCY:	shilling

From about the ninth century AD Arab traders visited the Kenyan coast in search of ivory and slaves, and gradually the local people were converted to Islam. Recent excavations on the island of Pate close to the Kenyan coast have revealed a group of locally made Islamic silver coins datable to the eleventh century. They are inscribed in Arabic: 'Mohammad he trusts in God' and 'The kingdom is God's and Abdullah trusts in him'. There have also been reports of bronze Islamic coins, issued on the Tanzanian coast during the next few centuries, found elsewhere on the Kenya coast.

During the sixteenth and seventeenth centuries the Kenyan coast was dominated by the Portuguese, who after 1593 used Mombasa as a base on their trade route around the Cape to India. They did not issue any coins for local use as they did in India and Malaya, but some coins were brought into the area during their occupation. Seventeenth-century gold coins from the Portuguese settlement at Goa and sixteenth-century silver coins from Spanish Mexico have been found around Mombasa.

MOMBASA COINAGE

During the eighteenth and early nineteenth centuries the Kenyan coast was under Arab control, and Mombasa was ruled by an Omani governor. The only coinage of this period are small tin coins inscribed in Arabic with the mint names of Lamu and Mombasa.

The name of Mombasa also appears on the next coins to be issued for the area. In 1888 the Calcutta and Birmingham mints began to make bronze pice and silver rupees for the Imperial British East Africa Company. The design on both denominations was a pan balance with the Arabic word 'adil (meaning 'just') between the pans, a symbol of fair trading borrowed from the 1830 Bombay coins of the former British East India Company. Both coins were inscribed with the name of Mombasa, the centre of the company's operations. On the pice the name Mombasa and the date were also written in Arabic. In place of the Arabic the rupee had the crowned sun symbol of the company. In 1890, 2 anna and ¼, ½ and 1 rupee silver coins, without the pan-balance design, were also issued.

BRITISH PROTECTORATE

In 1895 the British government bought out the East Africa Company and made Kenya a British protectorate, called British East Africa. Gradually this name came to include other British territories in the area: Uganda, Tanganyika and Somaliland. Coinage for the protectorate began to be made in 1897 with the issue of pice coins with a portrait of Queen Victoria. In 1906 these were replaced by a series of 10, 25 and 50 cent coins representing fractions of a rupee. This issue was continued until 1919; meanwhile ½, 1 and 5 cent denominations were added to the series. The lower denominations, up to 10 cents, had a central hole and were decorated with a crown and flowers on the front and four elephant tusks on the back; the higher denominations had the king's crowned head on the front and a lion and mountain design in a floral frame on the back.

In 1920 responsibility for the coinage was given to the East Africa Currency Board, which reorganized the coinage by replacing the rupee with first a florin and then in 1921 a shilling denomination. Coins with 1, 5, 10, 25 and 50 cent denominations continued to be issued with the earlier designs. A florin coin was issued, with the same design as the 50 cent coin, in 1920 and was replaced in 1921 by a shilling the same size and with the same designs.

INDEPENDENCE

The currency board continued to make Kenya's coins until after independence in 1963. The last issue, dated 1964, retained the inscription, EAST AFRICA, but omitted the name of the British monarch, replacing it with a Swahili version, *senti kuni* (10 cents) and *senti tano* (5 cents), of the denomination.

KENYA
1 SILVER RUPEE *of the Imperial British East Africa Company, Mombasa.*
2 BRONZE PICE *of the East Africa Protectorate.*
3 SILVER FLORIN *of East Africa.*
4 CUPRO-NICKEL 5 SHILLINGS *of the Republic.*

1 1888
2 1897
3 1921
4 1985

Kenya became a republic in 1964 and the republican coinage began in 1966. The cent-shilling system was retained and 5, 10, 25, 50 cent and 1 and 2 shilling coins with the portrait of President Jomo Kenyatta and the national arms were issued. Since 1980 the portrait has been that of President Arap Moi. In 1985 a heptagonal 5 shilling coin was added to the series. A few commemoratives have been issued and all, like the 1973 decagonal brass 5 shilling piece commemorating TEN YEARS OF FREEDOM, referring to national themes.

UGANDA

FIRST COINS:	1897
FIRST DECIMAL COINS:	1906
MAIN MINT:	Royal Mint
CURRENCY:	shilling

THE use of coinage in Uganda was introduced by the British administration which established a protectorate over the area between 1894 and 1896. The rupee and pice Mombasa coins of the

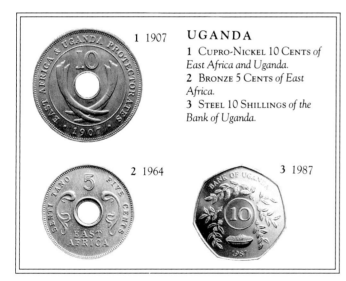

UGANDA
1 CUPRO-NICKEL 10 CENTS of East Africa and Uganda.
2 BRONZE 5 CENTS of East Africa.
3 STEEL 10 SHILLINGS of the Bank of Uganda.

Imperial British East Africa Company, issued since 1888, and 1 pice coins of the British East Africa Protectorate, issued from 1897, were used until replaced in 1906 by the coins of the British East Africa and Uganda Protectorates. This new coinage, made in England at the Royal Mint and in Birmingham, was denominated on a decimal basis (100 cents = 1 rupee). The lower denominations – ½, 1, 5 and 10 cents – were holed coins with a crown and flowers on the front and elephant tusks on the back. At first the ½ and 1 cent were issued in aluminium, but in 1909 they were made of cupro-nickel like the 10 cent. The ½ cent was dropped after 1909 and the 5 cent coin was only issued from 1913. Higher denominations in silver – 25 and 50 cents – had the portraits of English kings, Edward VII (1901–10) and George V (1910–36), on the front and a lion in front of Mount Kilimanjaro on the back.

In 1920 the rupee denomination was replaced by the florin, then the following year by the shilling, both equal to 100 cents. These new coins were issued for all the British territories of East Africa, which now included Tanganyika, by the East Africa Currency Board. The board's coins used the same designs as the earlier issue and were struck in the names of George V, Edward VIII (1936), George VI (1936–52) and Elizabeth II (1952–).

INDEPENDENCE

In 1962 Uganda gained its independence. The first coins of the republic were not issued until 1966, when 5, 10, 20 and 50 cents and 1 and 2 shilling coins were struck in England in the name of the Bank of Uganda. In 1972 these were joined by a heptagonal 5 shilling piece. The lower denominations retain the flower and elephant-tusk design used on the British issues, but the denominations above 50 cents have a new design featuring the national arms and a crowned crane in front of mountains. In 1987 a new series of clad-steel coins was struck for the Bank of Uganda at the Royal Mint: round copper-coated 1 and 2 shilling pieces with a cotton-plant design and nickel-coated seven-sided 5 and 10 shilling pieces with a coffee-plant design.

Since a UN Food and Agricultural Organization (FAO) issue in 1968, a small number of collectors' commemoratives have been issued.

TANZANIA

FIRST COINS:	eleventh century
FIRST DECIMAL COINS:	1904
MAIN MINT:	Royal Mint
CURRENCY:	shilingi

THE earliest-known coins from Tanzania are a large hoard of imported Islamic coins of the 'Abbasid caliphs of Baghdad (Iraq). The hoard contained ninth- and tenth-century coins. Gold coins of the Fatimid caliphs of Egypt from the tenth and eleventh centuries have also been recently found. All were found on the island of Pemba.

The first locally made coins were also Islamic. They have been found on the islands of Pemba and Zanzibar and on several mainland coastal sites. The largest number have been found during the excavation of the Islamic city of Kilwa. The earliest issues are thought to date from the eleventh century or soon after. A European traveller reported them still in use in the early sixteenth century. Both silver and copper coins have been found, with rhyming Arabic inscriptions which named a series of local Islamic rulers. Some of the later copper coins have an inscription suggesting influence from fourteenth-century Mamluk Egypt.

From this period many finds have also been made of Chinese coins, imported along with Chinese porcelain. Some of the Chinese coins date from the seventh century, but were imported during the thirteenth to fifteenth centuries.

No further coins have been reported from Tanzania until 1882 when the independent Sultan of Zanzibar issued his own coins. Sultan Barghash's coins were bronze pysa (pice) and silver ¼, ½ and 1 ryal and

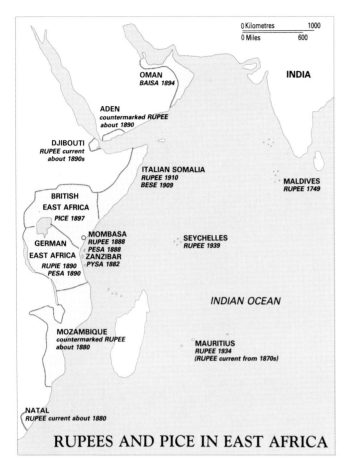

RUPEES AND PICE IN EAST AFRICA

The Great Mosque at Kilwa, Tanzania, fifteenth century. During recent excavations on this site contemporary local Islamic and imported Chinese coins have been found.

gold 2½ and 5 ryal, inscribed in Arabic. The first issue was struck in Belgium at the Brussels mint, but a second issue of bronze pysa with a shorter inscription was struck in Birmingham in 1887. Both issues of pysa have on their backs a pan-balance design, copied from the 1830 Bombay coins of the former British East India Company.

GERMAN PROTECTORATE

In 1891 the mainland of Tanzania became the German Protectorate of Tanganyika. In the previous year the German East Africa Company had begun to issue bronze pesa (pice) and silver rupees for circulation in the area. The pice, struck in Berlin in 1890, 1891 and 1892, were decorated with the German imperial eagle and inscribed in German and Arabic with the name of the company. The rupee and, from the following year, the ¼ and ½ rupee bore the helmeted portrait of the German Kaiser Wilhelm II on the front and the arms of the company on the back.

When the imperial government took over the issue of coins from the company in 1904, a decimal currency was devised for the colony with 100 heller equal to the rupee. Denominations of ½, 1, 5, 10 and 20

1 FIFTEENTH CENTURY

2 1870–88

3 1890

4 1913

5 1916

6 1987

TANZANIA

1 Bronze Coin *of Sulayman ibn al-Hasan, Sultan of Kilwa.*
2 Silver Ryal *of Barghash ibn Sa'id, Sultan of Zanzibar.*
3 Silver Rupee *of the German East Africa Company.*
4 Silver Rupee *of German East Africa.*
5 Gold 15 Rupees *of German East Africa, struck at Tabora.*
5 Cupro-Nickel 5 Shilingi *of the Republic.*

heller were struck at Berlin and Hamburg as small change to the ¼, ½ and 1 rupee coins which continued to be issued with a slightly modified design. In 1908 a decimal coinage was also made for Zanzibar: 1, 10 and 20 cent coins were struck at the Birmingham mint, with a palm tree and dolphins design. It is thought that the coins were not issued.

British and Belgian troops invaded the colony during the First World War and disrupted the supply of coins. An emergency issue of brass 5 heller and gold 15 rupee coins was made at the provincial town of Tabora in 1916. The gold coin has a dramatic elephant design on the back. After the war the colony became a British mandated territory and the coins of British East Africa (Kenya) were put into circulation.

INDEPENDENCE

The coins of the East Africa Currency Board were in circulation until Tanganyika became an independent republic in 1962. In the following year Zanzibar also achieved independence, but did so as a sultanate. When the sultan was overthrown in 1964, the new republican government united itself with Tanganyika to become the United Republic of Tanzania.

Tanzania's first coins were issued in 1966. They retained the cent and shilling denominations of the East Africa coinage, but renamed them as *senti* and *shilingi*, their Swahili names. The new coins all bore the portrait of President Julius Nyerere, and on the back either the torch of freedom, on the 1 shilingi, or a local animal on the lower denominations. A few commemoratives have been issued since 1971.

MOZAMBIQUE

FIRST COINS:	1725
FIRST DECIMAL COINS:	1935
MAIN MINTS:	Lisbon and Royal Mint
CURRENCY:	metical

THE section of the coast of East Africa now known as Mozambique was already regularly visited by Arab traders when Vasco da Gama 'discovered' it for Portugal in 1498, and the Portuguese made it a

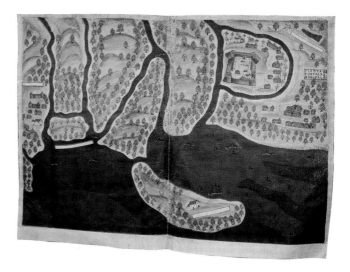

Seventeenth century Portuguese map showing the Portuguese fort and settlement at Sofala in Mozambique.

colony in 1505. The coins of the Islamic cities on the Tanzanian and Kenyan coasts have been found here, but the first coins made specifically for the region were not issued until 1725: a batch of crude copper and silver coins for the colony struck at Goa in Portuguese India. The bronze coins were decorated with the crowned arms of Portugal and the silver with only a cross. Before this issue the coins of the Portuguese settlement of Goa had been regularly imported.

In 1755 a second coinage of silver and gold coins was made for Mozambique at the Lisbon mint. On this issue the Portuguese King Jose I used the title 'Lord of East Africa'. The silver coins also had the emblem of the Portuguese colonies: a globe in the centre of a cross. This issue was inadequate for the colony's needs, and in 1765 an attempt was made to regularize the use of imported coins by counter-marking with an MR monogram all the foreign coins in circulation.

Coins were not made specifically for the colony again until 1840, when bronze coins struck in Lisbon were made for Mozambique. Denominations of 20, 40 and 80 reis (on the Portuguese system) were struck and in 1853 they were supplemented with a second issue of 1, 2, 5, 10 and 20 reis pieces. These all had the crowned arms of Portugal on the front and the denomination in a wreath on the back. Silver and

MOZAMBIQUE
1 COPPER COIN of the Portuguese colony, struck in Portuguese India.
2 SILVER ONCA of the Portuguese colony.
3 SILVER RUPEE of British India, countermarked in 1889 for use in Mozambique.
4 CUPRO-NICKEL ESCUDO of the Portuguese colony.

gold coins were not supplied, but from 1843 to 1851 locally made bar-shaped coins in these metals, stamped with an M and their weight, were issued. In 1874 a third batch of bronze coins, 5, 10 and 20 reis, were sent from the Lisbon mint. Foreign gold and silver continued to be used in the colony and in the 1880s and 1890s a renewed attempt at regulation by countermarking took place. The countermark consisted of a crown and the initials LM for Lourenço Marques, the capital, or PM for the Province of Mozambique. Foreign gold, British sovereigns and US eagles also circulated officially in the colony, but were not apparently countermarked.

In 1894 a coinage was made in Birmingham, England, for use in the northern part of Mozambique. The 10 and 20 reis bronze tokens were produced for the Portuguese Companhia do Nyasa. Silver pieces with a castle design were also made for the company, but not issued.

DECIMAL COINAGE

The establishment of the Republic of Portugal in 1910 brought about a change to a full decimal system for the coinage of Portugal and its colonies. New coins denominated in centavos and escudos (100 centavos = 1 escudo) were not issued for the colony until 1935–6. Silver 2½, 5 and 10 escudos, decorated with the arms of Portugal and the arms of Mozambique, mounted on the cross and globe emblem, were dated 1935. Bronze 10 and 20 centavos and cupro-nickel 50 centavos and 1 escudo with the arms of Mozambique alone were dated in the following year.

Sporadic centavo–escudo issues with slightly modified designs continued to be made for Mozambique until its independence in 1975. Until the 1951 issue the coins were inscribed COLONIA DE MOCAMBIQUE, but after that simply MOCAMBIQUE as the territory had been redesignated an overseas province of Portugal. From the same year the silver coins were gradually replaced by cupro-nickel ones and the sizes of the coins were reduced.

INDEPENDENCE

On independence the coinage system was reformed. An issue was made in 1975 of 1, 2, 5, 10, 20 and 50 centimos and 1 and 2½ meticas. Each coin portrayed the president of the new Republic of Mozambique and an example of local plantlife. In 1980 a new set of coins with a new spelling of the larger denomination – 50 centavos and 1, 2½, 5, 10 and 20 metical, each decorated with the national emblem and an industrial scene, was issued. The emblem, crossed rifle and hoe, sun and star within a wreath, also appears on a few commemoratives.

MALAWI

FIRST COINS:	1955
FIRST DECIMAL COINS:	1971
MAIN MINT:	Royal Mint
CURRENCY:	kwacha

Malawi's first contacts with coinage would have been through its northern and eastern neighbours, Tanzania and Mozambique, but its first officially recognized coinage was British, adopted in 1891

when the territory came under the control of the British South Africa Company. The company and from 1924 the British colonial authorities designated the area as Nyasaland after Lake Nyasa (now Lake Malawi), which dominates it. Alongside the British coins, South African and Southern Rhodesian coins also came into circulation.

In 1955 Nyasaland was given its own coinage as a constituent of the Federation of Rhodesia and Nyasaland. The new coins, denominated in pence and shillings, were based on the earlier issues of Southern Rhodesia.

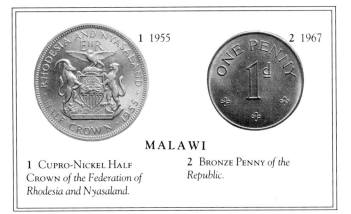

MALAWI

1 CUPRO-NICKEL HALF CROWN of the Federation of Rhodesia and Nyasaland.

2 BRONZE PENNY of the Republic.

INDEPENDENCE

Following the break-up of the Federation in 1963, new coins were issued in the name of the newly independent Republic of Malawi: 6 pence, 1 shilling, florin (2 shillings) and half-crown (2½ shillings) coins, dated 1964 and portraying Dr Hastings Banda, the first president. A commemorative crown (5 shillings) with the same portrait was also issued. The half-crown and crown had the arms of the republic on the back, but the smaller coins depicted local agriculture and wildlife: a cockerel, maize ears and an elephant cow and her calf. In 1967 a 1 penny coin was also issued, with an inscriptional design.

A decimal coinage was initiated in 1971, with a set of 1, 2, 5, 10 and 20 tambala coins, fractions of a kwacha. Some of the new coins readopted the designs of the 1964 issue, but the 2 and 5 cent coins had new wild bird designs. A collectors' set of these coins issued in the same year also contained a 1 kwacha coin with the same design as the earlier crown coin. Commemorative 1, 10 and 250 kwacha have also been issued, referring to national themes and wildlife conservation.

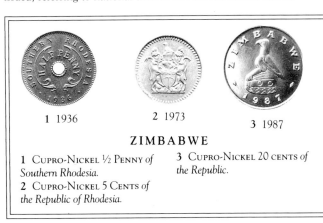

ZIMBABWE

1 CUPRO-NICKEL ½ PENNY of Southern Rhodesia.

2 CUPRO-NICKEL 5 CENTS of the Republic of Rhodesia.

3 CUPRO-NICKEL 20 CENTS of the Republic.

ZIMBABWE

FIRST COINS:	1932
FIRST DECIMAL COINS:	1964
MAIN MINT:	Royal Mint
CURRENCY:	dollar

ALTHOUGH the gold of Zimbabwe was long ago exported through Arab and Portuguese traders to be used in the coinages of the Middle East and Portugal, coinage did not circulate in this territory until about 100 years ago, when British adventurers penetrated the area. In 1888, under the leadership of Cecil Rhodes, the British South Africa Company began to operate in the area then known as Mashonaland. In 1891 the British authorities in South Africa brought this region into the Cape Colony currency area and British coins became its official currency. By 1894 the company and British currency had extended to include the rest of the territory, known as Matabeleland.

SOUTHERN RHODESIA
British coins continued to be officially acceptable in the area, known from 1924 as the British Protectorate of Southern Rhodesia, until 1939. Between 1923 and 1933 South African coins also circulated. From 1932, however, a new coinage was gradually introduced to replace them. The Southern Rhodesia Currency Board issued a series of coins, with the same denominations as the coins of South Africa, for use in the protectorate. The cupro-nickel ½ and 1 penny (bronze from 1942), like the contemporary coins of East Africa (Kenya), had a central hole, and therefore no royal portrait; both had a crowned-rose design. The silver 3 and 6 pence, 1 and 2 shillings and half-crown (all cupro-nickel from 1947), had a royal bust on the front. The back designs depicted local weapons (3 and 6 pence), the Zimbabwe eagle (1 shilling), an antelope (2 shillings) and the arms of the protectorate (half-crown).

FEDERATION OF RHODESIA AND NYASALAND
In 1953 Southern Rhodesia became part of the Federation of Rhodesia and Nyasaland and a new Central African Currency Board was established to issue its coinage. The coins, dated from 1955, had new designs, but the same denominations were struck. The ½ penny depicted a pair of giraffes, the penny a pair of elephants. The higher denominations had the royal bust on the front and a local plant or animal and the arms of the federation on the back. From 1956 the coins were issued by the Bank of Rhodesia and Nyasaland.

THE FIRST REPUBLIC
The federation was dissolved in 1963 so that its parts could become independent as the Republics of Rhodesia (Southern Rhodesia), Zambia (Northern Rhodesia) and Malawi (Nyasaland) in the following year. Rhodesia issued a new coinage, retaining the portrait of Queen Elizabeth II. Rhodesia's new coinage contained several changes. The lowest denomination issued was 3 pence, and collectors' sets of gold 10 shilling and 1 and 5 pound coins were also issued, all with the antelope design also used on the half-crown. In addition the coins had a dual denomination, expressed in both shillings and pence and in cents: (100 cents = 10 shillings = 1 dollar). From 1970 a fully decimal set of coins was introduced. Because Rhodesia had unlawfully revolted against British sovereignty and left the British Commonwealth, the queen's head was replaced by the national arms. The new coinage included ½, 1, 2½, 5, 10, 20 and 25 cent coins.

THE SECOND REPUBLIC
In 1980, after a civil war, the illegal regime was replaced by a democratic government which renamed the country after the ancient city ruins at Zimbabwe. The new republic's coins use the Zimbabwe eagle, a carving found at the ruins, as their main design. The ruins also appear on the dollar coin.

ZAMBIA

FIRST COINS:	1955
FIRST DECIMAL COINS:	1968
MAIN MINT:	Royal Mint
CURRENCY:	kwacha

COINS did not circulate in Zambia until traders of the British South Africa Company began to work in the area in 1889, establishing formal control from 1911. In line with other territories within the British sphere in South Africa, British coins circulated. These were joined from 1923 by South African and from 1932 by Southern Rhodesian coins. The territory was known as Northern Rhodesia from 1924, when it came under a British colonial administration.

In 1953, the Federation of Rhodesia and Nyasaland, linking Northern Rhodesia with its southern and eastern neighbours, was formed and the coinage of the federation was made the official currency of the territory. This new coinage was based on the earlier issues of Southern Rhodesia (*see* Zimbabwe).

INDEPENDENCE
The federation was disbanded in 1963, and in the following year Northern Rhodesia became independent as the Republic of Zambia.

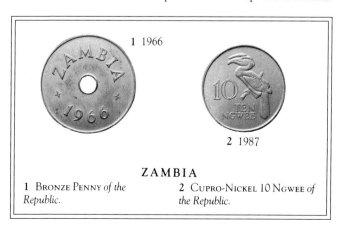

1 1966

2 1987

ZAMBIA

1 BRONZE PENNY *of the Republic.*

2 CUPRO-NICKEL 10 NGWEE *of the Republic.*

The first Zambian coinage, dated 1964, consisted of 6 pence and 1 and 2 shilling coins, decorated with the arms of the republic and local plants and animals. In 1965 a 5 shilling commemorative piece depicting the first president of Zambia, Kenneth Kaunda, and the arms of the republic was also issued. On a second issue of the lower denominations in the following year the president's portrait replaced the arms as the main design. As part of the 1966 issue a holed penny coin was introduced. This had a purely inscriptional design.

In 1968 a decimal coinage was introduced, with designs modified from the 1966 issue. Denominations of 1, 2, 5, 10 and 20 ngwee, fractions of a kwacha, were struck.

COMOROS

FIRST COINS:	1890
FIRST DECIMAL COINS:	1890
MAIN MINT:	Paris
CURRENCY:	franc

It is likely that coins first came to the Comoro Islands, situated off the East African coast between Mozambique and Madagascar, as the result of contacts with Islamic traders from the ports of Tanzania during the Middle Ages. The islands came under French control in 1886, and in 1890 the first coins were struck for the islands. The neighbouring island of Mayotte had already become a French possession in 1843, but the Comoros remained under the control of local sultans and it was in the name of one of these princes that the 1890 coins were issued.

The Paris mint struck bronze 5 and 10 centimes and silver 5 franc pieces for the sultan of the island of Anjouan. They were inscribed entirely in Arabic in the name of ''Ali bin Said 'Omar, Sultan of Anjouan, protected by the government of France the glorious'. The

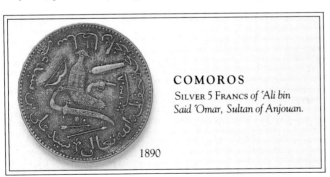

COMOROS
SILVER 5 FRANCS of 'Ali bin Said 'Omar, Sultan of Anjouan.

1890

bronze coins were decorated with a wreath design, borrowed from contemporary Tunisian coins (also struck in Paris), but the silver coin had a new design featuring a curved Arab dagger, sword, cannon, pistol, bow and arrow and flags.

DEPENDENCY OF MADAGASCAR
In 1912 the Comoros became a dependency of the French colony of Madagascar, and like it used French coins. In 1946 it became a separate

French possession once more, and in 1961 an autonomous territory, but coins were not issued specifically for it until 1964, when aluminium 1, 2 and 5 franc and bronze 10 and 20 franc coins in the name of the ARCHIPEL DES COMOROS were struck in Paris. All denominations had a female head representing the French Republic on the front. On their backs the aluminium coins had coconut palms, and the bronze coins had a composite scene representing the islands, including coconuts, boats, shells and the prehistoric caeleocanth fish.

The Comoros again became independent of French rule in 1975 and has since issued aluminium 5 franc and nickel 25, 50 and 100 franc coins. All the coins promote the FAO (United Nations Food and Agricultural Organization) and feature designs referring to the natural resources of the islands. In 1976 the island of Mayotte voted to remain under French rule and once again became separate from the other Comoros. French coins circulate there.

MADAGASCAR

FIRST COINS:	1943
FIRST DECIMAL COINS:	1943
MAIN MINT:	Royal Mint
CURRENCY:	ariary

During the nineteenth century French coins became widely used on the island of Madagascar, long before it became a French protectorate in 1886. French silver 5 franc pieces, particularly the issues of Louis-Philippe (1830–48), were introduced by French traders and readily accepted by the local people, but in the local markets they were soon cut up into tiny pieces paid out according to their weight. At the time of the establishment of French rule the possibility of a local coinage was considered. Pattern 10 centime and 5 franc coins in the name of Madagascar's local ruler, Queen Ranavalo, were made, but the idea was soon abandoned. French coins, no longer cut up, soon came to be the accepted currency of the island.

THE FIRST COINS
The first coins officially issued for Madagascar were made in South Africa. Because the German occupation of France in 1942 had cut off the supply of coins to Madagascar, the Free French, who controlled the island with British help, had bronze 50 centime and 1 franc coins struck at the Pretoria mint for the colony. Both denominations had a cockerel on the front and the cross of Lorraine on the back.

In 1948 the Paris mint made new aluminium coins for Madagascar, 1 and 2 franc pieces, both decorated with a female head representing the French Republic on the front and a double-horned buffalo on the back. An aluminium 5 franc coin with the same designs was also issued in 1953, together with bronze 10 and 20 franc coins with a map of Madagascar on the back.

INDEPENDENCE
Madagascar became the independent Malagasy Republic in 1960, but did not issue its own coins until 1965, when a set of stainless steel 1, 2

MADAGASCAR
1 SILVER 5 FRANCS *(fragments)* *of Louis Philippe, King of France.*
2 BRONZE PATTERN 10 CENTIMES *of Queen Ranavalo.*
3 ALUMINIUM-BRONZE 20 FRANCS *of French Madagascar.*

1 1830–48

3 1953

2 1883

and 5 franc coins was introduced. Each denomination had a flower on the front and a buffalo head on the back. A buffalo-head design also appeared on the bronze 10 and 20 franc pieces issued from 1970. Both denominations had local plants on the front.

In 1975 the island was renamed the Malagasy Democratic Republic, and this title appeared on two new denominations issued from 1978: nickel 50 and 100 franc coins issued for circulation, with designs which promoted the FAO (United Nations Food and Agricultural Organization). The fronts of both coins displayed the new national emblem, a star in a wreath, while the backs showed agricultural scenes. The denominations of both coins were expressed in terms of a new unit, the ariary, representing multiples of 5 francs. In 1988 gold and silver commemorative coins with these denominations were struck for Madagascar at the British Royal Mint.

MAURITIUS

FIRST COINS:	1723
FIRST DECIMAL COINS:	1877
MAIN MINT:	Royal Mint
CURRENCY:	rupee

IN 1715 the French East India Company established settlements in the Indian Ocean islands, now known as Mauritius and Réunion. They named the islands Île de France and Île de Bourbon respectively. The settlement was an important port of call for the French merchants trading with Pondichery, the French trading post in South India. This trade brought Spanish silver dollars and Indian gold and silver coins into the islands. In 1723 the French administration, based on Réunion, decided to issue copper coins, struck at the Company mint in Pondichery, for both islands (*see* Réunion).

Further issues of low denomination coins in the name of ILES DE

FRANCE ET DE BOURBON were made at the Paris mint in 1779, 1780 and 1781. The only silver coins made for Mauritius by the French were dollar-sized coins struck at Port Louis on Mauritius in 1810. They were denominated as 10 livre pieces and decorated with a crowned eagle, the emblem of Napoleon. In their inscription Mauritius was still called ILE DE FRANCE, but Réunion had been renamed Île de Bonaparte. A gold 40 livre piece was also planned. The silver dollars, however, did not circulate for long, as both Mauritius and Réunion were captured by the British later the same year.

BRITISH RULE
Réunion was returned to France and renamed the Île de Bourbon after the Treaty of Paris in 1814, but by the terms of the treaty Mauritius remained in British hands. Under British rule India continued to be the main source of coinage, but in 1820 there was an attempt to include Mauritius in a new currency system, based on the Spanish dollar. Silver coins denominated as fractions of the dollar were struck at London's Royal Mint for use in British colonial territories where the Spanish dollar already circulated. The first batch, consisting of $\frac{1}{16}$, $\frac{1}{8}$ and $\frac{1}{4}$ dollars, with an anchor design and dated 1820, were all sent to Mauritius. A second striking in 1822 also included $\frac{1}{2}$ dollars, but only part of it was sent to Mauritius; the remainder went to the British West Indies. The coins were not a great success and the scheme was abandoned in 1825, when the British government decreed that all British colonies should use only sterling.

Mauritius was linked too closely to the Indian currency system to be receptive to the establishment of a coinage system based on either the

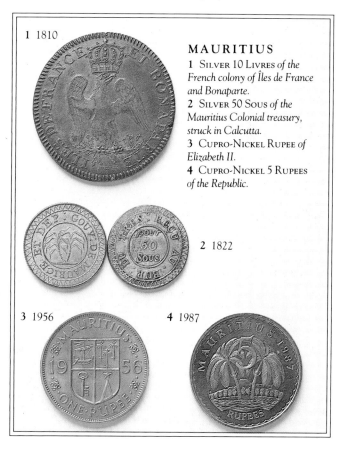

MAURITIUS
1 SILVER 10 LIVRES *of the French colony of Îles de France and Bonaparte.*
2 SILVER 50 SOUS *of the Mauritius Colonial treasury, struck in Calcutta.*
3 CUPRO-NICKEL RUPEE *of Elizabeth II.*
4 CUPRO-NICKEL 5 RUPEES *of the Republic.*

1 1810

2 1822

3 1956

4 1987

dollar or sterling. Already in 1822 an order has been placed with the British East India Company's Calcutta mint for a coinage of base-silver coins to the Madras standard. These were inscribed and denominated in French for the benefit of the local traders. 25 and 50 sou pieces were issued in the name of the GOUVERNEMENT DE MAURICE. The 50 sous was decorated with a picture of sugar canes, still the island's main commercial crop.

Although the British government sent large consignments of sterling coins to the island, including silver 1½ penny pieces specially issued for colonial use from 1834 until 1862, the island's administration kept its accounts in dollars and the local merchants used the Indian rupee as their standard.

RUPEE COINAGE

In 1877 the British government finally recognized the realities of the Mauritius coinage system and made the rupee the official standard, dividing it into 100 cents. No rupees were issued, but a set of bronze 1, 2 and 5 cent and silver 10 and 20 cent coins were struck in Birmingham, England, for the colony. Each denomination was decorated by Queen Victoria's crowned head on the front and a large numeral indicating the value on the back, a design which was adapted from the coinage of the British Straits Settlements (*see* Malaysia and Singapore).

Using these designs with the heads and titles of successive British monarchs, 1, 2 and 5 cent pieces were issued regularly from 1877 until 1986, but the 10 and 20 cents in their original form were only issued until 1897. The 20 cent denomination never reappeared, but a new scallop-edged 10 cent coin was introduced from 1947 to 1986.

From 1934 to 1986 a new series of higher denomination coins, including the first rupee, was struck in London for Mauritius. They were originally silver, but from 1950 cupro-nickel versions were issued. Like the smaller denominations they had a crowned portrait of the British monarch on the front, but a new set of designs was devised for their backs. The ¼ rupee had a design symbolizing the three main communities on the island: the British crown above a British rose, a French fleur-de-lis and an Indian lotus. The ½ rupee was decorated on its back with a stag and the rupee had the colony's arms on its back. Curiously, all the coins issued from 1978 until 1986 were dated 1978.

INDEPENDENCE

In 1968 Mauritius gained independence, but the British monarch remained head of state, so no immediate changes were made to the

coins as a result of this change. In 1971, however, a 10 rupee coin was issued to commemorate independence. This coin depicted the island's most famous emblem, the dodo. Other commemoratives have appeared since, but the pre-independence coin designs were retained until 1987 when, in its centenary year, the coinage system originated in 1877 was replaced by a new issue, including 1 and 20 cent and ½, 1 and 5 rupee pieces, all depicting the President.

RÉUNION

FIRST COINS:	1723
FIRST DECIMAL COINS:	1816
MAIN MINT:	Paris
CURRENCY:	franc

I N 1662 the uninhabited island of Réunion was settled by the French East India Company (Compagnie des Indes) as a staging post on its trade route round the Cape of Good Hope to India. The island was renamed the Île de Bourbon after the French royal family. The French traders introduced Spanish silver dollars and Indian gold and silver coins into the settlement. Small change was in the form of French billon and copper coins, countermarked with a B for Bourbon or ILR for Île de la Réunion, and French colonial issues of copper 9 denier pieces, made in 1721 primarily for use in the French West Indies.

In 1723 the Company had copper coins struck for use in the colony at its mint at Pondichery in South India. The coins were also to be current in the neighbouring island of Mauritius (Île de France), which was ruled by the French administration in Réunion. The new coppers were 1 and 2 sol pieces, decorated on the front with a crown and a pattern of fleurs-de-lis on the back. The same designs were used by the Pondichery mint for silver coins issued for use in French India.

In 1764 the Company handed over control of Réunion to the French Crown, but coins were not struck for the colony until 1779 when base-silver 3 sol pieces in the name of the French king Louis XVI were struck in Paris. Following the fall of the Bourbons in the French Revolution, the island was renamed Réunion in 1793, and then, in 1801, Bonaparte, after the First Consul, Napoleon. Coins using the second new name were struck in 1810 on the island of Mauritius (*see*

2 1779

3 1896

1 1723

4 1955

RÉUNION
1 COPPER 2 SOLS *of Îles de France and Bourbon, struck in Pondichery.*
2 BASE-SILVER 3 SOLS *of Îles de France and Bourbon.*
3 CUPRO-NICKEL FRANC *Token of the French Colonial Treasury.*
4 ALUMINIUM 5 FRANCS *of French Réunion.*

Mauritius). From 1810 until 1814 Réunion was captured by the British, but by the terms of the Treaty of Paris was restored to France, once again as the Île de Bourbon, under the restored Bourbon king Louis XVIII. In 1816 10 centime pieces in the name of Louis were issued for the colony, inscribed ILE DE BOURBON.

IMPORTED COINS

The second fall of the Bourbons in 1848 restored its original name to the island, but coins inscribed ILE DE LA REUNION were not issued until 50 centime and 1 franc cupro-nickel tokens were struck in 1896. The coinage of the colony, like that of its neighbour Mauritius, mostly consisted of imported coins brought in by traders. In 1859 there was such a shortage that a local landowner imported 227,000 Austrian base-silver 20 kreuzer coins for circulation on the island as francs. These coins proved to be so popular that another half-million were imported and continued to be used until 1879, when the colonial authorities made French coins the only official currency.

Apart from the 1896 tokens, French coins remained the only ones in use on Réunion until an issue of aluminium 1 and 2 franc coins was made in 1948. In 1946 Réunion had become an overseas department of the French Republic and these new coins had on the front a female head representing the Republic and on the back a sugar-cane design. In 1955 these were joined by an aluminium 5 franc coin with the same designs and bronze 10 and 20 franc pieces with the arms of the colony on the back. From 1962 and 1964 respectively nickel 50 and 100 franc coins, also with the arms of Réunion, have been issued.

SEYCHELLES

FIRST COINS:	1939
FIRST DECIMAL COINS:	1939
MAIN MINT:	Royal Mint
CURRENCY:	rupee

UNTIL 1903 the Seychelles Islands were a dependency of Mauritius, under French rule until captured by the British in 1810. In 1903 the Seychelles became a separate colony, but coinage continued to be the same as that used in Mauritius until 1939, when cupro-nickel 10 cent, silver 25 cent and ½ and 1 rupee coins were struck in London specifically for the Seychelles. The royal portrait from the Mauritian coinage was retained for the new coins, but on the back they all had the same new design, a floral frame containing the denomination. The 10 cent piece had a scalloped edge like the contemporary Indian 1 anna coin. The new coins were joined in 1948 by an issue for the Seychelles of bronze 1, 2 and 5 cent coins, which retained the Mauritian design both back and front. From 1951 all the higher denomination coins were struck in cupro-nickel.

The designs adopted in 1939 and 1948 were retained until 1974, except for the 10 cent piece which from 1953 was struck with twelve sides. In 1974 a new seven-sided 5 rupee coin with a palm tree and tortoise on the back was issued. In 1972 special 1 and 5 cent pieces with the inscription GROW MORE FOOD were made to promote the FAO

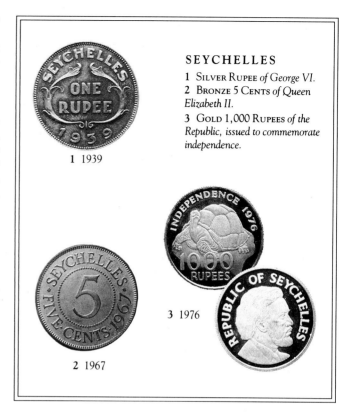

SEYCHELLES
1 SILVER RUPEE of George VI.
2 BRONZE 5 CENTS of Queen Elizabeth II.
3 GOLD 1,000 RUPEES of the Republic, issued to commemorate independence.

1 1939

3 1976

2 1967

(United Nations Food and Agriculture Organization). The 5 cent coin had a scalloped edge.

INDEPENDENCE

When the Seychelles gained independence as a republic in 1976 a new set of coins were issued, all portraying the first President on the front and local wildlife on the back. These were followed in 1977 by a set which replaced the presidential portrait with the national arms. In 1982 the use of shaped-edge coins was abandoned. The national arms was retained on the front of all the new round coins, but all the backs were redesigned, continuing to use the local wildlife theme. All the coins, apart from commemoratives, issued since 1982 have been dated in that year.

SOUTH AFRICA

FIRST COINS:	1802
FIRST DECIMAL COINS:	1961
MAIN MINT:	Pretoria
CURRENCY:	rand

COINAGE was not known in South Africa before the arrival of European settlers. Portuguese and Spanish coins found on the coast were probably lost during the sixteenth century, but the first intentional imports of coins were introduced in 1652, when the Dutch

243

under Jan van Riebeeck established a shipping and trading post at Cape Town. The Dutch did not issue coins for the colony, but imported coins made in the Netherlands. From the 1780s locally made paper money was also used. The Dutch settlement also imported the Spanish, Portuguese, Italian and Indian coins in regular use in international trade during the eighteenth century. Both the paper money and the imported coins circulated according to their value in Cape rixdaler, the local unit of account based on a Dutch coin.

In 1795 the Cape was captured by a British fleet and for the first time British gold and copper coins were officially imported. In 1802, following the Peace of Amiens, Britain handed the colony back to the Netherlands, but in 1806 retook it. During the brief Dutch repossession of the Cape, the mint at Enkhuizen in Holland struck the first coinage to be made for the colony. Silver $\frac{1}{8}$, $\frac{1}{4}$, $\frac{1}{2}$ and 1 guilder coins, dated 1802 and with a ship design, were sent to the Cape, but on their arrival it was decided that the continuing British threat made it unsafe to issue them. Most of the coins were forwarded to Java (Indonesia) and issued there. After the British reoccupation, a supply of the two smallest denomination ship coins was found and issued in 1806 for local use. However, the bulk of coins in use in South Africa was still imported. A proclamation of the British governor in 1806 listed British, Dutch, Spanish, Portuguese, Italian and Indian gold and silver coins in circulation.

The British administration remedied the chaotic effects of this mixed currency by importing British coins in bulk. From 1825 the official money of the Cape Colony was British. In 1866 Australian gold coins were included in the official currency. In 1867 the Australian gold was also made legal in the province of Natal, where British Indian rupees were the commonest coin. British coinage was not in fact made the official currency of this area until 1882, nor of Bechuanaland until 1885.

LOCAL COINAGE

During the first half of the nineteenth century European traders, missionaries and settlers began to move deeper into the interior, beyond the borders of the Cape Colony. This expansion brought about the issue of some local coinages in the territories not under British rule. These coins, however, were all denominated on the British system. The first issue was made for use by the local non-European people in a region to the north of the Cape Colony called Griqualand. Issued by the London Missionary Society to the Bastards of Griqua Town, $\frac{1}{2}$, 1, 5 and 10 penny pieces were struck in Birmingham with the dove and olive branch emblem of the society in 1815 and 1816.

TRANSVAAL AND ORANGE FREE STATE

In 1852 and 1854 respectively, Dutch settlers established the independent republics of the Transvaal and the Orange Free State north-east of the Cape. In 1874 the president of the Transvaal, Thomas Burgers, ordered a consignment of gold pond (pound) coins to be made at the Birmingham mint with his portrait and the arms of the Transvaal, named on the coin ZUID AFRIKAANSCHE REPUBLIEK. However, only 837 examples were delivered to the Transvaal.

After a brief attempt at British rule in the Transvaal (1877–81), the South African Republic was refounded in 1883 and its new president Paul Kruger, in order to make a coinage for Transvaal, established South Africa's first mint at Pretoria. From 1892 bronze 1 penny, silver

1 1802   2 1860   4 1874

3 1874

5 1892

SOUTH AFRICA

1 SILVER $\frac{1}{4}$ GUILDER *of Dutch Cape Colony.*
2 SILVER 6 PENCE *of the Durban Club, Natal.*
3 BRONZE PATTERN PENNY *of Orange Free State struck in Berlin by Otto Notte and Company.*
4 GOLD POND *of the South African Republic with the portrait of President Thomas Francis Burgers.*
5 BRONZE PENNY *of the South African Republic.*

Cape Coast Castle, the seventeenth century Dutch trading centre on the Gold Coast, Ghana, taken by the British in 1664. As well as being a local trading settlement the castle was an important staging post for Dutch ships heading for South Africa and further east.

3 and 6 pence, 1, 2, 2½ and 5 shilling and gold ½ and 1 pond coins were issued. A modified version of the design used for Burgers' pond was used for all the new coins, except the 3 and 6 pence and shilling, which used a wreath design on the back like the contemporary British coins of the same denomination. Because the Pretoria mint was not ready in time, some of the 1892 coins were made in Berlin.

In the Orange Free State a trial kroon (crown = 5 shillings) was produced dated 1874 and pennies dated 1888 and 1890 were made in Germany, but not adopted. Local traders' tokens, denominated in British money, were, however, in use.

The German manufacturer of some of the Orange Free State trial coins, Otto Nolte and Company of Berlin, also made suggested pieces for the Cape, Transvaal and Griqua Town.

British victory in the Boer War (1899–1902) brought the Kruger coinage to an end, but during the war two further issues were made within the Transvaal. A few gold blanks for pond coins, rescued from the mint during the British capture of Pretoria, were subsequently issued for circulation in Boer territory. In 1902, right at the end of the war, an emergency mint was set up at Pilgrim's Rest in the eastern Transvaal to strike gold coins in the name of the South African Republic. About 1000 pieces were struck, with crude handmade tools from a goldmine workshop, and inscribed simply with the initials of the Republic ZAR, the date 1902 and denomination EEN POND.

UNION OF SOUTH AFRICA

The end of the war allowed a unified currency system to be imposed by 1910 throughout the newly-established Union of South Africa. From 1923 part of the British coinage in circulation was made in South Africa at the reopened Pretoria mint, brought back into use as a branch of the British Royal Mint to turn locally mined gold into 1 pound and ½ pound coins, that is sovereigns and half-sovereigns.

At the same time it also began to issue a new coinage for the Union, with British denominations, but with new designs relating to South Africa. Each coin was inscribed in Latin on the front and English and Dutch on the back. There was a portrait of the British monarch on the front of each coin, and on the back the ¼ penny had two sparrows on a mimosa branch, the ½ and 1 penny a Dutch sailing ship, the 3 and 6 pence a mimosa wreath, the shilling the figure of Hope with an anchor and the 2 and 2½ shilling the arms of the union. The gold coins retained the English St George and dragon design, and were only distinguishable from British coins by the initials SA for South Africa; they were not issued after 1932. In 1925 the design on the 3 and 6 pence was changed to protea blossom, surrounded by bundles of sticks.

After a special issue to mark a royal visit in 1947, a 5 shilling coin was added to the series. It had a running springbok design. The same design was also used on ½ and 1 pound coins, when a gold coinage began to be made specifically as South African currency.

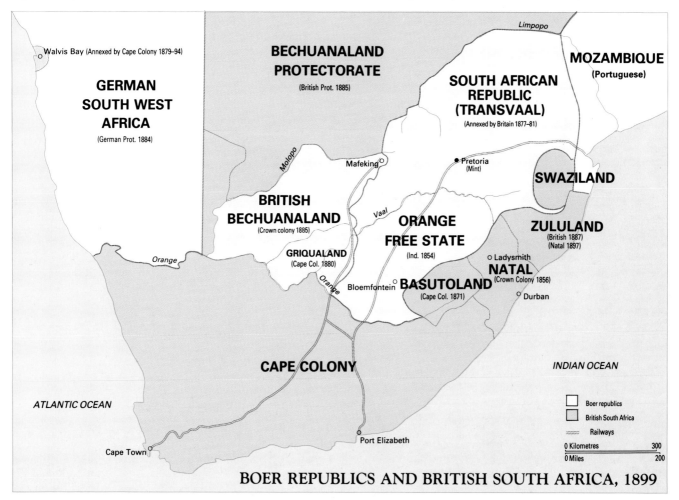

BOER REPUBLICS AND BRITISH SOUTH AFRICA, 1899

6 1902
7 1923
8 1947
9 1961
10 1986
11 1980

SOUTH AFRICA

6 GOLD POND *of the South African Republic.*
7 SILVER FLORIN *of the Union of South Africa.*
8 CUPRO-NICKEL 5 SHILLINGS *of the Union of South Africa.*
9 BRASS CENT *of the Republic.*
10 CUPRO-NICKEL 50 CENTS *of the Republic.*
11 GOLD KRUGERRAND *of the Republic.*

REPUBLIC OF SOUTH AFRICA

In 1961 South Africa became a republic and a new issue of coins was introduced, denominated on a new decimal system with a rand divided into 100 cents. The rand coin was equal to a $\frac{1}{2}$ pound under the British system. The front design of the new coins replaced the monarch's head with that of Jan van Riebeeck. The back designs were modified versions of those on the union coin, except for the 1 cent which had a new Boer wagon design.

A new smaller coinage was introduced in 1965, still with $\frac{1}{2}$, 1, 2, 5, 10, 20 and 50 cent and 1 rand coins, but with completely new designs featuring South African wild animals and plants. A new portrait of Riebeeck was used on the lower denominations until replaced by the portrait of President Swart in 1968, the national arms in 1970 and President Vorster from 1976. Between 1965 and 1969, instead of using the joint Dutch and English inscriptions, two concurrent issues, one in each language, were struck.

From 1961 until 1982 gold 1 and 2 rand coins continued to be issued as bullion coins, but not for circulation. In 1967 they were joined by another bullion piece, the krugerrand, and since 1980 by fractional krugerrand as well.

SWAZILAND

FIRST COINS:	1968
FIRST DECIMAL COINS:	1968
MAIN MINT:	Royal Mint
CURRENCY:	lilangeni

BRITISH and South African Republic coins were the first to circulate officially in Swaziland during the period of joint British and Transvaal rule from 1890 until 1894, and the subsequent sole rule of Transvaal until 1906. In 1906 the kingdom was made a British protectorate, and the coinage systems of the Cape Colony and subsequently the Union of South Africa were used.

Between 1961 and 1974 Republic of South Africa coins also circulated, but from 1968, when Swaziland achieved independence, a new denomination system was set up. The cent and rand were replaced by the cent and the luhlanga. A higher denomination, the lilangeni, worth 25 luhlanga, was also established. In 1968, however, only a collectors' set of coins commemorating independence was issued: silver 5, 10, 20 and 50 cents and 1 luhlanga and a gold lilangeni, depicting King Sobhuza II and Swazi weapons.

Swaziland's first currency coins were issued from 1974. They represented a change in the denomination system, with 100 cents = 1 lilangeni. The coins are distinguished by their shape: 1 lilangeni – round, 1 and 50 cent – dodecagonal, 2 cent – square, 5 and 20 cent – scalloped with 12 curves, and 10 cent – scalloped with 8 curves. They all show the king on the front and local plants and animals on the back.

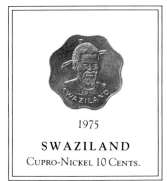

1975
SWAZILAND
CUPRO-NICKEL 10 CENTS.

1966
LESOTHO
CUPRO-NICKEL 20 LICENTE *of King Moshoeshoe II.*

LESOTHO

FIRST COINS:	1966
FIRST DECIMAL COINS:	1966
MAIN MINT:	Royal Mint
CURRENCY:	loti

IN 1868 the King of Lesotho, Moshoeshoe I, invited Britain to establish a protectorate over his realm. In 1871 it became part of the British Empire as Basutoland, but British coins did not become its official currency until 1884, when the currency system of the Cape Colony was extended to the area. From then until Basutoland became independent as the Kingdom of Lesotho under King Moshoeshoe II in 1966, the coinage circulating in South Africa continued to be used.

Lesotho's first coins were not made for issue, but as a souvenir of independence. They were denominated as cente (cent) and loti, equal in value to the contemporary South African cent and rand. The words used to indicate the denomination show an unusual feature of the Bantu languages; a prefix indicates the plural: *cente* = cent, but *licente* = cents. The 1966 set contained silver 5, 10, 20 and 50 licente and gold 1 loti and 2, 4 and 10 maloti pieces, all portraying King Moshoeshoe I. The first coins for circulation were made in Britain in 1979, brass 1, 2 and 5 lisente (the spelling was changed for this issue) and cupro-nickel 10, 25 and 50 lisente and 1 loti. These all portrayed King Moshoeshoe II.

BOTSWANA

FIRST COINS:	1966
FIRST DECIMAL COINS:	1966
MAIN MINT:	Royal Mint
CURRENCY:	pula

In 1885, when the region now called Botswana became the British Protectorate of Bechuanaland, it officially adopted the coinage system of the Cape Colony, and so British coins circulated there. From

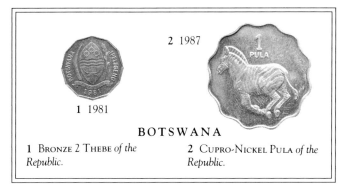

BOTSWANA

1 **BRONZE 2 THEBE** *of the Republic.*

2 **CUPRO-NICKEL PULA** *of the Republic.*

that date until its independence in 1966 the South African coinage was used.

For 10 years after independence South African cents and rands continued to be used, but a new currency system denominating these coins as cents and thebe was adopted from 1966 when a set of two commemorative coins with these denominations was made.

The first issue of coins for circulation, in 1976, were renamed, so that 100 thebe = 1 pula. The new coins made at the Royal Mint, 1, 5, 10, 25 and 50 thebe and 1 pula, all carried the arms of the Republic of Botswana, a decorated African shield between rampant zebras on the front and a local plant or animal on the back. A 1 pula coin was also issued in 1987.

NAMIBIA

FIRST COINS: No coins issued

ALTHOUGH coins have been used in Namibia since the nineteenth century, no specific issue has ever been made for the region. Coins were first intentionally brought to the area by British traders and military personnel in 1878, when the Walvis Bay port was developed as a British enclave. British coins continued to be the accepted currency of the port when it was placed under Cape Colony control in 1884, and when it was transferred to the Union of South Africa in 1910. Since then its currency has remained the same as that of South Africa.

In 1919 the rest of the territory now called Namibia became South West Africa, a League of Nations mandate under British rule, and subsequently in 1923 it passed to the Union of South Africa. British and later South African coins were authorized by these administrations. Before 1919 this territory had been ruled by Germany as a protectorate since 1880. German coins were acceptable, but British coins formed the bulk of the coinage in use.

When South Africa became a republic in 1961 it retained control of South West Africa in opposition to United Nations' wishes. Although the independence of Namibia is now becoming a reality, South African occupation and the circulation of South African coins continues for the time being.

ANGOLA

FIRST COINS:	1693
FIRST DECIMAL COINS:	1921
MAIN MINT:	Havana
CURRENCY:	kwanza

PORTUGAL's first African coinage was struck for Angola at the mint of Porto from 1693. On these coins the king of Portugal, Pedro II, was titled 'Lord of Ethiopia', to indicate that the coins were for use in Africa. They were copper pieces decorated with the crowned arms of Portugal and a cross, denominated according to the Portuguese system as 5, 10 and 20 reis. The coastal area of the territory now known as Angola, but then known simply as Portuguese Africa, had been under Portuguese control since 1482. Portuguese and Spanish coins had already been imported for use before the 1693 issue.

A second issue for the colony followed from 1715, when the copper coins were decorated with the globe emblem of Portugal's overseas empire. Around the globe they have a Latin inscription, PECUNIA TOTUM CIRCUMIT ORBEM ('money travels around the whole world'). At first only 10 and 20 reis pieces were struck, but, in 1749, 5 reis and, in 1753, 40 reis coins were added. These coins also circulated in Portugal's other African colonies: Mozambique (where they were countermarked for local use), Guinea, Cape Verde and Sao Tome and Principe. From 1752 the coin inscription gives the Portuguese King Jose I the title 'Lord of Guinea', meaning of West Africa in general.

The third issue for the colony was also struck in Portugal, but with a new denomination system specifically designed for use in Portugal's West African colonies, designated on the coins as AFRICA PORT-UGUEZA. They were denominated in macuta, a unit of account used in Angola for trade with the local people. Copper $\frac{1}{4}$, $\frac{1}{2}$ and 1 macuta, and silver 2, 4, 6, 8, 10 and 12 macuta coins were issued from 1762. They were all decorated with the crowned arms of Portugal, but the usual globe emblem was placed behind it on the copper pieces. As part of the issue, a copper 5 reis coin ($\frac{1}{8}$ macuta) with the same designs was struck in 1770. The macuta coinage continued until 1860, with only minor changes to its design.

In 1809, 1837 and 1853 a countermark in the form of the arms of Portugal was applied to the pre-macuta and macuta coins to make them valid for continued circulation. After the macuta coinage, Angola had to rely on old coins and imported ones. In 1871 a special consignment of Portuguese coins was imported.

In 1921 the Lisbon mint struck a new coinage for Angola, intending to bring its coinage system into line with the Portuguese republican system, with 100 centavos = 1 escudo. The arms on globe design was reused on 1, 2 and 5 centavo coins, and a female head wearing a cap of liberty, representing the republic, appeared on the 10, 20 and 50 centavo pieces. In 1927 a brief attempt was made to reuse the traditional macuta denomination, equated with 5 centavos. A modi-fied version of the arms and globe, occasionally adding a cross, was used on all the republican issues for Angola until independence was gained in 1975. Denominations of 1, 2½, 5, 10 and 20 escudo were added to the series from 1952.

INDEPENDENCE

Very few coins have been issued for Angola since independence. A new denomination system with 100 lwei = 1 kwanza was adopted and an undated set of 50 lwei, 1, 2, 5 and 10 kwanza coins was struck. This was followed by issues of 1, 10 and 20 kwanza dated 1978, and 50 lwei and 1 kwanza dated 1979.

ZAIRE

FIRST COINS:	1887
FIRST DECIMAL COINS:	1887
MAIN MINT:	Royal Mint
CURRENCY:	zaire

ALTHOUGH, from as early as the fifteenth century, many areas of the territory of Zaire had well-established monetary systems, based on the rich copper resources of the southeast, an official coinage came to the area only with the arrival of Belgian settlers in the 1880s. The first coins were struck in 1887 at the Brussels mint in the name of Leopold II, 'King of the Belgians'. Leopold, through the services of the American explorer Henry Stanley, and the agreement of the other European colonial powers, ruled Zaire as his personal possession. The coins, 1, 2, 5, 10, 20 and 50 centimes and 1, 2 and 5 francs were inscribed in French with Leopold's title 'Sovereign of the Independent State of the Congo'. In 1908 Leopold transferred this personal realm to the Belgian government and it was renamed the Belgian Congo. New coins inscribed with this name were issued from 1910.

The lower denominations of both the 1887 and the 1910 issue coins had central holes (a device which was adopted on Belgium's own coins from 1901 only).

The 1910 issue, like contemporary Belgian coins, was inscribed in both French and Flemish. It continued to be issued until 1928, although the 1 and 2 centime denominations were not issued after 1919. In 1917 the Belgian government in exile ordered coins for the Congo from the mint in Birmingham, England.

In 1921 cupro-nickel 50 centimes and 1 franc coins, with the portrait and name of King Albert on the front and with a palm tree on the back, were added to the coinage. Two series of these were issued, one inscribed in French, the other in Flemish. During the reign of his successor, Leopold III, coins for the Congo were issued only in the name of the Banque du Congo Belge. The first was a 5 franc piece issued in 1936 and 1937 with the king's portrait on the front and a lion on the back. During the Second World War, while Belgium was under German occupation, further issues of 1, 2, 5 and 50 franc pieces by this bank, without the royal portrait, were made, all depicting an elephant. The 1943 2 franc coin is a distinctive hexagonal shape. The bank's last

ANGOLA
1 COPPER 40 REIS of Joseph I, *King of Portugal*.
2 COPPER MACUTA of Joseph I, *King of Portugal*.
3 NICKEL-BRONZE 50 CENTA-VOS *of the Portuguese Colony*.

ZAIRE

1 Copper 10 Centimes of
Leopold II, King of the Belgians.
2 Cupro-Nickel Franc of
Albert, King of the Belgians.

3 Brass 5 Zaires of the Bank of
Zaire.
4 Bronze Franc of the National
Bank of Katanga.

issue was in 1949. No further coins were issued for the Belgian Congo.

INDEPENDENCE

In 1960 the Congo became the Democratic Republic of the Congo, but coins were not issued by the new republic until 1965, when the Brussels mint struck a set of gold commemoratives depicting President Joseph Kasavubu to celebrate the fifth anniversary of independence. In the same year a 10 franc (following the Belgian system) aluminium coin decorated with a lion's face was struck for issue in the name of the Banque Nationale du Congo. The issue was abandoned and in 1967 a new coinage was introduced, denominated in sengi and likuta: 100 sengi = 1 likuta, but on the larger coins the likuta became makuta, the plural of likuta. Denominations of 10 sengi, 1 likuta and 5 makuta coins were issued and in 1970 a presentation set of 25, 50 and 100 makuta coins, portraying President Joseph Mobuto, was also struck. The 100 makuta coin was called a zaire.

In 1971 the Congo was renamed Zaire and since then its coins have been issued in the name of the Banque du Zaire. The sengi denomination has been dropped and 10 and 20 makuta coins have been issued for circulation since 1973. In 1977 these were joined by a 5 makuta coin. In 1987 new 1 and 5 zaire coins were made in Britain at the Royal Mint for circulation in Zaire.

REPUBLIC OF KATANGA

During its early years the Democratic Republic of the Congo was fragmented by a fierce civil war. In the southeast one of the provinces of the Congo briefly declared itself independent as the Republic of Katanga. In 1961 the Banque Nationale du Katanga issued 1 and 5 franc pieces, decorated with a bunch of bananas on the front and a copper ingot on the back. The ingot, known as a Katanga cross, was of the type used locally as currency in the nineteenth century. A gold version of the 5 franc piece was also issued for collectors.

RWANDA

FIRST COINS:	1952
FIRST DECIMAL COINS:	1952
MAIN MINT:	Royal Mint
CURRENCY:	franc

Coinage was unknown in Rwanda 100 years ago. In 1898 it became a German protectorate and is likely to have become familiar with the coinage of neighbouring German East Africa (Tanzania). In 1916 Rwanda was occupied by Belgian troops and came within the currency area of the Belgian Congo (Zaire). In 1920 Belgian rule was confirmed by the League of Nations, which made Rwanda part of the Mandated Territory of Ruanda and Urundi. Coins were not made specifically for this territory until 1952 when the Central Bank of the Belgian Congo began to issue coins inscribed RUANDA-URUNDI. Between 1952 and 1960, 50 centime and 1 and 5 franc coins were struck, all decorated with a palm tree, like earlier Belgian Congo coins.

After the Belgian Congo became independent, Ruanda-Urundi was renamed Rwanda-Burundi and in 1961 its central bank issued 1 franc coins decorated with a lion design, struck at the Brussels mint. The issue continued until 1964, after Rwanda and Burundi had achieved independence as separate states in 1962.

In 1964 the joint coinage was replaced by a new issue of 1, 5 and 10 franc coins in the name of the national bank of the Republic of Rwanda and depicting the first president, Grégoire Kayibanda. A ½ franc piece issued by the national bank in 1970 has a different, non-pictorial, design, inscribed in both French and the local Kinyarwandu language. In 1974 a new series of 1, 5, 10, 20 and 50 franc coins, struck in France and later in Britain, was introduced.

RWANDA
Aluminium-Bronze Franc
Central Bank of Belgian Congo.

BURUNDI
Cupro-Nickel 10 Francs.

BURUNDI

FIRST COINS:	1952
FIRST DECIMAL COINS:	1952
MAIN MINT:	Brussels
CURRENCY:	franc

In 1898 Burundi became a protectorate within German East Africa and hence part of its currency area. It was similarly introduced to

Belgian Congo currency, when in 1920 it was made a mandated territory under Belgian control. The Belgian administration ruled it as a part of the joint territory of Ruanda-Urundi. A currency for the exclusive use of the territory was not issued until 1952, when the Central Bank of the Belgian Congo issued a 5 franc coin inscribed RUANDA-URUNDI. A second issue of 50 centimes, 1 and 5 franc pieces was struck between 1952 and 1960. In 1961, as preparations were made for granting the territory independence, the Central Bank of newly named Rwanda-Burundi also issued 1 franc coins.

INDEPENDENCE

In 1962 Burundi and Rwanda achieved independence as separate states. Burundi remained a kingdom and issued its first coins with a portrait of King Mwambutsa IV. These were a set of commemorative coins denominated in francs, struck at the Brussels mint in 1962. A second series commemorating the king's golden jubilee appeared in 1965. The only coin issued for circulation was a 1 franc piece made in the name of the Banque du Royaume du Burundi. In 1966 Mwambutsa IV was succeeded by King Ntare V, who was immediately overthrown.

The Republic of Burundi made commemorative coins from 1967, but only issued coins for circulation from 1968, when an aluminium 5 franc piece with the arms of the republic was struck at the Brussels mint. Since 1970 1 franc coins have also been issued. The coins are inscribed in French and the local language, Kirundi: BANQUE DE LA REPUBLIQUE DU BURUNDI, IBANKI YA REPUBLIKA Y'UBURUNDI.

CONGO

FIRST COINS:	1942
FIRST DECIMAL COINS:	1942
MAIN MINT:	Paris
CURRENCY:	franc

PORTUGUESE traders first brought coinage into this part of Africa and it is likely that the coins of the Portuguese colony of Angola came into the Congo during the eighteenth century. Portugal never made territorial claims in the area, so in 1883 the French, who had made use of the coastal area as a naval base, established a protectorate over the region. French coins were used in the area and it was not necessary to issue coins specifically for local use until 1942, when the German occupation of France cut off the supply of coinage. The new coins were issued for use throughout France's Central African possessions: Afrique Equatoriale Francaise (see Senegal). The coins were struck at the Pretoria mint in South Africa for the Free French rulers of the colonies and were decorated with the Free French cross of Lorraine and the republican cockerel: 50 centime and 1 franc pieces were issued. In the following year 5 and 10 centime pieces were also prepared, but not issued. After the Second World War a local coinage was continued with a Paris mint issue in 1948 of 1 and 2 franc pieces, with a female head representing the French Republic on the front and an antelope head representing Equatorial Africa on the back.

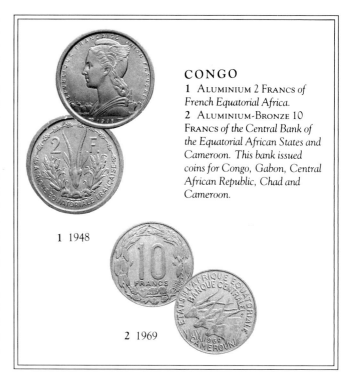

CONGO
1 ALUMINIUM 2 FRANCS of French Equatorial Africa.
2 ALUMINIUM-BRONZE 10 FRANCS of the Central Bank of the Equatorial African States and Cameroon. This bank issued coins for Congo, Gabon, Central African Republic, Chad and Cameroon.

1 1948

2 1969

INDEPENDENCE

In 1958 the Congo and the other French territories in the area – Gabon, Central Africa, Chad and Cameroon – were made self-ruling republics and in 1960 independent states. Up to the present day they have retained a joint coinage, from 1961 in the name of the ÉTATS DE L'AFRÌQUE EQUATORIALE and CAMEROON, and then from 1974 as the ÉTATS DE L'AFRIQUE CENTRALE. The 1, 5, 10, 25, 50 and 100 franc coins were issued by a joint bank and struck in Paris. The coins had a design incorporating three antelope heads. In 1971 the joint coinage combined with a set of local issues. The Congo began its own issues, still through the Banque des États de l'Afrique Centrale and retaining the three-antelope design. From 1971 only the 100 franc denomination was issued for circulation until a 500 franc with a new design featuring a woman's head was struck by the Paris mint in 1985. In 1976 a 500 franc and in 1978 a 50 franc coin of the joint issue were marked with a letter c for issue in the Congo.

GABON

FIRST COINS:	1942
FIRST DECIMAL COINS:	1942
MAIN MINT:	Paris
CURRENCY:	franc

ALTHOUGH official coins were only issued for Gabon from 1942, an unofficial coinage first circulated in this territory two years before it came under formal French rule in 1885. Coin-like tokens were issued at Franceville in 1883 for use in the local French trading station. The higher denominations representing 5, 25 and 50 francs were brass tokens inscribed OUEST AFRICAIN FRANÇAIS, struck in Paris. The lower denominations were locally made pieces of zinc plate stamped F for Franceville. They were distinguished simply by shape: hexagon (10 centimes), triangle (20 centimes), oblong (50 centimes), square (1 franc) and octagon (1½ francs). French and other European coins had entered the area in the early nineteenth century when French traders first arrived on the Gabon River.

In 1942 the currency of French Equatorial Africa was issued (*see* Congo). Gabon had been one of the four linked territories (the others were Congo, Central Africa and Chad) known since 1910 as French Equatorial Africa, and it continued to share a common coinage with them after it became an independent republic in 1960.

INDEPENDENCE

The initial issue of coins in the name of the République Gabonaise was a commemorative set of gold 10, 25, 50 and 100 franc pieces, celebrating independence, portraying the first president, Leon Mba, and the national arms. In 1969 and 1971 further commemorative gold sets were struck for Gabon.

Although commemorative coins were struck for Gabon from 1960, the first issue for circulation was not made until 1971, when nickel 100 franc pieces struck at the Paris mint began to be used. This retained the three-antelope design of the joint Equatorial Africa coins, and was still issued by the joint Banque Centrale. A cupro-nickel 500 franc piece with a female-head design shared with the other former French states of Central Africa (*see* Congo) came into circulation in 1985. Alongside the 100 and 500 franc coins, 5, 10, 25, 50 and 500 franc pieces issued for all the Central African States continue to circulate. From this series some 50 and 500 franc pieces issued between 1976 and 1985 are marked with a D. This indicated that they were struck for use specially in Gabon.

CENTRAL AFRICAN REPUBLIC

FIRST COINS:	1942
FIRST DECIMAL COINS:	1942
MAIN MINT:	Paris
CURRENCY:	franc

THIS territory was absorbed into the French Congo, as the district of Oubangui Chari, in 1894. From 1905 it was linked administratively with Chad, and in 1910 became a part of French Equatorial Africa. French coins circulated in the area until the German occupation of France during the Second World War stopped

the supply. French Equatorial Africa was under the control of the Free French, who had coins made for the region at the South African mint of Pretoria. These were issued in 1942 and after the war were replaced by a new set of coins struck in Paris (*see* Congo).

INDEPENDENCE

In 1960 French Equatorial Africa achieved independence and its constituent parts became autonomous republics. Oubangui Chari became the Central African Republic. The coinage of the Banque Centrale of what was now known as the States of Equatorial Africa continued to circulate in this territory until 1978, when the Central African Republic was abolished to form the Empire Centrafricain, ruled by Emperor Bokassa I. The States' 1, 5, 10, 25, 50 and 500 franc coins were used; 50 and 500 franc issues from 1976 to 1978 were marked with the letter B to indicate that they were for use in the Central African Republic, and 100 franc pieces were also issued by the Banque Centrale in the name of the republic.

In 1978 a 100 franc piece in the name of the empire was issued. The portrait of Bokassa had already appeared on a massive 20,000 franc gold coin issued in 1970 while he was still president. The gold issues of the empire struck in 1979 also portray him, on the 10,000 franc coin, together with the portraits of Caesar, Charlemagne and Napoleon, and, on the 25,000 franc coin, with the sun. After Bokassa was overthrown in September 1979, the republic, and the issues of the Banque Centrale, were restored. Since 1985 the 500 franc coin is also struck in the name of the republic.

CHAD

FIRST COINS:	1942
FIRST DECIMAL COINS:	1942
MAIN MINT:	Paris
CURRENCY:	franc

THE official use of coinage in Chad has been a very recent innovation. Even though coins have been in use for more than 25 centuries in its northern neighbour, the state of Libya, coins entered Chad only by chance before it became one of France's Equatorial African possessions, known in 1893 as Tchad. French currency circulated in the area until replaced during the Second World War by an issue made by the Free French specifically for use in French Equatorial Africa. The coins, dated 1942, were struck in South Africa (*see* Congo). After the war the Paris mint continued to supply coins in the name of l'Afrique Equatoriale Française.

Although Chad became independent in 1960, the first coins in the name of the République du Tchad were not issued until a set of commemoratives, celebrating famous men such as President Kennedy, Martin Luther King, President Nasser and General de Gaulle, appeared in 1970. Current 100 franc coins in the name of the republic commenced from 1971. A 100 franc issue was made too by the Banque des États de l'Afrique Centrale, which also issued a joint coinage for the former Equatorial African colonies. Since 1985 a 500 franc coin has been issued.

BRITISH AND FRENCH CURRENCY AREAS IN COLONIAL AFRICA

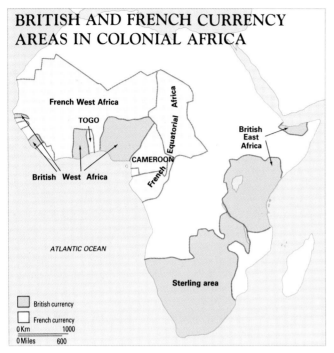

French West Africa

TOGO

French Equatorial Africa

CAMEROON

British East Africa

British West Africa

French

ATLANTIC OCEAN

Sterling area

British currency
French currency
0 Km   1000
0 Miles   600

became part of the Republic of Nigeria. An independence commemorative was issued in 1960 by the État du Cameroun. Current 100 franc coins were issued from 1966 with the Banque des États de l'Afrique Centrale design featuring three antelope heads. The bulk of the coins in circulation in Cameroon were issues (made since 1961) of this bank and of its earlier counterpart, named on 1958 coins as the INSTITUT D'ÉMISSION of AFRÌQUE EQUITORIALE FRANÇAISE and CAMEROUN.

In 1971 and 1972 the 100 franc coins were issued in the name of the République Fédérale du Cameroun, but since then they have been inscribed in both French and English with the name of CAMEROUN–CAMEROON. The 500 franc coin issued from 1985 used a similar two-language inscription.

CAMEROON
ALUMINIUM-BRONZE FRANC
of the French Mandated Territory of Cameroon.

1926

CAMEROON

FIRST COINS:	1924
FIRST DECIMAL COINS:	1924
MAIN MINT:	Paris
CURRENCY:	franc

THE first coins to enter Cameroon were Portuguese and Spanish, brought by Portuguese traders from the sixteenth century, but there was no official coinage until 1884, when this territory became the German protectorate of Kamerun and German imperial coins were introduced. Coins were not issued specifically for local use until after Kamerun had become a mandated territory, shared between Britain and France. British West African coins circulated in the British area, and from 1924 the Paris mint made coins for the French area in the name of the Territoire sous Mandate de la France: Cameroun. These were 50 centimes and 1 and 2 franc pieces decorated with a female head representing the French Republic and a leaf design. They were issued until 1926.

The next issue for the territory was in 1943, when coins in the name of Cameroun Français Libre were issued by the Free French: 50 centimes and 1 franc pieces with Free French cross of Lorraine designs. After the Second World War these were replaced by an issue of 1 and 2 franc pieces in the name of the Territoire du Cameroun. The representation of the French Republic was reused, with a facing antelope head within a floral spray on the back.

INDEPENDENCE

In 1960 French Cameroon became independent and was joined the following year in a federal republic by part of the British sector; the rest

EQUATORIAL GUINEA

FIRST COINS:	1969
FIRST DECIMAL COINS:	1969
MAIN MINT:	Madrid
CURRENCY:	ekwele

FROM the fifteenth century until 1778 the territory now known as Equatorial Guinea was administered by the Portuguese as part of their African colony of Angola. During this period it used the same coins as Angola. In 1778 Portugal transferred control to Spain, and Spanish American and Spanish coins became the predominant currency in local use. Spain in turn lost control of part of the colony, the island of Fernando Po, to Britain from 1827 until 1844. British coins became the legal currency there, although Spanish and Latin American silver dollars also remained in use.

Spain did not issue any coins specifically for Spanish Guinea, although in 1969, the year after it had become the Republic of Equatorial Guinea, 1, 5, 25 and 50 peseta coins dated 1969 were struck in Madrid for the country. Crossed elephant tusks appeared on all the denominations, except the 50 peseta which portrayed the first president, Francisco Macias.

In 1975 a new denomination system with coins denominated in ekuele was introduced: 1, 5 and 10 ekuele coins with the presidential portrait were issued. Five years later a fresh issue, with a new portrait of President Nkogo and with a different spelling of the denomination, was issued: 1 ekwele and 5, 25 and 50 bipkwele dated 1980 were struck (bipkwele is the plural of ekwele).

SAO TOME AND PRINCIPE

FIRST COINS:	1813
FIRST DECIMAL COINS:	1929
MAIN MINT:	Royal Mint
CURRENCY:	dobra

COINAGE came to these islands with their first inhabitants, Portuguese settlers, during the fifteenth century. The establishment of successful sugar plantations using convict and slave labour brought prosperity to the islands. At first Portuguese and, later, Portuguese African coins were used. A coinage specifically for the islands was not made until 1813 when a consignment of copper 20, 40 and 80 reis coins was sent to the island from the Rio de Janeiro mint. These coins had the usual Portuguese colonial designs of a crowned denomination numeral and a globe. In 1820 a similar batch was issued in Mozambique. A second issue of the same denominations with a slightly modified design was supplied to the island from 1819 by the Lisbon and Brazilian mints.

The supply stopped in 1825 and for the next 40 years no new coins were supplied, so a variety of imported coins were used. The colonial authority from 1853 countermarked the imported coins with a crown design to authorize their circulation. Copper coins from Portugal, Angola, Mozambique, Brazil and silver coins from Portugal, Brazil, Spain and Britain have been recorded with the countermark. In 1867 a fresh issue of coins specifically for the islands was sent from Lisbon: copper 5, 10 and 20 reis pieces in the name of King Luis I. Foreign coins, however, continued to be imported for local use as no new coins were made for the colony until 1928.

SAO TOME AND PRINCIPE
1 COPPER 80 REIS *made in Brazil for the Portuguese colony.*
2 NICKEL-BRONZE 50 CENTAVOS *of the Portuguese colony.*

1 1820

2 1929

From 1928 to 1929 a new set of 10, 20 and 50 centavo coins were struck for Sao Tome and Principe at the Lisbon mint, for the first time inscribed with the name of the islands. Like the contemporary coins of Portugal they were decorated with a female head with a cap of Liberty.

FURTHER ISSUES
Further issues were made in 1939 and 1948. These featured the arms on globe design also used on Portuguese coins, and were issued in the name of the COLONIA DE S. TOME E PRINCIPE; 1, 2½, 5 and 10 escudo coins were also included in the issue. From 1951 the colony was redesignated an overseas province and the word COLONIA was accordingly omitted from coins issued in that year. Similar issues followed in 1962 and 1971; the 1971 issue also including a 20 escudo denomination.

Since the islands became the Republica Democratica de Sao Tome e Principe in 1975, only commemorative coins have been struck. A new denomination system was adopted for the first issue: a set of 50 centimos and 1, 2, 5, 10 and 20 dobra FAO (United Nations Food and Agriculture Organization) coins dated 1977.

SENEGAL

FIRST COINS:	1944
FIRST DECIMAL COINS:	1944
MAIN MINT:	Paris
CURRENCY:	franc

DURING the eleventh century Senegal was occupied by Moroccan Berbers and was an important source for the gold used to strike the massive coin issues that also circulated in Europe. The al-Murabitun Berber rulers of Morocco and Spain originated in the Moroccan frontier forts which lined the Senegal River. From the fifteenth century the Portuguese operated trading stations in the area, both for gold and for slaves.

THE COLONIAL PERIOD
An official coinage, however, was not in use in the area until 1920, when Senegal became a French protectorate and the circulation of French coins was authorized. Before that, coinage in the area consisted of imported Portuguese, Spanish and British coins. During the first decades of French rule British West African coins circulated more widely than official French coins. In 1920 there were several issues of French tokens produced by the local French chambers of commerce. Denominated as 5, 10, 25 and 50 centime and 1 franc pieces, aluminium and brass tokens were issued in Dakar, Rufisque and Ziguinchor.

A distinct coinage for Senegal was first issued in 1944, when the Paris mint struck 50 centime and 1 franc pieces. The coins were issued in the name of Afrique Occidentale Française (French West Africa) and were also for use in the other French-controlled West African territories administered from Senegal. Apart from their inscription, they were identical in design to the regular French issues, with a female

SENEGAL
1 ALUMINIUM 25 CENTIMES
TOKEN *of the French Chamber of
Commerce, Rufisque.*
2 ALUMINIUM-BRONZE FRANC
of French West Africa.
3 ALUMINIUM-BRONZE 10
FRANCS *of the Institut d'Emission
of French West Africa.*
4 NICKEL 100 FRANCS *of the
Central Bank of the States of
West Africa.*

head, personifying the French Republic, on the front and two cornu-
copiae on the back. A new design, featuring an antelope head in a
floral wreath, was adopted for the next issues of 1 and 2 franc pieces
made in 1948 and 1955. In 1956 antelope-design 5, 10 and 25 franc
pieces were also struck.

INDEPENDENCE

In 1957, on the handing over by the French of limited self-rule to
Senegal and the other territories of French West Africa, a new
monetary authority was set up to take over the issue of coins from the
French government: new 10 and 25 franc pieces were issued in the
name of the Institut d'Émission of Afrique Occidentale Française –
Togo (Togo was a former German colony mandated under French
rule). On these coins the personification of the French Republic was
replaced by a fish mask representing West Africa.

When full independence was granted to Senegal and the other
French West African states in 1958, the monetary authority continued
to issue coins, but in the name of the Banque Centrale of the États de
l'Afrique de l'Ouest, and later in the name of the Union Monetaire
Ouest-Africaine. These coins circulated in Senegal and in the other
states served by the West African Monetary Union: Benin, Ivory
Coast, Burkina-Faso, Niger, Mauritania and Togo. Mali was originally
a member of the union, but left it in 1962. Former French Guinea,
which became independent as Guinea in 1957, never joined it. At first
the bank issued only 1, 5 and 10 franc coins, but a 100 franc piece has
been issued since 1963, a 25 franc since 1970 and a 50 franc since 1972.
The higher denominations have a floral frame in place of the antelope
design, and since 1976 the 1 franc coin has only its denomination on
the back.

MAURITANIA

FIRST COINS:	1944
FIRST DECIMAL COINS:	1944
MAIN MINT:	Paris
CURRENCY:	franc

FROM the eleventh century the territory now known as Mauritania
was within the sphere of the Islamic rulers of Morocco, and it
played a major role in the movement of West African gold into North
Africa. No Islamic coins were issued this far south, but they did
circulate in the Berber settlements on the Senegal River. From the
sixteenth century, European traders were active along the coast and in
the late nineteenth century the French government established control over the territory, making it one of their West African possessions
in 1903. Its coinage became that of French West Africa, and later the
West African Monetary Union (*see* Senegal).

INDEPENDENCE

In 1960 Mauritania became an independent republic and in 1966, as
the République Islamique de Mauritanie, broke its formal ties with the
French state. It nevertheless retained the currency of the Monetary
Union until 1973, when it began issuing its own coinage.

A new denomination system based on the ouguiya was introduced
in that year; 1, 5, 10 and 20 ouguiya coins inscribed in Arabic and
decorated with the star and crescent emblem were issued by the
Banque Centrale de Mauritanie. A khoum coin ($\frac{1}{5}$ ouguiya) was
also issued. The khoum was not made after 1974, but the other
denominations continue to be issued.

MAURITANIA
1 ALUMINIUM ⅕ OUGUIYA.
2 CUPRO-NICKEL 20 OUGUIYA.

MALI

FIRST COINS:	1944
FIRST DECIMAL COINS:	1944
MAIN MINT:	Paris
CURRENCY:	franc

DURING the Middle Ages Mali was probably the richest kingdom in
the world. It supplied gold to Egypt, Tunisia, Morocco, Algeria
and Libya, who in turn supplied it to Europe and the Middle East.

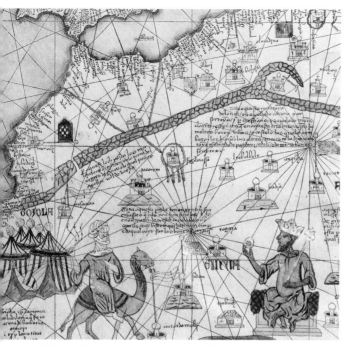

Map of West Africa from a fourteenth century Spanish atlas, showing the enthroned figure of King Mansu Masa of Mali holding his golden regalia.

Although Mali was an important centre of Islamic culture and was briefly conquered by the rulers of Morocco, the people of Mali had no coins of their own, preferring to use salt as money.

The first coinage to be officially used in the area was French, introduced by the French administration established in 1898. In 1920 Mali became the territory of French Sudan and in the same year the chamber of commerce in the town of Kayes issued aluminium 5, 10, 20 and 50 centime tokens for local circulation. Otherwise its currency was the same as that of the other parts of French West Africa (*see* Senegal) until it became an independent republic in 1960.

INDEPENDENCE

Unlike most of the former French West African states, Mali broke all its ties with the French and set up its own monetary system. In 1961 aluminium coins denominated in franc maliens were issued in the name of the République du Mali. Each denomination was decorated with the head of a local animal: 5 francs a hippopotamus; 10 francs a zebra; and 25 francs a lion. During 1975 and 1976 these were replaced by a new set of coins: 10, 25, 50 and 100 franc coins decorated with local crops, issued in the name of the Banque Centrale du Mali. In 1960 and 1967 commemorative coins were issued featuring the famous Mosque of Jenna above the rising sun.

MALI
1961   ALUMINIUM 5 FRANCS.

GUINEA

FIRST COINS:	1944
FIRST DECIMAL COINS:	1944
MAIN MINT:	Paris
CURRENCY:	syli

Although this country shares its name with the British guinea, struck at the British Royal Mint from West African gold during the late seventeenth century, Guinea did not have coins of its own until it came under French control in 1890. French coins were joined in circulation by British and later British West African issues imported from neighbouring Sierra Leone. After 1944 the coins issued for French West Africa were also used. Until 1958 the currency of Guinea was the same as that of the rest of French West Africa (*see* Senegal).

In 1958 Guinea broke all of its ties with France and became the independent Republic of Guinea. In the following year it issued its own coins, denominated in franc guineens and portraying Sekou Toure, the first president: 5, 10 and 25 franc pieces were produced and in 1962 a 1 franc was also made. In 1971 a new denomination system was introduced with coins denominated in cauri and syli (100 cauri = 1 syli). The 50 cauri coin was decorated with a picture of a money cowrie (the cowrie was an earlier form of currency); 1, 2 and 5 syli coins portrayed national heroes. Although commemorative coins denominated in syli were issued in 1977 and 1984, in 1985 a coinage of new 5 and 10 franc coins with the national arms was issued to replace the cauri–syli coinage.

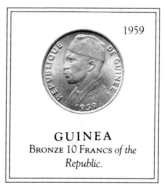

GUINEA
BRONZE 10 FRANCS *of the Republic.*

GUINEA BISSAU
COPPER ½ MACUTA *of Maria II, Queen of Portugal.*

GUINEA BISSAU

FIRST COINS:	1933
FIRST DECIMAL COINS:	1933
MAIN MINT:	Royal Mint
CURRENCY:	peso

Guinea, discovered by the Portuguese in 1446, was settled by them from 1558, but did not become a formally constituted territory until 1905. Portuguese African (Angolan) coins and European coins were used in the area until a coinage specifically for Portuguese Guinea was issued by the Portuguese Republic in 1933: 5, 10, 20 and 50 centavo and 1 escudo coins were struck in Lisbon in the name of Guine. All the denominations were decorated with a female head representing the Republic. The 50 centavos and 1 escudo also had the arms of Portugal on a globe representing Portugal's overseas territories. The designs were copied from contemporary Portuguese coins.

Further issues were made in 1946, 1952 and 1973, but no longer featured the head design. The arms on globe design appeared on all of the issues, while on the higher denominations, which eventually included 5, 10 and 20 escudo coins, this was joined by a second globe design including the arms of the colony.

When Guinea became an independent republic in 1974 it adopted the name Guinea Bissau, but it was 1977 before there was a new coinage in the name of the Republica da Guine-Bissau. A new denomination system was also adopted and 50 centavo, 1, 2½, 5 and 20 peso coins were struck at the Royal Mint. The first set were FAO (United Nations Food and Agriculture Organization) coins and featured local commercially grown plants. A second issue in 1978 had the same designs but was issued for circulation; the 250 and 1000 peso of 1984 are the only reported commemoratives.

IVORY COAST

FIRST COINS:	1944
FIRST DECIMAL COINS:	1944
MAIN MINT:	Paris
CURRENCY:	franc

ALTHOUGH Portuguese, Dutch and British traders operated along the Ivory Coast from the sixteenth to the early nineteenth centuries, French traders were the first to establish permanent stations and develop inland contacts which led in 1893 to formal French

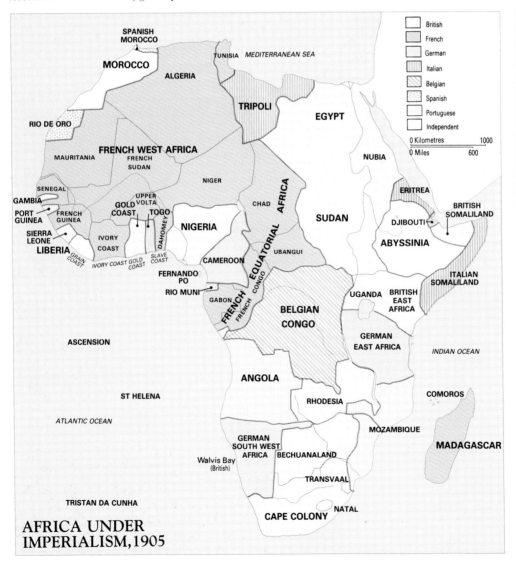

AFRICA UNDER IMPERIALISM, 1905

1966
IVORY COAST
SILVER 10 FRANCS.

1975
BURKINA FASO
BRASS 25 FRANCS of the Bank of the Central African States.

control. French coins were the legal currency of the territory, which became part of French West Africa in 1904. When a general coinage for French West Africa was made in 1944, it was also issued in the Ivory Coast. Later issues of the general coinage in 1948, 1955 and 1956 also circulated. In 1957 responsibility for the issue of the general coinage was passed by the French government to the Institut d'Émission of Afrique Occidentale Française, and in 1962 it was passed on to the Union Monetaire Ouest Africaine. Ivory Coast continues to be a member of this Monetary Union and to use its general coinage (*see* Senegal). The only coins issued in the name of the republic were commemoratives struck in 1966.

Market place in contemporary Ivory Coast. During the nineteenth century cowrie shells dominated the market economy of West Africa, but since the 1940s coins and paper money have become the accepted form of payment.

BURKINA-FASO

FIRST COINS:	1944
FIRST DECIMAL COINS:	1944
MAIN MINT:	Paris
CURRENCY:	franc

THE inland trade of French settlements in Senegal and the Ivory Coast brought French rule and French coinage into this region. A French protectorate was established in 1896, but it was not administered separately until it became the colony of Upper Volta in 1919. In 1932 the colony was divided between the Ivory Coast, Niger and the French Sudan (Mali). It became a distinct territory once again in 1948 and 10 years later a republic. In 1960 the Republic of Upper Volta gained independence and in 1984 it was renamed the Republic

of Burkina-Faso. Since 1944 the general coinage of French West Africa, and since 1962 of the West African Monetary Union, have circulated as the official coinage of this territory (*see* Senegal).

TOGO

FIRST COINS:	1924
FIRST DECIMAL COINS:	1924
MAIN MINT:	Paris
CURRENCY:	franc

IN 1884 the territory now known as Togo became a German protectorate and German imperial coins were introduced as the official currency. After the First World War German Togoland was made a mandated territory under Anglo–French rule. The British sector was administered from the Gold Coast (Ghana) and the coinage system of British West Africa (*see* Nigeria) was used there. The French sector was ruled as a separate territory and from 1924 was given its own coinage. Bronze 50 centime and 1 and 5 franc coins were struck at the Paris mint in the name of the Territoires sous Mandat de la France: Togo. The design used was the same as that adopted for the Cameroon.

A second issue, of aluminium 1, 2 and 5 franc pieces in the name of the Territoire du Togo, was made in 1948, also using the same design as the Cameroon coinage.

INDEPENDENCE

In 1957 the British sector became a formal part of the newly independent state of Ghana and the French sector became the République Togolaise. A new coinage of 10 and 25 franc coins, decorated with an African mask and an antelope, was issued in the name of the Institut d'Émission de l'Afrique Occidentale Française and Togo in the same year (*see* Senegal). From 1960 they were issued in the name of the Central Bank of the States of West Africa, which was regulated from 1962 by the West African Monetary Union. The coins of the union are still current in Togo.

The only coins issued in the name of the République Togolaise have been commemoratives, struck in 1977 to celebrate the 20th anniversary of independence.

BENIN

FIRST COINS:	1944
FIRST DECIMAL COINS:	1944
MAIN MINT:	Paris
CURRENCY:	franc

IN the seventeenth century the establishment of Porto Novo, a Portuguese trading post on the coast of Benin, first brought European coinage into this region. An official coinage was not, however, established until the French franc was put into circulation when Porto Novo and territory inland became a French protectorate in 1892. The area became a formal French possession, known as Dahomey, in 1904. From 1912 the coinage of British West Africa (*see* Nigeria) was also used locally.

As part of French West Africa Dahomey was administered from Senegal and in 1944 the coins struck at the Paris mint for general circulation in French West Africa were also issued in Dahomey. When Dahomey became an independent republic in 1960, the joint coinage of former French West Africa, now issued in the name of the Central Bank of the States of West Africa, continued to circulate. In 1962 responsibility for the joint coinage was taken over by the West African Monetary Union. Commemorative coins in the name of the republic were issued in 1971 to celebrate ten years of independence.

In 1975 Dahomey was renamed the Republic of Benin and the country continues to use the coins of the West African Monetary Union (*see* Senegal).

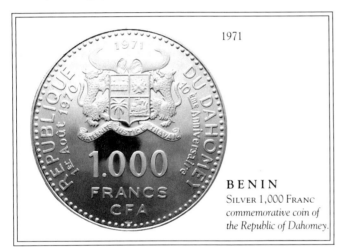

1971

BENIN
Silver 1,000 Franc *commemorative coin of the Republic of Dahomey.*

Fifteenth to sixteenth century bronze sculpture of a Portuguese musketeer, modelled and cast in the Benin Kingdom, Nigeria.

NIGER

FIRST COINS:	1944
FIRST DECIMAL COINS:	1944
MAIN MINT:	Paris
CURRENCY:	franc

COINAGE was introduced to this Saharan region by French traders in the late nineteenth century. It became a part of French West Africa in 1896 and until its independence in 1960 used the same currency as the other French West African territories. At first French coins were used, but from 1944 a general coinage made specifically for these territories was in use. It was administered after 1957 by the Institut d'Émission, and after 1962 by the West African Monetary Union. Niger, an independent republic since 1960, continues to use the coins of the Monetary Union (*see* Senegal).

Only commemorative coins have been issued in the name of the République du Niger itself.

NIGERIA

FIRST COINS:	1907
FIRST DECIMAL COINS:	1973
MAIN MINT:	Royal Mint
CURRENCY:	naira

BEFORE the nineteenth century European contacts with the territory now known as Nigeria were limited to the trade of slaves, which brought Spanish, Mexican and Austrian silver dollars into the area. British interest resulted in part from anti-slavery activities in West Africa, but missionary and trade contacts soon followed and in 1858 led to the first issue of European-style money for use in Nigeria. Coin-like tokens denominated as $\frac{1}{8}$ pence or $\frac{1}{400}$ dollar pieces were issued by a British trader, MacGregor Laird.

1 1858

2 1907

NIGERIA
1 Bronze ⅛ Penny Token *issued by Laird.*
2 Cupro-Nickel Penny *of Nigeria and British West Africa.*

'The Coining Press', a French cartoonist's view of the British imperialist policy in Africa.

From 1861, when the port of Lagos was taken under British control, until 1900, when Northern and Southern Nigeria became British protectorates, British silver coins were introduced in quantity into the territory and began to oust silver dollars as the main form of currency. British bronze coins were also imported but proved unpopular, as the local peoples still preferred to use cowrie shells or copper rings, known as manillas, as small change.

THE FIRST COINS

From 1907 small-change coins, pennies made of cupro-nickel, were struck at the Royal Mint for issue in Nigeria. These proved acceptable. They had a central hole, a star design (the Seal of Solomon) and were issued in the name of King Edward VII; their denomination was written in English and Arabic. An aluminium $\frac{1}{10}$ penny with the same design was also issued, but tropical conditions caused this metal to corrode. In 1908 a cupro-nickel coin replaced it. In 1911 a $\frac{1}{2}$ penny was added to the issue, in the name of George V, and struck in Birmingham. This coinage proved to be a success (except in the eastern part of Nigeria where manillas continued to be used until the 1940s), so in 1912 it was also issued for all British West African territories. The 1907 coins had been inscribed NIGERIA – BRITISH WEST AFRICA but NIGERIA was now omitted.

WEST AFRICAN CURRENCY BOARD

The new coins were issued by the West African Currency Board, which in 1913 added a set of silver coins to the issue; 3 and 6 pence and

1 and 2 shilling coins were made, all decorated with a crowned royal bust. A palm tree appeared on the back of the 1 and 2 shilling and a wreath on the 3 and 6 pence. British coins were gradually withdrawn as the new coins replaced them. In 1920 a rise in the international price of silver caused the board to use brass coins in place of the silver ones.

In 1938 the thickness of the 6 pence piece had to be increased to allow these coins to have a grooved edge to prevent forgery. A similar edge was applied to the 1 and 2 shilling without any change. At the same time the 3 pence became a larger cupro-nickel coin, also with a grooved edge. All were issued in the name of George VI and continued until the end of his reign, but only the $\frac{1}{10}$, 1 and 3 penny were issued by Elizabeth II before Nigeria achieved independence in 1960 as the Federation of Nigeria, with the queen as head of state. From 1952 the denominations formerly made of cupro-nickel were struck in bronze.

INDEPENDENCE

In preparation for independence a new set of coins in the name of the federation was minted in 1959. The $\frac{1}{2}$ and 1 penny coins retained the British West Africa coinage design, but the 3 and 6 pence and the 1 and 2 shilling pieces had new designs, featuring local plants on the back. The new 3 pence was a twelve-sided coin. In 1963 Nigeria broke its ties with the British Crown and became a republic, but the federation coins continued to be used. The last issue, still dated 1959, was of 6 pence pieces made at Birmingham in 1970. Coins in the name of the republic did not appear until 1973, when a new set of decimal coins was introduced. The coins were denominated in kobo – 100 kobo = 1 naire (equal to 10 shillings); $\frac{1}{2}$, 1, 5, 10 and 25 kobo coins were issued, all decorated on the front with the national arms. The designs on the back referred to Nigeria's national resources – oil, palm oil, groundnuts and cocoa.

BIAFRA

Commemorative coins have not been issued by the federal republic, but an issue was made in 1969 by the breakaway Republic of Biafra, which left the federation in 1967 and remained independent until it surrendered in 1970 after a bitter civil war. A set of commemoratives was issued to celebrate the second anniversary of independence. A series of aluminium coins, 3 pence, 1 and $2\frac{1}{2}$ shilling pieces, were also issued in the same year. They are decorated with a manilla, which was used in the Biafra region until the late 1940s.

3 1936

4 1959

5 1973

3 BRASS 6 PENCE *of British West Africa.*
4 BRASS 3 PENCE *of the Federation of Nigeria.*

5 BRONZE KOBO *of the Federal Republic.*

GHANA

FIRST COINS:	1796
FIRST DECIMAL COINS:	1965
MAIN MINT:	Royal Mint
CURRENCY:	cedi

GOLD brought European traders to the territory now known as Ghana. The area was such a rich source of the metal that it was known to British traders from the sixteenth century as the Gold Coast.

GHANA
1 Silver Ackey *of Gold Coast.*
2 Silver Ackey *of Gold Coast.*
3 Cupro-Nickel 50 Pesewas *of the Republic.*
4 Cupro-Nickel 2½ Pesewas *of the Republic.*

3 1965

1 1796

2 1818

4 1967

During the eighteenth century British and Dutch trading settlements were established along the coast. Spanish, Latin American and Dutch silver dollars entered the area, but most of the trade was conducted in accordance with local custom, by weighed amounts of gold dust reckoned in trade ounces.

British trade was conducted by the members of the Royal African Company, refounded as the Company of Merchants Trading to Africa by act of parliament in 1750. In 1796 the company had a silver coinage made for use in the Gold Coast in Birmingham. The coins were denominated by weight as $\frac{1}{16}$, $\frac{1}{8}$, $\frac{1}{4}$ and $\frac{1}{2}$ ounce pieces. Each ounce of silver coin was to be equal in value to $\frac{1}{16}$ ounce of gold dust. The $\frac{1}{2}$ ounce coin was known as a trade ackee and the $\frac{1}{16}$ as a trade taku. All denominations had the royal initials of George III in a wreath and the date 1796 on the front, and the company arms and the inscription FREE TRADE TO AFRICA, BY ACT OF PARLIAMENT, 1750 on the back. A second issue was made in 1801, but using the same designs and date.

In 1818 a new issue of silver coins, only $\frac{1}{2}$ and 1 ackee pieces, was struck, with the royal portrait replacing the monogram, and the denomination and date appearing below the king's head. Apparently the coins were used to reward native children for attendance at the company's school.

THE COLONIAL PERIOD

No further coins were issued, but British coins were regularly sent to the Gold Coast to circulate alongside the gold dust and cowries. By the end of the nineteenth century British control over the inland area had also been achieved and in 1901 the Gold Coast became a British colony. When a coinage for British West Africa began to be issued in 1912 (*see* Nigeria), it was also issued in the Gold Coast. The coins of the British West African Currency Board continued to be used until the colony became independent as Ghana in 1957.

INDEPENDENCE

New $\frac{1}{2}$, 1, 3 and 6 pence and 1 and 2 shilling coins were issued in the name of Ghana in 1958. They all had the portrait of Kwame Nkrumah on the front, with a Latin inscription, describing him as the founder of the state of Ghana, and a five-pointed star on the back. A commemorative silver 10 shilling coin with the same design was also issued. In 1960 Ghana became an independent republic and a gold 2 pound coin naming Nkrumah as the first president was also struck.

A decimal coinage consisting of 5, 10, 25 and 50 pesewa coins was issued in 1965, with the same design as the 1958 coinage, but after the overthrow of Nkrumah in 1966, a new coinage dated 1967 was issued to replace it. The new $\frac{1}{2}$, 1, 2$\frac{1}{2}$, 5, 10, 20 and 50 pesewa coins were decorated with a pair of drums or a cocoa plant. The two smallest coins retained the star design, but the others all had the national arms on the back. In 1979 a seven-sided 1 cedi coin (= 100 pesewas) was added to the series; with a cowrie shell depicted on its front. Since 1984 inflation has led to the issue of smaller coins denominated as 50 pesewas and 1 and 5 cedi pieces.

SIERRA LEONE

FIRST COINS:	1792
FIRST DECIMAL COINS:	1793
MAIN MINT:	Royal Mint
CURRENCY:	leone

Britain's first colonial coinage in Africa was struck in 1792 for Sierra Leone. Although this coast had been frequented by Portuguese and other European traders since the fifteenth century, it was not settled until Britain established the colony of Freetown for freed slaves in 1787. In 1791 the Sierra Leone Company was established to conduct trade from Freetown, and in 1792 the company had silver and copper coins struck in Birmingham. It was decided to base the coins on the Spanish dollar and so the silver coins were denominated as 1 dollar pieces and the coppers as 1 penny pieces. Both denominations were decorated on the front with a lion and on the back with clasped hands, representing British–African cooperation. The coins were dated 1791, the year of the foundation of the company. A second issue was made the following year, but the penny was replaced by a slightly smaller 1 cent piece, and silver 10, 20 and 50 cent coins were also made. Of the whole series only the 10 cent coins proved to be a success. Further issues were made until 1805 and these coins continued to circulate until 1809.

An attempt was made in 1813 to reuse the Sierra Leone Company copper cent; a large quantity was struck, but the issue failed. An issue of anti-slavery tokens struck in the following year was more successful and they circulated from their maker's trading station in Sierra Leone. They were inscribed in both English and Arabic with a declaration of the British abolition of slavery in 1807.

In 1823 the British government considered making copper $\frac{1}{50}$ and $\frac{1}{100}$ dollar pieces for use in Sierra Leone and the other colonies where silver dollars circulated. Copper coins inscribed COLONIAL and depicting George IV were prepared at the Royal Mint, but never issued. Instead British copper coins were sent to the colony in quantity, but it was also necessary to continue the import of Spanish silver dollars to provide an adequate coinage. The Spanish coins were cut into quarters for convenience in use. However, it soon became common for coins to be cut into fifths and dishonestly used as quarters, so in 1832 the colonial authorities stamped all full-weight quarters in use with a crowned WR stamp (for William IV Rex). This precaution however proved inadequate and in 1834 the circulation of dollars was no longer officially approved. British silver 1½, 2 and 3 pence coins were imported to take their place.

British and foreign coins continued to circulate in Sierra Leone until a coinage was supplied for the colony by the British West African Currency Board from 1912 (see Nigeria). British West Africa coins were used as currency in Sierra Leone until after it became independent in 1961.

INDEPENDENCE

Coins in the name of Sierra Leone, depicting local animals and plants, were issued from 1964 denominated on a decimal basis as ½, 1, 5, 10 and 20 cents. A collectors' version of the 1 leone coin (= 100 cents) was also issued in the same year, but not for circulation. The lion on the 20 cent piece was represented as a heraldic animal between two palm trees. In 1971 Sierra Leone became a republic and in the following year a 50 cent coin in the name of the republic and portraying President Siaka Stevens was issued for circulation.

SIERRA LEONE
1 SILVER DOLLAR *of the Sierra Leone Company.*
2 SPANISH DOLLAR *made in 1797 and countermarked in 1832 for circulation in the colony.*
3 SILVER 2 SHILLINGS *of British West Africa.*
4 CUPRO-NICKEL 20 CENTS *of independent Sierra Leone.*

GAMBIA

FIRST COINS:	1912
FIRST DECIMAL COINS:	1971
MAIN MINT:	Royal Mint
CURRENCY:	dalasi

THE Gambia, the first British settlement in Africa, was established in 1588 to exploit the local gold trade with the interior. British, Spanish and Portuguese coins were used in the settlement, but a standardized currency was not authorized until 1821 when the Gambia came under the control of the colonial authorities of Sierra Leone, and British coins became the accepted currency. However, the supply of British coins was not adequate and a variety of other coins was

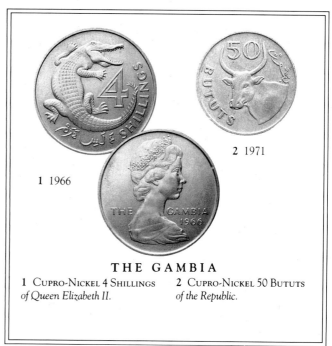

THE GAMBIA
1 CUPRO-NICKEL 4 SHILLINGS *of Queen Elizabeth II.*
2 CUPRO-NICKEL 50 BUTUTS *of the Republic.*

imported. US, Spanish and French gold coins, Spanish and Mexican silver dollars and Portuguese copper coins all circulated. Regular supplies of small British silver coins were sent to Sierra Leone and the Gambia, but foreign coins continued to play a role in the area into the present century.

In 1912 the issue of coins by the British West African Currency Board (see Nigeria) provided the Gambia with a new coinage, which it continued to use until it became an independent state, with the British queen as head of state, in 1965.

INDEPENDENCE

Coins in the name of The Gambia, with a portrait of Queen Elizabeth II were issued from 1966: 1, 3 and 6 penny and 1, 2 and 4 shilling coins, decorated on the back with a ship, guinea fowl, groundnuts, palm tree, bull and crocodile respectively. In 1970 a collectors' issue of an

8 shilling coin with a hippopotamus on the back was also produced. The 4 and 8 shilling coins had their denominations written in both English and Arabic.

In 1970 the Gambia became a republic and in the following year issued a new series of coins with the portrait of its president. The new coins were denominated in English and Arabic as 1, 5, 10, 25 and 50 bututs and 1 dalasi (= 100 bututs), and reused the designs from the 1966 coinage.

LIBERIA

FIRST COINS:	1833
FIRST DECIMAL COINS:	1833
MAIN MINT:	Royal Mint
CURRENCY:	dollar

Like its neighbour Sierra Leone, the state of Liberia was established as a settlement for freed black slaves. Its earliest coins were American dollars and cents carried to the area by the first Liberians, former slaves brought from the United States in 1822 by the American Colonization Society to settle on land purchased by the society from local chiefs.

The first coins produced for Liberia were private tokens made in 1833 in the United States by the American Colonization Society. They were copper cents, the same size as United States cents, but issued in the name of the society and Liberia.

Liberia did not have an official coinage of its own until 1896, when copper 1 and 2 cent and silver 10, 25 and 50 cent pieces were made for circulation in the territory by the Birmingham mint in England. A second, identical set was issued in 1906. All denominations had a female head on the front representing the Republic of Liberia, and either the badge of Liberia or a wreath on the back.

Before the 1896 issue several sets of suggested 1 and 2 cent copper coins were made for Liberia, but none was put into regular use. The first set was made in 1849 at a private mint in London to mark the establishment of the Republic of Liberia.

The next issue of coins for Liberia was not until 1937, when brass $\frac{1}{2}$, 1 and 2 cent coins were made. These were intended to circulate alongside British West African shillings and pence which had been in use in Liberia since about 1910. In 1941 a second issue of the new coins was made, but now in cupro-nickel. Both issues had an elephant on the front instead of the female head. In 1943 the British coins were banned and for large payments the official currency became the US dollar.

COINS SINCE 1960

In 1960 a new coinage was introduced, consisting of bronze 1 cent, cupro-nickel 5 cent and silver 10, 25, 50 cent and 1 dollar coins. The elephant design was retained on the 1 and 5 cent pieces, but a new female head with distinctive African features was used for the silver coins. The 1 and 5 cent coins had a new inscription: the motto of Liberia, recalling the former slavery of its founders, THE LOVE OF LIBERTY BROUGHT US HERE. These coins were made in London by the Royal Mint. The London mint continues to make Liberia's coins, but the current issues of 25 and 50 cent and 1 dollar coins are still dated 1968. In 1982 a seven-sided 5 dollar coin was also issued.

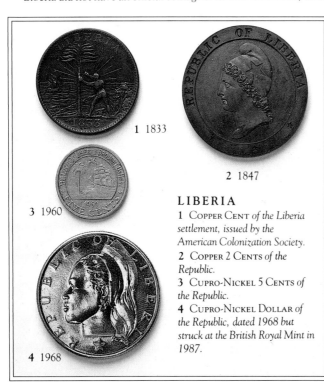

LIBERIA
1 COPPER CENT of the Liberia settlement, issued by the American Colonization Society.
2 COPPER 2 CENTS of the Republic.
3 CUPRO-NICKEL 5 CENTS of the Republic.
4 CUPRO-NICKEL DOLLAR of the Republic, dated 1968 but struck at the British Royal Mint in 1987.

1 1833
2 1847
3 1960
4 1968

CAPE VERDE

FIRST COINS:	1930
FIRST DECIMAL COINS:	1930
MAIN MINT:	Royal Mint
CURRENCY:	escudo

Cape Verde, Africa's smallest state, first became familiar with coins following contacts during the fifteenth century with Portuguese explorers and traders. Under Portuguese rule the islands became a staging post in the slave trade from West Africa, and during the following centuries they fell into British and Dutch hands. The coins used on the islands were imported Portuguese, Portuguese-African, Spanish, South American and British pieces until 1930 when the Portuguese republic had 5, 10, 20 and 50 centavo and 1 escudo coins struck in the name of CABO VERDE. All the coins were decorated with the symbol of the republic, a female head wearing the cap of liberty, copied from contemporary Portuguese issues.

In 1949, 1953 and 1967–8 further issues, all featuring the arms on globe design which symbolized Portugal's overseas possessions, were struck by the Lisbon mint for Cape Verde. The 5, 10 and 20 centavo pieces were not included in these issues and, during the last two issues, $2\frac{1}{2}$, 5 and 10 escudo coins were added to the series.

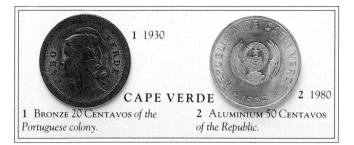

CAPE VERDE

1 Bronze 20 Centavos *of the Portuguese colony.*
2 Aluminium 50 Centavos *of the Republic.*

INDEPENDENCE

The denomination system of the Portuguese republic was retained when Cape Verde became an independent republic in 1975. The first issue of coins in the name of the REPUBLICA DE CABO VERDE was of commemorative coins to celebrate the first anniversary of independence. Coins for circulation were struck at the British Royal Mint in 1977. The new 20 and 50 centavo coins were decorated with the arms of the republic and a small fish motif. FAO (United Nations Food and Agriculture Organization) 1 and 2½ escudo coins were also made in the same year.

ST HELENA

FIRST COINS:	1716
FIRST DECIMAL COINS:	1973
MAIN MINT:	Royal Mint
CURRENCY:	pound

COINAGE first came to this island in the centre of the Atlantic Ocean in 1659, when it was settled as a permanent port of call by the British East India Company. The official coinage of the settlement was sterling, but the only coins to circulate in quantity were Spanish 8 reales imported by the company. In 1684 small change for local use was issued in the form of Japanese copper bars, stamped with their values in pence.

The settlement was continually running short of ready money and in 1713 even considered importing Chinese brass coins for use as farthings. The East India Company was not willing to do so; copper farthings and halfpennies and silver 3 pences were struck for St Helena at its mint in Madras, India, instead. The order for the coins was placed in 1714 and they arrived on the island in 1716. Dated 1714, they all have a rampant lion, the company crest, on the front and the company's trade mark, its initials in a heart-shaped frame, on the back. Alongside this new small change, imported coins – Indian gold pagodas and silver rupees, Venetian gold ducats and Spanish and Dutch silver dollars – continued to provide the bulk of the money that was in circulation.

The arrival of the exiled French emperor Napoleon, his retinue and guards on St Helena in 1815 brought even more foreign coins into use on the island. Although gold and silver coins were abundant, the shortage of copper coins for small change prompted the East India

Company to make a second issue of coins. Copper halfpennies, decorated with the company arms and dated 1821, were struck in Birmingham for St Helena. By the time the coins reached the island Napoleon was dead and his fellow exiles and their guards had left. There was no longer such a demand for coinage and most of the halfpennies were sent back to England.

STERLING COINS

Although a silver coinage, with the same designs as the 1821 halfpennies, was contemplated by the company in 1835, no more coins were made for St Helena until 1984, when a set of coins was struck in Britain for a joint issue with Ascension. Since 1834 St Helena had been under direct British rule and the new administration gradually replaced all earlier currency with British coins. The new coins of 1984 were

ST HELENA – ASCENSION

1 Copper ½ Penny *of the British East India Company.*
2 Copper ½ Penny *of the British East India Company.*
3 Cupro-Nickel 25 Pence.
4 Cupro-Nickel Crown *of Ascension.*

denominated in the same way as contemporary British coins: 1, 2, 5, 10 and 50 pence and 1 pound. Each denomination portrays Queen Elizabeth II on the front and local wildlife on the back. A few decimal 25 and 50 pence commemoratives have also been struck for St Helena alone since 1973.

ASCENSION

This tiny rocky outcrop 700 miles north-west of St Helena has been a dependency of St Helena since 1922. Although occupied by the British Navy since 1815, no coins were issued for its population of about 1000 until the 1984 joint issue with St Helena. Collectors' commemorative coins in the name of Ascension have also been struck since 1978.

TRISTAN DA CUNHA

Since 1938 this volcanic island in the South Atlantic has been St Helena's second dependency. British settlers have lived on the island since 1810, but apart from commemoratives, struck since 1977, no coins have been issued for its population of less than 300. The sterling currency of St Helena and Ascension is its only official money.

THE AMERICAS

SMALL 'MORGAN' DOLLAR *of the United States of America, 1879.*

OINAGE came to the Americas from Europe. Following the discovery of the New World by Christopher Columbus in 1492, the first coins to arrive were made in Spain, and the Spanish also established the first mints in the Americas at Mexico City in 1536, Santo Domingo in 1542 and Lima in 1565. Colonists also arrived from other European countries, notably the French and British in North America and the Caribbean and the Portuguese in Brazil. Many different imperial and colonial coinages were therefore used and in some regions, especially in the Caribbean, they circulated together.

Since the eighteenth century most of the countries in the Americas have gained their independence. The imperial and colonial coinages have largely been replaced by independent issues, but some European denominations have survived or been adapted. The old Spanish silver piece of eight reales, for example, developed into the US dollar and the peso of the republics of former Spanish America.

THE PRESENT-DAY DENOMINATIONS OF THE AMERICAS

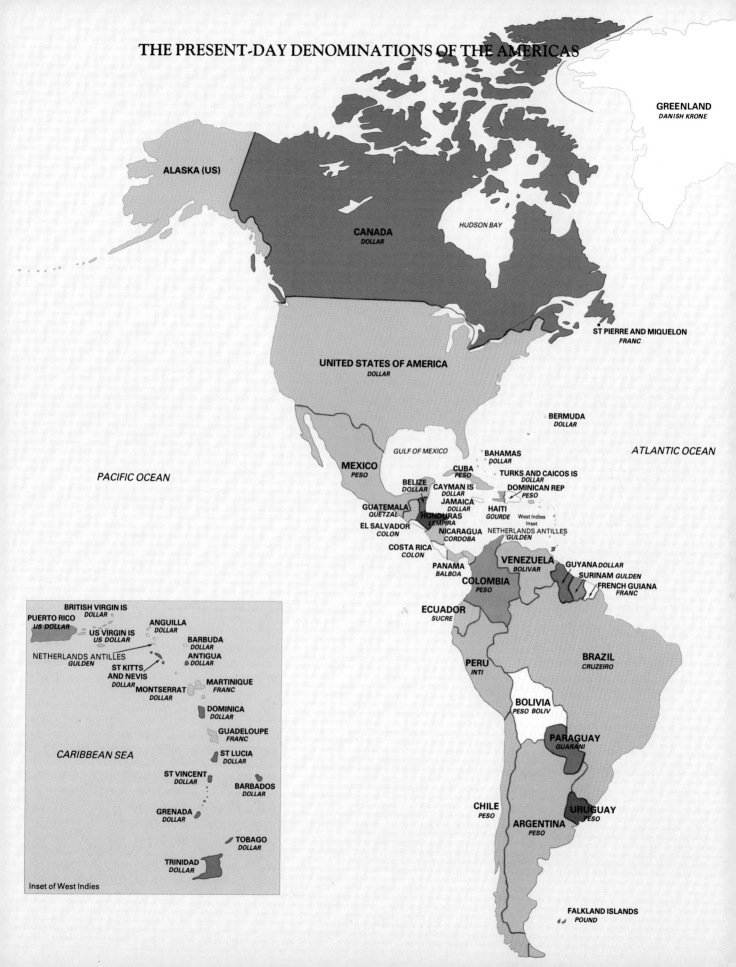

GREENLAND
DANISH KRONE

ALASKA (US)

CANADA
DOLLAR

HUDSON BAY

ST PIERRE AND MIQUELON
FRANC

UNITED STATES OF AMERICA
DOLLAR

PACIFIC OCEAN

GULF OF MEXICO

BERMUDA
DOLLAR

ATLANTIC OCEAN

BAHAMAS
DOLLAR

MEXICO
PESO

CUBA
PESO

TURKS AND CAICOS IS
DOLLAR

BELIZE
DOLLAR

CAYMAN IS
DOLLAR

DOMINICAN REP
PESO

JAMAICA
DOLLAR

GUATEMALA
QUETZAL

HONDURAS
LEMPIRA

HAITI
GOURDE

West Indies
Inset

EL SALVADOR
COLON

NICARAGUA
CORDOBA

NETHERLANDS ANTILLES
GULDEN

COSTA RICA
COLON

VENEZUELA
BOLIVAR

GUYANA *DOLLAR*

PANAMA
BALBOA

COLOMBIA
PESO

SURINAM *GULDEN*

FRENCH GUIANA
FRANC

ECUADOR
SUCRE

BRAZIL
CRUZEIRO

PERU
INTI

BOLIVIA
PESO BOLIV

PARAGUAY
GUARANI

CHILE
PESO

URUGUAY
PESO

ARGENTINA
PESO

FALKLAND ISLANDS
POUND

BRITISH VIRGIN IS
DOLLAR

PUERTO RICO
US DOLLAR

ANGUILLA
DOLLAR

US VIRGIN IS
US DOLLAR

BARBUDA
DOLLAR

NETHERLANDS ANTILLES
GULDEN

ANTIGUA
DOLLAR

ST KITTS
AND NEVIS
DOLLAR

MARTINIQUE
FRANC

MONTSERRAT
DOLLAR

DOMINICA
DOLLAR

GUADELOUPE
FRANC

CARIBBEAN SEA

ST LUCIA
DOLLAR

ST VINCENT
DOLLAR

BARBADOS
DOLLAR

GRENADA
DOLLAR

TOBAGO
DOLLAR

TRINIDAD
DOLLAR

Inset of West Indies

UNITED STATES OF AMERICA

FIRST COINS:	1652
FIRST DECIMAL COINS:	1787
MAIN MINTS:	Philadelphia, San Francisco, Denver
CURRENCY:	dollar

A Viking-age Norwegian coin discovered during archaeological excavations at an Indian site in Maine in 1957 confirms that the Norsemen were the first Europeans to discover America. The Americas were rediscovered by Christopher Columbus in 1492, and in the following century the eastern seaboard of what is now the USA was explored. The first permanent settlement was established by the English at Virginia in 1607, and by 1733 there were 13 separate English colonies in the eastern coastal region. Also colonizing the east coast, but far outnumbered and eclipsed by the English, were Dutch and Swedish settlers. French colonists, who had reached the Great Lakes via the St Lawrence River, ventured into the centre of the continent down the Mississippi River, and the Spanish, from their base in Mexico, pushed the frontier of their colony of New Spain north into the western USA. There were also Spanish settlements in Florida.

The wars between the European powers in the eighteenth century resulted in the French losing virtually all their North American territories, leaving the British dominant east of the Mississippi. However, in 1775 the 13 colonies rebelled, and in the War of American Independence, which continued until 1783, they eventually won their freedom from British rule, becoming the United States of America.

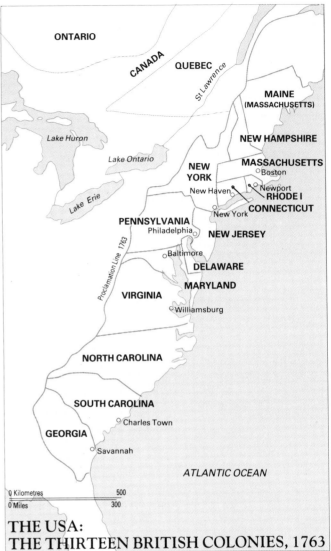

THE USA: THE THIRTEEN BRITISH COLONIES, 1763

The United States Mint at Philadelphia.

COLONIAL COINAGE

Before the arrival of European settlers the Indians of the eastern USA used wampum, made by stringing small sea-shells together into belts, as a form of ritual money. Wampum was accepted as legal tender in the British American colonies until 1670, and it continued to be used by the Indians until the late nineteenth century. Beaver and deer skins and, in Virginia, tobacco, were also used by the early colonists as money. However, coinage was needed to acquire foreign goods, and in the absence of an official coinage for the colonies the settlers made use of any foreign coins that came their way. These included French, Dutch and German, as well as English, coins, but the commonest of all were the Spanish coins, especially the silver 8 real, ancestor of the US dollar, which continued to circulate legally in the USA until 1857.

The first colonial coins issued in the USA were produced in Boston under the authority of the Massachusetts Bay Colony in 1652. They were crude silver pieces marked with the letters NE for New England and marks of value denoting threepence, sixpence and shilling. Later issues were inscribed MASATHUSETS IN NEW ENGLAND, and a tree was

UNITED STATES OF AMERICA
1 SILVER 'PINE TREE' SHILLING of the Massachusetts colony.
2 BRONZE 'ROSA AMERICANA' PENNY.
3 SILVER 'CONTINENTAL CONGRESS' PATTERN for a dollar coin.
4 COPPER HALFPENNY TOKEN of Vermont.

added to the design, at first a willow, then an oak, and finally a pine. Almost all the coins were dated 1652, though they were issued over a period of 30 years.

Other colonial issues also appeared. Lord Baltimore, 'Lord Proprietor of Maryland', had a series of coins struck in England for Maryland in 1658. The issue consisted of a very rare copper penny, plus a silver groat (4 pence), sixpence and shilling, all bearing Lord Baltimore's portrait on the front. In New Jersey, an issue of Irish halfpennies brought over by an immigrant, Mark Newby, was authorized to circulate as legal tender in 1682. These halfpennies have on their back a design depicting St Patrick so they are often known as 'St Patrick coins'. The Virginia colony had to wait until 1773 before it was granted its first issue of colonial coinage, consisting of halfpennies minted in England.

Only very rarely did the British government supply the American colonies with the official coinage they needed, and on one occasion the colonists rejected the coins provided. These were the issues of halfpennies, pennies and twopences produced by William Wood of London in the period 1722–3 and bearing the bust and titles of George I on the front, and a crowned rose and an inscription including the phrase ROSA AMERICANA on the back. The coins were unpopular because they were not made of pure copper; the colonists preferred unofficial copper tokens. The use of paper money, in denominations ranging from one penny to 100 pounds, was widespread. Paper money was also used by the French traders in the Mississippi region. A few of the French coins issued for the French American colonies between 1670 and 1767 must have reached the USA.

INDEPENDENCE
During the War of American Independence the 13 colonies were organized in a 'Continental Congress', and to finance the revolt against British rule they issued a 'continental currency' of paper money valued in Spanish dollars. Continental dollar coins in silver were also

proposed and proofs were struck in 1776, with a design on the front featuring a circular chain of 13 links symbolizing the unity of the colonies in the American Congress, but the coinage was never produced for circulation. Trial pieces for independent coinages for the states of Massachusetts and New Hampshire were also prepared in 1776, but again neither were issued for circulation. Various copper tokens, mostly struck in England, continued to circulate as coins.

After the war the states could not agree on a national coinage, and some states began producing their own issues. From 1785 to 1788, Vermont, Connecticut, New Jersey and Massachusetts authorized issues of copper coinage, produced by private contractors. The Connecticut and Vermont coins had designs similar to British halfpennies. Contemporary forgeries of the British halfpenny were common in this period in both Britain and the USA, and large quantities of these forgeries were produced in New York from 1784 to 1788.

THE FIRST FEDERAL COINAGE
The first issue of federally authorized coinage was struck under private contract in 1787. Only copper cents were issued, with designs based on those of the earlier continental dollar. They are referred to as 'fugio cents' because of the Latin word on the back, which, together with the design of a sundial on the front, represented the motto 'Time flies'. These coins are also commonly known as 'Franklin cents', because Benjamin Franklin is supposed to have been responsible for the designs and inscriptions. Meanwhile, various other coppers, including the individual state pieces and numerous private tokens, continued to circulate. One issue that first appeared in 1791 was produced in England and attempted to win favour by portraying the bust of George Washington on the front. However, Washington was one of those opposed to the introduction of a regal-style coinage.

In 1792 the Congress finally passed a mint act, authorizing an official coinage for the United States. A decimal system was adopted, with the dollar as the standard unit, divided into 100 cents. A mint was

Benjamin Franklin, portrayed on half-dollar coins.

George Washington, portrayed on quarter-dollar coins.

Gold mining in California in the 1860s.

established at Philadelphia, and regular production of the new coinage was under way by the mid-1790s.

DENOMINATIONS ISSUED UNDER THE 1792 MINT ACT

Denomination	Metal	Value
eagle	gold	$10.00
½-eagle	gold	5.00
¼-eagle	gold	2.50
dollar	silver	1.00
½-dollar	silver	0.50
¼-dollar	silver	0.25
disme (dime)	silver	0.10
½-disme	silver	0.05
cent	copper	0.01
½-cent	copper	0.005

The 1792 Mint Act decreed that the design on US coins should be 'emblematic of liberty', and for a long time only three designs were authorized: the head or figure of Liberty; the eagle, as on the State Seal; and the value within a wreath. There were, however, occasional changes in the style of design, particularly in the experimental early years. Thus, for instance, the silver ½-dollar began with a 'flowing hair' Liberty (1794–5) on the front, followed by a 'draped bust' Liberty (1796–1807), and the eagle in wreath on the back (1794–7) was replaced by an heraldic eagle in 1801. In 1807 Liberty was given a cap, but in 1839 the bust was replaced by a seated figure of Liberty holding her cap on a rod, and this design remained on the ½-dollar until 1891. Similar changes in design affected all the denominations, though not always at the same time.

THE NINETEENTH CENTURY

For the first 60 years, the output of US coinage was rarely sufficient to meet public needs, and some denominations were not issued for long periods, notably the silver dollar and gold eagle, which were not minted between 1804 and 1838. Consequently, foreign coinage continued to circulate widely. Spanish American silver coins were particularly common, and were accepted as legal tender until 1857.

Attempts were made to reform the coinage through legislation.

Laws of 1834 and 1837 changed metal standards and authorized new designs. Branch mints were also set up in the gold-mining states of Georgia and North Carolina. Then the discovery of gold in California in 1848 caused the famous Gold Rush of the American West, resulting in the production of numerous private and state gold issues (*see* table), mostly tolerated by the federal government, and the establishment of the important branch mint of San Francisco in 1854, and later that of Carson City (1870–9). In 1849 the gold dollar and double-eagle coins were introduced.

USA
5 BRONZE LARGE CENT.
6 SILVER DOLLAR.
7 GOLD EAGLE.

5 1793

6 1794

7 1795

PRIVATE OR STATE ISSUES OF GOLD
COINS OR INGOTS

Date	Issuer	Place of origin
1830–52	The Bechtlers	Rutherfordton, North Carolina
1830	Templeton Reid	Gainesville, Georgia
1849	Cincinnati Mining and Trading Co.	Cincinnati, Ohio
1849	Massachusetts and California Co.	San Francisco, California
1849	Miners' Bank	San Francisco, California
1849–53	Moffat and Co.	San Francisco, California
1849–50	Mormon	Salt Lake City, Utah
1849	Norris, Grieg and Norris	San Francisco, California
1849	Oregon Exchange Co.	Oregon City, Oregon
1849	J. S. Ormsby	Sacramento, California
1849	Pacific Co.	San Francisco, California
1849	Templeton Reid	San Francisco, California
1850	Baldwin and Co.	San Francisco, California
1850	Dubosq and Co.	San Francisco, California
1850	F. D. Kohler, California State Assayer	San Francisco, California
1851	Dunbar and Co.	San Francisco, California
1852–2	Augustus Humbert, US Assay Office	San Francisco, California
1851	Schultz and Co.	San Francisco, California
1852–82	California State	San Francisco, California
1852–3	US Assay Office of Gold	San Francisco, California
1852–3	Wass, Molitor and Co.	San Francisco, California
1854–5	Kellogg and Co.	San Francisco, California
1860–1	Clark, Gruber and Co.	Denver, Colorado
1861	J. J. Conway and Co.	Georgia Gulch, Colorado
1861	John Parsons and Co.	Tarryall Mines, Colorado

8 1852–3

USA

8 GOLD 50 DOLLARS *of the US Assay Office of Gold, San Francisco, one of tens of similar issues of the mid-nineteenth century.*

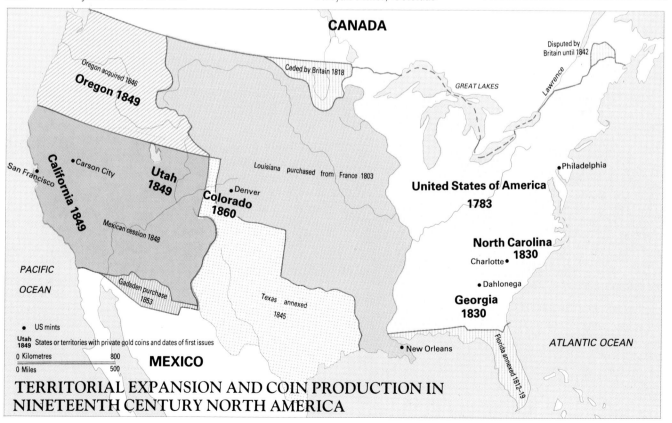

TERRITORIAL EXPANSION AND COIN PRODUCTION IN NINETEENTH CENTURY NORTH AMERICA

USA

9 Bronze Small Cent.
10 Silver Half Dollar.
11 Silver 'Barber' Half Dollar.
12 Cupro-Nickel 5 Cents ('Nickel').
13 Silver Commemorative Half Dollar *celebrating the Missouri centennial.*
14 Gold 20 Dollars *with designs by the artist Augustus St. Gaudens.*
15 Cupro-Nickel Clad Quarter-Dollar.
16 Cupro-Nickel Clad Dime (10 Cents), *portraying Franklin D. Roosevelt.*

9 1857

10 1861

11 1892

12 1915

13 1921

15 1979

14 1925

16 1980

The abundance of gold caused its value to fall in relation to that of silver and put further strain on the silver coinage. In 1853, a law was enacted reducing the weight of silver coins (other than the dollar), so enabling the recently introduced 3 cent, and the 5, 10, 25 and 50 cent pieces, to remain in circulation. At the same time production was stepped up and there was at last an adequate supply of silver coinage.

In 1857 the original copper large cent was replaced by a new small cent, made of an alloy of copper and nickel, and the old ½-cent was retired. Millions of the new cents were issued and exchanged for worn foreign silver coins, finally ending the circulation of the latter. The first small cents were given a flying eagle design on the front, but in 1859 this was replaced by the head of an Indian, similar to the design already used on the gold dollar and 3 dollars (introduced in 1854). The Indian head design was retained for the cent until 1909.

The American Civil War (1861–5) caused a crisis in the US currency, with coinage being hoarded and paper money and unofficial tokens and imitation coins circulating in abundance. New official small-change coins emerged from the chaos: a copper 2 cents (1864–73); a cupro-nickel 3 cents (1865–89); and a cupro-nickel 5 cents (the 'nickel' still issued today, introduced in 1866).

By a revision of the coinage laws in 1873 the silver 3 cents and ½-dime were retired. Production of the silver dollar also ceased for a period (1873–8), though trade dollars of increased weight were issued (1873–85) for commerce with China. Another new denomination, the 20 cent piece, was introduced in 1875, but it survived only until 1878. Production of the silver dollar resumed in 1878, with a new head of Liberty on the front designed by George Morgan, after whom the dollar of 1878–1921 is named. Similarly, the ½-dollars of 1892–1915 are known as 'Barber ½-dollars' after Charles Barber, the designer of the new Liberty head which appeared on them.

By the end of the nineteenth century the present boundaries of the USA were established. Westward expansion had opened up the whole continent from the Atlantic to the Pacific, and Alaska and Hawaii had also been acquired. Rapid economic development in the last decades of the century established the USA as one of the world's richest and most powerful nations and gave its currrency great influence.

NEW DESIGNS

In 1890 a law was passed restricting changes in coin design to periods of not less than 25 years. However, one of the most obvious features of US coinage since the beginning of the twentieth century has been the introduction of new designs, replacing the stereotyped images of the nineteenth century. The most outstanding designs ever to have appeared on US coins were those prepared by the artist Augustus St Gaudens for the gold 10 and 20 dollars in 1907, issued as currency until 1932. The facing figure of Liberty and the flying eagle on the 20 dollar coins are particularly impressive.

Other noteworthy designs from the early twentieth century include the Indian head and buffalo on the nickel (1913–38) and the winged Liberty head on the dime (1916–45). An extensive series of commemorative silver ½-dollars, issued mostly in the 1920s and 1930s, also includes some fine designs.

An important twentieth-century innovation has been the introduction of portraits of past presidents on the front: Abraham Lincoln on the cent since 1909; George Washington on the quarter since 1932; Thomas Jefferson on the nickel since 1938; Franklin D. Roosevelt on the dime since 1946; John F. Kennedy on the ½-dollar

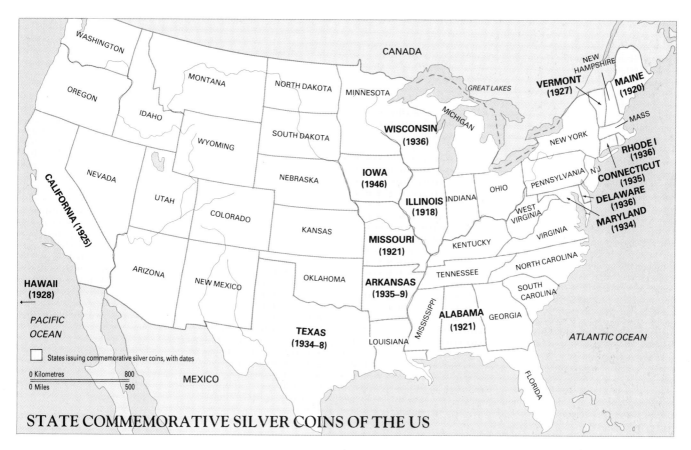

STATE COMMEMORATIVE SILVER COINS OF THE US

since 1964; and Dwight D. Eisenhower on the dollar since 1971. Also, Benjamin Franklin's portrait appeared on the front of the ½-dollar between 1948 and 1963, with a design which featured the Liberty Bell on the back.

MODERN COINAGE

The modern US coinage retains most of the regular denominations of the nineteenth century, but there have been significant changes in metals and in the function of the coinage. Paper money has replaced high-value coinage: gold currency coins have not been issued since 1932 and the Coinage Act of 1965 ended silver currency coinage. The former silver coins – the dime, quarter and ½-dollar – are now copper, clad with cupro-nickel. The dollar, which was last issued as a silver currency coin in 1935, was re-introduced in 1971 as a cupro-nickel clad, copper coin for the gaming industry and for vending machines, though issues in silver are also produced regularly for collectors. Special commemorative designs appeared on the backs of quarters, ½-dollars and dollars to mark the bicentenary of American Independence in 1976, and in recent years high-denomination commemorative coins in silver and gold have occasionally been issued, notably for the 1984 Los Angeles Olympic Games and the centenary of the building of the Statue of Liberty (1986).

HAWAII

The Hawaiian Islands were discovered in 1778 by Captain James Cook, who named them the Sandwich Islands. They were united as a single kingdom under King Kamehameha the Great (1795–1810). The

first coinage, consisting of copper *hapa haneri* (cents), was issued in 1847 and depicted on the front the ruler, King Kamehameha III (1825–54). The only other currency coinage produced for Hawaii was issued in 1883. It consisted of silver dimes, quarters, ½-dollars and dollars, on the model of contemporary US coinage. The head of King David Kalakaua (1874–91) appeared on the front and the arms of Hawaii on the back.

Hawaii became a republic in 1893, when the last monarch, Queen Liliuokalani (1891–3), was deposed. In 1898 the islands were annexed by the USA, becoming a territory in 1900, and finally a state in 1959. US coinage has been the official currency since the late nineteenth century.

USA

17 Silver Dollar of *Hawaii, portraying King Kalakaua I.*

17 1883

CANADA

FIRST COINS:	1670
FIRST DECIMAL COINS:	1858
MAIN MINT:	Royal Canadian Mint, Ottawa
CURRENCY:	dollar

THE first Europeans to discover Canada were probably Vikings, who arrived via Iceland and Greenland in the eleventh century AD, but the history of modern Canada began much later, following the discovery of Newfoundland by John Cabot, sailing on behalf of England in 1497, and the exploration of the St Lawrence River by the Frenchman Jacques Cartier in 1534 and 1535. Most of the subsequent early explorers and colonists were French or British. The French settled mainly in the St Lawrence River and Great Lakes regions, whereas the British colonized the Atlantic coastlands and Newfoundland and disputed the Hudson Bay area with the French.

Rival territorial claims in North America contributed to the wars between the European powers in the eighteenth century, and were only partially resolved when the British were granted Hudson Bay, Nova Scotia and Newfoundland by the Treaty of Utrecht (1713) and the rest of eastern and central Canada, except the islands of St Pierre and Miquelon, by the Treaty of Paris (1763).

In 1791 the territories acquired by the British from the French were divided into English-speaking Upper Canada (Ontario) and French-speaking Lower Canada (Quebec), but the provinces were reunited in 1840 as the colony of Canada. In 1858 the western colonies, formerly disputed between Spain, England and Russia, became the Crown Colony of British Columbia. Between 1867 and 1873 most of the British colonies joined a confederation to form the self-governing Dominion of Canada. The last member to join the Dominion was Newfoundland in 1949.

EARLY COINAGE

Until the nineteenth century various foreign coinages, including French, English, Dutch, Spanish (especially the silver 8 reales) and later US pieces, circulated in Canada. Even Chinese coins of the eighteenth and nineteenth centuries found their way to western Canada. A few issues of French coins – sols and deniers in silver, billon and copper – were produced for Canada between 1670 and 1760, but the first British colonial issues were not struck until 1858.

In the early nineteenth century, because of the general shortage of coins in circulation, there was widespread issuing of private bronze tokens by banks and traders. These were mostly produced by mints in Britain and they included issues in both decimal and sterling systems. The decimal system was based on the Spanish dollar (8 reales). Tokens of the period 1800 to 1858 are known from Quebec, Ontario, Nova Scotia, New Brunswick, Prince Edward Island and Newfoundland. The fur traders of the north also used tokens, sometimes denominated in beaver skins, issued by the Hudson's Bay Company, and by the North West Company (1820). Traders' tokens have been issued in Canada ever since.

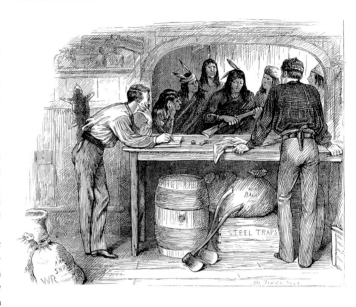

Nineteenth-century trading post in Manitoba, with Indians bartering furs for guns. The Canadian fur trade produced its own token coins.

PROVINCIAL COINAGE

Before the introduction of a general coinage for Canada in 1858, several provinces began issuing their own official coins, in some cases at first labelled tokens. Nova Scotia issued copper halfpenny and penny tokens between 1823 and 1856, and bronze ½-cents and cents from 1861 to 1864. New Brunswick issued copper halfpenny and penny pieces, marked TOKENS in 1843 and CURRENCY in 1854, and bronze ½-cents and cents, and silver 5, 10 and 20 cents from 1861 to 1864. Prince Edward Island issued bronze 1 cent coins in 1871.

CANADA
1 SILVER FRENCH 15 SOLS *issued for Canada.*
2 BRONZE PENNY TOKEN *issued by the Bank of Upper Canada (Ottawa).*
3 SILVER 20 CENTS *of Canada.*
4 SILVER 50 CENTS *of the Dominion of Canada.*
5 BRONZE LARGE CENT.
6 BRONZE NEWFOUNDLAND CENT.
7 BRONZE SMALL CENT.

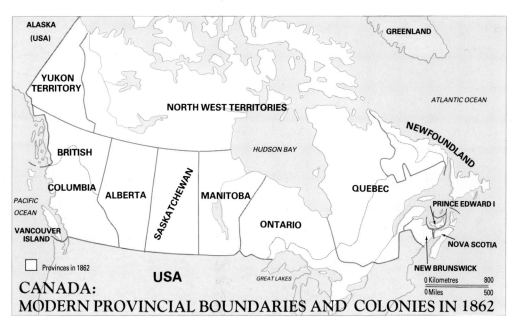

CANADA:
MODERN PROVINCIAL BOUNDARIES AND COLONIES IN 1862

CANADA
8 SILVER 'VOYAGEUR'
DOLLAR.

1935

Newfoundland issued by far the longest series of provincial coinage. Tokens were issued by Newfoundland traders between 1840 and 1860. In 1865 a regal currency was introduced, on the decimal system, which lasted until 1949. Its denominations were: bronze cents (1865–1947); silver 5 cents and 10 cents (1865–1947), 20 cents (1865–1912), 25 cents (1917, 1919) and 50 cents (1870–1919); and gold 2 dollars (1865–88). The designs on all these coins were similar, consisting of the monarch's bust on the front, and NEWFOUNDLAND, the date and the value on the back. The nineteenth-century issues of Newfoundland were minted in Britain, as were all the provincial coinages of Canada, but from 1917 most of the Newfoundland coins were minted in Ottawa.

CANADIAN COINAGE

The first coinage issued in the name of Canada, dated 1858, was in reality another provincial issue, since it was produced for the Province of Canada (Ontario and Quebec) before the formation of the Canadian Confederation. The monetary unit of the new coinage system was the dollar, though this was not yet issued as a coin, and it was given exactly the same value as the US dollar. The 1858 issue consisted of large bronze 1 cents and silver 5, 10 and 20 cents, with the bust of Queen Victoria on the front and the value, date and CANADA,

all within a wreath decoration, on the back. This was followed by further issues of bronze cents in 1859.

The first coins issued for the Dominion of Canada were dated 1870 and consisted of silver 5 and 10 cents and ¼- and ½-dollars, the ¼-dollar replacing the 20 cents because of the influence of the US ¼-dollar. Large bronze 1 cents were added in 1876. These denominations were all issued regularly, with the 1858 designs essentially unchanged, until 1920. The silver coins were struck to the sterling standard of 92.5 per cent fine, as opposed to the 90 per cent standard used in the USA, but Canada's silver coins were correspondingly smaller in size. From 1908 to 1919 a series of gold sovereigns was also issued. These were identical to contemporary British sovereigns, save for the mint mark. Between 1912 and 1914 they were accompanied by issues of gold 5- and 10-dollar pieces. Before 1908 all of Canada's coinage was struck in England, either at London or Birmingham, but from 1908 the Ottawa mint, later named the Royal Canadian Mint, was used.

REDUCTION IN FINENESS

In 1920 the Canadian cent was changed from a large to a small bronze coin, making it similar to the US cent. At the same time the designs on the cent and 5 cents were altered slightly, to look more up to date, and the fineness of the silver coinage was reduced to 80 per cent. The 5 cent piece remained a silver coin only until 1922, when nickel began to be used.

The next major changes took place in the 1930s. In 1935 Canada's first dollar coins were issued, in commemoration of George V's silver jubilee. Then, in 1937, there was a complete overhaul of the designs on the back of the coins, with the introduction of subjects appropriate to Canada: the maple leaf on the cent; the beaver on the 5 cents; a fishing schooner modelled on the famous *Bluenose* on the 10 cents; a caribou on the ¼-dollar; and the arms of Canada on the ½-dollar. The recently introduced silver dollar already had an appropriate design on the back, featuring a canoe paddled by an Indian and a colonist (giving it its name, the 'Voyageur dollar'). The bust of the reigning British

6 1917

7 1928

4 1870
5 1890

9 1937

10 1943

11 1967

12 1948

CANADA
9 Cupro-Nickel 5 Cents.
10 Tombac 5 Cents.
11 Silver Dollar *commemorating the centenary of the Canadian Confederation.*
12 Aluminium 2 Francs *of St Pierre and Miquelon.*

BERMUDA

FIRST COINS:	1616
FIRST DECIMAL COINS:	1970
MAIN MINT:	Royal Mint
CURRENCY:	dollar

monarch, head of state in Canada, remained on the front of all coins.

In the 1940s and 1950s there were further occasional changes to the coinage, principally in design, such as the v for victory on the 5 cents during the war years of 1943–5, and a design commemorating the bicentenary of the discovery of nickel (Canada is the world's leading producer) on the 5 cents of 1951. There were also changes to metals, notably the use of tombac, an alloy of copper and zinc, and then steel for the 5 cents of 1942–5, when nickel was required for military needs in the Second World War.

MODERN COINAGE
Since it was first introduced, the Canadian dollar has frequently been used to commemorate events of national importance, such as the visit of King George VI in 1939, Newfoundland joining the Canadian Confederation in 1949 and the centenary of British Columbia in 1958. In 1967 all the denominations were given special designs on the back, featuring Canadian animals, to commemorate the centenary of the Canadian Confederation. Since then issues of commemorative dollars have become much more frequent; different commemoratives are now produced each year.

There was a further reduction in the fineness of the silver coinage in 1967, but the new standard (50 per cent) was short lived, being replaced the following year by pure nickel for all denominations. Since 1968 only collectors' commemorative coins have been minted in silver. The most extensive series of these was produced for the Montreal Olympic Games in 1976. As well as dollars and 10 dollars in sterling silver, the Olympic commemorative issue included gold 100 dollar coins. A set of silver and gold commemorative coins was also produced for the 1988 Winter Olympics held at Calgary.

ST PIERRE AND MIQUELON
The archipelago of St Pierre and Miquelon, off the south coast of Newfoundland, is still a French overseas territory, the last remnant of France's once extensive North American colonies. The islands use French currrency, but on one occasion, in 1948, they were provided with their own coins, when an issue of aluminium 1 and 2 franc pieces was put into circulation.

This group of small islands in the Atlantic Ocean 580 miles east of North Carolina is named after the Spaniard, Juan de Bermudez, who first sighted them in about 1503, but they were uninhabited when a party of British colonists bound for Virginia were shipwrecked there in July 1609. The colonists were led by Sir George Somers, hence the islands' alternative name, Sommer Islands. A permanent settlement was established in 1612 by British colonists from Virginia, and the Bermudas became a British crown colony in 1684.

The earliest coins to circulate in Bermuda were struck for the islands in Britain in about 1616, the first named coinage minted for a British overseas possession. They were made of copper and given values of 2, 3, 6 and 12 pence. A pig appeared on the front, in recognition of the abundance of wild pigs on the islands, and a ship on the back. The inhabitants did not, it seems, think highly of this token coinage, which they referred to as *hogge money*, and it soon ceased to be used. In the later seventeenth century the local currency was tobacco, and Spanish silver coinage also circulated.

The second issue of coinage struck specifically for Bermuda was produced in Birmingham in 1793. The coins were copper pennies,

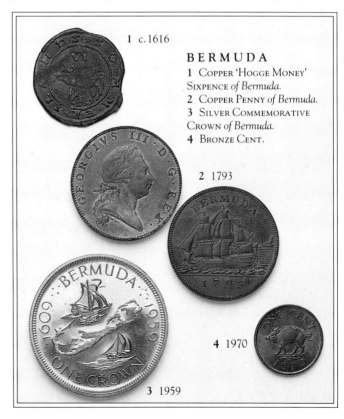

1 c.1616

BERMUDA
1 Copper 'Hogge Money' Sixpence *of Bermuda.*
2 Copper Penny *of Bermuda.*
3 Silver Commemorative Crown *of Bermuda.*
4 Bronze Cent.

2 1793

3 1959

4 1970

with the head of George III on the front and a sailing ship on the back. Again, they did not remain in circulation for long, and in 1842 all locally-circulating coinage was demonetized and the currency of the United Kingdom became standard.

In 1970 Bermuda changed from the British currency system to a decimal system of dollar and cents, equated to that of the USA. Regular issues of Bermudan coinage in bronze (1 cent) and cupro-nickel (5, 10, 25 and 50 cents) have since been produced by the Royal Mint, together with occasional commemorative issues of dollars and multiples in silver and gold.

BAHAMAS

FIRST COINS:	1806
FIRST DECIMAL COINS:	1966
MAIN MINTS:	Royal Mint, Franklin Mint
CURRENCY:	dollar

THE explorer Christopher Columbus discovered the New World when he sighted San Salvador in the Bahamas in 1492, but the Spanish did not at first make any attempt at colonization. The first settlement was established in 1629 at New Providence by British colonists from Carolina in North America. The British were twice removed by Spanish forces (in 1641 and 1703), but the islands were finally ceded to Britain by the Treaty of Versailles in 1783. The Bahamas remained a British crown colony until 1964, when the islands became self-governing. Full independence was gained on 10 July 1973. The Bahamas is a member of the British Commonwealth.

The earliest recorded coinage of the Bahamas was gold coinage which had already been plugged, clipped or otherwise mutilated (*see* Jamaica) on other islands and which was authorized to circulate by weight in 1788. Most of the gold coins were Portuguese 'Joes' (from the inscription JOHANNES), orginally from Brazil. The first coins minted for the Bahamas were issued in 1806 and 1807. These were copper pennies, made by the Soho Mint in Birmingham, England, and were intended as small change, though they failed to gain acceptance in the islands. They were the same size and weight as contemporary English halfpennies. On the front they had the bust and titles of George III; on the back was a design of a ship and the inscription COMMERCE RESTORED BY THE EXPULSION OF THE PIRATES, copied from the ceremonial seal of the islands.

MODERN COINAGE

The Bahamas used British coinage in the nineteenth century, and also in the present century until 1966, when the first full coinage for the

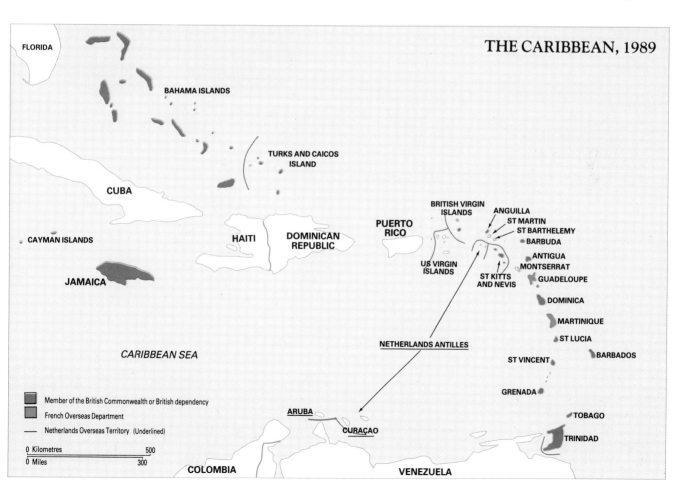

BAHAMAS
1 Copper Penny.
2 Nickel-Brass Cent.
3 Cupro-Nickel 10 Cents.
4 Cupro-Nickel Dollar.

islands was introduced. This initially consisted of nickel-brass 1 cent, cupro-nickel 5, 10 and 15 cent, nickel 25 cent, and silver 50 cent, 1, 2 and 5 dollar pieces. Gold dollar multiples were introduced in 1967. All denominations had the portrait of Queen Elizabeth II on the front and designs symbolizing the Bahamas (mostly local flora and fauna) on the back.

There have since been changes in metals, most significantly the replacement of the silver currency coins with cupro-nickel pieces. Silver and gold are now used only for proof issues and for the numerous special commemorative pieces produced for collectors.

TURKS AND CAICOS ISLANDS

FIRST COINS:	1969
FIRST DECIMAL COINS:	1969
MAIN MINT:	Royal Mint
CURRENCY:	dollar

LOCATED at the eastern end of the Bahamas, the Turks and Caicos Islands were visited by the Spanish explorer Juan Ponce de Leon in 1512, but the first European colonists were British settlers, who arrived from Bermuda in 1678. The islands were joined to the Bahamas in 1799, but in 1848 became a separate colony, administered from Jamaica. From 1958 to 1962 they were a territory of the Federation of the West Indies. Since the Federation's dissolution, they have been a British crown colony.

British and Jamaican coinage and, more recently, the coinage of the Bahamas has been used on the islands. The only coins produced in the name of Turks and Caicos have been commemorative issues for collectors, denominated in British crowns and minted in Britain by the

Royal Mint. These were first issued in 1969 and range from cupro-nickel crowns to gold 100 crown pieces.

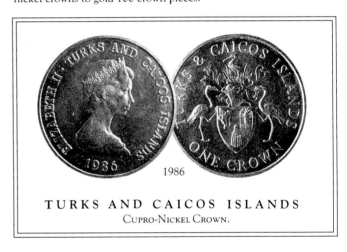

TURKS AND CAICOS ISLANDS
Cupro-Nickel Crown.

JAMAICA

FIRST COINS:	1758 (counterstamps); 1869
FIRST DECIMAL COINS:	1969
MAIN MINT:	Royal Mint
CURRENCY:	dollar

THE explorer Christopher Columbus discovered Jamaica during his second voyage to the New World in 1493–4, and the Spanish took possession in 1509. In 1655 a British expeditionary force sent by Oliver Cromwell conquered the island, and in 1670 British possession was confirmed by the Treaty of Madrid. Jamaica was the most important British colony in the Caribbean, and the base from which the British ruled their other possessions in the region. It became a crown colony in 1866, was part of the Federation of the West Indies between 1958 and 1962, and has been independent since 1962. Jamaica is a member of the British Commonwealth.

Map of the Americas dating from the early seventeenth century.

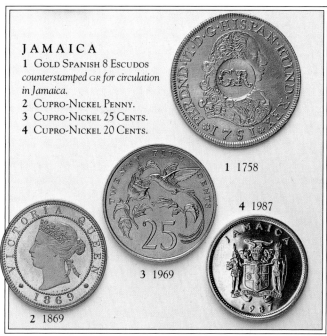

JAMAICA
1 GOLD SPANISH 8 ESCUDOS counterstamped GR for circulation in Jamaica.
2 CUPRO-NICKEL PENNY.
3 CUPRO-NICKEL 25 CENTS.
4 CUPRO-NICKEL 20 CENTS.

1 1758
4 1987
3 1969
2 1869

EARLY COINAGE IN THE BRITISH WEST INDIES

Before the nineteenth century, the dominant coinages in the Caribbean were Spanish gold and silver, particularly the silver 8 reales ('piece of eight'); Portuguese gold coins, known as 'Joes', mainly from Brazil; and French colonial base-metal coins popularly known as 'black dogs' and 'stampees' (see Guadeloupe). In the late eighteenth and early nineteenth centuries, these and other foreign coins circulating in the islands were frequently mutilated in some characteristic way to give them official local value. The four principal types of mutilation (often combined) were: cutting large coins into segments for smaller values ('bits'); removing a piece from the centre of a coin and giving this central section and the remaining outer ring separate values; inserting a small plug of metal into a coin (usually gold) to bring its weight up to the local standard; and counterstamping.

The first coins provided specifically for the British West Indies colonies were not issued until 1822. These were $\frac{1}{16}$, $\frac{1}{8}$ and $\frac{1}{4}$ dollar silver British colonial coins of the anchor type already used in Mauritius. In 1825 British sterling money was introduced throughout the colonies, and from 1834, at the request of Jamaica, the West Indies were supplied additionally with silver $1\frac{1}{2}$ pence and threepenny pieces, these being the local equivalent of the old Spanish $\frac{1}{4}$ and $\frac{1}{2}$ real.

JAMAICA'S COLONIAL COINAGE

Jamaica's first local coinage was produced in 1758 by the counterstamping of Spanish gold and silver coins. The stamp consisted of the letters GR (representing King George II). A GC counterstamp found on plugged gold coins of this period has also been attributed to Jamaica. Only silver and gold currency was acceptable to the Jamaicans, so when British colonial and later British imperial coins were introduced in the West Indies colonies the copper coins were rejected. The small-denomination silver coins first requested by Jamaica in 1834 were supplied until 1862 ($1\frac{1}{2}$ pence) and 1944 (threepence).

Colonial coinage produced specifically for Jamaica began in 1869, with an issue of cupro-nickel halfpennies and pennies. Farthings were added in 1880. These coins, which continued to be issued regularly until after independence, all bore the head of the British monarch on the front and the arms of Jamaica on the back. From 1937 they were made in nickel-brass.

MODERN COINAGE

In 1969 Jamaica changed its coinage, introducing a decimal currency system. Denominations issued since 1969 are the cent (either bronze or aluminium) and the 5, 10, 20, 25 and 50 cents and dollar (cupro-nickel). They use the arms of Jamaica on the front and local flora and fauna on the back. A large number of high-value silver and gold commemorative coins have also been issued in recent years with a wide variety of designs.

CAYMAN ISLANDS

FIRST COINS:	1972
FIRST DECIMAL COINS:	1972
MAIN MINT:	Royal Mint
CURRENCY:	dollar

THE three islands of this group, situated south of Cuba and north west of Jamaica, were discovered by Christopher Columbus in 1503. Ceded to Britain by Spain in 1670, they were governed as a

CAYMAN ISLANDS
1 Cupro-Nickel 5 Cents.
2 Cupro-Nickel 10 Cents.

1 1987

2 1987

dependency of Jamaica until 1959, when they joined the Federation of the West Indies. The islands are now a British dependency.

The Cayman Islands were colonized from Jamaica by the British, and for most of their history they have used the same currency as Jamaica. In 1972 a national coinage was introduced, on the decimal system like that of Jamaica, and consisting of bronze cents, cupro-nickel 5, 10 and 25 cents, and silver 50 cents, dollars and multiples. The coinage is produced mainly for the collectors' market and contains numerous high-value pieces in silver and also in gold, with commemorative designs. Queen Elizabeth II appears on the front of all coins; favoured subjects for the back are local flora and fauna and the British monarchy.

BRITISH VIRGIN ISLANDS

FIRST COINS:	1801 (counterstamps)
FIRST DECIMAL COINS:	1955
MAIN MINTS:	Royal Mint, Franklin Mint
CURRENCY:	dollar

THE Virgin Islands were discovered by the explorer Christopher Columbus in 1493 and following that were divided between Spain, Britain, Denmark and later the USA (see US Virgin Islands). The first British settlement was established on Tortola in 1666; the other major British islands are Anegada, Jost van Dyke and Virgin Garda. The British Virgin Islands became a crown colony in 1950. They remain a British dependency.

LOCAL COINAGE
The first local coinage of the British Virgin Islands was officially sanctioned by an Act of 1801, which established one copper and five silver denominations. For the coppers, French colonial 'black dogs' (see Guadeloupe) were counterstamped T; for the silver pieces Spanish 2 and 8 reales were cut into segments and stamped TORTOLA. From 1805 to 1824 the supply of these coins was maintained through private

sources. The cut coins of other islands were also put into circulation, the addition of the TORTOLA stamp producing double-stamped pieces. The circulation of this cut coinage continued until its recall in 1892.

From the late nineteenth century British coinage was the only official currency in the British Virgin Islands until 1955, when the first issues of the Eastern Caribbean Territories appeared (see Antigua).

MODERN COINAGE
The British Virgin Islands' own modern coinage was introduced in 1973. A decimal system was adopted, with the dollar as the standard unit, and denominations of 1 cent (bronze), 5, 10, 25 and 50 cents and 1 dollar (cupro-nickel). High-value commemorative coins have also been issued. Queen Elizabeth II appears on the front of all the coins; designs depicting local birds are usual for the back.

1 1801

2 1801

3 1973

4 1973

BRITISH VIRGIN ISLANDS
1 French Colonial Coin Of Cayenne, counterstamped T for circulation in Tortola after 1801.
2 Silver Spanish Cut 8 Reales, stamped for circulation in Tortola after 1801.
3 Bronze Cent.
4 Cupro-Nickel 50 cents.

ANGUILLA

FIRST COINS:	1955
FIRST DECIMAL COINS:	1955
MAIN MINT:	Royal Mint
CURRENCY:	dollar

DISCOVERED by the explorer Christopher Columbus in 1493, Anguilla became a British colony in 1650. For much of its colonial history, Anguilla has been linked administratively to St Kitts. From 1950 to 1965 Anguilla, with St Kitts and Nevis, was a member of the British Caribbean Territories (Eastern Group) Currency Board, which issued its own coinage (see Antigua). Anguilla unilaterally declared independence on two occasions, in 1967 and 1969. Since 1969, when direct British intervention ended the short-lived Republic of Anguilla, the island has remained under British rule, but with limited self-government since 1976.

In 1967 a nationalist coinage was produced by overstriking the inscription ANGUILLA . LIBERTY DOLLAR . JULY 11, 1967 on various dollar-sized foreign silver coins. Proof coins in silver and gold, in various denominations from the ½ dollar to the 100 dollar piece, were also produced, dated 1967, 1969 and 1970, in celebration of the 1967 declaration of independence. Anguilla has used the coinage of the East Caribbean States since 1981.

ST KITTS AND NEVIS

FIRST COINS:	1801 (counterstamps)
FIRST DECIMAL COINS:	1955
MAIN MINT:	Royal Mint
CURRENCY:	dollar

THE islands of St Kitts (St Christopher) and Nevis were discovered by the explorer Christopher Columbus in 1493. In 1623 St Kitts became the first island in the West Indies to be colonized by the British. French settlers, who first arrived in 1625, also laid claim to the island, but in 1783 it was formally ceded to Britain. Nevis was colonized by British settlers from St Kitts in 1628. It was captured by the French in 1782, but returned to British control the following year. For most of their colonial history the two islands were administered together, sometimes also with Anguilla. In 1967 the three islands were declared an associated state, but Anguilla quickly withdrew. St Kitts and Nevis became a fully independent state in 1983. It remains a member of the British Commonwealth.

LOCAL COINAGE
The first official coinages for St Kitts and Nevis were introduced at the beginning of the nineteenth century. On St Kitts Spanish silver dollars were cut into halves, quarters and eighths, and stamped s, and French colonial billon 'black dogs' (see Guadeloupe), counterstamped s, and later sk, provided small change. On Nevis the counterstamp NEVIS was applied to available silver and base issues, with a numeral added on the silver coins to indicate the value in multiples of the 'dog', which was a 1½ pence piece. These counterstamped coinages were withdrawn in 1849 in St Kitts and in 1858 in Nevis, giving way to British currency.

ST KITTS AND NEVIS

1 c.1800
1 BILLON FRENCH COLONIAL COIN of Cayenne counterstamped sk for circulation in St Kitts and Nevis.
2 WORN COIN counterstamped with the value of 6 BITS in Nevis.

2 c.1800

MODERN COINAGE
From 1950 St Kitts and Nevis, with Anguilla, were members of the British Caribbean Territories (Eastern Group) Currency Board and used its coinage, which was issued from 1955 to 1965 (see Antigua). The only modern coins issued in the name of St Kitts and Nevis have been high-value commemorative pieces aimed at collectors. The coinage of the East Caribbean States has been used since 1981.

ANTIGUA AND BARBUDA

FIRST COINS:	1955
FIRST DECIMAL COINS:	1955
MAIN MINT:	Royal Mint
CURRENCY:	dollar

THESE islands were discovered by the explorer Christopher Columbus in 1493. Antigua was first colonized by English settlers from St Kitts in 1632. It was captured by the French in 1666, but confirmed as a British possession by the Treaty of Breda the following year. The state

Drawing of a Spanish sailing ship of the 1490s, thought to be the Santa Maria, in which Christopher Columbus discovered America.

THE ISLANDS OF THE EASTERN CARIBBEAN

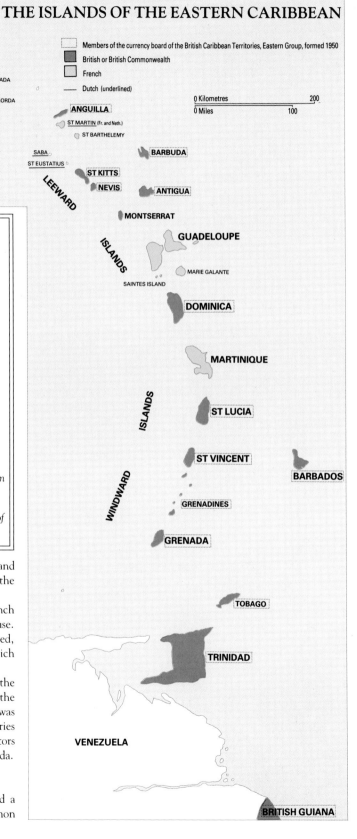

Members of the currency board of the British Caribbean Territories, Eastern Group, formed 1950

British or British Commonwealth

French

— Dutch (underlined)

0 Kilometres 200
0 Miles 100

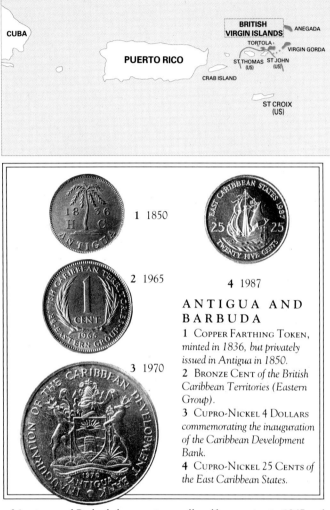

1 1850

2 1965

3 1970

4 1987

ANTIGUA AND BARBUDA

1 COPPER FARTHING TOKEN, *minted in 1836, but privately issued in Antigua in 1850.*
2 BRONZE CENT *of the British Caribbean Territories (Eastern Group).*
3 CUPRO-NICKEL 4 DOLLARS *commemorating the inauguration of the Caribbean Development Bank.*
4 CUPRO-NICKEL 25 CENTS *of the East Caribbean States.*

of Antigua and Barbuda became internally self-governing in 1967 and was granted full independence in 1981. It remains a member of the British Commonwealth.

In the early colonial period Spanish American silver and French colonial 'black dogs' (*see* Guadeloupe) were the main coinages in use. In 1822 the first British colonial anchor coins (*see* Jamaica) arrived, and these were followed by regular British imperial issues, which became the standard currency of the islands.

Since 1955 Antigua and Barbuda have used the coinage of the British Caribbean Territories (Eastern Group) and, from 1981, the East Caribbean States. The first coin to bear the name of Antigua was the 4 dollar commemorative issued by various east Caribbean countries in 1970. High-value commemorative pieces designed for collectors have more recently been issued in the name of Antigua and Barduda.

EAST CARIBBEAN COINAGES

In 1950 the British territories of the eastern Caribbean formed a currency board with the purpose of providing for themselves a common non-British currency. A decimal system was adopted, with a dollar of 100 cents. From 1955 to 1965 coins were struck at the Royal Mint in the name of the British Caribbean Territories (Eastern Group): in bronze, $\frac{1}{2}$, 1 and 2 cents; nickel-brass, 5 cents; and cupro-nickel, 10, 25 and 50 cents. The members of the board were the British Virgin Islands, Anguilla, St Kitts, Nevis, Antigua, Dominica, St Lucia, St Vincent, Grenada, Trinidad and Tobago, Barbados and British Guiana.

In 1970 a 4 dollar cupro-nickel coin, commemorating the inauguration of the Caribbean Development Bank, was issued as part of the United Nations Food and Agriculture Organization coinage programme by eight of these Caribbean states: Antigua, Barbados, Dominica, Grenada, Montserrat, St Kitts, St Lucia and St Vincent. Further commemorative issues (of 10 dollar pieces) followed in 1980 and 1981, and since 1981 the East Caribbean States have issued regular currency coins (aluminium 1, 2 and 5 cents, cupro-nickel 10 and 25 cents, and aluminium-bronze dollars, all struck at the Royal Mint) and high-value commemorative pieces.

MONTSERRAT

FIRST COINS:	c. 1800 (counterstamps)
FIRST DECIMAL COINS:	1955
MAIN MINT:	Royal Mint
CURRENCY:	dollar

Discovered by the explorer Christopher Columbus in 1493, Montserrat was first colonized by Irish settlers in 1632. The island was twice taken by the French, in 1664 and 1782, but was restored to Britain in 1783, and it remains a British crown colony today.

In the late eighteenth and early nineteenth centuries the coinage of Montserrat consisted mainly of Spanish silver and French colonial base-metal 'black dogs' (*see* Guadeloupe). Counterstamps of a cross design or the letter M were used to authorize continued circulation on the island of good-weight coins and cut pieces. From about 1811 to 1816 coins were countermarked with the letter M accompanied by a crowned numeral, representing the official value of the piece in multiples of the 'dog'. These local coins continued to circulate until the mid-nineteenth century, by which time British currency had become established as the legal tender.

Montserrat was a member of the currency board of the British Caribbean Territories (Eastern Group), formed in 1950, and has since used the coinage of the currency board and the East Caribbean States (*see* Antigua). The only coin issued in the name of Montserrat is the 4 dollar commemorative coin struck for the Caribbean Development Bank in 1970.

*c.*1800

MONTSERRAT
SILVER CUT SPANISH COIN *counter-stamped* M *for circulation in Montserrat.*

DOMINICA

FIRST COINS:	1760s (counterstamps)
FIRST DECIMAL COINS:	1955
MAIN MINT:	Royal Mint
CURRENCY:	dollar

The island of Dominica was discovered and named by the explorer Christopher Columbus in 1493. Initial colonization was by the French, who first arrived in 1632. Following British capture of the island in 1761, it changed hands between the French and British several times until 1805, after which it remained a British possession for the rest of its colonial history. Dominica became internally self-governing in 1967, and achieved full independence in 1978. It remains a member of the British Commonwealth.

THE FIRST COINS

The first coinage used in Dominica was Spanish silver, which was officially mutilated in the island as early as the 1760s. The first 'holey dollars' of Dominica were pierced with a heart-shaped hole; the next group, authorized in 1798, had a large circular, crenated hole, and the plugs, known locally as 'mocos', were stamped with a D; and further piercing, cutting and stamping (with value marks) took place in 1813 and later.

MODERN COINAGE

The local currency of mutilated Spanish silver coinage was not withdrawn until 1862, when British coinage became standard in the island. Dominica was a member of the currency board of the British Caribbean Territories (Eastern Group), which issued its own coinage from 1955 to 1965 (*see* Antigua), and it was one of the states which issued the 1970 commemorative 4 dollar coin for the Caribbean Development Bank. The only other modern coins issued by Dominica have been high-value commemorative pieces struck in silver and gold, in denominations from 10 to 150 dollars, celebrating events such as Dominica's independence (1978) and visits by Pope John Paul II (1979) and Queen Elizabeth II (1985). The coinage of the East Caribbean States has been used in Dominica since 1981.

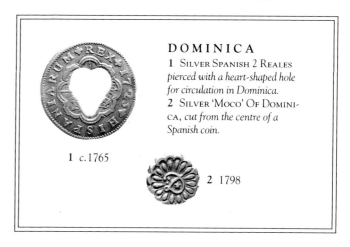

DOMINICA
1 SILVER SPANISH 2 REALES *pierced with a heart-shaped hole for circulation in Dominica.*
2 SILVER 'MOCO' OF DOMINICA, *cut from the centre of a Spanish coin.*

1 *c.*1765

2 1798

ST LUCIA

FIRST COINS:	1798 (counterstamps)
FIRST DECIMAL COINS:	1955
MAIN MINT:	Royal Mint
CURRENCY:	dollar

THE largest of the Windward Islands, St Lucia was discovered by the explorer Christopher Columbus in 1502. It was later claimed by both the British and the French, and it changed hands numerous times before finally passing to Britain in 1814. St Lucia became internally self-governing in 1967, and was granted full independence in 1979. It remains a member of the British Commonwealth.

THE FIRST COINS

The earliest marked coins of St Lucia were cut and counterstamped Spanish silver pieces (*see* Jamaica). Although issued when the island was under British rule, they were given values in terms of French currency (livres, sols and deniers) because this was the traditional money of account in the island. The earliest countermark, an sl monogram, appeared in about 1798. A later issue, dating from 1813, used segmented Spanish silver pieces stamped s. LUCIE. The copper coins used on the island, which circulated without counterstamps, were the French colonial 'black dogs' and 'stampees' (*see* Guadeloupe). The cut and counterstamped coinage of St Lucia was withdrawn in 1851 and replaced with British currency.

MODERN COINAGE

British coinage was used until the 1950s, when the British Caribbean Territories (Eastern Group) began issuing their own currency (*see* Antigua). The first modern coin issued in the name of St Lucia was the 4 dollar piece commemorating the inauguration of the Caribbean Development Bank in 1970. More recently, commemorative coins in values ranging from 5 dollars to 500 dollars have been issued by St Lucia. Since 1981 the coinage of the East Caribbean States has been used.

ST VINCENT

FIRST COINS:	*c.* 1800 (counterstamps)
FIRST DECIMAL COINS:	1955
MAIN MINT:	Royal Mint
CURRENCY:	dollar

THOUGHT to have been discovered by the explorer Christopher Columbus in 1498 but not colonized by the Spanish, St Vincent was later claimed by both the British and the French until formally ceded to Britain in 1783. The colony became internally self-governing in 1969 and was granted full independence under the name of St Vincent and the Grenadines in 1979.

1813

ST LUCIA
SILVER CUT SPANISH
COIN *stamped* s. LUCIE *for
circulation in St. Lucia.*

c. 1800

ST VINCENT
SILVER CUT SPANISH COIN
counterstamped with an sv
*monogram for circulation in
St Vincent.*

THE FIRST COINS

The earliest official coinage of St Vincent was produced towards the end of the eighteenth century by cutting and counterstamping the foreign coins already circulating in the colony (*see* Jamaica). From 1797 cut Spanish silver was stamped sv in monogram. Some pieces were plugged with extra silver to bring them to the correct authorized weight. Base-metal French colonial 'black dogs' and 'stampees' (*see* Guadeloupe) were also counterstamped. Portuguese 'Joes' provided most of the gold coinage for the island, and, because many of them had lost value through clipping, in 1798 an Act was passed which regulated the circulation of gold coin by weight and necessitated the plugging of underweight pieces with additional gold. The plugged pieces were counterstamped s.

Further cutting and counterstamping of silver coinage took place in the early nineteenth century, with a local 'holey dollar' coinage introduced in 1811, and numerals representing values added to the s counterstamps. The local coinages in gold and silver were withdrawn in 1818 (gold) and 1823 (silver), being replaced by British currency.

MODERN COINAGE

British coinage was used in St Vincent until the 1950s, when the island began using the coinage of the British Caribbean Territories (Eastern Group) and later of the East Caribbean States (*see* Antigua). The only modern coins issued for St Vincent have been commemorative pieces, the first a 4 dollar piece issued in the name of the Caribbean Development Bank in 1970, and more recently a 10 dollar piece issued in cupro-nickel, silver and gold, for the visit of Queen Elizabeth II in 1985.

GRENADA

FIRST COINS:	1787 (counterstamps)
FIRST DECIMAL COINS:	1955
MAIN MINT:	Royal Mint
CURRENCY:	dollar

GRENADA was discovered in 1498 by the explorer Christopher Columbus, who named it Conception. First colonization was by the French in the 1650s, but the British captured the island in 1762, and although the French re-took it in 1779, it was finally ceded to Britain in 1783. Grenada became internally self-governing with associated statehood in 1967, and achieved full independence in 1974, while remaining a member of the British Commonwealth. An internal revolt in 1983 prompted military intervention by US forces, which were withdrawn early in 1984.

THE FIRST COINS

The first local coinage of Grenada was authorized by an Act of 1787, which provided for the cutting of Spanish silver dollars (8 reales) into 11 segments, each valued at 1 bitt (9 pence) and counterstamped G. In 1798 the gold coinage in circulation, largely Portuguese 'Joes' (*see* Jamaica), was regulated so that underweight pieces had to be plugged with an additional piece of gold. Coins of confirmed weight were countermarked G. Further cutting and counterstamping of Spanish silver coins were authorized in 1814, with the addition of value marks and the initials of the counterstamper. These local coinages survived until 1840, when the sterling standard was adopted on the island.

MODERN COINAGE

British coinage was used until the 1950s, when Grenada, as a member of the currency board of the British Caribbean Territories (Eastern Group), used the coinage of the board and later of the East Caribbean States (*see* Antigua). Grenada was one of the states which shared in the issuing in 1970 of a 4 dollar commemorative coin for the Caribbean Development Bank. The only other modern issue of coinage of Grenada was produced in 1985 to commemorate the visit of Queen Elizabeth II.

GRENADA
SILVER CUT SPANISH 8 REALES *counterstamped for circulation in Grenada as a 4 bit piece.*

c.1814

BARBADOS

FIRST COINS:	1788 (tokens)
FIRST DECIMAL COINS:	1955
MAIN MINTS:	Royal Mint, Franklin Mint
CURRENCY:	dollar

DISCOVERED by the Portuguese in the sixteenth century, Barbados was not colonized until 1627, when the British established a settlement. The island was a British possession until independence was granted in 1966. It remains a member of the British Commonwealth.

THE COLONIAL PERIOD

No officially cut or counterstamped coinage (*see* Jamaica) was issued for colonial Barbados. In the eighteenth and early nineteenth centuries the coinage in circulation consisted largely of Spanish silver

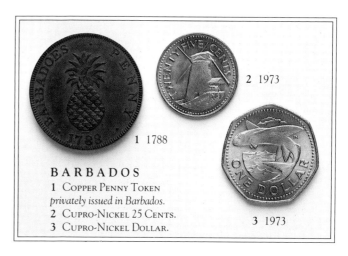

BARBADOS
1 COPPER PENNY TOKEN *privately issued in Barbados.*
2 CUPRO-NICKEL 25 CENTS.
3 CUPRO-NICKEL DOLLAR.

coins, privately cut into segments to provide much-needed small denominations. The coins most frequently cut were the 8 reales and the pistareen (Spanish provincial 2 reales). French colonial base-metal coins (*see* Guadeloupe) also circulated in the island. Copper tokens depicting a negro's head on the front and on the back a pineapple (dated 1788) or Neptune in a chariot (dated 1792) were issued in the name of Barbados, but these were private issues, by a plantation owner. Associated with these coins are silver plugged coins with a pineapple counterstamp. Other token issues were produced in Barbados in the nineteenth century.

In 1838 the cut coins still circulating in Barbados were withdrawn, and from 1848 the sterling system was adopted. British coinage was then the only legal tender until the 1950s, when the coinage and banknotes of the British Caribbean Territories (Eastern Group) became current (*see* Antigua).

INDEPENDENCE

Barbados began issuing its own decimal coinage in 1973. Coins issued regularly are the cent (bronze), 5 cents (brass), 10 and 25 cents, dollar and 2, 5 and 10 dollars (cupro-nickel). Various high-value commemorative coins in silver and gold have also been issued in recent years, in denominations from 25 to 250 dollars.

TRINIDAD AND TOBAGO

FIRST COINS:	1798 (Tobago counterstamps); 1811 (Trinidad counterstamps)
FIRST DECIMAL COINS:	1955
MAIN MINTS:	Royal Mint, Franklin Mint
CURRENCY:	dollar

DISCOVERED by the explorer Christopher Columbus in 1498, Tobago was subsequently occupied in turn by the English, Dutch and French, before finally being ceded to Britain in 1814. In the

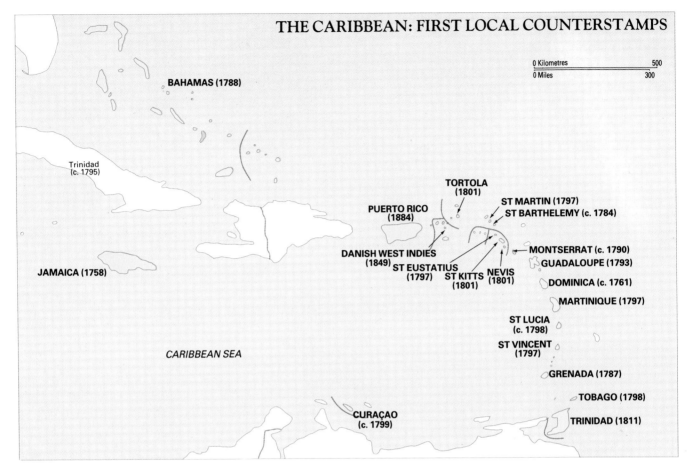

THE CARIBBEAN: FIRST LOCAL COUNTERSTAMPS

BAHAMAS (1788)

Trinidad (c. 1795)

TORTOLA (1801)

ST MARTIN (1797)
ST BARTHELEMY (c. 1784)

PUERTO RICO (1884)

DANISH WEST INDIES (1849)
ST EUSTATIUS (1797)
ST KITTS (1801)
NEVIS (1801)

MONTSERRAT (c. 1790)
GUADALOUPE (1793)
DOMINICA (c. 1761)
MARTINIQUE (1797)

JAMAICA (1758)

ST LUCIA (c. 1798)
ST VINCENT (1797)

CARIBBEAN SEA

GRENADA (1787)

TOBAGO (1798)
TRINIDAD (1811)

CURAÇAO (c. 1799)

eighteenth century the coinage in circulation in Tobago included Portuguese gold, Spanish silver and French colonial base-metal pieces (*see* Guadeloupe). In 1798 local coinages were created by piercing Spanish silver dollars with a crenated circular hole as in Dominica (the central segment or 'moco' was stamped with a stylized letter T), and by applying a TB counterstamp to the French colonial 'black dog' and 'stampee'. Gold coinage was regulated by weight, necessitating the plugging of underweight pieces (*see* Jamaica). These local coinages circulated until the second half of the nineteenth century.

TRINIDAD

Also discovered by Columbus in 1498, Trinidad was first settled by Spanish colonists in 1532, but suffered attacks from each of the other colonial nations – England, Holland and France – and in 1797 was captured by the British. The island was formally ceded to Britain by the Treaty of Amiens in 1802.

The Spanish brought the first coinage to Trinidad, and until the nineteenth century Spanish silver continued to be the main currency. Gold coins circulated by weight. Local coinage, produced by cutting Spanish silver pieces, was not officially sanctioned until an Act of 1804, and not until 1811 was the first distinctive local coinage for the island produced, when Spanish dollars were pierced with an octagonal hole. The resulting octagonal segment was stamped T and valued at 1 bit (1 shilling), the outer ring at 9 bits. These local coinages survived in circulation for much of the nineteenth century. Copper coins were

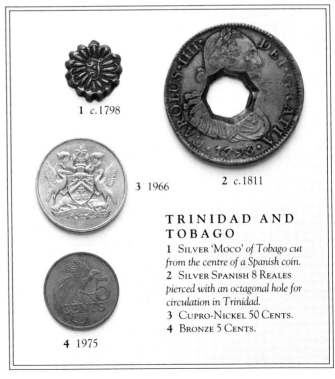

1 c.1798

3 1966

2 c.1811

4 1975

TRINIDAD AND TOBAGO

1 SILVER 'Moco' of Tobago cut from the centre of a Spanish coin.
2 SILVER SPANISH 8 REALES pierced with an octagonal hole for circulation in Trinidad.
3 CUPRO-NICKEL 50 CENTS.
4 BRONZE 5 CENTS.

not used in the island until after 1850, though in 1819 the British garrison was supplied with British copper coins, and private copper tokens were also in use in the middle of the century.

MODERN COINAGE

In 1888 Trinidad and Tobago were united to form a single colony. By this date British currency had been established and it continued as the main currency until the 1950s, when the decimal coinage and banknotes of the British Caribbean Territories (Eastern Group) became current (*see* Antigua). Trinidad and Tobago gained independence in 1962, and in 1976 became a republic, remaining a member of the British Commonwealth.

Trinidad and Tobago began issuing its own decimal coinage in 1966. The denominations that have since been issued regularly are the 1 and 5 cents (bronze) and the 10, 25 and 50 cents and dollar (cupronickel). High-value coins produced for collectors have also been issued frequently, in denominations ranging from 5 dollars to 200 dollars. The arms of Trinidad and Tobago and depictions of local flora and fauna are the dominant designs.

GUADELOUPE

FIRST COINS:	1793 (counterstamps)
FIRST DECIMAL COINS:	1903
MAIN MINT:	Paris
CURRENCY:	franc

Discovered by the explorer Christopher Columbus in 1493, Guadeloupe was colonized by the French in the seventeenth century. It was frequently attacked and occupied by British forces between 1759 and 1815, but since 1816 it has been a French possession.

FRENCH COLONIAL COINAGE

In the early colonial period, Guadeloupe and the other French possessions in the Caribbean were supplied with the general colonial issues of French coinage, first produced in 1670, and after 1731 with issues of French coinage specifically for the Caribbean colonies,

the first issue being a silver 12 sou piece inscribed on the back ISLES DU VENT.

One of the commonest coins in circulation in the French colonies and throughout the Caribbean in this period was the French billon 12 deniers, counterstamped with a fleur-de-lis to re-value it as a sol of 15 deniers in France. An Act of 1672 determined that this coin was to circulate in the French colonies with a value of 20 deniers. It was known to the French as the 'sol marque' and to the English as the 'black dog' (because of its colour).

In the eighteenth century another French coin, which came to be known as the 'stampee' (French *estampe*), emerged as a major coin in circulation throughout the Caribbean. This was originally produced in Paris by overstamping the French copper 2 sols of post-1738 with a crowned C (for *colonies*); later issues were struck in Paris on new flans. Because of the popularity of these coins in the West Indies and their overvaluation, numerous forgeries were put into circulation, many of which were minted in Birmingham, England.

OTHER COLONIAL COINAGE

In addition to the French colonial issues, silver Spanish American and gold Portuguese coinage circulated in Guadeloupe. In the late eighteenth and early nineteenth centuries, under both French and British administration, the cutting, plugging and counterstamping of coinage for local circulation was prevalent (*see* Jamaica). Counterstamps of a radiate G, a crowned G and marks of value were commonly used. Cut and counterstamped coinages were also produced for the smaller islands associated with Guadeloupe: Grand-Terre, Marie-Galante, Les Santes, Desirade and St Martin.

MODERN COINAGE

French coinage was established as the official currency of Guadeloupe in the nineteenth century. From 1825 to 1844 French colonial bronze coins of 5 and 10 centimes were issued for the West Indies, and, in 1903 and 1921, an issue of local coinage was provided for the island, of cupro-nickel 50 centime and 1 franc pieces.

SAINT BARTHELEMY

First occupied by France in the seventeenth century, this island was sold to Sweden in 1784 but later re-purchased by France (1877) and subsequently administered as a dependency of Guadeloupe. Under Sweden foreign coins, including Spanish American, French colonial, US and Swedish, were validated for internal circulation with a crown counterstamp and values reckoned in Dutch stivers.

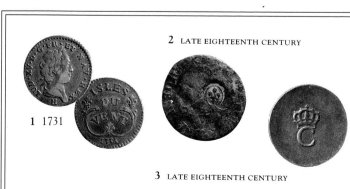

2 LATE EIGHTEENTH CENTURY

1 1731

3 LATE EIGHTEENTH CENTURY

GUADELOUPE
1 SILVER 12 SOLS *of the French West Indies.*
2 BILLON FRENCH COUNTERSTAMPED 15 DENIERS, *known locally as the 'sol marque' or 'black dog'.*
3 COPPER FRENCH COLONIAL STAMPEE.
4 CUPRO-NICKEL FRANC *of the colony of Guadeloupe.*

4 1903

MARTINIQUE

FIRST COINS:	1797–8 (cut coins and counterstamps)
FIRST DECIMAL COINS:	1897
MAIN MINT:	Paris
CURRENCY:	franc

Discovered by the explorer Christopher Columbus in 1502, the island was first colonized by the French in 1635. It has since remained a French possession, apart from two periods, 1793–1801 and 1809–16, when it was under British control.

In the early colonial period Martinique used French colonial coinage (*see* Guadeloupe), Spanish American silver and Portuguese gold. In the late eighteenth and early nineteenth centuries local island coinage was produced by the mutilation of existing currency. In the 1790s under the British, Spanish silver pieces were cut into segments with crenated edges, and Portuguese gold coins were plugged and stamped locally. In 1805 the French authorities ordered the stamping of Portuguese gold coins which featured marks of value relating to local money.

FRENCH CURRENCY

Following the withdrawal of the local cut coinage (1817) and later that of the counterstamped gold pieces, French currency became standard, and French colonial bronze coins (issued for the West Indies, 1825–44) also circulated in Martinique. In 1897 and 1922, a local coinage of cupro-nickel 50 centime and 1 franc pieces was issued for use on the islands.

1 1798

MARTINIQUE

1 GOLD PORTUGUESE 'JOHAN-NES', *plugged and counterstamped for circulation in Martinique.*
2 CUPRO-NICKEL FRANC *of the colony of Martinique.*

2 1897

NETHERLANDS ANTILLES

FIRST COINS:	1794
FIRST DECIMAL COINS:	1900
MAIN MINT:	Utrecht
CURRENCY:	gulden

The Netherlands Antilles, today an overseas territory of the Kingdom of the Netherlands, comprises two groups of islands: Curaçao, and Bonaire off the coast of Venezuela, and St Eustatius, Saba and part of St Martin in the Leeward Islands. The island of Aruba, near Curaçao, formerly part of the Netherlands Antilles, was recently granted separate administration. These islands first came under Dutch control in the 1630s and 1640s. In the seventeenth and eighteenth centuries the coinage circulating in these islands was the

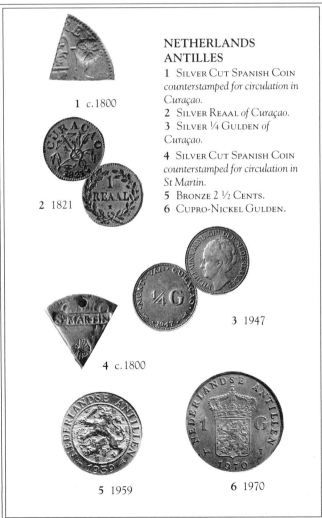

1 c.1800

2 1821

4 c.1800

3 1947

5 1959

6 1970

NETHERLANDS ANTILLES

1 SILVER CUT SPANISH COIN *counterstamped for circulation in Curaçao.*
2 SILVER REAAL *of Curaçao.*
3 SILVER ¼ GULDEN *of Curaçao.*
4 SILVER CUT SPANISH COIN *counterstamped for circulation in St Martin.*
5 BRONZE 2 ½ CENTS.
6 CUPRO-NICKEL GULDEN.

same as elsewhere in the Caribbean: Spanish silver, Portuguese gold and French colonial 'black dogs' and 'stampees' (*see* Guadeloupe), as well as an assortment of other European and colonial issues. The first coins issued directly for the Dutch West Indies colonies, comprising these islands and Dutch Guiana (*see* Surinam), were struck in 1794. They consisted of silver 2 stivers, ¼, 1 and 3 guilders, minted in Utrecht. The coins had the same designs as those of the Dutch East India Company, but with a large w added on the front. Some of the islands also had their own local coinages.

CURAÇAO

Discovered by explorer Alonso de Ojeda in 1499 and first settled by Spaniards in 1527, the Dutch West India Company took the island in 1634 and administered it until 1787, when it was handed over to the United Netherlands. During the Napoleonic Wars it was twice occupied by the British but was formally returned to the Dutch in 1816. Local coinages were produced for Curacao between 1799 and 1838 under both Dutch and British rule, by the counterstamping of Portuguese gold and cut Spanish silver coins and later cut Dutch guilders. New coins produced for Curaçao were also introduced in 1821 (silver 1 reaal, minted in the USA) and 1822 (silver 1 stuiver, also minted in the USA, re-struck in Utrecht 1840–1). The cut coinages of Curaçao continued to circulate until the late nineteenth century.

A new issue of coins for Curaçao was produced in 1900–1, consisting of silver $\frac{1}{10}$ and $\frac{1}{4}$ guilders, similar to contemporary 10 and 25 cent pieces of the Kingdom of the Netherlands. During the German occupation of the Netherlands (1940–5), Curaçao was supplied with coinage minted in the US mint at Denver, in denominations ranging from 1 cent to $2\frac{1}{2}$ guilders. Curaçao's final issues of coinage were produced in Utrecht in 1947–8.

ST EUSTATIUS AND ST MARTIN

St Eustatius has been a Dutch possession since 1635, though until 1814 it was frequently attacked and sometimes occupied by the British and the French. In the late eighteenth and early nineteenth centuries there was local countermarking (with stamps of the letters SE, and later P) of foreign copper coins (mainly French colonial: *see* Guadeloupe) and, to a lesser extent, of worn silver coins.

St Martin was a Spanish possession until 1648, when it was divided between the French and the Dutch. In the late eighteenth and early nineteenth centuries local coinages were created for the Dutch colony (the southern part of the island) by counter-stamping copper coins (mainly French colonial) and cut Spanish silver pieces.

MODERN COINAGE

Coinage in the name of the Netherlands Antilles has been issued regularly since 1952. The monetary system is the same as that of the Netherlands, with a gulden of 100 cents. Coins issued regularly have been the 1 and $2\frac{1}{2}$ cents (bronze until 1978, aluminium since), 5 cents (cupro-nickel), and 10 and 25 cents and 1 and $2\frac{1}{2}$ gulden (silver until 1970, nickel since). In recent years high-value commemorative coins intended for the collector have also been issued.

In 1986 Aruba was recognized as a state separate from the Netherlands Antilles, scheduled for full independence in 1996. A new coinage was also introduced, with a new unit of currency, the florin, and coins issued at 5, 10, 25 and 50 cents and 1 and $2\frac{1}{2}$ florins, all of nickel-bonded steel. A special commemorative silver 25 florin was also issued.

UNITED STATES VIRGIN ISLANDS

FIRST COINS:	1740
FIRST DECIMAL COINS:	1859
MAIN MINT:	US Mints
CURRENCY:	US dollar

PART of the Virgin Islands archipelago, including St Thomas and St John, was colonized by Danes and declared a Danish colony (the Danish West Indies) in 1674.

St Croix was bought from France in 1733 and added to the colony, which remained Danish until 1917. The first coins for the islands were issued in 1740 during the reign of Christian VI, and consisted of copper 1 and 2 skilling and silver 12 skilling pieces, all minted in Denmark. 6 and 12 skillings, both in silver, were added under Frederick V (1746–66). In 1816 a new coinage was introduced, consisting of silver 2, 10 and 20 skilling pieces. This coinage was issued intermittently until 1848. The next series was a counterstamped coinage, produced locally from 1849 to 1859. Various foreign coins, including US, British and Spanish American copper and silver, Portuguese gold, and Dutch and French silver, were counterstamped with a crowned FR VII monogram, representing King Frederick VII of Denmark.

In 1859 a decimal coinage was introduced. The new unit of currency was the franc of 100 cents, and coins issued at 1 cent (bronze) and 3, 5, 10 and 20 cents (silver) were produced at the Danish mints of Altona and Copenhagen. In 1904 a new monetary system was introduced, with the franc revalued at 20 cents (= 100 bits) and a new unit, the daler (= 5 francs). Coins were issued at $\frac{1}{2}$, 1 and 2 cents (bronze = $2\frac{1}{2}$, 5 and 10 bits); 5, 10, 20 and 40 cents (silver = 25 and 50 bits; 1 and 2 francs); and 4 and 10 dalers (gold = 20 and 50 francs).

US VIRGIN ISLANDS

In 1917 the USA purchased the islands from Denmark for $25 million, since when US currency has been used.

US VIRGIN ISLANDS
1 SILVER 12 SKILLING of the *Danish West Indies.*
2 SILVER 10 CENTS of the *Danish West Indies.*
3 NICKEL 5 CENTS of the *Danish West Indies.*

1 1748
2 1862
3 1906

PUERTO RICO

FIRST COINS:	1884 (counterstamps)
FIRST DECIMAL COINS:	1895
MAIN MINT:	US mints
CURRENCY:	US dollar

Discovered by the explorer Christopher Columbus in 1493, Puerto Rico was first colonized in 1508 by the Spanish under Juan Ponce de Leon, Deputy Governor of Hispaniola (*see* Dominican Republic). It remained a Spanish possession until 1898, when it was ceded to the USA under the terms of the peace treaty ending the Spanish American War. It became a US territory in 1917, and in 1952 a free commonwealth associated with the USA.

PUERTO RICO
SILVER 40 CENTAVOS *portraying the Spanish king Alphonso XIII.*

1895

Under Spanish rule the colony used Spanish American silver coinage and the usual mix of foreign coins in circulation in the Caribbean. In 1884 there was local counterstamping of Spanish, US and other coins with a fleur-de-lis. The offshore island of Vieque (Crab Island) had earlier used a counterstamp of a rayed sunburst to sanction the circulation of foreign coins. Puerto Rico's only named coinage was issued in 1895–6. It consisted of silver 5, 10, 20 and 40 centavo and 1 peso pieces, with the same designs as Spanish coins, but with ISLA DE PUERTO RICO included in the inscriptions.

Since 1898 US coinage has been used in Puerto Rico.

HAITI

FIRST COINS:	1802
FIRST DECIMAL COINS:	1813
MAIN MINT:	Paris
CURRENCY:	gourde

The Republic of Haiti occupies the western third of the large island of Hispaniola (Santo Domingo), which was discovered by the explorer Christopher Columbus in 1492. Hispaniola was colonized

HAITI
1 COPPER CENTIME of *President Henri Christophe.*
2 SILVER 30 SOLS.
3 SILVER 25 CENTIMES *of the Republic of Haiti, year 11.*
4 COPPER 6¼ CENTIMES *of Emperor Faustin 1.*
5 BRONZE 20 CENTIMES *of President Fabre Geffrard, minted in Birmingham.*
6 CUPRO-NICKEL 50 CENTIMES *portraying President Alexis.*
7 CUPRO-NICKEL 10 CENTIMES.

1 1807
2 1808
3 1823
4 1850
5 1863
6 1908
7 1953

early by the Spanish, who brought the first coinage to the island, and it became their initial base for further exploration of the Americas. The western part was evacuated by the Spanish in 1605 and in 1697 it was formally ceded to France as the colony of Saint Domingue.

FRENCH RULE
The coinage of Saint Domingue in the eighteenth century consisted of the usual French colonial issues (*see* Guadeloupe), Spanish American

silver, Portuguese gold and various other foreign coins. No local coinage was produced for the colony under the French until 1802, when the native leader from 1798 to 1802, Toussaint Louverture, issued silver ½, 1 and 2 escalin pieces in the names of Saint Domingue and the French Republic. There was also counterstamping of coinage under French authority in the period 1781–1809.

INDEPENDENCE

A native uprising, which began in 1804 with a declaration of independence, forced the French to abandon Saint Domingue, which adopted the Indian name Haiti. From 1821 to 1844 the Haitians also held the Spanish part of the island (Santo Domingo, now the Dominican Republic).

The first coins of independent Haiti were issued by President (later King) Henri Christophe in 1807. They were copper centimes and silver 7½, 15 and 30 sol pieces. The use of Christophe's portrait for the front of some coins set a precedent followed by most of Haiti's rulers. In 1813 a new monetary system was adopted. The coinage was super-ficially decimal, but with denominations of 6, 12 and 25 centimes (all silver) related to the contemporary Spanish colonial coins of ½, 1 and 2 reales. A new dating system was also introduced, using a national era counting back to 1804, following French revolutionary practice.

Under President Boyer in 1828–9 more new decimal denominations were introduced: the copper 1 and 2 centimes and the silver 50 and 100 centimes. But pre-decimal values still persisted, and in 1846 and 1850 issues of copper 6¼ centimes were produced, the 1850 coins being issued in the name of the self-styled Emperor Faustin I.

In 1863 bronze coins of 5, 10 and 20 centimes (minted in Birmingham, England) were introduced under the restored republic of President Geffrard; and in 1881–2 a new coinage series, minted in Paris, was inaugurated, with denominations of 1 and 2 centimes in bronze; 5 centimes in cupro-nickel; and 10, 20, 50 and 100 centimes (= 1 gourde) in silver. This series was minted until 1895.

MODERN COINAGE

The next coinage, beginning in 1904, consisted of cupro-nickel 5, 10, 20 and 50 centime pieces. These denominations, struck only in base-metal, have continued to the present day. No precious-metal currency coins have been issued for Haiti this century, though since 1967 there have been frequent issues of silver and gold commemorative coins aimed at collectors, in denominations ranging from 5 to 1000 gourdes. The currency of the USA is also legal tender in Haiti.

DOMINICAN REPUBLIC

FIRST COINS:	1542
FIRST DECIMAL COINS:	1877
MAIN MINT:	US mints
CURRENCY:	peso

THE island of Hispaniola, discovered by the explorer Christopher Columbus in 1492, was the site of the first Spanish settlement in the New World, called Santo Domingo. After the French took control of the western third of the island (see Haiti), the remaining eastern portion came to be known as Santo Domingo.

The first coinage to arrive in Santo Domingo was that of Spain, and a mint was established in the colony in about 1542 for production of Spanish silver and copper coinage. Further authorizations for the minting of Spanish silver and copper coinage in Santo Domingo were issued in 1573 and 1595, but from this early period only coins in the

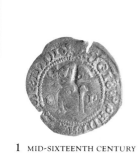

1 MID-SIXTEENTH CENTURY

2 1814–21

3 1891

4 1961

DOMINICAN REPUBLIC
1 COPPER SPANISH 4 MARAVEDIS minted in Santo Domingo.
2 COPPER ¼ REAL of Santo Domingo.
3 SILVER 5 FRANCOS.
4 BRONZE CENTAVO.
5 CUPRO-NICKEL ½ PESO.

5 1967

names of Carlos and Juana (1516–56) are known. The next coinage produced in Santo Domingo consisted of copper ¼ reales (quartillos) and silver 1 and 2 reales in the name of Fernando VII, all crudely struck and issued between 1814 and 1821. There was also counterstamping of foreign coinages in the colony at the beginning of the nineteenth century.

INDEPENDENCE

Santo Domingo was ruled by neighbouring Haiti from 1821 until 1844, when the Haitians were driven out by nationalists led by Juan Pablo Duarte and the independent Dominican Republic was established. The first coinage of the Dominican Republic, consisting only of brass ¼ reales, was issued in 1844. Decimal coinage was introduced in 1877. At first only base-metal low-value coins were issued: 1¼, 2½ and 5 centavos. In 1891 a new issue of currency appeared, minted in Paris and with new denominations of 5 and 10 centesimos (bronze), and 50 centesimos and 1 and 5 francos (silver). This was followed in 1897 by an issue of base-silver 10 and 20 centavos and ½ and 1 peso coins, also struck in Paris.

MODERN COINAGE

The Dominican Republic's next coinage did not begin until 1937, since when the regular currency coins have been made compatible with US coins, alongside which they circulate, the peso being equated with the dollar. In addition to the currency coins, a number of commemorative issues of high-value coinage have appeared since 1955, when the first gold coin of the republic, a 30 peso piece commemorating the 25th anniversary of the Trujillo regime, was struck. More recent commemoratives include an issue celebrating the centenary of Duarte's death in 1976, and an issue struck for the visit of Pope John Paul II in 1979, which included a gold 250 peso piece.

CUBA

FIRST COINS:	1915
FIRST DECIMAL COINS:	1915
MAIN MINT:	Havana
CURRENCY:	peso

Discovered by the explorer Christopher Columbus in 1492 and settled by the Spanish in the early sixteenth century, Cuba remained a Spanish possession until it was granted independence under US protection in 1902, following the Spanish American War of 1898. Cuba became a Communist republic in 1959.

SPANISH RULE

Under Spanish rule Cuba was never provided with its own coinage. Spanish coinage, at first from Spain and Santo Domingo, and later mainly from Mexico, provided the main circulating currency. The only counterstamps attributed to Cuba are a lattice stamp of the province of Trinidad on Spanish silver coins of the late eighteenth and early nineteenth centuries and a key stamp on Mexican coins applied by revolutionaries in the 1870s.

INDEPENDENCE

After 1898 US currency became legal tender in Cuba, and when Cuba's first national coinage appeared in 1915 most of the coins were devised to fit the US system. The full range of denominations comprised: 1, 2 and 5 centavos (cupro-nickel), 10, 20 and 40 centavos and 1 peso (silver), and 1, 2, 4, 5, 10 and 20 pesos (gold, issued only until 1916). The designs appearing most frequently were the arms of Cuba, which had first been seen on a souvenir silver peso minted in New York by nationalist sympathizers in 1897, and the portrait of José Marti, hero of the independence struggle. Silver coinage was issued until 1953, when the new denominations of 25 and 50 centavos appeared for the first and only time, replacing the 20 and 40 centavos. The designs celebrated the centenary of Marti's birth.

MODERN COINAGE

Since 1962 the regular coinage has been restricted to 1, 2 and 5 centavos (aluminium) and 20 and 40 centavos (cupro-nickel to 1968, then aluminium). The peso reappeared in 1980 as a cupro-nickel coin, and has since been issued regularly, with frequent changes of design on the back covering a wide range of national and international themes. In recent years silver and gold commemorative coins have also been issued for collectors, in denominations from 5 to 100 pesos.

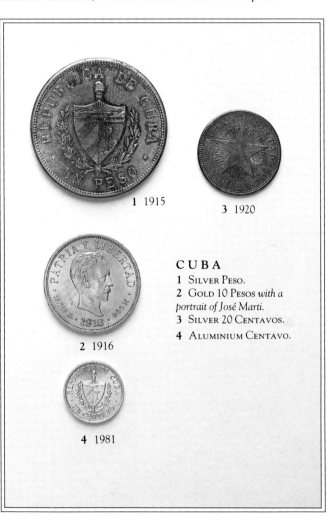

1 1915   3 1920

2 1916

4 1981

CUBA
1 SILVER PESO.
2 GOLD 10 PESOS *with a portrait of José Marti.*
3 SILVER 20 CENTAVOS.
4 ALUMINIUM CENTAVO.

MEXICO

FIRST COINS:	1536
FIRST DECIMAL COINS:	1863
MAIN MINT:	Mexico City
CURRENCY:	peso

THE Aztec Empire in Mexico was overthrown by a Spanish force under Hernando Cortés between 1519 and 1521. The conquered territory, which was given the name New Spain, became one of the four Spanish viceroyalties of the New World. For the next three centuries the frontiers of New Spain advanced until it at one time included all of Central America north of Panama and much of the western USA. Spanish rule was maintained until 1821, when an independent Mexican Empire was established, following a revolution which began in 1810.

Before the arrival of the Spanish, the Indian tribes of Mexico used copper ingots and cocoa beans for money. But the new rulers soon found that the land was rich in silver and gold, and in 1536 a mint, the first in the New World, was opened at Mexico City to convert these metals into coin. At first coinage of various denominations was struck in silver (reales), gold (escudos) and copper (maravedis), but copper coinage was soon discontinued.

All of Mexico's colonial coinage was struck at the Mexico City mint. The principal coins were the silver ½, 1, 2, 4 and 8 reales, and the gold ½, 1, 2, 4 and 8 escudos. The official exchange rate between the two precious-metal coinages was 16:1; one gold escudo equalled two 8 reales. The coins had similar designs to contemporary Spanish pieces, the name and titles of the ruling monarch and the Spanish coat of arms being the principal features. However, the earliest issues also included a new design, the pillars of Hercules, symbolizing Spanish interests in the New World.

From the second half of the sixteenth century until early in the eighteenth century the Mexican coins, called 'cobs', were struck crudely on irregularly shaped flans of metal. In 1732 new designs were introduced, coinciding with a lowering of silver fineness: on gold coins there appeared the bust of the reigning Spanish monarch, while on silver coins the pillars of Hercules reappeared, now flanking two hemispheres, representing the Old and New Worlds. In 1772, on the occasion of another minor debasement, the designs on the silver coins were again changed, to include the bust of the monarch.

The 8 reales or 'piece of eight' was by far the most important of the Spanish colonial coins. It circulated throughout the New World and in the Far East and it had a significant influence in these regions and in Europe. It was through the ubiquitous 8 reales that the pillars of Hercules design attained such familiarity that it eventually was turned into the dollar sign; and the 8 reales minted in Mexico were particularly important for Spain's trade with China, since each year a treasure fleet loaded with silver coins sailed from Acapulco in Mexico to Manila in the Philippines, where the Chinese trade was conducted.

THE FIRST MEXICAN EMPIRE
During the period of unrest following the revolution of 1810, numerous branch mints were opened in Mexico. The royalists struck coinage in the name of the imprisoned Fernando VII, who had been replaced as king of Spain by Napoléon Bonaparte's brother Joseph. There was also widespread counterstamping of existing coinage by both royalists and insurgents. The coinage of the First Mexican Empire, issued between 1822 and 1823, depicted the self-proclaimed emperor Augustin Iturbide on the front and another new design, showing an eagle perched on a cactus, on the back. However, the denominations of coinage remained the same as before.

THE REPUBLIC OF MEXICO
The Republic of Mexico was inaugurated in 1823 and its coinage also retained the colonial denominations, but the changed designs reflected the new political order. The front depicted the Aztec legend of Mexico City's foundation: that the city should be established where an eagle was found perched on a cactus and with a snake in its beak. The central feature on the back is the cap of liberty, surrounded by the sun's rays on the silver coinage, or held in a hand above a copy of the constitution on the gold coinage.

Some of the branch mints which opened in the period 1810–23 remained in production under the republic and other mints opened in the course of the nineteenth century, though some operated only briefly.

MEXICO
1 SILVER SPANISH 4 REALES *of Carlos I and Juana, Mexico City mint.*
2 SILVER SPANISH 8 REALES *('Pillar dollar').*
3 BASE SILVER 2 REALES *of General Morelos, minted at Oaxaxa during the Wars of Independence.*
4 SILVER 8 REALES *of Augustin Iturbide.*

1 1536–55

2 1745

3 1814

4 1822

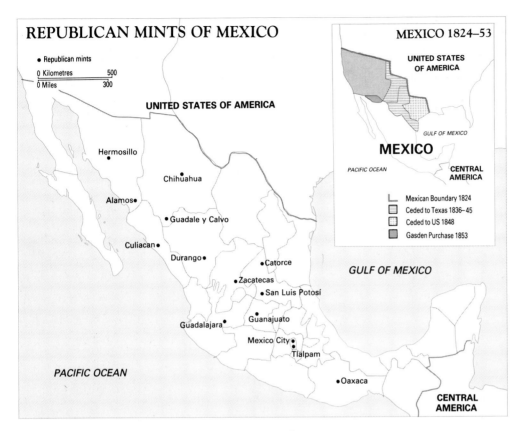

REPUBLICAN MINTS OF MEXICO

• Republican mints

0 Kilometres 500
0 Miles 300

UNITED STATES OF AMERICA

Hermosillo
Chihuahua
Alamos•
•Guadale y Calvo
Culiacan•
Durango•
•Catorce
•Zacatecas
•San Luis Potosí
Guadalajara•
Guanajuato•
Mexico City •
Tlalpam

PACIFIC OCEAN

•Oaxaca

GULF OF MEXICO

CENTRAL AMERICA

MEXICO 1824–53

UNITED STATES OF AMERICA

GULF OF MEXICO

MEXICO

PACIFIC OCEAN

CENTRAL AMERICA

Mexican Boundary 1824
Ceded to Texas 1836–45
Ceded to US 1848
Gasden Purchase 1853

5 1825

6 1835

MINTS OF THE MEXICAN REPUBLIC

	real system	decimal
Alamos	1862–63	1874–95
Catorce	1863	
Chihuahua	1831–71	1868–95
Culiacán	1846–70	1870–1905
Durango	1824–70	1870–95
Guadalajara	1825–70	
Guadale y Calvo	1843–52	
Guanajuato	1824–70	*1864–1900
Hermosillo	1835–73	1874–95
Mexico City	1823–69	*1863–
Oaxaca	1858–69	1869–93
San Luis Potosí	1827–70	*1863–93
Tlalpam	1828–30	
Zacatecas	1825–71	*1865–1905

* includes issues in the name of Maximilian

Bronze coinage was struck regularly at the Mexico mint only between 1829 and 1837; otherwise this was mostly left to the branch mints, which produced state coppers of varying sizes and designs. To add to the confusion numerous private tokens, often referred to as hacienda tokens, were also produced in this period.

TOWARDS DECIMAL COINAGE

Mexico's first decimal coinage was formally introduced in 1863 with an issue of bronze 1 centavos and silver 5 and 10 centavos for the republic.

This was quickly followed by the decimal issues of the Emperor Maximilian, installed as ruler of Mexico by French forces in the same year. Maximilian's coinage in copper (1 centavo), silver (5, 10 and 50 centavos and 1 peso) and gold (20 pesos) spans the brief period of his rule: 1864–67.

Following the overthrow and execution of the unfortunate Maximilian, the Mexican mints quickly reverted to striking silver reales

'The Execution of Emperor Maximilian', by Édouard Manet.

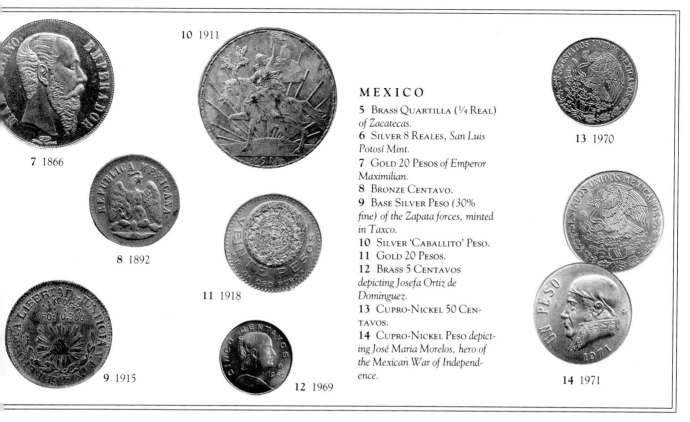

MEXICO
5 BRASS QUARTILLA (¼ REAL) *of Zacatecas.*
6 SILVER 8 REALES, *San Luis Potosí Mint.*
7 GOLD 20 PESOS *of Emperor Maximilian.*
8 BRONZE CENTAVO.
9 BASE SILVER PESO (30% *fine) of the Zapata forces, minted in Taxco.*
10 SILVER 'CABALLITO' PESO.
11 GOLD 20 PESOS.
12 BRASS 5 CENTAVOS *depicting Josefa Ortiz de Dominguez.*
13 CUPRO-NICKEL 50 CENTAVOS.
14 CUPRO-NICKEL PESO *depicting José Maria Morelos, hero of the Mexican War of Independence.*

and gold escudos for the republic. However, in 1869 a decimal coinage system was again introduced. The designs for the new coins featured prominently the Mexican eagle and the cap of liberty, continuing the tradition of the earlier republican issues. The new system included a full range of denominations, which could, to a large extent, be equated with the earlier real–escudo system.

REAL AND DECIMAL SYSTEMS

$\frac{1}{2}$ escudo = 8 reales = 1 peso
4 reales = 50 centavos
2 reales = 25 centavos
1, $\frac{1}{2}$, $\frac{1}{4}$ real = no decimal equivalent

The new decimal coinage was not, however, completely satisfactory. Between 1873 and 1898 the silver peso had to be replaced by the old 8 reales piece because the decimal coin was found to be much less acceptable for the Chinese trade, which still absorbed most of this denomination.

ABANDONING THE SILVER STANDARD
In the late nineteenth century a drastic fall in the value of silver caused turmoil in the world's currency, particularly hitting countries like Mexico which had coinage based on the silver standard. Mexico's response to the crisis finally came in 1905, when a major reform of the entire currency was introduced. The silver standard was abandoned, and the new currency system was based on a theoretical gold peso (= 50 US cents).

The new coinage had bronze 1 and 2 centavos and nickel 5 centavos (replacing the earlier silver 5 centavos). The silver pieces at 10, 20 and 50 centavos were reduced in fineness to enable them to circulate freely. The gold 5 and 10 pesos were smaller and finer, to be compatible with foreign gold coins, notably those of the USA. The new silver peso, whose design of Liberty on horseback gave it the nickname *caballito* ('little horse'), was not introduced until 1910. This piece retained the fineness of earlier Mexican silver coins since it was needed for the export trade with China. However, the old liberty-cap peso, successor to the 8 reales, was still much in demand in China, and issues were again struck in 1908, 1909 and finally in 1949, when a total of 8.25 million pieces, bearing the date 1898, were produced for the Republic of China.

Coinage production was centralized during the monetary reform of 1905. In the late nineteenth century the branch mints of Mexico had gradually been closing; the 1905 reform removed the last ones, at Culiacan and Zacatecas. Mexico City would now be the sole mint, aided when necessary by foreign mints.

Another period of revolution in Mexico between 1910 and 1917 caused a breakdown in the provision of official coinage. Various local authorities and revolutionary commanders, including Pancho Villa in the north and Emiliano Zapata south of Mexico City, had to produce and issue their own money. This included imitations of official coins and base-metal tokens substituting for silver and gold coins.

MODERN COINAGE
Since 1905 there have been many changes to the coinage of Mexico, affecting all denominations except the gold coins.

The silver peso was devalued many times, and gradually declined in fineness, metal composition, weight and size between 1910 and 1967. In 1970 the peso was struck in cupro-nickel and since 1984 in stainless steel. However, the frequent changes to metals, size and weight, have created a varied coinage, and opportunities have been taken to decorate the coins with interesting designs. Finely detailed representations of the Aztec Calendar Stone have appeared on various issues, notably the gold 20 pesos dated 1917–21 and 1959 (many of which were later re-strikes). The Mexican eagle has generally been retained, providing continuity with past coinage, but on modern issues it has more often been accompanied by portraits of famous people from Mexican history. These include figures from the independence movement: Father Miguel Hidalgo, José Maria Morelos and Josefa Ortiz de Dominguez; Presidents Benito Juarez and Francisco Madero and the last Aztec emperor Cuauhtemoc. In recent years designs have become even more varied as increasing numbers of large-denomination commemorative coins have been issued.

BELIZE

FIRST COINS:	1885
FIRST DECIMAL COINS:	1885
MAIN MINTS:	Royal Mint, Franklin Mint
CURRENCY:	dollar

BRITISH colonization of the Caribbean coast around the city of Belize dates from the seventeenth century, the first settlement being established by shipwrecked sailors in 1638. With the region situated on the Central American mainland and surrounded by Spanish colonies, Spain continued to claim sovereignty but the British retained control and in 1862 the colony gained recognition as British Honduras.

BELIZE
1 SILVER SPANISH 8 REALES, *counterstamped with a crowned GR for use in Belize.*
2 SILVER 25 CENTS *of British Honduras.*
3 CUPRO-NICKEL 25 CENTS.

1 1806
2 1897
3 1974

Until the nineteenth century Spanish coins were the accepted currency, but for the important timber trade with the native Indians, the colonists are said to have used cutlass blades stamped GR. A similar stamp, dating from about 1810 to 1818, appears on silver coins. Spanish coins continued to be standard currency in the colony after the collapse of the Spanish Empire, when they were joined by the silver peso of the newly independent Spanish American states which surrounded it. British copper coins were also in circulation.

In 1885, when British Honduras had become an independent crown colony, it was supplied with its own bronze coinage in the form of cents minted in London. The Guatemalan silver peso was declared the standard of value, but in 1894 the colony was switched to the gold standard and the US gold dollar took its place. At the same time silver coinage was minted in London for the colony on the model of the coinage provided for Canada, with 5, 10, 25 and 50 cent pieces joining the bronze cents.

The coins of British Honduras had uncomplicated designs: the bust and titles of the reigning British monarch on the front, and inscriptions on the back identifying country, date and, in the centre, denomination. From 1894 to 1973, when this coinage ceased, the only developments were minor adjustments to coin size and changes in metal composition, such as the replacement of silver with cupro-nickel coins.

INDEPENDENCE

In 1973 British Honduras became Belize, and in 1981 the country gained independence, though it remains a member of the Commonwealth and retains a British garrison for defence. The coinage system was not changed, but since 1974 a new feature has been the regular issuing of the dollar coin and its multiples. The Royal Mint has continued to produce coins for Belize with designs that have remained the same as on the earlier, British Honduran issues, except for the change of name. At the same time the Franklin mint (USA) has also made coins for Belize. These include both normal currency issues and special commemorative pieces aimed at collectors. The Franklin mint coins have much more varied designs, with an emphasis on local wildlife.

GUATEMALA

FIRST COINS:	1733
FIRST DECIMAL COINS:	1869
MAIN MINT:	Guatemala City
CURRENCY:	quetzal

CENTRAL America was discovered by Christopher Columbus on his last voyage in 1502, and by the end of the 1520s most of the region was under Spanish rule. In the Spanish colonial period the five modern Central American states of Guatemala, Honduras, El Salvador, Nicaragua and Costa Rica were provinces of the captaincy-general of Guatemala, which formed the southern portion of the much larger viceroyalty of New Spain (*see* Mexico).

In 1821 the captaincy-general of Guatemala declared its

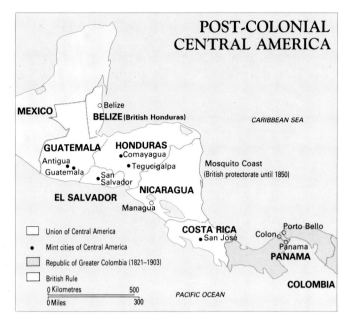

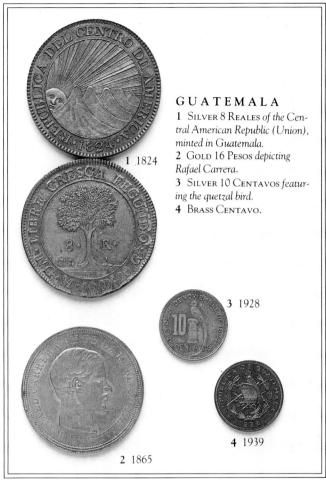

GUATEMALA
1 SILVER 8 REALES *of the Central American Republic (Union), minted in Guatemala.*
2 GOLD 16 PESOS *depicting Rafael Carrera.*
3 SILVER 10 CENTAVOS *featuring the quetzal bird.*
4 BRASS CENTAVO.

1 1824

2 1865

3 1928

4 1939

independence from Spain. After a brief period under the First Mexican Empire, in 1823 independence was regained and the five provinces formed the first Central American Union. This union lasted only until 1838, and other unions involving some of the states formed in 1842 and 1850 were similarly short-lived.

Between 1824 and 1851 coinage was issued in the name of the Republic (Union) of Central America. The coins followed the old Spanish system of silver reales and gold escudos, but had novel designs, with a sunrise over mountains on the front and a native ceiba tree on the back, symbolizing the new independent union.

MINTS OF THE CENTRAL AMERICAN UNION

	Dates	Mint mark
Guatemala City, Guatemala	1824–51	NG (G on ¼ real)
San José, Costa Rica	1825–50	CR
Tegucigalpa, Honduras	1830–32	T

COLONIAL GUATEMALA

Guatemala was conquered for Spain by Pedro de Alvarado, a lieutenant of Cortés, in the 1520s. The Spanish brought the first coinage to Guatemala. At first most of the circulating currency came from Mexico or the mints of Spanish South America, but in 1731 a mint for striking Spanish coinage in silver and gold was authorized for Guatemala City (now Antigua). In 1773 this city was largely destroyed by an earthquake and in 1776 the mint was moved to the new capital city being built 27 miles away, Nueva Guatemala. The transfer is marked on the coinage by a change in mint mark from G to NG.

THE REPUBLIC OF GUATEMALA

Guatemala was the leading state in the Central American Union, formed in 1823 following independence from Spain. It also provided the principal mint for the coinage of the Union, and after the Union broke up in 1838 Guatemala continued to issue coins of the organization until 1851.

The first coins issued in the name of the Republic of Guatemala date from 1859. Initially the coinage continued the old Spanish system of denominations except that the 8 reales was termed the peso and its multiples in gold were the 2, 4, 8 and 16 pesos. New designs were also introduced, with prominence given to the coat of arms of Guatemala and the portrait of the republic's first president, Rafael Carrera.

Coinage in the real–peso system was issued until 1912. Most was produced by the Guatemalan mint, but some issues between 1894 and 1901 were made in Birmingham, England. In 1894, in order to increase the quantity of silver coinage in circulation at minimum expense, the counterstamping of foreign silver coins was authorized. Small ½ real coin dies were used to produce the counterstamps. Meanwhile, attempts were made to introduce decimal coinage. Decimal issues in 1869 and 1870 failed for the silver coinage, but gold 5 and 20 peso pieces were issued until 1878, concurrent with silver coinage in the real system. A third, also short-lived, attempt to introduce decimal coinage in silver and bronze was made in 1881.

In the early twentieth century gold and silver coinage was no longer issued in Guatemala and very little remained in circulation. In 1912 the last cupro-nickel reales were produced, after which the only new coins put into circulation were 'provisional' issues made of aluminium–bronze between 1915 and 1923.

MODERN COINAGE

In 1924 a new coinage system was decreed. The new unit of currency, which was named after the country's national bird, the quetzal, was equated with the US dollar, and US gold coinage was made legal tender. The first issues appeared in 1925 and comprised base-metal coins (½, 1 and 2 centavos), silver coins (5, 10, 25 and 50 centavos and 1 quetzal) and gold coins (5, 10 and 20 quetzals). The gold coins were only issued in 1926. In 1965 the silver denominations still being issued (5, 10 and 25 centavos) also became base metal, made of nickel–brass or cupro-nickel. Issues of coinage for Guatemala since 1925 have been produced by mints in Britain and the USA, as well as by the Guatemalan mint.

The designs of Guatemala's modern coinage have been dominated by the arms of the republic and the quetzal bird. Other designs include the portrait of Fray Bartolome de la Casas, who championed Indian rights against the Spanish in the sixteenth century, and the Mayan monolith at Quirigua, the country's most famous archaeological monument.

HONDURAS

FIRST COINS:	1813
FIRST DECIMAL COINS:	1879
MAIN MINTS:	USA
CURRENCY:	lempira

CHRISTOPHER Columbus made his first landing on the Central American mainland at Cape Honduras in 1502, claiming the land for Spain. The first settlement was established by Cristobal de Olid, a lieutenant of Cortés, and in 1525 Cortés himself arrived. In 1539 Honduras was incorporated into the captaincy-general of Guatemala and it remained under Spanish rule until independence in 1821. Throughout this period Spanish coins, mostly minted in Mexico, circulated in Honduras. The only Spanish coins minted in Honduras were crudely made 8 reales struck at Tegucigalpa in 1813 during the wars of independence.

EARLY INDEPENDENCE

The next issues of coinage to be minted in Honduras were produced in 1823, during the brief rule of Augustin I's Mexican Empire. Minted at Tegucigalpa and Comayagua, these rare 1 and 2 reales have designs which include a crude portrait of Augustin and the Spanish and Mexican arms. From 1823 Honduras was a member state of the Central American Union (see Guatemala). Between 1830 and 1832 the mint of Tegucigalpa produced union coins. These were immediately followed by provisional issues in the name of Honduras as the union began to disintegrate. These provisional coins, which were of increasingly debased silver, were issued regularly until 1862. The denominations and designs of the earlier union coins were retained until 1861, but the last issue, dated 1862, consisted of copper pieces labelled 1, 2, 4 and 8 pesos and with a new design on the front featuring the Honduran national arms. It is believed that these coins were minted in Britain.

HONDURAS
1 COPPER 4 PESOS, *minted in Britain.*
2 CUPRO-NICKEL REAL, *minted in Paris.*
3 SILVER PESO.

1 1862
2 1869
3 1886

FIRST DECIMAL COINAGES

Between 1869 and 1870 an issue of cupro-nickel coinage, consisting of reales and fractions, was minted in Paris for Honduras. This was soon followed by the first decimal coinages. The earliest issues, produced in 1879, were struck from two sets of dies, both made in the USA. One of the sets, dated 1879, proved unsuitable and was replaced by the other, which was dated 1871 but had not previously been used for the production of regular coinage. These issues were soon replaced by a new series, which began in 1881 and continued intermittently until 1920, with the dies frequently being re-cut for continued use as an economy measure.

The early decimal coinages of Honduras consisted of a silver peso of 100 centavos and a gold peso and gold multiples of 5, 10 and 20 pesos. The major silver denominations have a design showing a standing figure of Liberty holding a flag and book. The head of Liberty appears on the front of the gold coins; on the back of the gold and most of the silver and bronze coins are the national arms of Honduras.

MODERN COINAGE

Another change was authorized in 1926, though the first issues of the new coinage were not struck until 1931. The new unit of currency was named the lempira, after the Indian chief who led the resistance against the Spanish conquistadores in the 1530s. It was valued at 50 US cents (= 100 centavos). The silver lempira coin was issued only in the 1930s. Small denomination pieces, mostly of bronze or cupro-nickel, have continued to the present time, though even these have been issued only intermittently. The principal element in the design has remained the arms of Honduras; the bust of Lempira appears on the back of the 20 and 50 centavos and the 1 lempira.

EL SALVADOR

FIRST COINS:	1828
FIRST DECIMAL COINS:	1889
MAIN MINTS:	USA
CURRENCY:	colon

E L Salvador was conquered for Spain by Pedro de Alvarado in 1525. It remained under Spanish rule, as part of the captaincy-general of Guatemala, until independence in 1821. During the colonial period Spanish currency circulated in El Salvador. Most of the coinage would have been minted in Mexico; the country had no mint of its own.

El Salvador was a member of the Central American Union (*see* Guatemala) from 1823 to 1838. It did not mint coins for the union, but between 1828 and 1835 it produced its own 'provisional' coins inscribed with the slogan POR LA LIVERTAD SALV ('For the freedom of Salvador') and with designs featuring a pillar crowned by a cap of liberty on the front and a volcano on the back. From this same period there are also counterstamped Spanish and foreign coins that have been attributed to El Salvador.

REPUBLIC OF EL SALVADOR

The first coins struck in the name of the Republic of Salvador were not produced until 1889, when an issue of cupro-nickel 1 and 3 centavo pieces, minted in Britain, was put into circulation. In 1892 a more comprehensive range of denominations was issued. The coinage system was decimal, comprising copper centavos, silver 5, 10, 20 and 50 centavos and 1 peso, and gold 2½, 5, 10 and 20 pesos, all minted in San Salvador. However, the only precious-metal coin issued regularly after 1892 was the peso, minted at San Salvador each year until 1896, and later issued intermittently between 1904 and 1914, though in this period minted overseas. The weakness of the new coinage was demonstrated by the issue as late as 1909 of ¼ reales, testifying to the continuing use of the old Spanish system of reckoning.

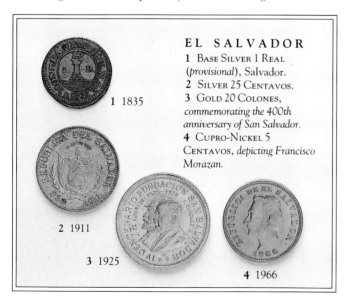

EL SALVADOR
1 BASE SILVER 1 REAL (*provisional*), Salvador.
2 SILVER 25 CENTAVOS.
3 GOLD 20 COLONES, *commemorating the 400th anniversary of San Salvador.*
4 CUPRO-NICKEL 5 CENTAVOS, *depicting Francisco Morazan.*

1 1835
2 1911
3 1925
4 1966

The designs on the coinage issued from 1889 are dominated by the national arms of Salvador. They also include portraits of Francisco Morazan, leading statesman of the Central American Union, on low-denomination coins, and Christopher Columbus on the 50 centavos and 1 peso.

MODERN COINAGE

A new unit of currency, the colon, named after Christopher Columbus, was established by decree in 1920. It was equated with 50 US cents and US currency was made legal tender. In 1925 a special issue of silver 1 colon pieces and gold 20 colones was produced by the Mexico mint to commemorate the 400th anniversary of the founding of the capital city, San Salvador. Apart from this and other commemorative issues produced in 1971 and 1977, the only modern coinage issued by El Salvador has been small change, mostly minted in the USA.

NICARAGUA

FIRST COINS:	1878
FIRST DECIMAL COINS:	1878
MAIN MINT:	Royal Mint
CURRENCY:	cordoba

T HE coast of Nicaragua was sighted by Christopher Columbus during his last voyage in 1502, but no European set foot on Nicaraguan soil until 1522, when conquistadores led by Gonzales Davila claimed the region for Spain. Soon the first settlements were established, under the successor to Gonzales, Francisco Hernandez de Cordoba, and Nicaragua was incorporated into the captaincy-general of Guatemala. The Spanish ruled Nicaragua until independence in 1821. Then a brief period under the Mexican Empire of Augustin I was followed by membership of the Central American Union, until in 1838 Nicaragua became an independent republic. The eastern coast of Nicaragua had since the seventeenth century contained British settlements and it was effectively governed as a British protectorate called the 'Mosquito Kingdom', but in 1850 this land was formally ceded to Nicaragua by the same treaty that confirmed British possession of Belize.

Nicaragua has never had its own mint. Spanish coinage, minted elsewhere in Spanish Central or South America, circulated throughout the colonial period and well into the nineteenth century, when it was joined by the coinage of the Central American Union (*see* Guatemala) and various foreign coins.

NICARAGUA'S FIRST COINS

The first coins issued in the name of Nicaragua were bronze centavos dated 1878. These were followed by issues of silver 5 centavos in 1880, 1887 and 1898–9 and silver 10 and 20 centavos in 1880 and 1887. Most of these coins were minted in Birmingham, England. The designs were purely functional: the arms of Nicaragua on the front and the denomination inscribed on the back.

NICARAGUA

1 Cupro-Nickel Centavo.   2 Cupro-Nickel 25
Centavos, *depicting Cordoba.*

MODERN COINAGE

In 1912 a coinage reform introduced a new unit of currency for
Nicaragua, the cordoba, named after the first conquistador-governor.
The silver cordoba was equated in value to the US dollar, and was
worth 100 centavos. It was issued only once, in 1912, but it later
reappeared in 1972 as a cupro-nickel coin. The lesser denominations
in silver (10, 25 and 50 centavos) were converted to cupro-nickel in
1939, since when no regular currency in precious metal has been
issued. These denominations are now made of aluminium. The lowest
value coins of the 1912 series, the bronze $\frac{1}{2}$ and 1 centavo, were issued
regularly at first but were abandoned in the 1940s, victims of devaluation and inflation.

The 1912 reform also introduced new designs for all denominations
above the centavo: the portrait of Cordoba was chosen for the front
and for the back the sunrise and mountains design copied from the
coinage of the Central American Union. A more recent change has
been the appearance of the portrait of the nineteenth-century revolutionary leader Sandino, which has been introduced as a coin design
since the Sandinistas came to power in 1979.

All of Nicaragua's coinage since 1912 has been minted in either
Britain or the USA, most of the recent coinage being provided by the
Royal Mint. Another recent feature of the coinage has been the
occasional issuing of large-denomination commemorative pieces.

COSTA RICA

FIRST COINS:	1825
FIRST DECIMAL COINS:	1864
MAIN MINTS:	USA
CURRENCY:	colon

Costa Rica gained its name ('rich coast') from a belief that the
region contained valuable gold mines. During his fourth voyage
in 1502, Christopher Columbus visited Costa Rica and attempted,
without success, to establish a settlement. Before long, however, the
country was conquered by the Spanish and incorporated into the
captaincy-general of Guatemala. It remained under Spanish rule until
Guatemala gained independence in 1821. Then followed a brief period
in the Mexican Empire of Augustin Iturbide. From 1823 to 1838 Costa

Rica was a member of the Central American Union, since when it has
been an independent republic.

Spanish currency, mostly from Mexico or elsewhere in the Spanish
Americas, was used in Costa Rica in the colonial period. There was no
mint in Costa Rica until the country joined the Central American
Union (*see Guatemala*). The mint at San José issued union coins in
both silver and gold until 1850, long after the union had ceased to
function. The first issue of coinage in the name of Costa Rica was
produced in 1842 and this was followed by other issues from 1847 to
1862. These early Costa Rican coins were struck to the old Spanish
colonial coinage system of reales and escudos. In the 1840s and 1850s
there was also widespread counterstamping of foreign coins to increase
the volume of currency in circulation.

In 1864 Costa Rica changed to a decimal coinage system. The new
peso contained 100 centavos and the denominations struck were: $\frac{1}{4}$ and
1 centavo (cupro-nickel); 5, 10, 25 and 50 centavos (silver); and 1, 2,
5, 10 and 20 pesos (gold). The principal designs, as on the earlier coins
of Costa Rica, were the country's national arms and the oak tree. This
coinage lasted until 1896; most was struck in Costa Rica, but between
1889 and 1893 the Heaton mint, Birmingham, was used. The year
1889 was also the occasion for another spate of official counterstamping of foreign currency.

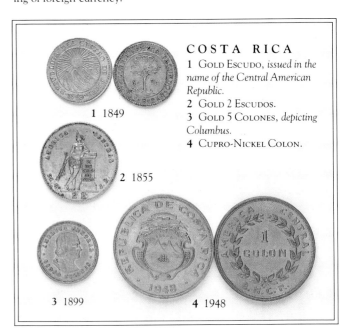

COSTA RICA

1 Gold Escudo, *issued in the
name of the Central American
Republic.*
2 Gold 2 Escudos.
3 Gold 5 Colones, *depicting
Columbus.*
4 Cupro-Nickel Colon.

MODERN COINAGE

Another coinage reform, in 1896, introduced a new coinage system
based on the gold standard. The new unit of currency was the colon
(= 100 centimos), named after Christopher Columbus. The only
coins of the new system issued before 1900 were gold 2, 5, 10 and 20
colones, which have on the back a portrait of Columbus. Of these
denominations, only the 2 colones continued to be issued after 1900.
The lesser denominations issued regularly in the present century are
the 5, 10, 25 and 50 centimos. These all originally contained silver,
but since the 1920s they have been base-metal coins. The devaluation
of the colon can also be seen in the history of the 2 colones piece,
which was a gold coin until 1928, but later re-emerged as cupro-nickel

in 1954. Costa Rica's twentieth-century coinage has so far been shared between three mints: San José, the US mint and the Royal Mint.

Since 1970 precious-metal coinage has returned to Costa Rica in the form of special commemorative coins, struck in silver and gold and in denominations ranging from 2 to 5000 colones. These coins have a variety of designs, relating to the subjects being commemorated, in contrast to the regular coinage, which has purely functional designs depicting the national arms and denomination.

PANAMA

FIRST COINS:	1904
FIRST DECIMAL COINS:	1904
MAIN MINTS:	USA, Royal Mint and Franklin Mint
CURRENCY:	balboa

The first coins to arrive in Panama came with the Spanish explorers and the colonists who settled on the northern coast between 1501 and 1510. Then in 1513 Vasco Nuñez de Balboa crossed the isthmus and made the first historic sighting of the Pacific Ocean, which he claimed in the name of the King of Spain. Henceforth, Panama was destined to occupy a vital position in communications, at first for the routing of Spanish American treasure and other goods bound for Spain, and, more recently, for international trade through the Panama Canal.

A paved track was built by the Spanish across the isthmus from the settlement of Panama on the Pacific coast to Porto Bello on the Caribbean. Since this was the route through which all the riches of Spanish South America travelled, it became a magnet for pirates seeking to capture treasure. Under Spanish rule Panama did not have its own mint, but vast quantities of gold and silver bullion and Spanish coinage minted in Peru, Bolivia, Colombia and elsewhere crossed the isthmus and circulated in Panama.

In 1718 Panama was incorporated into the Spanish viceroyalty of New Granada, administered from Bogotá in Colombia, and in 1821, following the wars of independence, Panama joined the Colombian federation. Panama did not achieve full independence until 1903, though attempts at secession from Colombia were made in 1841, 1853 and 1898. From 1821 until independence, Colombian coinage was used in Panama, the commonest piece in circulation being the ½ peso, known also as the 5 reales.

INDEPENDENCE

In 1904 the Panamanian government created a monetary system for the new republic. The gold balboa, which was not actually coined, was designated the country's monetary unit. It was equivalent in value to the US dollar, though its half piece, the silver 50 centesimos, virtually matched the US dollar in size and metal. Other fractions of the balboa also struck in silver were the 2½, 5, 10 and 25 centesimos. The tiny 2½ centesimo piece was nicknamed the Panama Pill. In 1907 it was replaced by a larger cupro-nickel coin. Balboa the explorer was portrayed on all the 1904 denominations and his image has remained

A statue of Vasco Nuñez de Balboa in Panama City. Balboa's name is used for the unit of currency.

on most coins of Panama to the present day. Panama's coat of arms has usually been used for designs on the back of coins.

Before 1930 Panama's coinage was not issued in large quantities and US coinage formed the chief circulating currency. The early coinage of Panama was all struck at the US mint at Philadelphia; since 1934 other overseas mints have been used, including the Royal Mint and the Franklin Mint (USA).

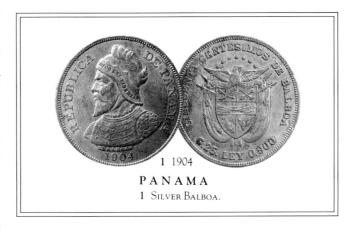

1 1904

PANAMA
1 SILVER BALBOA.

In 1930 a currency reform brought Panama's coinage into line with that of the United States. The new silver balboa exactly matched the US silver dollar, and new fractions ($\frac{1}{10}$, $\frac{1}{4}$ and $\frac{1}{2}$) equivalent to parallel US coins were also introduced. In 1935 the bronze 1 centesimo piece first appeared. Balboa was not portrayed on this coin; instead, it carried a representation of Urraca, the legendary Indian leader who led resistance against the Spaniards in Panama in the early sixteenth century.

PANAMA
BRONZE CENTESIMO, *depicting Urraca.*
2 1966

In the 1960s Panama's silver coins were replaced by pieces clad with silver or cupro-nickel. More recently, a wide variety of special large-denomination coins with commemorative designs has been issued. Notable among these coins, which are aimed at collectors, are the large gold pieces issued between 1975 and 1977, commemorating Balboa's discovery of the Pacific. For general-circulation purposes Panama, which has still not issued any national bank notes, remains heavily reliant on US currency.

THE CANAL ZONE

The Panama Canal Zone territory was leased in perpetuity to the United States in 1903, with the US dollar its official currency. By a treaty of 1977 the Canal Zone has now reverted to Panama, and the canal itself will become the property of Panama in the year 2000.

THE PALO SECO LEPER COLONY

This was established at Balboa in the Canal Zone in 1907. An issue of copper (1 cent), brass (5 cents) and aluminium (25 cents and 1 dollar) tokens was produced in 1919. In 1955 the tokens were officially destroyed and replaced by US currency.

COLOMBIA

FIRST COINS:	1620s
FIRST DECIMAL COINS:	1847
MAIN MINT:	Bogotá
CURRENCY:	peso

THE northern coast of Colombia was discovered by the Spanish in 1501–2 and further exploration soon followed. The first settlements were established on the northern coast at Santa Marta (1529) and Cartagena (1533), and in 1538, after the discovery and conquest of the interior by Gonzalo Jimenez de Quesada, Santa Fe de Bogotá was founded as the capital of the province of New Granada (Granada being the Spanish home of Quesada). New Granada became a viceroyalty in 1739.

The Spanish conquistadores first introduced coinage to the region and in the 1620s a mint for New Granada was established in Bogotá signing coins NR (Nuevo Reino). Cob coins were struck with the pillars of Hercules design (*see* Mexico). Both gold and silver were minted but the silver issues are rare. The royal bust design was introduced on the gold coinage of Bogotá in 1756 and on the silver coins from 1772. Output of silver coinage was mainly in denominations lower than the 8

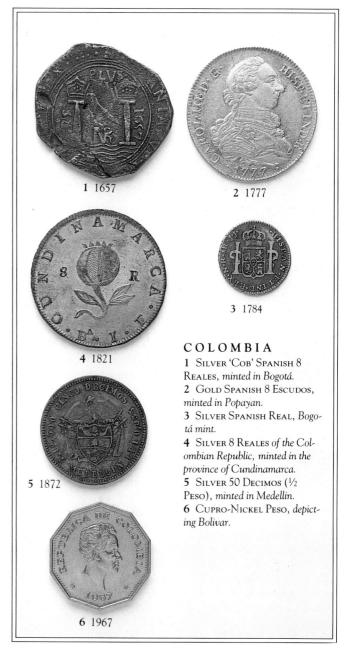

1 1657
2 1777
4 1821
3 1784
5 1872

COLOMBIA
1 SILVER 'COB' SPANISH 8 REALES, *minted in Bogotá.*
2 GOLD SPANISH 8 ESCUDOS, *minted in Popayan.*
3 SILVER SPANISH REAL, *Bogotá mint.*
4 SILVER 8 REALES *of the Colombian Republic, minted in the province of Cundinamarca.*
5 SILVER 50 DECIMOS (½ PESO), *minted in Medellin.*
6 CUPRO-NICKEL PESO, *depicting Bolivar.*

6 1967

reales. Meanwhile, in the south of Colombia another mint, authorized in 1729, was opened at Popayan, a gold-mining centre. The earliest known issue of Popayan is dated 1732. At first only gold coins were struck. All the gold issues of Popayan have the royal bust design and from the reign of Carlos III (1759–88) a full range of gold denominations was issued: ½, 1, 2, 4 and 8 escudos. Silver coinage at Popayan began with an 8 reales of 1769 with the pillars of Hercules design: all other issues had the royal bust design.

INDEPENDENCE

New Granada's struggle for independence from Spain began in 1811. The wars, which included Simon Bolivar's famous victory at the Battle

Simon Bolivar and Antonio José de Sucre, heroes of the independence movement, by an unknown artist. The names Bolivar and Sucre are used for coin denominations in Venezuela and Ecuador respectively.

of Boyacá (1819), continued until the early 1820s, when the Republic of Colombia was established (including Venezuela, Panama and Ecuador). Spanish colonial coins continued to be minted at Bogotá until 1820 and at Popayan until 1822. Royalist issues were also struck at Santa Marta between 1813 and 1820. Insurgents issued local coinage at Cartagena (1811–14) and Popayan (1813) and in the name of the Republic of Colombia and the state of Cundinamarca (1813–16 and 1820–2).

From 1822 to·1886 Colombia's coinage reflected the many constitutional changes of the developing republic. Coins were issued in the names of the Republic of Colombia (1822–37), Republic of New Granada (1837–59), Granadine Confederation (1859–62), United States of New Granada (1861–2) and United States of Colombia (1862–86). Until 1847 the old Spanish colonial coinage system of reales and escudos was retained. The principal change to the coinage was that the royal bust had been replaced by an idealized female bust personifying Colombia. All of Colombia's coinage in this period was minted at Bogotá and Popayan.

DECIMAL COINAGE

In 1847 a decimal coinage system was introduced, with a peso of 10 reales or decimos. The new system was similar to that of France, the silver peso being equivalent to the 5 franc piece. This coinage lasted until 1872. The smallest denominations, the copper $\frac{1}{2}$ decimo and decimo, were minted only in 1847 and 1848 and at Birmingham, England. All other coins – $\frac{1}{4}$ real to 10 reales in silver and the gold peso and its multiples – were struck at Bogotá and Popayan and from 1862 at a third mint at Medellin. The principal coin designs were the head of Colombia and the national arms.

In 1872 a new decimal system was introduced for the silver coinage with a peso of 100 centavos, and coins of $1\frac{1}{4}$ centavos (1874 only: cupro-nickel); $2\frac{1}{4}$ centavos (silver until 1881, then cupro-nickel); and 5, 10, 20 and 50 centavos (silver). The silver standard of these coins was lower than the earlier issues. The gold peso and multiples continued for a while to be struck as before. However, from the mid-

1880s the currency of Colombia suffered a severe decline in value. New issues of precious metal ceased. From 1907 to 1914 issues of paper-money coins (marked PM for *papel moneda*) were struck in cupro-nickel at 1, 2 and 5 pesos.

MODERN COINAGE

Since 1887 Colombia's coinage has again been issued in the name of the Republic of Colombia. Between 1911 and 1914 coinage standards were changed once more, with the new silver coins (10, 20 and 50 centavos) brought into line with US currency, and the gold 5 pesos matching the British pound. The head of Bolivar also began to appear as a coin design at this time, replacing the bust of Colombia.

Regular gold coinage was issued until 1930. The silver 10, 20 and 50 centavos survived until the 1950s (following a reduction of silver fineness in the 1940s), but they then became base-metal coins. The effects of modern inflation are clearly visible in the recent appearance of base-metal coins for the old gold denominations of 5, 10 and 20 pesos. Another recent feature of Colombia's coinage is the issuing of special commemorative coins in silver and especially gold, the most valuable of these so far being a 30,000 peso coin issued in 1980 for the 150th anniversary of the death of Bolivar.

COLOMBIA, VENEZUELA AND ECUADOR

VENEZUELA

FIRST COINS:	1802
FIRST DECIMAL COINS:	1843
MAIN MINTS:	Paris, Royal Mint, US mints
CURRENCY:	bolivar

THE coast of Venezuela was discovered by Christopher Columbus in 1498 and further explored in 1499–1500 by Alonso de Ojeda and Amerigo Vespucci. A Spanish settlement was founded in 1528 at

VENEZUELA
1 COPPER ¼ REAL, *issued from Caracas by royalists during the wars of independence.*
2 COPPER ¼ CENTAVO, *minted in Britain.*
3 GOLD 20 BOLIVARES.
4 COPPER-CLAD STEEL 5 CENTIMOS, *struck by the Royal Mint.*

1 1817   2 1843   3 1904   4 1977

Coro, and it became the base for Spanish and German exploration of the interior. In the colonial period the conquered areas of Venezuela were administered as part of the Spanish province (later viceroyalty) of New Granada. The future capital of Venezuela, Caracas, was founded in 1567.

Spanish coinage was the official and principal currency, but other foreign coins circulating in the Caribbean area also reached Venezuela. Another form of currency used by early European settlers was pearls. Venezuela had no mint for most of the period of Spanish rule, but in 1802 Caracas began issuing copper ⅛ and ¼ reales. During the wars of independence further issues of coinage were minted in Caracas by both the royalists and the insurgents, and between 1808 and 1813 coins were also issued by royalists in Maracaibo.

INDEPENDENCE

Venezuela played a significant part in the fight for independence from Spain, providing two of the key figures in the liberation movement, Simon Bolivar and Antonio José de Sucre. Venezuela's independence was achieved in 1821, after which the territory formed part of Greater Colombia until 1830. In this period most of the coinage circulating in Venezuela was colonial Spanish and Colombian, but in 1829 Caracas issued silver ¼ and ½ reales for Venezuela.

The first coins issued by Venezuela as an independent republic were copper centavos and fractions dated 1843. These coins were minted in Britain; similar issues followed in 1852 and 1858. Also in 1858 an issue of silver ½, 1, 2 and 5 reales was struck in Paris for Venezuela. The designs on the early coins of Venezuela show the national arms and a female head personifying Liberty.

MODERN COINAGE

In 1873 the first issues of a new coinage for Venezuela were produced. The new unit of currency was the venezolano, a silver coin equivalent to the French 5 franc piece (= 100 centavos). In 1879 another change introduced a new unit, the bolivar (= 100 centimos). The new 5 bolivar piece in silver matched the venezolano, and fractions were also issued in silver and cupro-nickel. Gold multiples of the venezolano and bolivar were struck from 1875, but they appeared only occasionally.

The designs for the coins introduced in the 1870s featured the portrait of Bolivar and Venezuela's national arms. This coinage has survived more or less intact to the present day, though gold coins intended for normal circulation have not been issued since 1930 and in the 1960s the silver bolivar and its surviving silver fractions and multiples were converted to nickel coins. The only coins now struck in precious metal are special commemorative pieces in high denominations, ranging from 10 to 75 bolivares in silver and 100 to 3000 bolivares in gold.

Between 1886 and 1889 a mint was operating in Caracas. Otherwise, all of the coinage issued by the Republic of Venezuela has been minted abroad, principally at the Paris and Philadelphia mints and in Britain.

ECUADOR

FIRST COINS:	1833
FIRST DECIMAL COINS:	1872
MAIN MINT:	Royal Mint
CURRENCY:	sucre

THE kingdom of Quito (modern Ecuador) was the most northerly province of the Inca Empire. It was first invaded by Spanish armies in 1532 and conquest was completed under Francisco Pizarro and his lieutenants by 1541. Ecuador was incorporated into the viceroyalty of Peru and later New Granada. It remained under Spanish rule until liberated by insurgent forces under Sucre in 1822 (*see* Venezuela). It was then a province of Greater Colombia until its withdrawal in 1830, officially becoming the Republic of Ecuador in 1835.

1 1841

2 1971

ECUADOR
1 GOLD 8 ESCUDOS.
2 NICKEL-CLAD STEEL SUCRE.

In the colonial period Spanish coinage was used in Ecuador, but none was minted locally. The first coining activity in Ecuador was the counterstamping of the letters M D Q (Moneda de Quito) on Colombian coins of about 1831. Then, in 1833, a mint opened at Quito, producing coins with the same designs as contemporary Colombian coins on the front but on the back a design for Ecuador of a sun between two mountains. Ecuador continued to issue reales and escudos according to the old colonial or Colombian coinage systems until the 1860s. Designs were copied from Colombian, Spanish and US coins, all of which circulated in Ecuador. A gold coin of Ecuador from this period is featured in Herman Melville's novel *Moby Dick* as the prize for the first seaman to sight the white whale that Captain Ahab is hunting.

MODERN COINAGE

In 1872 the coinage of Ecuador was changed to a decimal system. The new unit of currency was the sucre, named after the country's liberator, and this was divided into 100 centavos. Sucre's portrait has been the principal coin design, together with Ecuador's national arms, on most of the coins issued since 1872, but the portrait of another national hero, Jose Rocafuerte, appeared on 5 and 10 centavo coins in 1928 and 1929.

Since 1872 all of Ecuador's coinage has been minted abroad, mostly in Britain, the USA and Peru. None of the smallest base-metal coins ($\frac{1}{2}$, 1, 2 and $2\frac{1}{2}$ centavos) have been issued since 1928. The 5 centavos, 10 centavos (decimo), 20 and 50 centavos, 1 and 2 sucres were all silver coins at the beginning of this century; they are now base-metal coins. The most valuable coins issued by Ecuador have appeared only occasionally: 5 sucres (silver, 1943–4), 10 sucres (gold, 1899–1900) and 25 sucres or condor (gold, 1928).

The Galapagos Islands have been part of Ecuador since 1832. Some coins of Ecuador counterstamped with the initials RA late in the nineteenth century have been attributed to these islands.

PERU
1 GOLD SPANISH 8 ESCUDOS,
minted in Lima.

1588, with the arms of Spain on the front and a cross dividing castles and lions on the back.

The Lima mint was closed from 1589 to 1658 and again from 1660 to 1683. From 1658 to 1660 and after 1683 it struck cob silver coins with the pillars of Hercules design, and from 1696 gold cob coins also. The change to the royal bust design took place in 1751 on the gold coinage and in 1772 on the silver, the latter on the occasion of a change in metal fineness. For a brief period, 1698–9, a second mint operated at the city of Cuzco, formerly the Inca capital, producing gold Spanish colonial coins.

The remains of the Inca city of Machu Pichu, spectacularly sited high in the Andes. The conquest of the Inca Empire by the Spanish led to the introduction of coinage in western South America.

PERU

FIRST COINS:	1568
FIRST DECIMAL COINS:	1858
MAIN MINT:	Lima
CURRENCY:	inti

PERU was first explored by Spaniards based in Panama in the 1520s, and in 1532–3 the Inca Empire of Peru fell to conquistadores led by Francisco Pizarro. The city of Lima was founded in 1535 and became the capital of the viceroyalty of Peru, which until the eighteenth century administered all of Spanish South America from Panama to Argentina.

The Spanish were attracted to Peru by rumours of great riches in the Inca Empire and by the 1540s they were already exploiting the country's rich silver mines. In 1565 King Philip II authorized the setting up of a mint at Lima to produce Spanish silver coinage for the viceroyalty. The first coins, bearing the pillars of Hercules design, were minted between 1568 and 1570. Further silver issues followed until

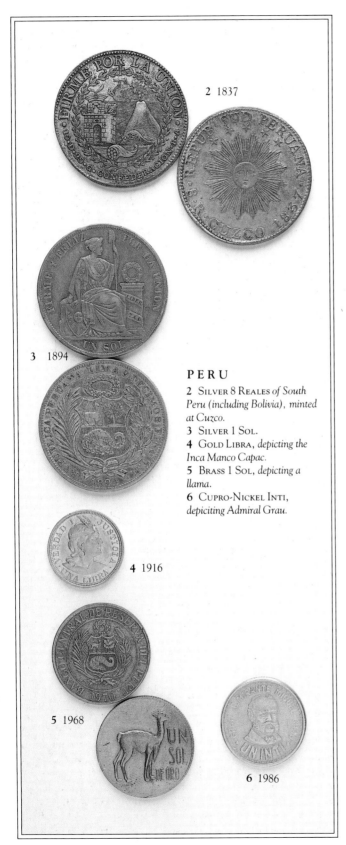

PERU

2 SILVER 8 REALES *of South Peru (including Bolivia), minted at Cuzco.*
3 SILVER 1 SOL.
4 GOLD LIBRA, *depicting the Inca Manco Capac.*
5 BRASS 1 SOL, *depicting a llama.*
6 CUPRO-NICKEL INTI, *depiciting Admiral Grau.*

INDEPENDENCE

During the struggle for independence from Spain, Peru was invaded by insurgent forces from two directions. In 1821 the Argentinian general José San Martin arrived from the south and liberated Lima, and in the following year Bolivar arrived, from the north. Fighting continued until 1824, when Bolivar's forces, led by Antonio José de Sucre, defeated the royalists at the Battle of Ayacucho. The mint of Lima changed hands several times during the wars, and production of coinage alternated between Spanish and republican issues. The royalists also counterstamped republican coins, and in 1824, when they had to abandon the Lima mint, they issued gold and silver coins from Cuzco.

From 1826 the Republic of Peru produced regular issues of coinage from both of the existing mints, Lima and Cuzco. The coinage system of silver reales and gold escudos was the same as in the colonial period, but inscriptions on the coins were now in Spanish, rather than Latin, and the coin designs reflected the country's independence, with Peru's national arms and the figure of Liberty prominent. From 1835 to 1839 Peru was divided into two regional republics and coinage production was organized accordingly, with the Lima mint issuing coins for North Peru and mints at Cuzco and Arequipo producing coins for South Peru (in confederation with Bolivia).

DECIMAL COINAGE

From 1858 a new coinage was issued which attempted to combine the old monetary system with a decimal system. This transitional coinage, with a silver real of $12\frac{1}{2}$ centimos and denominations ranging from $\frac{1}{2}$ real to 8 escudos, lasted only until 1861.

The conversion to a full decimal system, based on that of France, was made in 1863 with the establishment of a new unit of currency, the sol, divided into 10 dineros and 100 centavos, and exactly matching the 5 franc piece. Silver and base-metal fractions were also issued and gold multiples at 5, 10 and 20 soles, though these appeared only in 1863. The silver sol was issued in large quantities for a few decades and it became a familiar coin throughout the Americas and also in the Far East.

Between 1879 and 1883 Peru, Bolivia and Chile fought the War of the Pacific for control of the valuable Atacama Desert nitrate deposits. During these years a 'provisional' coinage was issued with different designs and new denominations of 5, 10 and 20 centavos in cupronickel and 1 and 5 pesetas (= 1 sol) in silver. Another mint, at Ayacucho, was temporarily opened.

MODERN COINAGE

Falling silver prices disrupted the coinage of Peru in the late nineteenth century. Production of the sol and its fractions in silver declined steadily from the 1890s and ceased altogether at the time of the First World War. When regular production of the $\frac{1}{2}$ and 1 sol was resumed in the 1920s their silver content was at first reduced to 50 per cent and later, from the 1930s, they became base-metal (brass) coins.

In 1898 regular production of gold coinage began again, with new denominations of $\frac{1}{5}$, $\frac{1}{2}$ and 1 libra, exactly matching the British sovereign. These coins, which were minted for the international gold trade, were issued fairly regularly until 1969. Their designs have Peru's national arms on the front and the bust of an Inca chief on the back. Gold 5, 10, 20, 50 and 100 sol coins have also been issued this century, mainly in the 1950s and 1960s, and more recently gold and silver

PERU, BOLIVIA AND CHILE PRE-1900

The Potosí silver mountain with mills for processing ore. The silver mountain, 15,381 feet high and covered with mineshafts, is believed to have produced £163 million worth of silver between 1545 and 1800.

commemorative coins in denominations as high as 100,000 soles have appeared. However, most of Peru's modern coinage has been issued in base-metal, and the decline in value of the currency is clearly shown by coins such as the 100 soles: a gold piece until 1970, it appeared as a silver commemorative coin in 1973, and then in the early 1980s returned as a brass currency coin.

Peru's latest coinage reform took place in 1985, with the introduction of a new unit of currency, the inti, a cupro-nickel coin divided into 100 centimos, with brass coins of 1, 5, 10, 20 and 50 centimos so far issued. All of these new coins carry the portrait of the Peruvian national hero Admiral Grau.

Most of Peru's modern coinage has been minted at Lima, though foreign mints, notably Philadelphia and San Francisco in the USA, have also been used. The Lima mint marked its 400th anniversary in 1965 by producing coins in various denominations with a design on the back imitating the pillars of Hercules design on its earliest coins.

BOLIVIA

FIRST COINS:	1574
FIRST DECIMAL COINS:	1864
MAIN MINT:	La Paz
CURRENCY:	peso boliviano

THE Spanish conquistadores, who gained control of Bolivia following their conquest of the Inca Empire in the 1530s, first brought coinage to the region. Known as Upper Peru, Bolivia was administered as part of the viceroyalty of Peru until 1776, after which it formed part of the new viceroyalty of the River Plate.

The Potosí silver mines were discovered in 1545 and were soon yielding unprecedented riches. The city of Potosí, which was founded in 1546, quickly grew into a major colonial centre, and the mint which began operating there in 1574 struck Spanish colonial coinage (*see* Mexico) for the next 250 years. For most of this period only silver coins were minted. From 1574 to 1773 cob silver coins were produced, at first with designs of the Spanish royal arms on the front and a cross with castles and lions on the back, and later (from 1651) with the pillars of Hercules design. From 1767 coins of finer workmanship were also produced, and in 1772 the royal bust design was introduced. Gold issues were not produced at Potosí until 1778, after which they appeared regularly.

INDEPENDENCE

The wars of independence in Bolivia lasted from 1809 to 1825, during which time there were invasions by liberating armies from Argentina and from Peru, as well as numerous uprisings within the country. From 1813 to 1815 the Potosí mint struck coins for the United Provinces of the River Plate (*see* Argentina), but following its recapture by royalist forces it resumed striking Spanish issues. When independence from Spain was finally secured in 1825, the new country was named after its liberator, Simon Bolivar, and the constitutional capital was named after his chief lieutenant, Sucre, who became first president.

Coinage was issued in the name of Bolivia from 1827. The old colonial monetary system of reales (named soles or sueldos in Bolivia) and escudos (scudos) was retained. The arms of Bolivia, featuring a tree flanked by llamas, and the portrait of Bolivar were the standard coin designs. Potosí continued to be the national mint, though in the 1850s coins were also minted at La Paz, and later in the century foreign mints were used (Birmingham and Paris). General Mariano Melgarejo, who ruled Bolivia from 1865 to 1871, issued a debased silver coinage. Melgarejo's coins, which carry his portrait, are dated 1865 and 1868. Two other Bolivian dictators who also made brief appearances on the coinage were Manuel Belzu (1848–55) and Hilarion Daza (1876–80).

DECIMAL COINAGE

In 1859 a new silver coin, the peso, replaced the 8 sueldos. Then, in 1864, the monetary system was completely changed, with the introduction of a new unit of currency, the boliviano = 100 centesimos (later centavos). When the next issue of gold currency was struck, in 1868, this conformed to the new standards of fineness introduced with the 1864 reform, but the old denominations of scudos were retained.

No gold coinage for circulation has been issued in the name of Bolivia since 1868. The silver boliviano was issued only until 1893; the silver 20 and 50 centavos were issued until 1909; and the smaller fractions were all base-metal coins by 1883. The only coins struck from 1909 until the 1940s were cupro-nickel 5, 10, 20 and 50 centavos, while British, US and Peruvian currency were all legal tender. When the boliviano returned in 1951, it was a small bronze coin accompanied by bronze multiples of 5 and 10 bolivianos. The fractions of the boliviano were no longer worth issuing.

MODERN COINAGE

In 1965 another new unit of currency was introduced: the peso boliviano = 100 centavos. Denominations of 5 and 10 centavos (copper-clad steel), 20, 25 and 50 centavos (nickel-clad steel) and 1

and 5 pesos bolivianos (nickel-clad steel) have since been issued. The modern circulating currency continues to feature the Bolivian arms as its main design, and the back simply identifies the denomination. Special commemorative issues of high-denomination coins have also appeared recently; they were introduced in 1975 for Bolivia's 150th anniversary (silver 100, 250 and 500 pesos bolivianos), and in 1979 for the International Year of the Child (silver 200 and gold 4000 pesos bolivianos).

CHILE

FIRST COINS:	1749
FIRST DECIMAL COINS:	1851
MAIN MINT:	Santiago
CURRENCY:	peso

NORTHERN Chile, which was part of the Inca Empire when the Spanish conquistadores arrived, was first explored in 1535–6 by a Spanish army led by Diego de Almagro. The conquest of the region by the Spanish was completed by Pedro de Valdivia, a lieutenant of Francisco Pizarro, who founded the city of Santiago in 1541. The native Araucanian Indians, however, continued to fight the invaders, and Valdivia himself was killed by them in 1553. Once the Spanish colony was properly established, it was administered from the viceroyalty of Peru until 1776, after which it became part of the new viceroyalty of the River Plate.

The Spanish conquistadores and early settlers of the sixteenth century brought the first coins to Chile. Because of a shortage of coined money in the isolated province, the colonists also used gold dust and gold and silver bits as currency. Following repeated appeals to the colonial government, in 1743 a private contractor was finally granted permission to establish a mint at Santiago. Regular minting of coins began in 1749, with production of gold 4 and 8 escudos bearing the bust of Fernando VI. Silver coinage was first produced in 1751, with an issue of 8 reales bearing the pillars of Hercules design. The full range of silver denominations (see Mexico) was later issued and from 1773 the royal bust design was used for all coins.

INDEPENDENCE

The wars of independence lasted from 1810 until 1818, when the liberating forces, led by the Argentinian San Martin and Bernardo O'Higgins, finally defeated the royalists at the Battle of Maipu. Spanish coinage continued to be struck until 1817, when the republicans took control of the mint and started to issue their own coins. At first the colonial denomination system of reales and escudos was retained, but the coins were now decorated with designs symbolic of the newly independent republic.

In 1833 the volume of official currency in circulation was increased by the counterstamping of Argentinian 4 and 8 reales. The counterstamps have the arms of Chile and the abbreviated name of the place of stamping: Chiloe, Concepción, Santiago, Serena, Valdivia or Valparaiso.

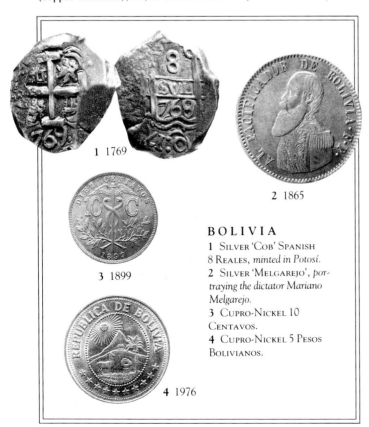

1 1769

2 1865

3 1899

BOLIVIA
1 Silver 'Cob' Spanish 8 Reales, *minted in Potosí.*
2 Silver 'Melgarejo', *portraying the dictator Mariano Melgarejo.*
3 Cupro-Nickel 10 Centavos.
4 Cupro-Nickel 5 Pesos Bolivianos.

4 1976

COLONIAL SOUTH AMERICA, 1776

CARIBBEAN SEA

Caracas

• Bogotá

Vice-royalty of New Granada

Guiana

• Popayán

○ Quito

Brazil (Portuguese)

Recife ○

Vice-royalty of Peru

• Lima
Cuzco

○ Bahia

• Potosí

Vice-royalty of River Plate

Rio de Janeiro ○

PACIFIC OCEAN

○ Asunción

Santiago •

○ Montevideo

Buenos Aires •

ATLANTIC OCEAN

PACIFIC OCEAN

ANTARCTIC OCEAN

• Spanish colonial mints

0 Kilometres 1500
0 Miles 1000

CARIBBEAN SEA

ATLANTIC OCEAN

VENEZUELA (1843)

GUYANA (1967)

SURINAM (1976)

FRENCH GUIANA

COLOMBIA (1813)

ECUADOR (1832)

BRAZIL (independent 1822, republic 1885)

PERU (1826)

BOLIVIA (1827)

PARAGUAY (1845)

PACIFIC OCEAN

CHILE (1817)

ARGENTINA (1813)

URUGUAY (1840)

ATLANTIC OCEAN

0 Kilometres 1500
0 Miles 1000

FIRST NATIONAL OR REPUBLICAN COINAGES

DECIMAL COINAGE

In 1851 the old coinage system was replaced by a decimal system, with a new unit of currency: 1 peso = 100 centavos. Denominations issued at first were the copper ½ and 1 centavo, the silver medio-decimo and decimo (10 centavos), the silver 20 and 50 centavos and 1 peso, and the gold 5 and 10 pesos. Other denominations were issued later in the century, including the 2 and 2½, 20 and 40 centavos and the gold 20 pesos. The designs on the decimal coins kept the same themes as the earlier republican issues.

In the later nineteenth century inflation and falling silver prices undermined the value of many national coinages, including that of Chile. The silver coinage was debased and reduced in size and the gold coinage was also changed in weight and fineness, equating it to the British pound.

MODERN COINAGE

In the present century the value of Chile's currency has continued to decline. The smallest denominations disappeared in the first two decades and the small silver pieces of 5, 10 and 20 centavos had their silver content reduced and then, in 1920, they were converted to cupro-nickel coins. In 1933 the peso also became a cupro-nickel coin. Gold coins for the international gold trade have been struck for most of

CHILE
1 GOLD 10 PESOS.
2 SILVER PESO (50% fine).
3 ALUMINIUM-BRONZE PESO, portraying Bernardo O'Higgins.

1 1872

2 1927

3 1979

this century and in 1926 new 50 and 100 peso gold coins, also known as 5 and 10 condores respectively, were introduced and were subsequently minted quite regularly until 1963.

In 1942 new coins of 20 and 50 centavos and 1 peso were introduced, all minted in copper and carrying the portrait of Bernardo O'Higgins for their main design. In the 1950s the 20 and 50 centavos disappeared and the peso, together with its new multiples of 5 and 10 pesos, was minted in aluminium.

In recent years there have been further changes to the coinage as inflation has caused revaluations and the introduction of new coins, such as the escudo and its multiples, minted between 1971 and 1975. The most recent revaluation introduced a new peso in 1975 (= 1000 escudos), divided into 100 centavos. By 1980 denominations of the new currency up to 50 centavos were no longer being issued; by the late 1980s only the peso and its multiples were minted as regular currency, all in base-metal. Occasional issues of high-value gold and silver commemorative coins have also been produced in recent years for collectors and for the bullion trade.

PARAGUAY

FIRST COINS:	1845
FIRST DECIMAL COINS:	1870
MAIN MINTS:	Royal Mint, Le Locle, Switzerland
CURRENCY:	guarani

COINAGE first arrived in Paraguay with the Spanish explorers of the sixteenth century. Sebastian Cabot arrived in 1527, sailing up from the River Plate estuary following reports of a rich inland country, and soon afterwards the settlement of Asunción was founded. The Spanish found a country rich in agricultural land, but not in minerals. The legendary silver and gold came from further west and north in Bolivia and Peru, and during the long period of Spanish rule most of the coinage circulating in Paraguay would have been minted at Potosí.

INDEPENDENCE
Independence was declared in 1811, but the first Paraguayan coinage was not struck until 1845, when bronze $\frac{1}{12}$ real coins, minted in Britain and in Asunción, were issued. Various trial pieces were struck in the 1850s and 1860s, including some gold 4 peso coins dated 1867, but the next regular currency issue did not appear until 1870. Consisting of copper 1, 2 and 4 centesimo pieces, it was mostly struck in Birmingham, England, though some 4 centesimo pieces of a recognizably cruder style were minted in Asunción.

It is clear that for most of the nineteenth century Paraguay relied heavily on coinage imported from neighbouring countries, and during the war of 1864–70 against the Triple Alliance of Brazil, Argentina and Uruguay, there was frequent countermarking of Spanish-American and Bolivian currency. Indeed, the 1870 copper issue was made to match Uruguayan coinage, and Paraguay's next issue, of silver peso pieces dated 1889, was based on Argentinian currency and minted in Buenos Aires.

1 1845
2 1870

The designs which were chosen for Paraguay's early coins include images derived from the country's coat of arms: the star in sunburst, the lion and the cap of liberty. The motto 'Peace and Justice' also features prominently.

Between 1900 and 1939 only base-metal coinage was issued in Paraguay. The decline in value of the coinage can be seen most clearly by comparing the small peso of 1925 (cupro-nickel) and 1938 (aluminium) with the large silver peso of 1889. Output remained sporadic and the coin designs stayed essentially the same.

MODERN COINAGE
In 1944 Paraguay issued a new coinage. The initial issue was restricted to base-metal, low-value coins, but it included a wider range of denominations than before: 1, 5, 10, 25 and 50 centimos. Further issues of these coins followed, but there have been none since 1953. The new large denomination, the guarani, did not appear in the form of a coin until more recently. In 1974 an issue of 1, 5, 10 and 50 guaranies, all minted in stainless steel, was produced. These coins had been preceded by a special issue of silver and gold 300 and 10,000 guaranies minted in 1968 to commemorate General Alfredo Stroessner's re-election as president.

URUGUAY

FIRST COINS:	1840
FIRST DECIMAL COINS:	1840
MAIN MINTS:	Santiago, Royal Mint
CURRENCY:	peso

JUAN Diaz de Solis, leading a Spanish expedition in 1515, is credited with being the first European to discover Uruguay and Argentina, though Portuguese ships had probably explored the River Plate earlier. Solis was killed by Charrua Indians when he set foot on the Uruguayan shore and it was a long time before permanent settlements were established, and therefore before coinage arrived, in Uruguay. The territory was disputed later between the Portuguese and the Spanish, who established Montevideo in 1726.

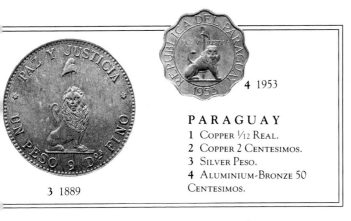

centesimos) was minted, displaying the coat of arms of Uruguay and commemorating the siege of Montevideo (1842–51).

Since 1857 all Uruguayan coins have been minted outside the country, at first in France, later at mints in Europe and the Americas, especially at Santiago in Chile. The 1857 issue had the same copper denominations and designs as the earlier issues. In 1869 the peso was revalued at 100 centesimos, and new bronze denominations of 1, 2 and 4 centesimos were introduced, again with similar designs.

Silver coins were issued again in 1877, in denominations of 10, 20 and 50 centesimos and 1 peso. Their designs were all similar, based on the *peso fuerte* of 1844, with the arms of Uruguay on the front and the denomination on the back.

MODERN COINAGE

Cupro-nickel coins first appeared in Uruguay in 1901. They were 1 and 5 centesimos, minted in Berlin; later issues were struck at other European mints. Designs continued unchanged until 1916 when the portrait of Artigas was introduced on the back of the silver 50 centesimos and, in 1917, on the peso. Artigas has since appeared on various denominations of Uruguayan coinage.

More new designs were introduced in 1930 to commemorate the centenary of the Uruguayan republic. Aluminium–bronze 10 centesimos depicted a puma against a sunrise, silver 20 centesimos had a seated figure symbolizing the republic on the front and a sheaf of cornstalks displayed in the shape of a sunrise within a laurel wreath. These coins were minted in Paris and the designs have an art deco style typical of French coins of the period.

Since the Second World War the coinage of Uruguay has changed dramatically. Economic difficulties, severe inflation and consequent devaluations caused the peso to decline from being a silver coin weighing 25 g in 1917 to an aluminium–bronze piece of only 2 g in 1969. By the early 1970s the peso was virtually worthless and completely inadequate as a measure of value, and in 1975 the new peso was introduced, worth 1000 old pesos. The new coins have some designs based on the arms of Uruguay and others derived from earlier coin designs.

Recently there has also been a proliferation of high-denomination commemorative issues, displaying a variety of topical designs covering such subjects as the World Fisheries Conference and the 25th Meeting of InterAmerican Bank Governors, both in 1984, and the visit of the Spanish king and queen in 1983.

PARAGUAY
1 Copper ¹⁄₁₂ Real.
2 Copper 2 Centesimos.
3 Silver Peso.
4 Aluminium-Bronze 50 Centesimos.

In 1811 the Uruguayans, led by Jose Gervasio Artigas, began their fight for independence. The wars included a period of annexation by Brazil, after which Uruguay joined the United Provinces of the River Plate, but eventually, following a declaration of independence in 1825, Uruguay was accepted as a free and independent state. Various foreign coinages, particularly imperial Spanish, circulated in Uruguay before and during the wars of independence.

INDEPENDENCE

In 1830 Uruguay was formally made a republic, which it remains to this day, though political turmoil, including civil and foreign wars, continued for much of the nineteenth century. From 1831 to 1840 the coinage of the United Provinces of the River Plate was the only legally authorized currency; then in 1840 Uruguay began to strike its own coins. The first issue, dated 1840, was produced by a private contractor in Montevideo. It consisted of copper 5 and 20 centesimo pieces, both with a design featuring the radiate sunface similar to that on the United Provinces and later Argentinian coinage. In 1844–5 and 1854–5 government mints operated in Montevideo, issuing 5, 20 and 40 centesimo copper pieces with designs similar to the 1840 issue. In addition, in 1844, a silver peso (*peso fuerte*) (valued at 8 reales = 800

URUGUAY
1 Silver 'Peso Fuerte', *with an inscription on the back meaning 'siege of Montevideo'.*
2 Copper Centesimo, *minted in Birmingham.*
3 Aluminium-Bronze New Peso, *portraying José Gervasio Artigas.*

ARGENTINA

FIRST COINS:	1813
FIRST DECIMAL COINS:	1881
MAIN MINT:	Buenos Aires
CURRENCY:	peso

THE first Spaniard to explore the River Plate estuary was Juan Diaz de Solis, in 1515. Other Spanish expeditions followed, and attempts were made to establish settlements in Argentina, at Rosario

ARGENTINA

1 Silver 8 Reales of the United Provinces of the River Plate, minted in Bogotá.
2 Silver 2 Reales of Rioja.
3 Silver 2 Reales of Rioja, portraying Juan Manuel de Rosas.
4 Copper 4 Centavos of the Argentine Confederation.
5 Gold 5 Pesos, depicting the head of Liberty.
6 Cupro-Nickel 25 Pesos.
7 Aluminium-Bronze 50 Pesos, with the portrait of José San Martin.

1 1815
2 1821
4 1854
7 1978
3 1842
5 1896
6 1966

(1527) and Buenos Aires (1535). Both failed, but later in the century colonists advancing from the opposite direction, overland from Bolivia and Paraguay, established permanent settlements and began developing the land's rich agricultural potential. At first the Argentinian colonies were administered from the viceroyalty of Peru, but in 1776 the viceroyalty of the River Plate was formed, with the seat of government in Buenos Aires.

The Spanish explorers and colonists brought the first coins to Argentina, but the province was never furnished with its own mint for producing Spanish colonial coinage (*see* Mexico). Foreign coins arrived in Argentina via illicit trade conducted through Buenos Aires and other ports in the River Plate estuary, and long after independence they continued to circulate in Argentina.

INDEPENDENCE

The independence movement in Argentina became active after the people of Buenos Aires successfully repelled British invasions in 1806 and 1807. In 1810 the Spanish viceroy was forced to resign and Buenos Aires came under the rule of a junta of Argentinian patriots. The struggle for independence was then carried to other parts of South America, notably to Bolivia and Chile, by armies led by Argentinian generals such as Manuel Belgrano and José San Martin. The first coins for the new republic, under the name 'Provinces of the River Plate', were struck at Potosí between 1813 and 1815.

In 1816 the United Provinces of the River Plate, consisting of most of modern Argentina, Paraguay and Uruguay, formally declared their independence from Spain. There followed years of political strife, during which the countries of Paraguay and Uruguay were formed and Argentina evolved as a confederation whose separate provinces retained a degree of self-government.

The early coinage of Argentina shows a clear lack of central organization. Republican issues with designs of a sunface and the arms of Argentina were produced at Potosí in 1813–15 and in the province of Rioja in the 1820s and 1830s, and a single issue of copper coins was minted in the name of the Argentine confederation in 1854. In addition, imitations of old-fashioned Spanish colonial cob coins were

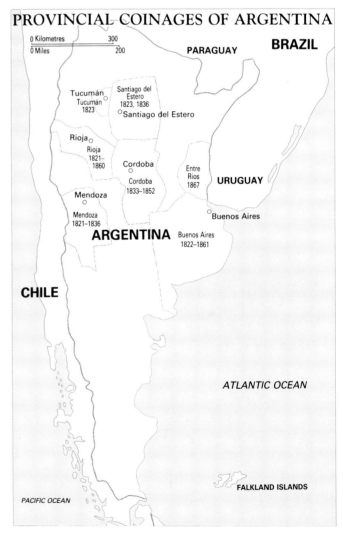

PROVINCIAL COINAGES OF ARGENTINA

0 Kilometres 300
0 Miles 200

PARAGUAY
BRAZIL
Tucumán
Tucumán
1823
Santiago del Estero
1823, 1836
Santiago del Estero
Rioja
Rioja
1821–1860
Cordoba
Cordoba
1833–1852
Entre Rios
1867
URUGUAY
Mendoza
Mendoza
1821–1836
Buenos Aires
ARGENTINA
Buenos Aires
1822–1861
CHILE
ATLANTIC OCEAN
FALKLAND ISLANDS
PACIFIC OCEAN

issued in Rioja, Mendoza and Tucuman between 1821 and 1824, and later several provinces, including Buenos Aires, Cordoba and Rioja, produced issues in their own names and with different designs. The first coins of Buenos Aires, copper pieces in a decimal system of small change, were minted in Birmingham (England) in 1822–3. The issues of Rioja include a series struck between 1836 and 1845 with designs and inscriptions celebrating the dictator Juan Manuel de Rosas.

In 1862 the provinces of Argentina were united in a republic, but a new coinage was not introduced until 1881. The system was decimal, with a peso of 100 centavos and an argentino of 5 pesos. The standards of the Latin Monetary Union (see France) were followed, and the original denominations were bronze 1 and 2 centavos, silver 10, 20 and 50 centavos and 1 peso, and gold ½ and 1 argentino. Designs were dominated by the arms of Argentina and the head of Liberty. In 1896 the cupro-nickel 5, 10 and 20 centavos were introduced and the small bronze pieces and the larger silver and gold coins were discontinued.

MODERN COINAGE

Since 1896 no regular currency coinage in gold or silver has been issued in Argentina, and there have been many changes in the size and metal of the base-metal issues. Nickel-clad steel, aluminium and various aluminium–bronze alloys have been used, and the denominations have risen as the peso has fallen in value.

Coin designs altered little at first, the only significant changes being the introduction of the portrait of San Martin in 1950 and the reintroduction in the 1960s of the sunface, copying Argentina's first independent coinage, to mark the 150th anniversary of the earlier coins.

Since the 1960s severe inflation has necessitated drastic revaluations of the currency. A monetary reform in 1970 introduced a new peso (= 100 old pesos), and in 1983 the peso argentino arrived (= 10,000 pesos). Coin designs have become more varied and topical, celebrating current events, notably the 1978 soccer World Cup held in Argentina, and anniversaries of historical events, such as the bicentenary of San Martin's birth (1978) and the centenary of the conquest of Patagonia (1979). Special silver commemorative coins were also issued for the World Cup.

FALKLAND ISLANDS

FIRST COINS:	1974
FIRST DECIMAL COINS:	1974
MAIN MINT:	Royal Mint
CURRENCY:	pound sterling

JOHN Davis, an English sea captain, is believed to have discovered the Falkland Islands in 1592. The first colonists did not arrive, however, until the 1760s, when both the French and British

attempted to establish settlements. In 1767 the French claim was ceded to Spain and later inherited by the Argentinians, who first attempted a settlement in 1829, when the islands once more had become uninhabited. The present colony was established by Britain in 1833. At first it was administered by the navy; then in 1842 the Falklands became a British crown colony.

British currency has been used in the Falklands since 1833. In 1974 a coinage was introduced specifically for the Falkland Islands. The first issue was announced by a set of commemorative gold coins, consisting of ½ sovereign, sovereign, 2 and 5 pounds, with the bust of Queen Elizabeth II on the front and a merino sheep on the back. The regular currency coins issued since 1974 include the same denominations as the United Kingdom, ranging from ½ penny to 50 pence. Various local animals are depicted on the backs of these coins, with the royal bust always on the front. In addition, special commemorative coins have also been issued. These include a special issue of 50 pence pieces in cupro-nickel, silver and gold commemorating the liberation of the Falklands from the Argentinian forces which briefly occupied the islands from April to June 1982.

FALKLAND ISLANDS
CUPRO-NICKEL 10 PENCE.

1974

BRAZIL

FIRST COINS:	1645
FIRST DECIMAL COINS:	1942
MAIN MINT:	Rio de Janeiro
CURRENCY:	cruzeiro

IN 1500 the lands that later became known as Brazil were claimed for Portugal by Pedro Alvares Cabral, whose fleet sighted the eastern tip of the South American mainland while sailing the Atlantic en route for India. In the following year an expedition piloted by Amerigo Vespucci made a detailed exploration of the Brazilian coastline, but organized colonization by the Portuguese did not begin until the 1530s, when land grants were made and the first cities were founded.

The first coins to arrive in Brazil were Portuguese issues brought by early settlers. Spanish coins also circulated. The first 'coins' to be made in Brazil were Spanish silver pieces counterstamped in 1643 with Portuguese denomination marks: 60, 120, 240 and 480 reis on 1, 2, 4 and 8 reales respectively. Later that century there was more counterstamping of Spanish and Portuguese silver and gold coins.

The Portuguese were not the only settlers in Brazil in the seventeenth century. In 1630 the Dutch West India Company established a colony in Pernambuco in the north east, based at the city of Recife. It fell to the Portuguese when Recife was recaptured in 1654. During their occupation the Dutch issued square coins in gold (3, 6 and 12 guilders), dated 1645–6, and in silver (10, 20, 30 and 40 stuivers) dated 1654.

In 1693 gold was discovered in the Minas Gerais region, and, once its mineral wealth began to be exploited, Brazil rapidly became a major producer of coinage. Regular minting of gold and silver Portuguese coins began in 1695 at Bahia, then the capital city of the colony. In 1699 Rio de Janeiro began to mint coins and from 1700 the mint operated for a short period at Pernambuco. For the remainder of the colonial period (until 1828) the principal mint in Brazil for production of gold and silver coinage was Rio, supported by Bahia, and from 1724 to 1734 gold coinage was also minted in Minas Gerais.

The gold coinage of colonial Brazil was issued in large quantities and it circulated widely in the Americas as well as in Portugal and in other Portuguese territories overseas. Two parallel series were produced, the national and the colonial, both of which could be equated to the Spanish monetary system. The national gold coinage, with denominations from 400 reis to 12,800 reis, bore the portrait of the

ruling Portuguese monarch on the front and the arms of Portugal on the back. The 12,800 reis coin or dobra (= Spanish 8 escudos) was popularly known as the 'Johannes' or 'Joe', after King Joao V (1707–50). The colonial coinage, minted at 1, 2, 4, 10 and 20 thousand reis, had the Portuguese arms on the front and a cross of Jerusalem on the back. The silver coinage of colonial Brazil also consisted of two separate series. The regular coinage had the Portuguese arms on the front and on the back a globe, representing the Portuguese overseas empire, imposed on the cross of Jerusalem. Denominations ranged from the 20 to 640 reis piece. A separate series issued for Minas Gerais from 1752 to 1774 had a crossed J on the front and was issued in denominations of 75, 150, 300 and 600 reis.

The earliest copper coinage of colonial Brazil was minted in Portugal between 1693 and 1729. Minas Gerais was supplied with a separate issue dated 1722. The design was usually a crown and denomination mark (5, 10, 20 and 40 reis) on the front and the crossed globe on the back. From 1729 the Brazilian mints issued copper coins, but mints in Portugal also continued to supply colonial coppers, some of which were intended for circulation in other colonies as well.

INDEPENDENCE

In 1807, as Napoleon advanced on Portugal, the prince regent, later Joao VI, moved his court to Brazil, and in 1815 Brazil was declared part

BRAZIL

1 GOLD 12 GUILDERS *of the Dutch colony of Pernambuco.*
2 GOLD 'JOHANNES' or 'JOE', (12,800 REIS) *of Portuguese Brazil, minted in Preto-Minas.*
3 GOLD 2,000 REIS, *minted in Bahia.*

4 SILVER 960 REIS *of Portuguese Brazil, minted in Rio de Janeiro.*
5 COPPER 80 REIS, *counterstamped for revaluation in Maranhao, 1834.*
6 GOLD 6,400 REIS *of Pedro II.*
7 SILVER 200 REIS *of Pedro II.*
8 GOLD 10,000 REIS.
9 SILVER 4,000 REIS, *commemorating the 400th anniversary of Cabral's discovery of Brazil.*
10 STAINLESS STEEL 20 CENTAVOS.

1 1646
2 1731
3 1723
4 1810
5 1825
6 1832
7 1868
8 1899
9 1900
10 1975

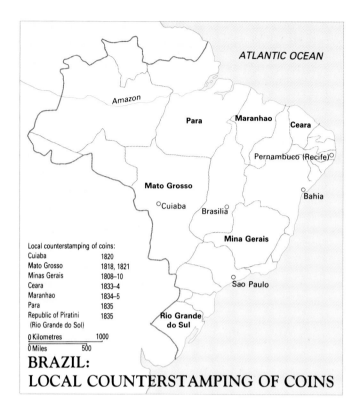

Local counterstamping of coins:
Cuiaba	1820
Mato Grosso	1818, 1821
Minas Gerais	1808–10
Ceara	1833–4
Maranhao	1834–5
Para	1835
Republic of Piratini (Rio Grande do Sol)	1835

0 Kilometres 1000
0 Miles 500

BRAZIL: LOCAL COUNTERSTAMPING OF COINS

federal republic, at first called the United States of Brazil, but since 1969 simply Brazil. After 1889 the only immediate changes to the coinage were in design, for example, female heads representing Liberty and Brazil were used instead of the royal portrait. In 1900 a special issue of coins was struck, including a huge 4000 reis silver piece, with designs commemorating the 400th anniversary of Cabral's discovery of Brazil. Further changes in design followed between 1922 and 1942, with various national figures and events commemorated on coins from the cupro-nickel 100 reis to the silver 5000 reis.

The effects of inflation can be seen clearly on the Brazilian coinage from the beginning of the twentieth century. Between 1889 and 1942 the lower-denomination base-metal coins from 20 to 200 reis declined in size and changed in metallic composition before disappearing altogether, and the standard silver coins of 400, 500, 1000 and 2000 reis were converted to base-metal pieces of cupro-nickel or aluminium–bronze. Gold 10,000 and 20,000 reis coins were issued regularly until 1922, since when no Brazilian gold coins have been produced as normal currency. An interesting feature of the early 1930s was another spate of counterstamping of circulating silver coinage, which took place during the revolution that brought President Getulio Vargas to power.

MODERN COINAGE

In 1942 a major coinage reform introduced a decimal system with a new unit of currency: 1 cruzeiro = 100 centavos. Denominations at first consisted of 10, 20 and 50 centavos minted in cupro-nickel and 1, 2 and 5 cruzeiros in aluminium–bronze. Inflation later led to the introduction of higher-denomination coins of 10, 20 and 50 cruzeiros.

Continuing inflation caused a coinage revaluation in 1967. A new cruzeiro was introduced, valued at 1000 old cruzeiros. Denominations issued since 1967 include 1, 2, 5, 10, 20 and 50 centavos and 1, 5, 10, 50, 100, 200 and 500 cruzeiros. All recently-issued coins have been struck in stainless steel. Various new designs have been introduced, including portraits of presidents and historical figures, maps of Brazil, topographical and industrial scenes and agricultural products. A commemorative issue was also struck in 1982 to mark the 150th anniversary of independence and consisting of silver 20 and gold 300 cruzeiros.

of a 'united kingdom' rather than a colony of Portugal. A further constitutional change took place in 1822 when, following the return of Joao VI to Portugal to quell a revolution, Brazil's independence was declared. Pedro I, son of Joao VI and regent in his father's absence, became the first emperor of independent Brazil.

The coinage of Brazil changed very little during the period covered by the regency of Joao VI, the United Kingdom (1815–22) and the early years following independence. The most striking feature of the coinage was the return of counterstamping. Beginning in 1808, various regions applied counterstamps to Spanish-American coins in order to increase the volume of silver currency in circulation. Counterstamps were also used to change the values of silver, and especially copper, coins between 1799 and 1835. Gold bars stamped by local-government assay offices also circulated as money in this period.

The second and last emperor of Brazil was Pedro II, who ruled from 1831 to 1889. During his reign the appearance of the coinage changed very little, except for the portrait of the emperor, at first shown as a child, later a full-bearded man. Other designs included the national arms of Brazil and the mark of denomination. However, there were changes to the monetary system, with new denominations introduced from 1834, and to metal fineness, as the gold and silver coinages were gradually debased. After 1834 the only base-metal coinage produced was an issue of 10 and 20 reis pieces dated 1868–70, some of which were minted in Brussels, and a series of 40 reis coins issued between 1873 and 1880. Cupro-nickel coinage was introduced in 1871 and was used for 50, 100 and 200 reis coins.

THE BRAZILIAN REPUBLIC

Pedro II was overthrown by a military coup in 1889 and Brazil became a

FRENCH GUIANA

FIRST COINS:	1780
FIRST DECIMAL COINS:	1818
MAIN MINT:	Paris
CURRENCY:	French

THE coast of what is now French Guiana was first explored by Europeans in the years 1499–1500. In the seventeenth century the French established settlements, including the trading post of Cayenne (founded 1635), and French Guiana became a colony of the

French crown in 1674. It briefly fell into British and Portuguese hands during the Napoleonic Wars but was restored to France in 1817. From 1852 to 1947 the French maintained a penal colony in French Guiana which included the notorious Devil's Island. Today French Guiana is administered as an overseas department within the French Union.

From the earliest days of European settlement a variety of coins were used, the principal trade coinage in the area being Spanish silver. Silver and bronze coins counterstamped for use in the French colonies in the seventeenth and eighteenth centuries, including the 'stampee' marked with a crowned c (for *colonies*), would also have been in circulation, as well as specially struck issues of French colonial coinage (*see* Guadeloupe and Martinique).

1 1789

2 1846

FRENCH GUIANA

1 BRONZE 2 SOUS *of the Colony of Cayenne.* 2 BILLON 10 CENTIMES.

The first coinage issued in the name of Cayenne was a series of 2 sou pieces in billon and bronze, minted in Paris between 1780 and 1789. Another issue of 2 sous for Cayenne was produced in 1816 and this was followed by issues of billon 10 centime coins in the name of French Guiana, again minted in Paris and dated 1818 and 1846. No coinage has since been minted specifically for use in French Guiana. French coinage is the official legal tender.

SURINAM

FIRST COINS:	1942
FIRST DECIMAL COINS:	1942
MAIN MINT:	Utrecht
CURRENCY:	gulden

THE coast of Surinam was discovered in 1499 by Alonso de Ojeda and Amerigo Vespucci. The first European settlers were Dutch, English and French traders, who began arriving at the end of the sixteenth century. The Surinam coastland was claimed by the British in the mid-seventeenth century, but was ceded to Holland by the Treaty of Breda in 1667 in exchange for New Amsterdam (New York) and became part of Dutch Guiana. It remained a colony of Holland after the other provinces of Dutch Guiana were relinquished to the British in 1814 (*see* Guyana).

Various coins, especially Dutch and Spanish issues, were used in trade by the early European settlers but because of the general shortage of coinage in the region, sugar was declared legal tender in 1669 and used as money into the eighteenth century. Only on two occasions in this period, in 1679 and 1764, were attempts made to provide a local currency, and the issues consisted simply of small quantities of low-denomination copper tokens with values given in Dutch doits.

The first true coins made specifically for circulation in Surinam were Dutch brass cent and silver 10 cent pieces dated 1942–3, when the Netherlands was under German occupation. The coins were struck in mints in the USA. Further issues of Dutch cents marked for Surinam were minted at Utrecht from 1957 to 1960.

MODERN COINAGE

Surinam was granted autonomy within the kingdom of the Netherlands in 1954 and finally gained full independence in 1975. Coins have been issued in the name of Surinam since 1962. The early issues included bronze cents, nickel–brass 5 cents, cupro-nickel 10 and 25 cents and silver guldens. The low-denomination coins had Surinam's national arms on the front and the mark of value on the back. The gulden had the national arms relegated to the back and the head of the Dutch queen on the front. After independence the gulden/cents coinage system was retained. Only 1, 5, 10 and 25 cent coins have since been issued as regular currency, still minted in Utrecht and with the same designs as before. The 1 and 5 cent coins are now minted in aluminium; the 10 and 25 cents are still cupro-nickel. In addition, a number of large-denomination commemorative coins in silver and gold have been issued in recent years.

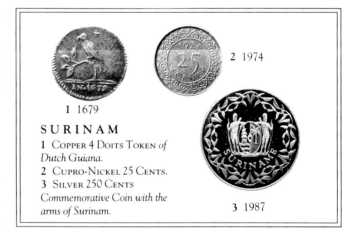

2 1974

1 1679

SURINAM

1 COPPER 4 DOITS TOKEN *of Dutch Guiana.*
2 CUPRO-NICKEL 25 CENTS.
3 SILVER 250 CENTS *Commemorative Coin with the arms of Surinam.*

3 1987

GUYANA

FIRST COINS:	1809
FIRST DECIMAL COINS:	1967
MAIN MINT:	Royal Mint
CURRENCY:	dollar

THE coast of what is now Guyana was sighted by Christopher Columbus in 1498 and again by Alonso de Ojeda and Amerigo Vespucci the following year. The first settlements were established by the Dutch 100 years later. Under Dutch administration there were

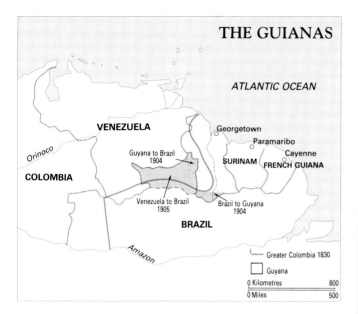

THE GUIANAS

ATLANTIC OCEAN

VENEZUELA

Georgetown
Paramaribo
Cayenne
SURINAM   FRENCH GUIANA

Guyana to Brazil
1904

COLOMBIA

Venezuela to Brazil
1905

Brazil to Guyana
1904

BRAZIL

Amazon

Greater Colombia 1830
Guyana
0 Kilometres 800
0 Miles 500

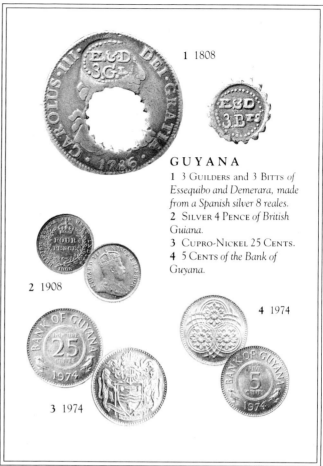

1 1808

2 1908

4 1974

3 1974

GUYANA
1 3 GUILDERS and 3 BITTS of
Essequibo and Demerara, made
from a Spanish silver 8 reales.
2 SILVER 4 PENCE of British
Guiana.
3 CUPRO-NICKEL 25 CENTS.
4 5 CENTS of the Bank of
Guyana.

three separate colonies, Essequibo, Demerara and Berbice. Between 1781 and 1803 the British took possession of the Dutch colonies three times and in 1814 they were formally ceded to Britain. In 1831 Berbice joined Essequibo and Demerara, which had been united administratively since 1814, to form British Guiana. In 1904 additional areas of disputed land formerly belonging to Venezuela and Brazil were added to British Guiana, following foreign arbitration.

EARLY COINAGE

The first coins to arrive in Guyana would have been Spanish coins brought by sixteenth-century explorers. In the Dutch colonies Dutch currency became standard, but shortages of coinage led to the use of paper money, a practice which was already widespread when the British arrived. In Essequibo and Demerara in the early years of British rule there were two attempts to provide official coinage by mutilating Portuguese gold and Spanish silver coinage. In 1798 gold Portuguese 'Joes' were stamped ED, and in 1808 Spanish silver 8 reales were pierced with a large hole and both the remains of the 8 real and the central plug were stamped with values (3 guilders and 3 'bitts' respectively) and E&D.

When the first coins were minted for the colony of Essequibo and Demerara by the British, the Dutch monetary system was retained. Between 1809 and 1836 issues included copper coins of $\frac{1}{2}$ stuiver and 1 stuiver and silver $\frac{1}{8}$, $\frac{1}{4}$, $\frac{1}{2}$, 1, 2 and 3 guilders. All had the bust of the British king on the front and the denomination on the back. Meanwhile, the Venezuelan province of Guayana, which was later joined to British Guiana, issued its own $\frac{1}{4}$ reales in copper between 1813 and 1817, at a time when Venezuela was fighting for independence from Spain.

BRITISH GUIANA

The final issue of coinage in the Dutch system was produced in 1836, with the coins now inscribed BRITISH GUIANA instead of DEMERARY & ESSEQUIBO. From 1839 accounts in British Guiana were reckoned in dollars and cents rather than guilders and stuivers, and Spanish, Mexican and Colombian coinage circulated as legal tender until 1876,

when British money became standard. Because the local population had continued to reckon in 'bitts' ($\frac{1}{4}$ guilders) the British silver fourpence, exactly equivalent to the 'bitt' in value, became the most popular coin in circulation and it was still requested in the colony after it ceased to be minted in England in 1856. An issue was produced specifically for British Guiana in 1888.

In 1891 a new colonial fourpence silver coin was introduced for British Guiana and the West Indies. This continued to be minted regularly until 1916, when it was decided that it was no longer required in the West Indies. Subsequent issues, from 1917 to 1945, were produced for British Guiana alone. After 1945 British Guiana was no longer provided with its own coins.

INDEPENDENCE

Guyana was granted full independence in 1966 and the following year its first independent coinage was issued. A decimal system of dollars and cents was adopted. Denominations of 1 and 5 cents (nickel–brass) and 10, 25 and 50 cents (cupro-nickel) were issued immediately, all with new designs including the arms of Guyana. The dollar coin was first issued in 1970 in cupro-nickel, and 5 and 10 dollar pieces (also cupro-nickel) have been issued since 1976. In 1976 designs on all denominations were changed, with prominence given to local wildlife. Special commemorative coins have also been issued since 1976, including, in 1976 and 1977, silver 50 dollars and gold 100 dollars.

AUSTRALASIA AND OCEANIA

NICKEL-ALLOY DOLLAR *of Australia, 1988.*

IN AUSTRALIA and the islands of the Pacific Ocean, coinage was unknown before European explorers and colonists arrived. In some of the more remote islands native forms of currency, such as shells, feathers and stone rings, were not replaced by coins and paper money until as recently as the Second World War.

The Spanish silver piece of eight reales was the first coin to achieve wide acceptance in the region. In the nineteenth century this was largely replaced by the coins of other European colonial powers, notably Britain, France and Germany, which established their own coinages as legal tender in their colonies. Many colonies were later provided with their own issues. In recent years, as many countries in the region have gained full independence, new national coinages have come to replace colonial issues and the dollar has become the new universal unit of currency in the region.

THE PRESENT-DAY DENOMINATIONS OF AUSTRALASIA

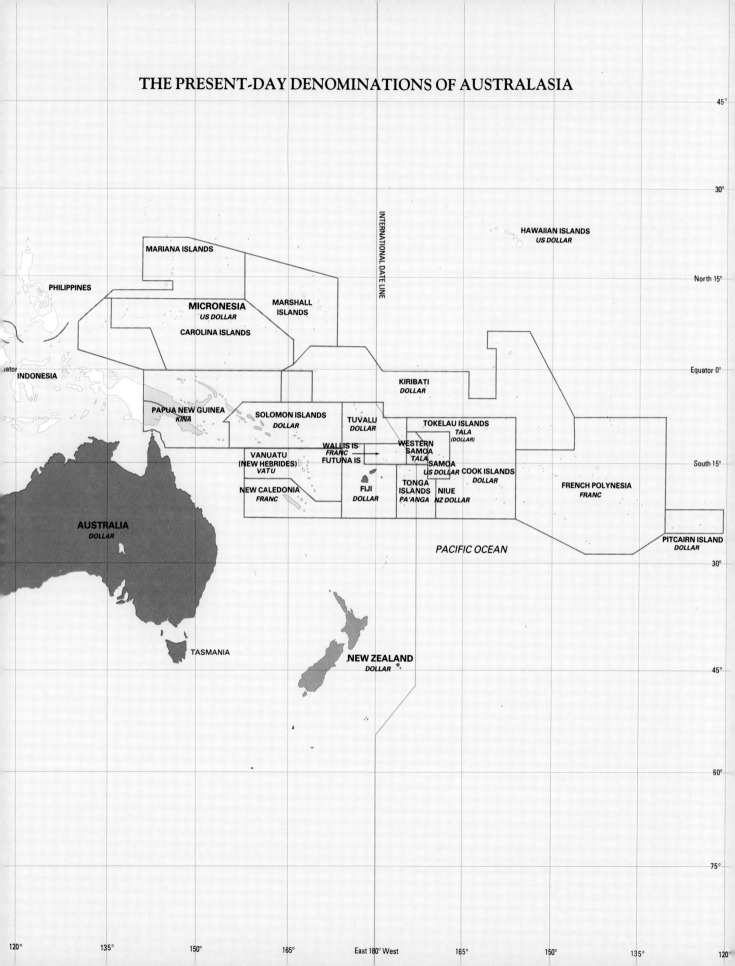

MARIANA ISLANDS

PHILIPPINES

MICRONESIA
US DOLLAR

MARSHALL ISLANDS

CAROLINA ISLANDS

INTERNATIONAL DATE LINE

HAWAIIAN ISLANDS
US DOLLAR

INDONESIA

Equator

KIRIBATI
DOLLAR

Equator 0°

PAPUA NEW GUINEA
KINA

SOLOMON ISLANDS
DOLLAR

TUVALU
DOLLAR

TOKELAU ISLANDS
TALA
(DOLLAR)

WALLIS IS
FRANC
FUTUNA IS

WESTERN SAMOA
TALA

VANUATU (NEW HEBRIDES)
VATU

SAMOA
US DOLLAR

COOK ISLANDS
DOLLAR

NEW CALEDONIA
FRANC

FIJI
DOLLAR

TONGA ISLANDS
PA'ANGA

NIUE
NZ DOLLAR

FRENCH POLYNESIA
FRANC

AUSTRALIA
DOLLAR

PITCAIRN ISLAND
DOLLAR

PACIFIC OCEAN

TASMANIA

NEW ZEALAND
DOLLAR

45°

30°

North 15°

South 15°

30°

45°

60°

75°

120°   135°   150°   165°   East 180° West   165°   150°   135°   120°

AUSTRALIA

FIRST COINS:	1813
FIRST DECIMAL COINS:	1966
MAIN MINT:	Royal Australian Mint, Canberra
CURRENCY:	dollar

THE Commonwealth of Australia today comprises the six former British colonies which were united in 1901 (New South Wales, Victoria, South Australia, Western Australia, Queensland and Tasmania) and the Northern Territory, which was administered from South Australia in 1901 but became a separate territory within the Commonwealth of Australia in 1911. It also possesses a number of Pacific and Indian Ocean islands administered as external territories. Australia is a member of the British Commonwealth.

NEW SOUTH WALES

Europeans were aware of the existence of Australia as early as the sixteenth century, but the first settlement was not attempted until 1788, when the British founded a colony, largely peopled by transported convicts, at Port Jackson (now part of Sydney), New South Wales.

No provision was made for the supply of coinage to the new colony. Many different coins arrived through trade, including Portuguese, Indian, Spanish and Dutch, as well as British, but because this coinage was also traded for much-needed goods there was always a chronic shortage of coinage in circulation. The colonists had to use foodstuffs and other commodities, notably rum, as currency.

In 1800 the governor, Philip Gidley King, issued a proclamation, fixing the values for the many different coins circulating in the colony, and at about the same time the first official shipment of coinage to Australia, consisting of 'cartwheel pennies', arrived from Britain.

The next attempt to deal with Australia's currency problem came in 1813, when the succeeding governor, Lachlan Macquarrie, authorized the mutilation of 40,000 Spanish dollars for coinage. Each dollar had a small round disc cut from its centre, the disc being valued at 15 pence, and the outer ring, known as the 'colonial dollar', at 5 shillings. Both pieces were stamped by the issuing authority, NEW SOUTH WALES, valued and dated. Production of these so-called 'holey dollars' was entrusted to a certain William Henshall, who had originally been transported to Australia for forging coins in England.

The holey dollars remained in circulation until 1829, when they ceased to be legal tender. In the meantime, in 1824 and 1825, £100,000 worth of British coinage had been imported, and in 1826 the Sterling Silver Money Act was passed by the British parliament, ending the use of the dollar standard. From 1829 to 1910 British coinage, mostly imported direct from Britain, was the only officially sanctioned coinage.

AUSTRALIA
1 SILVER 'HOLEY DOLLAR' (5 SHILLINGS) *of the New South Wales colony.*
2 COPPER PENNY TOKEN *privately issued in Melbourne, Victoria.*

1 1813
2 1862

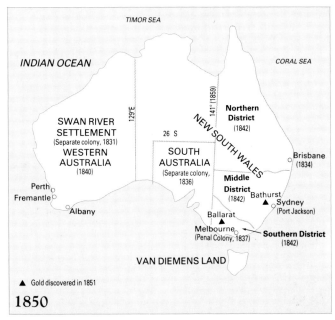

THE COLONIZATION OF AUSTRALIA

INDIAN OCEAN
CORAL SEA

New Holland
(1825 to NSW)
129°E
135°E (1788)
Queensland
Moreton Bay

Swan River Settlement
(Governed by NSW)
NEW SOUTH WALES
(British colony, 1788)

Perth
(Penal colony, 1829)
Port Jackson
(Penal colony, 1788)

Albany
(Penal colony, 1826)
Melbourne
(1837)
Botany Bay

Port Phillip
(Penal colony, 1803)

VAN DIEMENS LAND
(Penal colony, 1803)
(Separate colony, 1825)

1830

TIMOR SEA

INDIAN OCEAN
CORAL SEA

SWAN RIVER SETTLEMENT
(Separate colony, 1831)
WESTERN AUSTRALIA
(1840)
129°E
26 S
141° (1859)
Northern District
(1842)
NEW SOUTH WALES

Perth
Fremantle
SOUTH AUSTRALIA
(Separate colony, 1836)
Middle District
(1842)
Brisbane
(1834)

Albany
Bathurst
Sydney
(Port Jackson)

Ballarat
Melbourne
(Penal Colony, 1837)
Southern District
(1842)

VAN DIEMENS LAND

▲ Gold discovered in 1851

1850

NINETEENTH-CENTURY TOKENS

During this period more settlements were founded, bringing coinage to new areas of Australia, and the separate colonies of Tasmania (Van Diemens Land), Victoria, Queensland, South Australia and Western Australia were established. Shortages of official British coinage in the colonies occasioned production of privately issued tokens. The vast majority of these were copper or bronze pennies and halfpennies, needed for small change and issued mostly between 1855 and 1865 by numerous private traders, though an early (1823) silver shilling is known from Tasmania and a few silver threepence tokens were issued in New South Wales (1855–65). Over 500 different tokens were issued, some manufactured in Australia, others in Britain. However, an increase in the supply of British coinage to Australia in the 1860s caused a decline in the popularity of the tokens, and, starting with Victoria in 1863, they were outlawed by each of the colonies in turn.

GOLD COINAGE

In 1851 gold was discovered at Bathurst (New South Wales) and Ballarat (Victoria). The goldfields were soon crowded and there was increasing pressure to establish mints in Australia to convert the gold dust to coin. In 1852 gold ingots and later coins were issued under the authorization of the government of South Australia, and in 1853–4 an attempt was made to set up a private mint, the Kangaroo Office Mint, in Melbourne, though only trial pieces were ever made.

The British government eventually sanctioned the setting up of an official mint in Sydney, which began issuing gold coins in 1855. The early sovereigns and ½ sovereigns had designs which differed from British gold coins; they had the words SYDNEY MINT and AUSTRALIA inscribed on the back. But from 1871 the coins were given designs identical to contemporary British issues, except for the inclusion of a mint mark (s). Further branch mints were opened in 1872 in Melbourne (M) and in 1899 in Perth (P). In this period the Australian mints produced much more imperial gold coinage than the Royal Mint in London. They continued to strike British gold coins (sovereigns and ½ sovereigns) until 1926 (Sydney) and 1931 (Melbourne and Perth).

The Australian gold rush in the mid-nineteenth century.

THE AUSTRALIAN COMMONWEALTH

In 1901 the separate colonies of Australia joined together to form a federation, and in 1910 the first coins of the new Commonwealth of Australia were issued. All the coins bore the portrait of the British monarch on the front, and the British coinage system was used. For the first issue, in the name of Edward VII, only the silver coins (threepence, sixpence, shilling and florin) were produced. The bronze halfpenny and penny came into production the following year.

The halfpenny and penny continued to be issued regularly until 1964. From 1911 to 1939 the backs of these coins carried only an inscription, giving the authority, value and date, but from 1939 a kangaroo design was added. Mints in Britain (London and Birmingham) and India (Calcutta and Bombay) were sometimes employed for their production, as well as the three existing Australian mints. The regular silver denominations of threepence, sixpence,

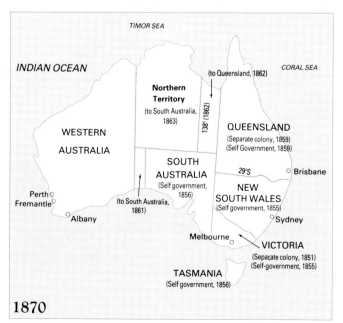

AUSTRALIA

3 GOLD 1 OUNCE PATTERN COIN *of the Kangaroo Office Mint, Port Phillip, Melbourne.*
4 GOLD SOVEREIGN, *Sydney mint.*
5 GOLD BRITISH SOVEREIGN *minted in Melbourne.*
6 SILVER FLORIN.
7 BRONZE PENNY.
8 CUPRO-NICKEL 10 CENTS.
9 NICKEL-ALLOY DOLLAR.
10 IVORY 5 CENTS TOKEN *of the Keeling-Cocos Islands, issued by J. S. Clunies Ross.*

shilling and florin were issued from 1910 to 1963 (the threepence until 1964). The British and Australian mints were again used, and, in the war years of 1942–4, the US mints of Denver and San Francisco. These coins were made of sterling silver (92.5 per cent fine) until 1946, when the standard was dropped to 50 per cent fine. The usual design on the back of most of them was the arms of Australia, but from 1938 the threepence used a design of three wheat stalks, and the shilling used a ram's head. In addition to the regular coinage, silver crowns, at first intended as commemorative coins, were issued in 1937–8, and special commemorative florins, celebrating anniversaries and other events, were issued in 1927, 1934–5, 1951 and 1954.

MODERN COINAGE

Australia's decimal coinage was introduced in 1966. The new unit of currency was the dollar (= 100 cents). The coins issued regularly since 1966 are the 1 and 2 cents (bronze) and 5, 10, 20 and 50 cents (cupro-nickel). The first 50 cent coins were made of 80 per cent fine-silver, but these were produced only in 1966 and the later 50 cent coins, issued since 1969, are cupro-nickel. Until 1984 banknotes supplied all values of a dollar and more, but in 1984 a 1 dollar currency coin was introduced, made of a mixture of nickel, aluminium and copper, followed in 1988 by a new 2 dollar coin. The new Royal Australian Mint in Canberra, opened 1966, has produced most of Australia's decimal coinage, but occasional assistance has been obtained from the mints in Melbourne and Perth, the Royal Mint in Britain and the Royal Canadian Mint.

The British monarch, still the country's head of state, remains on the front of all coins. On the backs are various Australian animals: the feather-tailed glider on the cent, the frilled-neck lizard on the 2 cents, the echidna (5 cents), the lyrebird (10 cents), the platypus (20 cents) and kangaroos (1 dollar), but on the 50 cents is the Australian coat of arms. In addition to the regular circulation coinage, proof decimal coins have also been issued for collectors, and in recent years these have been joined by issues of high-value commemorative coins in gold and silver, ranging from 10 to 100 dollars.

KEELING–COCOS ISLANDS

Now an Australian external territory, this group of islands in the Indian Ocean was discovered by Captain William Keeling of the British East India Company in 1609. British settlements were first established in the nineteenth century, and the islands were later administered from Ceylon (Sri Lanka) and the Straits Settlements before being attached to Australia in 1955.

An issue of coinage was produced in 1977 consisting of bronze 5, 10, 25 and 50 cents; cupro-nickel 1, 2 and 5 rupees; silver 10 and 25 rupees; and gold 150 rupees. This issue commemorated the 150th anniversary of the foundation of the permanent settlement on the islands in 1827, and it portrayed one of the founders, John Clunies Ross. The descendants of Clunies Ross had in 1913 issued private tokens made of ivory and valued in cents and rupees for use on their plantations on the islands.

NEW ZEALAND

FIRST COINS:	1933
FIRST DECIMAL COINS:	1967
MAIN MINT:	Royal Mint
CURRENCY:	dollar

IN 1642 the Dutch navigator, Abel Tasman, became the first European to discover New Zealand. Between 1769 and 1777 Captain Cook visited the islands on several occasions and claimed them for Britain, but colonization did not commence until the early nineteenth century. In 1840 the Waitangi Treaty, made between the native Maori people and the British, proclaimed British sovereignty. Discoveries of gold in the 1850s and 1860s accelerated the immigration of British settlers, and territorial disputes caused fighting with the Maoris until the 1870s. In 1907 the colony became the Dominion of New Zealand. New Zealand had already been effectively self-governing for many years when, in 1947, its full autonomy was formally recognized. New Zealand remains a member of the British Commonwealth and the British monarch is head of state.

Various foreign coins, including Spanish-American, French, Indian and British, arrived in New Zealand with the whalers and traders who visited in the early nineteenth century. British currency was proclaimed legal tender in 1850, but, because of the shortage of official coinage in the islands, there was widespread circulation of private traders' tokens in copper and bronze, first issued in 1857. Altogether, almost 150 varieties are known, mostly from the cities of Auckland, Christchurch, Wellington and Dunedin. They were issued until 1881 and continued to circulate until the end of the century, by which time the supply of British coinage was adequate.

FIRST LOCAL COINAGE

British, and later Australian, coins remained the only official coins until 1933, when New Zealand's first coinage was issued. The 1933 issue consisted of silver threepences, sixpences, shillings, florins and $\frac{1}{2}$ crowns (all 50 per cent fine, the same as contemporary British silver coinage). The crown, with a design on the back commemorating the Waitangi Treaty, was first issued in 1935, and bronze halfpennies and pennies followed in 1940. All the coins, which were minted in Britain, had the head of the British monarch on the front and designs symbolizing New Zealand on the back. Denominations from the halfpenny to the $\frac{1}{2}$ crown were issued regularly until 1965; the crown was issued only as a commemorative coin, in 1935, 1949 and 1953.

MODERN COINAGE

A new, decimal monetary system was introduced in 1967. The unit of currency was the dollar, and coins of 1 and 2 cents (bronze), 5, 10 and 20 cents (cupro-nickel) and 1 dollar (cupro-nickel) were issued. Plans to introduce a 2 dollar coin and to phase out 1 and 2 cent coins were announced in 1988. The head of Queen Elizabeth II has remained on the front of all coins; on the backs are designs of local flora and fauna and Maori art for coins up to 20 cents, and Captain Cook's ship, *Endeavour*, on the 50 cents. The arms of New Zealand were used on the dollar until 1976, as well as various special commemorative designs, which have continued in recent years. New Zealand's decimal coinage has been minted at the Royal Mint, the Royal Australian Mint and the Royal Canadian Mint.

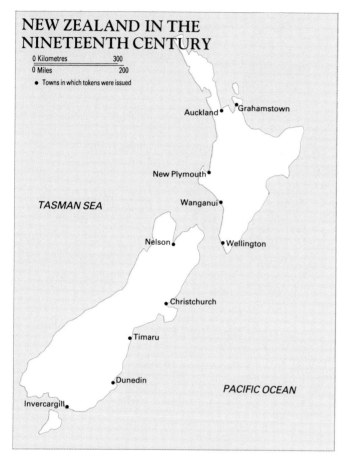

NEW ZEALAND IN THE NINETEENTH CENTURY

0 Kilometres   300
0 Miles   200
● Towns in which tokens were issued

Auckland ● ● Grahamstown

New Plymouth ●

Wanganui ●

TASMAN SEA

Nelson ●   ● Wellington

● Christchurch

● Timaru

● Dunedin

PACIFIC OCEAN

Invercargill ●

NEW ZEALAND

1 COPPER HALFPENNY TOKEN *privately issued in Auckland.*
2 SILVER FLORIN.
3 SILVER CROWN *commemorating the Waitangi treaty.*
4 BRONZE 2 CENTS.
5 CUPRO-NICKEL 50 CENTS.

1 1859
4 1968
3 1935
2 1933
5 1969

PAPUA NEW GUINEA

FIRST COINS:	1894
FIRST DECIMAL COINS:	1894
MAIN MINT:	Royal Mint
CURRENCY:	kina

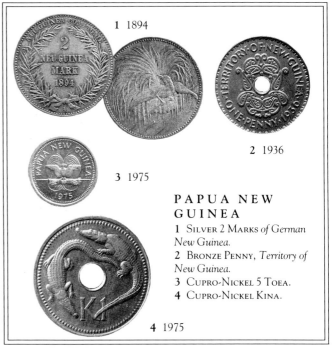

PAPUA NEW GUINEA
1 SILVER 2 MARKS of German New Guinea.
2 BRONZE PENNY, Territory of New Guinea.
3 CUPRO-NICKEL 5 TOEA.
4 CUPRO-NICKEL KINA.

Papua New Guinea occupies the eastern half of the island of New Guinea (see Indonesia), which was first discovered by Europeans in the sixteenth century. Various colonial powers – Spain, the Netherlands, Britain and Germany – laid territorial claim to the island. The northern part of what is now Papua New Guinea, including the islands of the Bismarck Archipelago and Bougainville, was annexed by Germany in 1884, but was invaded by Australian troops during the First World War and mandated to Australia in 1920 as the Territory of New Guinea. The southern part was a British protectorate (proclaimed 1888) administered from Australia. It was named British New Guinea until 1905, when it became the Territory of Papua. Papua and New Guinea were joined administratively in 1946 as an Australian trust territory, and became an independent state in 1975. Papua New Guinea remains a member of the Commonwealth, with the British monarch as head of state.

GERMAN NEW GUINEA

The German colony of New Guinea was provided with its own coinage, minted in Berlin. In 1894 copper coins of 1, 2 and 10 pfennigs were issued, together with silver ½, 1, 2 and 5 marks. In 1895 gold 10 and 20 mark pieces were minted. The two smallest denominations had designs consisting only of inscriptions, naming the authority, value and date. The larger denominations had inscriptions and a wreath on the front, and on the back a bird of paradise.

After the former German colony came under Australian administration, Australian coins gradually replaced the coins of German New Guinea in circulation until, in 1929, a new coinage was introduced for the territory. Issued intermittently until 1945, the coinage consisted of bronze halfpennies and pennies and cupro-nickel threepences, sixpences and shillings, all of which had a central hole.

MODERN COINAGE

The southern territories of British New Guinea and its successor, the Territory of Papua, were never supplied with their own coinages. British, and later Australian, coinage was used. Following the joining of Papua and New Guinea, Australian money became the usual currency throughout the country, but after independence in 1975 Papua New Guinea began issuing its own currency. A decimal system was adopted, similar to that of Australia but with local names for the denominations. The regular currency coins are the 1 and 2 toea (bronze) and 5, 10, 20 and 50 toea and 1, 5 and 10 kina (cupro-nickel). Local flora and fauna provide the coin designs. Commemorative coins in silver and gold have also been issued frequently in recent years, in denominations ranging from 5 to 100 kina.

SOLOMON ISLANDS

FIRST COINS:	1977
FIRST DECIMAL COINS:	1977
MAIN MINTS:	Royal Mint, Franklin Mint
CURRENCY:	dollar

A chain of islands east of New Guinea form the northern part of Melanesia. The most important islands of the Solomons are Guadalcanal (a famous Second World War battlefield), Malaita, New Georgia, Vella Lavella, Choiseul, San Cristobal, Santa Isabel, Makira and the Santa Cruz islands. They were discovered by the Spanish in the sixteenth century, but colonization did not begin in earnest until 1885, when the northern Solomon Islands were declared a German protectorate with German New Guinea. Britain claimed the southern islands in 1893, and in 1899 was given the protectorate of the northern islands by Germany in return for recognition of German claims in Western Samoa. German, British and, after 1910, Australian, currency was used in the Solomon Islands until the Second World War. The islands were occupied by the Japanese in 1942–3, but after the war they returned to the status of a British protectorate, becoming a self-governing dependency in 1976, and independent in 1978. The Solomon Islands remains a member of the Commonwealth, with the British monarch as head of state.

British and Australian currency continued to be used until 1977, when the first national coinage of the islands was introduced. The system is the same as that of Australia, consisting of bronze 1 and 2 cent, and cupro-nickel 5, 10, 20 cent and dollar pieces, all with Queen Elizabeth II's head on the front and designs depicting native art on the back. Higher-value commemorative coins have also been issued in recent years for collectors.

SOLOMON ISLANDS
1 BRONZE 2 CENTS.
2 CUPRO-NICKEL DOLLAR.
1 1977
2 1977

VANUATU

FIRST COINS:	1970
FIRST DECIMAL COINS:	1970
MAIN MINT:	Royal Mint
CURRENCY:	vatu

DISCOVERED by the Portuguese navigator Pedro de Quiros in 1606, these islands were visited in 1768 by Louis Antoine de Bougainville, the French explorer, and in 1774 by Captain Cook, who called them New Hebrides. The two claimants, Britain and France, declared the islands neutral in 1878, but in 1906 jointly accepted sovereignty and subsequently governed them as a condominium.

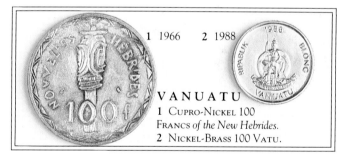

VANUATU
1 CUPRO-NICKEL 100 FRANCS of the New Hebrides.
2 NICKEL-BRASS 100 VATU.
1 1966
2 1988

Until independence the islands used a mixture of French, British and later Australian currency. The only coins issued in the name of New Hebrides date from the period 1966–79. These were French-style issues of nickel-brass 1, 2 and 5 francs, nickel 10, 20 and 50 francs and a silver 100 francs. The coins were all minted in Paris, had inscriptions in French, and for designs used the head of Liberty on the front and examples of native art on the back. Parallel issues were produced for New Caledonia and French Polynesia.

INDEPENDENCE

Independence was gained in 1980, and the islands took the name Vanuatu. New coinage was introduced in 1981 to celebrate the first

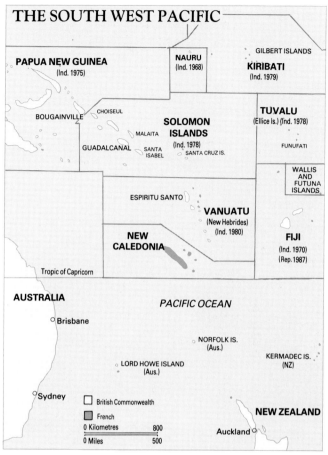

THE SOUTH WEST PACIFIC

PAPUA NEW GUINEA (Ind. 1975)
NAURU (Ind. 1968)
GILBERT ISLANDS
KIRIBATI (Ind. 1979)
BOUGAINVILLE
CHOISEUL
SOLOMON ISLANDS (Ind. 1978)
TUVALU (Ellice Is.) (Ind. 1978)
MALAITA
GUADALCANAL
SANTA ISABEL
SANTA CRUZ IS.
FUNUFATI
WALLIS AND FUTUNA ISLANDS
ESPIRITU SANTO
VANUATU (New Hebrides) (Ind. 1980)
NEW CALEDONIA
FIJI (Ind. 1970) (Rep. 1987)
Tropic of Capricorn
AUSTRALIA
PACIFIC OCEAN
Brisbane
NORFOLK IS. (Aus.)
KERMADEC IS. (NZ)
LORD HOWE ISLAND (Aus.)
Sydney
British Commonwealth
French
NEW ZEALAND
0 Kilometres 800
0 Miles 500
Auckland

anniversary of independence. The issue consisted of a nickel 50 vatu piece and two commemorative coins: a silver 50 vatu and a gold 10,000 vatu coin. Since 1983 coins have been struck regularly for Vanuatu by the Royal Mint in Britain in denominations of 1, 2 and 5 vatu (nickel-brass), 10, 20 and 50 vatu (cupro-nickel) and 100 vatu (nickel-brass). The arms of Vanuatu are used on the front of the coins with scenes symbolizing the islands on the back.

NEW CALEDONIA

FIRST COINS:	1949
FIRST DECIMAL COINS:	1949
MAIN MINT:	Paris
CURRENCY:	franc

THE islands of New Caledonia were discovered by Captain Cook in 1774, but were not colonized by Europeans until the French took possession in 1853. In 1946 New Caledonia became a French overseas territory.

Since 1853 French coinage has been the principal currency on the islands, though during the Second World War, when they were used as a base for Allied troops, there was an influx of other currencies. The first coins issued in the name of New Caledonia were dated 1949, and consisted of aluminium 50 centime and 1 and 2 franc pieces, all minted in Paris. These were followed by a 5 franc coin in 1952. The coinage was extended from 1967 to include 10, 20 and 50 franc nickel coins, matching the contemporary issues for the New Hebrides (see Vanuatu) and French Polynesia. A 100 franc nickel-bronze coin has also since been issued, in 1976 and 1979. For designs, the denominations introduced between 1949 and 1952 use a seated figure of Liberty on the front and a bird of paradise on the back; the denominations introduced since 1967 have the head of Liberty on the front and various island scenes on the back.

San Francisco and had a fineness of 90 per cent.

INDEPENDENCE

Fiji remained a British colony until 1970, when independence was granted to the islands. Fiji's sterling coinage was issued regularly until the islands changed to decimal currency in 1969. The decimal coinage of Fiji has consisted of bronze 1 and 2 cent, and cupro-nickel 5, 10, 20 and 50 cent and 1 dollar pieces, minted at the Royal Mint. Commemorative issues have also been produced, including silver and gold coins in denominations up to 250 dollars. The designs of the regular currency coinage, which was issued before the declaration of a republic following two military coups in 1987, feature the head of Queen Elizabeth II, combined with images symbolizing the islands. Fiji left the British Commonwealth in 1987.

NEW CALEDONIA
ALUMINIUM 50 CENTIMES.

FIJI
1 SILVER FLORIN.
2 CUPRO-NICKEL PENNY.
3 NICKEL-BRASS 3 PENCE.
4 BRONZE CENT.
5 CUPRO-NICKEL 50 CENTS.

FIJI

FIRST COINS:	1934
FIRST DECIMAL COINS:	1969
MAIN MINT:	Royal Mint
CURRENCY:	dollar

THE many islands which now comprise the Republic of Fiji were discovered by the Dutch navigator Abel Tasman in 1643, and later visited by Captain Cook in 1774. Colonization by Europeans began in the early nineteenth century and in 1874 the islands were voluntarily ceded to Britain by King Kacobau. Fiji's first coinage was that of Britain, made the sole legal tender in 1881. British coins and, after 1910, Australian coins continued to circulate in the islands until the introduction of a sterling coinage for Fiji in 1934. The new national coinage, produced by the Royal Mint in Britain, at first consisted of cupro-nickel halfpennies and pennies (with central holes), and silver sixpences, shillings and florins. A nickel-brass threepence was added in 1947. The denominations of threepence and above closely matched contemporary British coins in appearance (save for the designation to Fiji) and in metal composition, except for the issues of silver coins in 1942–3, which were minted in the US mint of

KIRIBATI

FIRST COINS:	1979
FIRST DECIMAL COINS:	1979
MAIN MINT:	Royal Mint
CURRENCY:	dollar

FORMERLY the Gilbert Islands, Kiribati was linked with the Ellice Islands as a British protectorate in 1892 and as a crown colony from 1915 to 1976 (with Fanning Island, Washington Island, Ocean, Christmas and other islands). Islands in the Gilbert and Ellice groups were sighted by Spanish mutineers in the sixteenth century and visited by British navigators in the eighteenth century. British interest in the islands dates from the early nineteenth century, since when British, and later Australian, currency was used.

The Gilbert Islands became a separate crown colony in 1976 and was granted independence as Kiribati in 1979. The islands' own national coinage was introduced in 1979. It is closely based on that of Australia, with bronze 1 and 2 cent and cupro-nickel 5, 10, 20 and 50 cent and 1 dollar coins. The arms of Kiribati appear on the front of the coins and local flora and fauna on the back. High-value commemorative coins in silver and gold have also been issued in recent years.

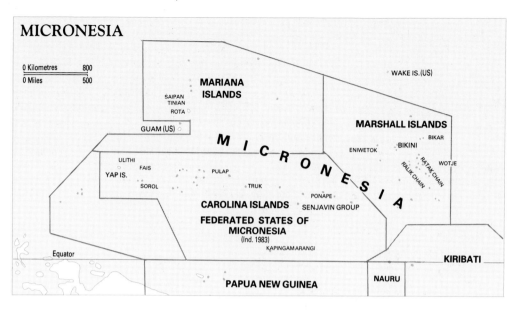

MICRONESIA

1973

COOK ISLANDS
Cupro-Nickel 7½ Dollar Commemorative Coin.

TUVALU

FIRST COINS:	1976
FIRST DECIMAL COINS:	1976
MAIN MINT:	Royal Mint
CURRENCY:	dollar

Formerly the Ellice Islands, discovered in 1764 by the British navigator John Byron, Tuvalu was later administered as a British colony together with the Gilbert Islands. Mainly British and later Australian coinage was used in the island until, in 1976, a national coinage was introduced when Tuvalu became a separate dependency, gaining full independence in 1978.

Tuvalu's coinage is closely modelled on that of Australia and consists of bronze 1 and 2 cent and cupro-nickel 5, 10, 20 and 50 cent and 1 dollar coins. The head of Queen Elizabeth II appears on the front of the coins; various sea creatures are used for the designs on the back. Silver and gold commemorative coins, in denominations from 5 to 50 dollars, have also been issued for collectors.

1 1976

TUVALU
1 Bronze 2 Cents.
2 Cupro-Nickel 20 Cents.

2 1976

COOK ISLANDS

FIRST COINS:	1972
FIRST DECIMAL COINS:	1972
MAIN MINTS:	Royal Mint, Royal Australian Mint, Franklin Mint
CURRENCY:	dollar

The first European to discover the Cook Islands was the Spanish navigator Alvaro de Mendada in 1595. They were later also visited by the Portuguese navigator Fernandes de Quieros in 1606 and by Captain Cook in the 1770s. The islands were declared a British protectorate in 1888 and became a territory of New Zealand in 1901. Since 1965 they have been internally self-governing.

Mainly British and, from 1933, New Zealand coinage was used in the Cook Islands until, in 1972, a national coinage was introduced. Based on the decimal coinage of New Zealand and at first minted by the Royal Mint in Britain, the Cook Islands coinage consisted of bronze 1 and 2 cent and cupro-nickel 5, 10, 20 and 50 cent and 1 dollar coins.

In 1987 a new coinage was issued, minted by the Royal Australian Mint, and including additional currency coins of 2 dollars (cupro-nickel) and 5 dollars (aluminium-bronze). The higher-denomination coins (1 and 5 dollars) were given various novel shapes. All of the coins of the Cook Islands have the head of Queen Elizabeth II on the front and local flora or fauna or native art on the back. A wide variety of commemorative issues have also been produced for circulation in the islands, including silver and gold coins minted in denominations up to 250 dollars.

NIUE

FIRST COINS:	1987
FIRST DECIMAL COINS:	1987
MAIN MINT:	Pobjoy Mint
CURRENCY:	New Zealand dollar

Discovered by Captain Cook in 1774, Niue, or Savage Island, became a British protectorate and was administered jointly with the Cook Islands after 1900. It later became a separate dependency of New Zealand, internally self-governing since 1974.

The coinage of New Zealand is in general use in Niue. The only coins issued in the name of Niue are commemorative pieces for collectors, of 5 dollars in cupro-nickel and 50, 100 and 200 dollars in silver, with the arms of Niue on the front and designs relating to tennis or soccer on the back.

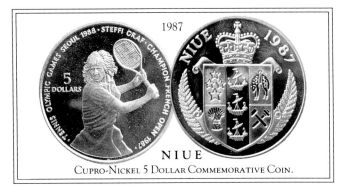

1987

NIUE
CUPRO-NICKEL 5 DOLLAR COMMEMORATIVE COIN.

TONGA

FIRST COINS:	1962
FIRST DECIMAL COINS:	1967
MAIN MINT:	Royal Mint
CURRENCY:	pa'anga

The islands which now comprise the kingdom of Tonga were discovered by Dutch navigators in the seventeenth century. Captain Cook visited in 1773 and named them the Friendly Islands. In

1880 treaties were signed between the King of Tonga, Britain and the USA, and in 1900 Tonga became a self-governing British protectorate. The Kingdom of Tonga became a fully independent state in 1970. It remains a member of the British Commonwealth.

BRITISH RULE

British currency was legal tender in Tonga from the late nineteenth century until the 1960s. In 1921 Tonga began issuing its own sterling banknotes, but its first coins were not minted until 1962, when gold coins valued at $\frac{1}{4}$, $\frac{1}{2}$ and 1 koula were issued, as well as proof pieces in platinum. The word *koula* means gold in Tonga, and each koula was worth 20 Tongan pounds in 1962. The gold coins were issued as currency, but were quickly bought up by collectors.

INDEPENDENCE

Tonga's present decimal coinage was introduced in 1967. The unit of currency is the pa'anga of 100 seniti, and there are 100 pa'anga in 1 hau. A full series of denominations has been issued: bronze 1 and 2 seniti; cupro-nickel 5, 10, 20 and 50 seniti and 1 and 2 pa'anga. The shape of the 1 pa'anga coin has been changed several times, being sometimes rectangular and multi-sided as well as round. Many commemorative coins have also been issued, including high-value pieces in silver and gold in denominations up to 5 hau (500 pa'anga). The usual designs are the head of the monarch of Tonga on the front – Queen Salote until 1967, King Taufa'ahau since 1968 – and either the arms of Tonga or other designs symbolizing the country on the back.

WESTERN SAMOA

FIRST COINS:	1967
FIRST DECIMAL COINS:	1967
MAIN MINT:	Royal Mint
CURRENCY:	tala (dollar)

First discovered by Europeans in the eighteenth century, the islands of Samoa were used as a base by whalers from the early nineteenth century, and they attracted the interest of Britain, the USA and Germany. In 1889 the three powers declared a tripartite protectorate

3 1974

TONGA
1 GOLD ½ KOULA.
2 CUPRO-NICKEL 20 SENITI.
3 BRONZE 2 SENITI.
4 CUPRO-NICKEL 50 SENITI.

1 1962   2 1967   4 1974

WESTERN SAMOA
1 BRONZE 5 SENE.
2 CUPRO-NICKEL COMMEMORATIVE DOLLAR.

over the islands, but in 1900 Britain withdrew, leaving the western islands to Germany (*see* Solomon Islands) and the eastern islands to the USA. In 1914 New Zealand troops occupied Western Samoa, and after the First World War the territory was mandated to New Zealand.

Until 1914, German, British and US coins were all used in Western Samoa. Thereafter British and, after 1933, New Zealand coinage was dominant.

INDEPENDENCE

Western Samoa became an independent state in 1962, but it remains a member of the British Commonwealth. Its first national coinage was introduced in 1967. The monetary system is decimal, with a tala (the local dollar) of 100 sene. The currency coins issued are bronze 1 and 2 sene and cupro-nickel 5, 10, 20 and 50 sene. The dominant coin designs are the head of Malietoa Tanumafili (the head of state), the arms of Western Samoa and local plants. Only two issues have appeared, dated 1967 and 1974, but production of commemorative dollars, which first appeared in 1967, has continued. Silver and gold commemorative multiples of the tala (minted in Singapore), in denominations up to 1000 tala, have also recently been issued.

TOKELAU ISLANDS

FIRST COINS:	1978
FIRST DECIMAL COINS:	1978
MAIN MINT:	Royal Australian Mint
CURRENCY:	tala (dollar)

First discovered by Europeans in the late eighteenth century, the Union Islands, as they were then known, became a British protectorate in 1893, and a British colony, under the Gilbert and Ellice Islands, in 1915. Since 1925 the island group, known as Tokelau since 1946, has been a dependency of New Zealand. British and, since 1933, New Zealand coins have been used. The only coins in the name of Tokelau are cupro-nickel and silver dollars; silver 5 dollars, issued since 1978, are intended mainly for collectors.

FRENCH POLYNESIA

FIRST COINS:	1949
FIRST DECIMAL COINS:	1949
MAIN MINT:	Paris
CURRENCY:	franc

French Polynesia comprises five separate archipelagos in the southern Pacific, the most important of which is the Society Islands, including Tahiti, claimed by France in 1768, and later visited by Captain Cook (1769) and the *Bounty* under Captain William Bligh (1788–9) (*see* Pitcairn Island). In 1903 the Society Islands were united with the Marquesas Islands, the Tuamotu Archipelago, the Gambier Islands and the Austral Islands to form the colony of French Oceania. In 1958 the group became an overseas territory of the French Republic under a new name: Territory of French Polynesia.

The official coinage of French Oceania and French Polynesia was and is that of France. The first issue of French colonial coinage produced specifically for the islands was dated 1949 and consisted of aluminium 50 centime and 1, 2 and 5 franc coins. The designs used were a seated Liberty on the front, identical to the figure on the parallel issue for New Caledonia, and an island landscape on the back. Both were retained for the coins of these denominations later issued in the name of French Polynesia, beginning in 1965. Higher denominations, introduced in 1967, and struck in nickel (10, 20 and 50 francs) and nickel-bronze (100 francs), used new designs, with a head of Liberty on the front and various images relating to the islands on the back. These coins were produced by the Paris mint along with the similar issues of New Caledonia and New Hebrides (*see* Vanuatu).

FRENCH POLYNESIA
ALUMINIUM FRANC.

PITCAIRN ISLAND

FIRST COINS:	1988
FIRST DECIMAL COINS:	1988
MAIN MINT:	Royal Mint
CURRENCY:	dollar

A remote South Pacific island first settled by the mutineers from the *Bounty*, a British ship sailing under Captain William Bligh, in 1790, Pitcairn Island was formally annexed by the British in 1838, and it remains today a British crown colony. The small population has had little use for coinage. British, and more recently New Zealand, currency has been the official legal tender. The only coins issued in the name of Pitcairn are special commemorative pieces, silver 50 dollars and gold 250 dollars, produced by the Royal Mint in Britain to celebrate the 150th anniversary of the drafting of the island's constitution in 1988 and the arrival of the *Bounty* respectively.

TRUST TERRITORY OF THE PACIFIC ISLANDS

THE island groups of the central and northern Pacific, including Micronesia (formerly the Carolina Islands), the Mariana Islands and the Marshall Islands were joined together in 1947 to form the Trust Territory of the Pacific Islands, administered by the USA. None has yet issued its own currency, but in recent years commemorative coins, intended for sale to collectors, have started to appear.

MICRONESIA

The Carolina Islands were discovered by the Spanish and the Portuguese in the sixteenth century, and were named after Charles II of Spain in 1686. The Spanish remained nominally in possession until the islands were ceded to Germany in 1899. They were later under Japanese control (1914–1945), and after the Second World War were administered by the USA until independence in 1983, when they took the name Federated States of Micronesia.

Various coinages, notably Spanish, German, Japanese and later US, have reached the islands, but until quite recently the native inhabitants had little use for them, preferring instead to use their own forms of money for largely ceremonial functions. The most famous island money is the huge stone money of Yap Island, widely used until the Second World War. US currency is now standard.

THE MARIANA ISLANDS AND MARSHALL ISLANDS

The Mariana Islands, discovered by the Portuguese Ferdinand Magellan in 1519, were Spanish until the end of the nineteenth century, when the largest island, Guam, was taken over by the USA, and the rest were sold to Germany (1899). The Mariana Islands were, like the Carolina Islands, occupied by the Japanese from 1914 to 1945 and subsequently administered by the USA. Spanish, German and Japanese coins were known, but now US currency is standard.

The Marshall Islands were discovered by the Spanish in the seventeenth century but named after the British sea captain, John Marshall, who explored them in 1788. They became a German colony in 1885. There was a period of Japanese occupation from 1914 to 1945, followed by US administration until independence was granted in 1986.

The German, and later Japanese, currency was replaced by the US dollar. No currency coins have been issued for the Marshall Islands, but recently commemorative coins have been produced for collectors. A series consisting of silver ½ and 1 dollar and gold 20, 50 and 200 dollar pieces celebrated the 1986 independence of the islands under the Compact of Free Association, and a cupro-nickel 5 dollars was issued to commemorate the US space shuttle *Discovery* in 1988.

The ceremonial stone money of Yap, widely used until the Second World War.

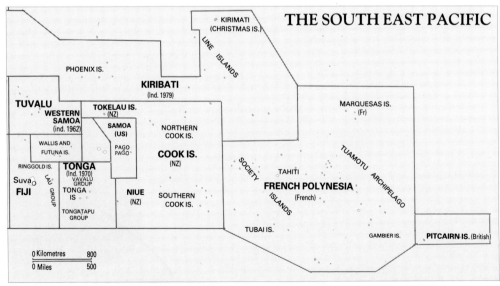

GLOSSARY

ANTONINIANUS *Double denarius coin introduced under Caracalla (211–17) and distinguished by a radiate crown on the emperor's head. Initially of relatively good silver, it was rapidly debased to about 3 per cent silver by 270. It was the predominant coin of the Roman Empire until its removal c. 300.*

BASE SILVER *Silver adulterated with some base metal, usually copper.*

BILLON *Silver adulterated with an equal or greater proportion of base metal, usually copper, and generally used for low denomination coins.*

BIMETALLISM *Monetary system involving coinage of both gold and silver. Bimetallic systems tend to be unstable because of the shifting relative values of gold and silver as supplies of the two metals fluctuate.*

BLACK MONEY *The name given to coinage of very base silver from about the thirteenth century, particularly in France and the Low Countries.*

BRACTEATE *The modern name for a type of penny or denar made in large parts of northern and eastern Europe in the middle ages, and in some regions until about 1700. The coin consisted of a very thin sheet of silver, with a design impressed on one side only and struck by a single die.*

BRASS *Alloy of copper and zinc, used for coinage in classical Greece and Rome and by the Chinese. It has played some role in modern coinage, but nowadays nickel-brass is more commonly encountered than brass itself, the copper-based alloy making the very hard nickel easier to work.*

BRONZE *Alloy traditionally of 90 per cent copper and 10 per cent tin, but for modern coinage of 95 per cent copper, 4 per cent tin and 1 per cent zinc, widely used for coinage since it is more durable than pure copper. A similar mixture was used in classical Greece and Rome and in China, but in the west it is only since the later nineteenth century that it has come to replace copper everywhere. Aluminium-bronze is also widely used in modern coinages.*

BULLION *Uncoined precious metal, usually in its purest form. Bullion coins are pieces of precious metal, usually gold, produced as a convenient way to acquire and store bullion. They usually state their fineness and metal content.*

CASH *Foreign name for the most common denomination of Chinese currency, a copper alloy piece with a square hole through the middle which changed little in appearance in two thousand years. Its Chinese name is ch'ien.*

CASTING *Method of coin manufacture involving the pouring of molten metal into moulds. Casting is a speedy and uncomplicated process, but maintaining consistent weights is always a problem, so the process has rarely been used for precious metal coins. Designs on cast coins are less well-defined than on struck ones.*

CLIPPING *Taking illegal profits by trimming or shaving material from the edge of precious-metal coins. An equivalent abuse is sweating, that is shaking gold coins together and accumulating the resultant gold dust. The development of edge-marking techniques put an end to clipping.*

COB *Coin struck on a crudely-cut, irregular flan. A common phenomenon of Spanish–American mints until the eighteenth century.*

COMMEMORATIVE *Coin issued with a design to commemorate an event or individual. These can be issued for currency when in base metal, but the majority are made in precious metal for sale at a profit to collectors. Their nominal face value usually bears no relation to their actual worth or sale price.*

COUNTERMARK (COUNTERSTAMP) *Distinctive mark punched or stamped into an existing coin by a public authority, usually to signify the currency of an existing coin at a new valuation, or to mark a foreign coin as legally current.*

COUNTERSTAMP *see countermark.*

CRENATE *To notch or mill the edge of a coin.*

CUPRO-NICKEL (COPPER-NICKEL) *Alloy of copper and nickel, with copper usually dominant. Modern cupro-nickel coins usually have a relatively high nickel content, about 25 per cent, to give the familiar silvery appearance. As nickel was only isolated in 1751, the large-scale use of cupro-nickel has been a modern phenomenon, beginning in Switzerland in 1850. It is more durable than silver or copper, but less hard than pure nickel, thus putting less pressure on coining dies. Also it does not tarnish easily.*

CURRENCY *General term referring to all forms of money actually circulating at a particular time and place. A currency coin is one issued for normal use in circulation, not as a souvenir, commemorative or piece of bullion.*

DEBASEMENT *The issuing of precious metal coinage with reduced standards of weight or fineness but at the original valuation with the intent to create profits for the coin-issuer.*

DECIMALIZATION *The introduction of a monetary system based on a unit subdivided into tenths or hundredths, and intended to simplify monetary calculations. Britain's was the world's last monetary system to become decimal, which it did in 1971.*

DENARIUS *The basic Roman silver coin from the late third century BC until the early third century AD.*

DENIER (DENARO, DENAR, DINEIRO, PENNY, PFENNIG, PENNING etc.) *The silver coin which was virtually the only coin struck in early medieval Europe. It took its title from the old Roman denarius, but its name, like its form, soon varied in the emerging countries of western Europe. It formed the basis of most medieval monetary systems, usually in a system of 12 deniers to the sol or shilling and 20 sols to the livre or pound.*

DENOMINATION *The name given to a coin, usually reflecting its value.*

DIE *Coins are most commonly manufactured by being struck between two dies, iron or steel implements which bear the design for the coin in reverse. These stamp both sides of the coin simultaneously.*

DINAR *General name for the standard gold coin of the Islamic world. Introduced in about 696, it established a standard of design and appearance for all later Islamic coinages.*

DIRHEM *General name for the most important silver coin of the Islamic world, beginning as a version of the Sasanian drachm.*

DOLLAR *In modern times the basic coin of the monetary system of the USA, the dollar was given this role because of the importance in the Americas of the Spanish piece of eight or 'pillar dollar'. The word itself comes from the anglicization of the German 'taler'.*

DOUBLOON *Name given to common Spanish gold coins: initially the double excelente, but from the seventeenth century the 8 escudos.*

DRACHM *Important silver coin of the ancient Greek world. Both multiples, particularly tetradrachms (= 4 drachms), and decadrachms (= 10 drachms), and fractions of the drachm were also commonly issued.*

DUCAT (ZECCHINO OR SEQUIN) *Introduced in 1284, the Venetian ducat came to dominate eastern Mediterranean trade in the later middle ages and it came to form a model for the gold coinages of many other countries, including the Ottoman empire and Persia. Gold ducats to the Venetian standard were produced by many European countries up to the twentieth century to serve as international trade coins.*

ELECTRUM (WHITE GOLD) *Mixture of silver and gold. Occurring naturally in Lydia, this was used to make the earliest known coins. As a man-made alloy it has only occasionally been openly used for coinage since then, for instance in the Byzantine empire, but when gold is debased, it is usually with silver, so many base-gold coins are technically electrum or 'white gold'.*

FINENESS *The proportion of precious metal contained in a coin.*

FLAN OR BLANK *Blank disc of metal of the correct fineness and weight which is stamped between dies to produce the finished coin.*

FLORIN *The Florentine florin was introduced in 1252. It soon became an important coin for international trade as well as providing the model for a number of other European gold coins, particularly in Italy, Hungary, Spain, the Low Countries and the Rhineland. The name was subsequently borrowed for silver coins in Austria, the Low Countries and Great Britain.*

FOLLIS *First introduced by Diocletian as a base-silver coin, the follis was later reintroduced to become the basic copper coin of the Byzantine empire.*

GOLD STANDARD *Monetary system based solely on the value of a country's gold coinage.*

GROS (GROSSO, GROSCHEN, GROAT, CROAT etc.) *Large silver coin introduced into most European countries in the later middle ages as a multiple of their traditional denier or penny.*

INCUSE *Coin designs stamped into metal in intaglio, rather than being made to rise in relief.*

INGOT *Bar or lump of precious metal, usually of a fixed standard of weight and fineness. Made in particular shapes or stamped with distinctive marks, ingots have sometimes functioned as high-value currency.*

LATIN MONETARY UNION *The countries of the Latin Monetary Union, founded in 1865, agreed to harmonize their gold and silver coinages in the hope of establishing an acceptable international currency. France took the lead in setting up the Union and her coinage was accepted as its model. The founding states were France, Belgium, Italy and Switzerland. Greece, Romania, Bulgaria, Finland and several Latin American states also joined later.*

LEGEND *The inscriptions running in a circle or arc around the outside of coins.*

MILLED COINS *Coins struck using mechanized means of manufacture, usually taken to refer to early methods, before the advent of steam power.*

MILLED EDGE *Mechanized manufacturing techniques made it possible to combat clipping by introducing edge markings onto coins, initially in the form of regular 'milling' or 'graining' but subsequently using inscriptions.*

MINT MARK *Mark included in the design of a coin to indicate the mint of origin. Other marks on coins can indicate its period of manufacture or the mintmaster or moneyer responsible.*

MONEYER *Individual given responsibility for the manufacture of coinage and the maintenance of official standards. Moneyers were particularly important in early medieval Europe when coin production was not centralized and many local mints were in operation. In later times the moneyer was normally the description given to the mint worker responsible for actually striking the coins.*

OBOL *A small, silver coin of the ancient Greek world, equal to 1/6 drachm. The name survived in the middle ages in the Latin form 'obolus' to designate the half of the medieval denier or penny.*

OBVERSE *The front of a coin, usually designated by portraying the image or symbol of the issuing authority.*

OVERSTRIKE *The technique of striking new coins over the top of old ones without melting the originals down. Often the original design can be made out under the overstrike.*

PATTERN *Coin produced in the mint to demonstrate or test possible new designs, materials and coining techniques. Patterns are not struck to any particular standard and have no currency role.*

PIECE OF EIGHT *Spanish coin worth 8 reales and equivalent to the taler. It became familiar and widely used throughout the Americas and the Far East as well as in Europe and was also known as the 'pillar dollar'.*

PLATE MONEY *Plates of copper stamped with coinage dies and used as currency. This unusual attempt to use copper for high-value coins with a face value reflecting intrinsic value was a particular phenomenon of early modern Sweden, but also occurred in neighbouring states and in Russia.*

PLUGGING *The insertion of a portion of one metal into a coin made of another metal.*

PROOF *Coin produced to an exceptionally high standard of finish from a specially-prepared die, usually for sale, or for commemorative or ceremonial purposes.*

PUNCH *Tool with all or part of a coin design in relief, used to create a coining die (see die).*

REFORM *As affecting coinage, the wholesale transformation of the coinage system of a country.*

REVERSE *The back of a coin. In modern times this side normally carries the value.*

SCYPHATE *Modern term used to designate coins which are 'dish-shaped', having one concave and one convex side, rather than being flat. The later Byzantine empire was the most prolific, but by no means the only, issuer of such coins.*

SEMI-BRACTEATE *Modern term designating a stage in the development of the bracteate in medieval Germany (see bracteate). It refers to a coin struck with an insufficient amount of metal to register both sides of the design. Usually the design on one side wholly or partially obliterates that on the other.*

SIEGE PIECE *Coin struck in a town or city under siege to pay the defenders. Siege pieces were usually crudely struck, sometimes in unusual shapes, and could employ a variety of metals.*

SOLIDUS *The standard gold coin of the late Roman and Byzantine empires, also known as the nomisma. It was imitated in several of the barbarian successor states in western Europe.*

STATER *The standard silver coin of the ancient Greek world and widely copied in the Celtic lands.*

TALER (THALER) *General name for the dominant large silver coin in German-speaking lands since the late fifteenth century. The name comes from the mint of St Joachimsthal in Bohemia, where the taler was first made. It provided the model for similar large silver coins throughout Europe which often had names taken from the original, such as daalder, daler, dollar and tallero (see dollar).*

TOKEN COIN *Coin with a face value which bears no relation to the actual value of the material of which it is composed. Its value comes from the guarantee of the issuing authority.*

TRIAL PIECE *Piece struck during the preparation of coining dies to check the progress of work.*

TUGHRA *Ornamental Turkish signature used to designate official imperial documents and found on many coins of Turkey and related states.*

UNIFACE COIN *Coin with a design on one side only (see bracteate).*

SELECT BIBLIOGRAPHY

D F Allen, *The Coins of the Ancient Celts*, Edinburgh 1979.

M Broome, *A Handbook of Islamic Coins*, London 1985.

C R Bruce et al. *The Standard Guide to South Asian Coins and Paper Money since 1556 AD*, Iola.

A Burnett, *Coinage in the Roman World*, London 1987.

T V Buttrey, *Coinage of the Americas*, New York 1973.

I Carradice and M Price, *Coinage in the Greek World*, London 1988.

R A G Carson, *Coins, Ancient, Mediaeval and Modern*, London 1962.

E E Clain-Stefanelli, *Select Numismatic Bibliography*, New York 1965.

E E and V Clain-Stefanelli, *Monnaies europeennes, 1450–1789*, Fribourg 1978.

W D Craig, *Coins of the World 1750–1850*, Racine 1976.

J Cribb (ed.) *Money, from Cowrie Shells to Credit Cards*, London 1986.

R G Doty, *Encyclopaedic Dictionary of Numismatics*, London 1982.

A Dowle and A de Clermont, *Monnaies modernes, 1789 a nos jours*, Fribourg 1972.

P Grierson, *Numismatics*, Oxford 1975.

P Grierson, *Bibliographie numismatique*, Brussels 1966.

P Grierson, *Monnaies au moyen age*, Fribourg 1976.

P Grierson, *Byzantine Coins*, London 1982.

B V Head, *Historia Numorum: A manual of Greek numismatics*, London 1911, repr. 1966.

C L Krause and C Mishler, *Standard Catalogue of World Coins*, Iola.

D Nash, *Coinage in the Celtic World*, London 1987.

R Plant, *Arabic Coins and how to read them*, London 1973.

J Porteous, *Coins in History*, London 1968.

M J Price (ed.) *Coins*, London 1980.

F Pridmore, *The Coins of the British Commonwealth of Nations* (4 vols.), London 1960–1975.

C Scholten, *The coins of the Dutch overseas territories, 1601–1948*, Amsterdam 1953.

INDEX